# Complete Solutions Manual
# for
# APPLIED FINITE
# MATHEMATICS
## FIFTH EDITION

## S. T. TAN
### Stonehill College

Brooks/Cole Publishing Company

I(T)P® An International Thomson Publishing Company

Pacific Grove • Albany • Belmont • Bonn • Boston • Cincinnati • Detroit • Johannesburg • London
Madrid • Melbourne • Mexico City • New York • Paris • Singapore • Tokyo • Toronto • Washington

COPYRIGHT© 1997 by Brooks/Cole Publishing Company
A division of International Thomson Publishing Inc.

 The ITP logo is a registered trademark under license.

*For more information, contact:*

BROOKS/COLE PUBLISHING COMPANY
511 Forest Lodge Road
Pacific Grove, CA  93950
USA

International Thomson Editores
Seneca 53
Col. Polanco
11560 México,  D. F., México

International Thomson Publishing Europe
Berkshire House 168-173
High Holborn
London WC1V 7AA
England

International Thomson Publishing GmbH
Königswinterer Strasse 418
53227 Bonn
Germany

Thomas Nelson Australia
102 Dodds Street
South Melbourne, 3205
Victoria, Australia

International Thomson Publishing Asia
221 Henderson Road
#05-10 Henderson Building
Singapore 0315

Nelson Canada
1120 Birchmount Road
Scarborough, Ontario
Canada M1K 5G4

International Thomson Publishing Japan
Hirakawacho Kyowa Building, 3F
2-2-1 Hirakawacho
Chiyoda-ku, Tokyo 102
Japan

Printed in the United States of America

5    4    3    2    1

ISBN 0-534-95563-0

# CONTENTS

## CHAPTER 1 STRAIGHT LINES AND LINEAR FUNCTIONS

## CHAPTER 2 SYSTEMS OF LINEAR EQUATIONS AND MATRICES

## CHAPTER 3 LINEAR PROGRAMMING: A GEOMETRIC APPROACH

## CHAPTER 4 LINEAR PROGRAMMING: AN ALGEBRAIC APPROACH

# CHAPTER 1

## EXERCISES 1.1, page 8

1.  The coordinates of A are (3,3) and it is located in Quadrant I.

2.  The coordinates of B are (−5,2) and it is located in Quadrant II.

3.  The coordinates of C are (2,−2) and it is located in Quadrant IV.

4.  The coordinates of D are (−2,5) and it is located in Quadrant II.

5.  The coordinates of E are (−4,−6) and it is located in Quadrant III.

6.  The coordinates of F are (8,−2) and it is located in Quadrant IV.

7.  A

8.  (−5,4)

9.  E, F, and G.

10. E

11. F

12. D

For Exercises 13-20, refer to the following figure.

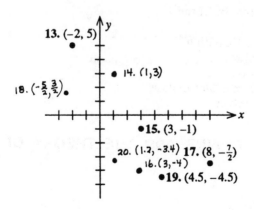

*1  Straight Lines and Linear Functions*

21. Using the distance formula, we find that

$$\sqrt{(4 - 1)^2 + (7 - 3)^2} = \sqrt{3^2 + 4^2} = \sqrt{25} = 5.$$

22. Using the distance formula, we find that

$$\sqrt{(4 - 1)^2 + (4 - 0)^2} = \sqrt{3^2 + 4^2} = \sqrt{25} = 5.$$

23. Using the distance formula, we find that

$$\sqrt{(4 - (-1))^2 + (9 - 3)^2} = \sqrt{5^2 + 6^2} = \sqrt{25 + 36} = \sqrt{61}.$$

24. Using the distance formula, we find that

$$\sqrt{(10 - (-2))^2 + (6 - 1)^2} = \sqrt{12^2 + 5^2} = \sqrt{144 + 25} = \sqrt{169}$$
$$= 13.$$

25. The coordinates of the points have the form $(x, -6)$. Since the points are 10 units away from the origin, we have

$$(x - 0)^2 + (-6 - 0)^2 = 10^2$$
$$x^2 = 64,$$

or $x = \pm 8$. Therefore, the required points are $(-8, -6)$ and $(8, -6)$.

26. The coordinates of the points have the form $(3, y)$. Since the points are 5 units away from the origin, we have

$$(3 - 0)^2 + (y - 0)^2 = 5^2$$
$$y^2 = 16,$$

or $x = \pm 4$. Therefore, the required points are $(3, 4)$ and $(3, -4)$.

27. The points are shown in the diagram on page 3.

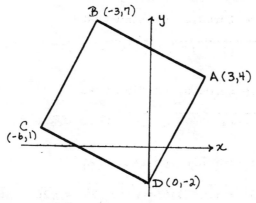

To show that the four sides are equal, we compute the following:

$$d(A,B) = \sqrt{(-3 - 3)^2 + (7 - 4)^2} = \sqrt{(-6)^2 + 3^2} = \sqrt{45}.$$

$$d(B,C) = \sqrt{[-6 - (-3)]^2 + (1 - 7)^2} = \sqrt{(-3)^2 + (-6)^2} = \sqrt{45}.$$

$$d(C,D) = \sqrt{[0 - (-6)]^2 + [(-2) - 1]^2} = \sqrt{(6)^2 + (-3)^2} = \sqrt{45}.$$

$$d(A,D) = \sqrt{(0 - 3)^2 + (-2 - 4)^2} = \sqrt{(3)^2 + (-6)^2} = \sqrt{45}.$$

Next, to show that $\triangle ABC$ is a right triangle, we show that it satisfies the Pythagorean theorem. Thus,

$$d(A,C) = \sqrt{(-6 - 3)^2 + [1 - 4]^2} = \sqrt{(-9)^2 + (-3)^2} = \sqrt{90} = 3\sqrt{10} .$$

and $\quad [d(A,B)]^2 + [d(B,C)]^2 = 90 = [d(A,C)]^2.$

Similarly, $d(B,D) = \sqrt{90} = 3\sqrt{10}$ , so $\triangle BAD$ is a right triangle as well. It follows that $\angle B$ and $\angle D$ are right angles, and we conclude that ADCB is a square.

28. The triangle is shown in the figure at the right. To prove that $\triangle ABC$ is a right triangle, we show that

$$[d(A,C)]^2 = [d(A,B)]^2 + [d(B,C)]^2$$

and the result will then follow from the Pythagorean Theorem.

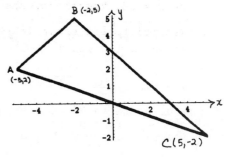

Now,

$$[d(A,C)]^2 = (-5 - 5)^2 + [2 - (-2)]^2 = 100 + 16 = 116.$$

Next, we find

$$[d(A,B)]^2 + [d(B,C)]^2 = [-2-(-5)]^2 + (5-2)^2 + [5-(-2)]^2 + (-2-5)^2$$
$$= 9 + 9 + 49 + 49 = 116,$$

and the result follows.

29. Referring to the diagram on page 9 of the text, we see that the distance from A to B is given by

$$d(A,B) = \sqrt{400^2 + 300^2} = \sqrt{250000} = 500.$$

The distance from B to C is given by

$$d(B,C) = \sqrt{(-800-400)^2 + (800-300)^2} = \sqrt{(-1200)^2 + (500)^2}$$
$$= \sqrt{1690000} = 1300.$$

The distance from C to D is given by

$$d(C,D) = \sqrt{[-800-(-800)]^2 + (800-0)^2} = \sqrt{0 + 800^2} = 800.$$

The distance from D to A is given by

$$d(D,A) = \sqrt{[(0-(-800)]^2 + (0-0)]}$$
$$= \sqrt{6400} = 800.$$

Therefore, the total distance covered on the tour, is

$$d(A,B) + d(B,C) + d(C,D) + d(D,A) = 500 + 1300 + 800 + 800$$
$$= 3400, \text{ or } 3400 \text{ miles.}$$

30. Suppose that the furniture store is located at the origin O so that your house is located at A(20,14). Since

$$d(O,A) = \sqrt{20^2 + (-14)^2} = \sqrt{596} = 24.4,$$

your house is located within a 25-mile radius of the store, you will not incur a delivery charge.

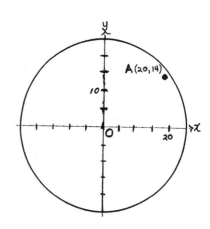

31. Referring to the following diagram,

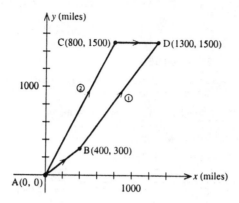

we see that the distance he would cover if he took Route (1) is given by

$$d(A,B) + d(B,D) = \sqrt{400^2 + 300^2} + \sqrt{(1300 - 400)^2 + (1500 - 300)^2}$$

$$= \sqrt{250000} + \sqrt{2250000} = 500 + 1500 = 2000,$$

or 2000 miles. On the other hand, the distance he would cover if he took Route (2) is given by

$$d(A,C) + d(C,D) = \sqrt{800^2 + 1500^2} + \sqrt{(1300 - 800)^2}$$

$$= \sqrt{2890000} + \sqrt{250000} = 1700 + 500 = 2200,$$

or 2200 miles. Comparing these results, we see that he should take Route (1).

32. Calculations to determine the cost of shipping by freight train:

$$(0.11)(2000)(100) = 22,000$$

or $22,000.

Calculations to determine the cost of shipping by truck:

$$(0.105)(2200)(100) = 23,100.$$

or $23,100.

Comparing these results we see that the automobiles should be shipped by freight train.

Net Savings:

$$23,100 - 22,000 = 1100, \text{ or } \$1100.$$

33. Calculations to determine VHF requirements:

$$d = \sqrt{25^2 + 35^2}$$

$$= \sqrt{625 + 1225} = \sqrt{1850}$$

$$= 43.01.$$

Models B through D satisfy this requirement.

Calculations to determine UHF requirements:

$$d = \sqrt{20^2 + 32^2} = \sqrt{400 + 1024} = \sqrt{1424} = 37.74.$$

Models C through D satisfy this requirement.
Therefore, Model C will allow him to receive both channels at the least cost.

34. Length of cable required on land:

$$d(P,Q) + d(Q,S) = \sqrt{(x - 10000)^2 + 800^2} + 10000$$

Length of cable required under water:

$$d(P,M) = \sqrt{x^2 + 2200^2}$$

Cost of laying cable:

$$2[\sqrt{(x - 10000)^2 + 800^2} + 10000] + 6\sqrt{x^2 + 2200^2}$$

If $x = 900$, then the cost is

$$2 [\sqrt{(900 - 10000)^2 + 800^2} + 10000] + 6\sqrt{900^2 + 2200^2}$$

$$= 52{,}543.03,$$

or approximately $52,543.
If $x = 1000$, then the cost is

$$2[\sqrt{(1000 - 10000)^2 + 800^2} + 10000] + 6\sqrt{1000^2 + 2200^2}$$

$$= 52{,}570.63,$$

or approximately $52,571.

35. a. Let $P(x,y)$ be any point in the plane. Draw a line through P parallel to the y-axis and a line through P parallel to the x-axis (see figure). The x-coordinate of P is the number corresponding to the point on the x-axis at which the line through P hits the

x-axis. Similarly y is the number that corresponds to the point on the y-axis at which the line parallel to the x-axis crosses the y-axis.

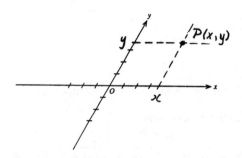

To show the converse, reverse the process.

b. You can use the Pythagorean Theorem in the Cartesian Coordinate System . This simplifies the computations greatly.

36. Referring to the figure in the text, we see that the distance between the two points is given by the length of the hypotenuse of the right triangle. That is,

$$d = \sqrt{(x_2 - x_1)^2 + (y_2 - y_1)^2}.$$

# EXERCISES 1.2, page 22

1. Referring to the figure shown in the text, we see that

$$m = \frac{2 - 0}{0 - (-4)} = \frac{1}{2}.$$

2. Referring to the figure shown in the text, we see that

$$m = \frac{4 - 0}{0 - 2} = -2.$$

3. This is a vertical line, and hence its slope is undefined.

4. This is a horizontal line, and hence its slope is 0.

5.      $m = \dfrac{y_2 - y_1}{x_2 - x_1} = \dfrac{8 - 3}{5 - 4} = 5.$

6.      $m = \dfrac{y_2 - y_1}{x_2 - x_1} = \dfrac{8 - 5}{3 - 4} = \dfrac{3}{(-1)} = -3.$

7.      $m = \dfrac{y_2 - y_1}{x_2 - x_1} = \dfrac{8 - 3}{4 - (-2)} = \dfrac{5}{6}.$

8.      $m = \dfrac{y_2 - y_1}{x_2 - x_1} = \dfrac{-4 - (-2)}{4 - (-2)} = \dfrac{-2}{6} = -\dfrac{1}{3}.$

9.      $m = \dfrac{y_2 - y_1}{x_2 - x_1} = \dfrac{d - b}{c - a}.$

10.     $m = \dfrac{y_2 - y_1}{x_2 - x_1} = \dfrac{-b - (b - 1)}{a + 1 - (-a + 1)} = \dfrac{-b - b + 1}{a + 1 + a - 1} = \dfrac{1 - 2b}{2a}.$

11. Since the equation is in the slope-intercept form, we read off the slope $m = 4$.
    a. If x increases by 1 unit, then y increases by 4 units.
    b. If x decreases by 2 unit, y decreases by $4(-2) = -8$.

12. Rewrite the given equation in slope-intercept form:

$$2x + 3y = 4$$

$$3y = 4 - 2x$$

$$y = \frac{4}{3} - \frac{2}{3}x.$$

   a. Since $m = -2/3$, we conclude that the slope is negative.
   b. Since the slope is negative, y decreases as x increases in value.
   c. If x decreases by 2 units, then y increases by $-(2/3)(-2) = 4/3$ units.

13. The slope of the line through A and B is

$$\frac{-10 - (-2)}{-3 - 1} = \frac{-8}{-4} = 2.$$

The slope of the line through C and D is

$$\frac{1 - 5}{-1 - 1} = \frac{-4}{-2} = 2.$$

Since the slopes of these two lines are equal, the lines are parallel.

14. The slope of the line through A and B is

$$\frac{-2 - 3}{2 - 2} \, .$$

Since this slope is undefined, we see that the line is vertical. The slope of the line through C and D is

$$\frac{5 - 4}{-2 - (-2)} \, .$$

Since this slope is undefined, we see that this line is also vertical. Furthermore, since the slopes of these two lines are equal, the lines are parallel.

15. The slope of the line through A and B is

$$\frac{2 - 5}{4 - (-2)} = \frac{-3}{6} = -\frac{1}{2} \, .$$

The slope of the line through C and D is

$$\frac{6 - (-2)}{3 - (-1)} = \frac{8}{4} = 2 \, .$$

Since the slopes of these two lines are the negative reciprocals of each other, the lines are perpendicular.

16. The slope of the line through A and B is

$$\frac{-2 - 0}{1 - 2} = \frac{-2}{-1} = 2 \, .$$

The slope of the line through C and D is

$$\frac{4 - 2}{-8 - 4} = \frac{2}{-12} = -\frac{1}{6} \, .$$

Since the slopes of these two lines are not the negative reciprocals of each other, the lines are not perpendicular.

17. The slope of the line through the point (1,a) and (4,−2) is

$$m_1 = \frac{-2 - a}{4 - 1}$$

and the slope of the line through (2,8) and (−7,a + 4) is

$$m_2 = \frac{a + 4 - 8}{-7 - 2} \, .$$

Since these two lines are parallel, $m_1$ is equal to $m_2$. Therefore,

$$\frac{-2 - a}{3} = \frac{a - 4}{-9}$$

$$-9(-2 - a) = 3(a - 4)$$

$$18 + 9a = 3a - 12$$

$$6a = -30 \quad \text{and} \quad a = -5.$$

18. The slope of the line through the point $(a,1)$ and $(5,8)$ is
$$m_1 = \frac{8 - 1}{5 - a}$$

and the slope of the line through $(4,9)$ and $(a + 2, 1)$ is
$$m_2 = \frac{1 - 9}{a + 2 - 4}.$$

Since these two lines are parallel, $m_1$ is equal to $m_2$. Therefore,

$$\frac{7}{5 - a} = \frac{-8}{a - 2}$$

$$7(a - 2) = -8(5 - a)$$

$$7a - 14 = -40 + 8a$$

$$a = 26$$

19. An equation of a horizontal line is of the form $y = b$. In this case $b = -3$, so $y = -3$ is an equation of the line.

20. An equation of a vertical line is of the form $x = a$. In this case $a = 0$, so $x = 0$ is an equation of the line.

21. e

22. c

23. a

24. d

25. f

26. b

27. We use the point-slope form of an equation of a line with the point $(3,-4)$ and slope $m = 2$. Thus

$$y - y_1 = m(x - x_1),$$

and
$$y - (-4) = 2(x - 3)$$

$$y + 4 = 2x - 6$$

$$y = 2x - 10.$$

28. We use the point-slope form of an equation of a line with the point (2,4) and slope m = -1. Thus

$$y - y_1 = m(x - x_1),$$

and $\qquad y - 4 = -1(x - 2)$

$$y - 4 = -x + 2$$

$$y = -x + 6.$$

29. Since the slope m = 0, we know that the line is a horizontal line of the form y = b. Since the line passes through (-3,2), we see that b = 2 and an equation of the line is y = 2.

30. We use the point-slope form of an equation of a line with the point (1,2) and slope m = -1/2. Thus

$$y - y_1 = m(x - x_1),$$

and $\qquad y - 2 = -\frac{1}{2}(x - 1)$

$$2y - 4 = -x + 1$$

$$2y = -x + 5$$

and $\qquad y = -\frac{1}{2}x + \frac{5}{2}.$

31. We first compute the slope of the line joining the points (2,4) and (3,7). Thus,

$$m = \frac{7 - 4}{3 - 2} = 1.$$

Using the point-slope form of an equation of a line with the point (2,4) and slope m = 3, we find

$$y - 4 = 3(x - 2)$$

$$y = 3x - 2.$$

32. We first compute the slope of the line joining the points (2,1) and (2,5). Thus,

$$m = \frac{5 - 1}{2 - 2} \ .$$

Since this slope is undefined, we see that the line must be a vertical line of the form x = a. Since it passes through (2,5), we see that x = 2 is the equation of the line.

33. We first compute the slope of the line joining the points (1,2) and (-3,-2). Thus,

$$m = \frac{-2 - 2}{-3 - 1} = \frac{-4}{-4} = 1.$$

Using the point-slope form of an equation of a line with the point (1,2) and slope m = 1, we find

$$y - 2 = x - 1$$
$$y = x + 1.$$

34. We first compute the slope of the line joining the points (-1,-2) and (3,-4). Thus,

$$m = \frac{-4 - (-2)}{3 - (-1)} = \frac{-2}{4} = -\frac{1}{2}.$$

Using the point-slope form of an equation of a line with the point (-1,-2) and slope m = -1/2, we find

$$y - (-2) = -\frac{1}{2}(x - (-1))$$
$$y + 2 = -\frac{1}{2}(x + 1).$$
$$y = -\frac{1}{2}x - \frac{5}{2}.$$

35. We use the slope-intercept form of an equation of a line: y = mx + b. Since m = 3, and b = 4, the equation is y = 3x + 4.

36. We use the slope-intercept form of an equation of a line: y = mx + b. Since m = -2, and b = -1, the equation is y = -2x - 1.

37. We use the slope-intercept form of an equation of a line: y = mx + b. Since m = 0, and b = 5, the equation is y = 5.

38. We use the slope-intercept form of an equation of a line: y = mx + b. Since m = -1/2, and b = 3/4, the equation is

$$y = -\frac{1}{2}x + \frac{3}{4}.$$

39. We first write the given equation in the slope-intercept form:

$$x - 2y = 0$$
$$-2y = -x$$
$$y = \frac{1}{2}x.$$

From this equation, we see that m = 1/2 and b = 0.

40. We write the equation in slope-intercept form:

$$y - 2 = 0$$
$$y = 2.$$

From this equation, we see that m = 0 and b = 2.

41. We write the equation in slope-intercept form:

$$2x - 3y - 9 = 0$$

$$-3y = -2x + 9$$

$$y = \frac{2}{3}x - 3.$$

From this equation, we see that m = 2/3 and b = −3.

42. We write the equation in slope-intercept form:

$$3x - 4y + 8 = 0$$

$$-4y = -3x - 8$$

$$y = \frac{3}{4}x + 2.$$

From this equation, we see that m = 3/4 and b = 2.

43. We write the equation in slope-intercept form:

$$2x + 4y = 14$$

$$4y = -2x + 14$$

$$y = -\frac{2}{4}x + \frac{14}{4}$$

$$= -\frac{1}{2}x + \frac{7}{2}.$$

From this equation, we see that m = −1/2 and b = 7/2.

44. We write the equation in the slope-intercept form:

$$5x + 8y - 24 = 0$$

$$8y = -5x + 24$$

$$y = -\frac{5}{8}x + 3.$$

From this equation, we conclude that m = −5/8 and b = 3.

45. We first write the equation 2x − 4y − 8 = 0 in slope-intercept form:

$$2x - 4y - 8 = 0$$

$$4y = 2x - 8$$

and
$$y = \frac{1}{2}x - 2.$$

Now the required line is parallel to this line, and hence has the same slope. Using the point-slope equation of a line with m = 1/2 and the point (−2,2), we have

$$y - 2 = \tfrac{1}{2}(x - (-2))$$

$$y = \tfrac{1}{2}x + 3.$$

46. We first write the equation $3x + 4y - 22 = 0$ in slope-intercept form:

$$3x + 4y - 22 = 0$$

$$4y = -3x + 22$$

and $$y = -\tfrac{3}{4}x + \tfrac{22}{4}.$$

Now the required line is perpendicular to this line, and hence has slope 4/3 (the negative reciprocal of -3/4). Using the point-slope equation of a line with m = 4/3 and the point (2,4), we have

$$y - 4 = \tfrac{4}{3}(x - 2)$$

$$y = \tfrac{4}{3}x + \tfrac{4}{3}.$$

47. A line parallel to the x-axis has slope 0 and is of the form $y = b$. Since the line is 6 units below the axis, it passes through (0,-6) and its equation is $y = -6$.

48. Since the required line is parallel to the line joining (2,4) and (4,7), it has slope

$$m = \frac{7 - 4}{4 - 2} = \frac{3}{2}.$$

We also know that the required line passes through (0,0) [the origin]. Using the point-slope form of an equation of a line, we find

$$y - 0 = \tfrac{3}{2}(x - 0)$$

or $$y = \tfrac{3}{2}x.$$

49. We use the point-slope form of an equation of a line to obtain

$$y - b = 0(x - a)$$

or $$y = b.$$

50. Since the line is parallel to the x-axis, its slope is 0 and it has the form $y = b$. We know that the line passes through $(-3,4)$, so the required equation is $y = 4$.

51. Since the required line is parallel to the line joining $(-3,2)$ and $(6,8)$, it has slope

$$m = \frac{8 - 2}{6 - (-3)} = \frac{6}{9} = \frac{2}{3}.$$

We also know that the required line passes through $(-5,-4)$. Using the point-slope form of an equation of a line, we find

$$y - (-4) = \frac{2}{3}(x - (-5)),$$

or
$$y = \frac{2}{3}x + \frac{10}{3} - 4$$

that is,
$$y = \frac{2}{3}x - \frac{2}{3}.$$

52. Since the slope of the line is undefined, it has the form $x = a$. Furthermore, since the line passes through $(a,b)$, the required equation is $x = a$.

53. Since the point $(-3,5)$ lies on the line $kx + 3y + 9 = 0$, it satisfies the equation. Substituting $x = -3$ and $y = 5$ into the equation gives

$$-3k + 15 + 9 = 0,$$

$$k = 8.$$

54. Since the point $(2,-3)$ lies on the line

$$-2x + ky + 10 = 0,$$

it satisfies the equation. Substituting $x = 2$ and $y = -3$ into the equation gives

$$-2(2) + (-3)k + 10 = 0$$

$$-4 - 3k + 10 = 0$$

$$-3k = -6$$

or
$$k = 2.$$

**55.** $3x - 2y + 6 = 0$

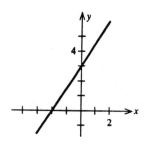

**56.** $2x - 5y + 10 = 0$

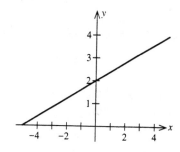

**57.** $x + 2y - 4 = 0$

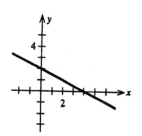

**58.** $2x + 3y - 15 = 0$

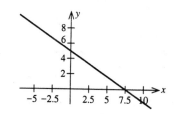

**59.** $y + 5 = 0$

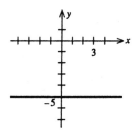

**60.** $-2x - 8y + 24 = 0$

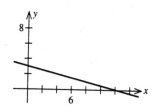

**61.** Since the line passes through the points $(a,0)$ and $(0,b)$, its slope is

$$m = \frac{b - 0}{0 - a} = -\frac{b}{a}.$$

Then, using the point-slope form of an equation of a line with the point $(a,0)$ we have

$$y - 0 = -\frac{b}{a}(x - a)$$

$$y = -\frac{b}{a}x + b$$

which may be written in the form

$$\frac{b}{a}x + y = b$$

Multiplying this last equation by $1/b$, we have

$$\frac{x}{a} + \frac{y}{b} = 1$$

62. Using the equation

$$\frac{x}{a} + \frac{y}{b} = 1$$

with $a = 3$ and $b = 4$, we have

$$\frac{x}{3} + \frac{y}{4} = 1.$$

Then $\qquad 4x + 3y = 12$

$$3y = 12 - 4x$$

and $\qquad y = -\frac{4}{3}x + 4.$

63. Using the equation

$$\frac{x}{a} + \frac{y}{b} = 1$$

with $a = -2$ and $b = -4$, we have

$$-\frac{x}{2} - \frac{y}{4} = 1.$$

Then $\qquad -4x - 2y = 8$

$$2y = -8 - 4x$$

and $\qquad y = -2x - 4.$

64. Using the equation

$$\frac{x}{a} + \frac{y}{b} = 1$$

with $a = -1/2$ and $b = 3/4$, we have

$$\frac{x}{-\frac{1}{2}} + \frac{y}{\frac{3}{4}} = 1.$$

$$\tfrac{3}{4}x - \tfrac{1}{2}y = \left(-\tfrac{1}{2}\right)\left(\tfrac{3}{4}\right)$$

$$-\tfrac{1}{2}y = -\tfrac{3}{4}x - \tfrac{3}{8}$$

$$y = 2\left(\tfrac{3}{4}x + \tfrac{3}{8}\right)$$

$$= \tfrac{3}{2}x + \tfrac{3}{4}.$$

65.  Using the equation

$$\frac{x}{a} + \frac{y}{b} = 1$$

with $a = 4$ and $b = -1/2$, we have

$$\frac{x}{4} + \frac{y}{-\tfrac{1}{2}} = 1.$$

$$-\tfrac{1}{4}x + 2y = -1$$

$$2y = \tfrac{1}{4}x - 1$$

$$y = \tfrac{1}{8}x - \tfrac{1}{2}.$$

66.  The slope of the line passing through A and B is

$$m = \frac{-2 - 7}{2 - (-1)} = -\frac{9}{3} = -3,$$

and the slope of the line passing through B and C is

$$m = \frac{-9 - (-2)}{5 - 2} = -\frac{7}{3}.$$

Since the slopes are not equal, the points do not lie on the same line.

67.  The slope of the line passing through A and B

$$m = \frac{7 - 1}{1 - (-2)} = \frac{6}{3} = 2,$$

and the slope of the line passing through B and C is

$$m = \frac{13 - 7}{4 - 1} = \frac{6}{3} = 2.$$

Since the slopes are equal, the points lie on the same line.

68. a. $y = 0.0765x$.

 b. \$0.0765

 c. $0.0765(35,000) = 2677.50$, or \$2677.50.

69. a. $y = 0.55x$

 b. Solving the equation

   $$1100 = 0.55x$$

   for x, we have

   $$x = \frac{1100}{0.55} = 2000$$

70. a. Substituting $L = 80$ into the given equation, we have

   $$W = 3.51(80) - 192$$

   $$= 280.8 - 192$$

   $$= 88.8, \qquad \text{or 88.8 British tons.}$$

 b.

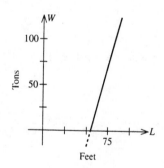

71. a. - b.

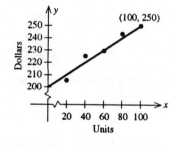

c. Using the points (0,200) and (100,250), we see that the slope of the required line is

$$m = \frac{250 - 200}{100} = \frac{1}{2}.$$

Therefore, the required equation is

$$y - 200 = \frac{1}{2}x$$

or

$$y = \frac{1}{2}x + 200.$$

d. The approximate cost for producing 54 units of the commodity is

$$\frac{1}{2}(54) + 200,$$

or $227.

72.  a. – b.

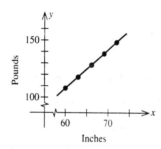

Inches

c. Using the points (60,108) and (72,152), we see that the slope of the required line is

$$m = \frac{152 - 108}{72 - 60} = \frac{44}{12} = \frac{11}{3}.$$

Therefore,

$$y - 108 = \frac{11}{3}(x - 60)$$

$$y = \frac{11}{3}x - \frac{11}{3}(60) + 108$$

$$= \frac{11}{3}x - 220 + 108$$

$$= \frac{11}{3}x - 112.$$

d. Using the equation of part (c), we find
$$y = \frac{11}{3}(65) - 112$$

$$\approx 126.33, \text{ or } 126\frac{1}{3} \text{ pounds.}$$

73. a. – b.

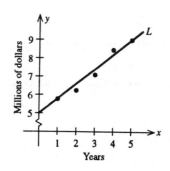

c. The slope of L is
$$m = \frac{9.0 - 5.8}{5 - 1} = \frac{3.2}{4} = 0.8$$

Using the point-slope form of an equation of a line, we have
$$y - 5.8 = 0.8(x - 1) = 0.8x - 0.8,$$

or
$$y = 0.8x + 5.$$

d. Using the equation of part (c) with x = 9, we have
$$y = 0.8(9) + 5 = 12.2, \qquad \text{or } \$12.2 \text{ million.}$$

74. Yes. A straight line with slope zero (m = 0) is a horizontal line, whereas a straight line whose slope doe not exist is a vertical line (m cannot be computed).

75. a. We obtain a family of parallel lines each having slope m.
b. We obtain a family of straight lines all of which pass through the point (0,b).

76. Writing each equation in the slope-intercept form, we have

$$y = -\frac{a_1}{b_1}x - \frac{c_1}{b_1} \ (b_1 \neq 0) \text{ and } y = -\frac{a_2}{b_2}x - \frac{c_2}{b_2} \ (b_2 \neq 0).$$

Since two lines are parallel if and only if their slopes are equal, we see that the lines are parallel if and only if

$$-\frac{a_1}{b_1} = -\frac{a_2}{b_2}$$

or $a_1b_2 - b_1a_2 = 0$.

77. The slope of $L_1$ is $m_1 = \dfrac{b - 0}{1 - 0} = b$. The slope of $L_2$ is $m_2 = \dfrac{c - 0}{1 - 0} = c$.

Applying the Pythagorean theorem to $\triangle OAC$ and $\triangle OCB$ gives

$$(OA)^2 = 1^2 + b^2 \quad \text{and} \quad (OB)^2 = 1^2 + c^2.$$

Adding these equations and applying the Pythagorean theorem to $\triangle OBA$ gives

$$(AB)^2 = (OA)^2 + (OB)^2 = 1^2 + b^2 + 1^2 + c^2 = 2 + b^2 + c^2.$$

Also $(AB)^2 = (b - c)^2$. Therefore,

$$(b - c)^2 = 2 + b^2 + c^2$$

$$b^2 - 2bc + c^2 = 2 + b^2 + c^2$$

$$-2bc = 2, \quad 1 = -bc.$$

Next, $\qquad m_1m_2 = b \cdot c = bc = -1,$

as was to be shown.

## USING TECHNOLOGY EXERCISES 1.2, page 29

1.

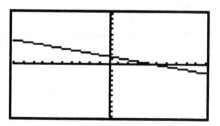

2.

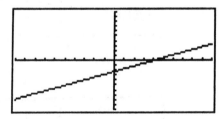

3.

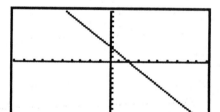

4.

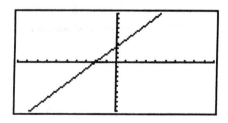

**5.**

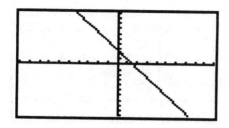

**6.**

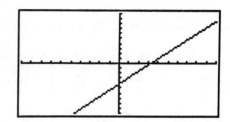

**7.  a.**

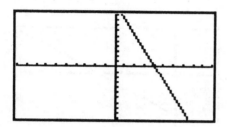

**b.**

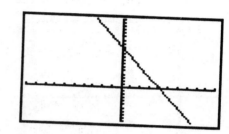

**8.  a.**

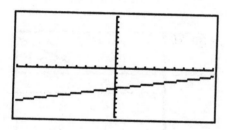

**b.**

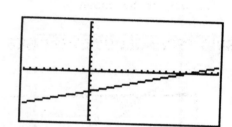

**9.  a.**

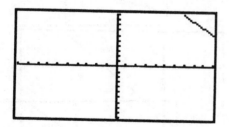

**b.**

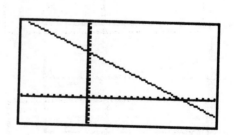

10. a.

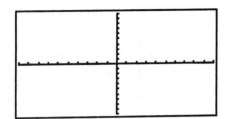

b.

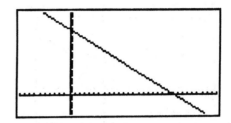

11.

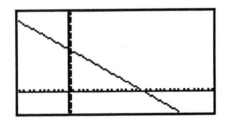

12.

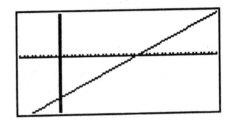

13.

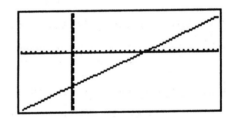

14.

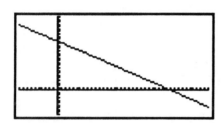

15.

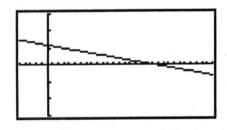

16.

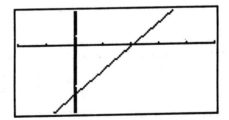

17.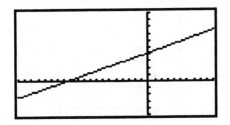

18.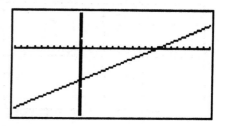

## EXERCISES 1.3, page 38

1. Yes. Solving for y in terms of x, we find
$$3y = -2x + 6, \quad \text{or} \quad y = -\frac{2}{3}x + 2.$$

2. Yes. Solving for y in terms of x, we find
$$4y = 2x + 7, \quad \text{or} \quad y = \frac{1}{2}x + \frac{7}{4}$$

3. Yes. Solving for y in terms of x, we find
$$2y = x + 4, \quad \text{or } y = \frac{1}{2}x + 2.$$

4. Yes. Solving for y in terms of x, we have
$$3y = 2x - 8, \quad \text{or} \quad y = \frac{2}{3}x - \frac{8}{3}.$$

5. Yes. Solving for y in terms of x, we have
$$4y = 2x + 9, \quad \text{or} \quad y = \frac{1}{2}x + \frac{9}{4}.$$

6. Yes. Solving for y in terms of x, we find
$$6y = 3x + 7, \quad \text{or} \quad \frac{1}{2}x + \frac{7}{6}.$$

7. y is not a linear function of x because of the quadratic term $2x^2$.

8. y is not a linear function of x because of the nonlinear term $3\sqrt{x}$.

9. y is not a linear function of x because of the term $-3y^2$.

10. y is not a linear function of x because of the term $\sqrt{y}$.

*1  Straight Lines and Linear Functions*

11. a. $C(x) = 8x + 40,000$, where x is the number of units produced.

 b. $R(x) = 12x$, where x is the number of units sold.

 c. $P(x) = R(x) - C(x) = 12x - (8x + 40,000) = 4x - 40,000$.

 d. $P(8,000) = 4(8,000) - 40,000 = -8,000$, or a loss of $8,000.

 $P(12,000) = 4(12,000) - 40,000 = 8,000$ or a profit of $8,000.

12. a. $C(x) = 14x + 100,000$

 b. $R(x) = 20x$

 c. $P(x) = R(x) - C(x) = 20x - (14x + 100,000) = 6x - 100,000$

 d. $P(12,000) = 6(12,000) - 100,000 = -28,000$,

  or a loss of $28,000.

  $P(20,000) = 6(20,000) - 100,000 = 20,000$,

  or a profit of $20,000.

13. $f(0) = 2$ gives $m(0) + b = 2$, or $b = 2$.

 So, $f(x) = mx + 2$.

 Next, $f(3) = -1$ gives $m(3) + 2 = -1$, or $m = -1$.

14. The fact that the straight line represented by $f(x) = mx + b$ has slope $-1$ tells us that $m = -1$ and so $f(x) = -x + b$. Next, the condition $f(2) = 4$ then gives $f(2) = -1(2) + b = 4$, or $b = 6$.

15. Let V be the book value of the office building after 1995. Since $V = 1,000,000$ when $t = 0$, the line passes through $(0, 1,000,000)$. Similarly, when $t = 50$, $V = 0$, so the line passes through $(50, 0)$. Then the slope of the line is given by

 $$m = \frac{0 - 1,000,000}{50 - 0} = -20,000.$$

 Using the point-slope form of the equation of a line with the point $(0, 1,000,000)$, we have

 $$V - 1,000,000 = -20,000(t - 0),$$

 or $\qquad V = -20,000t + 1,000,000.$

 In 2000, $t = 5$ and

 $$V = -20,000(5) + 1,000,000$$

 $$= 900,000, \qquad \text{or } \$900,000.$$

In 2005, t = 10 and

$$V = -20{,}000(10) + 1{,}000{,}000 = 800{,}000, \quad \text{or } \$800{,}000.$$

16. Let V be the book value of the automobile after 10 years. Since V = 14,000 when t = 0, and V = 0 when t = 5, the slope of the line L is

$$m = \frac{0 - 14{,}000}{5 - 0} = -2800.$$

Using the point-slope form of an equation of a line with the point (0, 5), we have

$$V - 0 = -2800(t - 5),$$

or $\qquad V = -2800t + 14{,}000.$

When t = 3

$$V = -2800(3) + 14{,}000$$

$$= 5600.$$

Therefore, the book value of the automobile at the end of three years will be $5600.

17. The consumption function is given by

$$C(x) = 0.75x + 6.$$

When x = 0, we have

$$C(0) = 0.75(0) + 6 = 6, \text{ or } \$6 \text{ billion dollars.}$$

When x = 50,

$$C(50) = 0.75(50) + 6 = 43.5, \quad \text{or } \$43.5 \text{ billion dollars.}$$

When x = 100,

$$C(100) = 0.75(100) + 6 = 81, \quad \text{or } \$81 \text{ billion dollars.}$$

18. a. T(x) = 0.06x.

b. T(200) = 0.06(200) = 12, $\qquad$ or $12.

c. T(5.60) = 0.06(5.60) = 0.34, $\qquad$ or $0.34.

19. a. y = 1.053x, where x is the monthly benefit before adjustment, and y is the adjusted monthly benefit.

b. His adjusted monthly benefit will be

$$(1.053)(620) = 652.86, \quad \text{or } \$652.86.$$

20.  a. $C(x) = 8x + 48{,}000$

   b. $R(x) = 14x$

   c. $P(x) = R(x) - C(x) = 14x - (8x + 48{,}000) = 6x - 48{,}000$

   d. $P(4{,}000) = 6(4{,}000) - 48{,}000 = -24{,}000$, or a loss of $\$24{,}000$.

   $P(6{,}000) = 6(6{,}000) - 48{,}000 = -12{,}000$, or a loss of $\$12{,}000$.

   $P(10{,}000) = 6(10{,}000) - 48{,}000 = 12{,}000$, or a profit of $\$12{,}000$.

21.  Let the number of tapes produced and sold be x.  Then

   $$C(x) = 12{,}100 + 0.60x$$

   $$R(x) = 1.15x$$

   and   $P(x) = R(x) - C(x) = 1.15x - (12{,}100 + 0.60x)$

   $$= 0.55x - 12{,}100.$$

22.  a. Let V denote the book value of the machine after t years. Since $V = 250{,}000$ when $t = 0$ and $V = 10{,}000$ when $t = 10$, the line passes through the points $(0, 250{,}000)$ and $(10, 10{,}000)$. Then the slope of the line through these points is given by

   $$m = \frac{10{,}000 - 250{,}000}{10 - 0} = \frac{-240{,}000}{10} = -24{,}000.$$

   Then, using the point-slope form of an equation of a line with the point $(10, 10{,}000)$, we have

   $$V - 10{,}000 = -24{,}000(t - 10)$$

   or   $V = -24{,}000t + 250{,}000.$

   b.

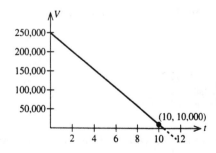

(10, 10,000)

c.   In 1994 t = 4 and

$$V = -24{,}000(4) + 250{,}000$$

$$= 154{,}000, \quad \text{or } \$154{,}000.$$

d. The rate of depreciation is given by −m or \$24,000/yr.

23.  Let the value of the minicomputer after t years be V. When t = 0, V = 60,000 and when t = 4, V = 12,000.

a. Since

$$m = \frac{12{,}000 - 60{,}000}{4} = -\frac{48{,}000}{4} = -12{,}000,$$

the rate of depreciation (−m) is \$12,000.

b. Using the point-slope form of the equation of a line with the point (4, 12,000), we have

$$V - 12{,}000 = -12{,}000(t - 4)$$

or

$$V = -12{,}000t + 60{,}000.$$

c.

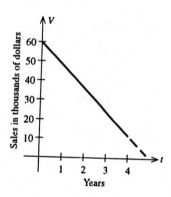

d.     When t = 3,

$$V = -12{,}000(3) + 60{,}000 = 24{,}000, \quad \text{or } \$24{,}000.$$

24.  The slope of the line passing through the points (0,C) and (N,S) is

$$m = \frac{S - C}{N - 0} = \frac{S - C}{N} = -\frac{C - S}{N}.$$

Using the point-slope form of an equation of a line with the point (0,C), we have

$$V - 0 = -\frac{C - S}{N} t + C$$

or

$$V = C - \frac{C - S}{N} t$$

25. The formula given in Exercise 24 is

$$V = C - \frac{C - S}{N} t.$$

Then, when $C = 1{,}000{,}000$, $N = 50$, and $S = 0$, we have

$$V = 1{,}000{,}000 - \frac{1{,}000{,}000 - 0}{50} t \text{ ,}$$

or $\qquad V = 1{,}000{,}000 - 20{,}000t.$

In 2000, $t = 5$ and

$$V = 1{,}000{,}000 - 20{,}000(5) = 900{,}000, \quad \text{or } \$900{,}000.$$

In 2005, $t = 10$ and

$$V = 1{,}000{,}000 - 20{,}000(10) = 800{,}000 \quad \text{or } \$800{,}000.$$

26. The formula given in Exercise 24 is

$$V = C - \frac{C - S}{N} t.$$

Then, when $C = 14{,}000$, $N = 5$, and $S = 0$, we have

$$V = 14{,}000 - \frac{14{,}000 - 0}{5} t \text{ ,}$$

$$= 14{,}000 - 2800 t.$$

When $t = 3$,

$$V = 14{,}000 - 2800(3) = 5600, \text{ or } \$5600.$$

27. a. $D(S) = \frac{Sa}{1.7}$ .

   If we think of D as having the form $D(S) = mS + b$, then $m = \frac{a}{1.7}$, $b = 0$, and D is a linear function of S.

   b. $D(0.4) = \frac{500(0.4)}{1.7} = 117.647,$ or approximately 117.6 mg.

28. a. $D(t) = (\frac{t + 1}{24})a = \frac{a}{24}t + \frac{a}{24}.$

   If we think of D as having the form $D(t) = mt + b$, then $m = \frac{a}{24}$, $b = \frac{a}{24}$, and D is a linear function of t.

   b. If $a = 500$ and $t = 4$,

$$D(4) = \left(\frac{4+1}{24}\right)(500) = 104.167, \quad \text{or approximately } 104.2 \text{ mg.}$$

29. a. Since the relationship is linear, we can write $F = mC + b$, where $m$ and $b$ are constants. Using the condition $C = 0$ when $F = 32$, we have $32 = b$, and so $F = mC + 32$. Next, using the condition $C = 100$ when $F = 212$, we have

$$212 = 100m + 32 \quad \text{or } m = \frac{9}{5}. \quad \text{Therefore, } F = \frac{9}{5}C + 32.$$

b. From (a), we see $F = \frac{9}{5}C + 32$. Next, when $C = 20$,

$$F = \frac{9}{5}(20) + 32 = 68$$

and so the temperature equivalent to 20°C is 68°F.

c. Solving for $C$ in terms of $F$, we find

$$\frac{9}{5}C = F - 32, \quad \text{or } C = \frac{5}{9}F - \frac{160}{9}.$$

When $F = 70$, $C = \frac{5}{9}(70) - \frac{160}{9} = \frac{190}{9}$, or approximately 21.1°C.

30. a. Since the relationship between $T$ and $N$ is linear, we can write

$$N = mT + b,$$

where $m$ and $b$ are constants. If $T = 70$, then $N = 120$ and this gives

$$120 = 70m + b. \tag{1}$$

If $T = 80$, then $N = 160$ and this gives

$$160 = 80m + b. \tag{2}$$

Subtracting Equation (1) from Equation (2) gives $40 = 10m$, or $m = 4$. Substituting this value of $m$ into either equation gives $b = -160$. Therefore,

$$N = 4T - 160.$$

b. From part (a), $N = 4T - 160$. If $T = 102$, we find

$$N = 4(102) - 160 = 248, \quad \text{or 248 chirps per minute.}$$

31. The slope of $L_2$ is greater than that of $L_1$. This tells us that if the manufacturer lowers the unit price for each model clock radio by the same amount, the quantity demanded of model B radios will be greater than that of the model A radios.

32. The slope of $L_2$ is greater than that of $L_1$. This tells us that if the unit price for each model clock radio is raised by the same amount, the manufacturer will make more model B than model A radios available in the market.

33. a. Setting $x = 0$, gives $3p = 18$, or $p = 6$. Next, setting $p = 0$, gives $2x = 18$, or $x = 9$.

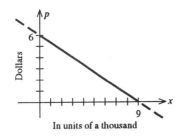

In units of a thousand

b.   When p = 4,

$$2x + 3(4) - 18 = 0$$

$$2x = 18 - 12 = 6$$

and x = 3. Therefore, the quantity demanded when p = 4 is 3000. (Remember x is given in units of a thousand.)

34.   a. Setting x = 0, gives p = 16.   Next, setting p = 0 gives x = 20.

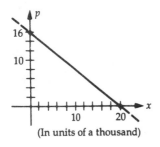

(In units of a thousand)

b.       $$5(1) + 4x - 80 = 0$$

$$4x = 80 - 50$$

$$x = 7\frac{1}{2},$$

or 7500 units (x represents the quantity demanded in units of 1000).

35.   a. When x = 0, p = 60 and when p = 0, -3x = -60, or x = 20.

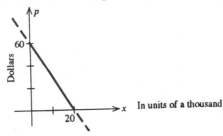

In units of a thousand

b. When p = 30,

$$30 = -3x + 60$$

$$3x = 30$$

and    x = 10.

Therefore, the quantity demanded when p = 30 is 10,000 units.

36.    a. When x = 0, p = 120, and when p = 0, −0.4x = −120, or x = 300.

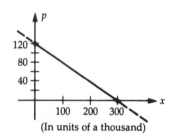

(In units of a thousand)

b. When p = 80,

$$80 = -0.4x + 120,$$

$$0.4x = 40,$$

or    x = 100.

Therefore, the quantity demanded when p = 80 is 100,000.

37.    When x = 1000, p = 55, and when x = 600, p = 85. Therefore, the graph of the linear demand equation is the straight line passing through the points (1000, 55) and (600, 85). The slope of the line is

$$\frac{85 - 55}{600 - 1000} = -\frac{3}{40}.$$

Using the point (1000, 55) and the slope just found, we find that the required equation is

$$p - 55 = -\frac{3}{40}(x - 1000)$$

$$p = -\frac{3}{40}x + 130.$$

When x = 0, p = 130 which means that there will be no demand above $130.  When p = 0, x = 1733, which means that 1733 units is the maximum quantity demanded.

38. When $x = 200$, $p = 90$, and when $x = 1200$, $p = 40$. Since the demand equation is linear, the slope of the line passing through $(200,90)$ and $(1200,40)$ is

$$m = \frac{40 - 90}{1200 - 200} = -\frac{50}{1000} = -0.05.$$

Using the point-slope form of the equation of a line with the point $(200, 90)$, we have

$$p - 90 = -0.05(x - 200)$$

or
$$p = -0.05x + 100.$$

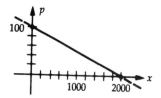

39. Since the demand equation is linear, we know that the line passes through the points $(1000,9)$ and $(6000,4)$. Therefore, the slope of the line is given by

$$m = \frac{4 - 9}{6000 - 1000} = -\frac{5}{5000} = -0.001.$$

Since the equation of the line has the form $p = ax + b$,

$$9 = -0.001(1000) + b$$

or
$$b = 10.$$

Therefore, the equation of the line is

$$p = -0.001x + 10.$$

If $p = 7.50$,

$$7.50 = -0.001x + 10$$

$$0.001x = 2.50$$

or
$$x = 2500.$$

So, the quantity demanded when the unit price is $7.50, is 2500 units.

40. When p = 0, x = 2000 and when x = 0, p = 50.

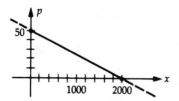

The highest price anyone would pay for the watch is $50 (x = 0).

41. a. Setting x = 0, we obtain

$$3(0) - 4p + 24 = 0$$

$$-4p = -24$$

or $$p = 6.$$

Setting p = 0, we obtain

$$3x - 4(0) + 24 = 0$$

$$3x = -8$$

or $$x = -8/3.$$

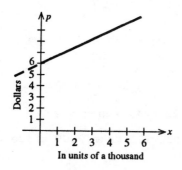

b. When p = 8

$$3x - 4(8) + 24 = 0$$

$$3x = 32 - 24 = 8$$

$$x = 8/3.$$

Therefore, 2667 units of the commodity would be supplied at a unit price of $8. (Here again x is measured in units of thousands.)

42.  a. When p = 0, x = −24, and when x = 0, p = 18.

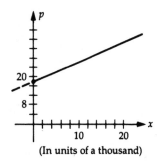

(In units of a thousand)

b.  $\frac{1}{2}x - \frac{2}{3}(24) + 12 = 0$

$$\frac{1}{2}x = 16 - 12 = 4$$

and  $x = 8,$  or 8000 units.

43.  a. When x = 0, p = 10, and when p = 0, x = −5.

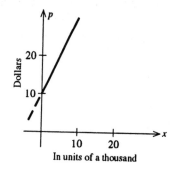

In units of a thousand

b.  p = 2x + 10, 14 = 2x + 10, 2x = 4, and x = 2.

Therefore, when p = 14, the supplier will make 2000 units of the commodity available.

**44.**  **a.** When x = 0, p = 20 and when p = 0, $\frac{1}{2}x$ = -10, or x = -20.

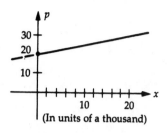

30
20
10

10     20
(In units of a thousand)

**b.** When p = 28,

$$28 = \frac{1}{2}x + 20,$$

$$\frac{1}{2}x = 8,$$

or                    x = 16.

Therefore, 16,000 units will be supplied at a unit price of $28.

**45.**  When x = 10,000, p = 45 and when x = 20,000, p = 50.  Therefore, the slope of the line passing (10,000, 45) and (20,000, 50) is

$$m = \frac{50 - 45}{20,000 - 10,000} = \frac{5}{10,000} = .0005.$$

Using the point-slope form of an equation of a line with the point (10,000, 45), we have

$$p - 45 = .0005(x - 10,000)$$

$$p = .0005x - 5 + 45$$

or                    $p = .0005x + 40.$

If p = 70,

$$70 = .0005x + 40$$

$$.0005x = 30$$

or                    $x = \frac{30}{.0005} = 60,000.$

**46.**  When x = 2000, p = 330; and when x = 6000, p = 390. Therefore, the graph of the linear equation passes through (2000, 330) and (6000, 390). The slope of the line is

$$\frac{390 - 330}{6000 - 2000} = \frac{3}{200}.$$

Using the point-slope form of an equation of a line with the point (2000, 330), we obtain

$$p - 330 = \frac{3}{200}(x - 2000),$$

or

$$p = \frac{3}{200}x + 300,$$

as the required supply equation.

When p = 450, we have

$$450 = \frac{3}{200}x + 300$$

$$\frac{3}{200}x = 150,$$

or x = 10,000, and the number of refrigerators marketed at this price is 10,000. When x = 0, p = 300, and the lowest price at which a refrigerator will be marketed is $300.

## USING TECHNOLOGY EXERCISES 1.3, page 43

1. 2.2875         2. 3.0125           3. 2.880952381           4. 0.7875

5. 7.2851648352         6. −26.82928836           7. 2.4680851064

8. 1.24375

## EXERCISES 1.4, page 52

1.   We solve the system

$$y = 3x + 4$$
$$y = -2x + 14.$$

Substituting the first equation into the second yields

$$3x + 4 = -2x + 14$$
$$5x = 10,$$

and x = 2. Substituting this value of x into the first equation yields

$$y = 3(2) + 4,$$

or y = 10. Thus, the point of intersection is (2,10).

2. We solve the system

$$y = -4x - 7$$

$$-y = 5x + 10.$$

Substituting the first equation into the second yields

$$-(-4x - 7) = 5x + 10$$

$$4x + 7 = 5x + 10$$

$$x = -3.$$

Substituting this value of x into the first equation, we obtain

$$y = -4(-3) - 7$$

$$= 12 - 7 = 5.$$

Therefore, the point of intersection is $(-3, 5)$.

3. We solve the system

$$2x - 3y = 6$$

$$3x + 6y = 16.$$

Solving the first equation for y, we obtain

$$3y = 2x - 6$$

$$y = \frac{2}{3}x - 2.$$

Substituting this value of y into the second equation, we obtain

$$3x + 6(\frac{2}{3}x - 2) = 16$$

$$3x + 4x - 12 = 16$$

$$7x = 28$$

and

$$x = 4.$$

Then

$$y = \frac{2}{3}(4) - 2 = \frac{2}{3}.$$

Therefore, the point of intersection is $(4, \frac{2}{3})$.

4. We solve the system

$$2x + 4y = 11$$

$$-5x + 3y = 5$$

Solving the first equation for x, we find

$$x = -2y + \frac{11}{2}.$$

Substituting this value into the second equation of the system, we have

$$-5\left(-2y + \frac{11}{2}\right) + 3y = 5$$

$$10y - \frac{55}{2} + 3y = 5$$

$$20y - 55 + 6y = 10$$

$$26y = 65,$$

or $y = 5/2$.

Substituting this value of y into the first equation, we have

$$2x + 4\left(\frac{5}{2}\right) = 11$$

$$2x = 1$$

or $x = 1/2$. Thus, the point of intersection is $\left(\frac{1}{2}, \frac{5}{2}\right)$.

5.  We solve the system

$$y = \frac{1}{4}x - 5$$

$$2x - \frac{3}{2}y = 1$$

Substituting the value of y given in the first equation into the second equation, we obtain

$$2x - \frac{3}{2}\left(\frac{1}{4}x - 5\right) = 1$$

$$2x - \frac{3}{8}x + \frac{15}{2} = 2$$

$$16x - 3x + 60 = 8$$

$$13x = -52,$$

or $x = -4$. Substituting this value of x in the first equation, we have

$$y = \frac{1}{4}(-4) - 5$$

$$= -1 - 5,$$

or $y = -6$. Therefore, the point of intersection is $(-4, -6)$.

6.  We solve the system

$$y = \frac{2}{3}x - 4$$

$$x + 3y + 3 = 0$$

Substituting the first equation into the second equation, we obtain

$$x + 3\left(\frac{2}{3}x - 4\right) + 3 = 0$$

$$x + 2x - 12 + 3 = 0$$

$$3x = 9$$

or

$$x = 3.$$

Substituting this value of $x$ in the first equation, we have

$$y = \frac{2}{3}(3) - 4 = -2.$$

Therefore, the point of intersection is $(3, -2)$.

7.  We solve the equation $R(x) = C(x)$, or $15x = 5x + 10{,}000$, obtaining

$$10x = 10{,}000,$$

or $x = 1000$. Substituting this value of $x$ into the equation $R(x) = 15x$, we find $R(1000) = 15{,}000$. Therefore, the breakeven point is $(1000, 15{,}000)$.

8.  We solve the equation $R(x) = C(x)$, or $21x = 15x + 12{,}000$, obtaining

$$6x = 12{,}000,$$

or $x = 2000$. Substituting this value of $x$ into the equation $R(x) = 21x$, we find $R(2000) = 42{,}000$. Therefore, the breakeven point is $(2000, 42{,}000)$.

9.  We solve the equation $R(x) = C(x)$, or $0.4x = 0.2x + 120$, obtaining

$$0.2x = 120,$$

or $x = 600$. Substituting this value of $x$ into the equation $R(x) = 0.4x$, we find $R(600) = 240$. Therefore, the breakeven point is $(600, 240)$.

10. We solve the equation $R(x) = C(x)$ or $270x = 150x + 20{,}000$, obtaining

$$120x = 20{,}000 \quad \text{or} \quad x = \frac{500}{3} \approx 167.$$

Substituting this value of x into the equation R(x) = 270x, we find

$$R(167) = 45,090.$$

Therefore, the breakeven point is (167, 45,090).

11. a.

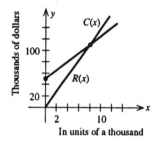

b. We solve the equation R(x) = C(x) or 14x = 8x + 48,000 , obtaining

$$6x = 48,000$$

or x = 8000. Substituting this value of x into the equation R(x) = 14x, we find R(8000) = 14(8000) = 112,000. Therefore, the breakeven point is (8000, 112,000).

c.

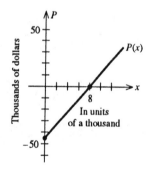

d.    P(x) = R(x) - C(x)

$$= 14x - 8x - 48,000$$

$$= 6x - 48,000.$$

The graph of the profit function crosses the x-axis when P(x) = 0, or

$$6x = 48,000$$

and x = 8000. This means that the revenue is equal to the cost when 8000 units are produced and consequently the company breaks even at this point.

12.   a. R(x) = 8x; C(x) = 25,000 + 3x

   P(x) = R(x) - C(x) = 5x - 25,000.


Next, the breakeven point occurs when P(x) = 0, that is,

   5x - 25,000 = 0

or                    x = 5000.

Then R(5000) = 40,000, so the breakeven point is (5000, 40,000).

b. If the division realizes a 15 percent profit over the cost of making the diaries, then

            P(x) = .15 C(x)

or      5x - 25,000 = .15(25,000 + 3x)

               4.55x = 28,750

and                 x = 6318.68, or approximately 6319 diaries.


13.   Let x denote the number of units sold. Then, the revenue function R is given by

      R(x) = 9x.

Since the variable cost is 40 percent of the selling price, and the monthly fixed costs are $50,000, the cost function C is given by

      C(x) = 0.4(9x) + 50,000

           = 3.6x + 50,000.

To find the breakeven point, we set R(x) = C(x), obtaining

         9x = 3.6x + 50,000

       5.4x = 50,000

         x ≈ 9259, or 9259 units.

Substituting this value of x into the equation R(x) = 9x gives

      R(9259) = 9(9259)

             = 83,331.

Thus, for a breakeven operation, the firm should manufacture 9259 bicycle pumps resulting in a breakeven revenue of $83,331.

14. a. The cost function associated with renting a truck from the Ace Truck Leasing Company is

$$C_1(x) = 30 + 0.15x.$$

The cost function associated with renting a truck from the Acme Truck Leasing Company is

$$C_2(x) = 25 + 0.20x.$$

b.

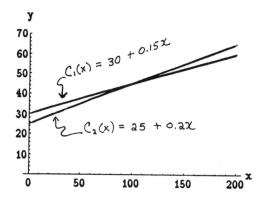

c. The cost of renting a truck from the Ace Truck Leasing Company for one day and driving 70 miles is

$$C_1(70) = 30 + 0.15(70)$$

$$= 40.50, \text{ or } \$40.50.$$

The cost of renting a truck from the Acme Truck Leasing Company for one day and driving it 70 miles is

$$C_2(70) = 25 + 0.20(70)$$

$$= 39, \text{ or } \$39.$$

Thus, the customer should rent the car from Acme Truck Leasing Company. This answer may also be obtained by inspecting the graph of the two functions and noting that the graph of $C_2(x)$ lies below that of $C_1(x)$ for $x \le 70$.

15. a. The cost function associated with using machine I is given by

$$C_1(x) = 18,000 + 15x.$$

The cost function associated with using machine II is given by

$$C_2(x) = 15,000 + 20x.$$

**b.**

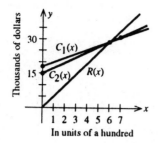

c. Comparing the cost of producing 450 units on each machine, we find

$$C_1(450) = 18,000 + 15(450)$$

$$= 24,750$$

or $24,750 on machine I, and

$$C_2(450) = 15,000 + 20(450)$$

$$= 24,000$$

or $24,000 on machine II. Therefore, machine II should be used in this case.

Next, comparing the costs of producing 550 units on each machine, we find

$$C_1(550) = 18,000 + 15(550)$$

$$= 26,250$$

or $26,250 on machine I, and

$$C_2(550) = 15,000 + 20(550)$$

$$= 26,000$$

on machine II. Therefore, machine II should be used in this instance. Once again, we compare the cost of producing 650 units on each machine and find that

$$C_1(650) = 18,000 + 15(650)$$

$$= 27,750$$

or $27,750 on machine I and

$$C_2(650) = 15,000 + 20(650)$$

$$= 28,000,$$

or \$28,000 on machine II. Therefore, machine I should be used in this case.

d. We use the equation $P(x) = R(x) - C(x)$ and find

$$P(450) = 50(450) - 24,000 = -1500,$$

or a loss of \$1500 when machine I is used to produce 450 units. Similarly,

$$P(550) = 50(550) - 26,000 = 1500,$$

or a profit of \$1500 when machine II is used to produce 550 units.

Finally,

$$P(650) = 50(650) - 27,750 = 4750,$$

or a profit of \$4750 when machine I is used to produce 650 units.

16. First, we find the point of intersection of the two straight lines. (This will give the time when the sales of both companies are the same). Substituting the first equation into the second gives

$$2.3 + 0.4t = 1.2 + 0.6t$$

$$1.1 = 0.2t$$

and

$$t = \frac{1.1}{0.2} = 5\frac{1}{2}.$$

From the observation that the sales of Cambridge Drug Store is increasing at a faster rate than that of the Crimson Drug Store (its trend line has the greater slope), we conclude that the sales of the Cambridge Drug Store will surpass the annual sales of the Crimson Drug Store in $5\frac{1}{2}$ years.

17. We solve the system

$$4x + 3p = 59$$

$$5x - 6p = -14.$$

Solving the first equation for $p$, we find

$$p = -\frac{4}{3}x + \frac{59}{3}.$$

Substituting this value of $p$ into the second equation, we have

$$5x - 6(-\frac{4}{3}x + \frac{59}{3}) = -14$$

$$5x + 8x - 118 = -14$$

$$13x = 104$$

$$x = 8.$$

Substituting this value of x into the equation

$$p = -\frac{4}{3}x + \frac{59}{3}$$

we have

$$p = -\frac{4}{3}(8) + \frac{59}{3} = \frac{27}{3} = 9.$$

Thus, the equilibrium quantity is 8000 units and the equilibrium price is $9.

18.  We solve the system

$$2x + 7p = 56$$

$$3x - 11p = -45$$

Solving the first equation for x, we obtain

$$2x = -7p + 56$$

or $\qquad x = -\frac{7}{2}p + 28.$

Substituting this value of x into the second equation, we obtain

$$3(-\frac{7}{2}p + 28) - 11p = -45$$

$$-\frac{21}{2}p + 84 - 11p = -45$$

$$-43p = -258$$

or $\qquad\qquad\qquad p = 6.$

Then

$$x = -\frac{7}{2}(6) + 28$$

$$= -21 + 28 = 7.$$

Therefore, the equilibrium quantity is 7000 units and the equilibrium price is $6.

19.  We solve the system

$$p = -2x + 22$$

$$p = 3x + 12.$$

Substituting the first equation into the second, we find

$$-2x + 22 = 3x + 12$$

$$5x = 10$$

and

$$x = 2.$$

Substituting this value of x into the first equation, we obtain

$$p = -2(2) + 22$$

$$= 18.$$

Thus, the equilibrium quantity is 2000 units and the equilibrium price is $18.

20. We solve the system

$$p = -0.3x + 6$$

$$p = 0.15x + 1.5.$$

Equating the two equations, we have

$$-0.3x + 6 = 0.15x + 1.5$$

$$-.45x = -4.5$$

$$x = 10.$$

Substituting this value of x into the fist equation gives

$$p = -0.3(10) + 6$$

and p = 3. Thus, the equilibrium quantity is 10,000 units, and the equilibrium price is $3.

21. Let x denote the number of VCR's produced per week, and p denote the price of each VCR.

a. The slope of the demand curve is given by

$$\frac{\Delta p}{\Delta x} = -\frac{20}{250} = -\frac{2}{25}.$$

Using the point-slope form of the equation of a line with the point (3000, 485), we have

$$p - 485 = -\frac{2}{25}(x - 3000)$$

$$p = -\frac{2}{25}x + 240 + 485$$

or $\qquad p = -0.08x + 725.$

b. From the given information, we know that the graph of the supply equation passes through the points (0, 300) and (2500, 525). Therefore, the slope of the supply curve is

$$m = \frac{525 - 300}{2500 - 0} = \frac{225}{2500} = 0.09.$$

Using the point-slope form of the equation of a line with the point (0,300), we find that

$$p - 300 = 0.09x$$

$$p = 0.09x + 300.$$

c. Equating the supply and demand equations, we have

$$-0.08x + 725 = 0.09x + 300$$

$$0.17x = 425$$

or $\qquad x = 2500.$

Then $\qquad p = -0.08(2500) + 725$

$$= 525.$$

We conclude that the equilibrium quantity is 2500 and the equilibrium price is $525.

22. We solve the system

$$x - 4p = 800$$

$$x - 20p = -1000.$$

Solving the first equation for x, we obtain

$$x = 4p + 800.$$

Substituting this value of x into the second equation, we obtain

$$4p + 800 - 20p = -1000$$

$$-16p = -1800$$

or $\qquad p = 112.50.$

Substituting this value of p into the first equation, we obtain

$$x - 4(112.50) = 800$$

or $\qquad x = 1250.$

Thus, the equilibrium quantity is 1250 and the equilibrium price is $112.50.

23. We solve the system

$$3x + p = 1500$$

$$2x - 3p = -1200.$$

Solving the first equation for p, we obtain

$$p = 1500 - 3x.$$

Substituting this value of p into the second equation, we obtain

$$2x - 3(1500 - 3x) = -1200$$

$$11x = 3300$$

or

$$x = 300.$$

Next,

$$p = 1500 - 3(300)$$

$$= 600.$$

Thus, the equilibrium quantity is 300 and the equilibrium price is $600.

24. Let x denote the number of espresso makers to be produced per month and let p denote the unit price of these espresso makers.

a. The slope of demand curve is given by

$$\frac{\Delta p}{\Delta x} = \frac{110 - 140}{1000 - 250} = -\frac{1}{25}.$$

Using the point-slope form of the equation of a line with the point (250, 140), we have

$$p - 140 = -\frac{1}{25}(x - 250)$$

$$p = -\frac{1}{25}x + 10 + 140$$

$$= -\frac{1}{25}x + 150.$$

b. The slope of the supply curve is given by

$$\frac{\Delta p}{\Delta x} = \frac{80 - 60}{2250 - 750} = \frac{20}{1500} = \frac{1}{75}.$$

Using the point-slope form of the equation of a line with the point (750, 60), we have

$$p - 60 = \frac{1}{75}(x - 750)$$

$$p = \frac{1}{75}x - 10 + 60$$

$$p = \frac{1}{75}x - 50.$$

c. Equating the demand equation and the supply equation, we have

$$-\frac{1}{25}x + 150 = \frac{1}{75}x + 50$$

$$-\frac{4}{75}x = -100$$

or
$$x = 1875.$$

Next,
$$p = \frac{1}{75}(1875) + 50$$

$$= 75.$$

Thus, the equilibrium quantity is 1875 espresso makers and the equilibrium price is $75.

25.  a. We solve the system of equations $p = cx + d$ and $p = ax + b$. Substituting the first into the second gives

$$cx + d = ax + b$$

$$(c - a)x = b - d$$

or
$$x = \frac{b - d}{c - a}.$$

Since $a < 0$ and $c > 0$, $c - a \neq 0$ and $x$ is well-defined. Substituting this value of $x$ into the second equation, we obtain

$$p = a\left(\frac{b - d}{c - a}\right) + b = \frac{ab - ad + bc - ab}{c - a} = \frac{bc - ad}{c - a}.$$

Therefore, the equilibrium quantity is $\frac{b - d}{c - a}$ and the equilibrium

price is $\frac{bc - ad}{c - a}$.

b. If $c$ is increased, the denominator in the expression for $x$ increases and so $x$ gets smaller. At the same time, the first term in the first equation for $p$ decreases and so $p$ gets larger. This analysis shows that if the unit price for producing the product is increased then the equilibrium quantity decreases while the equilibrium price increases.

c. If $b$ is decreased, the numerator of the expression for $x$ decreases while the denominator stays the same. Therefore $x$ decreases. The expression for $p$ also shows that $p$ decreases. This analysis shows that if the (theoretical) upper bound for the unit price of a commodity is lowered, then both the equilibrium quantity and the equilibrium price drops.

26.  The breakeven quantity is found by solving the equation

$$C(x) = R(x),$$

or $\quad\quad cx + F = sx$;

that is, $\quad\quad x = \dfrac{F}{s - c} \quad (s \neq c)$.

Substituting this value of x into $R(x) = sx$ gives the breakeven revenue as

$$R(x) = s\left(\dfrac{F}{s - c}\right) = \dfrac{sF}{s - c}.$$

Our analysis shows that for a breakeven operation, the breakeven quantity must be equal to the ratio of the fixed cost and the difference between the unit selling price and unit cost of production.

27. Solving the two equations simultaneously to find the point(s) of intersection of $L_1$ and $L_2$, we obtain

$$m_1x + b_1 = m_2x + b_2$$

$$(m_1 - m_2)x = b_2 - b_1 \quad\quad\quad\quad\quad\quad (1)$$

a. If $m_1 = m_2$ and $b_2 \neq b_1$, then there is no solution for (1) and in this case $L_1$ and $L_2$ do not intersect.

b. If $m_1 \neq m_2$, then Equation (1) can be solved (uniquely) for x and this shows that $L_1$ and $L_2$ intersect at precisely one point.

c. If $m_1 = m_2$ and $b_1 = b_2$, then (1) is satisfied for all values of x and this shows that $L_1$ and $L_2$ intersect at infinitely many points.

28. Rewrite the equations in the form

$$y = -\dfrac{a_1}{b_1}x + \dfrac{c_1}{b_1} \quad \text{and} \quad y = -\dfrac{a_2}{b_2} + \dfrac{c_2}{b_2}$$

and think of these equations as the equations of the lines $L_1$ and $L_2$, respectively. Using the results of Exercise 27, we see that the system

a. has no solution if and only if $-\dfrac{a_1}{b_1} = -\dfrac{a_2}{b_2}$, or $a_1b_2 - a_2b_1 = 0$

b. has a unique solution if and only if $a_1b_2 - a_2b_1 = 0$ and $\dfrac{c_1}{b_1} = \dfrac{c_2}{b_2}$, or $c_1b_2 - b_1c_2 = 0$.

## USING TECHNOLOGY EXERCISES 1.4, page 55

1. (0.6, 6.2)  2. (0.5273, 6.8327)  3. (3.8261, 0.1304)

4. (4.2246, −0.4007)  5. (386.9091, 145.3939)  6. (−1.5125, −3.5248)

1.  a. We first summarize the data:

| x | y | $x^2$ | xy |
|---|---|---|---|
| 1 | 4 | 1 | 4 |
| 2 | 6 | 4 | 12 |
| 3 | 8 | 9 | 24 |
| 4 | 11 | 16 | 44 |
| SUM 210 | 29 | 30 | 84 |

The normal equations are

$$4b + 10m = 29$$

$$10b + 30m = 84.$$

Solving this system of equations, we obtain m = 2.3, a and b = 1.5. So an equation is y = 2.3x + 1.5.

b. The scatter diagram and the least squares line for this data follow:

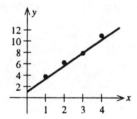

2.  a. We first summarize the data:

| x | y | $x^2$ | xy |
|---|---|---|---|
| 1 | 9 | 1 | 9 |
| 3 | 8 | 9 | 24 |
| 5 | 6 | 25 | 30 |
| 7 | 3 | 49 | 21 |
| 9 | 2 | 81 | 18 |
| SUM 25 | 28 | 165 | 102 |

The normal equations are

$$165m + 25b = 102$$

$$25m + 5b = 28$$

Solving, we find m = -0.95 and b = 10.35. The required equation is y = -0.95x + 10.35.

b. The scatter diagram and the least-squares line for these data follow:

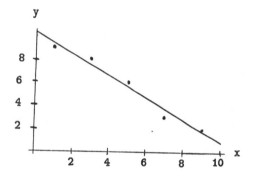

3.  a. We first summarize the data:

| x | y | $x^2$ | xy |
|---|---|---|---|
| 1 | 4.5 | 1 | 4.5 |
| 2 | 5 | 4 | 10 |
| 3 | 3 | 9 | 9 |
| 4 | 2 | 16 | 8 |
| 4 | 3.5 | 16 | 14 |
| 6 | 1 | 36 | 6 |
| SUM 20 | 19 | 82 | 51.5 |

The normal equations are

$$6b + 20m = 19$$

$$20b + 82m = 51.5.$$

The solutions are m ≈ −0.7717 and b ≈ 5.7391 and so a required equation is y = −0.772x + 5.739.

b. The scatter diagram and the least-squares line for these data follow.

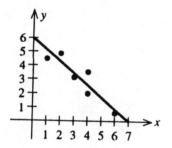

4.　　a. We first summarize the data:

| x | y | $x^2$ | xy |
|---|---|---|---|
| 1 | 2 | 1 | 2 |
| 1 | 3 | 1 | 3 |
| 2 | 3 | 4 | 6 |
| 3 | 3.5 | 9 | 10.5 |
| 4 | 3.5 | 16 | 14.0 |
| 4 | 4 | 16 | 16 |
| 5 | 5 | 25 | 25 |
| SUM 20 | 24 | 72 | 76.5 |

The normal equations are

$$72m + 20b = 76.5$$
$$20m + 7b = 24.$$

Solving, we find m = 0.53 and b = 1.91. The required equation is y = 0.53x + 1.91.

b. The scatter diagram and the least squares line for the given data are shown in the following figure.

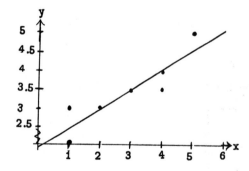

5.  a. We first summarize the data:

| x | y | $x^2$ | xy |
|---|---|-------|----|
| 1 | 3 | 1 | 3 |
| 2 | 5 | 4 | 10 |
| 3 | 5 | 9 | 15 |
| 4 | 7 | 16 | 28 |
| 5 | 8 | 25 | 40 |
| SUM 15 | 28 | 55 | 96 |

The normal equations are

$$55m + 15b = 96$$

$$15m + 5b = 28.$$

Solving, we find m = 1.2 and b = 2, so that the required equation is y = 1.2x + 2.

b. The scatter diagram and the least-squares line for the given data follow.

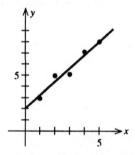

6.  a. We first summarize the data:

| x | y | $x^2$ | xy |
|---|---|-------|----|
| 1 | 8 | 1 | 8 |
| 2 | 6 | 4 | 12 |
| 5 | 6 | 25 | 30 |
| 7 | 4 | 49 | 28 |
| 10 | 1 | 100 | 10 |
| SUM 25 | 25 | 179 | 88 |

*1 Straight Lines and Linear Functions*

The normal equations are

$$5b + 25m = 25$$

$$25b + 179m = 88.$$

The solutions are m = -0.68519 and b = 8.4259 and so a required equation is y = -0.685x + 8.426.

b. The scatter diagram and least-squares line for the given data follow.

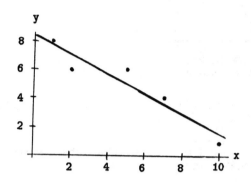

7. a. We first summarize the data:

| x | y | $x^2$ | xy |
|---|---|---|---|
| 4 | 0.5 | 16 | 2 |
| 4.5 | 0.6 | 20.25 | 2.7 |
| 5 | 0.8 | 25 | 4 |
| 5.5 | 0.9 | 30.25 | 4.95 |
| 6 | 1.2 | 36 | 7.2 |
| SUM 25 | 4 | 127.5 | 20.85 |

The normal equations are

$$5b + 25m = 4$$

$$25b + 127.5m = 20.85.$$

The solutions are m = 0.34 and b = -0.9 and so a required equation is y = 0.34x - 0.9.

b. The scatter diagram and the least-squares line for these data follow.

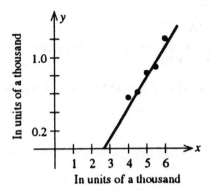

c. If x = 6.4, then y = 0.34(6.4) − 0.9 = 1.276 and so 1276 completed applications might be expected.

8.    a. We first summarize the data:

| x | y | $x^2$ | xy |
|---|---|---|---|
| 1 | 426 | 1 | 426 |
| 2 | 437 | 4 | 874 |
| 3 | 460 | 9 | 1380 |
| 4 | 473 | 16 | 1892 |
| 5 | 477 | 25 | 2385 |
| SUM  15 | 2273 | 55 | 6957 |

The normal equations are

$$55m + 15b = 6957$$

$$15m + 5b = 2273.$$

Solving, we find m = 13.8 and b = 413.2, so that the required equation is

$$y = 13.8x + 413.2.$$

b.

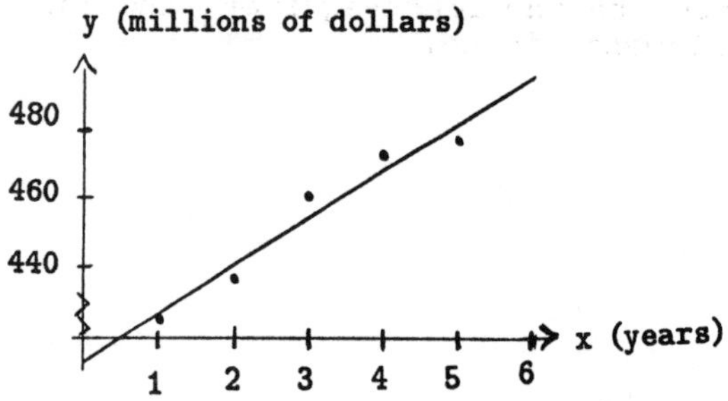

y (millions of dollars)

c. When x = 6, y = 13.8(6) + 413.2 = 496 and the predicted net sales for the upcoming year are $496 million.

9.    a. We first summarize the data:

| x | y | $x^2$ | xy |
|---|------|----|------|
| 1 | 436 | 1 | 436 |
| 2 | 438 | 4 | 876 |
| 3 | 428 | 9 | 1284 |
| 4 | 430 | 16 | 1720 |
| 5 | 426 | 25 | 2130 |
| SUM  15 | 2158 | 55 | 6446 |

The normal equations are

$$5b + 15m = 2158$$

$$15b + 55m = 6446.$$

Solving this system, we find

$$m = -2.8 \text{ and } b = 440.$$

Thus, the equation of the least-squares line is

$$y = -2.8x + 440.$$

b. The scatter diagram and the least-squares line for this data are shown in the following figure.

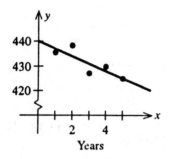

c. Two years from now, the average SAT verbal score in that area will be y = -2.8(7) + 440 = 420.4.

10.   a. We first summarize the data:

| x | y | $x^2$ | xy |
|---|---|---|---|
| 5 | 50.3 | 25 | 251.5 |
| 10 | 34.8 | 100 | 348 |
| 15 | 30.1 | 225 | 451.5 |
| 20 | 27.4 | 400 | 548 |
| 25 | 25.6 | 625 | 640 |
| 30 | 23.5 | 900 | 705 |
| SUM  105 | 191.7 | 2275 | 2944 |

The normal equations are

$$2275m + 105b = 2944$$

$$105m + 6b = 191.7.$$

Solving, we find m = -0.94 and b = 48.38, so that the required equation is

$$y = -0.94x + 48.38.$$

b. The scatter diagram and the least-squares line for the given data are shown in the following figure.

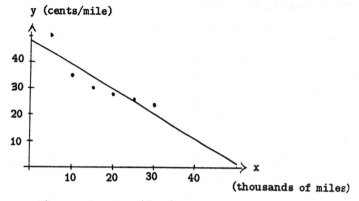

c. The cost per mile is

$$y = -0.94(8) + 48.38 = 40.86, \text{ or } 41 \text{ cents.}$$

11.  a. We first summarize the data:

| x | y | $x^2$ | xy |
|---|---|---|---|
| 0 | 168 | 0 | 0 |
| 10 | 213 | 100 | 2130 |
| 20 | 297 | 400 | 5940 |
| 30 | 374 | 900 | 11220 |
| 40 | 427 | 1600 | 17080 |
| 51 | 467 | 2601 | 23817 |
| SUM 151 | 1946 | 5601 | 60187 |

The normal equations are

$$6b + 151m = 1946$$

$$151b + 5601m = 60187.$$

The solutions are m = 6.2264 and b = 167.636 and so a required equation is y = 6.226x + 167.6.

b. In 2000, x = 60, y = 6.226(90) + 167.6 ≈ 541. Hence, the expected size of the average farm will be 541 acres.

12.  a. We first summarize the data:

| x | y | $x^2$ | xy |
|---|---|---|---|
| 0 | 1.550 | 0 | 0 |
| 1 | 1.662 | 1 | 1.662 |
| 2 | 1.786 | 4 | 3.572 |
| 3 | 1.888 | 9 | 5.664 |
| 4 | 2.009 | 16 | 8.036 |
| SUM 10 | 8.895 | 30 | 18.934 |

The normal equations are

$$5b + 10m = 8.895$$

$$10b + 30m = 18.934.$$

The solutions are m = 0.1144 and b = 1.5502 and so a required equation is y = 0.114x + 1.55.

b. In 1996, when x = 8, y = 0.114(8) + 1.55 = 2.462 and so the spending was expected to reach $2.462 billion.

13.  a. We first summarize the data:

| x | y | $x^2$ | xy |
|---|---|---|---|
| 1 | 20 | 1 | 20 |
| 2 | 24 | 4 | 48 |
| 3 | 26 | 9 | 78 |
| 4 | 28 | 16 | 112 |
| 5 | 32 | 25 | 160 |
| SUM 15 | 130 | 55 | 418 |

The normal equations are

$$5b + 15m = 130$$

$$15b + 55m = 418.$$

The solutions are m = 2.8 and b = 17.6, and so an equation of the line is y = 2.8x + 17.6.

b.   When x = 8, y = 2.8(8) + 17.6 = 40. Hence, the state subsidy is expected to be $40 million for the eighth year.

14.   a. We first summarize the data:

| x | y | $x^2$ | xy |
|---|---|---|---|
| 1 | 53.4 | 1 | 53.4 |
| 2 | 55.5 | 4 | 111 |
| 3 | 57.6 | 9 | 172.8 |
| 4 | 60.6 | 16 | 242.4 |
| 5 | 61.2 | 25 | 306 |
| 6 | 62.7 | 36 | 376.2 |
| SUM  21 | 351 | 91 | 1261.8 |

The normal equations are

$$6b + 21m = 351$$

$$21b + 91m = 1261.8.$$

The solutions are m = 1.90 and b = 51.84 and so an equation of the required line is y = 1.90x + 51.84.

b.   In the year 2000, x = 10 and y = 1.90(10) + 51.84 = 70.84. Hence the FICA wage base in 2000 can be expected to be $70,840.

15.   a. We first summarize the data:

| x | y | $x^2$ | xy |
|---|---|---|---|
| 1 | 16.7 | 1 | 16.7 |
| 3 | 26 | 9 | 78 |
| 5 | 33.3 | 25 | 166.5 |
| 7 | 48.3 | 49 | 338.1 |
| 9 | 57 | 81 | 513 |
| 11 | 65.8 | 121 | 723.8 |
| 13 | 74.2 | 169 | 964.6 |
| 15 | 83.3 | 225 | 1249.5 |
| **SUM** 64 | 404.6 | 680 | 4050.2 |

The normal equations are

$$8b + 64m = 404.6$$

$$64b + 680m = 4050.2.$$

The solutions are m = 4.8417 and b = 11.8417 and so a required equation is y = 4.842x + 11.842.

b. In 1993, x = 19, and so y = 4.842(19) + 11.842 = 103.83. Hence the estimated number of cans produced in 1993 is 103.8 billion.

16.  a. We first summarize the data:

| x | y | $x^2$ | xy |
|---|---|---|---|
| 4.25 | 178 | 18.0625 | 756.5 |
| 10 | 667 | 100 | 6670 |
| 14 | 1194 | 196 | 16716 |
| 15.5 | 1500 | 240.25 | 23250 |
| 17.8 | 1388 | 316.84 | 24706.4 |
| 19.5 | 1640 | 380.25 | 31980 |
| **SUM** 81.05 | 6567 | 1251.4025 | 104078.9 |

The normal equations are

$$6b + \quad 81.05m = 6567$$

$$81.05b + \quad 1251.4025m = 104078.9.$$

The solutions are m = 98.1761 and b = −231.696 and so a required equation is y = 98.176x − 231.7.

b. If x = 20, then y = 98.176(20) − 231.7 = 1731.82. Hence, if the health-spending in the U.S. were in line with OECD countries, it should only have been $1732 per capita.

## USING TECHNOLOGY EXERCISES 1.5, page 65

1. y = 2.3596x + 3.8639
2. y = 1.4068x − 2.1241

3. y = − 1.1948x + 3.5525
4. y = −2.07715x + 5.23847

5. a. y = 13.321x + 72.57
   b. 192 million tons

6. a. y = 3.295x + 63.073
   b. $115,800

## CHAPTER 1 REVIEW EXERCISES, page 68

1. The distance is

$$d = \sqrt{(6 - 2)^2 + (4 - 1)^2} = \sqrt{4^2 + 3^2} = \sqrt{25} = 5.$$

2. The distance is

$$d = \sqrt{(2 - 6)^2 + (6 - 9)^2} = \sqrt{4^2 + 3^2} = \sqrt{25} = 5.$$

3. The distance is

$$d = \sqrt{[1 - (-2)]^2 + [-7 - (-3)]^2} = \sqrt{3^2 + (-4)^2} = \sqrt{9 + 16} = \sqrt{25} = 5.$$

4. The distance is

$$d = \sqrt{(-1/2 - 1/2)^2 + (2\sqrt{3} - \sqrt{3})^2} = \sqrt{1 + 3} = \sqrt{4} = 2.$$

5. An equation is x = −2.

6. An equation is y = 4.

7. The slope of L is

$$m = \frac{\frac{7}{2} - 4}{3 - (-2)} = -\frac{1}{10}$$

and an equation of L is

$$y - 4 = -\frac{1}{10}[x - (-2)] = -\frac{1}{10}x - \frac{1}{5},$$

or $\qquad y = -\frac{1}{10}x + \frac{19}{5}.$

The general form of this equation is $x + 10y - 38 = 0$.

8. The line passes through the points $(-2,4)$ and $(3,0)$. So its slope is $m = (4 - 0)/(-2 - 3)$ or $m = -4/5$. An equation is

$$y - 0 = -\frac{4}{5}(x - 3) \quad \text{or} \quad y = -\frac{4}{5}x + \frac{12}{5}.$$

9. Writing the given equation in the form $y = \frac{5}{2}x - 3$, we see that the slope of the given line is 5/2. So a required equation is

$$y - 4 = \frac{5}{2}(x + 2) \quad \text{or} \quad y = \frac{5}{2}x + 9.$$

The general form of this equation is $5x - 2y + 18 = 0$.

10. Writing the given equation in the form $y = -\frac{4}{3}x + 2$, we see that the slope of the given line is $-4/3$. Therefore, the slope of the required line is 3/4 and an equation of the line is

$$y - 4 = \frac{3}{4}(x + 2) \quad \text{or} \quad y = \frac{3}{4}x + \frac{11}{2}.$$

11. Using the slope-intercept form of the equation of a line, we have

$$y = -\frac{1}{2}x - 3.$$

12. Rewriting the given equation in the slope-intercept form, we have

$$-5y = -3x + 6$$

or $\qquad y = \frac{3}{5}x - \frac{6}{5}.$

From this equation, we see that the slope of the line is 3/5 and its y-intercept is $-6/5$.

13. Rewriting the given equation in the slope-intercept form, we have

$$4y = -3x + 8$$

or

$$y = -\frac{3}{4}x + 2,$$

and conclude that the slope of the required line is −3/4. Using the point-slope form of the equation of a line with the point (2,3) and slope −3/4, we obtain

$$y - 3 = -\frac{3}{4}(x - 2)$$

$$y = -\frac{3}{4}x + \frac{6}{4} + 3$$

$$= -\frac{3}{4}x + \frac{9}{2}.$$

The general form of this equation is $3x + 4y - 18 = 0$.

14. The slope of the line joining the points (−3,4) and (2,1) is

$$m = \frac{1 - 4}{2 - (-3)} = \frac{-3}{5}.$$

Using the point-slope form of the equation of a line with the point (−1,3) and slope −3/5, we have

$$y - 3 = -\frac{3}{5}[x - (-1)]$$

$$y = -\frac{3}{5}(x + 1) + 3$$

$$= -\frac{3}{5}x + \frac{12}{5}.$$

15. Rewriting the given equation in the slope-intercept form

$$y = \frac{2}{3}x - 8.$$

we see that the slope of the line with this equation is 2/3. The slope of the required line is −3/2. Using the point-slope form of the equation of a line with the point (−2,−4) and slope −3/2, we have

$$y - (-4) = -\frac{3}{2}[x - (-2)]$$

or

$$y = -\frac{3}{2}x - 7.$$

The general form of this equation is $3x + 2y + 14 = 0$.

16. Setting x = 0 gives y = −6 as the y-intercept. Setting y = 0 gives x = 8 as the x-intercept. The graph of the equation 3x − 4y = 24 is shown below.

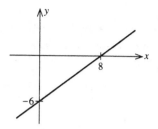

17. Setting x = 0, gives 5y = 15, or y = 3. Setting y = 0, gives −2x = 15, or x = −15/2. The graph of the equation −2x + 5y = 15 follows.

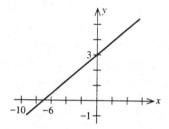

18. In 1998 (x = 5), we have

$$S(5) = 6000(5) + 30,000$$

$$= 60,000.$$

19. Let x denote the time in years. Since the function is linear, we know that it has the form f(x) = mx + b.

a. The slope of the line passing through (0, 2.4) and (5, 7.4) is

$$m = \frac{7.4 - 2.4}{5} = 1.$$

Since the line passes through (0, 2.4), we know that the y-intercept is 2.4. Therefore, the required function is

$$f(x) = x + 2.4.$$

b. In 1992 (x = 3), the sales were

$$f(3) = 3 + 2.4 = 5.4,$$

or $5.4 million dollars.

20. The slope of the line segment joining A and B is given by

$$m_1 = \frac{3-1}{5-1} = \frac{2}{4} = \frac{1}{2}.$$

The slope of the line segment joining B and C is

$$m_2 = \frac{5-3}{4-5} = \frac{2}{-1} = -2.$$

Since $m_1 = -1/m_2$, $\triangle ABC$ is a right triangle.

21. a. $D(w) = \frac{a}{150}w.$

The given equation can be expressed in the form $y = mx + b$, where

$$m = \frac{a}{150} \quad \text{and } b = 0.$$

b. If $a = 500$ and $w = 35$,

$$D(35) = \frac{500}{150}(35)$$

$$= 116\frac{2}{3}$$

or approximately 117 mg.

22. Let V denote the value of the building after t years.

a. The rate of depreciation is

$$-\frac{\Delta V}{\Delta t} = \frac{6,000,000}{30} = 200,000$$

or $200,000/year.

b. From part (a), we know that the slope of the line is −200,000. Using the point-slope form of the equation of a line, we have

$$V - 0 = -200,000(t - 30)$$

or $\qquad V = -200,000t + 6,000,000.$

In the year 2000 (t = 10), we have

$$V = -200,000(10) + 6,000,000$$

$$= 4,000,000 \quad \text{or } \$4,000,000.$$

23. Let V denote the value of the machine after t years.

a. The rate of depreciation is

$$-\frac{\Delta V}{\Delta t} = \frac{300,000 - 30,000}{12} = \frac{270,000}{12}$$

$$= 22,500, \quad \text{or } \$22,500/\text{year}.$$

b. Using the point-slope form of the equation of a line with the point (0, 300,000) and m = -22,500, we have

$$V - 300,000 = -22,500(t - 0)$$

$$V = -22,500t + 300,000.$$

24. Let x denote the number of units produced and sold.

a. The cost function is

$$C(x) = 6x + 30,000 \ .$$

b. The revenue function is

$$R(x) = 10x.$$

c. The profit function is

$$P(x) = R(x) - C(x) = 10x - (30,000 + 6x)$$

$$= 4x - 30,000.$$

d.  $\quad P(6000) = 4(6000) - 30,000 = -6,000$

or a loss of $6000.

$$P(8000) = 4(8000) - 30,000 = 2,000$$

or a profit of $2000.

$$P(12,000) = 4(12,000) - 30,000 = 18,000$$

or a profit of $18,000.

25. The slope of the demand curve is

$$\frac{\Delta p}{\Delta x} = -\frac{10}{200} = -0.05.$$

Using the point-slope form of the equation of a line with the point (0,200), we have

$$p - 200 = -0.05(x)$$

or  $\quad\quad\quad p = -0.05x + 200.$

The graph of the demand equation follows.

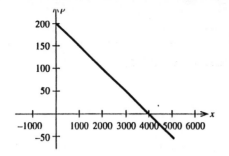

26.  The slope of the supply curve is

$$\frac{\Delta p}{\Delta x} = \frac{50}{1800} = \frac{1}{36}.$$

Using the point-slope form of the equation of a line with the point (200, 50), we have

$$p - 50 = \frac{1}{36}(x - 200),$$

$$p = \frac{1}{36}x - \frac{200}{36} + 50$$

$$= \frac{1}{36}x + \frac{1600}{36}$$

$$= \frac{1}{36}x + \frac{400}{9},$$

or $36p - x - 1600 = 0$.

27.  We solve the system

$$3x + 4y = -6$$

$$2x + 5y = -11.$$

Solving the first equation for x, we have

$$3x = -4y - 6$$

and       $x = -\frac{4}{3}y - 2.$

Substituting this value of x into the second equation yields

$$2(-\frac{4}{3}y - 2) + 5y = -11$$
$$-\frac{8}{3}y - 4 + 5y = -11$$
$$\frac{7}{3}y = -7$$

or              $y = -3.$

Then              $x = -\frac{4}{3}(-3) - 2$

$$= 4 - 2 = 2.$$

Therefore, the point of intersection is $(2,-3)$.

28. We solve the system

$$y = \frac{3}{4}x + 6$$

and

$$3x - 2y = -3.$$

Substituting the first equation into the second equation, we have

$$3x - 2\left(\frac{3}{4}x + 6\right) = -3$$

$$3x - \frac{3}{2}x - 12 = -3$$

$$\frac{3}{2}x = 9$$

$$x = 6.$$

Substituting this value of $x$ into the first equation, we have

$$y = \frac{3}{4}(6) + 6 = \frac{21}{2}.$$

Therefore, the point of intersection is $(6,\frac{21}{2})$

29. Setting $C(x) = R(x)$, we have

$$12x + 20,000 = 20x$$

$$8x = 20,000$$

or

$$x = 2500.$$

Next,     $R(2500) = 20(2500) = 50,000,$

and we conclude that the breakeven point is $(2500, 50,000)$.

30. We solve the system

$$3x + p = 40$$

$$2x - p = -10.$$

Solving the first equation for $p$, we obtain

$$p = 40 - 3x.$$

Substituting this value of $p$ into the second equation, we obtain

$$2x - (40 - 3x) = -10$$

$$5x - 40 = -10$$

$$5x = 30$$

or                      $x = 6.$

Next,                   $p = 40 - 3(6) = 40 - 18 = 22.$

We conclude that the equilibrium quantity is 6000 units and the equilibrium price is \$22.

31.  a. The slope of the line is

$$m = \frac{1 - 0.5}{4 - 2} = 0.25.$$

Using the point-slope form of an equation of a line, we have

$$y - 1 = 0.25(x - 4)$$

$$y = 0.25x$$

  b.                    $y = 0.25(6.4)$

$$= 1.6,$$

or 1600 applications.

   **GROUP DISCUSSION QUESTIONS**

**Page 6**

1.  a. Let $P_1 = (2,6)$ and $P_2 = (-4,3)$. Then we have

$$x_1 = 2, \; y_1 = 6, \; x_2 = -4, \; \text{and } y_2 = 3.$$

Using formula (1), we have

$$d = \sqrt{(-4 - 2)^2 + (3 - 6)^2}$$

$$= \sqrt{36 + 9} = \sqrt{45} = 3\sqrt{5},$$

as obtained in Example 1.

  b. Let $P_1(x_1,y_1)$ and $P_2(x_2,y_2)$ be any two points in the plane. Then the result follows from the equality

$$\sqrt{(x_2 - x_1)^2 + (y_2 - y_1)^2} = \sqrt{(x_1 - x_2)^2 + (y_1 - y_2)^2}.$$

1. Refer to the accompanying figure.
   Observe that the triangles $\triangle P_1 Q_1 P_2$
   and $\triangle P_3 Q_2 P_4$ are similar. From this
   we conclude that

$$m = \frac{Y_2 - Y_1}{x_2 - x_1} = \frac{Y_4 - Y_3}{x_4 - x_3} .$$

   Since $P_3$ and $P_4$ are arbitrary, the
   conclusion follows.

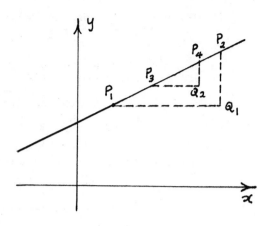

**Page 20**

1. In Example 11, we are told that the object is expected to
   appreciate in value at a given rate for the next five years, and
   the equation obtained in that example is based on this fact. Thus,
   the equation may not be used to predict the value of the object
   very much beyond five years from the date of purchase.

## EXPLORING WITH TECHNOLOGY QUESTIONS

**Page 18**

1. The straight lines $L_1$ and $L_2$ are shown in the following figure.

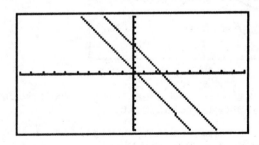

   a. $L_1$ and $L_2$ seem to be parallel to each other.

   b. Writing each equation in the slope-intercept form gives

$$y = -2x + 5 \quad \text{and} \quad y = -\frac{41}{20}x + \frac{11}{20}$$

   from which we see that the slopes of $L_1$ and $L_2$ are $-2$ and

-14/20 = -2.1, respectively. This shows that $L_1$ and $L_2$ are not parallel to each other.

2. The straight lines $L_1$ and $L_2$ are shown in the following figure.

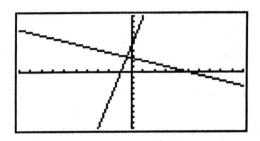

a. $L_1$ and $L_2$ seem to be perpendicular to each other.

b. The slopes of $L_2$ and $L_2$ are $m_1 = -1/2$ and $m_2 = 5$, respectively.

Since $\quad m_1 = -\frac{1}{2} \neq -\frac{1}{5} = -\frac{1}{m_2}$, we see that $L_1$ and $L_2$ are not perpendicular to each other.

**Page 19**

1. The straight lines with the given equations are shown in the following figure.

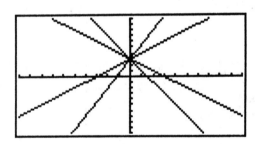

Changing the value of m in the equation $y = mx + b$ changes the slope of the line and thus rotates it.

2.    The straight lines of interest are shown in the following figure.

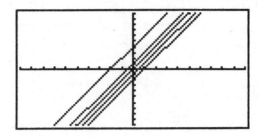

Changing the value of b in the equation y = mx + b changes the
y-intercept of the line and thus translates it (upwards if b > 0
and downwards if b < 0).

3.    Changing both m and b in the equation y = mx + b rotates as well
as translates the line.

## Page 45

1.    Plotting the straight lines $L_1$ and $L_2$ and using **TRACE** and **ZOOM**
repeatedly, you will see that the iterations approach the answer
(1,1). Using the "intersection" function of the graphing utility
gives the result x = 1 and y = 1, immediately.

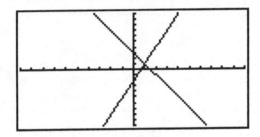

2.    Substituting the first equation into the second yields

$$3x - 2 = -2x + 3$$

$$5x = 5$$

and x = 1. Substituting this value of x into either equation
gives y = 1.

3.    The iterations obtained using **TRACE** and **ZOOM** converge to the
solution (1,1) with a little effort. The use of the "intersection"
function is clearly superior to the first method. The algebraic
method also yields the desired result accurately and with little
effort in the situation.

1.

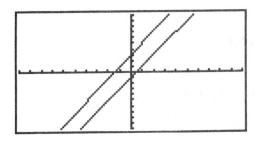

The lines seem to be parallel to each other and they appear to not intersect.

2.

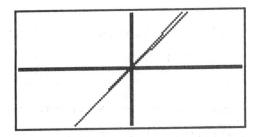

They appear to intersect. But finding the point of intersection using **TRACE** and **ZOOM** with any degree of accuracy seems to be an impossible task. Using the "intersection" function of the graphing utility yields the point of intersection (-40,-81) immediately.

3. Substituting the first equation into the second gives

$$2x - 1 = 2.1x + 3$$

$$-4 = 0.1x,$$

or x = -40. The corresponding y-value is -81.

4. The **Trace** and **Zoom** technique is not effective. The "intersection" function gives the desired result immediately. The algebraic method also yields the answer with little effort and without the use of a graphing utility.

# CHAPTER 2

## EXERCISES 2.1, page 78

1. Solving the first equation for x, we find

$$x = 3y - 1.$$

Substituting this value of x into the second equation yields

$$4(3y - 1) + 3y = 11$$
$$12y - 4 + 3y = 11$$

or

$$y = 1.$$

Substituting this value of y into the first equation gives

$$x = 3(1) - 1$$
$$= 2.$$

Therefore, the unique solution of the system is (2,1).

2. Solving the first equation for x, we have

$$2x = 4y + 5$$
$$x = 2y + \frac{5}{2}.$$

Substituting this value of x into the second equation, we have

$$3(2y + \frac{5}{2}) + 2y = 6$$
$$6y + \frac{15}{2} + 2y = 6$$
$$16y = -3$$

or

$$y = -\frac{3}{16}.$$

Then

$$x = 2(-\frac{3}{16}) + \frac{5}{2}.$$
$$= \frac{17}{8}.$$

Therefore, the solution is $(\frac{17}{8}, -\frac{3}{16})$.

3. Solving the first equation for x, we have

$$x = 7 - 4y.$$

Substituting this value of x into the second equation, we have

$$\frac{1}{2}(7 - 4y) + 2y = 5$$

$$7 - 4y + 4y = 10$$

$$7 = 10.$$

Clearly, this is impossible and we conclude that the system of equations has no solution.

4. Solving the first equation for x, we obtain

$$3x = 7 + 4y$$

$$x = \frac{7}{3} + \frac{4}{3}y.$$

Substituting this value of x into the second equation, we obtain

$$9\left(\frac{7}{3} + \frac{4}{3}y\right) - 12y = 14$$

$$\frac{63}{3} + 12y - 12y = 14$$

$$\frac{63}{3} = 14.$$

Since this is impossible, we conclude that the system of equations has no solution.

5. Solving the first equation for x, we obtain

$$x = 7 - 2y.$$

Substituting this value of x into the second equation, we have

$$2(7 - 2y) - y = 4$$

$$14 - 4y - y = 4$$

$$-5y = -10$$

and

$$y = 2.$$

Then

$$x = 7 - 2(2) = 7 - 4 = 3.$$

We conclude that the solution to the system is (3,2).

6. Solving the second equation for x, we obtain

$$x = -\frac{1}{3}y + 2.$$

Substituting this value of x into the first equation, gives

$$\frac{3}{2}(-\frac{1}{3}y + 2) - 2y = 4$$

$$-\frac{1}{2}y - 2y = 4 - 3$$

$$-\frac{5}{2}y = 1$$

$$y = -\frac{2}{5}.$$

Then
$$x = 2 - \frac{1}{3}(-\frac{2}{5}) = 2\frac{2}{15}.$$

Therefore, the solution of the system is $(\frac{32}{15}, -\frac{2}{5})$.

7. Solving the first equation for x, we have

$$2x = 5y + 10$$

and
$$x = \frac{5}{2}y + 5.$$

Substituting this value of x into the second equation, we have

$$6(\frac{5}{2}y + 5) - 15y = 30$$

$$15y + 30 - 15y = 30$$

or
$$0 = 0.$$

This result tells us that the second equation is equivalent to the first. Thus, any ordered pair of numbers (x,y) satisfying the equation

$$2x - 5y = 10 \text{ (or } 6x - 15y = 30)$$

is a solution to the system. In particular, by assigning the value t to x, where t is any real number, we find that

$$y = -2 + \frac{2}{5}t$$

so the ordered pair, $(t, \frac{2}{5}t - 2)$ is a solution to the system, and we conclude that the system has infinitely many solutions.

8. Solving the first equation for x, we have

$$5x = 6y + 8$$

$$x = \frac{6}{5}y + \frac{8}{5}.$$

Substituting this value of x into the second equation, gives

$$10\left(\frac{6}{5}y + \frac{8}{5}\right) - 12y = 16$$

$$12y + 16 - 12y = 16.$$

or $$0 = 0.$$

This result tells us that the second equation is equivalent to the first. Thus, any ordered pair of numbers (x,y) satisfying the equation

$$5x - 6y = 8 \text{ (or } 10x - 12y = 16)$$

is a solution to the system. In particular, by assigning the value t to x, where t is any real number, we find that

$$y = \frac{5}{6}t - \frac{4}{3}.$$

So the ordered pair, $(t, \frac{5}{6}t - \frac{4}{3})$ is a solution to the system, and we conclude that the system has infinitely many solutions.

9. Solving the first equation for x, we obtain

$$4x - 5y = 14$$

$$4x = 14 + 5y$$

$$x = \frac{14}{4} + \frac{5}{4}y = \frac{7}{2} + \frac{5}{4}y.$$

Substituting this value of x into the second equation gives

$$2\left(\frac{7}{2} + \frac{5}{4}y\right) + 3y = -4$$

$$7 + \frac{5}{2}y + 3y = -4$$

$$\frac{11}{2}y = -11,$$

or $$y = -2.$$

Then, $$x = \frac{7}{2} + \frac{5}{4}(-2)$$

$$= 1.$$

We conclude that the ordered pair $(1,-2)$ satisfies the given system of equations.

10. Solving the first equation for $x$, we have

$$\frac{5}{4}x - \frac{2}{3}y = 3$$

$$\frac{5}{4}x = \frac{2}{3}y + 3$$

$$x = \frac{4}{5}\left(\frac{2}{3}y + 3\right) = \frac{8}{15}y + \frac{12}{5}.$$

Substituting this value of $x$ into the second equation yields

$$\frac{1}{4}\left(\frac{8}{15}y + \frac{12}{5}\right) + \frac{5}{3}y = 6$$

$$\frac{2}{15}y + \frac{3}{5} + \frac{5}{3}y = 6$$

$$\frac{27}{15}y = \frac{27}{5}$$

or

$$y = 3.$$

Then

$$x = \frac{8}{15}(3) + \frac{12}{5} = \frac{20}{5} = 4.$$

Thus, the ordered pair $(4,3)$ satisfies the given equation.

11. Solving the first equation for $x$, we obtain

$$2x = 3y + 6$$

$$x = \frac{3}{2}y + 3.$$

Substituting this value of $x$ into the second equation gives

$$6\left(\frac{3}{2}y + 3\right) - 9y = 12$$

$$9y + 18 - 9y = 12$$

$$18 = 12$$

which is impossible. We conclude that the system of equations has no solution.

12. Solving the first equation for $y$, we obtain

$$\frac{2}{3}x + y = 5$$

$$y = -\frac{2}{3}x + 5.$$

Substituting this value of y into the second equation yields

$$\frac{1}{2}x + \frac{3}{4}(-\frac{2}{3}x + 5) = \frac{15}{4}$$

$$\frac{1}{2}x - \frac{1}{2}x + \frac{15}{4} = \frac{15}{4}.$$

or $$\frac{15}{4} = \frac{15}{4},$$

We conclude that the system of equations has infinitely many solutions of the form $(t, 5 - \frac{2}{3}t)$.

13. Solving the first equation for y, we obtain

$$y = 2x - 3.$$

Substituting this value of y into the second equation yields

$$4x + k(2x - 3) = 4,$$

$$4x + 2xk - 3k = 4$$

$$2x(2 + k) = 4 + 3k$$

$$x = \frac{4 + 3k}{2(2 + k)}.$$

Since x is not defined when the denominator of this last expression is zero, we conclude that the system has no solution when $k = -2$.

14. Solving the second equation for x, we have

$$x = 4 - ky.$$

Substituting this value of x into the first equation gives

$$3(4 - ky) + 4y = 12$$

$$12 - 3ky + 4y = 12$$

$$y(-3k + 4) = 0$$

Since this last equation is always true when $k = 4/3$, we see that the system has infinitely many solutions when $k = 4/3$. When $k = 4/3$,

$$x = 4 - ky = 4 - (4/3)y.$$

Then the set of all ordered pairs $(4 - \frac{4}{3}t, t)$, where t is a parameter satisfy the system when $k = 4/3$.

15. Let x and y denote the number of acres of corn and wheat planted respectively. Then x + y = 500. Since the cost of cultivating corn is $42/acre and that of wheat $30/acre and Mr. Johnson has $18,600 available for cultivation, we have 42x + 30y = 18600.
Thus, the solution is found by solving the system of equations

$$x \ + \ y = 500$$

$$42x \ + 30y = 18,600.$$

16. Let x = the amount of money Michael invested in the institution that pays interest at the rate of 6 percent per year and y = the amount of money invested in the institution paying 8 percent per year. Since his total investment is $2000, we have x + y = 2000. Next, since the interest earned during a one-year period was $144, we have

$$0.06x + 0.08y = 144.$$

Thus, the solution is found by solving the system of equations

$$x + \ y \ = 2000$$

and $\quad 0.06x + 0.08y = 144.$

17. Let x denote the number of pounds of the $2.50/lb coffee and y denote the number of pounds of the $3/lb coffee. Then x + y = 100. Since the blended coffee sells for $2.80/lb, we know that the blended mixture is worth

$$(2.80)(100) = \$280.$$

Therefore, $\quad 2.50x + 3y = 280.$

Thus, the solution is found by solving the system of equations

$$x + \ y = 100$$

$$2.50x + 3y = 280.$$

18. Let the amount of money invested in the bonds yielding 8% be x dollars and the amount of money invested in the bonds yielding 10% be y dollars. Then x + y = 30,000. Also, since the yield from both investments totals $2640, we have 0.08x + 0.10y = 2640. Thus, the solution to the problem can be found by solving the system of equations

$$x \ + \ y = 30,000$$

$$0.08x \ + 0.10y = \ 2,640.$$

19. Let x denote the number of children who rode the bus during the morning shift and y denote the number of adults who rode the bus

during the morning shift. Then x + y = 1000. Since the total fare collected was $650, we have 0.25x + 0.75y = 650. Thus, the solution to the problem can be found by solving the system of equations

$$x + y = 1000$$

$$0.25x + 0.75y = 650.$$

20.  Let x, y, and z denote the number of one-bedroom units, two-bedroom townhouses, and three-bedroom townhouses, respectively. Since the total number of units is 192, we have x + y + z = 192. Next, the number of family units is equal to the number of one-bedroom units, and this implies that

$$y + z = x \text{ or } x - y - z = 0.$$

Finally, the number of one-bedroom units is three times the number of three-bedroom units, and this implies that x = 3z or x - 3z = 0.

Summarizing, we have the system

$$x + y + z = 192$$

$$x - y - z = 0$$

$$x \qquad - 3z = 0.$$

21.  Let

> x = the amount of money invested at 6 percent in a savings account
>
> y = the amount of money invested at 8 percent in mutual funds

and  z = the amount of money invested at 12 percent in money market certificates.

Since the total interest was $21,600, we have

$$0.06x + 0.08y + 0.12z = 21,600.$$

Also, since the amount of Mr. Carrington's investment in money market certificates is twice the amount of the investment in the savings account, we have z = 2x. Finally, the interest earned from his investment in mutual funds was equal to the interest earned on his money market certificates, so .08y = 0.12z.

Thus, the solution to the problem can be found by solving the system of equations

$$0.06x + 0.08y + 0.12z = 21,600$$

$$2x \qquad - \qquad z = \quad 0$$

$$0.08y - 0.12z = \quad 0.$$

22.  Let

   $x$ = the number of tickets sold to the children

   $y$ = the number of tickets sold to students

   and    $z$ = the number of tickets sold to adults

at that particular screening. Since there was a full house at that screening, we have $x + y + z = 900$. Next, the number of adults present was equal to one-half the number of students and children present, and this implies $z = \frac{1}{2}(x + y)$. Finally, the receipts totaled $2800, and this implies that $2x + 3y + 4z = 2800$. Summarizing, we have the system

$$x + \quad y + \quad z = \quad 900$$

$$x + \quad y - 2z = \quad 0$$

$$2x + 3y + 4z = 2800.$$

23.  Let $x$, $y$, and $z$ denote the number of compact, intermediate, and full- size cars, respectively, to be purchased. The cost incurred in buying the specified number of cars is $8000x + 12000y + 16000z$. Since the budget is $1 million, we have the system

$$8000x + 12000y + 16000z = 1000000$$

$$x - \qquad 2y \qquad\qquad = 0$$

$$x + \qquad y \qquad + z = 100.$$

24.  Let

   $x$ = the amount of money invested in high-risk stocks

   $y$ = the amount of money invested in medium-risk stocks

   and    $z$ = the amount of money invested in low-risk stocks.

Since a total of $200,000 is to be invested, we have

$$x + y + z = 200,000.$$

Next, since the investment in low-risk stocks is to be twice the sum of the investments in high- and medium-risk stocks, we have

$$z = 2(x + y).$$

Finally, the expected return of the three investments is given by

$$0.15x + 0.10y + 0.06z$$

and the goal of the investment club is that an average return of 9 percent be realized on the total investment. If this goal is realized, then

$$0.15x + 0.10y + 0.06z = 0.09(x + y + z).$$

Summarizing, we have the following system of equations:

$$x + y + z = 200,000$$
$$2x + 2y - z = 0$$
$$6x + y - 3z = 0.$$

25. Let

$x$ = the number of ounces of Food I used in the meal

$y$ = the number of ounces of Food II used in the meal

and $z$ = the number of ounces of Food III used in the meal.

Since 100 percent of the daily requirement of proteins, carbohydrates, and iron is to be met by this meal, we have the following system of linear equations:

$$10x + 6y + 8z = 100$$
$$10x + 12y + 6z = 100$$
$$5x + 4y + 12z = 100.$$

## EXERCISES 2.2, page 93

1. $\begin{bmatrix} 2 & -3 & \vert & 7 \\ 3 & 1 & \vert & 4 \end{bmatrix}$

2. $\begin{bmatrix} 3 & 7 & -8 & \vert & 5 \\ 1 & 0 & 3 & \vert & -2 \\ 4 & -3 & 0 & \vert & 7 \end{bmatrix}$

3. $\begin{bmatrix} 0 & -1 & 2 & \vert & 6 \\ 2 & 2 & -8 & \vert & 7 \\ 0 & 3 & 4 & \vert & 0 \end{bmatrix}$

4. $\begin{bmatrix} 3 & 2 & 0 & \vert & 0 \\ 1 & -1 & 2 & \vert & 4 \\ 0 & 2 & -3 & \vert & 5 \end{bmatrix}$

5.　$3x + 2y = -4$

　　$x - y = 5$

6.　　　　$3y + 2z = 4$

　　　$x - y - 2z = -3$

　　$4x　　 + 3z = 2.$

7.　$x + 3y + 2z = 4$

　　$2x　　　 = 5$

　　$3x - 3y + 2z = 6$

8.　$2x + 3y + z = 6$

　　$4x + 3y + 2z = 5$

9.　Yes. Conditions 1-4 are satisfied (see page 85 of text).

10.　Yes. Conditions 1-4 are satisfied.

11.　No. Condition 3 is violated. The first nonzero entry in the second row does not lie to the right of the first nonzero entry 1 in row 1.

12.　Yes. Conditions 1-4 are satisfied.

13.　Yes. Conditions 1-4 are satisfied.

14.　No. Condition 2 is violated. The first nonzero entry in the third row is not a 1.

15.　No. Condition 2 and consequently condition 4 are not satisfied. The first nonzero entry in the last row is not a 1 and the column containing that entry does not have zeros elsewhere.

16.　Yes. Conditions 1-4 are satisfied.

17.　No. Condition 1 is violated. The first row consists entirely of zeros and it lies above row 2.

18.　No. Condition 1 is violated. The coefficient matrix of the third row consists entirely of zeros and it lies above the fourth row.

19.　$\begin{bmatrix} ②　4 & | & 8 \\ 3 & 1 & | & 2 \end{bmatrix} \xrightarrow{\frac{1}{2}R_1} \begin{bmatrix} 1 & 2 & | & 4 \\ ③ & 1 & | & 2 \end{bmatrix} \xrightarrow{R_2 - 3R_1} \begin{bmatrix} 1 & 2 & | & 4 \\ 0 & -5 & | & -10 \end{bmatrix}.$

20.　$\begin{bmatrix} 3 & 2 & | & 6 \\ ④ & 2 & | & 5 \end{bmatrix} \xrightarrow{\frac{1}{4}R_2} \begin{bmatrix} 3 & 2 & | & 6 \\ ① & \frac{1}{2} & | & \frac{5}{4} \end{bmatrix} \xrightarrow{R_1 - 3R_2} \begin{bmatrix} 0 & \frac{1}{2} & | & \frac{9}{4} \\ 1 & \frac{1}{2} & | & \frac{5}{4} \end{bmatrix}.$

21. $\begin{bmatrix} \text{\textcircled{$-1$}} & 2 & | & 3 \\ 6 & 4 & | & 2 \end{bmatrix} \xrightarrow{-R_1} \begin{bmatrix} 1 & -2 & | & -3 \\ 6 & 4 & | & 2 \end{bmatrix} \xrightarrow{R_2 - 6R_1} \begin{bmatrix} 1 & -2 & | & -3 \\ 0 & 16 & | & 20 \end{bmatrix}.$

22. $\begin{bmatrix} \text{\textcircled{$1$}} & 3 & | & 4 \\ 2 & 4 & | & 6 \end{bmatrix} \xrightarrow{R_2 - 2R_1} \begin{bmatrix} 1 & 3 & | & 4 \\ 0 & -2 & | & -2 \end{bmatrix}.$

23. $\begin{bmatrix} \text{\textcircled{$2$}} & 4 & 6 & | & 12 \\ 2 & 3 & 1 & | & 5 \\ 3 & -1 & 2 & | & 4 \end{bmatrix} \xrightarrow{\frac{1}{2}R_1} \begin{bmatrix} 1 & 2 & 3 & | & 6 \\ 2 & 3 & 1 & | & 5 \\ 3 & -1 & 2 & | & 4 \end{bmatrix} \xrightarrow[R_3 - 3R_1]{R_2 - 2R_1}$

$\begin{bmatrix} 1 & 2 & 3 & | & 6 \\ 0 & -1 & -5 & | & -7 \\ 0 & -7 & -7 & | & -14 \end{bmatrix}.$

24. $\begin{bmatrix} 1 & 3 & 2 & | & 4 \\ \text{\textcircled{$2$}} & 4 & 8 & | & 6 \\ -1 & 2 & 3 & | & 4 \end{bmatrix} \xrightarrow{\frac{1}{2}R_2} \begin{bmatrix} 1 & 3 & 2 & | & 4 \\ 1 & 2 & 4 & | & 3 \\ -1 & 2 & 3 & | & 4 \end{bmatrix} \xrightarrow[R_3 + R_2]{R_1 - R_2}$

$\begin{bmatrix} 0 & 1 & -2 & | & 1 \\ 1 & 2 & 4 & | & 3 \\ 0 & 4 & 7 & | & 7 \end{bmatrix}.$

25. $\begin{bmatrix} 0 & 1 & 3 & | & 4 \\ 2 & 4 & \text{\textcircled{$1$}} & | & 3 \\ 5 & 6 & 2 & | & -4 \end{bmatrix} \xrightarrow[R_3 - 2R_2]{R_1 - 3R_2} \begin{bmatrix} -6 & -11 & 0 & | & -5 \\ 2 & 4 & 1 & | & 3 \\ 1 & -2 & 0 & | & -10 \end{bmatrix}.$

**26.**
$$\begin{bmatrix} 1 & 2 & 3 & | & 5 \\ 0 & \boxed{-3} & 3 & | & 2 \\ 0 & 4 & -1 & | & 3 \end{bmatrix} \xrightarrow{-\frac{1}{3}R_2} \begin{bmatrix} 1 & 2 & 3 & | & 5 \\ 0 & 1 & -1 & | & -\frac{2}{3} \\ 0 & 4 & -1 & | & 3 \end{bmatrix} \xrightarrow[R_3 - 4R_2]{R_1 - 2R_2}$$

$$\begin{bmatrix} 1 & 0 & 5 & | & \frac{19}{3} \\ 0 & 1 & -1 & | & -\frac{2}{3} \\ 0 & 0 & 3 & | & \frac{17}{3} \end{bmatrix}.$$

**27.**
$$\begin{bmatrix} \boxed{3} & 9 & | & 6 \\ 2 & 1 & | & 4 \end{bmatrix} \xrightarrow{\frac{1}{3}R_1} \begin{bmatrix} 1 & 3 & | & 2 \\ 2 & 1 & | & 4 \end{bmatrix} \xrightarrow{R_2 - 2R_1} \begin{bmatrix} 1 & 3 & | & 2 \\ 0 & -5 & | & 0 \end{bmatrix} \xrightarrow{-\frac{1}{5}R_2}$$

$$\begin{bmatrix} 1 & 3 & | & 2 \\ 0 & 1 & | & 0 \end{bmatrix} \xrightarrow{R_1 - 3R_2} \begin{bmatrix} 1 & 0 & | & 2 \\ 0 & 1 & | & 0 \end{bmatrix}.$$

**28.**
$$\begin{bmatrix} 1 & 2 & | & 1 \\ 2 & 3 & | & -1 \end{bmatrix} \xrightarrow{R_2 - 2R_1} \begin{bmatrix} 1 & 2 & | & 1 \\ 0 & -1 & | & -3 \end{bmatrix} \xrightarrow{-R_2} \begin{bmatrix} 1 & 2 & | & 1 \\ 0 & 1 & | & 3 \end{bmatrix}$$

$$\xrightarrow{R_1 - 2R_2} \begin{bmatrix} 1 & 0 & | & -5 \\ 0 & 1 & | & 3 \end{bmatrix}.$$

**29.**
$$\begin{bmatrix} 1 & 3 & 1 & | & 3 \\ 3 & 8 & 3 & | & 7 \\ 2 & -3 & 1 & | & -10 \end{bmatrix} \xrightarrow[R_3 - 2R_1]{R_2 - 3R_1} \begin{bmatrix} 1 & 3 & 1 & | & 3 \\ 0 & -1 & 0 & | & -2 \\ 0 & -9 & -1 & | & -16 \end{bmatrix} \xrightarrow{-R_2}$$

$$\begin{bmatrix} 1 & 3 & 1 & | & 3 \\ 0 & 1 & 0 & | & 2 \\ 0 & -9 & -1 & | & -16 \end{bmatrix} \xrightarrow[R_3 + 9R_2]{R_1 - 3R_2} \begin{bmatrix} 1 & 0 & 1 & | & -3 \\ 0 & 1 & 0 & | & 2 \\ 0 & 0 & -1 & | & 2 \end{bmatrix} \xrightarrow[-R_3]{R_1 + R_3}$$

$$\begin{bmatrix} 1 & 0 & 0 & | & -1 \\ 0 & 1 & 0 & | & 2 \\ 0 & 0 & 1 & | & -2 \end{bmatrix}.$$

30. $\begin{bmatrix} 0 & 1 & 3 & | & -4 \\ 1 & 2 & 1 & | & 7 \\ 1 & -2 & 0 & | & 1 \end{bmatrix}$ $\xrightarrow{R_1 \leftrightarrow R_2}$ $\begin{bmatrix} 1 & 2 & 1 & | & 7 \\ 0 & 1 & 3 & | & -4 \\ 1 & -2 & 0 & | & 1 \end{bmatrix}$

$\xrightarrow{R_3 - R_1}$ $\begin{bmatrix} 1 & 2 & 1 & | & 7 \\ 0 & 1 & 3 & | & -4 \\ 0 & -4 & -1 & | & -6 \end{bmatrix}$ $\xrightarrow[R_3 + 4R_2]{R_1 + \frac{1}{2}R_3}$

$\begin{bmatrix} 1 & 0 & \frac{1}{2} & | & 4 \\ 0 & 1 & 3 & | & -4 \\ 0 & 0 & 11 & | & -22 \end{bmatrix}$ $\xrightarrow{\frac{1}{11}R_3}$ $\begin{bmatrix} 1 & 0 & \frac{1}{2} & | & 4 \\ 0 & 1 & 3 & | & -4 \\ 0 & 0 & 1 & | & -2 \end{bmatrix}$

$\xrightarrow[R_2 - 3R_3]{R_1 - \frac{1}{2}R_3}$ $\begin{bmatrix} 1 & 0 & 0 & | & 5 \\ 0 & 1 & 0 & | & 2 \\ 0 & 0 & 1 & | & -2 \end{bmatrix}$

31. The augmented matrix is equivalent to the system of linear equations

$$3x + 9y = 6$$
$$2x + y = 4.$$

The ordered pair (2,0) is the solution to the system.

32. The augmented matrix is equivalent to the system of linear equations

$$x + 2y = 1$$
$$2x + 3y = -1.$$

x = -5 and y = 3 is the solution to the system.

33. The augmented matrix is equivalent to the system of linear equations

$$x + 3y + z = 3$$
$$3x + 8y + 3z = 7$$
$$2x - 3y + z = -10.$$

Reading off the solution from the last augmented matrix, which is in row-reduced form,

$$\begin{bmatrix} 1 & 0 & 0 & | & -1 \\ 0 & 1 & 0 & | & 2 \\ 0 & 0 & 1 & | & -2 \end{bmatrix}$$

we have $x = -1$, $y = 2$, and $z = -2$.

34. The augmented matrix is equivalent to the system of linear equations

$$y + 3z = -4$$
$$x + 2y + z = 7$$
$$x - 2y = 1.$$

$x = 5$, $y = 2$, and $z = -2$ is the solution to the system.

35. Using the Gauss–Jordan method of solution, we have

$$\begin{bmatrix} 1 & -2 & | & 8 \\ 3 & 4 & | & 4 \end{bmatrix} \xrightarrow{R_2 - 3R_1} \begin{bmatrix} 1 & -2 & | & 8 \\ 0 & 10 & | & -20 \end{bmatrix} \xrightarrow{\frac{1}{10}R_2}$$

$$\begin{bmatrix} 1 & -2 & | & 8 \\ 0 & 1 & | & -2 \end{bmatrix} \xrightarrow{R_1 + 2R_2} \begin{bmatrix} 1 & 0 & | & 4 \\ 0 & 1 & | & -2 \end{bmatrix}$$

The solution is $(4, -2)$.

36. Using the Gauss–Jordan method of solution, we have

$$\begin{bmatrix} 3 & 1 & | & 1 \\ -7 & -2 & | & -1 \end{bmatrix} \xrightarrow{\frac{1}{3}R_1} \begin{bmatrix} 1 & \frac{1}{3} & | & \frac{1}{3} \\ -7 & -2 & | & -1 \end{bmatrix} \xrightarrow{R_2 + 7R_1} \begin{bmatrix} 1 & \frac{1}{3} & | & \frac{1}{3} \\ 0 & \frac{1}{3} & | & \frac{4}{3} \end{bmatrix} \xrightarrow{3R_2}$$

$$\begin{bmatrix} 1 & \frac{1}{3} & \bigm| & \frac{1}{3} \\ 0 & 1 & \bigm| & 4 \end{bmatrix} \xrightarrow{R_1 - \frac{1}{3}R_2} \begin{bmatrix} 1 & 0 & \bigm| & -1 \\ 0 & 1 & \bigm| & 4 \end{bmatrix}.$$

The solution is $(-1,4)$.

37. Using the Gauss-Jordan method of solution, we have

$$\begin{bmatrix} 2 & -3 & \bigm| & -8 \\ 4 & 1 & \bigm| & -2 \end{bmatrix} \xrightarrow{\frac{1}{2}R_1} \begin{bmatrix} 1 & -\frac{3}{2} & \bigm| & -4 \\ 4 & 1 & \bigm| & -2 \end{bmatrix} \xrightarrow{R_2 - 4R_1} \begin{bmatrix} 1 & -\frac{3}{2} & \bigm| & -4 \\ 0 & 7 & \bigm| & 14 \end{bmatrix} \xrightarrow{\frac{1}{7}R_2}$$

$$\begin{bmatrix} 1 & -\frac{3}{2} & \bigm| & -4 \\ 0 & 1 & \bigm| & 2 \end{bmatrix} \xrightarrow{R_1 + \frac{3}{2}R_2} \begin{bmatrix} 1 & 0 & \bigm| & -1 \\ 0 & 1 & \bigm| & 2 \end{bmatrix}.$$

The solution is $(-1,2)$.

38. Using the Gauss-Jordan method of solution, we have

$$\begin{bmatrix} 5 & 3 & \bigm| & 9 \\ -2 & 1 & \bigm| & -8 \end{bmatrix} \xrightarrow{\frac{1}{5}R_1} \begin{bmatrix} 1 & \frac{3}{5} & \bigm| & \frac{9}{5} \\ -2 & 1 & \bigm| & -8 \end{bmatrix} \xrightarrow{R_2 + 2R_1} \begin{bmatrix} 1 & \frac{3}{5} & \bigm| & \frac{9}{5} \\ 0 & \frac{11}{5} & \bigm| & -\frac{22}{5} \end{bmatrix} \xrightarrow{\frac{5}{11}R_2}$$

$$\begin{bmatrix} 1 & \frac{3}{5} & \bigm| & \frac{9}{5} \\ 0 & 1 & \bigm| & -2 \end{bmatrix} \xrightarrow{R_1 - \frac{3}{5}R_2} \begin{bmatrix} 1 & 0 & \bigm| & 3 \\ 0 & 1 & \bigm| & -2 \end{bmatrix}.$$

The solution is $(3,-2)$.

39. Using the Gauss-Jordan method of solution, we have

$$\begin{bmatrix} 1 & 1 & 1 & \bigm| & 0 \\ 2 & -1 & 1 & \bigm| & 1 \\ 1 & 1 & -2 & \bigm| & 2 \end{bmatrix} \xrightarrow[R_3 - R_1]{R_2 - 2R_1} \begin{bmatrix} 1 & 1 & 1 & \bigm| & 0 \\ 0 & -3 & -1 & \bigm| & 1 \\ 0 & 0 & -3 & \bigm| & 2 \end{bmatrix} \xrightarrow{-\frac{1}{3}R_2}$$

$$\begin{bmatrix} 1 & 1 & 1 & \bigm| & 0 \\ 0 & 1 & \frac{1}{3} & \bigm| & -\frac{1}{3} \\ 0 & 0 & -3 & \bigm| & 2 \end{bmatrix} \xrightarrow{R_1 - R_2} \begin{bmatrix} 1 & 0 & \frac{2}{3} & \bigm| & \frac{1}{3} \\ 0 & 1 & \frac{1}{3} & \bigm| & -\frac{1}{3} \\ 0 & 0 & -3 & \bigm| & 2 \end{bmatrix} \xrightarrow{-\frac{1}{3}R_3}$$

$$\begin{bmatrix} 1 & 0 & \frac{2}{3} & \Big| & \frac{1}{3} \\ 0 & 1 & \frac{1}{3} & \Big| & -\frac{1}{3} \\ 0 & 0 & 1 & \Big| & -\frac{2}{3} \end{bmatrix} \xrightarrow[R_2 \ - \ \frac{1}{3}R_3]{R_1 \ - \ \frac{2}{3}R_3} \begin{bmatrix} 1 & 0 & 0 & \Big| & \frac{7}{9} \\ 0 & 1 & 0 & \Big| & -\frac{1}{9} \\ 0 & 0 & 1 & \Big| & -\frac{2}{3} \end{bmatrix}$$

The solution is $(\frac{7}{9}, -\frac{1}{9}, -\frac{2}{3})$.

40. $$\begin{bmatrix} 2 & 1 & -2 & \Big| & 4 \\ 1 & 3 & -1 & \Big| & -3 \\ 3 & 4 & -1 & \Big| & 7 \end{bmatrix} \xrightarrow{R_1 \leftrightarrow R_2} \begin{bmatrix} 1 & 3 & -1 & \Big| & -3 \\ 2 & 1 & -2 & \Big| & 4 \\ 3 & 4 & -1 & \Big| & 7 \end{bmatrix} \xrightarrow[R_3 \ - \ 3R_1]{R_2 \ - \ 2R_1}$$

$$\begin{bmatrix} 1 & 3 & -1 & \Big| & -3 \\ 0 & -5 & 0 & \Big| & 10 \\ 0 & -5 & 2 & \Big| & 16 \end{bmatrix} \xrightarrow{-\frac{1}{5} R_2} \begin{bmatrix} 1 & 3 & -1 & \Big| & -3 \\ 0 & 1 & 0 & \Big| & -2 \\ 0 & -5 & 2 & \Big| & 16 \end{bmatrix} \xrightarrow[R_3 \ + \ 5R_2]{R_1 \ - \ 3R_2}$$

$$\begin{bmatrix} 1 & 0 & -1 & \Big| & 3 \\ 0 & 1 & 0 & \Big| & -2 \\ 0 & 0 & 2 & \Big| & 6 \end{bmatrix} \xrightarrow{\frac{1}{2} R_3} \begin{bmatrix} 1 & 0 & -1 & \Big| & 3 \\ 0 & 1 & 0 & \Big| & -2 \\ 0 & 0 & 1 & \Big| & 3 \end{bmatrix} \xrightarrow{R_1 \ + \ R_3}$$

$$\begin{bmatrix} 1 & 0 & 0 & \Big| & 6 \\ 0 & 1 & 0 & \Big| & -2 \\ 0 & 0 & 1 & \Big| & 3 \end{bmatrix} .$$

The solution is $(6, -2, 3)$.

41. $$\begin{bmatrix} 2 & 2 & 1 & \Big| & 9 \\ 1 & 0 & 1 & \Big| & 4 \\ 0 & 4 & -3 & \Big| & 17 \end{bmatrix} \xrightarrow{R_2 \leftrightarrow R_1} \begin{bmatrix} 1 & 0 & 1 & \Big| & 4 \\ 2 & 2 & 1 & \Big| & 9 \\ 0 & 4 & -3 & \Big| & 17 \end{bmatrix} \xrightarrow{R_2 \ - \ 2R_1}$$

$$\begin{bmatrix} 1 & 0 & 1 & 4 \\ 0 & 2 & -1 & 1 \\ 0 & 4 & -3 & 17 \end{bmatrix} \xrightarrow{\frac{1}{2}R_2} \begin{bmatrix} 1 & 0 & 1 & 4 \\ 0 & 1 & -\frac{1}{2} & \frac{1}{2} \\ 0 & 4 & -3 & 17 \end{bmatrix} \xrightarrow{R_3 - 4R_2}$$

$$\begin{bmatrix} 1 & 0 & 1 & 4 \\ 0 & 1 & -\frac{1}{2} & \frac{1}{2} \\ 0 & 0 & -1 & 15 \end{bmatrix} \xrightarrow{-R_3} \begin{bmatrix} 1 & 0 & 1 & 4 \\ 0 & 1 & -\frac{1}{2} & \frac{1}{2} \\ 0 & 0 & 1 & -15 \end{bmatrix}$$

$$\xrightarrow[R_2 + \frac{1}{2}R_3]{R_1 - R_3} \begin{bmatrix} 1 & 0 & 0 & 19 \\ 0 & 1 & 0 & -7 \\ 0 & 0 & 1 & -15 \end{bmatrix}.$$

The solution is $(19, -7, -15)$.

42. $$\begin{bmatrix} 2 & 3 & -2 & 10 \\ 3 & -2 & 2 & 0 \\ 4 & -1 & 3 & -1 \end{bmatrix} \xrightarrow{R_1 \leftrightarrow R_2} \begin{bmatrix} 3 & -2 & 2 & 0 \\ 2 & 3 & -2 & 10 \\ 4 & -1 & 3 & -1 \end{bmatrix} \xrightarrow{R_1 - R_2}$$

$$\begin{bmatrix} 1 & -5 & 4 & -10 \\ 2 & 3 & -2 & 10 \\ 4 & -1 & 3 & -1 \end{bmatrix} \xrightarrow[R_3 - 4R_1]{R_2 - 2R_1} \begin{bmatrix} 1 & -5 & 4 & -10 \\ 0 & 13 & -10 & 30 \\ 0 & 19 & -13 & 39 \end{bmatrix} \xrightarrow{\frac{1}{13}R_2}$$

$$\begin{bmatrix} 1 & -5 & 4 & -10 \\ 0 & 1 & -\frac{10}{13} & \frac{30}{13} \\ 0 & 19 & -13 & 39 \end{bmatrix} \xrightarrow[R_3 - 19R_2]{R_1 + 5R_2} \begin{bmatrix} 1 & 0 & \frac{2}{13} & \frac{20}{13} \\ 0 & 1 & -\frac{10}{13} & \frac{30}{13} \\ 0 & 0 & \frac{21}{13} & -\frac{63}{13} \end{bmatrix} \xrightarrow{\frac{13}{21}R_3}$$

$$\begin{bmatrix} 1 & 0 & \frac{2}{13} & \frac{20}{13} \\ 0 & 1 & -\frac{10}{13} & \frac{30}{13} \\ 0 & 0 & 1 & -3 \end{bmatrix} \xrightarrow[R_2 + \frac{10}{13}R_3]{R_1 - \frac{2}{13}R_3} \begin{bmatrix} 1 & 0 & 0 & 2 \\ 0 & 1 & 0 & 0 \\ 0 & 0 & 1 & -3 \end{bmatrix}.$$

The solution is $(2, 0, -3)$.

**43.**

$$\begin{bmatrix} 0 & -1 & 1 & | & 2 \\ 4 & -3 & 2 & | & 16 \\ 3 & 2 & 1 & | & 11 \end{bmatrix} \xrightarrow{R_1 \leftrightarrow R_2} \begin{bmatrix} 4 & -3 & 2 & | & 16 \\ 0 & -1 & 1 & | & 2 \\ 3 & 2 & 1 & | & 11 \end{bmatrix} \xrightarrow{R_1 - R_3}$$

$$\begin{bmatrix} 1 & -5 & 1 & | & 5 \\ 0 & -1 & 1 & | & 2 \\ 3 & 2 & 1 & | & 11 \end{bmatrix} \xrightarrow[R_3 - 3R_1]{-R_2} \begin{bmatrix} 1 & -5 & 1 & | & 5 \\ 0 & 1 & -1 & | & -2 \\ 0 & 17 & -2 & | & -4 \end{bmatrix} \xrightarrow[R_3 - 17R_2]{R_1 + 5R_2}$$

$$\begin{bmatrix} 1 & 0 & -4 & | & -5 \\ 0 & 1 & -1 & | & -2 \\ 0 & 0 & 15 & | & 30 \end{bmatrix} \xrightarrow{\frac{1}{15}R_3} \begin{bmatrix} 1 & 0 & -4 & | & -5 \\ 0 & 1 & -1 & | & -2 \\ 0 & 0 & 1 & | & 2 \end{bmatrix}$$

$$\xrightarrow[R_2 + R_3]{R_1 + 4R_3} \begin{bmatrix} 1 & 0 & 0 & | & 3 \\ 0 & 1 & 0 & | & 0 \\ 0 & 0 & 1 & | & 2 \end{bmatrix}.$$

The solution is $(3, 0, 2)$.

**44.**

$$\begin{bmatrix} 2 & 4 & -6 & | & 38 \\ 1 & 2 & 3 & | & 7 \\ 3 & -4 & 4 & | & -19 \end{bmatrix} \xrightarrow{R_2 \leftrightarrow R_1} \begin{bmatrix} 1 & 2 & 3 & | & 7 \\ 2 & 4 & -6 & | & 38 \\ 3 & -4 & 4 & | & -19 \end{bmatrix} \xrightarrow[R_3 - 3R_1]{R_2 - 2R_1}$$

$$\begin{bmatrix} 1 & 2 & 3 & | & 7 \\ 0 & 0 & -12 & | & 24 \\ 0 & -10 & -5 & | & -40 \end{bmatrix} \xrightarrow{R_2 \leftrightarrow R_3} \begin{bmatrix} 1 & 2 & 3 & | & 7 \\ 0 & -10 & -5 & | & -40 \\ 0 & 0 & -12 & | & 24 \end{bmatrix} \xrightarrow{-\frac{1}{10}R_2}$$

$$\begin{bmatrix} 1 & 2 & 3 & | & 7 \\ 0 & 1 & \frac{1}{2} & | & 4 \\ 0 & 0 & -12 & | & 24 \end{bmatrix} \xrightarrow{R_1 - 2R_2} \begin{bmatrix} 1 & 0 & 2 & | & -1 \\ 0 & 1 & \frac{1}{2} & | & 4 \\ 0 & 0 & -12 & | & 24 \end{bmatrix} \xrightarrow{-\frac{1}{12}R_3}$$

$$\begin{bmatrix} 1 & 0 & 2 & | & -1 \\ 0 & 1 & \frac{1}{2} & | & 4 \\ 0 & 0 & 1 & | & -2 \end{bmatrix} \xrightarrow[R_2 - \frac{1}{2}R_3]{R_1 - 2R_3} \begin{bmatrix} 1 & 0 & 0 & | & 3 \\ 0 & 1 & 0 & | & 5 \\ 0 & 0 & 1 & | & -2 \end{bmatrix}.$$

The solution is $(3,5,-2)$.

45. Using the Gauss-Jordan method of solution, we have

$$\begin{bmatrix} 1 & -2 & 1 & | & 6 \\ 2 & 1 & -3 & | & -3 \\ 1 & -3 & 3 & | & 10 \end{bmatrix} \xrightarrow[R_3 - R_1]{R_2 - 2R_1} \begin{bmatrix} 1 & -2 & 1 & | & 6 \\ 0 & 5 & -5 & | & -15 \\ 0 & -1 & 2 & | & 4 \end{bmatrix} \xrightarrow{\frac{1}{5}R_2}$$

$$\begin{bmatrix} 1 & -2 & 1 & | & 6 \\ 0 & 1 & -1 & | & -3 \\ 0 & -1 & 2 & | & 4 \end{bmatrix} \xrightarrow[R_3 + R_2]{R_1 + 2R_2} \begin{bmatrix} 1 & 0 & -1 & | & 0 \\ 0 & 1 & -1 & | & -3 \\ 0 & 0 & 1 & | & 1 \end{bmatrix} \xrightarrow[R_2 + R_3]{R_1 + R_3}$$

$$\begin{bmatrix} 1 & 0 & 0 & | & 1 \\ 0 & 1 & 0 & | & -2 \\ 0 & 0 & 1 & | & 1 \end{bmatrix}.$$

Therefore, the solution is $(1,-2,1)$.

46. Using the Gauss-Jordan method of solution, we have

$$\begin{bmatrix} 2 & 3 & -6 & | & -11 \\ 1 & -2 & 3 & | & 9 \\ 3 & 1 & 0 & | & 7 \end{bmatrix} \xrightarrow{R_1 \leftrightarrow R_2} \begin{bmatrix} 1 & -2 & 3 & | & 9 \\ 2 & 3 & -6 & | & -11 \\ 3 & 1 & 0 & | & 7 \end{bmatrix} \xrightarrow[R_3 - 3R_1]{R_2 - 2R_1}$$

$$\begin{bmatrix} 1 & -2 & 3 & | & 9 \\ 0 & 7 & -12 & | & -29 \\ 0 & 7 & -9 & | & -20 \end{bmatrix} \xrightarrow{\frac{1}{7}R_2} \begin{bmatrix} 1 & -2 & 3 & | & 9 \\ 0 & 1 & -\frac{12}{7} & | & -\frac{29}{7} \\ 0 & 7 & -9 & | & -20 \end{bmatrix} \xrightarrow[R_3 - 7R_2]{R_1 + 2R_2}$$

$$\begin{bmatrix} 1 & 0 & -\frac{3}{7} & \bigm| & \frac{5}{7} \\ 0 & 1 & -\frac{12}{7} & \bigm| & -\frac{29}{7} \\ 0 & 0 & 3 & \bigm| & 9 \end{bmatrix} \xrightarrow{\frac{1}{3}R_3} \begin{bmatrix} 1 & 0 & -\frac{3}{7} & \bigm| & \frac{5}{7} \\ 0 & 1 & -\frac{12}{7} & \bigm| & -\frac{29}{7} \\ 0 & 0 & 1 & \bigm| & 3 \end{bmatrix} \xrightarrow[R_2 + \frac{12}{7}R_3]{R_1 + \frac{3}{7}R_3}$$

$$\begin{bmatrix} 1 & 0 & 0 & \bigm| & 2 \\ 0 & 1 & 0 & \bigm| & 1 \\ 0 & 0 & 1 & \bigm| & 3 \end{bmatrix}.$$

Therefore, the solution is $(2,1,3)$.

47. $\begin{bmatrix} 2 & 0 & 3 & \bigm| & -1 \\ 3 & -2 & 1 & \bigm| & 9 \\ 1 & 1 & 4 & \bigm| & 4 \end{bmatrix} \xrightarrow{R_1 \leftrightarrow R_3} \begin{bmatrix} 1 & 1 & 4 & \bigm| & 4 \\ 3 & -2 & 1 & \bigm| & 9 \\ 2 & 0 & 3 & \bigm| & -1 \end{bmatrix} \xrightarrow[R_3 - 2R_1]{R_2 - 3R_1}$

$\begin{bmatrix} 1 & 1 & 4 & \bigm| & 4 \\ 0 & -5 & -11 & \bigm| & -3 \\ 0 & -2 & -5 & \bigm| & -9 \end{bmatrix} \xrightarrow{-\frac{1}{5}R_2} \begin{bmatrix} 1 & 1 & 4 & \bigm| & 4 \\ 0 & 1 & \frac{11}{5} & \bigm| & \frac{3}{5} \\ 0 & -2 & -5 & \bigm| & -9 \end{bmatrix} \xrightarrow[R_3 + 2R_2]{R_1 - R_2}$

$\begin{bmatrix} 1 & 0 & \frac{9}{5} & \bigm| & \frac{17}{5} \\ 0 & 1 & \frac{11}{5} & \bigm| & \frac{3}{5} \\ 0 & 0 & -\frac{3}{5} & \bigm| & -\frac{39}{5} \end{bmatrix} \xrightarrow{-\frac{5}{3}R_3} \begin{bmatrix} 1 & 0 & \frac{9}{5} & \bigm| & \frac{17}{5} \\ 0 & 1 & \frac{11}{5} & \bigm| & \frac{3}{5} \\ 0 & 0 & 1 & \bigm| & 13 \end{bmatrix} \xrightarrow[R_2 - \frac{11}{5}R_3]{R_1 - \frac{9}{5}R_3}$

$\begin{bmatrix} 1 & 0 & 0 & \bigm| & -20 \\ 0 & 1 & 0 & \bigm| & -28 \\ 0 & 0 & 1 & \bigm| & 13 \end{bmatrix}.$

Therefore, the solution is $(-20,-28,13)$.

48. $\begin{bmatrix} 2 & -1 & 3 & \bigm| & -4 \\ 1 & -2 & 1 & \bigm| & -1 \\ 1 & -5 & 2 & \bigm| & -3 \end{bmatrix} \xrightarrow{R_1 \leftrightarrow R_2} \begin{bmatrix} 1 & -2 & 1 & \bigm| & -1 \\ 2 & -1 & 3 & \bigm| & -4 \\ 1 & -5 & 2 & \bigm| & -3 \end{bmatrix} \xrightarrow[R_3 - R_1]{R_2 - 2R_1}$

$$\begin{bmatrix} 1 & -2 & 1 & | & -1 \\ 0 & 3 & 1 & | & -2 \\ 0 & -3 & 1 & | & -2 \end{bmatrix} \xrightarrow{\frac{1}{3}R_2} \begin{bmatrix} 1 & -2 & 1 & | & -1 \\ 0 & 1 & \frac{1}{3} & | & -\frac{2}{3} \\ 0 & -3 & 1 & | & -2 \end{bmatrix} \xrightarrow[R_3 + 3R_2]{R_1 + 2R_2}$$

$$\begin{bmatrix} 1 & 0 & \frac{5}{3} & | & -\frac{7}{3} \\ 0 & 1 & \frac{1}{3} & | & -\frac{2}{3} \\ 0 & 0 & 2 & | & -4 \end{bmatrix} \xrightarrow{\frac{1}{2}R_3} \begin{bmatrix} 1 & 0 & \frac{5}{3} & | & -\frac{7}{3} \\ 0 & 1 & \frac{1}{3} & | & -\frac{2}{3} \\ 0 & 0 & 1 & | & -2 \end{bmatrix} \xrightarrow[R_2 - \frac{1}{3}R_3]{R_1 - \frac{5}{3}R_3}$$

$$\begin{bmatrix} 1 & 0 & 0 & | & 1 \\ 0 & 1 & 0 & | & 0 \\ 0 & 0 & 1 & | & -2 \end{bmatrix}.$$

Therefore, the solution is $(1,0,-2)$.

49. $\begin{bmatrix} 1 & -1 & 3 & | & 14 \\ 1 & 1 & 1 & | & 6 \\ -2 & -1 & 1 & | & -4 \end{bmatrix} \xrightarrow[R_3 + 2R_1]{R_2 - R_1} \begin{bmatrix} 1 & -1 & 3 & | & 14 \\ 0 & 2 & -2 & | & -8 \\ 0 & -3 & 7 & | & 24 \end{bmatrix} \xrightarrow{\frac{1}{2}R_2}$

$\begin{bmatrix} 1 & -1 & 3 & | & 14 \\ 0 & 1 & -1 & | & -4 \\ 0 & -3 & 7 & | & 24 \end{bmatrix} \xrightarrow[R_3 + 3R_2]{R_1 + R_2} \begin{bmatrix} 1 & 0 & 2 & | & 10 \\ 0 & 1 & -1 & | & -4 \\ 0 & 0 & 4 & | & 12 \end{bmatrix} \xrightarrow{\frac{1}{4}R_3}$

$\begin{bmatrix} 1 & 0 & 2 & | & 10 \\ 0 & 1 & -1 & | & -4 \\ 0 & 0 & 1 & | & 3 \end{bmatrix} \xrightarrow[R_2 + R_3]{R_1 - 2R_3} \begin{bmatrix} 1 & 0 & 0 & | & 4 \\ 0 & 1 & 0 & | & -1 \\ 0 & 0 & 1 & | & 3 \end{bmatrix}.$

Therefore, the solution is $(4,-1,3)$.

50. Using the Gauss-Jordan method of solution, we have

$\begin{bmatrix} 2 & -1 & -1 & | & 0 \\ 3 & 2 & 1 & | & 7 \\ 1 & 2 & 2 & | & 5 \end{bmatrix} \xrightarrow{R_1 \leftrightarrow R_3} \begin{bmatrix} 1 & 2 & 2 & | & 5 \\ 3 & 2 & 1 & | & 7 \\ 2 & -1 & -1 & | & 0 \end{bmatrix} \xrightarrow[R_3 - 2R_1]{R_2 - 3R_1}$

$$\begin{bmatrix} 1 & 2 & 2 & \bigm| & 5 \\ 0 & -4 & -5 & \bigm| & -8 \\ 0 & -5 & -5 & \bigm| & -10 \end{bmatrix} \xrightarrow{-\frac{1}{4}R_2} \begin{bmatrix} 1 & 2 & 2 & \bigm| & 5 \\ 0 & 1 & \frac{5}{4} & \bigm| & 2 \\ 0 & -5 & -5 & \bigm| & -10 \end{bmatrix} \xrightarrow[R_3 + 5R_2]{R_1 - 2R_2}$$

$$\begin{bmatrix} 1 & 0 & -\frac{1}{2} & \bigm| & 1 \\ 0 & 1 & \frac{5}{4} & \bigm| & 2 \\ 0 & 0 & \frac{5}{4} & \bigm| & 0 \end{bmatrix} \xrightarrow{\frac{4}{5}R_3} \begin{bmatrix} 1 & 0 & -\frac{1}{2} & \bigm| & 1 \\ 0 & 1 & \frac{5}{4} & \bigm| & 2 \\ 0 & 0 & 1 & \bigm| & 0 \end{bmatrix} \xrightarrow[R_2 - \frac{5}{4}R_3]{R_1 + \frac{1}{2}R_3}$$

$$\begin{bmatrix} 1 & 0 & 0 & \bigm| & 1 \\ 0 & 1 & 0 & \bigm| & 2 \\ 0 & 0 & 1 & \bigm| & 0 \end{bmatrix}.$$

Therefore, the solution is (1, 2, 0).

51. We wish to solve the system of equations

$$\begin{aligned} x \quad + \quad y &= \quad 500 \qquad &&(x = \text{the number of acres of corn planted}) \\ 42x \quad + \quad 30y &= 18{,}600 \qquad &&(y = \text{the number of acres of wheat planted}) \end{aligned}$$

Using the Gauss–Jordan method of elimination, we find

$$\begin{bmatrix} 1 & 1 & \bigm| & 500 \\ 42 & 30 & \bigm| & 18600 \end{bmatrix} \xrightarrow{R_2 - 42R_1} \begin{bmatrix} 1 & 1 & \bigm| & 500 \\ 0 & -12 & \bigm| & -2400 \end{bmatrix} \xrightarrow{-\frac{1}{12}R_2}$$

$$\begin{bmatrix} 1 & 1 & \bigm| & 500 \\ 0 & 1 & \bigm| & 200 \end{bmatrix} \xrightarrow{R_1 - R_2} \begin{bmatrix} 1 & 0 & \bigm| & 300 \\ 0 & 1 & \bigm| & 200 \end{bmatrix}.$$

The solution to this system of equations is $x = 300$ and $y = 200$. We conclude that Mr. Johnson should plant 300 acres of corn and 200 acres of wheat.

52. We wish to solve the system of equations

$$x + y = 2000 \qquad (x = \text{the amount invested at 6 percent})$$

$$0.06x + 0.08y = 144 \qquad (y = \text{the amount invested at 8 percent})$$

Using the Gauss-Jordan method of elimination, we find

$$\begin{bmatrix} 1 & 1 & | & 2000 \\ 0.06 & 0.08 & | & 144 \end{bmatrix} \xrightarrow{R_2 - 0.06R_1} \begin{bmatrix} 1 & 1 & | & 2000 \\ 0 & 0.02 & | & 24 \end{bmatrix} \xrightarrow{50R_2}$$

$$\begin{bmatrix} 1 & 1 & | & 2000 \\ 0 & 1 & | & 1200 \end{bmatrix} \xrightarrow{R_1 - R_2} \begin{bmatrix} 1 & 0 & | & 800 \\ 0 & 1 & | & 1200 \end{bmatrix}.$$

The solution to this system of equations is x = 800 and y = 1200. We conclude that Michael should invest $800 at 6 percent per year and $1200 at 8 percent per year.

53. Let x denote the number of pounds of the $2.50/lb coffee and y denote the number of pounds of the $3.00/lb coffee. Then we are required to solve the system

$$x + y = 100$$

$$2.50x + 3.00y = 280.$$

Using the Gauss-Jordan method of elimination, we have

$$\begin{bmatrix} 1 & 1 & | & 100 \\ 2.5 & 3 & | & 280 \end{bmatrix} \xrightarrow{R_2 - 2.5R_1} \begin{bmatrix} 1 & 1 & | & 100 \\ 0 & 0.5 & | & 30 \end{bmatrix} \xrightarrow{2R_2}$$

$$\begin{bmatrix} 1 & 1 & | & 100 \\ 0 & 1 & | & 60 \end{bmatrix} \xrightarrow{R_1 - R_2} \begin{bmatrix} 1 & 0 & | & 40 \\ 0 & 1 & | & 60 \end{bmatrix}.$$

Therefore, 40 pounds of the $2.50/lb coffee and 60 pounds of the $3.00/lb coffee should be used in the 100 lb mixture.

54. Let the amount of money invested in the bonds yielding 8% be x dollars and the amount of money invested in the bonds yielding 10% be y dollars. Then the solution to the problem can be found by solving the system of equations

$$x + y = 30{,}000$$

$$0.08x + 0.10y = 2{,}640.$$

Using the Gauss–Jordan method of elimination, we have

$$
\begin{bmatrix} 1 & 1 & \bigm| & 30{,}000 \\ 0.08 & 0.10 & \bigm| & 2{,}640 \end{bmatrix}
\xrightarrow{R_2 - 0.08R_1}
\begin{bmatrix} 1 & 1 & \bigm| & 30{,}000 \\ 0 & 0.02 & \bigm| & 240 \end{bmatrix}
\xrightarrow{50R_2}
$$

$$
\begin{bmatrix} 1 & 1 & \bigm| & 30{,}000 \\ 0 & 1 & \bigm| & 12{,}000 \end{bmatrix}
\xrightarrow{R_1 - R_2}
\begin{bmatrix} 1 & 0 & \bigm| & 18{,}000 \\ 0 & 1 & \bigm| & 12{,}000 \end{bmatrix}.
$$

Then the amount she has invested in bonds yielding 8% is $18,000 and the amount she has invested in bonds yielding 10% is $12,000.

55. Let $x$ and $y$ denote the number of children and adults who rode the bus during the morning shift, respectively. Then the solution to the problem can be found by solving the system of equations

$$x + y = 1000$$

$$0.25x + 0.75y = 650.$$

Using the Gauss–Jordan elimination method, we have

$$
\begin{bmatrix} 1 & 1 & \bigm| & 1000 \\ 0.25 & 0.75 & \bigm| & 650 \end{bmatrix}
\xrightarrow{R_2 - 0.25R_1}
\begin{bmatrix} 1 & 1 & \bigm| & 1000 \\ 0 & 0.5 & \bigm| & 400 \end{bmatrix}
\xrightarrow{2R_2}
$$

$$
\begin{bmatrix} 1 & 1 & \bigm| & 1000 \\ 0 & 1 & \bigm| & 800 \end{bmatrix}
\xrightarrow{R_1 - R_2}
\begin{bmatrix} 1 & 0 & \bigm| & 200 \\ 0 & 1 & \bigm| & 800 \end{bmatrix}.
$$

We conclude that there 800 adults and 200 children rode the bus during the morning shift.

56. Let $x$, $y$, and $z$ denote the number of one-bedroom units, two-bedroom townhouses, and three-bedroom townhouses, respectively. Then we are required to solve the system

$$x + y + z = 192$$

$$x - y - z = 0$$

$$x \quad\ - 3z = 0.$$

Using the Gauss-Jordan method of elimination, we find that

$$\begin{bmatrix} 1 & 1 & 1 & | & 192 \\ 1 & -1 & -1 & | & 0 \\ 1 & 0 & -3 & | & 0 \end{bmatrix} \xrightarrow[\;R_3 \;-\; R_1\;]{R_2 \;-\; R_1} \begin{bmatrix} 1 & 1 & 1 & | & 192 \\ 0 & -2 & -2 & | & -192 \\ 0 & -1 & -4 & | & -192 \end{bmatrix} \xrightarrow{\frac{-1}{2}R_2}$$

$$\begin{bmatrix} 1 & 1 & 1 & | & 192 \\ 0 & 1 & 1 & | & 96 \\ 0 & -1 & -4 & | & -192 \end{bmatrix} \xrightarrow[\;R_3 \;+\; R_2\;]{R_1 \;-\; R_2} \begin{bmatrix} 1 & 0 & 0 & | & 96 \\ 0 & 1 & 1 & | & 96 \\ 0 & 0 & -3 & | & -96 \end{bmatrix} \xrightarrow{-\frac{1}{3}R_3}$$

$$\begin{bmatrix} 1 & 0 & 0 & | & 96 \\ 0 & 1 & 1 & | & 96 \\ 0 & 0 & 1 & | & 32 \end{bmatrix} \xrightarrow{R_2 \;-\; R_3} \begin{bmatrix} 1 & 0 & 0 & | & 96 \\ 0 & 1 & 0 & | & 64 \\ 0 & 0 & 1 & | & 32 \end{bmatrix}.$$

Therefore, 96 one-bedroom, 64 two-bedroom, and 32 three-bedroom units should be built.

57.  Let x, y, and z, denote the amount of money he should invest in a savings account, in mutual funds, and in money market certificates respectively. Then, we are required to solve the system

$$0.06x + 0.08y + 0.12z = 21,600$$

$$2x \qquad\quad - \quad z = \quad 0$$

$$0.08y - 0.12z = \quad 0.$$

Using the Gauss-Jordan method of elimination, we find

$$\begin{bmatrix} 0.06 & 0.08 & 0.12 & | & 21,600 \\ 2 & 0 & -1 & | & 0 \\ 0 & 0.08 & -0.12 & | & 0 \end{bmatrix} \xrightarrow[\;\frac{1}{0.08} R_3\;]{\frac{1}{0.06} R_1} \begin{bmatrix} 1 & \frac{4}{3} & 2 & | & 360,000 \\ 2 & 0 & -1 & | & 0 \\ 0 & 1 & -\frac{3}{2} & | & 0 \end{bmatrix}$$

$$\xrightarrow{R_2 \;-2R_1} \begin{bmatrix} 1 & \frac{4}{3} & 2 & | & 360,000 \\ 0 & -\frac{8}{3} & -5 & | & -720,000 \\ 0 & 1 & -\frac{3}{2} & | & 0 \end{bmatrix} \xrightarrow{-\frac{3}{8}R_2} \begin{bmatrix} 1 & \frac{4}{3} & 2 & | & 360,000 \\ 0 & 1 & \frac{15}{8} & | & 270,000 \\ 0 & 1 & -\frac{3}{2} & | & 0 \end{bmatrix}$$

$$\begin{array}{c} R_2 - \frac{4}{3}R_2 \\ \xrightarrow{\hspace{1.5cm}} \\ R_3 - R_2 \end{array} \left[\begin{array}{ccc|c} 1 & 0 & -\frac{1}{2} & 0 \\ 0 & 1 & \frac{15}{8} & 270,000 \\ 0 & 0 & -\frac{27}{8} & -270,000 \end{array}\right] \xrightarrow{-\frac{8}{27}R_3} \left[\begin{array}{ccc|c} 1 & 0 & -\frac{1}{2} & 0 \\ 0 & 1 & \frac{15}{8} & 270,000 \\ 0 & 0 & 1 & 80,000 \end{array}\right]$$

$$\begin{array}{c} R_1 + \frac{1}{2}R_3 \\ \xrightarrow{\hspace{1.5cm}} \\ R_2 - \frac{15}{8}R_3 \end{array} \left[\begin{array}{ccc|c} 1 & 0 & 0 & 40,000 \\ 0 & 1 & 0 & 120,000 \\ 0 & 0 & 1 & 80,000 \end{array}\right]$$

Therefore, Mr. Carrington should invest \$40,000 in a savings account, \$120,000 in mutual funds, and \$80,000 in money-market certificates.

58. Let $x$, $y$, and $z$ denote the number of tickets sold to children, students and adults, respectively. Then the solution to the problem can be found by solving the system

$$x + y + z = 900$$

$$x + y - 2z = 0$$

$$2x + 3y + 4z = 2800.$$

Using the Gauss-Jordan elimination method, we have

$$\left[\begin{array}{ccc|c} 1 & 1 & 1 & 900 \\ 1 & 1 & -2 & 0 \\ 2 & 3 & 4 & 2800 \end{array}\right] \begin{array}{c} R_2 - R_1 \\ \xrightarrow{\hspace{1cm}} \\ R_3 - 2R_1 \end{array} \left[\begin{array}{ccc|c} 1 & 1 & 1 & 900 \\ 0 & 0 & -3 & -900 \\ 0 & 1 & 2 & 1000 \end{array}\right] \xrightarrow{R_2 \leftrightarrow R_3}$$

$$\left[\begin{array}{ccc|c} 1 & 1 & 1 & 900 \\ 0 & 1 & 2 & 1000 \\ 0 & 0 & -3 & -900 \end{array}\right] \xrightarrow{R_1 - R_2} \left[\begin{array}{ccc|c} 1 & 0 & -1 & -100 \\ 0 & 1 & 2 & 1000 \\ 0 & 0 & -3 & -900 \end{array}\right] \xrightarrow{-\frac{1}{3}R_3}$$

$$\left[\begin{array}{ccc|c} 1 & 0 & -1 & -100 \\ 0 & 1 & 2 & 1000 \\ 0 & 0 & 1 & 300 \end{array}\right] \begin{array}{c} R_1 + R_3 \\ \xrightarrow{\hspace{1cm}} \\ R_2 - 2R_3 \end{array} \left[\begin{array}{ccc|c} 1 & 0 & 0 & 200 \\ 0 & 1 & 0 & 400 \\ 0 & 0 & 1 & 300 \end{array}\right].$$

We conclude that 200 children attended the show.

59. Let x, y, and z denote the number of compact, intermediate, and full-size cars, respectively, to be purchased. Then the problem can be solved by solving the system

$$8000x + 12000y + 16000z = 1000000$$
$$x - 2y = 0$$
$$x + y + z = 100.$$

Using the Gauss-Jordan method of elimination, we have

$$\begin{bmatrix} 8000 & 12000 & 16000 & | & 1000000 \\ 1 & -2 & 0 & | & 0 \\ 1 & 1 & 1 & | & 100 \end{bmatrix} \quad R_1 \longleftrightarrow R_3$$

$$\begin{bmatrix} 1 & 1 & 1 & | & 100 \\ 1 & -2 & 0 & | & 0 \\ 8000 & 12000 & 16000 & | & 1000000 \end{bmatrix} \quad \xrightarrow[R_3 - 8000R_1]{R_2 - R_1}$$

$$\begin{bmatrix} 1 & 1 & 1 & | & 100 \\ 0 & -3 & -1 & | & -100 \\ 0 & 4000 & 8000 & | & 200000 \end{bmatrix} \quad \xrightarrow{-\frac{1}{3}R_2}$$

$$\begin{bmatrix} 1 & 1 & 1 & | & 100 \\ 0 & 1 & \frac{1}{3} & | & \frac{100}{3} \\ 0 & 4000 & 8000 & | & 200000 \end{bmatrix} \quad \xrightarrow[R_3 - 4000R_2]{R_1 - R_2}$$

$$\begin{bmatrix} 1 & 0 & \frac{2}{3} & | & \frac{200}{3} \\ 0 & 1 & \frac{1}{3} & | & \frac{100}{3} \\ 0 & 0 & \frac{20000}{3} & | & \frac{200000}{3} \end{bmatrix} \quad \xrightarrow{\frac{3}{20000}R_3}$$

$$\begin{bmatrix} 1 & 0 & \frac{2}{3} & | & \frac{200}{3} \\ 0 & 1 & \frac{1}{3} & | & \frac{100}{3} \\ 0 & 0 & 1 & | & 10 \end{bmatrix} \quad \xrightarrow[R_2 - \frac{1}{3}R_3]{R_1 - \frac{2}{3}R_3}$$

$$\begin{bmatrix} 1 & 0 & 0 & 60 \\ 0 & 1 & 0 & 30 \\ 0 & 0 & 1 & 10 \end{bmatrix}.$$

We conclude that 60 compact cars, 30 intermediate-size cars, and 10 full-size cars will be purchased.

60. Let x, y, and z denote the amount of money invested in high-risk stocks, medium-risk stocks, and low-risk stocks, respectively. Then the problem   can be solved by solving the system

$$x + y + z = 200,000$$

$$2x + 2y - z = 0$$

~~6x + y - 3z = 0.~~    $.15x + .10y + .06z = 18000$

Using the Gauss-Jordan method of elimination, we have

$$\begin{bmatrix} 1 & 1 & 1 & | & 200000 \\ 2 & 2 & -1 & | & 0 \\ 6 & 1 & -3 & | & 0 \end{bmatrix} \xrightarrow[\begin{array}{c} R_2 - 2R_1 \\ R_3 - 6R_1 \end{array}]{} \begin{bmatrix} 1 & 1 & 1 & | & 200000 \\ 0 & 0 & -3 & | & -400000 \\ 0 & -5 & -9 & | & -1200000 \end{bmatrix} \xrightarrow{R_2 \leftrightarrow R_3}$$

$$\begin{bmatrix} 1 & 1 & 1 & | & 200000 \\ 0 & -5 & -9 & | & -1200000 \\ 0 & 0 & -3 & | & -400000 \end{bmatrix} \xrightarrow{-\frac{1}{5}R_2} \begin{bmatrix} 1 & 1 & 1 & | & 200000 \\ 0 & 1 & \frac{9}{5} & | & 240000 \\ 0 & 0 & -3 & | & -400000 \end{bmatrix} \xrightarrow{R_1 - R_2}$$

$$\begin{bmatrix} 1 & 0 & -\frac{4}{5} & | & -40000 \\ 0 & 1 & \frac{9}{5} & | & 240000 \\ 0 & 0 & -3 & | & -400000 \end{bmatrix} \xrightarrow{-\frac{1}{3}R_3} \begin{bmatrix} 1 & 0 & -\frac{4}{5} & | & -40000 \\ 0 & 1 & \frac{9}{5} & | & 240000 \\ 0 & 0 & 1 & | & \frac{-400,000}{3} \end{bmatrix} \xrightarrow[\begin{array}{c} R_1 + \frac{4}{5}R_3 \\ R_2 - \frac{9}{5}R_3 \end{array}]{}$$

$$\begin{bmatrix} 1 & 0 & 0 & | & \frac{200000}{3} \\ 0 & 1 & 0 & | & 0 \\ 0 & 0 & 1 & | & \frac{400000}{3} \end{bmatrix}.$$

We conclude that the investment club should invest \$66,666.67 in high risk stocks, \$0 in medium risk stocks, and \$133,333.33 in low risk stocks.

61. Let x, y, and z, represent the number of ounces of Food I, Food II, and Food III used in the meal, respectively. Then the problem reduces to solving the following system of linear equations:

$$10x + 6y + 8z = 100$$

$$10x + 12y + 6z = 100$$

$$5x + 4y + 12z = 100.$$

Using the Gauss-Jordan method of elimination, we obtain

$$\begin{bmatrix} 10 & 6 & 8 & | & 100 \\ 10 & 12 & 6 & | & 100 \\ 5 & 4 & 12 & | & 100 \end{bmatrix} \xrightarrow{\frac{1}{10}R_1} \begin{bmatrix} 1 & \frac{3}{5} & \frac{4}{5} & | & 10 \\ 10 & 12 & 6 & | & 100 \\ 5 & 4 & 12 & | & 100 \end{bmatrix} \xrightarrow[R_3 - 5R_1]{R_2 - 10R_1}$$

$$\begin{bmatrix} 1 & \frac{3}{5} & \frac{4}{5} & | & 10 \\ 0 & 6 & -2 & | & 0 \\ 0 & 1 & 8 & | & 50 \end{bmatrix} \xrightarrow{\frac{1}{6}R_2} \begin{bmatrix} 1 & \frac{3}{5} & \frac{4}{5} & | & 10 \\ 0 & 1 & -\frac{1}{3} & | & 0 \\ 0 & 1 & 8 & | & 50 \end{bmatrix} \xrightarrow[R_3 - R_2]{R_1 - \frac{3}{5}R_2}$$

$$\begin{bmatrix} 1 & 0 & 1 & | & 10 \\ 0 & 1 & -\frac{1}{3} & | & 0 \\ 0 & 0 & \frac{25}{3} & | & 50 \end{bmatrix} \xrightarrow{\frac{3}{25}R_3} \begin{bmatrix} 1 & 0 & 1 & | & 10 \\ 0 & 1 & -\frac{1}{3} & | & 0 \\ 0 & 0 & 1 & | & 6 \end{bmatrix} \xrightarrow[R_2 + \frac{1}{3}R_3]{R_1 - R_3}$$

$$\begin{bmatrix} 1 & 0 & 0 & | & 4 \\ 0 & 1 & 0 & | & 2 \\ 0 & 0 & 1 & | & 6 \end{bmatrix}.$$

We conclude that 4 oz of Food I, 2 oz of Food II, and 6 oz of Food III should be used to prepare the meal.

62. Let x, y, and z denote the amount of money invested in stocks, bonds, and a money-market account, respectively. Then the problem can be solved by solving the system

$$x + y + z = 100,000$$

$$12x + 8y + 4z = 1,000,000$$

$$20x + 10y - 100z = 0.$$

Using the Gauss–Jordan method of elimination, we have

$$
\begin{bmatrix}
1 & 1 & 1 & 100000 \\
12 & 8 & 4 & 1000000 \\
20 & 10 & -100 & 0
\end{bmatrix}
\xrightarrow[R_3\ -\ 20R_1]{R_2\ -\ 12R_1}
\begin{bmatrix}
1 & 1 & 1 & 100000 \\
0 & -4 & -8 & -200000 \\
0 & -10 & -120 & -2000000
\end{bmatrix}
\xrightarrow{-\frac{1}{4}R_2}
$$

$$
\begin{bmatrix}
1 & 1 & 1 & 100000 \\
0 & 1 & 2 & 50000 \\
0 & -10 & -120 & -2000000
\end{bmatrix}
\xrightarrow{R_1\ -\ R_2}
\begin{bmatrix}
1 & 0 & -1 & 50000 \\
0 & 1 & 2 & 50000 \\
0 & 0 & -100 & -1500000
\end{bmatrix}
\xrightarrow{-\frac{1}{100}R_3}
$$

$$
\begin{bmatrix}
1 & 0 & -1 & 50000 \\
0 & 1 & 2 & 50000 \\
0 & 0 & 1 & 15000
\end{bmatrix}
\xrightarrow[R_2\ -\ 2R_3]{R_1\ +\ R_3}
\begin{bmatrix}
1 & 0 & 0 & 65000 \\
0 & 1 & 0 & 20000 \\
0 & 0 & 1 & 15000
\end{bmatrix}
$$

We conclude that the Garcias should invest $65,000 in stocks, $20,000 in bonds, and $15,000 in a money-market account.

63.  Let

$x$ = the number of front orchestra seats sold

$y$ = the number of rear orchestra seats sold

and  $z$ = the number of front balcony seats sold for this performance.

Then, we are required to solve the system

$$
\begin{aligned}
x + y + z &= 1{,}000 \\
80x + 60y + 50z &= 62{,}800 \\
x + y - 2z &= 400.
\end{aligned}
$$

Using the Gauss–Jordan method of elimination, we find

$$
\begin{bmatrix}
1 & 1 & 1 & 1000 \\
80 & 60 & 50 & 62800 \\
1 & 1 & -2 & 400
\end{bmatrix}
\xrightarrow[R_3\ -\ R_1]{R_2\ -\ 80R_1}
\begin{bmatrix}
1 & 1 & 1 & 1000 \\
0 & -20 & -30 & -17200 \\
0 & 0 & -3 & -600
\end{bmatrix}
\xrightarrow[-\frac{1}{3}R_3]{-\frac{1}{20}R_2}
$$

$$\begin{bmatrix} 1 & 1 & 1 & \bigm| & 1000 \\ 0 & 1 & \frac{3}{2} & \bigm| & 860 \\ 0 & 0 & 1 & \bigm| & 200 \end{bmatrix} \xrightarrow{R_1 - R_2} \begin{bmatrix} 1 & 0 & -\frac{1}{2} & \bigm| & 140 \\ 0 & 1 & \frac{3}{2} & \bigm| & 860 \\ 0 & 0 & 1 & \bigm| & 200 \end{bmatrix} \xrightarrow[R_2 - \frac{3}{2}R_3]{R_1 + \frac{1}{2}R_3}$$

$$\begin{bmatrix} 1 & 0 & 0 & \bigm| & 240 \\ 0 & 1 & 0 & \bigm| & 560 \\ 0 & 0 & 1 & \bigm| & 200 \end{bmatrix}.$$

We conclude that tickets for 240 front orchestra seats, 560 rear orchestra seats, and 200 front balcony seats were sold.

64. Let

   $x$ = the number of dozens of sleeveless blouses produced per day

   $y$ = the number of dozens of short-sleeve blouses produced per day

and $z$ = the number of dozens of long-sleeve blouses produced per day.

Then, we want to solve the system

$$9x + 12y + 15z = 4800$$

$$22x + 24y + 28z = 9600$$

$$6x + 8y + 8z = 2880.$$

Using the Gauss-Jordan method of elimination, we find

$$\begin{bmatrix} 9 & 12 & 15 & \bigm| & 4800 \\ 22 & 24 & 28 & \bigm| & 9600 \\ 6 & 8 & 8 & \bigm| & 2880 \end{bmatrix} \xrightarrow{\frac{1}{9}R_1} \begin{bmatrix} 1 & \frac{4}{3} & \frac{5}{3} & \bigm| & \frac{1600}{3} \\ 22 & 24 & 28 & \bigm| & 9600 \\ 6 & 8 & 8 & \bigm| & 2880 \end{bmatrix} \xrightarrow[R_3 - 6R_1]{R_2 - 22R_1}$$

$$\begin{bmatrix} 1 & \frac{4}{3} & \frac{5}{3} & \bigm| & \frac{1600}{3} \\ 0 & \frac{-16}{3} & \frac{-26}{3} & \bigm| & \frac{-6400}{3} \\ 0 & 0 & -2 & \bigm| & -320 \end{bmatrix} \xrightarrow{-\frac{3}{16}R_2} \begin{bmatrix} 1 & \frac{4}{3} & \frac{5}{3} & \bigm| & \frac{1600}{3} \\ 0 & 1 & \frac{13}{8} & \bigm| & 400 \\ 0 & 0 & -2 & \bigm| & -320 \end{bmatrix} \xrightarrow[-\frac{1}{2}R_3]{R_1 - \frac{4}{3}R_2}$$

$$\begin{bmatrix} 1 & 0 & -\frac{1}{2} & | & 0 \\ 0 & 1 & \frac{13}{8} & | & 400 \\ 0 & 0 & 1 & | & 160 \end{bmatrix} \xrightarrow[R_2 - \frac{13}{8}R_3]{R_1 + \frac{1}{2}R_3} \begin{bmatrix} 1 & 0 & 0 & | & 80 \\ 0 & 1 & 0 & | & 140 \\ 0 & 0 & 1 & | & 160 \end{bmatrix}$$

Therefore, the manufacturer should produce 80 dozen sleeveless, 140 dozen short-sleeve and 160 dozen long-sleeve blouses per day.

## USING TECHNOLOGY EXERCISES 2.2, page 98

1.  $(3,1,-1,2)$  2.  $(1,0,-2,-1)$  3.  $(5,4,-3,-4)$

4.  $(-256,-33,-12,167)$  5.  $(1,-1,2,0,3)$

6.  $(1.2,-0.8,3.6,4.7,2.1)$

## EXERCISES 2.3, page 108

1.  a. The system has one solution.  b. The solution is $(3,-1,2)$.

2.  a. The system has one solution.  b. The solution is $(3,-2,1)$.

3.  a. The system has one solution.  b. The solution is $(2,4)$.

4.  a. The system has one solution.  b. The solution is $(3,1)$.

5.  a. The system has infinitely many solutions.

    b. Letting $x_3 = t$, we see that the solutions are given by $(4-t,-2,t)$, where $t$ is a parameter.

6.  a. The system has infinitely many solutions.

    b. Letting $x_3 = t$, we see that the solutions are given by $(3,-1-t,t,2)$, where $t$ is a parameter.

7.  a. The system has no solution. The last row contains all zeros to the left of the vertical line and a nonzero number (1) to its right.

8.  a. The system has no solution. The last row contains all zeros to the left of the vertical line and a nonzero number (1) to its right.

9.  a. The system has infinitely many solutions.

    b. Letting $x_4 = t$, we see that the solutions are given by

$(2,-1,2-t,t)$, where t is a parameter.

10.  a. The system has infinitely many solutions.

   b. Letting $x_1$ = s and $x_4$ = t, we see that the solutions are given by $(s,3-t,4+2t,t)$, where s and t are parameters.

11.  a. The system has infinitely many solutions.

   b. Letting $x_3$ = s and $x_4$ = t, the solutions are given by $(2-3s,1+s,s,t)$, where s and t are parameters.

12.  a. The system has infinitely many solutions.

   b. Letting $x_3$ = s and $x_4$ = t, we see that the solutions are given by $(4-3s+t,2+2s-3t,s,t)$, where s and t are parameters.

13.  Using the Gauss-Jordan method of solution, we have

$$\left[\begin{array}{cc|c} 2 & -1 & 3 \\ 1 & 2 & 4 \\ 2 & 3 & 7 \end{array}\right] \xrightarrow{R_1 \leftrightarrow R_3} \left[\begin{array}{cc|c} 1 & 2 & 4 \\ 2 & -1 & 3 \\ 2 & 3 & 7 \end{array}\right] \xrightarrow[R_3 - 2R_1]{R_2 - 2R_1}$$

$$\left[\begin{array}{cc|c} 1 & 2 & 4 \\ 0 & -5 & -5 \\ 0 & -1 & -1 \end{array}\right] \xrightarrow{-\frac{1}{5}R_2} \left[\begin{array}{cc|c} 1 & 2 & 4 \\ 0 & 1 & 1 \\ 0 & -1 & -1 \end{array}\right] \xrightarrow[R_3 + R_2]{R_1 - 2R_2}$$

$$\left[\begin{array}{cc|c} 1 & 0 & 2 \\ 0 & 1 & 1 \\ 0 & 0 & 0 \end{array}\right].$$

The solution is $(2,1)$.

14.  Using the Gauss-Jordan method of solution, we have

$$\left[\begin{array}{cc|c} 1 & 2 & 3 \\ 2 & -3 & -8 \\ 1 & -4 & -9 \end{array}\right] \xrightarrow[R_3 - R_1]{R_2 - 2R_1} \left[\begin{array}{cc|c} 1 & 2 & 3 \\ 0 & -7 & -14 \\ 0 & -6 & -12 \end{array}\right] \xrightarrow{-\frac{1}{7}R_2} \left[\begin{array}{cc|c} 1 & 2 & 3 \\ 0 & 1 & 2 \\ 0 & -6 & -12 \end{array}\right]$$

$$\xrightarrow[R_3 + 6R_2]{R_1 - 2R_2} \left[\begin{array}{cc|c} 1 & 0 & -1 \\ 0 & 1 & 2 \\ 0 & 0 & 0 \end{array}\right].$$

We conclude that the solution is $(-1,2)$.

15.  Using the Gauss–Jordan method, we have

$$\begin{bmatrix} 3 & -2 & -3 \\ 2 & 1 & 3 \\ 1 & -2 & -5 \end{bmatrix} \xrightarrow{R_1 \leftrightarrow R_3} \begin{bmatrix} 1 & -2 & -5 \\ 2 & 1 & 3 \\ 3 & -2 & -3 \end{bmatrix} \xrightarrow[R_3 \,-\, 3R_1]{R_2 \,-\, 2R_1} \begin{bmatrix} 1 & -2 & -5 \\ 0 & 5 & 13 \\ 0 & 4 & 12 \end{bmatrix} \xrightarrow{\frac{1}{5}R_2}$$

$$\begin{bmatrix} 1 & -2 & -5 \\ 0 & 1 & \frac{13}{5} \\ 0 & 4 & 12 \end{bmatrix} \xrightarrow[R_3 \,-\, 4R_2]{R_1 \,+\, 2R_2} \begin{bmatrix} 1 & 0 & \frac{1}{5} \\ 0 & 1 & \frac{13}{5} \\ 0 & 0 & \frac{8}{5} \end{bmatrix}.$$

Since the last row implies the $0 = 8/5$, we conclude that the system of equations is inconsistent and has no solution.

16.  Using the Gauss–Jordan method, we have

$$\begin{bmatrix} 2 & 3 & 2 \\ 1 & 3 & -2 \\ 1 & -1 & 3 \end{bmatrix} \xrightarrow{R_1 \leftrightarrow R_2} \begin{bmatrix} 1 & 3 & -2 \\ 2 & 3 & 2 \\ 1 & -1 & 3 \end{bmatrix} \xrightarrow[R_3 \,-\, R_1]{R_2 \,-\, 2R_1} \begin{bmatrix} 1 & 3 & -2 \\ 0 & -3 & 6 \\ 0 & -4 & 5 \end{bmatrix} \xrightarrow{-\frac{1}{3}R_2}$$

$$\begin{bmatrix} 1 & 3 & -2 \\ 0 & 1 & -2 \\ 0 & -4 & 5 \end{bmatrix} \xrightarrow[R_3 \,+\, 4R_2]{R_1 \,-\, 3R_2} \begin{bmatrix} 1 & 0 & 4 \\ 0 & 1 & -2 \\ 0 & 0 & -3 \end{bmatrix}.$$

This last row implies that $0 = -3$, which is impossible. We conclude that the system of equations is inconsistent and has no solution.

17.

$$\begin{bmatrix} 3 & -2 & 5 \\ -1 & 3 & -4 \\ 2 & -4 & 6 \end{bmatrix} \xrightarrow{R_1 \leftrightarrow R_2} \begin{bmatrix} -1 & 3 & -4 \\ 3 & -2 & 5 \\ 2 & -4 & 6 \end{bmatrix} \xrightarrow{-R_1} \begin{bmatrix} 1 & -3 & 4 \\ 3 & -2 & 5 \\ 2 & -4 & 6 \end{bmatrix} \xrightarrow[R_3 \,-2R_1]{R_2 \,-3R_1}$$

$$\begin{bmatrix} 1 & -3 & 4 \\ 0 & 7 & -7 \\ 0 & 2 & -2 \end{bmatrix} \xrightarrow{\frac{1}{7}R_2} \begin{bmatrix} 1 & -3 & 4 \\ 0 & 1 & -1 \\ 0 & 2 & -2 \end{bmatrix} \xrightarrow[R_3 \,-\, 2R_2]{R_1 \,+\, 3R_2} \begin{bmatrix} 1 & 0 & 1 \\ 0 & 1 & -1 \\ 0 & 0 & 0 \end{bmatrix}.$$

We conclude that the solution is $(1,-1)$.

**18.**

$$\begin{bmatrix} 4 & 6 & | & 8 \\ 3 & -2 & | & -7 \\ 1 & 3 & | & 5 \end{bmatrix} \xrightarrow{R_1 \leftrightarrow R_3} \begin{bmatrix} 1 & 3 & | & 5 \\ 3 & -2 & | & -7 \\ 4 & 6 & | & 8 \end{bmatrix} \xrightarrow[R_3 - 4R_1]{R_2 - 3R_1} \begin{bmatrix} 1 & 3 & | & 5 \\ 0 & -11 & | & -22 \\ 0 & -6 & | & -12 \end{bmatrix} \xrightarrow{-\frac{1}{11}R_2}$$

$$\begin{bmatrix} 1 & 3 & | & 5 \\ 0 & 1 & | & 2 \\ 0 & -6 & | & -12 \end{bmatrix} \xrightarrow[R_3 + 6R_2]{R_1 - 3R_2} \begin{bmatrix} 1 & 0 & | & -1 \\ 0 & 1 & | & 2 \\ 0 & 0 & | & 0 \end{bmatrix}.$$

We conclude that the solution is $(-1,2)$.

**19.**

$$\begin{bmatrix} 1 & -2 & | & 2 \\ 7 & -14 & | & 14 \\ 3 & -6 & | & 6 \end{bmatrix} \xrightarrow[R_3 - 3R_1]{R_2 - 7R_1} \begin{bmatrix} 1 & -2 & | & 2 \\ 0 & 0 & | & 0 \\ 0 & 0 & | & 0 \end{bmatrix}.$$

We conclude that the infinitely many solutions are given by $(2t+2,t)$, where $t$ is a parameter.

**20.**

$$\begin{bmatrix} 1 & 2 & 1 & | & -2 \\ -2 & -3 & -1 & | & 1 \\ 2 & 4 & 2 & | & -4 \end{bmatrix} \xrightarrow[R_3 - 2R_1]{R_2 + 2R_1} \begin{bmatrix} 1 & 2 & 1 & | & -2 \\ 0 & 1 & 1 & | & -3 \\ 0 & 0 & 0 & | & 0 \end{bmatrix} \xrightarrow{R_1 - 2R_2}$$

$$\begin{bmatrix} 1 & 0 & -1 & | & 4 \\ 0 & 1 & 1 & | & -3 \\ 0 & 0 & 0 & | & 0 \end{bmatrix}.$$

Let $x_3 = t$ and we find that $x_1 = 4 + t$ and $x_2 = -3 - t$. The infinitely many solutions are given by $(4 + t, -3 - t, t)$.

**21.**

$$\begin{bmatrix} 3 & 2 & | & 4 \\ -\frac{3}{2} & -1 & | & -2 \\ 6 & 4 & | & 8 \end{bmatrix} \xrightarrow{\frac{1}{3}R_1} \begin{bmatrix} 1 & \frac{2}{3} & | & \frac{4}{3} \\ -\frac{3}{2} & -1 & | & -2 \\ 6 & 4 & | & 8 \end{bmatrix} \xrightarrow[R_3 - 6R_1]{R_2 + \frac{3}{2}R_1} \begin{bmatrix} 1 & \frac{2}{3} & | & \frac{4}{3} \\ 0 & 0 & | & 0 \\ 0 & 0 & | & 0 \end{bmatrix}.$$

We conclude that the infinitely many solutions are given by $(\frac{4}{3} - \frac{2}{3}t, \ t)$, where $t$ is a parameter.

22.
$$\begin{bmatrix} 0 & 3 & 2 & | & 4 \\ 2 & -1 & -3 & | & 3 \\ 2 & 2 & -1 & | & 7 \end{bmatrix} \xrightarrow{R_1 \leftrightarrow R_2} \begin{bmatrix} 2 & -1 & -3 & | & 3 \\ 0 & 3 & 2 & | & 4 \\ 2 & 2 & -1 & | & 7 \end{bmatrix} \xrightarrow{\frac{1}{2}R_1}$$

$$\begin{bmatrix} 1 & -\frac{1}{2} & -\frac{3}{2} & | & \frac{3}{2} \\ 0 & 3 & 2 & | & 4 \\ 2 & 2 & -1 & | & 7 \end{bmatrix} \xrightarrow{R_3 \ - \ 2R_1} \begin{bmatrix} 1 & -\frac{1}{2} & -\frac{3}{2} & | & \frac{3}{2} \\ 0 & 3 & 2 & | & 4 \\ 0 & 3 & 2 & | & 4 \end{bmatrix} \xrightarrow{\frac{1}{3}R_2}$$

$$\begin{bmatrix} 1 & -\frac{1}{2} & -\frac{3}{2} & | & \frac{3}{2} \\ 0 & 1 & \frac{2}{3} & | & \frac{4}{3} \\ 0 & 3 & 2 & | & 4 \end{bmatrix} \begin{array}{c} \xrightarrow{R_1 \ + \ \frac{1}{2}R_2} \\ \xrightarrow{R_3 \ - \ 3R_2} \end{array} \begin{bmatrix} 1 & 0 & -\frac{7}{6} & | & \frac{13}{6} \\ 0 & 1 & \frac{2}{3} & | & \frac{4}{3} \\ 0 & 0 & 0 & | & 0 \end{bmatrix}.$$

Letting $z = t$, we see that the infinitely many solutions are given by $(\frac{13}{6} + \frac{7t}{6}, \ \frac{4}{3} - \frac{2t}{3}, \ t)$.

23.
$$\begin{bmatrix} 2 & -1 & 1 & | & -4 \\ 3 & -\frac{3}{2} & \frac{3}{2} & | & -6 \\ -6 & 3 & -3 & | & 12 \end{bmatrix} \xrightarrow{\frac{1}{2}R_1} \begin{bmatrix} 1 & -\frac{1}{2} & \frac{1}{2} & | & -2 \\ 3 & -\frac{3}{2} & \frac{3}{2} & | & -6 \\ -6 & 3 & -3 & | & 12 \end{bmatrix} \begin{array}{c} \xrightarrow{R_2 \ - \ 3R_1} \\ \xrightarrow{R_3 \ + \ 6R_1} \end{array}$$

$$\begin{bmatrix} 1 & -\frac{1}{2} & \frac{1}{2} & | & -2 \\ 0 & 0 & 0 & | & 0 \\ 0 & 0 & 0 & | & 0 \end{bmatrix}$$

We conclude that the infinitely many solutions are given by $(-2 + \frac{1}{2}s - \frac{1}{2}t, \ s, \ t)$, where $s$ and $t$ are parameters.

24.
$$\begin{bmatrix} 1 & 1 & -2 & | & -3 \\ 2 & -1 & 3 & | & 7 \\ 1 & -2 & 5 & | & 0 \end{bmatrix} \begin{array}{c} \xrightarrow{R_2 \ - \ 2R_1} \\ \xrightarrow{R_3 \ - \ R_1} \end{array} \begin{bmatrix} 1 & 1 & -2 & | & -3 \\ 0 & -3 & 7 & | & 13 \\ 0 & -3 & 7 & | & 3 \end{bmatrix} \xrightarrow{-\frac{1}{3}R_2}$$

$$\begin{bmatrix} 1 & 1 & -2 & | & -3 \\ 0 & 1 & -\frac{7}{3} & | & -\frac{13}{3} \\ 0 & -3 & 7 & | & 3 \end{bmatrix} \xrightarrow[\substack{R_3 + 3R_2}]{R_1 - R_2} \begin{bmatrix} 1 & 0 & \frac{1}{3} & | & \frac{4}{3} \\ 0 & 1 & -\frac{7}{3} & | & -\frac{13}{3} \\ 1 & 0 & 0 & | & -10 \end{bmatrix}.$$

This last row implies that $0 = -10$, which is impossible. We conclude that the system of equations is inconsistent and has no solution.

25. $\begin{bmatrix} 1 & -2 & 3 & | & 4 \\ 2 & 3 & -1 & | & 2 \\ 1 & 2 & -3 & | & -6 \end{bmatrix} \xrightarrow[\substack{R_3 - R_1}]{R_2 - 2R_1} \begin{bmatrix} 1 & -2 & 3 & | & 4 \\ 0 & 7 & -7 & | & -6 \\ 0 & 4 & -6 & | & -10 \end{bmatrix} \xrightarrow{\frac{1}{7}R_2}$

$\begin{bmatrix} 1 & -2 & 3 & | & 4 \\ 0 & 1 & -1 & | & -\frac{6}{7} \\ 0 & 4 & -6 & | & -10 \end{bmatrix} \xrightarrow[\substack{R_3 - 4R_2}]{R_1 + 2R_2} \begin{bmatrix} 1 & 0 & 1 & | & \frac{16}{7} \\ 0 & 1 & -1 & | & -\frac{6}{7} \\ 0 & 0 & -2 & | & -\frac{46}{7} \end{bmatrix} \xrightarrow{-\frac{1}{2}R_3}$

$\begin{bmatrix} 1 & 0 & 1 & | & \frac{16}{7} \\ 0 & 1 & -1 & | & -\frac{6}{7} \\ 0 & 0 & 1 & | & \frac{23}{7} \end{bmatrix} \xrightarrow[\substack{R_2 + R_3}]{R_1 - R_3} \begin{bmatrix} 1 & 0 & 0 & | & -1 \\ 0 & 1 & 0 & | & \frac{17}{7} \\ 0 & 0 & 1 & | & \frac{23}{7} \end{bmatrix}$

We conclude that the solution is $(-1, \frac{17}{7}, \frac{23}{7})$

26. $\begin{bmatrix} 1 & -2 & 1 & | & -3 \\ 2 & 1 & -2 & | & 2 \\ 1 & 3 & -3 & | & 5 \end{bmatrix} \xrightarrow[\substack{R_3 - R_1}]{R_2 - 2R_1} \begin{bmatrix} 1 & -2 & 1 & | & -3 \\ 0 & 5 & -4 & | & 8 \\ 0 & 5 & -4 & | & 8 \end{bmatrix} \xrightarrow{\frac{1}{5}R_2}$

$\begin{bmatrix} 1 & -2 & 1 & | & -3 \\ 0 & 1 & -\frac{4}{5} & | & \frac{8}{5} \\ 0 & 5 & -4 & | & 8 \end{bmatrix} \xrightarrow[\substack{R_3 - 5R_2}]{R_1 + 2R_2} \begin{bmatrix} 1 & 0 & -\frac{3}{5} & | & \frac{1}{5} \\ 0 & 1 & -\frac{4}{5} & | & \frac{8}{5} \\ 0 & 0 & 0 & | & 0 \end{bmatrix}.$

We conclude that the infinitely many solutions to this system are $(\frac{1}{5} + \frac{3}{5}t, \frac{8}{5} + \frac{4}{5}t, t)$.

27. $\begin{bmatrix} 4 & 1 & -1 & | & 4 \\ 8 & 2 & -2 & | & 8 \end{bmatrix} \xrightarrow{\frac{1}{4}R_1} \begin{bmatrix} 1 & \frac{1}{4} & -\frac{1}{4} & | & 1 \\ 8 & 2 & -2 & | & 8 \end{bmatrix} \xrightarrow{R_2 - 8R_1}$

$$\begin{bmatrix} 1 & \frac{1}{4} & -\frac{1}{4} & \Big| & 1 \\ 0 & 0 & 0 & \Big| & 0 \end{bmatrix}$$

We conclude that the infinitely many solutions are given by

$(1 - \frac{1}{4}s + \frac{1}{4}t, \ s, \ t)$, where s and t are parameters.

28. $\begin{bmatrix} 1 & 2 & 4 & \Big| & 2 \\ 1 & 1 & 2 & \Big| & 1 \end{bmatrix} \xrightarrow{R_2 - R_1} \begin{bmatrix} 1 & 2 & 4 & \Big| & 2 \\ 0 & -1 & -2 & \Big| & -1 \end{bmatrix} \xrightarrow{-R_2}$

$\begin{bmatrix} 1 & 2 & 4 & \Big| & 2 \\ 0 & 1 & 2 & \Big| & 1 \end{bmatrix} \xrightarrow{R_1 - 2R_2} \begin{bmatrix} 1 & 0 & 0 & \Big| & 0 \\ 0 & 1 & 2 & \Big| & 1 \end{bmatrix}.$

We conclude that the infinitely many solutions are given by
$(0, \ 1-2t, \ t)$, where t is a parameter.

29. $\begin{bmatrix} 2 & 1 & -3 & \Big| & 1 \\ 1 & -1 & 2 & \Big| & 1 \\ 5 & -2 & 3 & \Big| & 6 \end{bmatrix} \xrightarrow{R_1 \longleftrightarrow R_2} \begin{bmatrix} 1 & -1 & 2 & \Big| & 1 \\ 2 & 1 & -3 & \Big| & 1 \\ 5 & -2 & 3 & \Big| & 6 \end{bmatrix} \begin{array}{c} \xrightarrow{R_2 - 2R_1} \\ \xrightarrow{R_3 - 5R_1} \end{array}$

$\begin{bmatrix} 1 & -1 & 2 & \Big| & 1 \\ 0 & 3 & -7 & \Big| & -1 \\ 0 & 3 & -7 & \Big| & 1 \end{bmatrix} \xrightarrow{\frac{1}{3}R_2} \begin{bmatrix} 1 & -1 & 2 & \Big| & 1 \\ 0 & 1 & -\frac{7}{3} & \Big| & -\frac{1}{3} \\ 0 & 3 & -7 & \Big| & 1 \end{bmatrix} \begin{array}{c} \xrightarrow{R_1 + R_2} \\ \xrightarrow{R_3 - 3R_2} \end{array}$

$\begin{bmatrix} 1 & 0 & -\frac{1}{3} & \Big| & \frac{2}{3} \\ 0 & 1 & -\frac{7}{3} & \Big| & -\frac{1}{3} \\ 0 & 0 & 0 & \Big| & 2 \end{bmatrix}.$

This last row implies that 0 = 2, which is impossible. We conclude
that the system of equations is inconsistent and has no solution.

30. $\begin{bmatrix} 3 & -9 & 6 & \Big| & -12 \\ 1 & -3 & 2 & \Big| & -4 \\ 2 & -6 & 4 & \Big| & 8 \end{bmatrix} \xrightarrow{R_1 \longleftrightarrow R_2} \begin{bmatrix} 1 & -3 & 2 & \Big| & -4 \\ 3 & -9 & 6 & \Big| & -12 \\ 2 & -6 & 4 & \Big| & 8 \end{bmatrix} \begin{array}{c} \xrightarrow{R_2 - 3R_1} \\ \xrightarrow{R_3 - 2R_1} \end{array}$

$\begin{bmatrix} 1 & -3 & 2 & \Big| & -4 \\ 0 & 0 & 0 & \Big| & 0 \\ 0 & 0 & 0 & \Big| & 16 \end{bmatrix}$

This last row implies that $0 = 16$, which is impossible. We conclude that the system of equations is inconsistent and has no solution.

31.
$$\begin{bmatrix} 1 & 2 & -1 & -4 \\ 2 & 1 & 1 & 7 \\ 1 & 3 & 2 & 7 \\ 1 & -3 & 1 & 9 \end{bmatrix} \xrightarrow[\substack{R_2 - 2R_1 \\ R_3 - R_1 \\ R_4 - R_1}]{} \begin{bmatrix} 1 & 2 & -1 & -4 \\ 0 & -3 & 3 & 15 \\ 0 & 1 & 3 & 11 \\ 0 & -5 & 2 & 13 \end{bmatrix} \xrightarrow{-\frac{1}{3}R_2}$$

$$\begin{bmatrix} 1 & 2 & -1 & -4 \\ 0 & 1 & -1 & -5 \\ 0 & 1 & 3 & 11 \\ 0 & -5 & 2 & 13 \end{bmatrix} \xrightarrow[\substack{R_1 - 2R_2 \\ R_3 - R_2 \\ R_4 + 5R_2}]{} \begin{bmatrix} 1 & 0 & 1 & 6 \\ 0 & 1 & -1 & -5 \\ 0 & 0 & 4 & 16 \\ 0 & 0 & -3 & -12 \end{bmatrix} \xrightarrow{\frac{1}{4}R_3}$$

$$\begin{bmatrix} 1 & 0 & 1 & 6 \\ 0 & 1 & -1 & -5 \\ 0 & 0 & 1 & 4 \\ 0 & 0 & -3 & -12 \end{bmatrix} \xrightarrow[\substack{R_1 + \frac{1}{3}R_3 \\ R_2 + R_3 \\ R_4 + 3R_3}]{} \begin{bmatrix} 1 & 0 & 0 & 2 \\ 0 & 1 & 0 & -1 \\ 0 & 0 & 1 & 4 \\ 0 & 0 & 0 & 0 \end{bmatrix}.$$

We conclude that the solution of the system is $(2,-1,4)$.

32.
$$\begin{bmatrix} 3 & -2 & 1 & 4 \\ 1 & 3 & -4 & -3 \\ 2 & -3 & 5 & 7 \\ 1 & -8 & 9 & 10 \end{bmatrix} \xrightarrow{R_1 \leftrightarrow R_2} \begin{bmatrix} 1 & 3 & -4 & -3 \\ 3 & -2 & 1 & 4 \\ 2 & -3 & 5 & 7 \\ 1 & -8 & 9 & 10 \end{bmatrix} \xrightarrow[\substack{R_2 - 3R_1 \\ R_3 - 2R_1 \\ R_4 - R_1}]{}$$

$$\begin{bmatrix} 1 & 3 & -4 & -3 \\ 0 & -11 & 13 & 13 \\ 0 & -9 & 13 & 13 \\ 0 & -11 & 13 & 13 \end{bmatrix} \xrightarrow{-\frac{1}{11}R_2} \begin{bmatrix} 1 & 3 & -4 & -3 \\ 0 & 1 & -\frac{13}{11} & -\frac{13}{11} \\ 0 & -9 & 13 & 13 \\ 0 & -11 & 13 & 13 \end{bmatrix} \xrightarrow[\substack{R_1 - 3R_2 \\ R_3 + 9R_2 \\ R_4 + 11R_2}]{}$$

$$\begin{bmatrix} 1 & 0 & -\frac{5}{11} & \frac{6}{11} \\ 0 & 1 & -\frac{13}{11} & -\frac{13}{11} \\ 0 & 0 & \frac{26}{11} & \frac{26}{11} \\ 0 & 0 & 0 & 0 \end{bmatrix} \xrightarrow{\frac{11}{26}R_3} \begin{bmatrix} 1 & 0 & -\frac{5}{11} & \frac{6}{11} \\ 0 & 1 & -\frac{13}{11} & -\frac{13}{11} \\ 0 & 0 & 1 & 1 \\ 0 & 0 & 0 & 0 \end{bmatrix} \xrightarrow[R_2 + \frac{13}{11}R_3]{R_1 + \frac{5}{11}R_3}$$

$$\begin{bmatrix} 1 & 0 & 0 & 1 \\ 0 & 1 & 0 & 0 \\ 0 & 0 & 1 & 1 \\ 0 & 0 & 0 & 0 \end{bmatrix}.$$

We conclude that the solution of the system is $(1,0,1)$.

33. Let $x$, $y$, and $z$ represent the number of compact, mid-sized, and full-size cars, respectively, to be purchased. Then the problem can be solved by solving the system

$$x + y + z = 60$$

$$10000x + 16000y + 22000z = 840000$$

Using the Gauss-Jordan method of elimination, we have

$$\begin{bmatrix} 1 & 1 & 1 & 60 \\ 10000 & 16000 & 22000 & 840000 \end{bmatrix} \xrightarrow{R_2 - 10000R_1}$$

$$\begin{bmatrix} 1 & 1 & 1 & 60 \\ 0 & 6000 & 12000 & 240000 \end{bmatrix} \xrightarrow{\frac{1}{6000}R_2}$$

$$\begin{bmatrix} 1 & 1 & 1 & 60 \\ 0 & 1 & 2 & 40 \end{bmatrix} \xrightarrow{R_1 - R_2}$$

$$\begin{bmatrix} 1 & 0 & -1 & 20 \\ 0 & 1 & 2 & 40 \end{bmatrix}$$

and we conclude that the solution is $(20+z, 40-2z, z)$. Letting $z = 5$, we see that one possible solution is $(25,30,5)$; that is Hartman should buy 25 compact, 30 mid-sized cars, and 5 full-sized cars. Letting $z = 10$, we see that another possible solution is $(30,20,10)$; that is, 30 compact cars, 20 mid-sized cars, and 10 full-sized cars.

34. Let $x$, $y$, and $z$ denote the number of ounces of Food I, Food II, and Food III, respectively, that the dietician includes in the meal. Then the problem can be solved by solving the system

$$400x + 1200y + 800z = 8800$$

$$110x + 570y + 340z = 3380$$

$$90x + 30y + 60z = 1020.$$

Using the Gauss-Jordan method of elimination, we have

$$
\begin{bmatrix}
400 & 1200 & 800 & 8800 \\
110 & 570 & 340 & 3380 \\
90 & 30 & 60 & 1020
\end{bmatrix}
\xrightarrow{\frac{1}{400}R_1}
\begin{bmatrix}
1 & 3 & 2 & 22 \\
110 & 570 & 340 & 3380 \\
90 & 30 & 60 & 1020
\end{bmatrix}
\xrightarrow[R_3 - 90R_1]{R_2 - 110R_1}
$$

$$
\begin{bmatrix}
1 & 3 & 2 & 22 \\
0 & 240 & 120 & 960 \\
0 & -240 & -120 & -960
\end{bmatrix}
\xrightarrow{\frac{1}{240}R2}
\begin{bmatrix}
1 & 3 & 2 & 22 \\
0 & 1 & \frac{1}{2} & 4 \\
0 & -240 & -120 & -960
\end{bmatrix}
\xrightarrow[R_3 + 240R_2]{R_1 - 3R_2}
$$

$$
\begin{bmatrix}
1 & 0 & \frac{1}{2} & 10 \\
0 & 1 & \frac{1}{2} & 4 \\
0 & 0 & 0 & 0
\end{bmatrix},
$$

and we conclude that the solution is $(10 - \frac{1}{2}z, 4 - \frac{1}{2}z, z)$. Letting $z = 2$, we see that one possible solution is a meal prepared with 9 ounces of Food I, 3 ounces of Food II, and 2 ounces of Food III. Another possible solution is obtained by letting $z = 4$, In this case, 8 ounces of Food I, 2 ounces of Food II, and 4 ounces of Food III would be used to prepare the meal.

35. Let $x$, $y$, and $z$ denote the number of ounces of Food I, Food II, and Food III, respectively, that the dietician includes in the meal. Then the problem can be solved by solving the system

$$400x + 1200y + 800z = 8800$$

$$110x + 570y + 340z = 2160$$

$$90x + 30y + 60z = 1020.$$

Using the Gauss-Jordan method of elimination, we have

$$\begin{bmatrix} 400 & 1200 & 800 & | & 8800 \\ 110 & 570 & 340 & | & 2160 \\ 90 & 30 & 60 & | & 1020 \end{bmatrix} \xrightarrow{\frac{1}{400}R_1} \begin{bmatrix} 1 & 3 & 2 & | & 22 \\ 110 & 570 & 340 & | & 2160 \\ 90 & 30 & 60 & | & 1020 \end{bmatrix} \xrightarrow[R_3 - 90R_1]{R_2 - 110R_1}$$

$$\begin{bmatrix} 1 & 3 & 2 & | & 22 \\ 0 & 240 & 120 & | & -260 \\ 0 & -240 & -120 & | & -960 \end{bmatrix} \xrightarrow{\frac{1}{240}R_2} \begin{bmatrix} 1 & 3 & 2 & | & 22 \\ 0 & 1 & \frac{1}{2} & | & -\frac{13}{12} \\ 0 & -240 & -120 & | & -960 \end{bmatrix} \xrightarrow[R_3 + 240R_2]{R_1 - 3R_2}$$

$$\begin{bmatrix} 1 & 0 & \frac{1}{2} & | & \frac{225}{12} \\ 0 & 1 & \frac{1}{2} & | & -\frac{13}{12} \\ 0 & 0 & 0 & | & -1220 \end{bmatrix}.$$

This last row implies that $0 = -1220$, which is impossible. We conclude that the system of equations is inconsistent and has no solution--that is, the dietician cannot prepare a meal from these foods and meet the given requirements.

36.  Let x, y, and z denote the amount of money invested in stocks, bonds, and a money-market account, respectively. Then the problem can be solved by solving the system

$$x + y + z = 100,000$$

$$12x + 8y + 4z = 1,000,000$$

$$x - y - 3z = 0.$$

Using the Gauss-Jordan method of elimination, we have

$$\begin{bmatrix} 1 & 1 & 1 & | & 100000 \\ 12 & 8 & 4 & | & 1000000 \\ 1 & -1 & -3 & | & 0 \end{bmatrix} \xrightarrow[R_3 - R_1]{R_2 - 12R_1} \begin{bmatrix} 1 & 1 & 1 & | & 100000 \\ 0 & -4 & -8 & | & -200000 \\ 0 & -2 & -4 & | & -100000 \end{bmatrix} \xrightarrow{-\frac{1}{4}R_2}$$

$$
\begin{bmatrix}
1 & 1 & 1 & | & 100000 \\
0 & 1 & 2 & | & 50000 \\
0 & -2 & -4 & | & -100000
\end{bmatrix}
\xrightarrow[R_3 + 2R_2]{R_1 - R_2}
\begin{bmatrix}
1 & 0 & -1 & | & 50000 \\
0 & 1 & 2 & | & 50000 \\
0 & 0 & 0 & | & 0
\end{bmatrix}.
$$

We conclude that the solution is $(50000 + z,\ 50000 - 2z,\ z)$. Therefore, one possible solution for the Garcias is to invest $10,000 in a money-market account, $60,000 in stocks and $30,000 in bonds. Another possible solution is for the Garcias to invest $20,000 in a money-market account, $70,000 in stocks and $10,000 in bonds.

37.  a. 
$$
\begin{aligned}
x_1 - x_2 &&&&&= 200 \\
x_1 &&&- x_5 &&= 100 \\
-x_2 + x_3 &&&+ x_6 &&= 600 \\
-x_3 + x_4 &&&&&= 200 \\
x_4 - x_5 + x_6 &&&&&= 700.
\end{aligned}
$$

b.

$$
\begin{bmatrix}
1 & -1 & 0 & 0 & 0 & 0 & | & 200 \\
1 & 0 & 0 & 0 & -1 & 0 & | & 100 \\
0 & -1 & 1 & 0 & 0 & 1 & | & 600 \\
0 & 0 & -1 & 1 & 0 & 0 & | & 200 \\
0 & 0 & 0 & 1 & -1 & 1 & | & 700
\end{bmatrix}
\xrightarrow{R_2 - R_1}
\begin{bmatrix}
1 & -1 & 0 & 0 & 0 & 0 & | & 200 \\
0 & 1 & 0 & 0 & -1 & 0 & | & -100 \\
0 & -1 & 1 & 0 & 0 & 1 & | & 600 \\
0 & 0 & -1 & 1 & 0 & 0 & | & 200 \\
0 & 0 & 0 & 1 & -1 & 1 & | & 700
\end{bmatrix}
\xrightarrow[R_1 + R_2]{R_3 + R_2}
$$

$$
\begin{bmatrix}
1 & 0 & 0 & 0 & -1 & 0 & | & 100 \\
0 & 1 & 0 & 0 & -1 & 0 & | & -100 \\
0 & 0 & 1 & 0 & -1 & 1 & | & 500 \\
0 & 0 & -1 & 1 & 0 & 0 & | & 200 \\
0 & 0 & 0 & 1 & -1 & 1 & | & 700
\end{bmatrix}
\xrightarrow{R_4 + R_3}
\begin{bmatrix}
1 & 0 & 0 & 0 & -1 & 0 & | & 100 \\
0 & 1 & 0 & 0 & -1 & 0 & | & -100 \\
0 & 0 & 1 & 0 & -1 & 1 & | & 500 \\
0 & 0 & 0 & 1 & -1 & 1 & | & 700 \\
0 & 0 & 0 & 1 & -1 & 1 & | & 700
\end{bmatrix}
\xrightarrow{R_5 - R_4}
$$

$$\begin{bmatrix} 1 & 0 & 0 & 0 & -1 & 0 & | & 100 \\ 0 & 1 & 0 & 0 & 1 & 0 & | & -100 \\ 0 & 0 & 1 & 0 & -1 & 1 & | & 500 \\ 0 & 0 & 0 & 1 & -1 & 1 & | & 700 \\ 0 & 0 & 0 & 0 & 0 & 0 & | & 0 \end{bmatrix}.$$

We conclude that the solution is

$$(s + 100, \ s - 100, \ s - t + 500, \ s - t + 700, \ s, \ t).$$

Taking $s = 150$ and $t = 50$, we see that one possible traffic pattern is

$$(250, \ 50, \ 600, \ 800, \ 150, \ 50).$$

Similarly, taking $s = 200$, and $t = 100$, we see that another possible traffic pattern is

$$(300, \ 100, \ 600, \ 800, \ 200, \ 100).$$

c. Taking $t = 0$ and $s = 200$, we see that another possible traffic pattern is $(300, \ 100, \ 700, \ 900, \ 200, \ 0)$.

38. a.
$$\begin{aligned}
x_1 \qquad\qquad\qquad\qquad + x_6 \qquad &= 1700 \\
x_1 - x_2 \qquad\qquad\qquad\quad + x_7 &= 700 \\
x_2 - x_3 \qquad\qquad\qquad &= 300 \\
- x_3 + x_4 \qquad\qquad &= 400 \\
- x_4 + x_5 \qquad + x_7 &= 700 \\
x_5 + x_6 \qquad &= 1800.
\end{aligned}$$

b.

$$\begin{bmatrix} 1 & 0 & 0 & 0 & 0 & 1 & 0 & | & 1700 \\ 1 & -1 & 0 & 0 & 0 & 0 & 1 & | & 700 \\ 0 & 1 & -1 & 0 & 0 & 0 & 0 & | & 300 \\ 0 & 0 & -1 & 1 & 0 & 0 & 0 & | & 400 \\ 0 & 0 & 0 & -1 & 1 & 0 & 1 & | & 700 \\ 0 & 0 & 0 & 0 & 1 & 1 & 0 & | & 1800 \end{bmatrix} \xrightarrow{R_2 - R_1} \begin{bmatrix} 1 & 0 & 0 & 0 & 0 & 1 & 0 & | & 1700 \\ 0 & -1 & 0 & 0 & 0 & -1 & 1 & | & -1000 \\ 0 & 1 & -1 & 0 & 0 & 0 & 0 & | & 300 \\ 0 & 0 & -1 & 1 & 0 & 0 & 0 & | & 400 \\ 0 & 0 & 0 & -1 & 1 & 0 & 1 & | & 700 \\ 0 & 0 & 0 & 0 & 1 & 1 & 0 & | & 1800 \end{bmatrix}$$

$$
\xrightarrow{-R_2}
\begin{bmatrix}
1 & 0 & 0 & 0 & 0 & 1 & 0 & 1700 \\
0 & 1 & 0 & 0 & 0 & 1 & -1 & 1000 \\
0 & 1 & -1 & 0 & 0 & 0 & 0 & 300 \\
0 & 0 & -1 & 1 & 0 & 0 & 0 & 400 \\
0 & 0 & 0 & -1 & 1 & 0 & 1 & 700 \\
0 & 0 & 0 & 0 & 1 & 1 & 0 & 1800
\end{bmatrix}
\xrightarrow{R_3 - R_2}
$$

$$
\begin{bmatrix}
1 & 0 & 0 & 0 & 0 & 1 & 0 & 1700 \\
0 & 1 & 0 & 0 & 0 & 1 & -1 & 1000 \\
0 & 0 & -1 & 0 & 0 & -1 & 1 & -700 \\
0 & 0 & -1 & 1 & 0 & 0 & 0 & 400 \\
0 & 0 & 0 & -1 & 1 & 0 & 1 & 700 \\
0 & 0 & 0 & 0 & 1 & 1 & 0 & 1800
\end{bmatrix}
\xrightarrow{-R_3}
$$

$$
\begin{bmatrix}
1 & 0 & 0 & 0 & 0 & 1 & 0 & 1700 \\
0 & 1 & 0 & 0 & 0 & 1 & -1 & 1000 \\
0 & 0 & 1 & 0 & 0 & 1 & -1 & 700 \\
0 & 0 & -1 & 1 & 0 & 0 & 0 & 400 \\
0 & 0 & 0 & -1 & 1 & 0 & 1 & 700 \\
0 & 0 & 0 & 0 & 1 & 1 & 0 & 1800
\end{bmatrix}
\xrightarrow{R_4 + R_3}
$$

$$
\begin{bmatrix}
1 & 0 & 0 & 0 & 0 & 1 & 0 & 1700 \\
0 & 1 & 0 & 0 & 0 & 1 & -1 & 1000 \\
0 & 0 & 1 & 0 & 0 & 1 & -1 & 700 \\
0 & 0 & 0 & 1 & 0 & 1 & -1 & 1100 \\
0 & 0 & 0 & -1 & 1 & 0 & 1 & 700 \\
0 & 0 & 0 & 0 & 1 & 1 & 0 & 1800
\end{bmatrix}
\xrightarrow{R_5 + R_4}
$$

$$\begin{bmatrix} 1 & 0 & 0 & 0 & 0 & 1 & 0 & | & 1700 \\ 0 & 1 & 0 & 0 & 0 & 1 & -1 & | & 1000 \\ 0 & 0 & 1 & 0 & 0 & 1 & -1 & | & 700 \\ 0 & 0 & 0 & 1 & 0 & 1 & -1 & | & 1100 \\ 0 & 0 & 0 & 0 & 1 & 1 & 0 & | & 1800 \\ 0 & 0 & 0 & 0 & 1 & 1 & 0 & | & 1800 \end{bmatrix} \xrightarrow{\;R_6 - R_5\;}$$

$$\begin{bmatrix} 1 & 0 & 0 & 0 & 0 & 1 & 0 & | & 1700 \\ 0 & 1 & 0 & 0 & 0 & 1 & -1 & | & 1000 \\ 0 & 0 & 1 & 0 & 0 & 1 & -1 & | & 700 \\ 0 & 0 & 0 & 1 & 0 & 1 & -1 & | & 1100 \\ 0 & 0 & 0 & 0 & 1 & 1 & 0 & | & 1800 \\ 0 & 0 & 0 & 0 & 0 & 0 & 0 & | & 0 \end{bmatrix}$$

We conclude that the solution of the system is

$(1700 - s,\ 1000 - s + t,\ 700 - s + t,\ 1100 - s + t,\ 1800 - s,\ s,\ t)$.

Two possible traffic patterns are

$(900,\ 1000,\ 700,\ 1100,\ 1000,\ 800,\ 800)$

and    $(1000,\ 1100,\ 800,\ 1200,\ 1100,\ 700,\ 800)$,

c. $x_6$ must have at least 300 cars/hour.

39.  We solve the given system by using the Gauss–Jordan elimination method. We have

$$\begin{bmatrix} 2 & 3 & | & 2 \\ 1 & 4 & | & 6 \\ 5 & k & | & 2 \end{bmatrix} \xrightarrow{\;R_1 \leftrightarrow R_2\;} \begin{bmatrix} 1 & 4 & | & 6 \\ 2 & 3 & | & 2 \\ 5 & k & | & 2 \end{bmatrix} \begin{array}{c} \xrightarrow{\;R_2 - 2R_1\;} \\ R_3 - 4R_1 \end{array}$$

$$\begin{bmatrix} 1 & 4 & | & 6 \\ 0 & -5 & | & -10 \\ 0 & k-20 & | & -28 \end{bmatrix} \xrightarrow{\;-\frac{1}{5}R_2\;} \begin{bmatrix} 1 & 4 & | & 6 \\ 0 & 1 & | & 2 \\ 0 & k-20 & | & -28 \end{bmatrix} \begin{array}{c} \xrightarrow{\;R_1 - 4R_2\;} \\ R_3 + aR_2 \end{array}$$

$$\begin{bmatrix} 1 & 0 & \bigm| & -2 \\ 0 & 1 & \bigm| & 2 \\ 0 & k+a-20 & \bigm| & -28+2a \end{bmatrix} .$$

From the last matrix, we see that the system has a solution if and only if x = -2, y = 2, and

$$-28 + 2a = 0, \text{ or } a = 14$$

and   $k + a - 20 = k - 6 = 0$, or $k = 6$.

(All the entries in the last row of the matrix must be equal to zero.)

40.  We solve the given system by using the Gauss-Jordan elimination method. We have

$$\begin{bmatrix} 3 & -2 & 4 & \bigm| & 12 \\ -9 & 6 & -12 & \bigm| & k \end{bmatrix} \xrightarrow{\frac{1}{3}R_1} \begin{bmatrix} 1 & -\frac{2}{3} & \frac{4}{3} & \bigm| & 4 \\ -9 & 6 & -12 & \bigm| & k \end{bmatrix} \xrightarrow{R_1 + 9R_2}$$

$$\begin{bmatrix} 1 & -\frac{2}{3} & \frac{4}{3} & \bigm| & 4 \\ 0 & 0 & 0 & \bigm| & k+36 \end{bmatrix} .$$

Since this system has a solution only if the last row has all zero entries, we see that k = -36.  We conclude that the solution

is $(4+\frac{2}{3}y - \frac{4}{3}z, y, z)$ and k = -36.

## USING TECHNOLOGY EXERCISES 2.3, page 111

1.   (1+t, 2+t, t); t, a parameter          2.   No solution

3.   $(-\frac{17}{7} + \frac{6}{7}t, 3 - t, -\frac{18}{7} + \frac{1}{7}t, t)$          4.   (2t, 1 - t, 1 + t, t)

5.   No solution

6.   (2.5810-0.0406t, 3.2462- 3.8226t, 1.6619-2.1548t, 0.2942+0.3531t)

# EXERCISES 2.4, page 120

1. The size of A is 4 x 4; the size of B is 4 x 3; the size of C is 1 x 5, and the size of D is 4 x 1.

2. $a_{14} = -4$; $a_{21} = -11$; $a_{31} = 6$; $a_{43} = 5$.

3. These are entries of the matrix B. The entry $b_{13}$ refers to the entry in  the first row and third column and is equal to 2. Similarly, $b_{31} = 3$, and $b_{43} = 8$.

4. The row matrix is the matrix C. The transpose of the matrix C is

$$C^T = \begin{bmatrix} 1 \\ 0 \\ 3 \\ 4 \\ 5 \end{bmatrix} .$$

5. The column matrix is the matrix D. The transpose of the matrix D is

$$D^T = [1 \quad 3 \quad -2 \quad 0].$$

6. The square matrix is A. The transpose is

$$A^T = \begin{bmatrix} 2 & -11 & 6 & 5 \\ -3 & 2 & 0 & 1 \\ 9 & 6 & 2 & 5 \\ -4 & 7 & 9 & -8 \end{bmatrix}.$$

7. A is of size 3 x 2; B is of size 3 x 2; C and D are of size 3 x 3.

8. A is of size 3 x 2 and C is of size 3 x 3; therefore, their sum does not exist.

9.
$$A + B = \begin{bmatrix} -1 & 2 \\ 3 & -2 \\ 4 & 0 \end{bmatrix} + \begin{bmatrix} 2 & 4 \\ 3 & 1 \\ -2 & 2 \end{bmatrix} = \begin{bmatrix} 1 & 6 \\ 6 & -1 \\ 2 & 2 \end{bmatrix}$$

10.
$$2A - 3B = \begin{bmatrix} -2 & 4 \\ 6 & -4 \\ 8 & 0 \end{bmatrix} - \begin{bmatrix} 6 & 12 \\ 9 & 3 \\ -6 & 6 \end{bmatrix} = \begin{bmatrix} -8 & -8 \\ -3 & -7 \\ 14 & -6 \end{bmatrix}$$

11. $\begin{bmatrix} 3 & -1 & 0 \\ 2 & -2 & 3 \\ 4 & 6 & 2 \end{bmatrix} - \begin{bmatrix} 2 & -2 & 4 \\ 3 & 6 & 2 \\ -2 & 3 & 1 \end{bmatrix} = \begin{bmatrix} 1 & 1 & -4 \\ -1 & -8 & 1 \\ 6 & 3 & 1 \end{bmatrix}$

12. $\begin{bmatrix} 8 & -8 & 16 \\ 12 & 24 & 8 \\ -8 & 12 & 4 \end{bmatrix} + \begin{bmatrix} -6 & 2 & 0 \\ -4 & 4 & -6 \\ -8 & -12 & -4 \end{bmatrix} = \begin{bmatrix} 2 & -6 & 16 \\ 8 & 28 & 2 \\ -16 & 0 & 0 \end{bmatrix}$.

13. $\begin{bmatrix} 6 & 3 & 8 \\ 4 & 5 & 6 \end{bmatrix} - \begin{bmatrix} 3 & -2 & -1 \\ 0 & -5 & -7 \end{bmatrix} = \begin{bmatrix} 3 & 5 & 9 \\ 4 & 10 & 13 \end{bmatrix}$.

14. $\begin{bmatrix} 2 & -3 & 4 & -1 \\ 3 & 1 & 0 & 0 \end{bmatrix} + \begin{bmatrix} 4 & 3 & -2 & -4 \\ 6 & 2 & 0 & -3 \end{bmatrix} = \begin{bmatrix} 6 & 0 & 2 & -5 \\ 9 & 3 & 0 & -3 \end{bmatrix}$.

15. $\begin{bmatrix} 1 & 4 & -5 \\ 3 & -8 & 6 \end{bmatrix} + \begin{bmatrix} 4 & 0 & -2 \\ 3 & 6 & 5 \end{bmatrix} - \begin{bmatrix} 2 & 8 & 9 \\ -11 & 2 & -5 \end{bmatrix}$

$= \begin{bmatrix} 3 & -4 & -16 \\ 17 & -4 & 16 \end{bmatrix}$ .

16. $3 \begin{bmatrix} 1 & 1 & -3 \\ 3 & 2 & 3 \\ 7 & -1 & 6 \end{bmatrix} + 4 \begin{bmatrix} -2 & -1 & 8 \\ 4 & 2 & 2 \\ 3 & 6 & 3 \end{bmatrix} = \begin{bmatrix} 3 & 3 & -9 \\ 9 & 6 & 9 \\ 21 & -3 & 18 \end{bmatrix} + \begin{bmatrix} -8 & -4 & 32 \\ 16 & 8 & 8 \\ 12 & 24 & 12 \end{bmatrix}$

$= \begin{bmatrix} -5 & -1 & 23 \\ 25 & 14 & 17 \\ 33 & 21 & 30 \end{bmatrix}$ .

17. $\begin{bmatrix} 1.2 & 4.5 & -4.2 \\ 8.2 & 6.3 & -3.2 \end{bmatrix} - \begin{bmatrix} 3.1 & 1.5 & -3.6 \\ 2.2 & -3.3 & -4.4 \end{bmatrix} = \begin{bmatrix} -1.9 & 3.0 & -0.6 \\ 6.0 & 9.6 & 1.2 \end{bmatrix}$.

18.
$$\begin{bmatrix} 0.06 & 0.12 \\ 0.43 & 1.11 \\ 1.55 & -0.43 \end{bmatrix} - \begin{bmatrix} 0.77 & -0.75 \\ 0.22 & -0.65 \\ 1.09 & -0.57 \end{bmatrix} = \begin{bmatrix} -0.71 & 0.87 \\ 0.21 & 1.76 \\ 0.46 & 0.14 \end{bmatrix}.$$

19.
$$\frac{1}{2}\begin{bmatrix} 1 & 0 & 0 & -4 \\ 3 & 0 & -1 & 6 \\ -2 & 1 & -4 & 2 \end{bmatrix} + \frac{4}{3}\begin{bmatrix} 3 & 0 & -1 & 4 \\ -2 & 1 & -6 & 2 \\ 8 & 2 & 0 & -2 \end{bmatrix} - \frac{1}{3}\begin{bmatrix} 3 & -9 & -1 & 0 \\ 6 & 2 & 0 & -6 \\ 0 & 1 & -3 & 1 \end{bmatrix}$$

$$= \begin{bmatrix} \frac{7}{2} & 3 & -1 & \frac{10}{3} \\ -\frac{19}{6} & \frac{2}{3} & -\frac{17}{2} & \frac{23}{3} \\ \frac{29}{3} & \frac{17}{6} & -1 & -2 \end{bmatrix}.$$

20.
$$0.5\begin{bmatrix} 1 & 3 & 5 \\ 5 & 2 & -1 \\ -2 & 0 & 1 \end{bmatrix} - 0.2\begin{bmatrix} 2 & 3 & 4 \\ -1 & 1 & -4 \\ 3 & 5 & -5 \end{bmatrix} + 0.6\begin{bmatrix} 3 & 4 & -1 \\ 4 & 5 & 1 \\ 1 & 0 & 0 \end{bmatrix}$$

$$= \begin{bmatrix} 1.9 & 3.3 & 1.1 \\ 5.1 & 3.8 & 0.9 \\ -1 & -1 & 1.5 \end{bmatrix}.$$

21.
$$\begin{bmatrix} 2x - 2 & 3 & 2 \\ 2 & 4 & y - 2 \\ 2z & -3 & 2 \end{bmatrix} = \begin{bmatrix} 3 & u & 2 \\ 2 & 4 & 5 \\ 4 & -3 & 2 \end{bmatrix}$$

Now, by the definition of equality of matrices,

$u = 3$

$2x - 2 = 3$ and $2x = 5$, or $x = 5/2$,

$y - 2 = 5$, and $y = 7$,

$2z = 4$, and $z = 2$.

22.
$$\begin{bmatrix} x & -2 \\ 3 & y \end{bmatrix} + \begin{bmatrix} -2 & z \\ -1 & 2 \end{bmatrix} = \begin{bmatrix} 4 & -2 \\ 2u & 4 \end{bmatrix}.$$

$$\begin{bmatrix} x - 2 & -2 + z \\ 2 & y + 2 \end{bmatrix} = \begin{bmatrix} 4 & -2 \\ 2u & 4 \end{bmatrix}.$$

Now, by the definition of equality of matrices,

$$x - 2 = 4, \text{ so } x = 6$$

$$-2 + z = -2, \text{ so } z = 0$$

$$2 = 2u, \text{ so } u = 1$$

$$y + 2 = 4, \text{ so } y = 2.$$

23.
$$\begin{bmatrix} 1 & x \\ 2y & -3 \end{bmatrix} - 4 \begin{bmatrix} 2 & -2 \\ 0 & 3 \end{bmatrix} = \begin{bmatrix} 3z & 10 \\ 4 & -u \end{bmatrix}.$$

$$\begin{bmatrix} -7 & x + 8 \\ 2y & -15 \end{bmatrix} = \begin{bmatrix} 3z & 10 \\ 4 & -u \end{bmatrix}.$$

Now, by the definition of equality of matrices,

$$-u = -15, \text{ so } u = 15$$

$$x + 8 = 10, \text{ so } x = 2$$

$$2y = 4, \text{ so } y = 2$$

$$3z = -7, \text{ so } z = -7/3.$$

24.
$$\begin{bmatrix} 1 & 2 \\ 3 & 4 \\ x & -1 \end{bmatrix} - 3 \begin{bmatrix} y - 1 & 2 \\ 1 & 2 \\ 4 & 2z + 1 \end{bmatrix} = 2 \begin{bmatrix} -4 & -u \\ 0 & -1 \\ 4 & 4 \end{bmatrix}.$$

$$\begin{bmatrix} -3y + 4 & -4 \\ 0 & -2 \\ x - 12 & -6z - 4 \end{bmatrix} = \begin{bmatrix} -8 & -2u \\ 0 & -2 \\ 8 & 8 \end{bmatrix}.$$

Now, by the definition of equality of matrices,

$$-2u = -4, \text{ so } u = 2$$

$$x - 12 = 8, \text{ so } x = 20$$

$$-3y + 4 = -8, \text{ so } -3y = -12, \ y = 4$$

$$-6z - 4 = 8, \text{ so } -6z = 12, \text{ and } z = -2.$$

25. To verify the Commutative Law for matrix addition, let us show that

$$A + B = B + A.$$

Now,

$$A + B = \begin{bmatrix} 2 & -4 & 3 \\ 4 & 2 & 1 \end{bmatrix} + \begin{bmatrix} 4 & -3 & 2 \\ 1 & 0 & 4 \end{bmatrix} = \begin{bmatrix} 6 & -7 & 5 \\ 5 & 2 & 5 \end{bmatrix}$$

$$= \begin{bmatrix} 4 & -3 & 2 \\ 1 & 0 & 4 \end{bmatrix} + \begin{bmatrix} 2 & -4 & 3 \\ 4 & 2 & 1 \end{bmatrix} = B + A.$$

26. To verify the Associative Law for matrix addition, let us show that

$$A + (B + C) = (A + B) + C.$$

Now,

$$B + C = \begin{bmatrix} 4 & -3 & 2 \\ 1 & 0 & 4 \end{bmatrix} + \begin{bmatrix} 1 & 0 & 2 \\ 3 & -2 & 1 \end{bmatrix} = \begin{bmatrix} 5 & -3 & 4 \\ 4 & -2 & 5 \end{bmatrix}$$

and

$$A + (B + C) = \begin{bmatrix} 2 & -4 & 3 \\ 4 & 2 & 1 \end{bmatrix} + \begin{bmatrix} 5 & -3 & 4 \\ 4 & -2 & 5 \end{bmatrix} = \begin{bmatrix} 7 & -7 & 7 \\ 8 & 0 & 6 \end{bmatrix}$$

Now,

$$A + B = \begin{bmatrix} 2 & -4 & 3 \\ 4 & 2 & 1 \end{bmatrix} + \begin{bmatrix} 4 & -3 & 2 \\ 1 & 0 & 4 \end{bmatrix} = \begin{bmatrix} 6 & -7 & 5 \\ 5 & 2 & 5 \end{bmatrix}$$

and

$$(A + B) + C = \begin{bmatrix} 6 & -7 & 5 \\ 5 & 2 & 5 \end{bmatrix} + \begin{bmatrix} 1 & 0 & 2 \\ 3 & -2 & 1 \end{bmatrix} = \begin{bmatrix} 7 & -7 & 7 \\ 8 & 0 & 6 \end{bmatrix} .$$

**27.**

$$(3 + 5)A = 8A = 8 \begin{bmatrix} 3 & 1 \\ 2 & 4 \\ -4 & 0 \end{bmatrix} = \begin{bmatrix} 24 & 8 \\ 16 & 32 \\ -32 & 0 \end{bmatrix} = 3 \begin{bmatrix} 3 & 1 \\ 2 & 4 \\ -4 & 0 \end{bmatrix} + 5 \begin{bmatrix} 3 & 1 \\ 2 & 4 \\ -4 & 0 \end{bmatrix}$$

$$= 3A + 5A.$$

**28.**

$$2(4A) = 2(4) \begin{bmatrix} 3 & 1 \\ 2 & 4 \\ -4 & 0 \end{bmatrix} = 2 \begin{bmatrix} 12 & 4 \\ 8 & 16 \\ -16 & 0 \end{bmatrix} = \begin{bmatrix} 24 & 8 \\ 16 & 32 \\ -32 & 0 \end{bmatrix}$$

$$= (2 \cdot 4) \begin{bmatrix} 3 & 1 \\ 2 & 4 \\ -4 & 0 \end{bmatrix} = 8 \begin{bmatrix} 3 & 1 \\ 2 & 4 \\ -4 & 0 \end{bmatrix}.$$

**29.**

$$4(A + B) = 4 \left[ \begin{bmatrix} 3 & 1 \\ 2 & 4 \\ -4 & 0 \end{bmatrix} + \begin{bmatrix} 1 & 2 \\ -1 & 0 \\ 3 & 2 \end{bmatrix} \right] = 4 \begin{bmatrix} 4 & 3 \\ 1 & 4 \\ -1 & 2 \end{bmatrix} = \begin{bmatrix} 16 & 12 \\ 4 & 16 \\ -4 & 8 \end{bmatrix}$$

$$4A + 4B = 4 \begin{bmatrix} 3 & 1 \\ 2 & 4 \\ -4 & 0 \end{bmatrix} + 4 \begin{bmatrix} 1 & 2 \\ -1 & 0 \\ 3 & 2 \end{bmatrix} = \begin{bmatrix} 16 & 12 \\ 4 & 16 \\ -4 & 8 \end{bmatrix}.$$

**30.**

$$2(A - 3B) = 2 \left[ \begin{bmatrix} 3 & 1 \\ 2 & 4 \\ -4 & 0 \end{bmatrix} -3 \begin{bmatrix} 1 & 2 \\ -1 & 0 \\ 3 & 2 \end{bmatrix} \right] = 2 \begin{bmatrix} 0 & -5 \\ 5 & 4 \\ -13 & -6 \end{bmatrix} = \begin{bmatrix} 0 & -10 \\ 10 & 8 \\ -26 & -12 \end{bmatrix}$$

$$2A - 6B = 2 \begin{bmatrix} 3 & 1 \\ 2 & 4 \\ -4 & 0 \end{bmatrix} - 6 \begin{bmatrix} 1 & 2 \\ -1 & 0 \\ 3 & 2 \end{bmatrix} = \begin{bmatrix} 0 & -10 \\ 10 & 8 \\ -26 & -12 \end{bmatrix}.$$

31.

$$[3 \quad 2 \quad -1 \quad 5]^T = \begin{bmatrix} 3 \\ 2 \\ -1 \\ 5 \end{bmatrix}.$$

32. $\begin{bmatrix} 4 & 2 & 0 & -1 \\ 3 & 4 & -1 & 5 \end{bmatrix}^T = \begin{bmatrix} 4 & 3 \\ 2 & 4 \\ 0 & -1 \\ -1 & 5 \end{bmatrix}.$

33. $\begin{bmatrix} 1 & -1 & 2 \\ 3 & 4 & 2 \\ 0 & 1 & 0 \end{bmatrix}^T = \begin{bmatrix} 1 & 3 & 0 \\ -1 & 4 & 1 \\ 2 & 2 & 0 \end{bmatrix}.$

34. $\begin{bmatrix} 1 & 2 & 6 & 4 \\ 2 & 3 & 2 & 5 \\ 6 & 2 & 3 & 0 \\ 4 & 5 & 0 & 2 \end{bmatrix}^T = \begin{bmatrix} 1 & 2 & 6 & 4 \\ 2 & 3 & 2 & 5 \\ 6 & 2 & 3 & 0 \\ 4 & 5 & 0 & 2 \end{bmatrix}$

35.

|  | 1 | 2 | 3 | 4 |
|---|---|---|---|---|
| Mr. Cross | 220 | 215 | 210 | 205 |
| Mr. Jones | 220 | 210 | 200 | 195 |
| Mr. Smith | 215 | 205 | 195 | 190 |

36. a.

| | Text. | Fict. | Non-fict. | Ref. |
|---|---|---|---|---|
| Hard | 5280 | 1680 | 2320 | 1890 |
| Paper | 1940 | 2810 | 1490 | 2070 |

$A = $ (above)

b.

| | Text. | Fict. | Non-fict. | Ref. |
|---|---|---|---|---|
| Hard | 6340 | 2220 | 1790 | 1980 |
| Paper | 2050 | 3100 | 1720 | 2710 |

$B = $ (above)

c.

$$C = \begin{array}{c} \\ \text{Hard} \\ \\ \text{Paper} \end{array} \begin{array}{cccc} \text{Text.} & \text{Fict.} & \text{Non-fict.} & \text{Ref.} \\ \begin{bmatrix} 11620 & 3900 & 4110 & 3870 \\ 3990 & 5910 & 3210 & 4780 \end{bmatrix} \end{array}.$$

37.  a. D = A + B − C =

$$\begin{bmatrix} 2820 & 1470 & 1120 \\ 1030 & 520 & 480 \\ 1170 & 540 & 460 \end{bmatrix} + \begin{bmatrix} 260 & 120 & 110 \\ 140 & 60 & 50 \\ 120 & 70 & 50 \end{bmatrix} - \begin{bmatrix} 120 & 80 & 80 \\ 70 & 30 & 40 \\ 60 & 20 & 40 \end{bmatrix}$$

$$= \begin{bmatrix} 2960 & 1510 & 1150 \\ 1100 & 550 & 490 \\ 1230 & 590 & 470 \end{bmatrix}.$$

b.

$$E = 1.1D = 1.1 \begin{bmatrix} 2960 & 1510 & 1150 \\ 1100 & 550 & 490 \\ 1230 & 590 & 470 \end{bmatrix} = \begin{bmatrix} 3256 & 1661 & 1265 \\ 1210 & 605 & 539 \\ 1353 & 649 & 517 \end{bmatrix}.$$

## USING TECHNOLOGY EXERCISES 2.4, page 123

1.  $$\begin{bmatrix} 15 & 38.75 & -67.5 & 33.75 \\ 51.25 & 40 & 52.5 & -38.75 \\ 21.25 & 35 & -65 & 105 \end{bmatrix}$$

2.  $$\begin{bmatrix} -52.08 & 26.88 & -11.76 & 10.08 \\ -26.04 & -22.68 & 10.08 & -14.28 \\ -10.08 & 11.76 & 14.28 & -23.52 \end{bmatrix}$$

3.  $$\begin{bmatrix} -5 & 6.3 & -6.8 & 3.9 \\ 1 & .5 & 5.4 & -4.8 \\ .5 & 4.2 & -3.5 & 5.6 \end{bmatrix}$$

4.
$$\begin{bmatrix} 5 & -6.3 & 6.8 & -3.9 \\ -1 & -0.5 & -5.4 & 4.8 \\ -.5 & -4.2 & 3.5 & -5.6 \end{bmatrix}$$

5.
$$\begin{bmatrix} 16.44 & -3.65 & -3.66 & .63 \\ 12.77 & 10.64 & 2.58 & .05 \\ 5.09 & .28 & -10.84 & 17.64 \end{bmatrix}$$

6.
$$\begin{bmatrix} -8.02 & 11.95 & -13.72 & 7.71 \\ 3.34 & 2.13 & 10.86 & -9.4 \\ 1.53 & 8.26 & -8.03 & 12.88 \end{bmatrix}$$

7.
$$\begin{bmatrix} 7.4 & 7.2 & 2.9 \\ -0.1 & 5.9 & 1.4 \\ -4 & 3 & -6.9 \\ 1.5 & -1.4 & 11.2 \end{bmatrix}$$

8.
$$\begin{bmatrix} 28.4 & 24.7 & 9.9 \\ -3.5 & 20.4 & 2.8 \\ -10.6 & 7.8 & -22.4 \\ 3.3 & -2.5 & 36.4 \end{bmatrix}$$

## EXERCISES 2.5, page 133

1.    (2 x 3)(3 x 5)    so AB has order 2 x 5.
         ↑  ↑
         ⌊ = ⌋

      (3 x 5 (2 x 3)    so BA is not defined.
         ↑  ↑
         ⌊ ≠ ⌋

2.  (3 x 4) (4 x 3)    so AB has order 3 x 3.

    (4 x 3) (3 x 4)    so BA has order 4 x 4.

3.  (1 x 7) (7 x 1)    so AB has order 1 x 1.

    (7 x 1) (1 x 7)    so AB has order 7 x 7.

4.  (4 x 4) (4 x 4)    so AB has order 4 x 4.

    (4 x 4) (4 x 4)    so BA has order 4 x 4.

5.  If AB and BA are defined then n = s and m = t.

6.  A must be a square matrix. Then the order of A is n x n so that the order of $A^2$ is also n x n.

7.  $\begin{bmatrix} 1 & 2 \\ 3 & 0 \end{bmatrix} \begin{bmatrix} 1 \\ -1 \end{bmatrix} = \begin{bmatrix} -1 \\ 3 \end{bmatrix}.$

8.  $\begin{bmatrix} -1 & 3 \\ 5 & 0 \end{bmatrix} \begin{bmatrix} 7 \\ 2 \end{bmatrix} = \begin{bmatrix} -1 \\ 35 \end{bmatrix}.$

9.  $\begin{bmatrix} 3 & 1 & 2 \\ -1 & 2 & 4 \end{bmatrix} \begin{bmatrix} 4 \\ 1 \\ -2 \end{bmatrix} = \begin{bmatrix} 9 \\ -10 \end{bmatrix}.$

10. $\begin{bmatrix} 3 & 2 & -1 \\ 4 & -1 & 0 \\ -5 & 2 & 1 \end{bmatrix} \begin{bmatrix} 3 \\ -2 \\ 0 \end{bmatrix} = \begin{bmatrix} 5 \\ 14 \\ -19 \end{bmatrix}.$

11. $\begin{bmatrix} -1 & 2 \\ 3 & 1 \end{bmatrix} \begin{bmatrix} 2 & 4 \\ 3 & 1 \end{bmatrix} = \begin{bmatrix} 4 & -2 \\ 9 & 13 \end{bmatrix}.$

12. $\begin{bmatrix} 1 & 3 \\ -1 & 2 \end{bmatrix} \begin{bmatrix} 1 & 3 & 0 \\ 3 & 0 & 2 \end{bmatrix} = \begin{bmatrix} 10 & 3 & 6 \\ 5 & -3 & 4 \end{bmatrix}.$

13. $\begin{bmatrix} 2 & 1 & 2 \\ 3 & 2 & 4 \end{bmatrix} \begin{bmatrix} -1 & 2 \\ 4 & 3 \\ 0 & 1 \end{bmatrix} = \begin{bmatrix} 2 & 9 \\ 5 & 16 \end{bmatrix}.$

14. $\begin{bmatrix} -1 & 2 \\ 4 & 3 \\ 0 & 1 \end{bmatrix} \begin{bmatrix} 2 & 1 & 2 \\ 3 & 2 & 4 \end{bmatrix} = \begin{bmatrix} 4 & 3 & 6 \\ 17 & 10 & 20 \\ 3 & 2 & 4 \end{bmatrix}.$

15. $\begin{bmatrix} 0.1 & 0.9 \\ 0.2 & 0.8 \end{bmatrix} \begin{bmatrix} 1.2 & 0.4 \\ 0.5 & 2.1 \end{bmatrix} =$

$$= 2 \begin{bmatrix} 0.1(1.2) + 0.9(0.5) & 0.1(0.4) + 0.9(2.1) \\ 0.2(1.2) + 0.8(0.5) & 0.2(0.4) + 0.8(2.1) \end{bmatrix}$$

$$= \begin{bmatrix} 0.57 & 1.93 \\ 0.64 & 1.76 \end{bmatrix}.$$

16. $\begin{bmatrix} 1.2 & 0.3 \\ 0.4 & 0.5 \end{bmatrix} \begin{bmatrix} 0.2 & 0.6 \\ 0.4 & -0.5 \end{bmatrix} = \begin{bmatrix} 0.36 & 0.57 \\ 0.28 & -0.01 \end{bmatrix}$

17. $\begin{bmatrix} 6 & -3 & 0 \\ -2 & 1 & -8 \\ 4 & -4 & 9 \end{bmatrix} \begin{bmatrix} 1 & 0 & 0 \\ 0 & 1 & 0 \\ 0 & 0 & 1 \end{bmatrix} = \begin{bmatrix} 6 & -3 & 0 \\ -2 & 1 & -8 \\ 4 & -4 & 9 \end{bmatrix}.$

18. $\begin{bmatrix} 2 & 4 \\ -1 & -5 \\ 3 & -1 \end{bmatrix} \begin{bmatrix} 2 & -2 & 4 \\ 1 & 3 & -1 \end{bmatrix} = \begin{bmatrix} 8 & 8 & 4 \\ -7 & -13 & 1 \\ 5 & -9 & 13 \end{bmatrix}.$

19. $\begin{bmatrix} 3 & 0 & -2 & 1 \\ 1 & 2 & 0 & -1 \end{bmatrix} \begin{bmatrix} 2 & 1 & -1 \\ -1 & 2 & 0 \\ 0 & 0 & 1 \\ -1 & -2 & 2 \end{bmatrix} = \begin{bmatrix} 5 & 1 & -3 \\ 1 & 7 & -3 \end{bmatrix}.$

20. $\begin{bmatrix} 2 & 1 & -3 & 0 \\ 4 & -2 & -1 & 1 \\ -1 & 2 & 0 & 1 \end{bmatrix} \begin{bmatrix} 2 & -1 \\ 1 & 4 \\ 3 & -3 \\ 0 & -5 \end{bmatrix} = \begin{bmatrix} -4 & 11 \\ 3 & -14 \\ 0 & 4 \end{bmatrix}.$

21. $4\begin{bmatrix} 1 & -2 & 0 \\ 2 & -1 & 1 \\ 3 & 0 & -1 \end{bmatrix} \begin{bmatrix} 1 & 3 & 1 \\ 1 & 4 & 0 \\ 0 & 1 & -2 \end{bmatrix} = \begin{bmatrix} -4 & -20 & 4 \\ 4 & 12 & 0 \\ 12 & 32 & 20 \end{bmatrix}.$

22. $3\begin{bmatrix} 2 & -1 & 0 \\ 2 & 1 & 2 \\ 1 & 0 & -1 \end{bmatrix} \begin{bmatrix} 2 & 3 & 1 \\ 3 & -3 & 0 \\ 0 & 1 & -1 \end{bmatrix} = \begin{bmatrix} 3 & 27 & 6 \\ 21 & 15 & 0 \\ 6 & 6 & 6 \end{bmatrix}.$

23. $\begin{bmatrix} 1 & 0 \\ 0 & 1 \end{bmatrix} \begin{bmatrix} 4 & -3 & 2 \\ 7 & 1 & -5 \end{bmatrix} \begin{bmatrix} 1 & 0 & 0 \\ 0 & 1 & 0 \\ 0 & 0 & 1 \end{bmatrix} = \begin{bmatrix} 1 & 0 \\ 0 & 1 \end{bmatrix} \begin{bmatrix} 4 & -3 & 2 \\ 7 & 1 & -5 \end{bmatrix}$

$= \begin{bmatrix} 4 & -3 & 2 \\ 7 & 1 & -5 \end{bmatrix}.$

24. $2\begin{bmatrix} 3 & 2 & -1 \\ 0 & 1 & 3 \\ 2 & 0 & 3 \end{bmatrix} \begin{bmatrix} 1 & 0 & 0 \\ 0 & 1 & 0 \\ 0 & 0 & 1 \end{bmatrix} \begin{bmatrix} 1 & 2 & 0 \\ 0 & -1 & -2 \\ 1 & 3 & 1 \end{bmatrix}$

$$= 2 \begin{bmatrix} 3 & 2 & -1 \\ 0 & 1 & 3 \\ 2 & 0 & 3 \end{bmatrix} \begin{bmatrix} 1 & 2 & 0 \\ 0 & -1 & -2 \\ 1 & 3 & 1 \end{bmatrix} = 2 \begin{bmatrix} 2 & 1 & -5 \\ 3 & 8 & 1 \\ 5 & 13 & 3 \end{bmatrix}$$

$$= \begin{bmatrix} 4 & 2 & -10 \\ 6 & 16 & 2 \\ 10 & 26 & 6 \end{bmatrix} .$$

25. To verify the associative law for matrix multiplication, we will show that (AB)C = A(BC).

$$(AB) = \begin{bmatrix} 1 & 0 & -2 \\ 1 & -3 & 2 \\ -2 & 1 & 1 \end{bmatrix} \begin{bmatrix} 3 & 1 & 0 \\ 2 & 2 & 0 \\ 1 & -3 & -1 \end{bmatrix} = \begin{bmatrix} 1 & 7 & 2 \\ -1 & -11 & -2 \\ -3 & -3 & -1 \end{bmatrix}$$

$$(AB)C = \begin{bmatrix} 1 & 7 & 2 \\ -1 & -11 & -2 \\ -3 & -3 & -1 \end{bmatrix} \begin{bmatrix} 2 & 1 & 0 \\ 1 & -1 & 2 \\ 3 & -2 & 1 \end{bmatrix} = \begin{bmatrix} 15 & -12 & 16 \\ -19 & 16 & -24 \\ -12 & 8 & -7 \end{bmatrix} .$$

$$(BC) = \begin{bmatrix} 3 & 1 & 0 \\ 2 & 2 & 0 \\ 1 & -3 & -1 \end{bmatrix} \begin{bmatrix} 2 & -1 & 0 \\ 1 & -1 & 2 \\ 3 & -2 & 1 \end{bmatrix} = \begin{bmatrix} 7 & -4 & 2 \\ 6 & -4 & 4 \\ -4 & 4 & -7 \end{bmatrix}$$

$$A(BC) = \begin{bmatrix} 1 & 0 & -2 \\ 1 & -3 & 2 \\ -2 & 1 & 1 \end{bmatrix} \begin{bmatrix} 7 & -4 & 2 \\ 6 & -4 & 4 \\ -4 & 4 & -7 \end{bmatrix} = \begin{bmatrix} 15 & -12 & 16 \\ -19 & 16 & -24 \\ -12 & 8 & -7 \end{bmatrix} .$$

26. To verify the distributive law for matrix multiplication , we will show that A(B + C) = AB + AC.

$$A(B + C) = \begin{bmatrix} 1 & 0 & -2 \\ 1 & -3 & 2 \\ -2 & 1 & 1 \end{bmatrix} \cdot \begin{bmatrix} 5 & 0 & 0 \\ 3 & 1 & 2 \\ 4 & -5 & 0 \end{bmatrix} = \begin{bmatrix} -3 & 10 & 0 \\ 4 & -13 & -6 \\ -3 & -4 & 2 \end{bmatrix}$$

$$AB + AC = \begin{bmatrix} 1 & 7 & 2 \\ -1 & -11 & -2 \\ -3 & -3 & -1 \end{bmatrix} + \begin{bmatrix} -4 & 3 & -2 \\ 5 & -2 & -4 \\ 0 & -1 & 3 \end{bmatrix} = \begin{bmatrix} -3 & 10 & 0 \\ 4 & -13 & -6 \\ -3 & -4 & 2 \end{bmatrix}$$

27.
$$AB = \begin{bmatrix} 1 & 2 \\ 3 & 4 \end{bmatrix} \begin{bmatrix} 2 & 1 \\ 4 & 3 \end{bmatrix} = \begin{bmatrix} 10 & 7 \\ 22 & 15 \end{bmatrix}.$$

$$BA = \begin{bmatrix} 2 & 1 \\ 4 & 3 \end{bmatrix} \begin{bmatrix} 1 & 2 \\ 3 & 4 \end{bmatrix} = \begin{bmatrix} 5 & 8 \\ 13 & 20 \end{bmatrix}.$$

Therefore, AB ≠ BA and matrix multiplication is not commutative.

28. a.
$$\begin{bmatrix} 0 & 3 & 0 \\ 1 & 0 & 1 \\ 0 & 2 & 0 \end{bmatrix} \begin{bmatrix} 2 & 4 & 5 \\ 3 & -1 & -6 \\ 4 & 3 & 4 \end{bmatrix} = \begin{bmatrix} 9 & -3 & -18 \\ 6 & 7 & 9 \\ 6 & -2 & -12 \end{bmatrix}$$

b.
$$\begin{bmatrix} 0 & 3 & 0 \\ 1 & 0 & 1 \\ 0 & 2 & 0 \end{bmatrix} \begin{bmatrix} 4 & 5 & 6 \\ 3 & -1 & -6 \\ 2 & 2 & 3 \end{bmatrix} = \begin{bmatrix} 9 & -3 & -18 \\ 6 & 7 & 9 \\ 6 & -2 & -12 \end{bmatrix}.$$

c.    From the results of (a) and (b), we see that AB = AC does not
imply that B = C.

29.
$$AB = \begin{bmatrix} 3 & 0 \\ 8 & 0 \end{bmatrix} \begin{bmatrix} 0 & 0 \\ 4 & 5 \end{bmatrix} = \begin{bmatrix} 0 & 0 \\ 0 & 0 \end{bmatrix}.$$

AB = 0, but neither A nor B is the zero matrix. Therefore, AB = 0,
does not imply that A or B is the zero matrix.

30.
$$A^2 = \begin{bmatrix} 2 & 2 \\ -2 & -2 \end{bmatrix} \begin{bmatrix} 2 & 2 \\ -2 & -2 \end{bmatrix} = \begin{bmatrix} 0 & 0 \\ 0 & 0 \end{bmatrix} = 0.$$

Thus, for matrices, $A^2 = 0$ does not imply A = 0.
If $a^2 = 0$, where a is a real number, then a = 0.

**31.**

$$\begin{bmatrix} a & b \\ c & d \end{bmatrix} \begin{bmatrix} 1 & 0 \\ -1 & 3 \end{bmatrix} = \begin{bmatrix} a-b & 3b \\ c-d & 3d \end{bmatrix} = \begin{bmatrix} -1 & -3 \\ 3 & 6 \end{bmatrix}.$$

Then $\qquad$ $3b = -3$, and $b = -1$.

$3d = 6$, and $d = 2$

$a - b = -1$, and $a = b - 1 = -2$.

$c - d = 3$, and $c = d + 3 = 5$.

Therefore,

$$A = \begin{bmatrix} -2 & -1 \\ 5 & 2 \end{bmatrix}.$$

**32.** a.

$$(A + B)^2 = \begin{bmatrix} 7 & -1 \\ 2 & 3 \end{bmatrix} \begin{bmatrix} 7 & -1 \\ 2 & 3 \end{bmatrix} = \begin{bmatrix} 47 & -10 \\ 20 & 7 \end{bmatrix}$$

b.

$$A^2 + 2AB + B^2 = \begin{bmatrix} 9 & 5 \\ 0 & 4 \end{bmatrix} + \begin{bmatrix} 28 & -10 \\ 8 & 4 \end{bmatrix} + \begin{bmatrix} 12 & -10 \\ 10 & -3 \end{bmatrix} = \begin{bmatrix} 49 & -15 \\ 18 & 5 \end{bmatrix}$$

c. From the results of (a) and (b), we see that, in general,
$(A + B)^2 \neq A^2 + 2AB + B^2$

**33.** a.

$$A^T = \begin{bmatrix} 2 & 5 \\ 4 & -6 \end{bmatrix} \text{ and } (A^T)^T = \begin{bmatrix} 2 & 4 \\ 5 & -6 \end{bmatrix} = A.$$

b.

$$(A + B)^T = \begin{bmatrix} 6 & 12 \\ -2 & -3 \end{bmatrix}^T = \begin{bmatrix} 6 & -2 \\ 12 & -3 \end{bmatrix}.$$

$$A^T + B^T = \begin{bmatrix} 2 & 5 \\ 4 & -6 \end{bmatrix} + \begin{bmatrix} 4 & -7 \\ 8 & 3 \end{bmatrix} = \begin{bmatrix} 6 & -2 \\ 12 & -3 \end{bmatrix} = (A + B)^T.$$

c.

$$AB = \begin{bmatrix} 2 & 4 \\ 5 & -6 \end{bmatrix} \begin{bmatrix} 4 & 8 \\ -7 & 3 \end{bmatrix} = \begin{bmatrix} -20 & 28 \\ 62 & 22 \end{bmatrix}$$

so $(AB)^T = \begin{bmatrix} -20 & 62 \\ 28 & 22 \end{bmatrix}$.

$B^T A^T = \begin{bmatrix} 4 & -7 \\ 8 & 3 \end{bmatrix} \begin{bmatrix} 2 & 5 \\ 4 & -6 \end{bmatrix} = \begin{bmatrix} -20 & 62 \\ 28 & 22 \end{bmatrix} = (AB)^T$.

34.  a.

$A^T = \begin{bmatrix} 1 & -2 \\ 3 & -1 \end{bmatrix}$ and $(A^T)^T = \begin{bmatrix} 1 & 3 \\ -2 & -1 \end{bmatrix} = A$.

b.

$(A + B)^T = \begin{bmatrix} 4 & -1 \\ 0 & -3 \end{bmatrix}^T = \begin{bmatrix} 4 & 0 \\ -1 & -3 \end{bmatrix}$.

$A^T + B^T = \begin{bmatrix} 1 & -2 \\ 3 & -1 \end{bmatrix} + \begin{bmatrix} 3 & 2 \\ -4 & -2 \end{bmatrix} = \begin{bmatrix} 4 & 0 \\ -1 & -3 \end{bmatrix} = (A + B)^T$.

c.

$(AB) = \begin{bmatrix} 1 & 3 \\ -2 & -1 \end{bmatrix} \begin{bmatrix} 3 & -4 \\ 2 & -2 \end{bmatrix} = \begin{bmatrix} 9 & -10 \\ -8 & 10 \end{bmatrix}$

so $(AB)^T = \begin{bmatrix} 9 & -8 \\ -10 & 10 \end{bmatrix}$.

$B^T A^T = \begin{bmatrix} 3 & 2 \\ -4 & -2 \end{bmatrix} \begin{bmatrix} 1 & -2 \\ 3 & -1 \end{bmatrix} = \begin{bmatrix} 9 & -8 \\ -10 & 10 \end{bmatrix} = (AB)^T$.

35.  The given system of linear equations can be represented by the matrix equation AX = B, where

$$A = \begin{bmatrix} 2 & -3 \\ 3 & -4 \end{bmatrix} \quad X = \begin{bmatrix} x \\ y \end{bmatrix} \quad \text{and } B = \begin{bmatrix} 7 \\ 8 \end{bmatrix} .$$

36.  The given system of linear equations can be represented by the matrix equation AX = B, where

$$A = \begin{bmatrix} 2 & 0 \\ 3 & -2 \end{bmatrix} \quad X = \begin{bmatrix} x \\ y \end{bmatrix} \quad \text{and } B = \begin{bmatrix} 7 \\ 12 \end{bmatrix} .$$

37. The given system of linear equations can be represented by the matrix equation AX = B, where

$$A = \begin{bmatrix} 2 & -3 & 4 \\ 0 & 2 & -3 \\ 1 & -1 & 2 \end{bmatrix}, \quad X = \begin{bmatrix} x \\ y \\ z \end{bmatrix}, \quad \text{and } B = \begin{bmatrix} 6 \\ 7 \\ 4 \end{bmatrix}.$$

38. The given system of linear equations can be represented by the matrix equation AX = B, where

$$A = \begin{bmatrix} 1 & -2 & 3 \\ 3 & 4 & -2 \\ 2 & -3 & 7 \end{bmatrix}, \quad X = \begin{bmatrix} x \\ y \\ z \end{bmatrix}, \quad \text{and } B = \begin{bmatrix} -1 \\ 1 \\ 6 \end{bmatrix}.$$

39. The given system of linear equations can be represented by the matrix equation AX = B, where

$$A = \begin{bmatrix} -1 & 1 & 1 \\ 2 & -1 & -1 \\ -3 & 2 & 4 \end{bmatrix}, \quad X = \begin{bmatrix} x_1 \\ x_2 \\ x_3 \end{bmatrix}, \quad \text{and } B = \begin{bmatrix} 0 \\ 2 \\ 4 \end{bmatrix}.$$

40. The given system of linear equations can be represented by the matrix equation AX = B, where

$$A = \begin{bmatrix} 3 & -5 & 4 \\ 4 & 2 & -3 \\ -1 & 0 & 1 \end{bmatrix}, \quad X = \begin{bmatrix} x_1 \\ x_2 \\ x_3 \end{bmatrix}, \quad \text{and } B = \begin{bmatrix} 10 \\ -12 \\ -2 \end{bmatrix}.$$

41. a.

$$AB = \begin{bmatrix} 200 & 300 & 100 & 200 \\ 100 & 200 & 400 & 0 \end{bmatrix} \begin{bmatrix} 54 \\ 48 \\ 98 \\ 82 \end{bmatrix} = \begin{bmatrix} 51,400 \\ 54,200 \end{bmatrix}$$

b. The first entry shows that William's total stock holdings are $51,400, while Michael's stockholdings are $54,200.

42. The column vector that represents the admission prices is

$$B = \begin{bmatrix} 2 \\ 3 \\ 4 \end{bmatrix} .$$

The column vector that gives the gross receipts for each theater is

$$AB = \begin{bmatrix} 225 & 110 & 50 \\ 75 & 180 & 225 \\ 280 & 85 & 110 \\ 0 & 250 & 225 \end{bmatrix} \begin{bmatrix} 2 \\ 3 \\ 4 \end{bmatrix} = \begin{bmatrix} 980 \\ 1590 \\ 1255 \\ 1650 \end{bmatrix}$$

The total revenue collected is given by

$$980 + 1590 + 1255 + 1650,$$

or \$5475.

43. The column vector that represents the profit for each type of house is

$$B = \begin{bmatrix} 20,000 \\ 22,000 \\ 25,000 \\ 30,000 \end{bmatrix}$$

The column vector that gives the total profit for Bond Brothers is

$$AB = \begin{bmatrix} 60 & 80 & 120 & 40 \\ 20 & 30 & 60 & 10 \\ 10 & 15 & 30 & 5 \end{bmatrix} \begin{bmatrix} 20,000 \\ 22,000 \\ 25,000 \\ 30,000 \end{bmatrix}$$

$$= \begin{bmatrix} 7,160,000 \\ 2,860,000 \\ 1,430,000 \end{bmatrix} .$$

Therefore, Bond Brothers expects to make \$7,160,000 in New York, \$2,860,000 in Connecticut, and 1,430,000 in Massachusetts, and the total profit is \$11,450,000.

**44.**

$$BA = [\ 30{,}000 \quad 40{,}000 \quad 20{,}000\ ] \begin{bmatrix} & D & R & I \\ .50 & .30 & .20 \\ .45 & .40 & .15 \\ .40 & .50 & .10 \end{bmatrix}$$

$$= \begin{matrix} D & R & I \\ [41{,}000 & 35{,}000 & 14{,}000] \end{matrix}.$$

**45.**

$$AB = \begin{bmatrix} 2700 & 3000 \\ 800 & 700 \\ 500 & 300 \end{bmatrix} \begin{bmatrix} .25 & .20 & .30 & .25 \\ .30 & .35 & .25 & .10 \end{bmatrix} = \begin{bmatrix} 1575 & 1590 & 1560 & 975 \\ 410 & 405 & 415 & 270 \\ 215 & 205 & 225 & 155 \end{bmatrix}$$

**46. a.**

$$PA = \begin{bmatrix} 700 & 1000 & 800 \\ 500 & 800 & 600 \end{bmatrix} \begin{bmatrix} 1.3 & 20 & 12 \\ 1.5 & 30 & 5 \\ 2.5 & 25 & 15 \end{bmatrix} = \begin{bmatrix} 4410 & 64000 & 25400 \\ 3350 & 49000 & 19000 \end{bmatrix}$$

**b.**

$$PAC = \begin{bmatrix} 4410 & 64000 & 25400 \\ 3350 & 49000 & 19000 \end{bmatrix} \begin{bmatrix} 4.50 \\ 0.10 \\ 0.25 \end{bmatrix} = \begin{bmatrix} 32{,}595 \\ 24{,}725 \end{bmatrix}.$$

c. The total cost of materials incurred by Ace Novelty in filling the order is 32,595 + 24,725 = 57320, or $57,320.

**47. a.**

$$AC = \begin{bmatrix} 320 & 280 & 460 & 280 \\ 480 & 360 & 580 & 0 \\ 540 & 420 & 200 & 880 \end{bmatrix} \begin{bmatrix} 120 \\ 180 \\ 260 \\ 500 \end{bmatrix} = \begin{bmatrix} 348{,}400 \\ 273{,}200 \\ 632{,}400 \end{bmatrix}$$

The entries give the total production costs at locations I, II, and III for the month of May as $348,000, $273,200, and $632,400, respectively.

**b.**

$$AD = \begin{bmatrix} 320 & 280 & 460 & 280 \\ 480 & 360 & 580 & 0 \\ 540 & 420 & 200 & 880 \end{bmatrix} \begin{bmatrix} 160 \\ 250 \\ 350 \\ 700 \end{bmatrix} = \begin{bmatrix} 478{,}200 \\ 369{,}800 \\ 877{,}400 \end{bmatrix}$$

The total revenue realized at locations I, II, and III for the month of May are $478,200, $369,800, $877,400, respectively.

c.

$$BC = \begin{bmatrix} 210 & 180 & 330 & 180 \\ 400 & 300 & 450 & 40 \\ 420 & 280 & 180 & 740 \end{bmatrix} \begin{bmatrix} 120 \\ 180 \\ 260 \\ 500 \end{bmatrix} = \begin{bmatrix} 233,400 \\ 239,000 \\ 517,600 \end{bmatrix}$$

The total production costs at locations I, II, and III for the month of June are $233,400, $239,000, and $517,600, respectively.

d.

$$BD = \begin{bmatrix} 210 & 180 & 330 & 180 \\ 400 & 300 & 450 & 40 \\ 420 & 280 & 180 & 740 \end{bmatrix} \begin{bmatrix} 160 \\ 250 \\ 350 \\ 700 \end{bmatrix} = \begin{bmatrix} 320,100 \\ 324,500 \\ 718,200 \end{bmatrix}$$

The total revenue realized at locations I, II, and III for the month of June are $320,100, $324,500, and $718,200, respectively.

e.

$$(A + B)C = \begin{bmatrix} 530 & 460 & 790 & 460 \\ 880 & 660 & 1030 & 40 \\ 960 & 700 & 380 & 1620 \end{bmatrix} \begin{bmatrix} 120 \\ 180 \\ 500 \\ 700 \end{bmatrix} = \begin{bmatrix} 581,800 \\ 512,200 \\ 1,150,000 \end{bmatrix}$$

The total production costs in May and June are Locations I, II, and III are $581,800, $512,200, and $1,150,000, respectively.

f.

$$(A + B)D = \begin{bmatrix} 530 & 460 & 790 & 460 \\ 880 & 660 & 1030 & 40 \\ 960 & 700 & 380 & 1620 \end{bmatrix} \begin{bmatrix} 160 \\ 250 \\ 350 \\ 700 \end{bmatrix} = \begin{bmatrix} 798,300 \\ 694,300 \\ 1,595,600 \end{bmatrix}$$

The total revenue realized in May and June in Locations I, II, and III are $798,300, $694,300, and $1,595,600, respectively.

g.

$$A(D - C) = \begin{bmatrix} 320 & 280 & 460 & 280 \\ 480 & 360 & 580 & 0 \\ 540 & 420 & 200 & 880 \end{bmatrix} \begin{bmatrix} 40 \\ 70 \\ 90 \\ 200 \end{bmatrix} = \begin{bmatrix} 129,800 \\ 96,600 \\ 245,000 \end{bmatrix}$$

The profits in Locations I, II, and III in May are $129,800, $96,600, and $245,000, respectively.

h. $B(D - C) = \begin{bmatrix} 86,700 \\ 85,500 \\ 200,600 \end{bmatrix}$    i. $(A + B)(D - C) = \begin{bmatrix} 216,500 \\ 182,100 \\ 445,500 \end{bmatrix}$

The profits in Locations I, II, and III in June are $86,700, $85,500, and $200,600, respectively.

The profits in Locations I, II, and III in May and June are $216,500, $182,100, $445,600, respectively.

48. a. $MA^T = \begin{bmatrix} 400 & 1200 & 800 \\ 110 & 570 & 340 \\ 90 & 30 & 60 \end{bmatrix} \begin{bmatrix} 7 \\ 1 \\ 6 \end{bmatrix} = \begin{bmatrix} 8800 \\ 3380 \\ 1020 \end{bmatrix}$

The amount of vitamin A, vitamin C, and calcium taken by Patricia in the first meal are 8800, 3380, and 1020 units respectively.

b. $MB^T = \begin{bmatrix} 400 & 1200 & 800 \\ 110 & 570 & 340 \\ 90 & 30 & 60 \end{bmatrix} \begin{bmatrix} 9 \\ 4 \\ 8 \end{bmatrix} = \begin{bmatrix} 14800 \\ 5990 \\ 1410 \end{bmatrix}$

The amount of vitamin A, vitamin C, and calcium taken by Patricia in the second meal is 14,800, 5990, and 1410 units, respectively.

c. $M(A + B) = \begin{bmatrix} 400 & 1200 & 800 \\ 110 & 570 & 340 \\ 90 & 30 & 60 \end{bmatrix} \begin{bmatrix} 16 \\ 4 \\ 8 \end{bmatrix} = \begin{bmatrix} 17,600 \\ 6,760 \\ 2,040 \end{bmatrix}$

The amount of vitamin A, vitamin C, and calcium taken by Patricia in the two meals are 17,600, 6,760, and 2,040 units respectively.

## USING TECHNOLOGY EXERCISES 2.5, page 137

1. $\begin{bmatrix} 18.66 & 15.2 & -12 \\ 24.48 & 41.88 & 89.82 \\ 15.39 & 7.16 & -1.25 \end{bmatrix}$

2. $\begin{bmatrix} -11.38 & 4.87 & 51.85 & 49.02 \\ -14.97 & -6.81 & 19.92 & 7.68 \\ 9.22 & 6.95 & 5.06 & 5.92 \\ 33.03 & 16.15 & -21.56 & -15.12 \end{bmatrix}$

3. $\begin{bmatrix} 20.09 & 20.61 & -1.3 \\ 44.42 & 71.6 & 64.89 \\ 20.97 & 7.17 & -60.65 \end{bmatrix}$

4. $\begin{bmatrix} 41.61 & 46.63 & 8.1 \\ 108.78 & 172.92 & 104.85 \\ 47.52 & 14.35 & -180.7 \end{bmatrix}$

5.
$$\begin{bmatrix} 32.89 & 13.63 & -57.17 \\ -12.85 & -8.37 & 256.92 \\ 13.48 & 14.29 & 181.64 \end{bmatrix}$$

6.
$$\begin{bmatrix} 83.37 & 156.39 & 173.82 & 169.23 \\ -49.67 & 16.07 & 37.79 & 87.89 \\ 72.60 & 57.67 & 27.60 & 9.52 \\ 145.26 & 51.24 & -39.26 & -92.93 \end{bmatrix}$$

7.
$$\begin{bmatrix} 18.66 & 24.48 & 15.39 \\ 15.2 & 41.88 & 7.16 \\ -12 & 89.82 & -1.25 \end{bmatrix}$$

8.
$$\begin{bmatrix} 57.04 & -.84 & 20.52 & 18.84 \\ 67.05 & 18.03 & 16.87 & -0.21 \\ 3.76 & -12.36 & 5.43 & 14.16 \\ 5.89 & 30.15 & -4.49 & -21.21 \end{bmatrix}$$

9.
$$\begin{bmatrix} 87 & 68 & 110 & 82 \\ 119 & 176 & 221 & 143 \\ 51 & 128 & 142 & 94 \\ 28 & 174 & 174 & 112 \end{bmatrix}$$

$$\begin{bmatrix} 113 & 117 & 72 & 101 & 90 \\ 72 & 85 & 36 & 72 & 76 \\ 81 & 69 & 76 & 87 & 30 \\ 133 & 157 & 56 & 121 & 146 \\ 154 & 157 & 94 & 127 & 122 \end{bmatrix}$$

10.
$$\begin{bmatrix} 107.81 & -58.81 & 158.45 & 98.36 & 175.89 \\ 135.54 & -20.23 & 143.96 & 44.58 & 121.12 \\ 88.31 & 125.79 & 147.64 & 199.69 & 126.11 \\ 184.91 & 27.29 & 227.45 & 142.01 & 224.24 \\ 211.68 & -102.14 & 201.81 & -39.29 & 228.33 \end{bmatrix}$$

$$\begin{bmatrix} 243.56 & 196.98 & 153.97 & 20.36 & 311.72 \\ 148.25 & 101.54 & 71.07 & 152.12 & 113.96 \\ 213.16 & 203.26 & 147.46 & 33.67 & 268.89 \\ 212.75 & 185.59 & 155.87 & 11.05 & 278.86 \\ 65.57 & 38.57 & -46.63 & 21.51 & 101.95 \end{bmatrix} ; \text{No}$$

11. $$\begin{bmatrix} 170 & 18.1 & 133.1 & -106.3 & 341.3 \\ 349 & 226.5 & 324.1 & 164 & 506.4 \\ 245.2 & 157.7 & 231.5 & 125.5 & 312.9 \\ 310 & 245.2 & 291 & 274.3 & 354.2 \end{bmatrix}$$

12. a. $$\begin{bmatrix} 113.6 & 103.3 & 60.2 & -118.3 & 254.6 \\ 217.2 & 202.2 & 134.7 & -1 & 319.6 \\ 144.4 & 130.9 & 96.4 & 13.3 & 188.8 \\ 173 & 165.8 & 93.9 & 93 & 181.9 \end{bmatrix}$$

b. $$\begin{bmatrix} 56.4 & -85.2 & 72.9 & 12 & 86.7 \\ 131.8 & 24.3 & 189.4 & 165 & 186.8 \\ 100.8 & 26.8 & 135.1 & 112.2 & 124.1 \\ 137 & 79.4 & 197.1 & 181.3 & 172.3 \end{bmatrix}$$

c. $$\begin{bmatrix} 170 & 18.1 & 133.1 & -106.3 & 341.3 \\ 349 & 226.5 & 324.1 & 164 & 506.4 \\ 245.2 & 157.7 & 231.5 & 125.5 & 312.9 \\ 310 & 245.2 & 291 & 274.3 & 354.2 \end{bmatrix}$$

d. Yes

**EXERCISES 2.6, page 149**

1. $\begin{bmatrix} 1 & -3 \\ 1 & -2 \end{bmatrix} \begin{bmatrix} -2 & 3 \\ -1 & 1 \end{bmatrix} = \begin{bmatrix} 1 & 0 \\ 0 & 1 \end{bmatrix}$ ; $\begin{bmatrix} -2 & 3 \\ -1 & 1 \end{bmatrix} \begin{bmatrix} 1 & -3 \\ 1 & -2 \end{bmatrix} = \begin{bmatrix} 1 & 0 \\ 0 & 1 \end{bmatrix}$.

2. $\begin{bmatrix} 4 & 5 \\ 2 & 3 \end{bmatrix} \begin{bmatrix} \frac{3}{2} & -\frac{5}{2} \\ -1 & 2 \end{bmatrix} = \begin{bmatrix} 1 & 0 \\ 0 & 1 \end{bmatrix}$ ; $\begin{bmatrix} \frac{3}{2} & -\frac{5}{2} \\ 1 & 2 \end{bmatrix} \begin{bmatrix} 4 & 5 \\ 2 & 3 \end{bmatrix} = \begin{bmatrix} 1 & 0 \\ 0 & 1 \end{bmatrix}$.

3. $\begin{bmatrix} 3 & 2 & 3 \\ 2 & 2 & 1 \\ 2 & 1 & 1 \end{bmatrix} \begin{bmatrix} -\frac{1}{3} & -\frac{1}{3} & \frac{4}{3} \\ 0 & 1 & -1 \\ \frac{2}{3} & -\frac{1}{3} & -\frac{2}{3} \end{bmatrix} = \begin{bmatrix} 1 & 0 & 0 \\ 0 & 1 & 0 \\ 0 & 0 & 1 \end{bmatrix}$ and

$\begin{bmatrix} -\frac{1}{3} & -\frac{1}{3} & \frac{4}{3} \\ 0 & 1 & -1 \\ \frac{2}{3} & -\frac{1}{3} & -\frac{2}{3} \end{bmatrix} \begin{bmatrix} 3 & 2 & 3 \\ 2 & 2 & 1 \\ 2 & 1 & 1 \end{bmatrix} = \begin{bmatrix} 1 & 0 & 0 \\ 0 & 1 & 0 \\ 0 & 0 & 1 \end{bmatrix}$

4. $\begin{bmatrix} 2 & 4 & -2 \\ -4 & -6 & 1 \\ 3 & 5 & -1 \end{bmatrix} \begin{bmatrix} \frac{1}{2} & -3 & -4 \\ -\frac{1}{2} & 2 & 3 \\ -1 & 1 & 2 \end{bmatrix} = \begin{bmatrix} 1 & 0 & 0 \\ 0 & 1 & 0 \\ 0 & 0 & 1 \end{bmatrix}$ and

$\begin{bmatrix} \frac{1}{2} & -3 & -4 \\ -\frac{1}{2} & 2 & 3 \\ -1 & 1 & 2 \end{bmatrix} \begin{bmatrix} 2 & 4 & -2 \\ -4 & -6 & 1 \\ 3 & 5 & -1 \end{bmatrix} = \begin{bmatrix} 1 & 0 & 0 \\ 0 & 1 & 0 \\ 0 & 0 & 1 \end{bmatrix}$.

5. Using Formula (13), we find

$$A^{-1} = \frac{1}{(2)(3) - (1)(5)} \begin{bmatrix} 3 & -5 \\ -1 & 2 \end{bmatrix} = \begin{bmatrix} 3 & -5 \\ -1 & 2 \end{bmatrix}.$$

6. Using Formula (13), we find

$$A^{-1} = \frac{1}{(2)(5) - (3)(3)} \begin{bmatrix} 5 & -3 \\ -3 & 2 \end{bmatrix} = \begin{bmatrix} 5 & -3 \\ -3 & 2 \end{bmatrix}.$$

7. Since $ad - bc = (3)(2) - (-2)(-3) = 6 - 6 = 0$, the inverse does not exist.

8. Since $ad - bc = (4)(3) - (6)(2) = 12 - 12 = 0$, the inverse does not exist.

9.
$$\left[\begin{array}{ccc|ccc} 2 & -3 & -4 & 1 & 0 & 0 \\ 0 & 0 & -1 & 0 & 1 & 0 \\ 1 & -2 & 1 & 0 & 0 & 1 \end{array}\right] \xrightarrow{R_1 \leftrightarrow R_3} \left[\begin{array}{ccc|ccc} 1 & -2 & 1 & 0 & 0 & 1 \\ 0 & 0 & -1 & 0 & 1 & 0 \\ 2 & -3 & -4 & 1 & 0 & 0 \end{array}\right] \xrightarrow{R_3 - 2R_1}$$

$$\left[\begin{array}{ccc|ccc} 1 & -2 & 1 & 0 & 0 & 1 \\ 0 & 0 & -1 & 0 & 1 & 0 \\ 0 & 1 & -6 & 1 & 0 & -2 \end{array}\right] \xrightarrow{R_2 \leftrightarrow R_3} \left[\begin{array}{ccc|ccc} 1 & -2 & 1 & 0 & 0 & 1 \\ 0 & 1 & -6 & 1 & 0 & -2 \\ 0 & 0 & -1 & 0 & 1 & 0 \end{array}\right] \xrightarrow[-R_3]{R_1 + 2R_2}$$

$$\left[\begin{array}{ccc|ccc} 1 & 0 & -11 & 2 & 0 & -3 \\ 0 & 1 & -6 & 1 & 0 & -2 \\ 0 & 0 & 1 & 0 & -1 & 0 \end{array}\right] \xrightarrow[R_2 + 6R_3]{R_1 + 11R_3} \left[\begin{array}{ccc|ccc} 1 & 0 & 0 & 2 & -11 & -3 \\ 0 & 1 & 0 & 1 & -6 & -2 \\ 0 & 0 & 1 & 0 & -1 & 0 \end{array}\right].$$

Therefore, the required inverse is

$$\begin{bmatrix} 2 & -11 & -3 \\ 1 & -6 & -2 \\ 0 & -1 & 0 \end{bmatrix}.$$

**10.**

$$\begin{bmatrix} 1 & -1 & 3 & | & 1 & 0 & 0 \\ 2 & 1 & 2 & | & 0 & 1 & 0 \\ -2 & -2 & 1 & | & 0 & 0 & 1 \end{bmatrix} \xrightarrow[R_3 + 2R_1]{R_2 - 2R_1} \begin{bmatrix} 1 & -1 & 3 & | & 1 & 0 & 0 \\ 0 & 3 & -4 & | & -2 & 1 & 0 \\ 0 & -4 & 7 & | & 2 & 0 & 1 \end{bmatrix} \xrightarrow{\frac{1}{3}R_2}$$

$$\begin{bmatrix} 1 & -1 & 3 & | & 1 & 0 & 0 \\ 0 & 1 & -\frac{4}{3} & | & -\frac{2}{3} & \frac{1}{3} & 0 \\ 0 & -4 & 7 & | & 2 & 0 & 1 \end{bmatrix} \xrightarrow[R_3 + 4R_2]{R_1 + R_2} \begin{bmatrix} 1 & 0 & \frac{5}{3} & | & \frac{1}{3} & \frac{1}{3} & 0 \\ 0 & 1 & -\frac{4}{3} & | & -\frac{2}{3} & \frac{1}{3} & 0 \\ 0 & 0 & \frac{5}{3} & | & -\frac{2}{3} & \frac{4}{3} & 1 \end{bmatrix} \xrightarrow{\frac{3}{5}R_3}$$

$$\begin{bmatrix} 1 & 0 & \frac{5}{3} & | & \frac{1}{3} & \frac{1}{3} & 0 \\ 0 & 1 & -\frac{4}{3} & | & -\frac{2}{3} & \frac{1}{3} & 0 \\ 0 & 0 & 1 & | & -\frac{2}{5} & \frac{4}{5} & \frac{3}{5} \end{bmatrix} \xrightarrow[R_2 + \frac{4}{3}R_3]{R_1 - \frac{5}{3}R_3} \begin{bmatrix} 1 & 0 & 0 & | & 1 & -1 & -1 \\ 0 & 1 & 0 & | & -\frac{6}{5} & \frac{7}{5} & \frac{4}{5} \\ 0 & 0 & 1 & | & -\frac{2}{5} & \frac{4}{5} & \frac{3}{5} \end{bmatrix}.$$

**11.**

$$\begin{bmatrix} 4 & 2 & 2 & | & 1 & 0 & 0 \\ -1 & -3 & 4 & | & 0 & 1 & 0 \\ 3 & -1 & 6 & | & 0 & 0 & 1 \end{bmatrix} \xrightarrow{R_1 - R_3} \begin{bmatrix} 1 & 3 & -4 & | & 1 & 0 & -1 \\ -1 & -3 & 4 & | & 0 & 1 & 0 \\ 3 & -1 & 6 & | & 0 & 0 & 1 \end{bmatrix}$$

$$\xrightarrow[R_3 + 5R_1]{R_2 + R_1} \begin{bmatrix} 1 & 3 & -4 & | & 1 & 0 & -1 \\ 0 & 0 & 0 & | & 1 & 1 & -1 \\ 3 & -1 & 6 & | & 0 & 0 & 1 \end{bmatrix}.$$

Because there is a row of zeros to the left of the vertical line, we see that the inverse does not exist.

**12.**

$$\begin{bmatrix} 1 & 2 & 0 & | & 1 & 0 & 0 \\ -3 & 4 & -2 & | & 0 & 1 & 0 \\ -5 & 0 & -2 & | & 0 & 0 & 1 \end{bmatrix} \xrightarrow[R_3 + 5R_1]{R_2 + 3R_1} \begin{bmatrix} 1 & 2 & 0 & | & 1 & 0 & 0 \\ 0 & 10 & -2 & | & 3 & 1 & 0 \\ 0 & 10 & -2 & | & 5 & 0 & 1 \end{bmatrix}$$

$$R_3 - R_2 \quad \begin{bmatrix} 1 & 2 & 0 & | & 1 & 0 & 0 \\ 0 & 10 & -2 & | & 3 & 1 & 0 \\ 0 & 0 & 0 & | & 2 & -1 & 1 \end{bmatrix}.$$

Since the last row of the 3 x 3 submatrix comprising the left-hand side of the last augmented matrix is comprised of all zero entries, we conclude that the given matrix is singular and does not possess an inverse.

13.
$$\begin{bmatrix} 1 & 4 & -1 & | & 1 & 0 & 0 \\ 2 & 3 & -2 & | & 0 & 1 & 0 \\ -1 & 2 & 3 & | & 0 & 0 & 1 \end{bmatrix} \xrightarrow[R_3 + R_1]{R_2 - 2R_1} \begin{bmatrix} 1 & 4 & -1 & | & 1 & 0 & 0 \\ 0 & -5 & 0 & | & -2 & 1 & 0 \\ 0 & 6 & 2 & | & 1 & 0 & 1 \end{bmatrix}$$

$$\xrightarrow{R_2 + R_3}$$

$$\begin{bmatrix} 1 & 4 & -1 & | & 1 & 0 & 0 \\ 0 & 1 & 2 & | & -1 & 1 & 1 \\ 0 & 6 & 2 & | & 1 & 0 & 1 \end{bmatrix} \xrightarrow[R_3 - 6R_2]{R_1 - 4R_2} \begin{bmatrix} 1 & 0 & -9 & | & 5 & -4 & -4 \\ 0 & 1 & 2 & | & -1 & 1 & 1 \\ 0 & 0 & -10 & | & 7 & -6 & -5 \end{bmatrix} \xrightarrow{-\frac{1}{10}R_3}$$

$$\begin{bmatrix} 1 & 0 & -9 & | & 5 & -4 & -4 \\ 0 & 1 & 2 & | & -1 & 1 & 1 \\ 0 & 0 & 1 & | & -\frac{7}{10} & \frac{3}{5} & \frac{1}{2} \end{bmatrix} \xrightarrow[R_2 - 2R_3]{R_1 + 9R_3} \begin{bmatrix} 1 & 0 & 0 & | & -\frac{13}{10} & \frac{7}{5} & \frac{1}{2} \\ 0 & 1 & 0 & | & \frac{2}{5} & -\frac{1}{5} & 0 \\ 0 & 0 & 1 & | & -\frac{7}{10} & \frac{3}{5} & \frac{1}{2} \end{bmatrix}.$$

So,

$$A^{-1} = \begin{bmatrix} -\frac{13}{10} & \frac{7}{5} & \frac{1}{2} \\ \frac{2}{5} & -\frac{1}{5} & 0 \\ -\frac{7}{10} & \frac{3}{5} & \frac{1}{2} \end{bmatrix}.$$

14. Starting with the matrix

$$\begin{bmatrix} 3 & -2 & 7 & | & 1 & 0 & 0 \\ -2 & 1 & 4 & | & 0 & 1 & 0 \\ 6 & -5 & 8 & | & 0 & 0 & 1 \end{bmatrix}$$

we use the sequence of row operations

1. $R_1 + R_2$      2. $R_2 + 2R_1,\ R_3 - 6R_1$

3. $-R_2$      4. $R_1 + R_2,\ R_3 - R_2$

5. $-\dfrac{1}{32}R_3$      6. $R_1 + 15R_3,\ R_2 + 26R_3$

to find that

$$A^{-1} = \begin{bmatrix} \dfrac{7}{8} & -\dfrac{19}{32} & -\dfrac{15}{32} \\[2mm] \dfrac{5}{4} & -\dfrac{9}{16} & -\dfrac{13}{16} \\[2mm] \dfrac{1}{8} & \dfrac{3}{32} & -\dfrac{1}{32} \end{bmatrix}.$$

15.
$$\left[\begin{array}{cccc|cccc} 1 & 1 & -1 & 1 & 1 & 0 & 0 & 0 \\ 2 & 1 & 1 & 0 & 0 & 1 & 0 & 0 \\ 2 & 1 & 0 & 1 & 0 & 0 & 1 & 0 \\ 2 & -1 & -1 & 3 & 0 & 0 & 0 & 1 \end{array}\right] \xrightarrow[\substack{R_3 - 2R_1 \\ R_4 - 2R_1}]{R_2 - 2R_1}$$

$$\left[\begin{array}{cccc|cccc} 1 & 1 & -1 & 1 & 1 & 0 & 0 & 0 \\ 0 & -1 & 3 & -2 & -2 & 1 & 0 & 0 \\ 0 & -1 & 2 & -1 & -2 & 0 & 1 & 0 \\ 0 & -3 & 1 & 1 & -2 & 0 & 0 & 1 \end{array}\right] \xrightarrow{-R_2}$$

$$\left[\begin{array}{cccc|cccc} 1 & 1 & -1 & 1 & 1 & 0 & 0 & 0 \\ 0 & 1 & -3 & 2 & 2 & -1 & 0 & 0 \\ 0 & -1 & 2 & -1 & -2 & 0 & 1 & 0 \\ 0 & -3 & 1 & 1 & -2 & 0 & 0 & 1 \end{array}\right] \xrightarrow[\substack{R_3 + R_2 \\ R_4 + 3R_2}]{R_1 - R_2}$$

$$\left[\begin{array}{cccc|cccc} 1 & 0 & 2 & -1 & -1 & 1 & 0 & 0 \\ 0 & 1 & -3 & 2 & 2 & -1 & 0 & 0 \\ 0 & 0 & -1 & 1 & 0 & -1 & 1 & 0 \\ 0 & 0 & -8 & 7 & 4 & -3 & 0 & 1 \end{array}\right] \xrightarrow{-R_3}$$

$$\begin{bmatrix} 1 & 0 & 2 & -1 & | & -1 & 1 & 0 & 0 \\ 0 & 1 & -3 & 2 & | & 2 & -1 & 0 & 0 \\ 0 & 0 & 1 & -1 & | & 0 & 1 & -1 & 0 \\ 0 & 0 & -8 & 7 & | & 4 & -3 & 0 & 1 \end{bmatrix} \quad \begin{array}{c} \xrightarrow{\begin{array}{c} R_1 - 2R_3 \\ R_2 + 3R_3 \\ R_4 + 8R_3 \end{array}} \end{array}$$

$$\begin{bmatrix} 1 & 0 & 0 & 1 & | & -1 & -1 & 2 & 0 \\ 0 & 1 & 0 & -1 & | & 2 & 2 & -3 & 0 \\ 0 & 0 & 1 & -1 & | & 0 & 1 & -1 & 0 \\ 0 & 0 & 0 & -1 & | & 4 & 5 & -8 & 1 \end{bmatrix} \quad \begin{array}{c} \xrightarrow{\begin{array}{c} R_1 + R_4 \\ R_2 - R_4 \\ R_3 - R_4 \\ -R_4 \end{array}} \end{array}$$

$$\begin{bmatrix} 1 & 0 & 0 & 0 & | & 3 & 4 & -6 & 1 \\ 0 & 1 & 0 & 0 & | & -2 & -3 & 5 & -1 \\ 0 & 0 & 1 & 0 & | & -4 & -4 & 7 & -1 \\ 0 & 0 & 0 & 1 & | & -4 & -5 & 8 & -1 \end{bmatrix}.$$

So the required inverse is

$$A^{-1} = \begin{bmatrix} 3 & 4 & -6 & 1 \\ -2 & -3 & 5 & -1 \\ -4 & -4 & 7 & -1 \\ -4 & -5 & 8 & -1 \end{bmatrix}.$$

We can verify our result by showing that $A^{-1}A = A$. Thus,

$$\begin{bmatrix} 3 & 4 & -6 & 1 \\ -2 & -3 & 5 & -1 \\ -4 & -4 & 7 & -1 \\ -4 & -5 & 8 & -1 \end{bmatrix} \begin{bmatrix} 1 & 1 & -1 & 1 \\ 2 & 1 & 1 & 0 \\ 2 & 1 & 0 & 1 \\ 2 & -1 & -1 & 3 \end{bmatrix} = \begin{bmatrix} 1 & 0 & 0 & 0 \\ 0 & 1 & 0 & 0 \\ 0 & 0 & 1 & 0 \\ 0 & 0 & 0 & 1 \end{bmatrix}.$$

16. Starting with the matrix

$$\begin{bmatrix} 1 & 1 & 2 & 3 & | & 1 & 0 & 0 & 0 \\ 2 & 3 & 0 & -1 & | & 0 & 1 & 0 & 0 \\ 0 & 2 & -1 & 1 & | & 0 & 0 & 1 & 0 \\ 1 & 2 & 1 & 1 & | & 0 & 0 & 0 & 1 \end{bmatrix}$$

we use the sequence of row operations

1. $R_2 - 2R_1$, $R_4 - R_1$  2. $R_1 - R_2$, $R_3 - 2R_2$, $R_4 - R_2$

3. $R_3 - 2R_4$  4. $R_1 - 6R_3$, $R_2 + 4R_3$, $R_4 - 3R_3$

5. $-\frac{1}{10}R_4$  6. $R_1 + 20R_4$, $R_2 - 13R_4$, $R_3 - 5R_4$

to find that

$$A^{-1} = \begin{bmatrix} 1 & 1 & 0 & -2 \\ -\frac{1}{2} & -\frac{3}{10} & \frac{1}{10} & \frac{11}{10} \\ -\frac{1}{2} & -\frac{1}{2} & -\frac{1}{2} & \frac{3}{2} \\ \frac{1}{2} & \frac{1}{10} & \frac{3}{10} & -\frac{7}{10} \end{bmatrix}.$$

17. a. $A = \begin{bmatrix} 2 & 5 \\ 1 & 3 \end{bmatrix}$, $X = \begin{bmatrix} x \\ y \end{bmatrix}$, $B = \begin{bmatrix} 3 \\ 2 \end{bmatrix}$;

b. $X = A^{-1}B = \begin{bmatrix} 3 & -5 \\ -1 & 2 \end{bmatrix}\begin{bmatrix} 3 \\ 2 \end{bmatrix} = \begin{bmatrix} -1 \\ 1 \end{bmatrix}.$

18. a. $A = \begin{bmatrix} 2 & 3 \\ 3 & 5 \end{bmatrix}$, $X = \begin{bmatrix} x \\ y \end{bmatrix}$, $B = \begin{bmatrix} 5 \\ 8 \end{bmatrix}$;

b. $X = A^{-1}B = \begin{bmatrix} 5 & -3 \\ -3 & 2 \end{bmatrix}\begin{bmatrix} 5 \\ 8 \end{bmatrix} = \begin{bmatrix} 1 \\ 1 \end{bmatrix}.$

19. a.
$$A = \begin{bmatrix} 2 & -3 & -4 \\ 0 & 0 & -1 \\ 1 & -2 & 1 \end{bmatrix}, \quad X = \begin{bmatrix} x \\ y \\ z \end{bmatrix}, \quad B = \begin{bmatrix} 4 \\ 3 \\ -8 \end{bmatrix} \quad ;$$

b.
$$X = A^{-1}B = \begin{bmatrix} 2 & -11 & -3 \\ 1 & -6 & -2 \\ 0 & -1 & 0 \end{bmatrix} \begin{bmatrix} 4 \\ 3 \\ -8 \end{bmatrix} = \begin{bmatrix} -1 \\ 2 \\ -3 \end{bmatrix} .$$

20. a.
$$A = \begin{bmatrix} 1 & -1 & 3 \\ 2 & 1 & 2 \\ -2 & -2 & 1 \end{bmatrix}, \quad X = \begin{bmatrix} x \\ y \\ z \end{bmatrix}, \quad B = \begin{bmatrix} 2 \\ 2 \\ 3 \end{bmatrix} \quad ;$$

b.
$$X = A^{-1}B = \begin{bmatrix} 1 & -1 & -1 \\ -\frac{6}{5} & \frac{7}{5} & \frac{4}{5} \\ -\frac{2}{5} & \frac{4}{5} & \frac{3}{5} \end{bmatrix} \begin{bmatrix} 2 \\ 2 \\ 3 \end{bmatrix} = \begin{bmatrix} -3 \\ \frac{14}{5} \\ \frac{13}{5} \end{bmatrix} .$$

21. a.
$$A = \begin{bmatrix} 1 & 4 & -1 \\ 2 & 3 & -2 \\ -1 & 2 & 3 \end{bmatrix}, \quad X = \begin{bmatrix} x \\ y \\ z \end{bmatrix}, \quad B = \begin{bmatrix} 3 \\ 1 \\ 7 \end{bmatrix} \quad ;$$

b.
$$X = A^{-1}B = \begin{bmatrix} -\frac{13}{10} & \frac{7}{5} & \frac{1}{2} \\ \frac{2}{5} & -\frac{1}{5} & 0 \\ -\frac{7}{10} & \frac{3}{5} & \frac{1}{2} \end{bmatrix} \begin{bmatrix} 3 \\ 1 \\ 7 \end{bmatrix} = \begin{bmatrix} 1 \\ 1 \\ 2 \end{bmatrix} .$$

22. a.
$$A = \begin{bmatrix} 3 & -2 & 7 \\ -2 & 1 & 4 \\ 6 & -5 & 8 \end{bmatrix}, \quad X = \begin{bmatrix} x \\ y \\ z \end{bmatrix}, \quad B = \begin{bmatrix} 6 \\ 4 \\ 4 \end{bmatrix} \quad ;$$

b.

$$X = A^{-1}B = \begin{bmatrix} \frac{7}{8} & -\frac{19}{32} & -\frac{15}{32} \\ \frac{5}{4} & -\frac{9}{16} & -\frac{13}{16} \\ \frac{1}{8} & \frac{3}{32} & -\frac{1}{32} \end{bmatrix} \begin{bmatrix} 6 \\ 4 \\ 4 \end{bmatrix} = \begin{bmatrix} 1 \\ 2 \\ 1 \end{bmatrix}.$$

23. a.

$$A = \begin{bmatrix} 1 & 1 & -1 & 1 \\ 2 & 1 & 1 & 0 \\ 2 & 1 & 0 & 1 \\ 2 & -1 & -1 & 3 \end{bmatrix}, \quad X = \begin{bmatrix} x_1 \\ x_2 \\ x_3 \\ x_4 \end{bmatrix}, \quad B = \begin{bmatrix} 6 \\ 4 \\ 7 \\ 9 \end{bmatrix}$$

b.

$$X = A^{-1}B = \begin{bmatrix} 3 & 4 & -6 & 1 \\ -2 & -3 & 5 & 1 \\ -4 & -4 & 7 & -1 \\ -4 & -5 & 8 & -1 \end{bmatrix} \begin{bmatrix} 6 \\ 4 \\ 7 \\ 9 \end{bmatrix} = \begin{bmatrix} 1 \\ 2 \\ 0 \\ 3 \end{bmatrix}.$$

24. a.

$$A = \begin{bmatrix} 1 & 1 & 2 & 3 \\ 2 & 3 & 0 & -1 \\ 0 & 2 & -1 & 1 \\ 1 & 2 & 1 & 1 \end{bmatrix}, \quad X = \begin{bmatrix} x_1 \\ x_2 \\ x_3 \\ x_4 \end{bmatrix}, \quad B = \begin{bmatrix} 4 \\ 11 \\ 7 \\ 6 \end{bmatrix}$$

b.

$$X = A^{-1}B = \begin{bmatrix} 1 & 1 & 0 & -2 \\ -\frac{1}{2} & -\frac{3}{10} & \frac{1}{10} & \frac{11}{10} \\ -\frac{1}{2} & -\frac{1}{2} & -\frac{1}{2} & \frac{3}{2} \\ \frac{1}{2} & \frac{1}{10} & \frac{3}{10} & -\frac{7}{10} \end{bmatrix} \begin{bmatrix} 4 \\ 11 \\ 7 \\ 6 \end{bmatrix} = \begin{bmatrix} 3 \\ 2 \\ -2 \\ 1 \end{bmatrix}.$$

25. a. $A = \begin{bmatrix} 1 & 2 \\ 2 & -1 \end{bmatrix}, \quad X = \begin{bmatrix} x \\ y \end{bmatrix}, \quad B = \begin{bmatrix} b_1 \\ b_2 \end{bmatrix};$

b. $X = A^{-1}B = \begin{bmatrix} .2 & .4 \\ .4 & -.2 \end{bmatrix} \begin{bmatrix} 14 \\ 5 \end{bmatrix} = \begin{bmatrix} 4.8 \\ 4.6 \end{bmatrix}$

and we conclude that x = 4.8 and y = 4.6.

$$X = A^{-1}B = \begin{bmatrix} .2 & .4 \\ .4 & -.2 \end{bmatrix} \begin{bmatrix} 4 \\ -1 \end{bmatrix} = \begin{bmatrix} 0.4 \\ 1.8 \end{bmatrix}$$

and we conclude that x = 0.4 and y = 1.8.

26. a. $A = \begin{bmatrix} 3 & -2 \\ 4 & 3 \end{bmatrix}$, $X = \begin{bmatrix} x \\ y \end{bmatrix}$, $B = \begin{bmatrix} b_1 \\ b_2 \end{bmatrix}$;

b. $X = A^{-1}B = \begin{bmatrix} \frac{3}{17} & \frac{2}{17} \\ -\frac{4}{17} & \frac{3}{17} \end{bmatrix} \begin{bmatrix} -6 \\ 10 \end{bmatrix} = \begin{bmatrix} \frac{2}{17} \\ \frac{54}{17} \end{bmatrix}$ ,

and we conclude that x = 2/17 and y = 54/17.

$$X = A^{-1}B = \begin{bmatrix} \frac{3}{17} & \frac{2}{17} \\ -\frac{4}{17} & \frac{3}{17} \end{bmatrix} \begin{bmatrix} 3 \\ -2 \end{bmatrix} = \begin{bmatrix} \frac{5}{17} \\ -\frac{18}{17} \end{bmatrix}$$ ,

and we conclude that x = 5/17 and y = -18/17.

27. First we find $A^{-1}$.

$$\begin{bmatrix} 1 & 2 & 1 & | & 1 & 0 & 0 \\ 1 & 1 & 1 & | & 0 & 1 & 0 \\ 3 & 1 & 1 & | & 0 & 0 & 1 \end{bmatrix} \xrightarrow[\;R_3\,-\,3R_1\;]{R_2\,-\,R_1} \begin{bmatrix} 1 & 2 & 1 & | & 1 & 0 & 0 \\ 0 & -1 & 0 & | & -1 & 1 & 0 \\ 0 & -5 & -2 & | & -3 & 0 & 1 \end{bmatrix} \xrightarrow{-R_2}$$

$$\begin{bmatrix} 1 & 2 & 1 & | & 1 & 0 & 0 \\ 0 & 1 & 0 & | & 1 & -1 & 0 \\ 0 & -5 & -2 & | & -3 & 0 & 1 \end{bmatrix} \xrightarrow[\;R_3\,+\,5R_2\;]{R_1\,-\,2R_2} \begin{bmatrix} 1 & 0 & 1 & | & -1 & 2 & 0 \\ 0 & 1 & 0 & | & 1 & -1 & 0 \\ 0 & 0 & -2 & | & 2 & -5 & 1 \end{bmatrix} \xrightarrow{-\frac{1}{2}R_3}$$

$$\begin{bmatrix} 1 & 0 & 1 & | & -1 & 2 & 0 \\ 0 & 1 & 0 & | & 1 & -1 & 0 \\ 0 & 0 & 1 & | & -1 & \frac{5}{2} & -\frac{1}{2} \end{bmatrix} \xrightarrow{R_1\,-\,R_3} \begin{bmatrix} 1 & 0 & 0 & | & 0 & -\frac{1}{2} & \frac{1}{2} \\ 0 & 1 & 0 & | & 1 & -1 & 0 \\ 0 & 0 & 1 & | & -1 & \frac{5}{2} & -\frac{1}{2} \end{bmatrix}.$$

$$\begin{bmatrix} 1 & 2 & 1 \\ 1 & 1 & 1 \\ 3 & 1 & 1 \end{bmatrix} \begin{bmatrix} x \\ y \\ z \end{bmatrix} = \begin{bmatrix} b_1 \\ b_2 \\ b_3 \end{bmatrix}.$$

a.
$$\begin{bmatrix} x \\ y \\ z \end{bmatrix} = \begin{bmatrix} 0 & -\frac{1}{2} & \frac{1}{2} \\ 1 & -1 & 0 \\ -1 & \frac{5}{2} & -\frac{1}{2} \end{bmatrix} \begin{bmatrix} 7 \\ 4 \\ 2 \end{bmatrix} = \begin{bmatrix} -1 \\ 3 \\ 2 \end{bmatrix}.$$

and we conclude that $x = -1$, $y = 3$, and $z = 2$.

b.
$$\begin{bmatrix} x \\ y \\ z \end{bmatrix} = \begin{bmatrix} 0 & -\frac{1}{2} & \frac{1}{2} \\ 1 & -1 & 0 \\ -1 & \frac{5}{2} & -\frac{1}{2} \end{bmatrix} \begin{bmatrix} 5 \\ -3 \\ -1 \end{bmatrix} = \begin{bmatrix} 1 \\ 8 \\ -12 \end{bmatrix}.$$

and we conclude that $x = 1$, $y = 8$, and $z = -12$.

28.

a.
$$\begin{bmatrix} 1 & 1 & 1 \\ 1 & -1 & 1 \\ 1 & -2 & -1 \end{bmatrix} \begin{bmatrix} x_1 \\ x_2 \\ x_3 \end{bmatrix} = \begin{bmatrix} b_1 \\ b_2 \\ b_3 \end{bmatrix}.$$

b.
$$\begin{bmatrix} x_1 \\ x_2 \\ x_3 \end{bmatrix} = \begin{bmatrix} \frac{3}{4} & -\frac{1}{4} & \frac{1}{2} \\ \frac{1}{2} & -\frac{1}{2} & 0 \\ -\frac{1}{4} & \frac{3}{4} & -\frac{1}{2} \end{bmatrix} \begin{bmatrix} 5 \\ -3 \\ -1 \end{bmatrix} = \begin{bmatrix} 4 \\ 4 \\ -3 \end{bmatrix}.$$

and we conclude that $x_1 = 4$, $x_2 = 4$, and $x_3 = -3$.

$$\begin{bmatrix} x_1 \\ x_2 \\ x_3 \end{bmatrix} = \begin{bmatrix} \frac{3}{4} & -\frac{1}{4} & \frac{1}{2} \\ \frac{1}{2} & -\frac{1}{2} & 0 \\ -\frac{1}{4} & \frac{3}{4} & -\frac{1}{2} \end{bmatrix} \begin{bmatrix} 1 \\ 4 \\ -2 \end{bmatrix} = \begin{bmatrix} -\frac{5}{4} \\ -\frac{3}{2} \\ \frac{15}{4} \end{bmatrix}.$$

and we conclude that $x_1 = -5/4$, $x_2 = -3/2$, and $x_3 = 15/4$.

29. $\begin{bmatrix} 3 & 2 & -1 & | & 1 & 0 & 0 \\ 2 & -3 & 1 & | & 0 & 1 & 0 \\ 1 & -1 & -1 & | & 0 & 0 & 1 \end{bmatrix} \xrightarrow{R_1 \leftrightarrow R_3} \begin{bmatrix} 1 & -1 & -1 & | & 0 & 0 & 1 \\ 2 & -3 & 1 & | & 0 & 1 & 0 \\ 3 & 2 & -1 & | & 1 & 0 & 0 \end{bmatrix} \xrightarrow[\displaystyle R_3 - 3R_1]{\displaystyle R_2 - 2R_1}$

$$\begin{bmatrix} 1 & -1 & -1 & | & 0 & 0 & 1 \\ 0 & -1 & 3 & | & 0 & 1 & -2 \\ 0 & 5 & 2 & | & 1 & 0 & -3 \end{bmatrix} \xrightarrow{-R_2} \begin{bmatrix} 1 & -1 & -1 & | & 0 & 0 & 1 \\ 0 & 1 & -3 & | & 0 & -1 & 2 \\ 0 & 5 & 2 & | & 1 & 0 & -3 \end{bmatrix} \xrightarrow[\;R_3 - 5R_2\;]{R_1 + R_2}$$

$$\begin{bmatrix} 1 & 0 & -4 & | & 0 & -1 & 3 \\ 0 & 1 & -3 & | & 0 & -1 & 2 \\ 0 & 0 & 17 & | & 1 & 5 & -13 \end{bmatrix} \xrightarrow{\frac{1}{17}R_3} \begin{bmatrix} 1 & 0 & -4 & | & 0 & -1 & 3 \\ 0 & 1 & -3 & | & 0 & -1 & 2 \\ 0 & 0 & 1 & | & \frac{1}{17} & \frac{5}{17} & -\frac{13}{17} \end{bmatrix}$$

$$\xrightarrow[\;R_2 + 3R_3\;]{R_1 + 4R_3} \begin{bmatrix} 1 & 0 & 0 & | & \frac{4}{17} & \frac{3}{17} & -\frac{1}{17} \\ 0 & 1 & 0 & | & \frac{3}{17} & -\frac{2}{17} & -\frac{5}{17} \\ 0 & 0 & 1 & | & \frac{1}{17} & \frac{5}{17} & -\frac{13}{17} \end{bmatrix}.$$

Therefore,

$$A^{-1} = \begin{bmatrix} \frac{4}{17} & \frac{3}{17} & -\frac{1}{17} \\ \frac{3}{17} & -\frac{2}{17} & -\frac{5}{17} \\ \frac{1}{17} & \frac{5}{17} & -\frac{13}{17} \end{bmatrix}.$$

$$\begin{bmatrix} 3 & 2 & -1 \\ 2 & -3 & 1 \\ 1 & -1 & -1 \end{bmatrix} \begin{bmatrix} x \\ y \\ z \end{bmatrix} = \begin{bmatrix} b_1 \\ b_2 \\ b_3 \end{bmatrix}.$$

a.

$$\begin{bmatrix} x \\ y \\ z \end{bmatrix} = \begin{bmatrix} \frac{4}{17} & \frac{3}{17} & -\frac{1}{17} \\ \frac{3}{17} & -\frac{2}{17} & -\frac{5}{17} \\ \frac{1}{17} & \frac{5}{17} & -\frac{13}{17} \end{bmatrix} \begin{bmatrix} 2 \\ -2 \\ 4 \end{bmatrix} = \begin{bmatrix} -\frac{2}{17} \\ -\frac{10}{17} \\ -\frac{60}{17} \end{bmatrix}.$$

We conclude that $x = -2/17$, $y = -10/17$, and $z = -60/17$.

b.

$$\begin{bmatrix} x \\ y \\ z \end{bmatrix} = \begin{bmatrix} \frac{4}{17} & \frac{3}{17} & -\frac{1}{17} \\ \frac{3}{17} & -\frac{2}{17} & -\frac{5}{17} \\ \frac{1}{17} & \frac{5}{17} & -\frac{13}{17} \end{bmatrix} \begin{bmatrix} 8 \\ -3 \\ 6 \end{bmatrix} = \begin{bmatrix} 1 \\ 0 \\ -5 \end{bmatrix}$$

We conclude that $x = 1$, $y = 0$, and $z = -5$.

30. $\begin{bmatrix} 2 & 1 & 1 & | & 1 & 0 & 0 \\ 1 & -3 & 4 & | & 0 & 1 & 0 \\ -1 & 0 & 1 & | & 0 & 0 & 1 \end{bmatrix} \xrightarrow{R_1 \leftrightarrow R_3} \begin{bmatrix} -1 & 0 & 1 & | & 0 & 0 & 1 \\ 1 & -3 & 4 & | & 0 & 1 & 0 \\ 2 & 1 & 1 & | & 1 & 0 & 0 \end{bmatrix} \xrightarrow{-R_1}$

$\begin{bmatrix} 1 & 0 & -1 & | & 0 & 0 & -1 \\ 1 & -3 & 4 & | & 0 & 1 & 0 \\ 2 & 1 & 1 & | & 1 & 0 & 0 \end{bmatrix} \xrightarrow[R_3 - 2R_1]{R_2 - R_1} \begin{bmatrix} 1 & 0 & -1 & | & 0 & 0 & -1 \\ 0 & -3 & 5 & | & 0 & 1 & 1 \\ 0 & 1 & 3 & | & 1 & 0 & 2 \end{bmatrix} \xrightarrow{R_2 \leftrightarrow R_3}$

$\begin{bmatrix} 1 & 0 & -1 & | & 0 & 0 & -1 \\ 0 & 1 & 3 & | & 1 & 0 & 2 \\ 0 & -3 & 5 & | & 0 & 1 & 1 \end{bmatrix} \xrightarrow{R_3 + 3R_2} \begin{bmatrix} 1 & 0 & -1 & | & 0 & 0 & -1 \\ 0 & 1 & 3 & | & 1 & 0 & 2 \\ 0 & 0 & 14 & | & 3 & 1 & 7 \end{bmatrix} \xrightarrow{\frac{1}{14}R_3}$

$\begin{bmatrix} 1 & 0 & -1 & | & 0 & 0 & -1 \\ 0 & 1 & 3 & | & 1 & 0 & 2 \\ 0 & 0 & 1 & | & \frac{3}{14} & \frac{1}{14} & \frac{1}{2} \end{bmatrix} \xrightarrow[R_2 - 3R_3]{R_1 + R_3} \begin{bmatrix} 1 & 0 & 0 & | & \frac{3}{14} & \frac{1}{14} & -\frac{1}{2} \\ 0 & 1 & 0 & | & \frac{5}{14} & -\frac{3}{14} & \frac{1}{2} \\ 0 & 0 & 1 & | & \frac{3}{14} & \frac{1}{14} & \frac{1}{2} \end{bmatrix}$ .

$$\begin{bmatrix} 2 & 1 & 1 \\ 1 & -3 & 4 \\ -1 & 0 & 1 \end{bmatrix} \begin{bmatrix} x_1 \\ x_2 \\ x_3 \end{bmatrix} = \begin{bmatrix} b_1 \\ b_2 \\ b_3 \end{bmatrix}.$$

a. $\begin{bmatrix} x_1 \\ x_2 \\ x_3 \end{bmatrix} = \begin{bmatrix} -\frac{3}{14} & \frac{1}{14} & -\frac{1}{2} \\ \frac{5}{14} & -\frac{3}{14} & \frac{1}{2} \\ \frac{3}{14} & \frac{1}{14} & \frac{1}{2} \end{bmatrix} \begin{bmatrix} 1 \\ 4 \\ -3 \end{bmatrix} = \begin{bmatrix} 2 \\ -2 \\ -1 \end{bmatrix}$ .

b. $\begin{bmatrix} x \\ y \\ z \end{bmatrix} = \begin{bmatrix} \frac{3}{14} & \frac{1}{14} & -\frac{1}{2} \\ \frac{5}{14} & -\frac{3}{14} & \frac{1}{2} \\ \frac{3}{14} & \frac{1}{14} & \frac{1}{2} \end{bmatrix} \begin{bmatrix} 2 \\ -5 \\ 0 \end{bmatrix} = \begin{bmatrix} \frac{1}{14} \\ \frac{25}{14} \\ \frac{1}{14} \end{bmatrix}$ .

31. $AX = B_1$ and $AX = B_2$, where

$$A = \begin{bmatrix} 1 & 1 & 1 & 1 \\ 1 & -1 & -1 & 1 \\ 0 & 1 & 2 & 2 \\ 1 & 2 & 1 & -2 \end{bmatrix}, \quad X = \begin{bmatrix} x_1 \\ x_2 \\ x_3 \\ x_4 \end{bmatrix}, \quad B_1 = \begin{bmatrix} 1 \\ -1 \\ 4 \\ 0 \end{bmatrix} \quad \text{and} \quad \begin{bmatrix} 2 \\ 8 \\ 4 \\ -1 \end{bmatrix}.$$

We first find $A^{-1}$.

$$\left[\begin{array}{cccc|cccc} 1 & 1 & 1 & 1 & 1 & 0 & 0 & 0 \\ 1 & -1 & -1 & 1 & 0 & 1 & 0 & 0 \\ 0 & 1 & 2 & 2 & 0 & 0 & 1 & 0 \\ 1 & 2 & 1 & -2 & 0 & 0 & 0 & 1 \end{array}\right] \quad \begin{array}{c} R_2 - R_1 \\ \xrightarrow{\hspace{1cm}} \\ R_4 - R_1 \end{array}$$

$$\left[\begin{array}{cccc|cccc} 1 & 1 & 1 & 1 & 1 & 0 & 0 & 0 \\ 0 & -2 & -2 & 0 & -1 & 1 & 0 & 0 \\ 0 & 1 & 2 & 2 & 0 & 0 & 1 & 0 \\ 0 & 1 & 0 & -3 & -1 & 0 & 0 & 1 \end{array}\right] \quad R_2 \leftrightarrow R_3$$

$$\left[\begin{array}{cccc|cccc} 1 & 1 & 1 & 1 & 1 & 0 & 0 & 0 \\ 0 & 1 & 2 & 2 & 0 & 0 & 1 & 0 \\ 0 & -2 & -2 & 0 & -1 & 1 & 0 & 0 \\ 0 & 1 & 0 & -3 & -1 & 0 & 0 & 1 \end{array}\right] \quad \begin{array}{c} R_1 - R_2 \\ \xrightarrow{\hspace{1cm}} \\ R_3 + 2R_2 \\ R_4 - R_2 \end{array}$$

$$\left[\begin{array}{cccc|cccc} 1 & 0 & -1 & -1 & 1 & 0 & -1 & 0 \\ 0 & 1 & 2 & 2 & 0 & 0 & 1 & 0 \\ 0 & 0 & 2 & 4 & -1 & 1 & 2 & 0 \\ 0 & 0 & -2 & -5 & -1 & 0 & -1 & 1 \end{array}\right] \quad \xrightarrow{\frac{1}{2}R_3}$$

$$\left[\begin{array}{cccc|cccc} 1 & 0 & -1 & -1 & 1 & 0 & -1 & 0 \\ 0 & 1 & 2 & 2 & 0 & 0 & 1 & 0 \\ 0 & 0 & 1 & 2 & -\frac{1}{2} & \frac{1}{2} & 1 & 0 \\ 0 & 0 & -2 & -5 & -1 & 0 & -1 & 1 \end{array}\right] \quad \begin{array}{c} R_1 + R_3 \\ \xrightarrow{\hspace{1cm}} \\ R_2 - 2R_3 \\ R_4 + 2R_3 \end{array}$$

$$\left[\begin{array}{cccc|cccc} 1 & 0 & 0 & 1 & \frac{1}{2} & \frac{1}{2} & 0 & 0 \\ 0 & 1 & 0 & -2 & 1 & -1 & -1 & 0 \\ 0 & 0 & 1 & 2 & -\frac{1}{2} & \frac{1}{2} & 1 & 0 \\ 0 & 0 & 0 & -1 & -2 & 1 & 1 & 1 \end{array}\right] \begin{array}{l} R_1 + R_4 \\ \xrightarrow{\phantom{R_2 - 2R_4}} \\ R_2 - 2R_4 \\ R_3 + 2R_4 \\ -R_4 \end{array}$$

$$\left[\begin{array}{cccc|cccc} 1 & 0 & 0 & 0 & -\frac{3}{2} & \frac{3}{2} & 1 & 1 \\ 0 & 1 & 0 & 0 & 5 & -3 & -3 & -2 \\ 0 & 0 & 1 & 0 & -\frac{9}{2} & \frac{5}{2} & 3 & 2 \\ 0 & 0 & 0 & 1 & 2 & -1 & -1 & -1 \end{array}\right].$$

So

$$A^{-1} = \begin{bmatrix} -\frac{3}{2} & \frac{3}{2} & 1 & 1 \\ 5 & -3 & -3 & -2 \\ -\frac{9}{2} & \frac{5}{2} & 3 & 2 \\ 2 & -1 & -1 & -1 \end{bmatrix}.$$

a.
$$\begin{bmatrix} x_1 \\ x_2 \\ x_3 \\ x_4 \end{bmatrix} = \begin{bmatrix} -\frac{3}{2} & \frac{3}{2} & 1 & 1 \\ 5 & -3 & -3 & -2 \\ -\frac{9}{2} & \frac{5}{2} & 3 & 2 \\ 2 & -1 & -1 & -1 \end{bmatrix} \begin{bmatrix} 1 \\ -1 \\ 4 \\ 0 \end{bmatrix} = \begin{bmatrix} 1 \\ -4 \\ 5 \\ -1 \end{bmatrix}$$

and we conclude that $x_1 = 1$, $x_2 = -4$, $x_3 = 5$, and $x_4 = -1$.

b.
$$\begin{bmatrix} x_1 \\ x_2 \\ x_3 \\ x_4 \end{bmatrix} = \begin{bmatrix} -\frac{3}{2} & \frac{3}{2} & 1 & 1 \\ 5 & -3 & -3 & -2 \\ -\frac{9}{2} & \frac{5}{2} & 3 & 2 \\ 2 & -1 & -1 & -1 \end{bmatrix} \begin{bmatrix} 2 \\ 8 \\ 4 \\ -1 \end{bmatrix} = \begin{bmatrix} 12 \\ -24 \\ 21 \\ -7 \end{bmatrix}$$

and we conclude that $x_1 = 12$, $x_2 = -24$, $x_3 = 21$, and $x_4 = -7$.

32. a.

$$\begin{bmatrix} 1 & 1 & 2 & 1 \\ 4 & 5 & 9 & 1 \\ 3 & 4 & 7 & 1 \\ 2 & 3 & 4 & 2 \end{bmatrix} \begin{bmatrix} x_1 \\ x_2 \\ x_3 \\ x_4 \end{bmatrix} = \begin{bmatrix} b_1 \\ b_2 \\ b_3 \\ b_4 \end{bmatrix}.$$

$$\begin{bmatrix} x_1 \\ x_2 \\ x_3 \\ x_4 \end{bmatrix} = \begin{bmatrix} 0 & 5 & -7 & 1 \\ -2 & 0 & 0 & 1 \\ 1 & -2 & 3 & -1 \\ 1 & -1 & 1 & 0 \end{bmatrix} \begin{bmatrix} 3 \\ 6 \\ 5 \\ 7 \end{bmatrix} = \begin{bmatrix} 2 \\ 1 \\ -1 \\ 2 \end{bmatrix}$$

and we conclude that $x_1 = 2$, $x_2 = 1$, $x_3 = -1$, and $x_4 = 2$.

b.

$$\begin{bmatrix} x_1 \\ x_2 \\ x_3 \\ x_4 \end{bmatrix} = \begin{bmatrix} 0 & 5 & -7 & 1 \\ -2 & 0 & 0 & 1 \\ 1 & -2 & 3 & -1 \\ 1 & -1 & 1 & 0 \end{bmatrix} \begin{bmatrix} 1 \\ -1 \\ 0 \\ -4 \end{bmatrix} = \begin{bmatrix} -9 \\ -6 \\ 7 \\ 2 \end{bmatrix}$$

and we conclude that $x_1 = -9$, $x_2 = -6$, $x_3 = 7$, and $x_4 = 2$.

33. a. Using Formula (13), we find

$$A^{-1} = \frac{1}{(2)(-5) - (-4)(3)} \begin{bmatrix} -5 & -3 \\ 4 & 2 \end{bmatrix} = \begin{bmatrix} -\frac{5}{2} & -\frac{3}{2} \\ 2 & 1 \end{bmatrix}.$$

b. Using Formula (13) once again, we find

$$(A^{-1})^{-1} = \frac{1}{(-\frac{5}{2})(1) - 2(-\frac{3}{2})} \begin{bmatrix} 1 & \frac{3}{2} \\ -2 & -\frac{5}{2} \end{bmatrix} = \begin{bmatrix} 2 & 3 \\ -4 & -5 \end{bmatrix} = A.$$

34.

$$AB = \begin{bmatrix} 6 & -4 \\ -4 & 3 \end{bmatrix} \begin{bmatrix} 3 & -5 \\ 4 & -7 \end{bmatrix} = \begin{bmatrix} 2 & -2 \\ 0 & -1 \end{bmatrix}.$$

a. Using Formula (13), we find

$$A^{-1} = \frac{1}{(6)(3) - (-4)(-4)} \begin{bmatrix} 3 & 4 \\ 4 & 6 \end{bmatrix} = \begin{bmatrix} \frac{3}{2} & 2 \\ 2 & 3 \end{bmatrix}$$

$$B^{-1} = \frac{1}{(3)(-7) - (4)(-5)} \begin{bmatrix} -7 & 5 \\ -4 & 3 \end{bmatrix} = \begin{bmatrix} 7 & -5 \\ 4 & -3 \end{bmatrix}$$

**b.** Using Formula (13),

$$(AB)^{-1} = \frac{1}{(2)(-1) - 0} \begin{bmatrix} -1 & 2 \\ 0 & 2 \end{bmatrix} = \begin{bmatrix} \frac{1}{2} & -1 \\ 0 & -1 \end{bmatrix}.$$

Also,

$$B^{-1}A^{-1} = \begin{bmatrix} 7 & -5 \\ 4 & -3 \end{bmatrix} \begin{bmatrix} \frac{3}{2} & 2 \\ 0 & 2 \end{bmatrix} = \begin{bmatrix} \frac{1}{2} & -1 \\ 0 & -1 \end{bmatrix} = (AB)^{-1}.$$

**35. a.**

$$ABC = \begin{bmatrix} 2 & -5 \\ 1 & -3 \end{bmatrix} \begin{bmatrix} 4 & 3 \\ 1 & 1 \end{bmatrix} \begin{bmatrix} 2 & 3 \\ -2 & 1 \end{bmatrix}$$

$$= \begin{bmatrix} 2 & -5 \\ 1 & -3 \end{bmatrix} \begin{bmatrix} 2 & 15 \\ 0 & 4 \end{bmatrix} = \begin{bmatrix} 4 & 10 \\ 2 & 3 \end{bmatrix}.$$

Using the formula for finding the inverse of a 2 x 2 matrix, we find

$$A^{-1} = \begin{bmatrix} 3 & -5 \\ 1 & -2 \end{bmatrix} \qquad B^{-1} = \begin{bmatrix} 1 & -3 \\ -1 & 4 \end{bmatrix} \qquad C^{-1} = \begin{bmatrix} \frac{1}{8} & -\frac{3}{8} \\ \frac{1}{4} & \frac{1}{4} \end{bmatrix}.$$

**b.** Using the formula for finding the inverse of a 2 x 2 matrix, we find

$$(ABC)^{-1} = \begin{bmatrix} -\frac{3}{8} & \frac{5}{4} \\ \frac{1}{4} & -\frac{1}{2} \end{bmatrix}.$$

Next,

$$C^{-1}B^{-1}A^{-1} = \begin{bmatrix} \frac{1}{8} & -\frac{3}{8} \\ \frac{1}{4} & \frac{1}{4} \end{bmatrix} \begin{bmatrix} 1 & -3 \\ -1 & 4 \end{bmatrix} \begin{bmatrix} 3 & -5 \\ 1 & -2 \end{bmatrix}$$

$$= \begin{bmatrix} \frac{1}{8} & -\frac{3}{8} \\ \frac{1}{4} & \frac{1}{4} \end{bmatrix} \begin{bmatrix} 0 & 1 \\ 1 & -3 \end{bmatrix} = \begin{bmatrix} -\frac{3}{8} & \frac{5}{4} \\ \frac{1}{4} & -\frac{1}{2} \end{bmatrix}.$$

Therefore, $(ABC)^{-1} = C^{-1}B^{-1}A^{-1}.$

36. Let x denote the number of adults who took the cruise and y the number of children who took the cruise. Then the number of adults and children who took the cruise on Saturday is found by solving the system

$$x + y = 1000$$

$$8x + 4y = 6400$$

and the number of adults and children who took the cruise on Sunday is found by solving the system

$$x + y = 800$$

$$8x + 4y = 4800.$$

These systems may be written in the form $AX = B_1$ and $AX = B_2$ where

$$A = \begin{bmatrix} 1 & 1 \\ 8 & 4 \end{bmatrix}, \quad B_1 = \begin{bmatrix} 1000 \\ 6400 \end{bmatrix}, \text{ and } B_2 = \begin{bmatrix} 800 \\ 4800 \end{bmatrix}.$$

Using the formula for finding the inverse of a 2 x 2 matrix, we find

$$A^{-1} = \begin{bmatrix} -1 & \frac{1}{4} \\ 2 & -\frac{1}{4} \end{bmatrix}.$$

Then the number of adults and children who took the cruise on Saturday may be found by computing

$$\begin{bmatrix} x \\ y \end{bmatrix} = \begin{bmatrix} -1 & \frac{1}{4} \\ 2 & -\frac{1}{4} \end{bmatrix} \begin{bmatrix} 1000 \\ 6400 \end{bmatrix} = \begin{bmatrix} 600 \\ 400 \end{bmatrix}.$$

We conclude that 600 adults and 400 children took the cruise on Saturday. Similarly, the number of adults and children who took the cruise on Sunday may be found by computing

$$\begin{bmatrix} x \\ y \end{bmatrix} = \begin{bmatrix} -1 & \frac{1}{4} \\ 2 & -\frac{1}{4} \end{bmatrix} \begin{bmatrix} 800 \\ 4800 \end{bmatrix} = \begin{bmatrix} 400 \\ 400 \end{bmatrix}.$$

We conclude that there were 400 adults and 400 children on the Sunday cruise.

37. Let x denote the number of copies of the deluxe edition and y the number of copies of the deluxe edition demanded per month when the unit prices are p and q dollars, respectively. Then the three systems of linear equations

$$5x + y = 20000 \qquad 5x + y = 25000 \qquad 5x + y = 25000$$

$$x + 3y = 15000 \qquad x + 3y = 15000 \qquad x + 3y = 20000$$

give the quantity demanded of each edition at the stated price. These systems may be written in the form $AX = B_1$, $AX = B_2$, and $AX = B_3$, where

$$A = \begin{bmatrix} 5 & 1 \\ 1 & 3 \end{bmatrix}, \quad B_1 = \begin{bmatrix} 20000 \\ 15000 \end{bmatrix}, \quad B_2 = \begin{bmatrix} 25000 \\ 15000 \end{bmatrix}, \text{ and } B_3 = \begin{bmatrix} 25000 \\ 20000 \end{bmatrix}.$$

Using the formula for finding the inverse of a 2 x 2 matrix, with $a = 5$, $b = 1$, $c = 1$, $d = 3$, and $D = ad - bc = (5)(3) - (1)(1) = 14$, we find that

$$A^{-1} = \begin{bmatrix} \frac{3}{14} & -\frac{1}{14} \\ -\frac{1}{14} & \frac{5}{14} \end{bmatrix}.$$

a. $$\begin{bmatrix} x \\ y \end{bmatrix} = \begin{bmatrix} \frac{3}{14} & -\frac{1}{14} \\ -\frac{1}{14} & \frac{5}{14} \end{bmatrix} \begin{bmatrix} 20,000 \\ 15,000 \end{bmatrix} = \begin{bmatrix} 3,214 \\ 3,929 \end{bmatrix}.$$

b. $$\begin{bmatrix} x \\ y \end{bmatrix} = \begin{bmatrix} \frac{3}{14} & -\frac{1}{14} \\ -\frac{1}{14} & \frac{5}{14} \end{bmatrix} \begin{bmatrix} 25,000 \\ 15,000 \end{bmatrix} = \begin{bmatrix} 4,286 \\ 3,571 \end{bmatrix}.$$

c. $$\begin{bmatrix} x \\ y \end{bmatrix} = \begin{bmatrix} \frac{3}{14} & -\frac{1}{14} \\ -\frac{1}{14} & \frac{5}{14} \end{bmatrix} \begin{bmatrix} 25,000 \\ 20,000 \end{bmatrix} = \begin{bmatrix} 3,929 \\ 5,357 \end{bmatrix}.$$

38. Let x denote the number of ounces of food A, food B, and food C, respectively, in a meal. Then we can find the number of ounces of each food needed in Susan's and Tom's diets by solving the systems

$$30x + 25y + 20z = 400 \qquad 30x + 25y + 20z = 350$$

$$x + y + 2z = 20 \qquad x + y + 2z = 15$$

$$2x + 5y + 4z = 50 \qquad 2x + 5y + 4z = 40$$

These systems may be written in the form $AX = B_1$ and $AX = B_2$, where

$$A = \begin{bmatrix} 30 & 25 & 20 \\ 1 & 1 & 2 \\ 2 & 5 & 4 \end{bmatrix}, \quad X = \begin{bmatrix} x \\ y \\ z \end{bmatrix}, \quad B_1 \begin{bmatrix} 400 \\ 20 \\ 50 \end{bmatrix} \text{ and } B_2 = \begin{bmatrix} 350 \\ 15 \\ 40 \end{bmatrix}.$$

To find $A^{-1}$, we compute

$$\left[\begin{array}{ccc|ccc} 30 & 25 & 20 & 1 & 0 & 0 \\ 1 & 1 & 2 & 0 & 1 & 0 \\ 2 & 5 & 4 & 0 & 0 & 1 \end{array}\right] \xrightarrow{R_1 \leftrightarrow R_2} \left[\begin{array}{ccc|ccc} 1 & 1 & 2 & 0 & 1 & 0 \\ 30 & 25 & 20 & 1 & 0 & 0 \\ 2 & 5 & 4 & 0 & 0 & 1 \end{array}\right]$$

$$\xrightarrow[\begin{array}{c} R_2 - 30R_1 \\ R_3 - 2R_1 \end{array}]{}$$

$$\left[\begin{array}{ccc|ccc} 1 & 1 & 2 & 0 & 1 & 0 \\ 0 & -5 & -40 & 1 & -30 & 0 \\ 0 & 3 & 0 & 0 & -2 & 1 \end{array}\right] \xrightarrow{-\frac{1}{5}R_2} \left[\begin{array}{ccc|ccc} 1 & 1 & 2 & 0 & 1 & 0 \\ 0 & 1 & 8 & -\frac{1}{5} & 6 & 0 \\ 0 & 3 & 0 & 0 & -2 & 1 \end{array}\right]$$

$$\xrightarrow[\begin{array}{c} R_1 - R_2 \\ R_3 - 3R_2 \end{array}]{}$$

$$\left[\begin{array}{ccc|ccc} 1 & 0 & -6 & \frac{1}{5} & -5 & 0 \\ 0 & 1 & 8 & -\frac{1}{5} & 6 & 0 \\ 0 & 0 & -24 & \frac{3}{5} & -20 & 1 \end{array}\right] \xrightarrow{-\frac{1}{24}R_3} \left[\begin{array}{ccc|ccc} 1 & 0 & -6 & \frac{1}{5} & -5 & 0 \\ 0 & 1 & 8 & -\frac{1}{5} & 6 & 0 \\ 0 & 0 & 1 & -\frac{1}{40} & \frac{5}{6} & -\frac{1}{24} \end{array}\right]$$

$$\xrightarrow[\begin{array}{c} R_1 + 6R_3 \\ R_2 - 8R_3 \end{array}]{}$$

$$\left[\begin{array}{ccc|ccc} 1 & 0 & 0 & \frac{1}{20} & 0 & -\frac{1}{4} \\ 0 & 1 & 0 & 0 & -\frac{2}{3} & \frac{1}{3} \\ 0 & 0 & 1 & -\frac{1}{40} & \frac{5}{6} & -\frac{1}{24} \end{array}\right].$$

Therefore,

$$A^{-1} = \begin{bmatrix} \frac{1}{20} & 0 & -\frac{1}{4} \\ 0 & -\frac{2}{3} & \frac{1}{3} \\ -\frac{1}{40} & \frac{5}{6} & -\frac{1}{24} \end{bmatrix} .$$

Next,

$$\begin{bmatrix} x \\ y \\ z \end{bmatrix} = \begin{bmatrix} \frac{1}{20} & 0 & -\frac{1}{4} \\ 0 & -\frac{2}{3} & \frac{1}{3} \\ -\frac{1}{40} & \frac{5}{6} & -\frac{1}{24} \end{bmatrix} \begin{bmatrix} 400 \\ 20 \\ 50 \end{bmatrix} = \begin{bmatrix} \frac{15}{2} \\ \frac{10}{3} \\ \frac{55}{12} \end{bmatrix}$$

and,

$$\begin{bmatrix} x \\ y \\ z \end{bmatrix} = \begin{bmatrix} \frac{1}{20} & 0 & -\frac{1}{4} \\ 0 & -\frac{2}{3} & \frac{1}{3} \\ -\frac{1}{40} & \frac{5}{6} & -\frac{1}{24} \end{bmatrix} \begin{bmatrix} 350 \\ 15 \\ 40 \end{bmatrix} = \begin{bmatrix} \frac{15}{2} \\ \frac{10}{3} \\ \frac{25}{12} \end{bmatrix}$$

We conclude that Susan's meals should contain $7\frac{1}{2}$ ounces of food A, $3\frac{1}{3}$ ounces of food B, and $4\frac{7}{12}$ ounces of food C.

Tom's meals should contain $7\frac{1}{2}$ ounces of food A, $3\frac{1}{3}$ ounces of food B, $2\frac{1}{12}$ ounces of food C.

39.  Let x, y, and z (in millions of dollars) be the amount awarded to organization I, II, and III, respectively. Then we have

$$0.6x + 0.4y + 0.2z = 9.2 \qquad (8.2)$$

$$0.3x + 0.3y + 0.6z = 9.6 \qquad (7.2)$$

$$0.1x + 0.3y + 0.2z = 5.2 \qquad (3.6).$$

The quantities within the brackets are for part (b). We can rewrite the systems as $AX = B_1$, and $AX = B2$. Put

$$X = \begin{bmatrix} x \\ y \\ z \end{bmatrix}, \quad A = \begin{bmatrix} 6 & 4 & 2 \\ 3 & 3 & 6 \\ 1 & 3 & 2 \end{bmatrix}, \quad B_1 = \begin{bmatrix} 92 \\ 96 \\ 52 \end{bmatrix}, \quad B_2 = \begin{bmatrix} 82 \\ 72 \\ 36 \end{bmatrix}.$$

To find $A^{-1}$, we use the Gauss method:

$$\left[\begin{array}{ccc|ccc} 6 & 4 & 2 & 1 & 0 & 0 \\ 3 & 3 & 6 & 0 & 1 & 0 \\ 1 & 3 & 2 & 0 & 0 & 1 \end{array}\right] \xrightarrow{R_1 \leftrightarrow R_3} \left[\begin{array}{ccc|ccc} 1 & 3 & 2 & 0 & 0 & 1 \\ 3 & 3 & 6 & 0 & 1 & 0 \\ 6 & 4 & 2 & 1 & 0 & 0 \end{array}\right] \xrightarrow[R_3 - 6R_1]{R_2 - 3R_1}$$

$$\left[\begin{array}{ccc|ccc} 1 & 3 & 2 & 0 & 0 & 1 \\ 0 & -6 & 0 & 0 & 1 & -3 \\ 0 & -14 & -10 & 1 & 0 & -6 \end{array}\right] \xrightarrow{-\frac{1}{6}R_2} \left[\begin{array}{ccc|ccc} 1 & 3 & 2 & 0 & 0 & 1 \\ 0 & 1 & 0 & 0 & -\frac{1}{6} & \frac{1}{2} \\ 0 & -14 & -10 & 1 & 0 & -6 \end{array}\right] \xrightarrow[R_3 + 14R_2]{R_1 - 3R_2}$$

$$\left[\begin{array}{ccc|ccc} 1 & 0 & 2 & 0 & \frac{1}{2} & -\frac{1}{2} \\ 0 & 1 & 0 & 0 & -\frac{1}{6} & \frac{1}{2} \\ 0 & 0 & -10 & 1 & -\frac{7}{3} & 1 \end{array}\right] \xrightarrow{-\frac{1}{10}R_3} \left[\begin{array}{ccc|ccc} 1 & 0 & 2 & 1 & \frac{1}{2} & -\frac{1}{2} \\ 0 & 1 & 0 & 0 & -\frac{1}{6} & \frac{1}{2} \\ 0 & 0 & 1 & -\frac{1}{10} & \frac{7}{30} & -\frac{1}{10} \end{array}\right] \xrightarrow{R_1 - 2R_3}$$

$$\left[\begin{array}{ccc|ccc} 1 & 0 & 0 & \frac{1}{5} & \frac{1}{30} & -\frac{3}{10} \\ 0 & 1 & 0 & 0 & -\frac{1}{6} & \frac{1}{2} \\ 0 & 0 & 1 & -\frac{1}{10} & \frac{7}{30} & -\frac{1}{10} \end{array}\right].$$

a.

$$X = A^{-1}B_1 = \left[\begin{array}{ccc} \frac{1}{5} & \frac{1}{30} & -\frac{3}{10} \\ 0 & -\frac{1}{6} & \frac{1}{2} \\ -\frac{1}{10} & \frac{7}{30} & -\frac{1}{10} \end{array}\right] \left[\begin{array}{c} 92 \\ 96 \\ 52 \end{array}\right] = \left[\begin{array}{c} 6 \\ 10 \\ 8 \end{array}\right].$$

that is, $x = 6$, $y = 10$, and $z = 8$, and Organization I will receive $6 million, Organization II will receive $10 million, and Organization III will receive $8 million.

b.

$$X = A^{-1}B_1 = \left[\begin{array}{ccc} \frac{1}{5} & \frac{1}{30} & -\frac{3}{10} \\ 0 & -\frac{1}{6} & \frac{1}{2} \\ -\frac{1}{10} & \frac{7}{30} & -\frac{1}{10} \end{array}\right] \left[\begin{array}{c} 82 \\ 72 \\ 36 \end{array}\right] = \left[\begin{array}{c} 8 \\ 6 \\ 5 \end{array}\right].$$

that is, $x = 8$, $y = 6$, and $z = 5$, and Organization I will receive $8 million, Organization II will receive \$6 million, and Organization III will receive \$5 million.

40. Case 1: $a \neq 0$.

$$\left[\begin{array}{cc|cc} a & b & 1 & 0 \\ c & d & 0 & 1 \end{array}\right] \xrightarrow{\frac{1}{a}R_1} \left[\begin{array}{cc|cc} 1 & \frac{b}{a} & \frac{1}{a} & 0 \\ c & d & 0 & 1 \end{array}\right] \xrightarrow{R_2 - cR_1} \left[\begin{array}{cc|cc} 1 & \frac{b}{a} & \frac{1}{a} & 0 \\ 0 & d - \frac{bc}{a} & -\frac{c}{a} & 1 \end{array}\right]$$

$$\xrightarrow{\frac{a}{ad-bc}R_2} \left[\begin{array}{cc|cc} 1 & \frac{b}{a} & \frac{1}{a} & 0 \\ 0 & 1 & -\frac{c}{ad-bc} & \frac{a}{ad-bc} \end{array}\right] \xrightarrow{R_1 - \frac{b}{a}R_2}$$

$$\left[\begin{array}{cc|cc} 1 & 0 & \frac{d}{ad-bc} & \frac{-b}{ad-bc} \\ 0 & 1 & -\frac{c}{ad-bc} & \frac{a}{ad-bc} \end{array}\right]$$

since $\dfrac{1}{a} - \dfrac{b}{a}\left(-\dfrac{c}{ad-bc}\right) = \dfrac{ad-bc+bc}{a(ad-bc)} = \dfrac{d}{ad-bc}$

provided $ad - bc \neq 0$.

Case 2: $a = 0$

$$\left[\begin{array}{cc|cc} 0 & b & 1 & 0 \\ c & d & 0 & 1 \end{array}\right] \xrightarrow{R_1 \leftrightarrow R_2} \left[\begin{array}{cc|cc} c & d & 0 & 1 \\ 0 & b & 1 & 0 \end{array}\right] \xrightarrow[\frac{1}{b}R_2]{\frac{1}{c}R_1}$$

$$\left[\begin{array}{cc|cc} 1 & \frac{d}{c} & 0 & \frac{1}{c} \\ 0 & 1 & \frac{1}{b} & 0 \end{array}\right] \xrightarrow{R_1 - \frac{d}{c}R_2} \left[\begin{array}{cc|cc} 1 & 0 & -\frac{d}{bc} & \frac{1}{c} \\ 0 & 1 & \frac{1}{b} & 0 \end{array}\right]$$

provided $ad - bc \neq 0$.

## USING TECHNOLOGY EXERCISES 2.6, page 153

1. $$\left[\begin{array}{ccc} 0.36 & 0.04 & -0.36 \\ 0.06 & 0.05 & 0.20 \\ -0.19 & 0.10 & 0.09 \end{array}\right]$$

2. $$\left[\begin{array}{ccc} 0.12 & 0.25 & -0.01 \\ 0 & -0.10 & 0.11 \\ 0.11 & -0.15 & -0.08 \end{array}\right]$$

3.
$$\begin{bmatrix} 0.01 & -0.09 & 0.31 & -0.11 \\ -0.25 & 0.58 & -0.15 & -0.02 \\ 0.86 & -0.42 & 0.07 & -0.37 \\ -0.27 & 0.01 & -0.05 & 0.31 \end{bmatrix}$$

4.
$$\begin{bmatrix} -3.18 & -0.28 & 2.49 & -1.76 \\ -2.06 & -0.32 & 1.84 & -1 \\ 5.44 & 0.76 & -4.47 & 2.81 \\ -6.84 & -0.84 & 5.42 & -3.38 \end{bmatrix}$$

5.
$$\begin{bmatrix} 0.30 & 0.85 & -0.10 & -0.77 & -0.11 \\ -0.21 & 0.10 & 0.01 & -0.26 & 0.21 \\ 0.03 & -0.16 & 0.12 & -0.01 & 0.03 \\ -0.14 & -0.46 & 0.13 & 0.71 & -0.05 \\ 0.10 & -0.05 & -0.10 & -0.03 & 0.11 \end{bmatrix}.$$

6.
$$\begin{bmatrix} -0.07 & 0.11 & 0.17 & 0.09 & -0.16 \\ 0.28 & 0.09 & -0.14 & 0.08 & -0.17 \\ 0.09 & -0.09 & 0.01 & -0.26 & 0.16 \\ 0.04 & -0.23 & 0.29 & -0.06 & 0.10 \\ -0.26 & 0.28 & -0.35 & 0.20 & 0.13 \end{bmatrix}.$$

## EXERCISES 2.7, page 163

1. a. The amount of agricultural products consumed in the production of $100 million worth of manufactured goods is given by (100)(0.10), or $10 million.

b. The amount of manufactured goods required to produce $200 million of all goods in the economy is given by $200(0.1 + 0.4 + 0.3) = 160$, or $160 million.

c. From the input-output matrix, we see that the agricultural sector consumes the greatest amount of agricultural products, namely, 0.4 units, in the production of each unit of goods in that sector. The manufacturing and transportation sectors consume the least, 0.1 units each.

2. a. 0.2 units

   b. $(0.1 + 0.2 + 0.3 + 0.2)(3) = 2.4$ units.

   c. agricultural

   d. transportation

3. Multiplying both sides of the given equation on the left by $(I - A)^{-1}$, we see that

   $$X = (I - A)^{-1}D.$$

   Now

   $$(I - A) = \begin{bmatrix} 1 & 0 \\ 0 & 1 \end{bmatrix} - \begin{bmatrix} .4 & .2 \\ .3 & .1 \end{bmatrix} = \begin{bmatrix} .6 & -.2 \\ -.3 & .9 \end{bmatrix}$$

   Using the formula for finding the inverse of a 2 x 2 matrix, we find

   $$(I - A)^{-1} = \begin{bmatrix} 1.875 & .417 \\ .625 & 1.25 \end{bmatrix}.$$

   $$(I - A)^{-1}X = \begin{bmatrix} 1.875 & .417 \\ .625 & 1.25 \end{bmatrix} \begin{bmatrix} 10 \\ 12 \end{bmatrix} = \begin{bmatrix} 23.754 \\ 21.25 \end{bmatrix}.$$

4. Multiplying both sides of the given equation on the left by $(I - A)^{-1}$, we see that

   $$X = (I - A)^{-1}D.$$

   Now

   $$(I - A) = \begin{bmatrix} 1 & 0 \\ 0 & 1 \end{bmatrix} - \begin{bmatrix} .2 & .3 \\ .5 & .2 \end{bmatrix} = \begin{bmatrix} .8 & -.3 \\ -.5 & .8 \end{bmatrix}$$

   Using the formula for finding the inverse of a 2 x 2 matrix, we find

   $$(I - A)^{-1} = \begin{bmatrix} 1.63 & .61 \\ 1.02 & 1.63 \end{bmatrix}.$$

   Then

   $$(I - A)^{-1}D = \begin{bmatrix} 1.63 & .61 \\ 1.02 & 1.63 \end{bmatrix} \begin{bmatrix} 4 \\ 8 \end{bmatrix} = \begin{bmatrix} 11.4 \\ 17.1 \end{bmatrix}.$$

5. We first compute

$$(I - A) = \begin{bmatrix} 1 & 0 \\ 0 & 1 \end{bmatrix} - \begin{bmatrix} .5 & .2 \\ .2 & .5 \end{bmatrix} = \begin{bmatrix} .5 & -.2 \\ -.2 & .5 \end{bmatrix}.$$

Using the formula for finding the inverse of a 2 x 2 matrix, we find

$$(I - A)^{-1} = \begin{bmatrix} 2.381 & .952 \\ .952 & 2.381 \end{bmatrix}.$$

Then

$$\begin{bmatrix} x \\ y \end{bmatrix} = \begin{bmatrix} 2.381 & .952 \\ .952 & 2.381 \end{bmatrix} \begin{bmatrix} 10 \\ 20 \end{bmatrix} = \begin{bmatrix} 42.85 \\ 57.14 \end{bmatrix}.$$

6. Proceeding as in Exercise 4, we first compute

$$(I - A) = \begin{bmatrix} 1 & 0 \\ 0 & 1 \end{bmatrix} - \begin{bmatrix} .6 & .2 \\ .1 & .4 \end{bmatrix} = \begin{bmatrix} .4 & -.2 \\ -.1 & .6 \end{bmatrix}.$$

Using the formula for finding the inverse of a 2 x 2 matrix, we find

$$(I - A)^{-1} = \begin{bmatrix} 2.727 & .909 \\ .455 & 1.818 \end{bmatrix}.$$

Then

$$\begin{bmatrix} x \\ y \end{bmatrix} = \begin{bmatrix} 2.727 & .909 \\ .455 & 1.818 \end{bmatrix} \begin{bmatrix} 8 \\ 12 \end{bmatrix} = \begin{bmatrix} 32.72 \\ 25.46 \end{bmatrix}.$$

7. We verify

$$(I - A)(I - A)^{-1} = \begin{bmatrix} .92 & -.60 & -.30 \\ -.04 & .98 & -.01 \\ -.02 & 0 & .94 \end{bmatrix} \begin{bmatrix} 1.13 & .69 & .37 \\ .05 & 1.05 & .03 \\ .02 & .02 & 1.07 \end{bmatrix}$$

$$= \begin{bmatrix} 1 & 0 & 0 \\ 0 & 1 & 0 \\ 0 & 0 & 1 \end{bmatrix}.$$

8. a. 
$$A = \begin{bmatrix} .2 & .4 \\ .3 & .3 \end{bmatrix}$$

and

$$(I - A) = \begin{bmatrix} 1 & 0 \\ 0 & 1 \end{bmatrix} - \begin{bmatrix} .2 & .4 \\ .3 & .3 \end{bmatrix} = \begin{bmatrix} .8 & -.4 \\ -.3 & .7 \end{bmatrix}.$$

Using the formula for finding the inverse of a 2 x 2 matrix, we find

$$(I - A)^{-1} = \begin{bmatrix} 1.591 & .909 \\ .682 & 1.818 \end{bmatrix}.$$

Then

$$\begin{bmatrix} x \\ y \end{bmatrix} = \begin{bmatrix} 1.591 & .909 \\ .682 & 1.818 \end{bmatrix} \begin{bmatrix} 100 \\ 150 \end{bmatrix} = \begin{bmatrix} 295.45 \\ 340.90 \end{bmatrix}.$$

To fulfill consumer demand, \$295.5 million worth of agricultural goods and \$340.9 million worth of manufactured goods should be produced.

b. The net value of goods consumed in the internal process of production is

$$AX = X - D = \begin{bmatrix} 295.45 \\ 340.90 \end{bmatrix} - \begin{bmatrix} 100 \\ 150 \end{bmatrix} = \begin{bmatrix} 195.45 \\ 190.90 \end{bmatrix},$$

or \$195.5 million of agricultural goods and \$190.9 million worth of manufactured goods.

9.    a.

$$A = \begin{bmatrix} .2 & .4 \\ .3 & .3 \end{bmatrix}$$

and

$$(I - A) = \begin{bmatrix} 1 & 0 \\ 0 & 1 \end{bmatrix} - \begin{bmatrix} .2 & .4 \\ .3 & .3 \end{bmatrix} = \begin{bmatrix} .8 & -.4 \\ -.3 & .7 \end{bmatrix}.$$

Using the formula for finding the inverse of a 2 x 2 matrix, we find

$$(I - A)^{-1} = \begin{bmatrix} 1.591 & .909 \\ .682 & 1.818 \end{bmatrix}.$$

Then

$$\begin{bmatrix} x \\ y \end{bmatrix} = \begin{bmatrix} 1.591 & .909 \\ .682 & 1.818 \end{bmatrix} \begin{bmatrix} 120 \\ 140 \end{bmatrix} = \begin{bmatrix} 318.18 \\ 336.36 \end{bmatrix}.$$

To fulfill consumer demand, \$318.2 million worth of agricultural goods and \$336.4 million worth of manufactured goods should be produced.

b. The net value of goods consumed in the internal process of production is

$$AX = X - D = \begin{bmatrix} 318.18 \\ 336.36 \end{bmatrix} - \begin{bmatrix} 120 \\ 140 \end{bmatrix} = \begin{bmatrix} 198.18 \\ 196.36 \end{bmatrix},$$

or \$198.2 million of agricultural goods and \$196.4 million worth of manufactured goods.

10. The matrix representing consumer demand is

$$D = \begin{bmatrix} (1.1)200 \\ (1.2)800 \\ (1.1)120 \end{bmatrix} = \begin{bmatrix} 220 \\ 960 \\ 132 \end{bmatrix}.$$

Then

$$X = (I - A)^{-1}D = \begin{bmatrix} 1.13 & 0.69 & 0.37 \\ 0.05 & 1.05 & 0.03 \\ 0.02 & 0.02 & 1.07 \end{bmatrix} \begin{bmatrix} 220 \\ 960 \\ 132 \end{bmatrix} = \begin{bmatrix} 959.84 \\ 1022.96 \\ 164.84 \end{bmatrix}.$$

To fulfill demand, \$959.8 million worth of raw rubber, \$1023 million worth of tires, and \$164.8 million worth of rubber-based goods should be produced.

11. a.

$$(I - A) = \begin{bmatrix} 1 & 0 & 0 \\ 0 & 1 & 0 \\ 0 & 0 & 1 \end{bmatrix} - \begin{bmatrix} .4 & .1 & .1 \\ .1 & .4 & .3 \\ .2 & .2 & .2 \end{bmatrix} = \begin{bmatrix} .6 & -.1 & -.1 \\ -.1 & .6 & -.3 \\ -.2 & -.2 & .8 \end{bmatrix}.$$

Using the methods of Section 2.6 we next compute the inverse of $(1 - A)^{-1}$ and use this value to find

$$X = (I - A)^{-1}D = \begin{bmatrix} 1.875 & 0.446 & 0.402 \\ 0.625 & 2.054 & 0.848 \\ 0.625 & 0.625 & 1.563 \end{bmatrix} \begin{bmatrix} 200 \\ 100 \\ 60 \end{bmatrix} = \begin{bmatrix} 443.7 \\ 381.3 \\ 281.3 \end{bmatrix}.$$

Therefore, to fulfill demand, \$443.7 million worth of agricultural products, \$381.3 million worth of manufactured products, and \$281.3 million worth of transportation services should be produced.

b. To meet the gross output, the value of goods and transportation consumed in the internal process of production is

$$AX = X - D = \begin{bmatrix} 443.7 \\ 381.3 \\ 281.3 \end{bmatrix} - \begin{bmatrix} 200 \\ 100 \\ 60 \end{bmatrix} = \begin{bmatrix} 243.7 \\ 281.3 \\ 221.3 \end{bmatrix},$$

or \$243.7 million worth of agricultural products, \$281.3 million worth of manufactured services, and \$221.3 million worth of transportation services.

12. The input-output matrix is

$$A = \begin{bmatrix} .4 & .1 & .3 \\ .2 & .2 & .1 \\ .2 & .3 & .1 \end{bmatrix}.$$

The required level of production is

$$(I - A) = \begin{bmatrix} 1 & 0 & 0 \\ 0 & 1 & 0 \\ 0 & 0 & 1 \end{bmatrix} - \begin{bmatrix} .4 & .1 & .3 \\ .2 & .2 & .1 \\ .2 & .3 & .1 \end{bmatrix} = \begin{bmatrix} .6 & -.1 & -.3 \\ -.2 & .8 & -.1 \\ -.2 & -.3 & .9 \end{bmatrix}.$$

Using the methods of Section 2.6 we next compute the inverse of $(1 - A)^{-1}$ and use this value to find

$$X = (I - A)^{-1}D = \begin{bmatrix} 2.104 & 0.549 & 0.762 \\ 0.610 & 1.463 & 0.366 \\ 0.671 & 0.610 & 1.402 \end{bmatrix} \begin{bmatrix} 100 \\ 30 \\ 250 \end{bmatrix} = \begin{bmatrix} 417.4 \\ 196.4 \\ 435.9 \end{bmatrix}.$$

Therefore, to fulfill demand, \$417.4 million worth of agricultural products, \$196.4 million worth of manufactured products, and \$435.9 million worth of transportation services should be produced.

13. We want to solve the equation

$$(I - A)X = D$$

for X, the total output matrix. First, we compute

$$(I - A) = \begin{bmatrix} 1 & 0 \\ 0 & 1 \end{bmatrix} - \begin{bmatrix} 0.4 & 0.2 \\ 0.3 & 0.5 \end{bmatrix} = \begin{bmatrix} 0.6 & -0.2 \\ -0.3 & 0.5 \end{bmatrix}.$$

Using the formula for finding the inverse of a 2 x 2 matrix, we find

$$(I - A)^{-1} = \begin{bmatrix} 2.08 & 0.833 \\ 1.25 & 2.4 \end{bmatrix}.$$

Therefore,

$$X = (I - A)^{-1}D = \begin{bmatrix} 2.08 & 0.833 \\ 1.25 & 2.5 \end{bmatrix} \begin{bmatrix} 12 \\ 24 \end{bmatrix} = \begin{bmatrix} 45 \\ 75 \end{bmatrix}.$$

We conclude that \$45 million worth of goods of one industry and \$75 million worth of goods of the other industry must be produced.

14. We want to solve the equation

$$(I - A)X = D$$

for X, the total output matrix. First, we compute

$$(I - A) = \begin{bmatrix} 1 & 0 \\ 0 & 1 \end{bmatrix} - \begin{bmatrix} 0.1 & 0.4 \\ 0.3 & 0.2 \end{bmatrix} = \begin{bmatrix} 0.9 & -0.4 \\ -0.3 & 0.8 \end{bmatrix}.$$

Using the formula for finding the inverse of a 2 x 2 matrix, we find

$$(I - A)^{-1} = \begin{bmatrix} 1.33 & .67 \\ 0.50 & 1.50 \end{bmatrix}.$$

Therefore,

$$X = (I - A)^{-1}D = \begin{bmatrix} 1.33 & .67 \\ 0.50 & 1.50 \end{bmatrix} \begin{bmatrix} 5 \\ 10 \end{bmatrix} = \begin{bmatrix} 13.35 \\ 17.50 \end{bmatrix}.$$

We conclude that \$13.35 million worth of goods of one industry and \$17.50 million worth of goods of the other industry must be produced.

15. First, we compute

$$(I - A) = \begin{bmatrix} 1 & 0 & 0 \\ 0 & 1 & 0 \\ 0 & 0 & 1 \end{bmatrix} - \begin{bmatrix} .2 & .4 & .2 \\ .5 & 0 & .5 \\ 0 & .2 & 0 \end{bmatrix} = \begin{bmatrix} .8 & -.4 & -.2 \\ -.5 & 1 & -.5 \\ 0 & -.2 & 1 \end{bmatrix}.$$

Next, using the Gauss-Jordan method of elimination, we find

$$(I - A)^{-1} = \begin{bmatrix} 1.8 & 0.88 & 0.80 \\ 1 & 1.6 & 1 \\ 0.2 & 0.32 & 1.20 \end{bmatrix}.$$

Then

$$\begin{bmatrix} x \\ y \\ z \end{bmatrix} = \begin{bmatrix} 1.8 & 0.88 & 0.80 \\ 1 & 1.6 & 1 \\ 0.2 & 0.32 & 1.20 \end{bmatrix} \begin{bmatrix} 10 \\ 5 \\ 15 \end{bmatrix} = \begin{bmatrix} 34.4 \\ 33 \\ 21.6 \end{bmatrix}.$$

We conclude that $34.4 million worth of goods of one industry, $33 million worth of a second industry, and $21.6 million worth of a third industry should be produced.

16. First, we compute

$$(I - A) = \begin{bmatrix} 1 & 0 & 0 \\ 0 & 1 & 0 \\ 0 & 0 & 1 \end{bmatrix} - \begin{bmatrix} .2 & .4 & .1 \\ .3 & .2 & .1 \\ .1 & .2 & .2 \end{bmatrix} = \begin{bmatrix} .8 & -.4 & -.1 \\ -.3 & .8 & -.1 \\ -.1 & -.2 & .8 \end{bmatrix}.$$

Next, using the Gauss-Jordan method of elimination, we find

$$(I - A)^{-1} = \begin{bmatrix} 1.623 & .890 & .314 \\ .654 & 1.649 & .288 \\ .366 & .524 & 1.361 \end{bmatrix}.$$

Then

$$\begin{bmatrix} x \\ y \\ z \end{bmatrix} = \begin{bmatrix} 1.623 & .890 & .314 \\ .654 & 1.649 & .288 \\ .366 & .524 & 1.361 \end{bmatrix} \begin{bmatrix} 6 \\ 8 \\ 10 \end{bmatrix} = \begin{bmatrix} 20 \\ 20 \\ 20 \end{bmatrix}.$$

We conclude that $20 million worth of goods of each industry should be produced.

## USING TECHNOLOGY EXERCISES 2.7, page 164

1. The final outputs of the first, second, third, and fourth industries are 602.62, 502.30, 572.57, and 523.46 units, respectively.

2. The final outputs of the first, second, third, and fourth industries are 219.89, 194.39, 182.1, and 208.04 units, respectively.

3. The final outputs of the first, second, third, and fourth industries are 143.06, 132.98, 188.59, and 125.53 units, respectively.

4. The final outputs of the first, second, third, and fourth industries are 193.59, 131.73, 150.64, and 169.87, respectively.

## CHAPTER 2, REVIEW EXERCISES, page 169

1. $\begin{bmatrix} 1 & 2 \\ -1 & 3 \\ 2 & 1 \end{bmatrix} + \begin{bmatrix} 1 & 0 \\ 0 & 1 \\ 1 & 2 \end{bmatrix} = \begin{bmatrix} 2 & 2 \\ -1 & 4 \\ 3 & 3 \end{bmatrix}.$

2. $\begin{bmatrix} -1 & 2 \\ 3 & 4 \end{bmatrix} - \begin{bmatrix} 1 & 2 \\ 5 & -2 \end{bmatrix} = \begin{bmatrix} -2 & 0 \\ -2 & 6 \end{bmatrix}.$

3. $\begin{bmatrix} -3 & 2 & 1 \end{bmatrix} \begin{bmatrix} 2 & 1 \\ -1 & 0 \\ 2 & 1 \end{bmatrix} = \begin{bmatrix} -6 & -2 \end{bmatrix}.$

4. $\begin{bmatrix} 1 & 3 & 2 \\ -1 & 2 & 3 \end{bmatrix} \begin{bmatrix} 1 \\ 4 \\ 2 \end{bmatrix} = \begin{bmatrix} 17 \\ 13 \end{bmatrix}.$

5.  By the equality of matrices,

$$x = 2, \ z = 1, \ y = 3 \text{ and } w = 3.$$

6.  $3(1) + 2x = 7, \ 2x = 4, \text{ or } x = 2.$

$y + 6 = 4, \text{ or } y = -2$

7.  By the equality of matrices,

$a + 3 = 6, \quad \text{or } a = 3.$

$-1 = e + 2, \text{ or } e = -3; \ b = 4.$

$c + 1 = -1, \text{ or } c = -2; \ d = 2.$

$e + 2 = -1, \text{ and } e = -3.$

8.  $x + 3(3) + 4 = 12, \text{ or } x = -1.$

$x + 3z + 2 = 4, \text{ or } 3z + 1 = 4, \ 3z = 3, \text{ and } z = 1.$

$0(1) + y(3) + 2(4) = 2, \ 3y = -6, \text{ or } y = -2.$

$0(1) + y(z) + 2(2) = -2 + 4 = 2.$

9.

$$2A + 3B = 2 \begin{bmatrix} 1 & 3 & 1 \\ -2 & 1 & 3 \\ 4 & 0 & 2 \end{bmatrix} + 3 \begin{bmatrix} 2 & 1 & 3 \\ -2 & -1 & -1 \\ 1 & 4 & 2 \end{bmatrix}$$

$$= \begin{bmatrix} 2 & 6 & 2 \\ -4 & 2 & 6 \\ 8 & 0 & 4 \end{bmatrix} + \begin{bmatrix} 6 & 3 & 9 \\ -6 & -3 & -3 \\ 3 & 12 & 6 \end{bmatrix}$$

$$= \begin{bmatrix} 8 & 9 & 11 \\ -10 & -1 & 3 \\ 11 & 12 & 10 \end{bmatrix}.$$

10.

$$3A - 2B = 3 \begin{bmatrix} 1 & 3 & 1 \\ -2 & 1 & 3 \\ 4 & 0 & 2 \end{bmatrix} - 2 \begin{bmatrix} 2 & 1 & 3 \\ -2 & -1 & -1 \\ 1 & 4 & 2 \end{bmatrix}$$

$$= \begin{bmatrix} 3 & 9 & 3 \\ -6 & 3 & 9 \\ 12 & 0 & 6 \end{bmatrix} - \begin{bmatrix} 4 & 2 & 6 \\ -4 & -2 & -2 \\ 2 & 8 & 4 \end{bmatrix}$$

$$= \begin{bmatrix} -1 & 7 & -3 \\ -2 & 5 & 11 \\ 10 & -8 & 2 \end{bmatrix}.$$

11.

$$3A = \begin{bmatrix} 1 & 3 & 1 \\ -2 & 1 & 3 \\ 4 & 0 & 2 \end{bmatrix} = \begin{bmatrix} 3 & 9 & 3 \\ -6 & 3 & 9 \\ 12 & 0 & 6 \end{bmatrix}$$

and

$$2(3A) = 2 \begin{bmatrix} 3 & 9 & 3 \\ -6 & 3 & 9 \\ 12 & 0 & 6 \end{bmatrix} = \begin{bmatrix} 6 & 18 & 6 \\ -12 & 6 & 18 \\ 24 & 0 & 12 \end{bmatrix}.$$

12.

$$3A - 4B = 3 \begin{bmatrix} 1 & 3 & 1 \\ -2 & 1 & 3 \\ 4 & 0 & 2 \end{bmatrix} - 4 \begin{bmatrix} 2 & 1 & 3 \\ -2 & -1 & -1 \\ 1 & 4 & 2 \end{bmatrix}$$

$$= \begin{bmatrix} 3 & 9 & 3 \\ -6 & 3 & 9 \\ 12 & 0 & 6 \end{bmatrix} - \begin{bmatrix} 8 & 4 & 12 \\ -8 & -4 & -4 \\ 4 & 16 & 8 \end{bmatrix}$$

$$= \begin{bmatrix} -5 & 5 & -9 \\ 2 & 7 & 13 \\ 8 & -16 & -2 \end{bmatrix}.$$

Therefore,

$$2(3A - 4B) = 2 \begin{bmatrix} -5 & 5 & -9 \\ 2 & 7 & 13 \\ 8 & -16 & -2 \end{bmatrix} = \begin{bmatrix} -10 & 10 & -18 \\ 4 & 14 & 26 \\ 16 & -32 & -4 \end{bmatrix}.$$

13.

$$B - C = \begin{bmatrix} 2 & 1 & 3 \\ -2 & -1 & -1 \\ 1 & 4 & 2 \end{bmatrix} - \begin{bmatrix} 3 & -1 & 2 \\ 1 & 6 & 4 \\ 2 & 1 & 3 \end{bmatrix} = \begin{bmatrix} -1 & 2 & 1 \\ -3 & -7 & -5 \\ -1 & 3 & -1 \end{bmatrix}$$

and so

$$A(B - C) = \begin{bmatrix} 1 & 3 & 1 \\ -2 & 1 & 3 \\ 4 & 0 & 2 \end{bmatrix} \begin{bmatrix} -1 & 2 & 1 \\ -3 & -7 & -5 \\ -1 & 3 & -1 \end{bmatrix} = \begin{bmatrix} -11 & -16 & -15 \\ -4 & -2 & -10 \\ -6 & 14 & 2 \end{bmatrix}.$$

14. Observe that $AB + AC = A(B + C)$. Now

$$B + C = \begin{bmatrix} 2 & 1 & 3 \\ -2 & -1 & -1 \\ 1 & 4 & 2 \end{bmatrix} + \begin{bmatrix} 3 & -1 & 2 \\ 1 & 6 & 4 \\ 2 & 1 & 3 \end{bmatrix} = \begin{bmatrix} 5 & 0 & 5 \\ -1 & 5 & 3 \\ 3 & 5 & 5 \end{bmatrix}$$

and so

$$A(B + C) = \begin{bmatrix} 1 & 3 & 1 \\ -2 & 1 & 3 \\ 4 & 0 & 2 \end{bmatrix} \begin{bmatrix} 5 & 0 & 5 \\ -1 & 5 & 3 \\ 3 & 5 & 5 \end{bmatrix} = \begin{bmatrix} 5 & 20 & 19 \\ -2 & 20 & 8 \\ 26 & 10 & 30 \end{bmatrix}.$$

15.

$$BC = \begin{bmatrix} 2 & 1 & 3 \\ -2 & -1 & -1 \\ 1 & 4 & 2 \end{bmatrix} \begin{bmatrix} 3 & -1 & 2 \\ 1 & 6 & 4 \\ 2 & 1 & 3 \end{bmatrix} = \begin{bmatrix} 13 & 7 & 17 \\ -9 & -5 & -11 \\ 11 & 25 & 24 \end{bmatrix}$$

$$ABC = \begin{bmatrix} 1 & 3 & 1 \\ -2 & 1 & 3 \\ 4 & 0 & 2 \end{bmatrix} \begin{bmatrix} 13 & 7 & 17 \\ -9 & -5 & -11 \\ 11 & 25 & 24 \end{bmatrix} = \begin{bmatrix} -3 & 17 & 8 \\ -2 & 56 & 27 \\ 74 & 78 & 116 \end{bmatrix}.$$

**16.**

$$A - B = \begin{bmatrix} 1 & 3 & 1 \\ -2 & 1 & 3 \\ 4 & 0 & 2 \end{bmatrix} - \begin{bmatrix} 2 & 1 & 3 \\ -2 & -1 & -1 \\ 1 & 4 & 2 \end{bmatrix} = \begin{bmatrix} -1 & 2 & -2 \\ 0 & 2 & 4 \\ 3 & -4 & 0 \end{bmatrix}.$$

So

$$\frac{1}{2}(C)(A - B) = \frac{1}{2} \begin{bmatrix} 3 & -1 & 2 \\ 1 & 6 & 4 \\ 2 & 1 & 3 \end{bmatrix} \begin{bmatrix} -1 & 2 & -2 \\ 0 & 2 & 4 \\ 3 & -4 & 0 \end{bmatrix}$$

$$= \frac{1}{2} \begin{bmatrix} 3 & -4 & -10 \\ 11 & -2 & 22 \\ 7 & -6 & 0 \end{bmatrix} = \begin{bmatrix} \frac{3}{2} & -2 & -5 \\ \frac{11}{2} & -1 & 11 \\ \frac{7}{2} & -3 & 0 \end{bmatrix}.$$

**17.** Using the Gauss–Jordan elimination method, we find

$$\begin{bmatrix} 2 & -3 & | & 5 \\ 3 & 4 & | & -1 \end{bmatrix} \xrightarrow{\frac{1}{2}R_1} \begin{bmatrix} 1 & -\frac{3}{2} & | & \frac{5}{2} \\ 3 & 4 & | & -1 \end{bmatrix} \xrightarrow{R_2 - 3R_1} \begin{bmatrix} 1 & -\frac{3}{2} & | & \frac{5}{2} \\ 0 & \frac{17}{2} & | & -\frac{17}{2} \end{bmatrix} \xrightarrow{\frac{2}{17}R_2}$$

$$\begin{bmatrix} 1 & -\frac{3}{2} & | & \frac{5}{2} \\ 0 & 1 & | & -1 \end{bmatrix} \xrightarrow{R_1 + \frac{3}{2}R_2} \begin{bmatrix} 1 & 0 & | & 1 \\ 0 & 1 & | & -1 \end{bmatrix}.$$

We conclude that $x = 1$ and $y = -1$.

**18.**

$$\begin{bmatrix} 3 & 2 & | & 3 \\ 2 & -4 & | & -14 \end{bmatrix} \xrightarrow{R_1 - R_2} \begin{bmatrix} 1 & 6 & | & 17 \\ 2 & -4 & | & -14 \end{bmatrix} \xrightarrow{R_2 - 2R_1} \begin{bmatrix} 1 & 6 & | & 17 \\ 0 & -16 & | & -48 \end{bmatrix} \xrightarrow{-\frac{1}{16}R_2}$$

$$\begin{bmatrix} 1 & 6 & | & 17 \\ 0 & 1 & | & 3 \end{bmatrix} \xrightarrow{R_1 - 6R_2} \begin{bmatrix} 1 & 0 & | & -1 \\ 0 & 1 & | & 3 \end{bmatrix}.$$

So $x = -1$ and $y = 3$.

**19.**

$$\begin{bmatrix} 1 & -1 & 2 & \bigm| & 5 \\ 3 & 2 & 1 & \bigm| & 10 \\ 2 & -3 & -2 & \bigm| & -10 \end{bmatrix} \xrightarrow[\;R_3\;-\;2R_1\;]{R_2\;-\;3R_1} \begin{bmatrix} 1 & -1 & 2 & \bigm| & 5 \\ 0 & 5 & -5 & \bigm| & -5 \\ 0 & -1 & -6 & \bigm| & -20 \end{bmatrix} \xrightarrow{\frac{1}{5}R_2} \begin{bmatrix} 1 & -1 & 2 & \bigm| & 5 \\ 0 & 1 & -1 & \bigm| & -1 \\ 0 & -1 & -6 & \bigm| & -20 \end{bmatrix}$$

$$\xrightarrow[\;R_3\;+\;R_2\;]{R_1\;+\;R_2} \begin{bmatrix} 1 & 0 & 1 & \bigm| & 4 \\ 0 & 1 & -1 & \bigm| & -1 \\ 0 & 0 & -7 & \bigm| & -21 \end{bmatrix} \xrightarrow{-\frac{1}{7}R_3} \begin{bmatrix} 1 & 0 & 1 & \bigm| & 4 \\ 0 & 1 & -1 & \bigm| & -1 \\ 0 & 0 & 1 & \bigm| & 3 \end{bmatrix} \xrightarrow[\;R_2\;+\;R_3\;]{R_1\;-\;R_3}$$

$$= \begin{bmatrix} 1 & 0 & 0 & \bigm| & 1 \\ 0 & 1 & 0 & \bigm| & 2 \\ 0 & 0 & 1 & \bigm| & 3 \end{bmatrix} .$$

Therefore, $x = 1$, $y = 2$, and $z = 3$.

**20.**

$$\begin{bmatrix} 3 & -2 & 4 & \bigm| & 16 \\ 2 & 1 & -2 & \bigm| & -1 \\ 1 & 4 & -8 & \bigm| & -18 \end{bmatrix} \xrightarrow{R_1 \leftrightarrow R_3} \begin{bmatrix} 1 & 4 & -8 & \bigm| & -18 \\ 2 & 1 & -2 & \bigm| & -1 \\ 3 & -2 & -4 & \bigm| & 16 \end{bmatrix} \xrightarrow[\;R_3\;-\;3R_1\;]{R_2\;-\;2R_1} \begin{bmatrix} 1 & 4 & -8 & \bigm| & -18 \\ 0 & -7 & 14 & \bigm| & 35 \\ 0 & -14 & 28 & \bigm| & 70 \end{bmatrix}$$

$$\xrightarrow{-\frac{1}{7}R_2} \begin{bmatrix} 1 & 4 & -8 & \bigm| & -18 \\ 0 & 1 & -2 & \bigm| & -5 \\ 0 & -14 & 28 & \bigm| & 70 \end{bmatrix} \xrightarrow[\;R_3\;+\;14R_2\;]{R_1\;-\;4R_2} \begin{bmatrix} 1 & 0 & 0 & \bigm| & 2 \\ 0 & 1 & -2 & \bigm| & -5 \\ 0 & 0 & 0 & \bigm| & 0 \end{bmatrix} .$$

The solutions are $(2, 2t - 5, t)$, $t$, a parameter.

**21.**

$$\begin{bmatrix} 3 & -2 & 4 & \bigm| & 11 \\ 2 & -4 & 5 & \bigm| & 4 \\ 1 & 2 & -1 & \bigm| & 10 \end{bmatrix} \xrightarrow{R_1 \;-\; R_2} \begin{bmatrix} 1 & 2 & -1 & \bigm| & 7 \\ 2 & -4 & 5 & \bigm| & 4 \\ 1 & 2 & -1 & \bigm| & 10 \end{bmatrix} \xrightarrow[\;R_3\;-\;R_1\;]{R_2\;-\;2R_1} \begin{bmatrix} 1 & 2 & -1 & \bigm| & 7 \\ 0 & -8 & 7 & \bigm| & -10 \\ 0 & 0 & 0 & \bigm| & 3 \end{bmatrix}$$

Since this last row implies that $0 = 3!$, we conclude that the system
has no solution.

**22.**

$$\begin{bmatrix} 1 & -2 & 3 & 4 & | & 17 \\ 2 & 1 & -2 & -3 & | & -9 \\ 3 & -1 & 2 & -4 & | & 0 \\ 4 & 2 & -3 & 1 & | & -2 \end{bmatrix} \xrightarrow[\substack{R_3 - 3R_1 \\ R_4 - 4R_1}]{R_2 - 2R_1} \begin{bmatrix} 1 & -2 & 3 & 4 & | & 17 \\ 0 & 5 & -8 & -11 & | & -43 \\ 0 & 5 & -7 & -16 & | & -51 \\ 0 & 10 & -15 & -15 & | & -70 \end{bmatrix} \xrightarrow{\frac{1}{5}R_2}$$

$$\begin{bmatrix} 1 & -2 & 3 & 4 & | & 17 \\ 0 & 1 & -\frac{8}{5} & -\frac{11}{5} & | & -\frac{43}{5} \\ 0 & 5 & -7 & -16 & | & -51 \\ 0 & 10 & -15 & -15 & | & -70 \end{bmatrix} \xrightarrow[\substack{R_3 - 5R_2 \\ R_4 - 10R_2}]{R_1 + 2R_2} \begin{bmatrix} 1 & 0 & -\frac{1}{5} & -\frac{2}{5} & | & -\frac{1}{5} \\ 0 & 1 & -\frac{8}{5} & -\frac{11}{5} & | & -\frac{43}{5} \\ 0 & 0 & 1 & -5 & | & -8 \\ 0 & 0 & 1 & 7 & | & 16 \end{bmatrix} \xrightarrow[\substack{R_2 + \frac{8}{5}R_3 \\ R_4 - R_3}]{R_1 + \frac{1}{5}R_3}$$

$$\begin{bmatrix} 1 & 0 & 0 & -\frac{7}{5} & | & -\frac{9}{5} \\ 0 & 1 & 0 & -\frac{51}{5} & | & -\frac{107}{5} \\ 0 & 0 & 1 & -5 & | & -8 \\ 0 & 0 & 0 & 12 & | & 24 \end{bmatrix} \xrightarrow{\frac{1}{12}R_4} \begin{bmatrix} 1 & 0 & 0 & -\frac{7}{5} & | & -\frac{9}{5} \\ 0 & 1 & 0 & -\frac{51}{5} & | & -\frac{107}{5} \\ 0 & 0 & 1 & -5 & | & -8 \\ 0 & 0 & 0 & 1 & | & 2 \end{bmatrix} \xrightarrow[\substack{R_2 + \frac{51}{5}R_4 \\ R_3 + 5R_4}]{R_1 + \frac{7}{5}R_4}$$

$$\begin{bmatrix} 1 & 0 & 0 & 0 & | & 1 \\ 0 & 1 & 0 & 0 & | & -1 \\ 0 & 0 & 1 & 0 & | & 2 \\ 0 & 0 & 0 & 1 & | & 2 \end{bmatrix}.$$

Therefore, x = 1, y = -1, z = 2, and w = 2.

**23.**

$$\begin{bmatrix} 3 & -2 & 1 & | & 4 \\ 1 & 3 & -4 & | & -3 \\ 2 & -3 & 5 & | & 7 \\ 1 & -8 & 9 & | & 10 \end{bmatrix} \xrightarrow{R_1 - R_3} \begin{bmatrix} 1 & 1 & -4 & | & -3 \\ 1 & 3 & -4 & | & -3 \\ 2 & -3 & 5 & | & 7 \\ 1 & -8 & 9 & | & 10 \end{bmatrix} \xrightarrow[\substack{R_3 - 2R_1 \\ R_4 - R_1}]{R_2 - R_1}$$

$$\begin{bmatrix} 1 & 1 & -4 & | & -3 \\ 0 & 2 & 0 & | & 0 \\ 0 & -5 & 13 & | & 13 \\ 0 & -9 & 13 & | & 13 \end{bmatrix} \xrightarrow{\frac{1}{2}R_2} \begin{bmatrix} 1 & 1 & -4 & | & -3 \\ 0 & 1 & 0 & | & 0 \\ 0 & -5 & 13 & | & 13 \\ 0 & -9 & 13 & | & 13 \end{bmatrix} \xrightarrow[\substack{R_3 + 5R_2 \\ R_4 + 9R_2}]{R_1 - R_2}$$

$$\begin{bmatrix} 1 & 0 & -4 & | & -3 \\ 0 & 1 & 0 & | & 0 \\ 0 & 0 & 13 & | & 13 \\ 0 & 0 & 13 & | & 13 \end{bmatrix} \xrightarrow{\frac{1}{13}R_3} \begin{bmatrix} 1 & 0 & -4 & | & -3 \\ 0 & 1 & 0 & | & 0 \\ 0 & 0 & 1 & | & 1 \\ 0 & 0 & 13 & | & 13 \end{bmatrix} \xrightarrow[R_4 - 13R_3]{R_1 + 4R_3}$$

$$\begin{bmatrix} 1 & 0 & 0 & | & 1 \\ 0 & 1 & 0 & | & 0 \\ 0 & 0 & 1 & | & 1 \\ 0 & 0 & 0 & | & 0 \end{bmatrix}.$$

Therefore, $x = 1$, $y = 0$, and $z = 1$.

24. Using the formula for finding the inverse of a 2 x 2 matrix with $a = 2$, $b = 4$, $c = 1$, $d = 6$, we find that

$$D = ad - bc = (2)(6) - (4)(1) = 8,$$

and

$$A^{-1} = \begin{bmatrix} \frac{3}{4} & -\frac{1}{2} \\ -\frac{1}{8} & \frac{1}{4} \end{bmatrix}.$$

We can verify that this is correct by computing

$$\begin{bmatrix} 2 & 4 \\ 1 & 6 \end{bmatrix}\begin{bmatrix} \frac{3}{4} & -\frac{1}{2} \\ -\frac{1}{8} & \frac{1}{4} \end{bmatrix} = \begin{bmatrix} 1 & 0 \\ 0 & 1 \end{bmatrix}.$$

25. $$A^{-1} = \frac{1}{(3)(2) - (1)(1)} \begin{bmatrix} 2 & -1 \\ -1 & 3 \end{bmatrix} = \begin{bmatrix} \frac{2}{5} & -\frac{1}{5} \\ -\frac{1}{5} & \frac{3}{5} \end{bmatrix}.$$

26. $$A^{-1} = \frac{1}{(2)(-2) - (1)(4)} \begin{bmatrix} -2 & -4 \\ -1 & 2 \end{bmatrix} = \begin{bmatrix} \frac{1}{4} & \frac{1}{2} \\ \frac{1}{8} & -\frac{1}{4} \end{bmatrix}.$$

27. $$A^{-1} = \frac{1}{(3)(2) - (2)(4)} \begin{bmatrix} 2 & -4 \\ -2 & 3 \end{bmatrix} = \begin{bmatrix} -1 & 2 \\ 1 & -\frac{3}{2} \end{bmatrix}.$$

**28.**

$$\begin{bmatrix} 1 & 2 & 4 & | & 1 & 0 & 0 \\ 2 & 1 & 3 & | & 0 & 1 & 0 \\ -1 & 0 & 2 & | & 0 & 0 & 1 \end{bmatrix} \xrightarrow[\;R_3 + R_1\;]{R_2 - 2R_1} \begin{bmatrix} 1 & 2 & 4 & | & 1 & 0 & 0 \\ 0 & -3 & -5 & | & -2 & 1 & 0 \\ 0 & 2 & 6 & | & 1 & 0 & 1 \end{bmatrix} \xrightarrow{R_2 + 2R_3}$$

$$\begin{bmatrix} 1 & 2 & 4 & | & 1 & 0 & 0 \\ 0 & 1 & 7 & | & 0 & 1 & 2 \\ 0 & 2 & 6 & | & 1 & 0 & 1 \end{bmatrix} \xrightarrow[\;R_3 - 2R_2\;]{R_1 - 2R_2} \begin{bmatrix} 1 & 0 & -10 & | & 1 & -2 & -4 \\ 0 & 1 & 7 & | & 0 & 1 & 2 \\ 0 & 0 & -8 & | & 1 & -2 & -3 \end{bmatrix} \xrightarrow{-\frac{1}{8}R_3}$$

$$\begin{bmatrix} 1 & 0 & -10 & | & 1 & -2 & -4 \\ 0 & 1 & 7 & | & 0 & 1 & 2 \\ 0 & 0 & 1 & | & -\frac{1}{8} & \frac{1}{4} & \frac{3}{8} \end{bmatrix} \xrightarrow[\;R_2 - 7R_3\;]{R_1 + 10R_3} \begin{bmatrix} 1 & 0 & 0 & | & -\frac{1}{4} & \frac{1}{2} & -\frac{1}{4} \\ 0 & 1 & 0 & | & \frac{7}{8} & -\frac{3}{4} & -\frac{5}{8} \\ 0 & 0 & 1 & | & -\frac{1}{8} & \frac{1}{4} & \frac{3}{8} \end{bmatrix}.$$

**29.**

$$\begin{bmatrix} 2 & 3 & 1 & | & 1 & 0 & 0 \\ 1 & -1 & 2 & | & 0 & 1 & 0 \\ 1 & 2 & 1 & | & 0 & 0 & 1 \end{bmatrix} \xrightarrow{R_1 - R_2} \begin{bmatrix} 1 & 4 & -1 & | & 1 & -1 & 0 \\ 0 & -1 & 2 & | & 0 & 1 & 0 \\ 1 & 2 & 1 & | & 0 & 0 & 1 \end{bmatrix} \xrightarrow[\;R_3 - R_1\;]{R_2 - R_1}$$

$$\begin{bmatrix} 1 & 4 & -1 & | & 1 & -1 & 0 \\ 0 & -5 & 3 & | & -1 & 2 & 0 \\ 0 & -2 & 2 & | & -1 & 1 & 1 \end{bmatrix} \xrightarrow{R_2 - 3R_3} \begin{bmatrix} 1 & 4 & -1 & | & 1 & -1 & 0 \\ 0 & 1 & -3 & | & 2 & -1 & -3 \\ 0 & -2 & 2 & | & -1 & 1 & 1 \end{bmatrix} \xrightarrow[\;R_3 + 2R_2\;]{R_1 - 4R_2}$$

$$\begin{bmatrix} 1 & 0 & 11 & | & -7 & 3 & 12 \\ 0 & 1 & -3 & | & 2 & -1 & -3 \\ 0 & 0 & -4 & | & 3 & -1 & -5 \end{bmatrix} \xrightarrow{-\frac{1}{4}R_3} \begin{bmatrix} 1 & 0 & 11 & | & -7 & 3 & 12 \\ 0 & 1 & -3 & | & 2 & -1 & -3 \\ 0 & 0 & 1 & | & -\frac{3}{4} & \frac{1}{4} & \frac{5}{4} \end{bmatrix} \xrightarrow[\;R_2 + 3R_3\;]{R_1 - 11R_3}$$

$$\begin{bmatrix} 1 & 0 & 0 & | & \frac{5}{4} & \frac{1}{4} & -\frac{7}{4} \\ 0 & 1 & 0 & | & -\frac{1}{4} & -\frac{1}{4} & \frac{3}{4} \\ 0 & 0 & 1 & | & -\frac{3}{4} & \frac{1}{4} & \frac{5}{4} \end{bmatrix} \quad \text{So } A^{-1} = \begin{bmatrix} \frac{5}{4} & \frac{1}{4} & -\frac{7}{4} \\ -\frac{1}{4} & -\frac{1}{4} & \frac{3}{4} \\ -\frac{3}{4} & \frac{1}{4} & \frac{5}{4} \end{bmatrix}.$$

30.

$$\begin{bmatrix} 2 & 1 & -3 & | & 1 & 0 & 0 \\ 1 & 2 & -4 & | & 0 & 1 & 0 \\ 3 & 1 & -2 & | & 0 & 0 & 1 \end{bmatrix} \xrightarrow{R_1 - R_2} \begin{bmatrix} 1 & -1 & 1 & | & 1 & -1 & 0 \\ 1 & 2 & -4 & | & 0 & 1 & 0 \\ 3 & 1 & -2 & | & 0 & 0 & 1 \end{bmatrix} \xrightarrow[R_3 - 3R_1]{R_2 - R_1}$$

$$\begin{bmatrix} 1 & -1 & 1 & | & 1 & -1 & 0 \\ 0 & 3 & -5 & | & -1 & 2 & 0 \\ 0 & 4 & -5 & | & -3 & 3 & 1 \end{bmatrix} \xrightarrow{R_2 \leftrightarrow R_3} \begin{bmatrix} 1 & -1 & 1 & | & 1 & -1 & 0 \\ 0 & 4 & -5 & | & -3 & 3 & 1 \\ 0 & 3 & -5 & | & -1 & 2 & 0 \end{bmatrix} \xrightarrow{R_2 - R_3}$$

$$\begin{bmatrix} 1 & -1 & 1 & | & 1 & -1 & 0 \\ 0 & 1 & 0 & | & -2 & 1 & 1 \\ 0 & 3 & -5 & | & -1 & 2 & 0 \end{bmatrix} \xrightarrow[R_3 - 3R_2]{R_1 + R_2} \begin{bmatrix} 1 & 0 & 0 & | & -1 & 0 & 1 \\ 0 & 1 & 0 & | & -2 & 1 & 1 \\ 0 & 0 & -5 & | & 5 & -1 & -3 \end{bmatrix} \xrightarrow{-\frac{1}{5}R_3}$$

$$\begin{bmatrix} 1 & 0 & 1 & | & -1 & 0 & 1 \\ 0 & 1 & 0 & | & -2 & 1 & 1 \\ 0 & 0 & 1 & | & -1 & \frac{1}{5} & \frac{3}{5} \end{bmatrix} \xrightarrow{R_1 - R_3} \begin{bmatrix} 1 & 0 & 0 & | & 0 & -\frac{1}{5} & \frac{2}{5} \\ 0 & 1 & 0 & | & -2 & 1 & 1 \\ 0 & 0 & 1 & | & -1 & \frac{1}{5} & \frac{3}{5} \end{bmatrix}.$$

So

$$A^{-1} = \begin{bmatrix} 0 & -\frac{1}{5} & \frac{2}{5} \\ -2 & 1 & 1 \\ -1 & \frac{1}{5} & \frac{3}{5} \end{bmatrix}.$$

31.

$$\begin{bmatrix} 1 & 2 & 4 & | & 1 & 0 & 0 \\ 3 & 1 & 2 & | & 0 & 1 & 0 \\ 1 & 0 & -6 & | & 0 & 0 & 1 \end{bmatrix} \xrightarrow[R_3 - R_1]{R_2 - 3R_1} \begin{bmatrix} 1 & 2 & 4 & | & 1 & 0 & 0 \\ 0 & -5 & -10 & | & -3 & 1 & 0 \\ 0 & -2 & -10 & | & -1 & 0 & 1 \end{bmatrix} \xrightarrow{R_2 - 3R_3}$$

$$\begin{bmatrix} 1 & 2 & 4 & | & 1 & 0 & 0 \\ 0 & 1 & 20 & | & 0 & 1 & -3 \\ 0 & -2 & -10 & | & -1 & 0 & 1 \end{bmatrix} \xrightarrow[R_3 + 2R_2]{R_1 - 2R_2} \begin{bmatrix} 1 & 0 & -36 & | & 1 & -2 & 6 \\ 0 & 1 & 20 & | & 0 & 1 & -3 \\ 0 & 0 & 30 & | & -1 & 2 & -5 \end{bmatrix} \xrightarrow{\frac{1}{30}R_3}$$

$$\begin{bmatrix} 1 & 0 & -36 & | & 1 & -2 & 6 \\ 0 & 1 & 20 & | & 0 & 1 & -3 \\ 0 & 0 & 1 & | & -\frac{1}{30} & \frac{1}{15} & -\frac{1}{6} \end{bmatrix} \xrightarrow[\ R_2 - 20R_3\ ]{\ R_1 + 36R_3\ } \begin{bmatrix} 1 & 0 & 0 & | & -\frac{1}{5} & \frac{2}{5} & 0 \\ 0 & 1 & 0 & | & \frac{2}{3} & -\frac{1}{3} & \frac{1}{3} \\ 0 & 0 & 1 & | & -\frac{1}{30} & \frac{1}{15} & -\frac{1}{6} \end{bmatrix}$$

So

$$A^{-1} = \begin{bmatrix} -\frac{1}{5} & \frac{2}{5} & 0 \\ \frac{2}{3} & -\frac{1}{3} & \frac{1}{3} \\ -\frac{1}{30} & \frac{1}{15} & -\frac{1}{6} \end{bmatrix}.$$

32.

$$AB = \begin{bmatrix} 1 & 2 \\ -1 & 2 \end{bmatrix} \begin{bmatrix} 3 & 1 \\ 4 & 2 \end{bmatrix} = \begin{bmatrix} 11 & 5 \\ 5 & 3 \end{bmatrix}.$$

$$ABC = \begin{bmatrix} 11 & 5 \\ 5 & 3 \end{bmatrix} \begin{bmatrix} 1 & 1 \\ -1 & 2 \end{bmatrix} = \begin{bmatrix} 6 & 21 \\ 2 & 11 \end{bmatrix}.$$

$$(ABC)^{-1} = \frac{1}{(6)(11) - 2(21)} \begin{bmatrix} 11 & -21 \\ -2 & 6 \end{bmatrix} = \begin{bmatrix} \frac{11}{24} & -\frac{7}{8} \\ -\frac{1}{12} & \frac{1}{4} \end{bmatrix}.$$

33.  $(A^{-1}B)^{-1} = B^{-1}(A^{-1})^{-1} = B^{-1}A.$ Now

$$B^{-1} = \frac{1}{(3)(2) - 4(1)} \begin{bmatrix} 2 & -1 \\ -4 & 3 \end{bmatrix} = \begin{bmatrix} 1 & -\frac{1}{2} \\ -2 & \frac{3}{2} \end{bmatrix}.$$

$$B^{-1}A = \begin{bmatrix} 1 & -\frac{1}{2} \\ -2 & \frac{3}{2} \end{bmatrix} \begin{bmatrix} 1 & 2 \\ -1 & 2 \end{bmatrix} = \begin{bmatrix} \frac{3}{2} & 1 \\ -\frac{7}{2} & -1 \end{bmatrix}.$$

34.

$$A + B = \begin{bmatrix} 1 & 2 \\ -1 & 2 \end{bmatrix} + \begin{bmatrix} 3 & 1 \\ 4 & 2 \end{bmatrix} = \begin{bmatrix} 4 & 3 \\ 3 & 4 \end{bmatrix}.$$

$$(A + B)^{-1} = \frac{1}{(4)(4) - 3(3)} \begin{bmatrix} 4 & -3 \\ -3 & 4 \end{bmatrix} = \begin{bmatrix} \frac{4}{7} & -\frac{3}{7} \\ -\frac{3}{7} & \frac{4}{7} \end{bmatrix}.$$

35.

$$2A - C = \begin{bmatrix} 2 & 4 \\ -2 & 4 \end{bmatrix} - \begin{bmatrix} 1 & 1 \\ -1 & 2 \end{bmatrix} = \begin{bmatrix} 1 & 3 \\ -1 & 2 \end{bmatrix}$$

$$(2A - C)^{-1} = \frac{1}{(1)(2) - (-1)(3)} \begin{bmatrix} 2 & -3 \\ 1 & 1 \end{bmatrix} = \begin{bmatrix} \frac{2}{5} & -\frac{3}{5} \\ \frac{1}{5} & \frac{1}{5} \end{bmatrix}.$$

36.

$$A = \begin{bmatrix} 1 & -3 \\ 2 & 4 \end{bmatrix}, \quad X = \begin{bmatrix} x \\ y \end{bmatrix}, \quad B = \begin{bmatrix} -1 \\ 8 \end{bmatrix}$$

$$A^{-1} = \frac{1}{(1)(4) - (2)(-3\ )} \begin{bmatrix} 4 & 3 \\ -2 & 1 \end{bmatrix} = \begin{bmatrix} \frac{2}{5} & \frac{3}{10} \\ -\frac{1}{5} & \frac{1}{10} \end{bmatrix}.$$

$$\begin{bmatrix} x \\ y \end{bmatrix} = A^{-1}B = \begin{bmatrix} \frac{2}{5} & \frac{3}{10} \\ -\frac{1}{5} & \frac{1}{10} \end{bmatrix} \begin{bmatrix} -1 \\ 8 \end{bmatrix} = \begin{bmatrix} 2 \\ 1 \end{bmatrix}.$$

37.

$$A = \begin{bmatrix} 2 & 3 \\ 1 & -2 \end{bmatrix}, \quad X = \begin{bmatrix} x \\ y \end{bmatrix}, \quad B = \begin{bmatrix} -8 \\ 3 \end{bmatrix}$$

$$A^{-1} = \frac{1}{(-2)(2) - (1)(3)} \begin{bmatrix} -2 & -3 \\ -1 & 2 \end{bmatrix} = \begin{bmatrix} \frac{2}{7} & \frac{3}{7} \\ \frac{1}{7} & -\frac{2}{7} \end{bmatrix}.$$

$$\begin{bmatrix} x \\ y \end{bmatrix} = A^{-1}B = \begin{bmatrix} \frac{2}{7} & \frac{3}{7} \\ \frac{1}{7} & -\frac{2}{7} \end{bmatrix} \begin{bmatrix} -8 \\ 3 \end{bmatrix} = \begin{bmatrix} -1 \\ -2 \end{bmatrix}.$$

38. Put

$$X = \begin{bmatrix} x \\ y \\ z \end{bmatrix}, \quad A = \begin{bmatrix} 2 & -3 & 4 \\ 1 & 2 & -4 \\ 3 & -1 & 2 \end{bmatrix}, \quad C = \begin{bmatrix} 17 \\ -7 \\ 14 \end{bmatrix}.$$

Then AX = C and X = A⁻¹C. To find A⁻¹,

$$\left[\begin{array}{ccc|ccc} 2 & -3 & 4 & 1 & 0 & 0 \\ 1 & 2 & -4 & 0 & 1 & 0 \\ 3 & -1 & 2 & 0 & 0 & 1 \end{array}\right] \xrightarrow{R_1 \leftrightarrow R_2} \left[\begin{array}{ccc|ccc} 1 & 2 & -4 & 0 & 1 & 0 \\ 2 & -3 & 4 & 1 & 0 & 0 \\ 3 & -1 & 2 & 0 & 0 & 1 \end{array}\right] \xrightarrow[R_3 - 3R_1]{R_2 - 2R_1}$$

$$\left[\begin{array}{ccc|ccc} 1 & 2 & -4 & 0 & 1 & 0 \\ 0 & -7 & 12 & 1 & -2 & 0 \\ 0 & -7 & 14 & 0 & -3 & 1 \end{array}\right] \xrightarrow{-\frac{1}{7}R_2} \left[\begin{array}{ccc|ccc} 1 & 2 & -4 & 0 & 1 & 0 \\ 0 & 1 & -\frac{12}{7} & -\frac{1}{7} & \frac{2}{7} & 0 \\ 0 & -7 & 14 & 0 & -3 & 1 \end{array}\right] \xrightarrow[R_3 + 7R_2]{R_1 - 2R_2}$$

$$\left[\begin{array}{ccc|ccc} 1 & 0 & -\frac{4}{7} & \frac{2}{7} & \frac{3}{7} & 0 \\ 0 & 1 & -\frac{12}{7} & -\frac{1}{7} & \frac{2}{7} & 0 \\ 0 & 0 & 2 & -1 & -1 & 1 \end{array}\right] \xrightarrow{\frac{1}{2}R_3} \left[\begin{array}{ccc|ccc} 1 & 0 & -\frac{4}{7} & \frac{2}{7} & \frac{3}{7} & 0 \\ 0 & 1 & -\frac{12}{7} & -\frac{1}{7} & \frac{2}{7} & 0 \\ 0 & 0 & 1 & -\frac{1}{2} & -\frac{1}{2} & \frac{1}{2} \end{array}\right] \xrightarrow[R_2 + \frac{12}{7}R_3]{R_1 + \frac{4}{7}R_3}$$

$$\left[\begin{array}{ccc|ccc} 1 & 0 & 0 & 0 & \frac{1}{7} & \frac{2}{7} \\ 0 & 1 & 0 & -1 & -\frac{4}{7} & \frac{6}{7} \\ 0 & 0 & 1 & -\frac{1}{2} & -\frac{1}{2} & \frac{1}{2} \end{array}\right].$$

Therefore,

$$X = A^{-1}C = \begin{bmatrix} 0 & \frac{1}{7} & \frac{2}{7} \\ -1 & -\frac{4}{7} & \frac{6}{7} \\ -\frac{1}{2} & -\frac{1}{2} & \frac{1}{2} \end{bmatrix} \begin{bmatrix} 17 \\ -7 \\ 14 \end{bmatrix} = \begin{bmatrix} 3 \\ -1 \\ 2 \end{bmatrix}$$

that is, x = 3, y = -1, and z = 2.

39. Put

$$X = \begin{bmatrix} x \\ y \\ z \end{bmatrix}, \quad A = \begin{bmatrix} 1 & -2 & 4 \\ 2 & 3 & -2 \\ 1 & 4 & -6 \end{bmatrix}, \quad C = \begin{bmatrix} 13 \\ 0 \\ -15 \end{bmatrix}.$$

Then AX = C and X = A$^{-1}$C. To find A$^{-1}$,

$$\begin{bmatrix} 1 & -2 & 4 & | & 1 & 0 & 0 \\ 2 & 3 & -2 & | & 0 & 1 & 0 \\ 1 & 4 & -6 & | & 0 & 0 & 1 \end{bmatrix} \xrightarrow[R_3\ -\ R_1]{R_2\ -2R_1} \begin{bmatrix} 1 & -2 & 4 & | & 1 & 0 & 0 \\ 0 & 7 & -10 & | & -2 & 1 & 0 \\ 0 & 6 & -10 & | & -1 & 0 & 1 \end{bmatrix} \xrightarrow{R_2\ -\ R_3}$$

$$\begin{bmatrix} 1 & -2 & 4 & | & 1 & 0 & 0 \\ 0 & 1 & 0 & | & -1 & 1 & -1 \\ 0 & 6 & -10 & | & -1 & 0 & 1 \end{bmatrix} \xrightarrow[R_3\ -\ 6R_2]{R_1\ +\ 2R_2} \begin{bmatrix} 1 & 0 & 4 & | & -1 & 2 & -2 \\ 0 & 1 & 0 & | & -1 & 1 & -1 \\ 0 & 0 & -10 & | & 5 & -6 & 7 \end{bmatrix} \xrightarrow{-\frac{1}{10}R_3}$$

$$\begin{bmatrix} 1 & 0 & 4 & | & -1 & 2 & -2 \\ 0 & 1 & 0 & | & -1 & 1 & -1 \\ 0 & 0 & 1 & | & -\frac{1}{2} & \frac{3}{5} & -\frac{7}{10} \end{bmatrix} \xrightarrow{R_1\ -\ 4R_3} \begin{bmatrix} 1 & 0 & 0 & | & 1 & -\frac{2}{5} & \frac{4}{5} \\ 0 & 1 & 0 & | & -1 & 1 & -1 \\ 0 & 0 & 1 & | & -\frac{1}{2} & \frac{3}{5} & -\frac{7}{10} \end{bmatrix}.$$

So A$^{-1}$ =
$$\begin{bmatrix} 1 & -\frac{2}{5} & \frac{4}{5} \\ -1 & 1 & -1 \\ -\frac{1}{2} & \frac{3}{5} & -\frac{7}{10} \end{bmatrix}.$$

Therefore,

$$X = A^{-1}C = \begin{bmatrix} 1 & -\frac{2}{5} & \frac{4}{5} \\ -1 & 1 & -1 \\ -\frac{1}{2} & \frac{3}{5} & -\frac{7}{10} \end{bmatrix} \begin{bmatrix} 13 \\ 0 \\ -15 \end{bmatrix} = \begin{bmatrix} 1 \\ 2 \\ 4 \end{bmatrix}$$

that is, x = 1, y = 2, and z = 4.

40.  Write Mr. Spaulding's holdings as the row vector

$$[10000 \quad 20000 \quad 30000].$$

His holdings initially are worth,

$$[10000 \quad 20000 \quad 30000] \begin{bmatrix} 20 \\ 30 \\ 50 \end{bmatrix} = 2,300,000$$

or $2,300,000. His holding 6 months later are worth

$$[10000 \quad 20000 \quad 30000] \begin{bmatrix} 22 \\ 35 \\ 51 \end{bmatrix} = 2,450,000$$

or $2,450,000, an increase of $150,000.

41.
$$\begin{bmatrix} x \\ y \\ z \end{bmatrix} = \begin{bmatrix} 600 & 1000 & 800 & 1400 \\ 700 & 800 & 600 & 1200 \\ 1200 & 800 & 1000 & 900 \end{bmatrix} \begin{bmatrix} 1.60 \\ 1.20 \\ 1.50 \\ 1.30 \end{bmatrix} = \begin{bmatrix} 5180 \\ 4540 \\ 5550 \end{bmatrix}.$$

The total revenue is $5180 at station A, $4540 at station B, and $5550 at station C.

42.  Suppose the amount at the Houston refinery is x gallons and the amount produced at the Tulsa refinery is y gallons. Then

$$0.6x + 0.3y = 240,000$$

$$0.4x + 0.7y = 460,000$$

or    $6x + 3y = 2,400,000$

$4x + 7y = 4,600,000.$

Write the system in matrix form, AX = B with

$$A = \begin{bmatrix} 6 & 3 \\ 4 & 7 \end{bmatrix} \quad X = \begin{bmatrix} x \\ y \end{bmatrix} \text{ and } B = \begin{bmatrix} 2,400,000 \\ 4,600,000 \end{bmatrix}$$

$$A^{-1} = \frac{1}{(6)(7) - (4)(3)} \begin{bmatrix} 7 & -3 \\ -4 & 6 \end{bmatrix} = \begin{bmatrix} \frac{7}{30} & -\frac{1}{10} \\ -\frac{2}{15} & \frac{1}{5} \end{bmatrix}.$$

$$\begin{bmatrix} x \\ y \end{bmatrix} = A^{-1}B = \begin{bmatrix} \frac{7}{30} & -\frac{1}{10} \\ -\frac{2}{15} & \frac{1}{5} \end{bmatrix} \begin{bmatrix} 2,400,000 \\ 4,600,000 \end{bmatrix} = \begin{bmatrix} 100,000 \\ 600,000 \end{bmatrix}.$$

So x = 100,000 and y = 600,000. Therefore, the Houston refinery produced 100,000 gallons and the Tulsa refinery produced 600,000 gallons.

43. We wish to solve the system of equations

$$2x + 2y + 3z = 210$$

$$2x + 3y + 4z = 270$$

$$3x + 4y + 3z = 300.$$

Using the Gauss-Jordan method of elimination, we find

$$\begin{bmatrix} 2 & 2 & 3 & | & 210 \\ 2 & 3 & 4 & | & 270 \\ 3 & 4 & 3 & | & 300 \end{bmatrix} \xrightarrow{\frac{1}{2}R_1} \begin{bmatrix} 1 & 1 & \frac{3}{2} & | & 105 \\ 2 & 3 & 4 & | & 270 \\ 3 & 4 & 3 & | & 300 \end{bmatrix} \xrightarrow[R_3 - 3R_1]{R_2 - 2R_1} \begin{bmatrix} 1 & 1 & \frac{3}{2} & | & 105 \\ 0 & 1 & 1 & | & 60 \\ 0 & 1 & -\frac{3}{2} & | & -15 \end{bmatrix}$$

$$\xrightarrow[R_3 - R_2]{R_1 - R_2}$$

$$\begin{bmatrix} 1 & 0 & \frac{1}{2} & | & 45 \\ 0 & 1 & 1 & | & 60 \\ 0 & 0 & -\frac{5}{2} & | & -75 \end{bmatrix} \xrightarrow{-\frac{2}{5}R_3} \begin{bmatrix} 1 & 0 & \frac{1}{2} & | & 45 \\ 0 & 1 & 1 & | & 60 \\ 0 & 0 & 1 & | & 30 \end{bmatrix} \xrightarrow[R_2 - R_3]{R_1 - \frac{1}{2}R_3} \begin{bmatrix} 1 & 0 & 0 & | & 30 \\ 0 & 1 & 0 & | & 30 \\ 0 & 0 & 1 & | & 30 \end{bmatrix}.$$

So x = y = z = 30 . Therefore, Desmond should produce 30 of each type of pendant.

## GROUP DISCUSSION QUESTIONS

**Page 73**

1.  The system has a unique solution if and only if all three lines
    intersect at a point. There are infinitely many solutions if all
    three lines coalesce. In all other cases, the system has no solution.
    The results are the same in the case of n lines defined by n
    equations.

**Page 75**

1.  No. Geometrically, you can verify that the two straight lines with
    the given linear equations intersect at exactly one point or they are
    coincident. Thus, a system comprising two linear equations can only
    have one solution or infinitely many solutions (or none).

2.  The system can have no solution, exactly *any* finite number of
    solutions, and infinitely many solutions. Some possibilities are
    illustrated below.

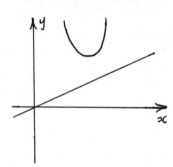

No solution

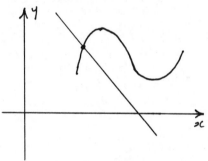

Exactly one solution

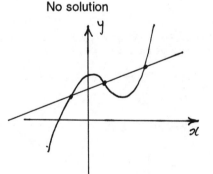

Exactly three solutions

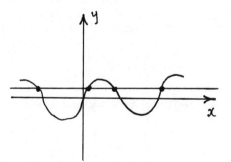

Infinitely many solutions

**Page 77**

1.  Here are some possibilities.

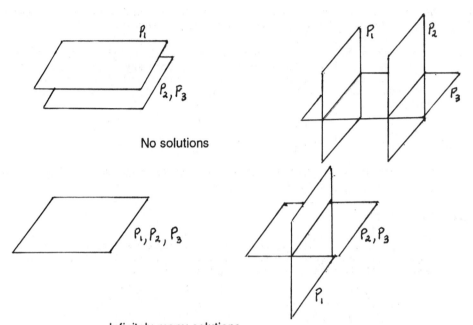

No solutions

Infinitely many solutions

**Page 91**

1.  No. Consider the system

$$2x - y = 1$$
$$3x + 2y = 12 \ .$$

It was shown that this system has the unique solution (2,3). (See page 73.) The augmented matrix for this system is

$$\begin{bmatrix} 2 & -1 & | & 1 \\ 3 & 2 & | & 12 \end{bmatrix} \ .$$

If we replace the second row of the augmented matrix by zero times itself, we obtain

$$\begin{bmatrix} 2 & -1 & | & 1 \\ 0 & 0 & | & 0 \end{bmatrix} \xrightarrow{\frac{1}{2}R_1} \begin{bmatrix} 1 & -\frac{1}{2} & | & \frac{1}{2} \\ 0 & 0 & | & 0 \end{bmatrix}$$

and the last augmented matrix tells us that there are infinitely many solutions of the form $(\frac{1}{2} + \frac{1}{2}t, t)$, where t is a parameter.

2. No. Consider the system of 1. Suppose we add 1 to each element in the first row of the augmented matrix, we obtain

$$\begin{bmatrix} 3 & 0 & | & 2 \\ 3 & 2 & | & 12 \end{bmatrix} \xrightarrow{\frac{1}{3}R_1} \begin{bmatrix} 1 & 0 & | & \frac{2}{3} \\ 3 & 2 & | & 12 \end{bmatrix} \xrightarrow{R_2 - 3R_1}$$

$$\begin{bmatrix} 1 & 0 & | & \frac{2}{3} \\ 0 & 2 & | & 10 \end{bmatrix} \xrightarrow{\frac{1}{2}R_2} \begin{bmatrix} 1 & 0 & | & \frac{2}{3} \\ 0 & 1 & | & 5 \end{bmatrix}$$

and the solution here is $(\frac{2}{3}, 5)$. Of course, the solution of the original system is $(2, 3)$!

**Page 103**

1. Suppose there are three linear equations in the system. These equations represent three lines $L_1$, $L_2$, and $L_3$ in the plane. The results of Theorem 1a are illustrated below.

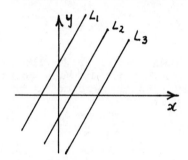

No solution

Exactly one solution

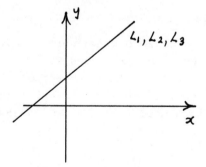

Infinitely many solutions

Next, suppose there are four linear equations in the system, and suppose the equations represent the straight lines $L_1$, $L_2$, $L_3$, and $L_4$. The results of Theorem 1a are illustrated below.

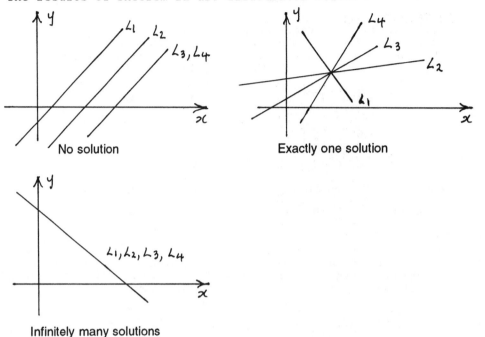

No solution

Exactly one solution

Infinitely many solutions

Finally, suppose there is only one linear equation in the system. Then according to Theorem 1b, there are infinitely many solutions. In this case, the infinitely many solutions correspond to the infinitely many points lying on the line.

## Page 141

1.  Both A and $A^{-1}$ must be square so that the products $A^{-1}A$ and $AA^{-1}$ are defined.

## Page 145

1.  If one row in the square matrix A is a nonzero constant multiple of another row, then $A^{-1}$ does not exist. For, in this case, we can obtain an equivalent augmented matrix in which a row to the left of the augmented matrix contains all zeros and, using the criterion on page 145, we conclude that the matrix A does not have an inverse.

# CHAPTER 3

## EXERCISES 3.1, page 180

1. $4x - 8 < 0$ implies $x < 2$. The graph of the inequality follows.

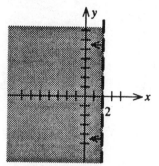

2. $3y + 2 > 0$ implies $y > -2/3$. The graph of the inequality follows.

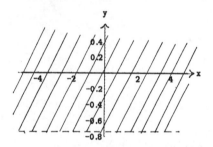

3. $x - y \leq 0$ implies $x \leq y$. The graph of the inequality follows.

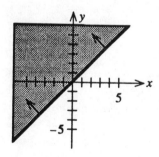

4. We first sketch the straight line with equation $3x + 4y = -2$. Next, picking $(0,0)$ as the test point, we see that

$$3(0) + 4(0) = 0 \not\leq -2.$$

Therefore, the half-plane not containing the origin is the required half-plane. The graph of the inequality follows.

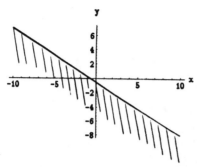

5.  The graph of the inequality x ≤ -3 is shown below.

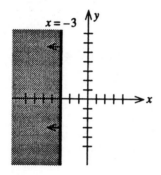

6.  The graph of the inequality y ≥ -1 is shown below.

7. We first sketch the straight line with equation 2x + y = 4. Next, picking the test point (0,0), we have 2(0) + (0) = 0 < 4. We conclude that the half-plane containing the origin is the required half-plane.

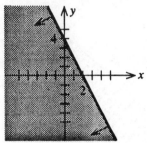

8. We first sketch the straight line with equation −3x + 6y = 12. Next, picking the test point (0,0), we see that −3(0) + 6(0) = 0 ≯ 12. Therefore, the half-plane not containing the origin is the required half-plane. The graph of this inequality follows.

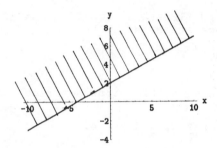

9. We first sketch the graph of the straight line 4x − 3y = −24. Next, picking the test point (0,0), we see that

$$4(0) - 3(0) = 0 \nless -24.$$

We conclude that the half-plane not containing the origin is the required half-plane. The graph of this inequality follows.

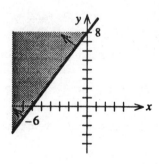

10. We first sketch the graph of the straight line $5x - 3y = 15$. Next, we pick the test point $(0,0)$. Since $5(0) - 3(0) = 0 \not> 15$, we conclude that the half-plane not containing the origin is the required half-plane.

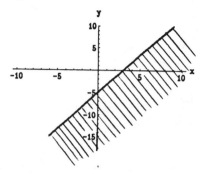

11. The system of linear inequalities that describes the shaded region is

$$x \geq 1, \ x \leq 5, \ y \geq 2, \text{ and } y \leq 4.$$

We may also combine the first and second inequalities and the third and fourth inequalities and write

$$1 \leq x \leq 5 \quad \text{and} \quad 2 \leq y \leq 4.$$

12. The system of linear inequalities that describes the shaded region is

$$x + y \geq 3, \ y - x \geq 0, \text{ and } y \leq 4.$$

13. The system of linear inequalities that describes the shaded region is

$$2x - y \geq 2, \ 5x + 7y \geq 35, \text{ and } x \leq 4.$$

14. The system of linear inequalities that describes the shaded region is

$$5x + 2y \leq 20, \ x + 2y \leq 8, \ x \geq 0, \text{ and } y \geq 0.$$

15. The system of linear inequalities that describes the shaded region is

$$7x + 4y \leq 140, \ x + 3y \geq 30, \text{ and } x - y \geq -10.$$

16. The system of linear inequalities that describes the shaded region is

$$x + y \geq 2, \ 9x + 5y \leq 90, \ 3x + 5y \leq 60, \ x \geq 0, \text{ and } y \geq 0.$$

17. The system of linear inequalities that describes the shaded region is

$$x + y \geq 7, \; x \geq 2, \; y \geq 3, \; \text{and} \; y \leq 7.$$

18. The system of linear inequalities that describes the shaded region is

$$5x + 4y \geq 40, \; x + 5y \geq 20, \; \text{and} \; 4x + y \geq 16, \; x \geq 0, \; \text{and} \; y \geq 0.$$

19. The required solution set is shown in the following figure.

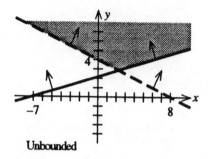

To find the coordinates of A, we solve the system

$$2x + 4y = 16$$

$$-x + 3y = \;\;\; 7,$$

giving A = (2,3). Observe that a dotted line is used to show that no point on the line constitutes a solution to the given problem. Observe that this is an unbounded solution set.

20. The required solution set is shown in the following figure.

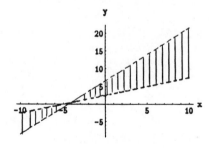

To find the coordinates of A, we solve

$$3x - 2y = -13$$

$$-x + 2y = \;\;\; 5$$

giving A = $(-4, \frac{1}{2})$. Observe that the dotted lines are shown in the figure to indicate that no point on the line constitutes a solution to the problem. Also observe that the solution set is unbounded.

21. The solution set is shown in the following figure. Observe that the set is unbounded.

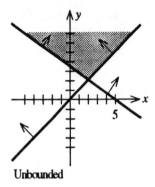

Unbounded

To find the coordinates of A, we solve the system

$$x - y = 0$$

and     $2x + 3y = 10,$

giving A = (2,2). Observe that this is an unbounded solution set.

22. The solution set is shown in the following figure. Observe that the set is unbounded.

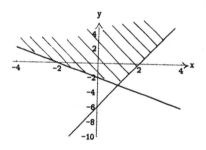

To find the coordinates of A, we solve the system

$$x + y = -2$$

and     $3x - y = 6,$

giving A = (1,-3).

23. The half-planes defined by the two inequalities are shown in the following figure.

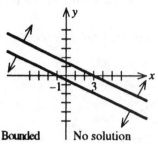

**Bounded** | No solution

Since the two half-planes have no points in common, we conclude that the given system of inequalities has no solution. (The empty set is a bounded set.)

24. The half-planes defined by the two inequalities are shown in the following figure.

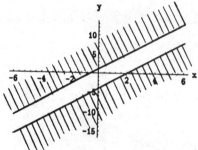

Since the two half-planes have no points in common, we conclude that the given system of inequalities has no solution, The (empty) set is bounded.

25. The half-planes defined by the three inequalities are shown in the following figure.

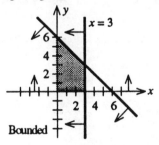

The point A is found by solving the system

$$x + y = 6$$
$$x = 3,$$

giving A = (3,3). Observe that this is a bounded solution set.

26. The half-planes defined by the given inequalities are shown in the following figure.

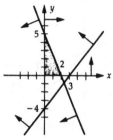

   The coordinates of A are found by solving the system

   $$4x - 3y = 12$$
   $$5x + 2y = 10,$$

   giving A = $(\frac{54}{23}, -\frac{20}{23})$. The solution set is bounded.

27. The half-planes defined by the given inequalities are shown in the following figure.

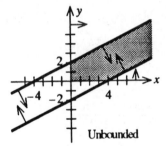

Unbounded

   Observe that the two lines described by the equations $3x - 6y = 12$ and $-x + 2y = 4$ do not intersect because they are parallel. The solution set is unbounded.

28. The half-planes defined by the given inequalities are shown in the following figure.

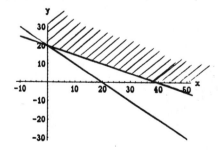

The vertex A(0,20) is found by solving the system

$$x + 2y = 40$$

$$x + y = 20$$

The solution set is unbounded.

29. The required solution set is shown in the following figure.

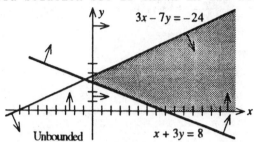

The coordinates A are found by solving the system

$$3x - 7y = -24$$

and     $x + 3y = 8,$

giving (-1,3). The solution set is unbounded.

30. The required solution set is shown in the following figure.

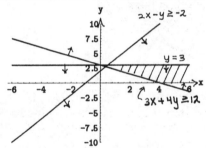

The coordinates of A are $(\frac{4}{11},\frac{30}{11})$. The solution set is unbounded.

31. The required solution set is shown in the following figure.

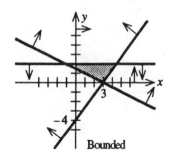

The solution set is bounded.

32. The required solution set is shown in the following figure.

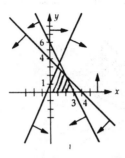

The corners of this solution set are (0,0), (0,1), (1,3), (2,2), and (3,0). The solution set is bounded.

33. The required solution set is shown in the following figure.

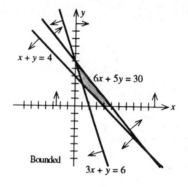

The solution set has vertices at (0,6), (5,0), (4,0), and (1,3). The solution set is bounded.

34. The required solution set is shown in the following figure.

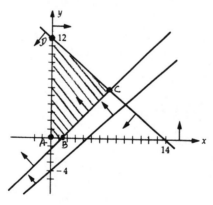

The bounded solution set has vertices at (0,0), (0,12), (7,6) and (1.5, 0).

35.  The required solution set is shown in the following figure.

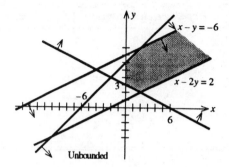

The unbounded solution set has vertices at (2,8), (0,6), (0,3), and (2,2).

36.  The required solution set is shown in the following figure.

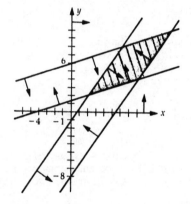

The bounded solution set has vertices at (2,2), (8,4), (12,10), and (6,8).

1. We tabulate the given information

|  | Product A | Product B | Time available |
|---|---|---|---|
| Machine I | 6 | 9 | 300 |
| Machine II | 5 | 4 | 180 |
| Profit per unit ($) | 3 | 4 | |

Let x and y denote the number of units of Product A and Product B to be produced. Then the required linear programming problem is:

Maximize the objective function

$$P = 3x + 4y$$

subject to the constraints

$$6x + 9y \le 300$$

$$5x + 4y \le 180$$

$$x \ge 0, \ y \ge 0$$

2. Let x denote the number of model A hibachis to be produced and y denote the number of model B hibachis to be produced. Since only 1000 pounds of cast iron are available, we must have

$$3x + 4y \le 1000.$$

The restriction that only 20 hours of labor are available per day implies that

$$6x + 3y \le 1200. \quad \text{(time in minutes)}$$

Then the profit on the production of these hibachis is given by

$$P = 2x + 1.5y.$$

Summarizing, we have the following linear programming problem:

Maximize P = 2x + 1.5y subject to

$$3x + 4y \leq 1000$$

$$6x + 3y \leq 1200$$

$$x \geq 0, \ y \geq 0.$$

3.  Let x denote the number of model A hibachis to be produced and y denote the number of model B hibachis to be produced. Since only 1000 pounds of cast iron are available, we must have

$$3x + 4y \leq 1000.$$

The restriction that only 20 hours of labor are available per day implies that

$$6x + 3y \leq 1200. \qquad \text{(time in minutes)}$$

Then the profit on the production of these hibachis is given by

$$P = 2x + 1.5y.$$

The additional restriction that at least 150 model A hibachis be produced each day implies that

$$x \geq 150.$$

Summarizing, we have the following linear programming problem:

Maximize P = 2x + 1.5y subject to

$$3x + 4y \leq 1000$$

$$6x + 3y \leq 1200$$

and $\qquad x \geq 150, \ y \geq 0.$

4.  Suppose the company extends x million dollars in homeowner loans and y million dollars in automobile loans. Then, the returns on these loans are given by P = 0.1x + 0.12y million dollars. Since the company has a total of $20 million for these loans, we have x + y ≤ 20. Furthermore, since the total amount of homeowner loans should be greater than or equal to four times the total amount of automobile loans, we have x ≥ 4y. Therefore, the required linear programming problem is

Maximize P = 0.1x + 0.12y subject to

$$x + y \leq 20$$

$$x - 4y \geq 0$$

$$x \geq 0, \ y \geq 0.$$

5.  Let x and y denote the amount of food A and food B, respectively, used to prepare a meal. Then the requirement that the meal contain a minimum of 400 mg of calcium implies

$$30x + 25y \geq 400.$$

Similarly, the requirements that the meal contain at least 10 mg of iron and 40 mg of vitamin C imply that

$$x + 0.5y \geq 10$$

$$2x + 5y \geq 40.$$

The cholesterol content is given by

$$C = 2x + 5y.$$

Therefore, the linear programming problem is

Minimize $C = 2x + 5y$ subject to

$$30x + 25y \geq 400$$

$$x + 0.5y \geq 10$$

$$2x + 5y \geq 40$$

$$x \geq 0, \ y \geq 0.$$

6.  Let x denote the number of acres of crop A that will be planted and y the number of acres of crop B that will be planted. Since there are a total of 150 acres of land available, $x + y \leq 150$. Then the restriction on the amount of money available for land cultivation implies $40x + 60y \leq 7400$. Similarly, the restriction regarding the amount of time available for labor implies that $20x + 25y \leq 3300$. Since the profit on crop A is $150 per acre and the profit on crop B is $200 per acre, we have $P = 150x + 200y$.

Summarizing, we have the following linear programming problem:

Maximize $P = 150x + 200y$ subject to

$$x + y \leq 150$$

$$40x + 60y \leq 7400$$

$$20x + 25y \leq 3300$$

$$x \geq 0, \ y \geq 0.$$

7.  Let x denote the number of picture tubes shipped from location I to city A and let y denote the number of picture tubes shipped from location I to city B. Since the number of picture tubes

required by the two factories in city A and city B are 3000 and 4000, respectively, the number of picture tubes shipped from location II to city A and city B, are (3000 − x) and (4000 − y), respectively. These numbers are shown in the following schematic,

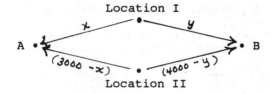

Location I

A

B

Location II

Referring to the schematic and the shipping schedule, we find that the total shipping costs incurred by the company are given by

$$C = 3x + 2y + 4(3000 - x) + 5(4000 - y)$$

$$= 32000 - x - 3y.$$

The production constraints on location I and II lead to the inequalities

$$x + y \leq 6000$$

$$(3000 - x) + (4000 - y) \leq 5000.$$

This last inequality simplifies to

$$x + y \geq 2000.$$

The requirements of the two factories lead to the inequalities

$$x \geq 0, \; y \geq 0, \; 3000 - x \geq 0, \; \text{and} \; 4000 - y \geq 0.$$

These last two inequalities may be written as

$$x \leq 3000 \quad \text{and} \quad y \leq 4000.$$

Summarizing, we have the following linear programming problem:

Minimize $C = 32,000 - x - 3y$ subject to

$$x + y \leq 6000$$

$$x + y \geq 2000$$

$$x \leq 3000$$

$$y \leq 4000$$

$$x \geq 0, \; y \geq 0.$$

8.   Let x and y denote the amount of money given in aid to country A

and country B, respectively. Then the requirement that country A receives between $1 and $1.5 million, inclusive, in aid, implies

$$1 \leq x \leq 2.5.$$

Similarly, the requirement that country B receive at least $0.75 million in aid implies

$$y \geq 0.75.$$

The condition that between $2 and $2.5 million dollars in aid has been earmarked for these two countries implies that

$$x + y \leq 2.5$$

and $\qquad x + y \geq 2.$

Therefore, we have the following linear programming problem:

Maximize $P = 0.6x + 0.8y$ subject to

$$x + y \leq 2.5$$

$$x + y \geq 2$$

$$1 \leq x \leq 1.5$$

$$y \geq 0.75.$$

9. Let $x$, $y$, and $z$ denote the number of units produced of products A, B, and C, respectively. From the given information, we formulate the following linear programming problem:

Maximize $P = 18x + 12y + 15z$ subject to

$$2x + \phantom{2}y + 2z \leq 900$$

$$3x + \phantom{2}y + 2z \leq 1080$$

$$2x + 2y + \phantom{2}z \leq 840$$

$$x \geq 0, \ y \geq 0, \ z \geq 0.$$

10. Let $x$ denote the number of minutes of morning television advertising time, $y$ denote the number of minutes of afternoon advertising time, and $z$ denote the number of minutes of evening advertising time that Excelsior should buy. Then the budget restrictions imply that

$$3000x + 1000y + 12{,}000z \leq 102{,}000.$$

Next, the restrictions regarding the availability of time at Station KAOS imply that

$$x + y + z \leq 25 \text{ and } z \leq 6.$$

The data regarding the exposure of these commercials imply that the function we wish to maximize is

$$P = 200{,}000x + 100{,}000y + 600{,}000z.$$

Summarizing, we have the following linear programming problem:

Maximize $P = 200{,}000x + 100{,}000y + 600{,}000z$ subject to

$$3000x + 1000y + 12{,}000z \leq 102{,}000$$

$$x + y + z \leq 25$$

$$z \leq 6$$

$$x \geq 0, \ y \geq 0, \text{ and } z \geq 0.$$

11. We first tabulate the given information:

**MODELS**

| Dept. | A | B | C | Time available |
|-------|-----|-----|-----|----------------|
| Fabrication | $\frac{5}{4}$ | $\frac{3}{2}$ | $\frac{3}{2}$ | 310 |
| Assembly | 1 | 1 | $\frac{3}{4}$ | 205 |
| Finishing | 1 | 1 | $\frac{1}{2}$ | 190 |

Let $x$, $y$, and $z$ denote the number of units of model A, model B, and model C to be produced, respectively. Then the required linear programming problem is

Maximize $P = 26x + 28y + 24z$ subject to

$$\frac{5}{4}x + \frac{3}{2}y + \frac{3}{2}z \leq 310$$

$$x + y + \frac{3}{4}z \leq 205$$

$$x + y + \frac{1}{2}z \leq 190$$

$$x \geq 0, \ y \geq 0, \ z \geq 0.$$

12. The shipping costs per loudspeaker system in dollars are given in the following table.

| | Warehouse | | |
| | A | B | C |
|---|---|---|---|
| Plant I | 16 | 20 | 22 |
| Plant II | 18 | 16 | 14 |

Letting $x_1$ denote the number of loudspeaker systems shipped from plant I to warehouse A, $x_2$ the number of loudspeaker systems shipped from plant I to warehouse B, and so on we have

| | Warehouse | | | Max. Production |
| | A | B | C | |
|---|---|---|---|---|
| Plant I | $x_1$ | $x_2$ | $x_3$ | 800 |
| Plant II | $x_4$ | $x_5$ | $x_6$ | 600 |
| Min. Req. | 500 | 400 | 400 | |

From the two tables we see that the total monthly shipping cost incurred by Acrosonic is given by

$$C = 16x_1 + 20x_2 + 22x_3 + 18x_4 + 16x_5 + 14x_6.$$

Next, the production constraints on plants I and II lead to the inequalities

$$x_1 + x_2 + x_3 \leq 800$$

$$x_4 + x_5 + x_6 \leq 600.$$

Also, the minimum requirements of each warehouse leads to the three inequalities

$$x_1 + x_4 \geq 500$$

$$x_2 + x_5 \geq 400$$

$$x_3 + x_6 \geq 400.$$

Summarizing we have the following linear programming problem:

Minimize $C = 16x_1 + 20x_2 + 22x_3 + 18x_4 + 16x_5 + 14x_6$

subject to

$$x_1 + x_2 + x_3 \leq 800$$

$$x_4 + x_5 + x_6 \leq 600.$$

$$x_1 + x_4 \geq 500$$

$$x_2 + x_5 \geq 400$$

$$x_3 + x_6 \geq 400.$$

$$x_1 \geq 0, \ x_2 \geq 0, \ \ldots, \ x_6 \geq 0.$$

13. The shipping costs are tabulated in the following table.

|  | Warehouse A | Warehouse B | Warehouse C |
|---|---|---|---|
| Plant I | 60 | 60 | 80 |
| Plant II | 80 | 70 | 50 |

Letting $x_1$ denote the number of pianos shipped from plant I to warehouse A, $x_2$ the number of pianos shipped from plant I to warehouse B, and so we have

| | Warehouse | | | Max. Production |
|---|---|---|---|---|
| | A | B | C | |
| Plant I | $x_1$ | $x_2$ | $x_3$ | 300 |
| Plant II | $x_4$ | $x_5$ | $x_6$ | 250 |
| Min. Req. | 200 | 150 | 200 | |

From the two tables we see that the total monthly shipping cost is given by

$$C = 60x_1 + 60x_2 + 80x_3 + 80x_4 + 70x_5 + 50x_6.$$

Next, the production constraints on plants I and II lead to the inequalities

$$x_1 + x_4 \geq 200$$

$$x_2 + x_5 \geq 150$$

$$x_3 + x_6 \geq 200.$$

Summarizing we have the following linear programming problem:

Minimize $C = 60x_1 + 60x_2 + 80x_3 + 80x_4 + 70x_5 + 50x_6$

subject to

$$x_1 + x_2 + x_3 \leq 300$$

$$x_4 + x_5 + x_6 \leq 250.$$

$$x_1 + x_4 \geq 200$$

$$x_2 + x_5 \geq 150$$

$$x_3 + x_6 \geq 200.$$

$$x_1 \geq 0, \ x_2 \geq 0, \ \ldots, \ x_6 \geq 0.$$

14. Let x, y, and z denote the number of standard, deluxe, and luxury models to be completed. Then, the required linear programming problem is

Maximize $P = 3400x + 4000y + 5000z$ subject to

$$6x + 8y + 10z \leq 8200$$

$$24x + 22y + 20z \leq 21800$$

$$18x + 21y + 30z \leq 23700$$

$$x \geq 0, \ y \geq 0, \ z \geq 0.$$

(Note that we have divided the first inequality by 1000 and the second and third inequalities by 10 in order to simplify our work later on.)

15. Let x, y, and z denote the number (in thousands) of bottles of formula I, formula II, and formula III, respectively, produced. Then the profit function to be maximized is

$$P = 180x + 200y + 300z.$$

Next, the limitation on time implies that

$$2.5x + 3y + 4z \leq 70.$$

Similarly, the restrictions on the amount of ingredients available imply that

$$x \leq 9, \ y \leq 12 \text{ and } z \leq 6.$$

Summarizing, we have the following linear programming problem:

Maximize $P = 180x + 200y + 300z$ subject to

$$\frac{5}{2}x + 3y + 4z \leq 70$$
$$x \leq 9$$
$$y \leq 12$$
$$z \leq 6$$

$$x \geq 0, \ y \geq 0, \text{ and } z \geq 0.$$

## EXERCISES 3.3, page 201

1.  Evaluating the objective function at each of the corner points we obtain the following table.

| Vertex | Z = 2x + 3y |
|--------|-------------|
| (1,1)  | 5           |
| (8,5)  | 31          |
| (4,9)  | 35          |
| (2,8)  | 28          |

From the table, we conclude that the maximum value of Z is 35 and it occurs at the vertex (4,9). The minimum value of Z is 5 and it occurs at the vertex (1,1).

2.  Evaluating the objective function at each of the corner points we obtain the following table.

| Vertex  | Z = 3x - y |
|---------|------------|
| (2,2)   | 4          |
| (10,1)  | 29         |
| (7,9)   | 12         |
| (2,6)   | 0          |

From the table, we conclude that the maximum value of Z is 29 and it occurs at the vertex (10,1). The minimum value of Z is 0 and it occurs at the vertex (2,6).

3.   Evaluating the objective function at each of the corner points we obtain the following table.

| Vertex | Z = 3x + 4y |
|--------|-------------|
| (0,20) | 80 |
| (3,10) | 49 |
| (4,6)  | 36 |
| (9,0)  | 27 |

From the graph, we conclude that there is no maximum value since Z is unbounded. The minimum value of Z is 27 and it occurs at the vertex (9,0).

4.   Evaluating the objective function at each of the corner points we obtain the following table.

| Vertex | Z = 7x + 9y |
|--------|-------------|
| (0,7)  | 63 |
| (1,5)  | 52 |
| (4,2)  | 46 |
| (8,0)  | 56 |

From the graph, we conclude that there is no maximum value since Z is unbounded. The minimum value of Z is 46 and it occurs at the vertex (4,2).

5.   Evaluating the objective function at each of the corner points we obtain the following table.

| Vertex | Z = x + 4y |
|--------|------------|
| (0,6)  | 24 |
| (4,10) | 44 |
| (12,8) | 44 |
| (15,0) | 15 |

From the table, we conclude that the maximum value of Z is 44 and it occurs at every point on the line segment joining the points (4,10) and (12,8). The minimum value of Z is 15 and it occurs at the vertex (15,0).

6. Evaluating the objective function at each of the corner points we obtain the following table.

| Vertex | Z = 3x + 2y |
|--------|-------------|
| (1,4)  | 11 |
| (3,1)  | 11 |
| (5,4)  | 23 |
| (3,6)  | 21 |

From the table, we conclude that the maximum value of Z is 23 and it occurs at the vertex (5,4). The minimum value of Z is 11 and it occurs at every point on the line segment joining the points (1,4) and (3,1).

7. The problem is to maximize P = 2x + 3y subject to

$$x + y \le 6$$

$$x \le 3$$

$$x \ge 0, \ y \ge 0.$$

The feasible set S for the problem is shown in the following figure, and the values of the function P at the vertices of S are summarized in the accompanying table.

| Vertex | P = 2x + 3y |
|--------|-------------|
| A(0,0) | 0 |
| B(3,0) | 6 |
| C(3,3) | 15 |
| D(0,6) | 18 |

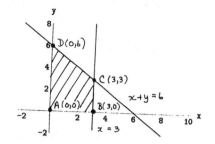

We conclude that P attains a maximum
value of 18 when x = 0 and y = 6.


8.   The problem is to maximize P = 3x − 4y subject to

$$x + 3y \le 15$$

$$4x + y \le 16$$

$$x \ge 0, \ y \ge 0.$$

The feasible set S for the problem is shown in the following
figure, and the values of the function P at the vertices of S are
summarized in the accompanying table.

| Vertex | P = 3x − 4y |
|--------|-------------|
| A(0,0) | 0 |
| B(4,0) | 12 |
| C(3,4) | −7 |
| D(0,5) | −20 |

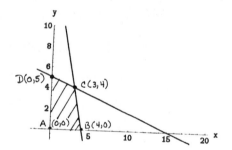

We conclude that P attains a maximum value
of 12 when x = 4 and y = 0.


9.   The problem is to minimize C = 2x + 10y subject to

$$5x + 2y \ge 40$$

$$x + 2y \ge 20$$

$$y \ge 3, \ x \ge 0.$$

The feasible set S for the problem is shown in the following figure and the values of the function C at the vertices of S are summarized in the accompanying table.

| Vertex | C = 2x + 10y |
|--------|--------------|
| A(0,20) | 200 |
| B(5,$\frac{15}{2}$) | 85 |
| C(14,3) | 58 |

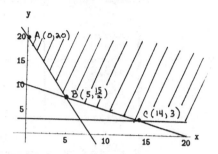

We conclude that C attains a minimum value of 58 when x = 14 and y = 3.

10. The problem is to minimize C = 2x + 5y subject to

$$4x + y \geq 40$$

$$2x + y \geq 30$$

$$x + 3y \geq 30$$

$$x \geq 0, \; y \geq 0.$$

The feasible set S is shown in the following figure, and the values of C at each of the vertices of S are shown in the accompanying table.

| Vertex | C = 2x + 5y |
|--------|-------------|
| A(0,40) | 200 |
| B(5,20) | 110 |
| C(12,6) | 54 |
| D(30,0) | 60 |

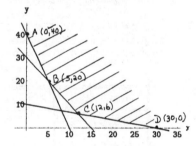

We conclude that C attains a minimum value of 54 when x = 12 and y = 6.

11. The problem is to minimize C = 6x + 3y subject to

$$4x + y \geq 40$$

$$2x + y \geq 30$$

$$x + 3y \geq 30$$

$$x \geq 0, \; y \geq 0.$$

The feasible set S is shown in the following figure, and the values of C at each of the vertices of S are shown in the accompanying table.

| Vertex | C = 6x + 3y |
|--------|-------------|
| A(0,40) | 120 |
| B(5,20) | 90 |
| C(12,6) | 90 |
| D(30,0) | 180 |

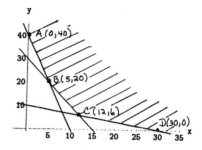

We conclude that C attains a minimum value of 90 at any point (x,y) lying on the line segment joining (5,20) to (12,6).

12. The problem is to maximize P = 2x + 5y subject to

$$2x + y \le 16$$

$$2x + 3y \le 24$$

$$y \le 6$$

$$x \ge 0, \ y \ge 0.$$

The feasible set S for the problem is shown in the following figure, and the values of the function P at the vertices of S are summarized in the accompanying table.

| Vertex | P = 2x + 5y |
|--------|-------------|
| A(0,0) | 0 |
| B(8,0) | 16 |
| C(6,4) | 32 |
| D(3,6) | 36 |
| E(0,6) | 30 |

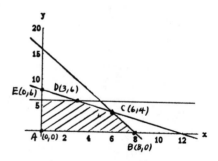

We conclude that P attains a maximum value of 36 when x = 3 and y = 6.

13. The problem is to minimize C = 10x + 15y subject to

$$x + y \leq 10$$

$$3x + y \geq 12$$

$$-2x + 3y \geq 3$$

$$x \geq 0, \; y \geq 0.$$

The feasible set is shown in the following figure, and the values of C at each of the vertices of S are shown in the accompanying table.

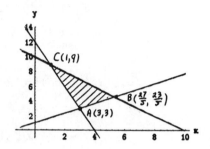

| Vertex | C = 10x + 15y |
|--------|---------------|
| A(3,3) | 75 |
| B($\frac{27}{5}$,$\frac{23}{5}$) | 123 |
| C(1,9) | 145 |

We conclude that C attains a minimum value of 75 when x = 3 and y = 3.

14. The problem is to maximize P = 2x + 5y subject to the constraints of Exercise 13. Since the graph of the feasible set S has already been sketched (see Exercise 13), we need only compute the value of P at each of the vertices of the feasible set S. Thus,

| Vertex | P = 2x + 5y |
|--------|-------------|
| A(3,3) | 21 |
| B($\frac{27}{5}$,$\frac{23}{5}$) | 33.8 |
| C(1,9) | 47 |

We conclude that P attains a maximum value of 47 when x = 1 and y = 9.

15. The problem is to maximize P = 3x + 4y subject to

$$x + 2y \leq 50$$

$$5x + 4y \leq 145$$

$$2x + y \geq 25$$

$$y \geq 5, \; x \geq 0.$$

The feasible set S is shown in the following figure, and the values of P at each of the vertices of S are shown in the accompanying table.

| Vertex | C = 3x + 4y |
|--------|-------------|
| A(10,5) | 50 |
| B(25,5) | 95 |
| C(15,$\frac{35}{2}$) | 115 |
| D(0,25) | 100 |

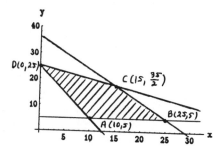

We conclude that P attains a maximum value of 115 when x = 15 and y = 35/2.

16.  The problem is to maximize P = 4x − 3y subject to

$$x + 2y \leq 50$$

$$5x + 4y \leq 145$$

$$2x + y \geq 25$$

$$y \geq 5, \quad x \geq 0.$$

The feasible set S is shown in the following figure, and the values of P at each of the vertices of S are shown in the accompanying table.

| Vertex | C = 4x − 3y |
|--------|-------------|
| A(10,5) | 25 |
| B(25,5) | 85 |
| C(15,$\frac{35}{2}$) | $\frac{15}{2}$ |
| D(0,25) | −75 |

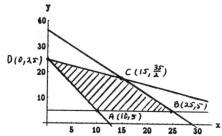

We conclude that P attains a maximum value of 85 when x = 25 and y = 5.

17.  The problem is to maximize P = 2x + 3y subject to

$$x + y \leq 48$$

$$x + 3y \geq 60$$

$$9x + 5y \leq 320$$

$$x \geq 10, \quad y \geq 0.$$

The feasible set S is shown in the figure that follows, and the values of P at each of the vertices of S are shown in the accompanying table.

| Vertex | C = 2x + 3y |
|--------|-------------|
| $A(10, \frac{50}{3})$ | 70 |
| B(30,10) | 90 |
| C(20,28) | 124 |
| D(10,38) | 134 |

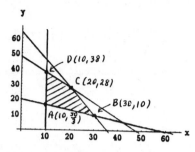

We conclude that P attains a maximum value of 134 when x = 10 and y = 38.

18. The problem is to minimize C = 5x + 3y subject to the constraints of Exercise 17. The feasible set is below. The table of values for the objective function follows.

| Vertex | C = 5x + 3y |
|--------|-------------|
| $A(10, \frac{50}{3})$ | 100 |
| B(30,10) | 180 |
| C(20,28) | 184 |
| D(10,38) | 164 |

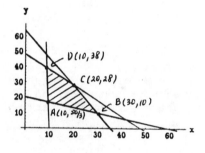

We conclude that P attains a minimum value of 100 when x = 10 and y = 50/3.

19. The problem is to find the maximum and minimum value of P = 10x + 12y subject to

$$5x + 2y \geq 63$$

$$x + y \geq 18$$

$$3x + 2y \leq 51$$

$$x \geq 0, \ y \geq 0.$$

The feasible set is shown on the next page and the value of P at each of the vertices of S are shown in the accompanying table.

| Vertex | P = 10x + 12y |
|--------|---------------|
| A(9,9) | 198 |
| B(15,3) | 186 |
| C(6,$\frac{33}{2}$) | 258 |

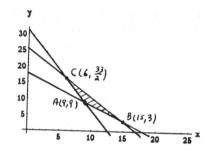

P attains a maximum value of 258 when x = 6
and y = 33/2. The minimum value of P is 186.
It is attained when x = 15 and y = 3.

20. The problem is to find the maximum and minimum value of
P = 4x + 3y subject to

$$3x + 5y \geq 20$$

$$3x + y \leq 16$$

$$-2x + y \leq 1$$

$$x \geq 0, \ y \geq 0.$$

The feasible set is shown in the following
figure at the right and the value of P
at each of the vertices of S are shown
in the accompanying table.

| Vertex | P = 4x + 3y |
|--------|-------------|
| A($\frac{15}{13},\frac{43}{13}$) | $14\frac{7}{13}$ |
| B(5,1) | 23 |
| C(3,7) | 33 |

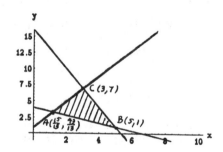

P attains a maximum value of 33 when x = 3
and y = 7. The minimum value of P is $14\frac{7}{13}$.
It is attained when x = 15/13 and y = 43/13.

21. The problem is to find the maximum and minimum value of P = 2x + 4y subject to

$$x + y \leq 20$$

$$-x + y \leq 10$$

$$x \leq 10$$

$$x + y \geq 5$$

$$y \geq 5, \ x \geq 0.$$

The feasible set is shown in the figure at the right, and the value of P at each of the vertices of S are shown in the following table.

| Vertex | P = 2x + 4y |
|--------|-------------|
| A(0,5) | 20 |
| B(10,5) | 40 |
| C(10,10) | 60 |
| D(5,15) | 70 |
| E(0,10) | 40 |

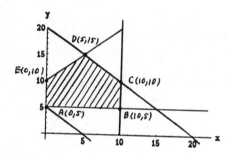

P attains a maximum value of 70 when x = 5 and y = 15. The minimum value of P is 20. It is attained when x = 0 and y = 5.

22. Refer to the solution of Exercise 1, Section 3.2, The problem is

Maximize P = 3x + 4y subject to

$$6x + 9y \leq 300$$

$$5x + 4y \leq 180$$

$$x \geq 0, \ y \geq 0.$$

The graph of the feasible set S and the associated table of values of P follow.

| Vertex | C = 3x + 4y |
|--------|-------------|
| A(0,0) | 0 |
| B(36,0) | 108 |
| C(20,20) | 140 |
| D(0,$\frac{100}{3}$) | $133\frac{1}{3}$ |

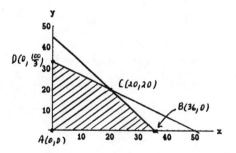

P attains a maximum value of 140 when x = y = 20.
Thus, by producing 20 units of each product in each
shift, the company will realize an optimal profit
of $140.

23. Let x and y denote the number of model A and model B fax machines
produced in each shift. Then the restriction on manufacturing
costs implies

$$200x + 300y \leq 600,000,$$

and the limitation on the number produced implies

$$x + y \leq 2,500.$$

The total profit is P = 25x + 40y. Summarizing, we have the
following linear programming problem.

Maximize P = 25x + 40y subject to

$$200x + 300y \leq 600,000$$

$$x + y \leq 2,500$$

$$x \geq 0, \ y \geq 0.$$

The graph of the feasible set S and the
associated table of values of P follow.

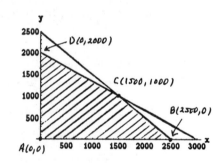

| Vertex | C = 25x + 40y |
|--------|---------------|
| A(0,0) | 0 |
| B(2500,0) | 62,500 |
| C(1500,1000) | 77,500 |
| D(0,2000) | 80,000 |

P attains a maximum value of 80,000 when x = 0
and y = 2000.
Thus, by producing 2000 model B fax machines in
each shift, the company will realize an optimal
profit of $80,000.

24. Let x and y denote the number of luxury and standard model
steppers, respectively, produced each day. Then we have the
following linear programming problem:

Maximize P = 40x + 30y subject to

$$10x + 16y \leq 6000$$

$$10x + 8y \leq 3600$$

$$x \geq 0, \ y \geq 0.$$

The graph of the feasible set S and the associated table of values of P follow.

| Vertex | C = 40x + 30y |
|--------|---------------|
| A(0,0) | 0 |
| B(360,0) | 14400 |
| C(120,300) | 13800 |
| D(0,375) | 11250 |

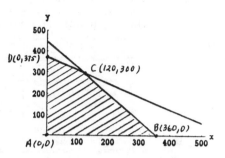

P attains a maximum value of 14400 when x = 360 and y = 0. Therefore, Bata should produce 360 luxury steppers per day in order to maximize its profits.

25. Refer to the solution of Exercise 2, Section 3.2, The problem is

Maximize P = 2x + 1.5y subject to

$$3x + 4y \leq 1000$$

$$6x + 3y \leq 1200$$

$$x \geq 0, \ y \geq 0.$$

The graph of the feasible set S and the associated table of values of P follow.

| Vertex | C = 2x + 1.5y |
|--------|---------------|
| A(0,0) | 0 |
| B(200,0) | 400 |
| C(120,160) | 480 |
| D(0,250) | 375 |

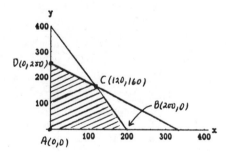

P attains a maximum value of 480 when x = 120 and y = 160.
Thus, by producing 120 model A hibachis and 160 model B hibachis in each shift, the company will realize an optimal profit of $480.

26. Refer to the solution of Exercise 3, Section 3.2. The problem is
    Maximize P = 2x + 1.5y subject to

    $$3x + 4y \leq 1000$$

    $$6x + 3y \leq 1200$$

    and    x ≥ 150, y ≥ 0.

The graph of the feasible set S and the associated table of values of P follow.

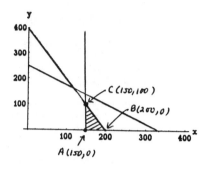

| Vertex | C = 2x + 1.5y |
|--------|---------------|
| A(150,0) | 300 |
| B(200,0) | 400 |
| C(150,100) | 450 |

P attains a maximum value of 450 when x = 150
and y = 100.
Thus, by producing 150 model A hibachis and 100
model B hibachis in each shift, the company will
realize an optimal profit of $450.

27. Refer to the solution of Exercise 4, Section 3.2. The linear
    programming problem is

    Maximize  P = 0.1x + 0.12y subject to

    $$x + y \leq 20$$

    $$x - 4y \geq 0$$

    $$x \geq 0, \ y \geq 0.$$

The feasible set S for the problem is
shown in the figure at the right, and
the value of P at each of the vertices
of S is shown in the accompanying table.

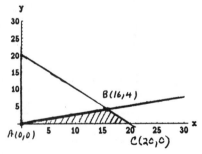

| Vertex | C = 0.1x + 0.12y |
|--------|------------------|
| A(0,0) | 0 |
| B(16,4) | 2.08 |
| C(20,0) | 2.00 |

The maximum value of P is attained when x = 16
and y = 4. Thus, by extending $16 million in
housing loans and $4 million in automobile loans,
the company will realize a return of $2.08 million
on its loans.

28. Refer to Exercise 5, Section 3.2. The problem is

Minimize C = 2x + 5y subject to

$$30x + 25y \geq 400$$

$$x + 0.5y \geq 10$$

$$2x + 5y \geq 40$$

$$x \geq 0, \quad y \geq 0.$$

The graph of the feasible set S and the associated table of values of C follow.

| Vertex | C = 2x + 5y |
|--------|-------------|
| A(0,20) | 100 |
| B(5,10) | 60 |
| C(10,4) | 40 |
| D(20,0) | 40 |

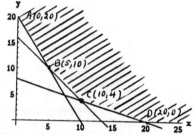

C attains a minimum value of 40 when x = 10 and y = 4 and x = 20, and y = 0. This means that any point lying on the line joining the points (10,4) and (20,0) will satisfy these constraints. For example, we could use 10 ounces of food A and 4 ounces of food B, or we could use 20 ounces of food A and zero ounces of food B.

29. Refer to Exercise 6, Section 3.2. The problem is

Maximize P = 150x + 200y subject to

$$40x + 60y \leq 7400$$

$$20x + 25y \leq 3300$$

$$x \geq 0, \quad y \geq 0.$$

The graph of the feasible set S and the associated table of values of P follow.

| Vertex | P = 150x + 200y |
|--------|-----------------|
| A(0,0) | 0 |
| B(165,0) | 24750 |
| C(65,80) | 25750 |
| D(0,123) | 24600 |

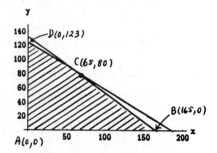

P attains a maximum value of 25,750 when x = 65 and y = 80. Thus, by producing 65 acres of crop A and 80 acres of crop B, the farmer will realize a maximum profit of $25,750.

30. The problem is

Minimize C = 14,500 − 20x − 10y subject to

$x + y \geq 40$

$x + y \leq 100$

$0 \leq x \leq 80$

$0 \leq y \leq 70.$

The feasible set S for the problem is shown in the following figure, and the value of C at each of the vertices of S is given in the accompanying table.

| Vertex | C = 14,500 − 20x − 10y |
|--------|------------------------|
| A(40,0) | 13,700 |
| B(80,0) | 12,900 |
| C(80,20) | 12,700 |
| D(30,70) | 13,200 |
| E(0,70) | 13,800 |
| F(0,40) | 14,100 |

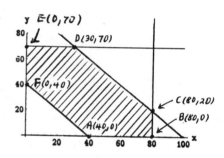

We conclude that the minimum value of C occurs when x = 80 and y = 20. Thus, 80 engines should be shipped from plant I to assembly plant A, and 20 engines should be shipped from plant I to assembly plant B;  whereas

(80 − x) = 80 − 80 = 0, and (70 − y) = 70 − 20 = 50

engines should be shipped from plant II to assembly plants A and B, respectively, at a total cost of $12,700.

31. Refer to the solution of Exercise 7, Section 3.2.

Minimize C = 32,000 - x - 3y subject to

$x + y \le 6000$

$x + y \ge 2000$

$x \le 3000$

$y \le 4000$

$x \ge 0, y \ge 0.$

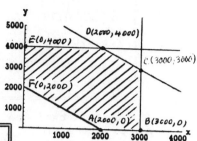

| Vertex | C = 32,000 - x - 3y |
|--------|---------------------|
| A(2000,0) | 30,000 |
| B(3000,0) | 29,000 |
| C(3000,3000) | 20,000 |
| D(2000,4000) | 18,000 |
| E(0,4000) | 20,000 |
| F(0,2000) | 26,000 |

Since x denotes the number of picture tubes shipped from location I to city A and y denotes the number of picture tubes shipped from location I to city B, we see that the company should ship 2000 tubes from location I to city A and 4000 tubes from location I to city B. Since the number of picture tubes required by the two factories in city A and city B are 3000 and 4000, respectively, the number of picture tubes shipped from location II to city A and city B, are

(3000 - x) = 3000 - 2000 = 1000   and   (4000 - y) = 4000 - 4000 = 0

respectively. The minimum shipping cost will then be $18,000.

32. Refer to the solution of Exercise 8, Section 3.2. The problem is

Maximize P = 0.6x + 0.8y subject to

$x + y \le 2.5$

$x + y \ge 2$

$1 \le x \le 1.5$

$y \ge 0.75.$

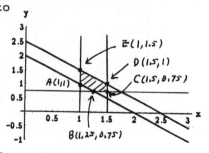

The feasible set S for the problem is shown in the figure at the right, and the value of P at each of the vertices of S is given in the table that follows.

| Vertex | P = 0.6x + 0.8y |
|---|---|
| A(1,1) | 1.4 |
| B(1.25,0.75) | 1.35 |
| C(1.5,0.75) | 1.5 |
| D(1.5,1) | 1.7 |
| E(1,1.5) | 1.8 |

We conclude that the maximum value of P occurs when x = 1 and
y = 1.5. Therefore, AntiFam should give $1 million in aid to
country A and $1.5 million in aid to country B.

33. Let x denote Patricia's investment in growth stocks and y denote
the value of her investment in speculative stocks, where both x
and y are measured in thousands of dollars. Then the return on her
investments is given by P = 0.15x + 0.25y. Since her investment
may not exceed $30,000, we have the constraint x + y < 30. The
condition that her investment in growth stocks be at least 3 times
as much as her investment in speculative stocks translates into
the inequality x ≥ 3y. Thus, we have the following linear
programming problem:

$$\text{Maximize } P = 0.15x + 0.25y \text{ subject to}$$

$$x + y \leq 30$$

$$x - 3y \geq 0$$

$$x \geq 0, \ y \geq 0.$$

The graph of the feasible set S is shown in the following figure,
and the value of P at each of the vertices of S is shown in the
accompanying table. The maximum value of P occurs when x = 22.5
and y = 7.5. Thus, by investing $22,500 in growth stocks and
$7,500 in speculative stocks. Patricia will realize a return of
$5250 on her investments.

| Vertex | C = 0.15x + 0.25 |
|---|---|
| A(0,0) | 0 |
| B(30,0) | 4.5 |
| C($\frac{45}{2}, \frac{15}{2}$) | 5.25 |

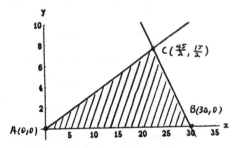

34. Let x and y denote the number of ounces of brand A and brand B dog food to be used in each serving. Then the cost of each serving is given by C = 3x + 4y cents. Since the size of each serving must not exceed 8 ounces, we have x + y ≤ 8. Furthermore, since each serving must contain at least 29 units of nutrient I and at least 20 units of nutrient II, we have 3x + 5y ≥ 29 and 4x + 2y ≥ 20. Therefore, we have the following linear programming problem.

Minimize C = 3x + 4y subject to

$$x + y \leq 8$$

$$3x + 5y \geq 29$$

$$4x + 2y \geq 20$$

$$x \geq 0, \ y \geq 0.$$

The graph of the feasible set S is shown figure that follows and the value of C at each of the vertices of S is given in the accompanying table.

| Vertex | C = 3x + 4y |
|--------|-------------|
| A(2,6) | 30 |
| B(3,4) | 25 |
| C($\frac{11}{2}, \frac{5}{2}$) | $26\frac{1}{2}$ |

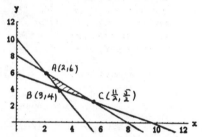

We conclude that the cost will be minimized when x = 3 and y = 4. Therefore, 3 ounces of brand A dog food and 4 ounces of brand B dog food can be prepared with the required nutrients at a minimum cost of 25 cents per serving.

35. Let x denote the number of urban families and let y denote the number of suburban families interviewed by the company. Then, the amount of money paid to Trendex will be

P = 1500 + 2(x + y) − 1.1x − 1.25y = 1500 + 0.9x + 0.75y.

Since a maximum of 1500 families are to be interviewed, we have

x + y ≤ 1500.

Next, the condition that at least 500 urban families are to be interviewed translates into the condition x ≥ 500. Finally the condition that at least half of the families interviewed must be from the suburban area gives

$$y \geq \frac{1}{2}(x + y) \quad \text{or} \quad y - x \geq 0.$$

Thus, we are led to the following programming problem:

Maximize P = 1500 + 0.9x + 0.75y subject to

$$x + y \leq 1500$$

$$y - x \geq 0$$

$$x > 500$$

$$y \geq 0.$$

The graph of the feasible set S for this problem follows and the value of P at each of the vertices of S is given in the accompanying table.

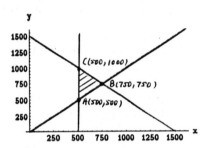

| Vertex | P = 1500 + 0.9x + 0.75y |
|--------|--------------------------|
| A(500,500) | 2325 |
| B(750,750) | 2737.50 |
| C(500,1000) | 2700 |

Using the method of corners, we conclude that the profit will be maximized when x = 750 and y = 750. Thus, a maximum profit of $2,737.50 will be realized when 750 urban and 750 suburban families are interviewed.

36. Since the point $Q(x_1, y_1)$ lies in the interior of the feasible set S, it is possible to find another point $P(x_1, y_2)$ lying to the right and above the point Q and contained in S. (See accompanying figure on page 241.) Clearly, $x_2 > x_1$ and $y_2 > y_1$. Therefore, $ax_2 + by_2 > ax_1 + by_1$, since a > 0 and b > 0 and this shows

that the objective function P = ax + by takes on a larger value at
P than it does at Q. Therefore, the optimal solution cannot occur
at Q.

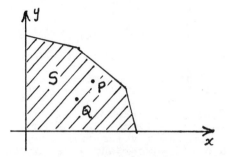

37.  a.   True. Since a > 0, the term ax can be made as large as we
     please by taking x sufficiently large (because S is unbounded) and
     therefore P is unbounded as well.

     b.   True. Maximizing P = ax + by on S is the same as minimizing

$$Q = -P - (ax + by) = -ax - by = AX + By,$$

where A $\geq$ 0 and B $\geq$ 0. Since x $\geq$ 0 and y $\geq$ 0, the linear function
Q, and therefore P, has at least one optimal solution.


38.  Let $A(x_1, y_1)$ and $B(x_2, y_2)$. Then you can verify that $Q(\overline{x}, \overline{y})$, where

$$\overline{x} = x_1 + t(x_2 - x_1) \quad \text{and} \quad \overline{y} = y_1 + t(y_2 - y_1)$$

and t is a number satisfying 0 < t < 1. Therefore, the value of P
at Q is

$$P = a\overline{x} + b\overline{y} = a[x_1 + t(x_2 - x_1)] + b[y_1 + t(y_2 - y_1)]$$

$$= ax_1 + by_1 + [a(x_2 - x_1) + b(y_2 - y_1)]t.$$

Now, if $c = a(x_2 - x_1) + b(y_2 - y_1) = 0$, then P has the (maximum)
value $ax_1 + by_1$ on the line segment joining A and B; that is, the
infinitely many solutions lie on this line segment. If c > 0, then
a point a little to the right of Q will give a larger value of P.
Thus, P is not maximal at Q. (Such a point can be found because
Q lies in the interior of the line segment). A similar statement
holds for the case c < 0. Thus, the maximum of P cannot occur at Q
unless it occurs in every point on the line segment joining A
and B.


## CHAPTER 3 REVIEW, page 208

1.   Evaluating Z at each of the corners of the feasible set S, we
     obtain the following table.

| Vertex | Z = 2x + 3y |
|--------|-------------|
| (0,0)  | 0           |
| (5,0)  | 10          |
| (3,4)  | 18          |
| (0,6)  | 18          |

We conclude that Z attains a minimum value of 0 when x = 0 and y = 0, and a maximum value of 18 when x and y lie on the line segment joining (3,4) and (0,6).

2.  Evaluating Z at each of the corners of the feasible set S, we obtain the following table.

| Vertex | Z = 4x + 3y |
|--------|-------------|
| (1,1)  | 7           |
| (1,6)  | 22          |
| (3,5)  | 27          |
| (1,3)  | 13          |

We conclude that Z attains a minimum value of 7 at (1,1) and a maximum value of 27 at (3,5).

3.  The graph of the feasible set S is shown at the right.

| Vertex   | C = 3x + 5y |
|----------|-------------|
| A(0,0)   | 0           |
| B(5,0)   | 15          |
| C(3,2)   | 19          |
| D(0,4)   | 20          |

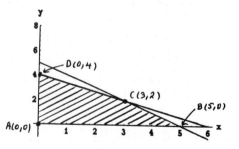

We conclude that the maximum value of P is 20 when x = 0 and y = 4.

4. The graph of the feasible set S is shown at the right.

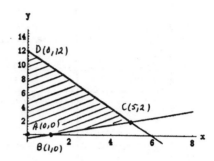

| Vertex | P = 2x + 3y |
|--------|-------------|
| A(0,0) | 0 |
| B(1,0) | 2 |
| C(5,2) | 16 |
| D(0,12) | 36 |

We conclude that the maximum value of P is 36 when x = 0 and y = 12.

5. The values of the objective function C = 3x + 4y at the corners of the feasible set are given in the following table. The graph of the feasible set S follows.

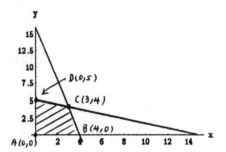

| Vertex | C = 2x + 5y |
|--------|-------------|
| A(0,0) | 0 |
| B(4,0) | 8 |
| C(3,4) | 26 |
| D(0,5) | 25 |

We conclude that the minimum value of C is 0 when x = 0 and y = 0.

6. The values of the objective function C = 3x + 4y at the vertices of the feasible set are given in the following table.

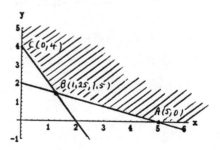

| Vertex | C = 3x + 4y |
|--------|-------------|
| A(5,0) | 15 |
| B(1.25,1.5) | 9.75 |
| C(0,4) | 16 |

The graph of the feasible set is shown at the right.

We conclude that the minimum value of C is 9.75
when x = 1.25 and y = 1.5.

7.  The values of the objective function P = 3x + 2y at the vertices
    of the feasible set are given in the following table.

| Vertex | P = 3x + 2y |
|--------|-------------|
| $A(0,\frac{28}{5})$ | $\frac{56}{5}$ |
| B(7,0) | 21 |
| C(8,0) | 24 |
| D(3,10) | 29 |
| E(0,12) | 24 |

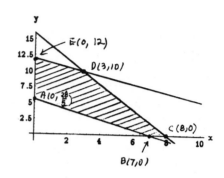

The graph of the feasible set is shown
at the right. We conclude that P attains
a maximum value of 29 when x = 3 and y = 10.

8.  The graph of the feasible set S follows.

| Vertex | P = 6x + 2y |
|--------|-------------|
| A(3,0) | 18 |
| B(8,0) | 48 |
| C(6,2) | 40 |

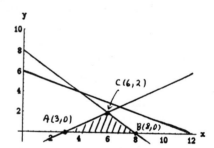

We conclude that the maximum value of P
is 48 when x = 8 and y = 0.

9.  The graph of the feasible set S is
    shown at the right. The values of the
    objective function C = 2x + 7y at each
    of the corner points of the feasible
    set S are shown in the table that
    follows.

| Vertex | C = 2x + 7y |
|--------|-------------|
| A(20,0) | 40 |
| B(10,3) | 41 |
| C(0,9) | 63 |

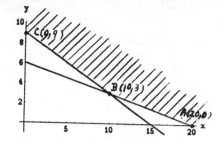

We conclude that C attains a minimum value of 40 when x = 20 and y = 0.

10. The graph of the feasible set S is shown at the right. The values of the objective function C = 4x + y at each of the corner points of the feasible set S are shown in the following table.

| Vertex | C = 4x + y |
|--------|------------|
| A(0,18) | 18 |
| B(2,6) | 14 |
| C(4,2) | 18 |
| D(12,0) | 48 |

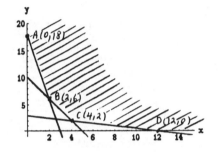

We conclude that C attains a minimum value of 14 when x = 2 and y = 6.

11. The graph of the feasible set S is shown in the following figure. We conclude that Q attains a maximum value of 22 when x = 22 and y = 0, and a minimum value of $5\frac{1}{2}$ when x = 3 and y = $\frac{5}{2}$.

| Vertex | Q = x + y |
|--------|-----------|
| A(2,5) | 7 |
| B(3,$\frac{5}{2}$) | $5\frac{1}{2}$ |
| C(8,0) | 8 |
| D(22,0) | 22 |

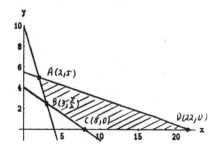

12. The graph of the feasible set S is shown
    in the following figure. We conclude that
    Q attains a maximum value of 54 when x = 12
    and y = 6, and a minimum value of 8 when
    x = 4 and y = 0.

| Vertex | Q = 2x + 5y |
|--------|-------------|
| A(4,0) | 8 |
| B(12,0) | 24 |
| C(12,6) | 54 |
| D(3,9) | 51 |
| E(0,6) | 30 |
| F(0,4) | 20 |

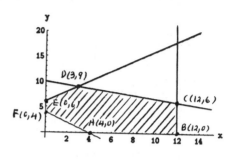

13. Suppose the investor puts x and y thousand dollars into the stocks
    of company A and company B, respectively. Then the mathematical
    formulation leads to the linear programming problem:

    Maximize P = 0.14x + 0.20y subject to

    $$x + \phantom{0.04}y \leq 80$$

    $$0.01x + 0.04y \leq 2$$

    $$x \geq 0, \ y \geq 0.$$

    The feasible set S for this problem is shown in
    figure at the right and the values at each
    cornerpoint  are given in the accompanying table.

| Vertex | P = .14x + .20y |
|--------|------------------|
| A(0,0) | 0 |
| B(80,0) | 11.2 |
| C(40,40) | 13.6 |
| D(0,50) | 10 |

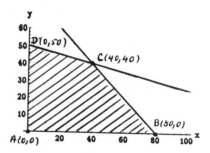

    P attains a maximum value of 13.6 when
    x = 40 and y = 40. Thus, by investing

$40,000 in the stocks of each company,
the investor will achieve a maximum
return of $13,600.

14. The given information is summarized in the following table.

| Assembly Line | Model A | Model B | Time available (in minutes) |
|---|---|---|---|
| I | 15 | 10 | 1500 |
| II | 10 | 12 | 1320 |
| Profit per unit ($) | 12 | 10 | |

Let x and y denote the number of units of model A and model B
clock- radios to be produced. Then the required linear programming
problem is

Maximize P = 12x + 10y subject to

$$15x + 10y \leq 1500$$

$$10x + 12y \leq 1320$$

$$x \geq 0, \ y \geq 0.$$

The graph of the feasible set S is shown
in the figure which follows.

| Vertex | P = 12x + 10y |
|---|---|
| A(0,0) | 0 |
| B(100,0) | 1200 |
| C(60,60) | 1320 |
| D(0,110) | 1100 |

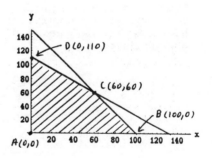

Thus, the maximum value of P occurs at
x = 60 and y = 60; that is, the company
should produce 60 model A clock-radios and
60 model B clock-radios for a maximum profit
of $1320.

15. Let x denote the number of model A hibachis and y the number of required is

$$3x + 4y \leq 1000$$

and the number of minutes of labor used each day is

$$6x + 3y \leq 1200.$$

One additional constraint specifies that y > 180. The daily profit is P = 2x + 1.5y. Therefore, we have the following linear programming problem:

Maximize P = 2x + 1.5y subject to

$$3x + 4y \leq 1000$$

$$6x + 3y \leq 1200$$

$$x \geq 0$$

and                           $$y \geq 180.$$

The graph of the feasible set S is shown in the figure which follows.

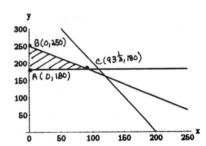

| Vertex | P = 2x + 1.5y |
|--------|---------------|
| A(0,180) | 270 |
| B(0,250) | 375 |
| C($\frac{931}{3}$,180) | $456\frac{2}{3}$ |

Thus, the optimal profit of $456 is realized when 93 units of model A hibachis and 180 units of model B hibachis are produced.

# GROUP DISCUSSION QUESTIONS

**Page 196**

1.   a. – b.

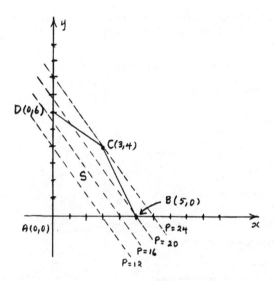

Each of the isoprofit lines has slope $-\frac{4}{3}$ as can be seen by writing each equation in the slope-intercept form.

c.   Solving the system comprising the equations $2x + y = 10$ and $2x + 3y = 18$ gives $(3,4)$ as the points of intersection of the lines represented by these equations. The values of P at the vertices of S are given in the table that follows.

| Vertex | P = 4x + 3y |
|--------|-------------|
| A(0,0) | 0 |
| B(5,0) | 20 |
| C(3,4) | 24 |
| D(0,6) | 18 |

From the table, we see that the solution of the linear programming problem occurs at C(3,4) as observed in part (b).

1.  a. – b.

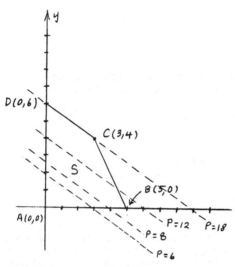

Each of the isoprofit lines has slope $-\frac{2}{3}$.

c.  From the following table

| Vertex | P = 2x + 3y |
|--------|-------------|
| A(0,0) | 0 |
| B(5,0) | 10 |
| C(3,4) | 18 |
| D(0,6) | 18 |

we see that there are infinitely many solutions represented by the points lying on the line segment joining C and D. This is as predicted by the geometric results of part (b).

# CHAPTER 4

## EXERCISES 4.1, page 227

1. All entries in the last row of the simplex tableau are nonnegative and an optimal solution has been reached. We find

   $x = \dfrac{30}{7}$, $y = \dfrac{20}{7}$, $u = 0$, $v = 0$, and $P = \dfrac{220}{7}$.

2. All entries in the last row of the simplex tableau are nonnegative and an optimal solution has been reached. We find

   $x = 0$, $y = 6$, $u = 0$, $v = 2$, and $P = 30$.

3. The simplex tableau is not in final form because there is an entry in the last row which is negative. The entry in the first row, second column is the next pivot element and has a value of 1/2.

4. All entries in the last row of the simplex tableau are nonnegative and an optimal solution has been reached. We find

   $x = 0$, $y = 16$, $z = 0$, $u = 28$, $v = 0$, $w = 0$ and $P = 48$.

5. The simplex tableau is in final form. We find

   $x = 1/3$, $y = 0$, $z = 13/3$, $u = 0$, $v = 6$, $w = 0$ and $P = 17$.

6. The simplex tableau is not in final form because there is an entry in the last row which is negative. The entry in the third row, first column, is the pivot element and has a value of 2.

7. The simplex tableau is not in final form because there is an entry in the last row which is negative. The entry in the third row, second column, is the pivot element and has a value of 1.

8. The simplex tableau is not in final form because there is an entry in the last row which is negative. The entry in the second row, sixth column, is the pivot element and has a value of 6/5.

9. The simplex tableau is in final form. The solutions are

$$x = 30, \ y = 0, \ z = 0, \ u = 10, \ v = 0, \text{ and } P = 60,$$

and $\quad x = 0, \ y = 30, \ z = 0, \ u = 10, \ v = 0, \text{ and } P = 60.$

(There are infinitely many answers).

10. The initial tableau is

| x | y | u | v | P | Const. |
|---|---|---|---|---|--------|
| 1 | 1 | 1 | 0 | 0 | 80 |
| 3 | 0 | 0 | 1 | 0 | 90 |
| -5 | -3 | 0 | 0 | 1 | 0 |

Using the sequence of operations

1. $\frac{1}{3}R_2$ 　　　　　　　　　2. $R_1 - R_2; \ R_3 + 5R_2$

3. $R_3 + 3R_1$

we obtain the final tableau

| x | y | u | v | P | Const. |
|---|---|---|---|---|--------|
| 0 | 1 | 1 | $-\frac{1}{3}$ | 0 | 50 |
| 1 | 0 | 0 | $\frac{1}{3}$ | 0 | 30 |
| 0 | 0 | 3 | $\frac{2}{3}$ | 1 | 300 |

from which we conclude that $x = 30, \ y = 50, \ u = 0, \ v = 0,$
and $P = 300$.

11.

| | x | y | u | v | P | Const. | Ratio |
|---|---|---|---|---|---|--------|-------|
| p.r.→ | 1 | ②  | 1 | 0 | 0 | 12 | 12/2 = 6 |
| | 3 | 2 | 0 | 1 | 0 | 24 | 24/2 = 12 |
| | -10 | -12 | 0 | 0 | 1 | 0 | |

　　　　　　　↑
　　　　　p.c.

| | x | y | u | v | P | Const. |
|---|---|---|---|---|---|--------|
| $\frac{1}{2}R_1$ → | $\frac{1}{2}$ | 1 | $\frac{1}{2}$ | 0 | 0 | 6 |
| | 3 | 2 | 0 | 1 | 0 | 24 |
| | -10 | -12 | 0 | 0 | 1 | 0 |

$$\xrightarrow{\begin{array}{c} R_2 - 2R_1 \\ R_3 + 12R_1 \end{array}}$$

| x | y | u | v | P | Const. | Ratio |
|---|---|---|---|---|--------|-------|
| $\frac{1}{2}$ | 1 | $\frac{1}{2}$ | 0 | 0 | 6 | $6/(1/2) = 12$ |
| ② | 0 | -1 | 1 | 0 | 12 | $12/2 = 6$ |
| -4 | 0 | 6 | 0 | 1 | 72 | |

p.r.→ points to ②; p.c. ↑ under x

$\frac{1}{2}R_2$

| x | y | u | v | P | Const. |
|---|---|---|---|---|--------|
| $\frac{1}{2}$ | 1 | $\frac{1}{2}$ | 0 | 0 | 6 |
| 1 | 0 | $-\frac{1}{2}$ | $\frac{1}{2}$ | 0 | 6 |
| -4 | 0 | 6 | 0 | 1 | 72 |

$$\xrightarrow[R_3 + 4R_2]{R_1 - \frac{1}{2}R_2}$$

| x | y | u | v | P | Const. |
|---|---|---|---|---|--------|
| 0 | 1 | $\frac{3}{4}$ | $-\frac{1}{4}$ | 0 | 3 |
| 1 | 0 | $-\frac{1}{2}$ | $\frac{1}{2}$ | 0 | 6 |
| 0 | 0 | 4 | 2 | 1 | 96 |

The last tableau is in final form. We find that x = 6, y = 3, u = 0, v = 0, and P = 96.

12. Starting with the initial tableau

| x | y | u | v | P | Const. | Ratio |
|---|---|---|---|---|--------|-------|
| 3 | 5 | 1 | 0 | 0 | 78 | $78/3 = 26$ |
| ④ | 1 | 0 | 1 | 0 | 36 | $36/4 = 9$ |
| -5 | -4 | 0 | 0 | 1 | 0 | |

p.r.→ points to ④; p.c. ↑ under x

we use the sequence of row operations

1. $\frac{1}{4}R_2$

2. $R_1 - 3R_2;\ R_3 + 5R_2$

3. $\frac{4}{17}R_1$

4. $R_2 - \frac{1}{4}R_1;\ R_3 + \frac{11}{4}R_1$

to obtain the final tableau

| x | y | u | v | P | Const. |
|---|---|---|---|---|---|
| 0 | 1 | $\frac{4}{17}$ | $-\frac{3}{17}$ | 0 | 12 |
| 1 | 0 | $-\frac{1}{17}$ | $\frac{5}{17}$ | 0 | 6 |
| 0 | 0 | $\frac{11}{17}$ | $\frac{13}{17}$ | 1 | 78 |

and conclude that $x = 6$, $y = 12$, $u = 0$, $v = 0$, and $P = 78$.

13. We obtain the following sequence of tableaus:

| | x | y | u | v | w | P | Const. | Ratio |
|---|---|---|---|---|---|---|---|---|
| | 3 | 1 | 1 | 0 | 0 | 0 | 24 | 24 |
| | 2 | 1 | 0 | 1 | 0 | 0 | 18 | 18 |
| p.r.→ | 1 | ③ | 0 | 0 | 1 | 0 | 24 | 8 |
| | -4 | -6 | 0 | 0 | 0 | 1 | 0 | |

p.c. (under y column)   $\frac{1}{3}R_3 \longrightarrow$

| x | y | u | v | w | P | Const. |
|---|---|---|---|---|---|---|
| 3 | 1 | 1 | 0 | 0 | 0 | 24 |
| 2 | 1 | 0 | 1 | 0 | 0 | 18 |
| $\frac{1}{3}$ | 1 | 0 | 0 | $\frac{1}{3}$ | 0 | 8 |
| -4 | -6 | 0 | 0 | 0 | 1 | 0 |

$$\begin{array}{c} R_1 - R_3 \\ R_2 - R_3 \\ R_4 + 6R_3 \end{array} \longrightarrow$$

| | x | y | u | v | w | P | Const. | Ratio |
|---|---|---|---|---|---|---|---|---|
| p.r.→ | $\frac{8}{3}$ | 0 | 1 | 0 | $-\frac{1}{3}$ | 0 | 16 | 6 |
| | $\frac{5}{3}$ | 0 | 0 | 1 | $-\frac{1}{3}$ | 0 | 10 | 6 |
| | $\frac{1}{3}$ | 1 | 0 | 0 | $\frac{1}{3}$ | 0 | 8 | 24 |
| | -2 | 0 | 0 | 0 | 2 | 1 | 48 | |

p.c. (under x column)   $\frac{3}{8}R_1 \longrightarrow$

(Observe that we have a choice here.)

| x | y | u | v | w | P | Const. |
|---|---|---|---|---|---|---|
| 1 | 0 | $\frac{3}{8}$ | 0 | $-\frac{1}{8}$ | 0 | 6 |
| $\frac{5}{3}$ | 0 | 0 | 1 | $-\frac{1}{3}$ | 0 | 10 |
| $\frac{1}{3}$ | 1 | 0 | 0 | $\frac{1}{3}$ | 0 | 8 |
| $-2$ | 0 | 0 | 0 | 2 | 1 | 48 |

$$\xrightarrow[\substack{R_3 \ - \ \frac{1}{3}R_1 \\ R_4 \ + \ 2R_1}]{R_2 \ - \ \frac{5}{3}R_1}$$

| x | y | u | v | w | P | Const. |
|---|---|---|---|---|---|---|
| 1 | 0 | $\frac{3}{8}$ | 0 | $-\frac{1}{8}$ | 0 | 6 |
| 0 | 0 | $-\frac{5}{8}$ | 1 | $-\frac{1}{8}$ | 0 | 0 |
| 0 | 1 | $-\frac{1}{8}$ | 0 | $\frac{3}{8}$ | 0 | 6 |
| 0 | 0 | $\frac{3}{4}$ | 0 | $\frac{7}{4}$ | 1 | 60 |

We deduce that $x = 6$, $y = 6$, $u = 0$, $v = 0$, $w = 0$, and $P = 60$.

14. The initial simplex tableaux is

| x | y | u | v | w | P | Const. |
|---|---|---|---|---|---|---|
| 1 | 1 | 1 | 0 | 0 | 0 | 12 |
| 3 | 1 | 0 | 1 | 0 | 0 | 20 |
| 10 | 7 | 0 | 0 | 1 | 0 | 70 |
| $-15$ | $-12$ | 0 | 0 | 0 | 1 | 0 |

Using the sequence of row operations

1. $\frac{1}{10}R_3$

2. $R_1 - R_3$; $R_2 - 3R_3$; $R_4 + 15R_3$

3. $\frac{10}{7}R_3$

4. $R_1 - \frac{3}{10}R_3$; $R_2 + \frac{11}{10}R_3$; $R_4 + \frac{3}{2}R_3$

we obtain the final simplex tableau

| x | y | u | v | w | P | Const. |
|---|---|---|---|---|---|---|
| 0 | 0 | 1 | 0 | $-\frac{1}{7}$ | 0 | 2 |
| $\frac{11}{7}$ | 0 | 0 | 1 | $-\frac{1}{7}$ | 0 | 20 |
| $\frac{10}{7}$ | 1 | 0 | 0 | $\frac{1}{7}$ | 0 | 10 |
| $\frac{15}{7}$ | 0 | 0 | 0 | $\frac{12}{7}$ | 1 | 120 |

from which we deduce that $x = 0$, $y = 10$, $u = 2$, $v = 20$, and $P = 120$.

15.  We obtain the following sequence of tableaus:

| x | y | z | u | v | P | Const. |  | -Ratio-- |
|---|---|---|---|---|---|---|---|---|
| 1 | 1 | 1 | 1 | 0 | 0 | 8 |  | 8/1 = 8 |
| 3 | 2 | (4) | 0 | 1 | 0 | 24 |  | 24/4 = 6 |
| -3 | -4 | -5 | 0 | 0 | 1 | 0 |  |  |

p.r.→ (row 2)  p.c. (z column)  $\frac{1}{4}R_2$ →

| x | y | z | u | v | P | Const. |
|---|---|---|---|---|---|---|
| 1 | 1 | 1 | 1 | 0 | 0 | 8 |
| $\frac{3}{4}$ | $\frac{1}{2}$ | 1 | 0 | $\frac{1}{4}$ | 0 | 6 |
| -3 | -4 | -5 | 0 | 0 | 1 | 0 |

$R_1 - R_2$
$R_3 + 5R_2$ →

| x | y | z | u | v | P | Const. |  | --Ratio---- |
|---|---|---|---|---|---|---|---|---|
| $-\frac{1}{4}$ | $\left(\frac{1}{2}\right)$ | 0 | 1 | $-\frac{1}{4}$ | 0 | 2 |  | 2/(1/2) = 4 |
| $\frac{3}{4}$ | $\frac{1}{2}$ | 1 | 0 | $\frac{1}{4}$ | 0 | 6 |  | 6/(1/2) = 12 |
| $\frac{3}{4}$ | $-\frac{3}{2}$ | 0 | 0 | $\frac{5}{4}$ | 1 | 30 |  |  |

p.r.→ (row 1)  p.c. (y column)  $2R_1$ →

| x | y | z | u | v | P | Const. |
|---|---|---|---|---|---|---|
| $\frac{1}{2}$ | 1 | 0 | 2 | $-\frac{1}{2}$ | 0 | 4 |
| $\frac{3}{4}$ | $\frac{1}{2}$ | 1 | 0 | $\frac{1}{4}$ | 0 | 6 |
| $\frac{3}{4}$ | $-\frac{3}{2}$ | 0 | 0 | $\frac{5}{4}$ | 1 | 30 |

$R_2 - \frac{1}{2}R_1$
$R_3 + \frac{3}{2}R_1$ →

| x | y | z | u | v | P | Const. |
|---|---|---|---|---|---|---|
| $\frac{1}{2}$ | 1 | 0 | 2 | $-\frac{1}{2}$ | 0 | 4 |
| $\frac{1}{2}$ | 0 | 1 | -1 | $\frac{1}{2}$ | 0 | 4 |
| $\frac{3}{2}$ | 0 | 0 | 3 | $\frac{1}{2}$ | 1 | 36 |

This last tableau is in final form. We find that $x = 0$, $y = 4$, $z = 4$, $u = 0$, $v = 0$, and $P = 36$.

16.  The initial tableau is

| x | y | z | u | v | P | Const. |
|---|---|---|---|---|---|---|
| 1 | 1 | 3 | 1 | 0 | 0 | 15 |
| 4 | 4 | 3 | 0 | 1 | 0 | 65 |
| -3 | -3 | -4 | 0 | 0 | 1 | 0 |

Using the following sequence of row operations

1. $\frac{1}{3}R_1$

2. $R_2 - 3R_1$; $R_3 + 4R_1$

3. $3R_1$

4. $R_2 - 3R_1$; $R_3 + \frac{5}{3}R_1$

we obtain the final tableau

| x | y | z | u | v | P | Const. |
|---|---|---|---|---|---|---|
| 1 | 1 | 3 | 1 | 0 | 0 | 15 |
| 0 | 0 | -9 | -4 | 1 | 0 | 5 |
| 0 | 0 | 5 | 3 | 0 | 1 | 45 |

we find that the solutions are $x = 15$, $y = 0$, $z = 0$, $u = 0$, $v = 5$, and $P = 45$; and $x = 0$, $y = 15$, $z = 0$, $u = 0$, $v = 5$, and $P = 45$.

17.

| | x | y | z | u | v | w | P | Const. | Ratio | |
|---|---|---|---|---|---|---|---|---|---|---|
| | 3 | 10 | 5 | 1 | 0 | 0 | 0 | 120 | $120/10 = 12$ | |
| p.r.→ | 5 | ② | 8 | 0 | 1 | 0 | 0 | 6 | $6/2 = 3$ | $\frac{1}{2}R_2$ → |
| | 8 | 10 | 3 | 0 | 0 | 1 | 0 | 105 | $105/10 = 21/2$ | |
| | -3 | -4 | -1 | 0 | 0 | 0 | 1 | 0 | | |

p.c.

| x | y | z | u | v | w | P | Const. |
|---|---|---|---|---|---|---|--------|
| 3 | 10 | 5 | 1 | 0 | 0 | 0 | 120 |
| $\frac{5}{2}$ | 1 | 4 | 0 | $\frac{1}{2}$ | 0 | 0 | 3 |
| 8 | 10 | 3 | 0 | 0 | 1 | 0 | 105 |
| -3 | -4 | -1 | 0 | 0 | 0 | 1 | 0 |

$$\xrightarrow{\begin{array}{c} R_1 - 10R_2 \\ R_3 - 10R_2 \\ R_4 + 4R_2 \end{array}}$$

| x | y | z | u | v | w | P | Const. |
|---|---|---|---|---|---|---|--------|
| -22 | 0 | -35 | 1 | -5 | 0 | 0 | 90 |
| $\frac{5}{2}$ | 1 | 4 | 0 | $\frac{1}{2}$ | 0 | 0 | 3 |
| -17 | 0 | -37 | 0 | -5 | 1 | 0 | 75 |
| 7 | 0 | 15 | 0 | 2 | 0 | 1 | 12 |

The last tableau is in final form. We find that $x = 0$, $y = 3$, $z = 0$, $u = 90$, $w = 75$, and $P = 12$.

18.  From the initial tableau

| x | y | z | u | v | w | P | Const. |
|---|---|---|---|---|---|---|--------|
| 2 | 1 | 1 | 1 | 0 | 0 | 0 | 14 |
| 4 | 2 | 3 | 0 | 1 | 0 | 0 | 28 |
| 2 | 5 | 5 | 0 | 0 | 1 | 0 | 30 |
| -1 | -2 | 1 | 0 | 0 | 0 | 1 | 0 |

we use the following row operations

1. $\frac{1}{5}R_3$
2. $R_1 - R_3$; $R_2 - 2R_3$; $R_4 + 2R_3$
3. $\frac{5}{8}R_1$
4. $R_2 - \frac{16}{5}R_1$; $R_3 - \frac{2}{5}R_1$; $R_4 + \frac{1}{5}R_1$

to obtain the final tableau

| x | y | z | u | v | w | P | Const. |
|---|---|---|---|---|---|---|--------|
| 1 | 0 | 0 | $\frac{5}{8}$ | 0 | $-\frac{1}{8}$ | 0 | 5 |
| 0 | 0 | 1 | -2 | 1 | 0 | 0 | 0 |
| 0 | 1 | 1 | $-\frac{1}{4}$ | 0 | $\frac{1}{4}$ | 0 | 4 |
| 0 | 0 | 3 | $\frac{1}{8}$ | 0 | $\frac{3}{8}$ | 1 | 13 |

and conclude that P attains an optimal value of 13 when $x = 5$, $y = 4$, $z = 0$, $u = 0$, $v = 0$, and $w = 0$.

19. We obtain the following sequence of tableaus:

| | x | y | z | u | v | w | P | Const. | --Ratio-- |
|---|---|---|---|---|---|---|---|---|---|
| | 1 | 1 | 1 | 1 | 0 | 0 | 0 | 20 | 20 |
| p.r.→ | 2 | ④ | 3 | 0 | 1 | 0 | 0 | 42 | $10\frac{1}{2}$ |
| | 2 | 0 | 3 | 0 | 0 | 1 | 0 | 30 | -- |
| | -4 | -6 | -5 | 0 | 0 | 0 | 1 | 0 | |

p.c. (under y)

$\xrightarrow{\frac{1}{4}R_2}$

| | x | y | z | u | v | w | P | Const. |
|---|---|---|---|---|---|---|---|---|
| | 1 | 1 | 1 | 1 | 0 | 0 | 0 | 20 |
| | $\frac{1}{2}$ | 1 | $\frac{3}{4}$ | 0 | $\frac{1}{4}$ | 0 | 0 | $\frac{21}{2}$ |
| | 2 | 0 | 3 | 0 | 0 | 1 | 0 | 30 |
| | -4 | -6 | -5 | 0 | 0 | 0 | 1 | 0 |

$\xrightarrow[R_4 + 6R_2]{R_1 - R_2}$

| | x | y | z | u | v | w | P | Const. | --Ratio-- |
|---|---|---|---|---|---|---|---|---|---|
| | $\frac{1}{2}$ | 0 | $\frac{1}{4}$ | 1 | $-\frac{1}{4}$ | 0 | 0 | $\frac{19}{2}$ | 19 |
| | $\frac{1}{2}$ | 1 | $\frac{3}{4}$ | 0 | $\frac{1}{4}$ | 0 | 0 | $\frac{21}{2}$ | 21 |
| p.r.→ | ② | 0 | 3 | 0 | 0 | 1 | 0 | 30 | 15 |
| | -1 | 0 | $-\frac{1}{2}$ | 0 | $\frac{3}{2}$ | 0 | 1 | 63 | |

p.c. (under x)

$\xrightarrow{\frac{1}{2}R_3}$

| | x | y | z | u | v | w | P | Const. |
|---|---|---|---|---|---|---|---|---|
| | $\frac{1}{2}$ | 0 | $\frac{1}{4}$ | 1 | $-\frac{1}{4}$ | 0 | 0 | $\frac{19}{2}$ |
| | $\frac{1}{2}$ | 1 | $\frac{3}{4}$ | 0 | $\frac{1}{4}$ | 0 | 0 | $\frac{21}{2}$ |
| | 1 | 0 | $\frac{3}{2}$ | 0 | 0 | $\frac{1}{2}$ | 0 | 15 |
| | -1 | 0 | $-\frac{1}{2}$ | 0 | $\frac{3}{2}$ | 0 | 1 | 63 |

$\xrightarrow[\substack{R_2 - \frac{1}{2}R_3 \\ R_4 + R_3}]{R_1 - \frac{1}{2}R_3}$

| x | y | z | u | v | w | P | Const. |
|---|---|---|---|---|---|---|---|
| 0 | 0 | $-\frac{1}{2}$ | 1 | $-\frac{1}{4}$ | $-\frac{1}{4}$ | 0 | 2 |
| 0 | 1 | 0 | 0 | $\frac{1}{4}$ | $-\frac{1}{4}$ | 0 | 3 |
| 1 | 0 | $\frac{3}{2}$ | 0 | 0 | $\frac{1}{2}$ | 0 | 15 |
| 0 | 0 | 1 | 0 | $\frac{3}{2}$ | $\frac{1}{2}$ | 1 | 78 |

So the solution is x = 15, y = 3, z = 0, u = 2, v = 0, w = 0, and P = 78.

20.  From the initial tableau

| x | y | z | u | v | w | P | Const. |
|---|---|---|---|---|---|---|---|
| 3 | 1 | -1 | 1 | 0 | 0 | 0 | 80 |
| 2 | 1 | -1 | 0 | 1 | 0 | 0 | 40 |
| -1 | 1 | 1 | 0 | 0 | 1 | 0 | 80 |
| -1 | -4 | 2 | 0 | 0 | 1 | 1 | 0 |

we use the following row operations

1. $R_1 - R_2$; $R_3 - R_2$; $R_4 + 4R_2$      2. $\frac{1}{2}R_3$

3. $R_2 + R_3$; $R_4 + 2R_3$

to obtain the final simplex tableau

| x | y | z | u | v | w | P | Const. |
|---|---|---|---|---|---|---|---|
| 1 | 0 | 0 | 1 | -1 | 0 | 0 | 40 |
| $\frac{1}{2}$ | 1 | 0 | 0 | $\frac{1}{2}$ | $\frac{1}{2}$ | 0 | 60 |
| $-\frac{3}{2}$ | 0 | 1 | 0 | $-\frac{1}{2}$ | $\frac{1}{2}$ | 0 | 20 |
| 4 | 0 | 0 | 0 | 3 | 1 | 1 | 200 |

and conclude that the solution is x = 0, y = 60, z = 20, u = 40, v = 0, w = 0, and P = 200.

21. We obtain the following sequence of tableaus:

| | x | y | z | u | v | w | P | Const. | Ratio |
|---|---|---|---|---|---|---|---|---|---|
| p.r. → | (2) | 1 | 1 | 1 | 0 | 0 | 0 | 10 | 10/2 = 5 |
| | 3 | 5 | 1 | 0 | 1 | 0 | 0 | 45 | 45/3 = 15 |
| | 2 | 5 | 1 | 0 | 0 | 1 | 0 | 40 | 40/2 = 20 |
| | -12 | -10 | -5 | 0 | 0 | 0 | 1 | 0 | |

p.c. (under x)

$\frac{1}{2}R_1 \longrightarrow$

| x | y | z | u | v | w | P | Const. | |
|---|---|---|---|---|---|---|---|---|
| 1 | $\frac{1}{2}$ | $\frac{1}{2}$ | $\frac{1}{2}$ | 0 | 0 | 0 | 5 | |
| 3 | 5 | 1 | 0 | 1 | 0 | 0 | 45 | $R_2 - 3R_1$ |
| 2 | 5 | 1 | 0 | 0 | 1 | 0 | 40 | $R_3 - 2R_1$ |
| -12 | -10 | -5 | 0 | 0 | 0 | 1 | 0 | $R_4 + 12R_1$ |

$\longrightarrow$

| | x | y | z | u | v | w | P | Const. | Ratio |
|---|---|---|---|---|---|---|---|---|---|
| | 1 | $\frac{1}{2}$ | $\frac{1}{2}$ | $\frac{1}{2}$ | 0 | 0 | 0 | 5 | 5/(1/2) = 10 |
| | 0 | $\frac{7}{2}$ | $-\frac{1}{2}$ | $-\frac{3}{2}$ | 1 | 0 | 0 | 30 | 30/(7/2) = 60/7 |
| p.r. → | 0 | (4) | 0 | -1 | 0 | 1 | 0 | 30 | 30/4 = 15/2 |
| | 0 | -4 | 1 | 6 | 0 | 0 | 1 | 60 | |

p.c. (under y)

$\frac{1}{4}R_3 \longrightarrow$

| x | y | z | u | v | w | P | Const. | |
|---|---|---|---|---|---|---|---|---|
| 1 | $\frac{1}{2}$ | $\frac{1}{2}$ | $\frac{1}{2}$ | 0 | 0 | 0 | 5 | $R_1 - \frac{1}{2}R_3$ |
| 0 | $\frac{7}{2}$ | $-\frac{1}{2}$ | $-\frac{3}{2}$ | 1 | 0 | 0 | 30 | $R_2 - \frac{7}{2}R_3$ |
| 0 | 1 | 0 | $-\frac{1}{4}$ | 0 | $\frac{1}{4}$ | 0 | $\frac{15}{2}$ | $R_4 + 4R_3$ |
| 0 | -4 | 1 | 6 | 0 | 0 | 1 | 60 | |

| x | y | z | u | v | w | P | Const. |
|---|---|---|---|---|---|---|---|
| 1 | 0 | $\frac{1}{2}$ | $\frac{5}{8}$ | 0 | $-\frac{1}{8}$ | 0 | $\frac{5}{4}$ |
| 0 | 0 | $-\frac{1}{2}$ | $-\frac{5}{8}$ | 1 | $-\frac{7}{8}$ | 0 | $\frac{15}{4}$ |
| 0 | 1 | 0 | $-\frac{1}{4}$ | 0 | $\frac{1}{4}$ | 0 | $\frac{15}{2}$ |
| 0 | 0 | 1 | 5 | 0 | 1 | 1 | 90 |

This last tableau is in final form, and we conclude that
x = 5/4, y =15/2, z = 0, u = 0, v = 15/4, w = 0, and P = 90.

22. We obtain the following sequence of tableaus, where t, u, v and w are slack variables.

| x | y | z | t | u | v | w | P | Const. | Ratio | |
|---|---|---|---|---|---|---|---|---|---|---|
| 2 | (1) | 3 | 1 | 0 | 0 | 0 | 0 | 10 | 10 | $R_2 - R_1$ |
| 4 | 1 | 2 | 0 | 1 | 0 | 0 | 0 | 56 | 56 | $R_3 - 4R_1$ |
| 6 | 4 | 3 | 0 | 0 | 1 | 0 | 0 | 126 | $31\frac{1}{2}$ | $R_4 - R_1$  $R_5 + 6R_1$ |
| 2 | 1 | 1 | 0 | 0 | 0 | 1 | 0 | 32 | 32 | |
| -2 | -6 | -6 | 0 | 0 | 0 | 0 | 1 | 0 | | |

| x | y | z | t | u | v | w | P | Const. |
|---|---|---|---|---|---|---|---|---|
| 2 | 1 | 3 | 1 | 0 | 0 | 0 | 0 | 10 |
| 2 | 0 | -1 | -1 | 1 | 0 | 0 | 0 | 46 |
| -2 | 0 | -9 | -4 | 0 | 1 | 0 | 0 | 86 |
| 0 | 0 | -2 | -1 | 0 | 0 | 1 | 0 | 22 |
| 10 | 0 | 12 | 6 | 0 | 0 | 0 | 1 | 60 |

The last simplex tableau is in final form, and we have the
solution x = 0, y = 10, z = 0, t = 0, u = 46, v = 86,
w = 22, and P = 60.

23.

|        | x | y | z | s | t | u | v | P | Const. |
|--------|---|---|---|---|---|---|---|---|--------|
| p.r.→  | 1 | 2 | ⑤ | 1 | 0 | 0 | 0 | 0 | 30 |
|        | 2 | 1 | 1 | 0 | 1 | 0 | 0 | 0 | 10 |
|        | 3 | 2 | 1 | 0 | 0 | 1 | 0 | 0 | 12 |
|        | 1 | 1 | 1 | 0 | 0 | 0 | 1 | 0 | 8 |
|        | -4 | -1 | -5 | 0 | 0 | 0 | 0 | 1 | 0 |

┌─Ratio─┐
│ 30/5 = 6 │   $\frac{1}{5}R_1$  →
│ 10 │
│ 12 │
│ 8 │
└────┘

p.c. (under z)

| x | y | z | s | t | u | v | P | Const. |
|---|---|---|---|---|---|---|---|--------|
| $\frac{1}{5}$ | $\frac{2}{5}$ | 1 | $\frac{1}{5}$ | 0 | 0 | 0 | 0 | 6 |
| 2 | 1 | 1 | 0 | 1 | 0 | 0 | 0 | 10 |
| 3 | 2 | 1 | 0 | 0 | 1 | 0 | 0 | 12 |
| 1 | 1 | 1 | 0 | 0 | 0 | 1 | 0 | 8 |
| -4 | -1 | -5 | 0 | 0 | 0 | 0 | 1 | 0 |

$R_2 - R_1$
$R_3 - R_1$
$R_4 - R_1$
$R_5 + 5R_1$

|        | x | y | z | s | t | u | v | P | Const. |
|--------|---|---|---|---|---|---|---|---|--------|
|        | $\frac{1}{5}$ | $\frac{2}{5}$ | 1 | $\frac{1}{5}$ | 0 | 0 | 0 | 0 | 6 |
|        | $\frac{9}{5}$ | $\frac{3}{5}$ | 0 | $-\frac{1}{5}$ | 1 | 0 | 0 | 0 | 4 |
| p.r.→  | ⑭⁄₅ | $\frac{8}{5}$ | 0 | $-\frac{1}{5}$ | 0 | 1 | 0 | 0 | 6 |
|        | $\frac{4}{5}$ | $\frac{3}{5}$ | 0 | $-\frac{1}{5}$ | 0 | 0 | 1 | 0 | 2 |
|        | -3 | 1 | 0 | 1 | 0 | 0 | 0 | 1 | 30 |

┌──Ratio── ──┐
│ 6/(1/5) = 30 │
│ 4/(9/5) = 20/9 │
│ 6/(14/5) =15/7 │
│ 2/(4/5) =5/2 │
└────────┘

p.c. (under x)

$\dfrac{5}{14}R_3$
⟶

| x | y | z | s | t | u | v | P | Const. |
|---|---|---|---|---|---|---|---|---|
| $\frac{1}{5}$ | $\frac{2}{5}$ | 1 | $\frac{1}{5}$ | 0 | 0 | 0 | 0 | 6 |
| $\frac{9}{5}$ | $\frac{3}{5}$ | 0 | $-\frac{1}{5}$ | 1 | 0 | 0 | 0 | 4 |
| 1 | $\frac{4}{7}$ | 0 | $-\frac{1}{14}$ | 0 | $\frac{5}{14}$ | 0 | 0 | $\frac{15}{7}$ |
| $\frac{4}{5}$ | $\frac{3}{5}$ | 0 | $-\frac{1}{5}$ | 0 | 0 | 1 | 0 | 2 |
| $-3$ | 1 | 0 | 1 | 0 | 0 | 0 | 1 | 30 |

| | x | y | z | s | t | u | v | P | Const. |
|---|---|---|---|---|---|---|---|---|---|
| $R_1 - \frac{1}{5}R_3$ | 0 | $\frac{2}{7}$ | 1 | $\frac{3}{14}$ | 0 | $-\frac{1}{14}$ | 0 | 0 | $\frac{39}{7}$ |
| $R_2 - \frac{9}{5}R_3$ | 0 | $-\frac{3}{7}$ | 0 | $-\frac{1}{14}$ | 1 | $-\frac{9}{14}$ | 0 | 0 | $\frac{1}{7}$ |
| $R_4 - \frac{4}{5}R_3$ | 1 | $\frac{4}{7}$ | 0 | $-\frac{1}{14}$ | 0 | $\frac{5}{14}$ | 0 | 0 | $\frac{15}{7}$ |
| $R_5 + 3R_3$ | 0 | $\frac{1}{7}$ | 0 | $-\frac{1}{7}$ | 0 | $-\frac{2}{7}$ | 1 | 0 | $\frac{2}{7}$ |
| | 0 | $\frac{19}{7}$ | 0 | $\frac{11}{14}$ | 0 | $\frac{15}{14}$ | 0 | 1 | $\frac{255}{7}$ |

The last tableau is in final form. We see that x = 15/7, y = 0, z = 39/7, s = 0, t = 1/7, u = 0, v = 2/7, and P = 255/7.

24. From the initial tableau

| x | y | z | u | v | w | P | Const. |
|---|---|---|---|---|---|---|---|
| 2 | 1 | 2 | 1 | 0 | 0 | 0 | 14 |
| 2 | 4 | 1 | 0 | 1 | 0 | 0 | 26 |
| 1 | 2 | 3 | 0 | 0 | 1 | 0 | 28 |
| $-2$ | $-2$ | $-1$ | 0 | 0 | 0 | 1 | 0 |

we use the following row operations

1. $\frac{1}{4}R_2$

2. $R_1 - R_2;\ R_3 - 2R_2;\ R_4 + 2R_2$

3. $\frac{2}{3}R_1$

4. $R_2 - \frac{1}{2}R_1;\ R_3 - \frac{1}{2}R_1;\ R_4 + R_1$

to obtain the final tableau

| x | y | z | u | v | w | P | Const. |
|---|---|---|---|---|---|---|--------|
| 1 | 0 | $\frac{7}{6}$ | $\frac{2}{3}$ | $-\frac{1}{6}$ | 0 | 0 | 5 |
| 0 | 1 | $-\frac{1}{3}$ | $-\frac{1}{3}$ | $\frac{1}{3}$ | 0 | 0 | 4 |
| 0 | 0 | $\frac{5}{2}$ | 0 | $-\frac{1}{2}$ | 1 | 0 | 15 |
| 0 | 0 | $\frac{2}{3}$ | $\frac{2}{3}$ | $\frac{1}{3}$ | 0 | 1 | 18 |

to obtain the solution is x = 5, y = 4, z = 0, u = 0, v = 0, w = 15, and P = 18.

25. Pivoting about the x-column in the initial simplex tableau, we have

| | x | y | z | u | v | P | Const. | --Ratio-- |
|-----|---|---|----|---|---|---|--------|-----------|
| | 3 | 3 | -2 | 1 | 0 | 0 | 100 | 100/3 |
| p.r.→ | ⑤ | 5 | 3 | 0 | 1 | 0 | 150 | 150/5 |
| | -2 | -2 | 4 | 0 | 0 | 1 | 0 | |

p.c.

$\xrightarrow{\frac{1}{5}R_2}$

| x | y | z | u | v | P | Const. |
|---|---|----|---|---|---|--------|
| 3 | 3 | -2 | 1 | 0 | 0 | 100 |
| 1 | 1 | $\frac{3}{5}$ | 0 | $\frac{1}{5}$ | 0 | 30 |
| -2 | -2 | 4 | 0 | 0 | 1 | 0 |

$\xrightarrow[R_3 + 2R_2]{R_1 - 3R_2}$

| x | y | z | u | v | P | Const. |
|---|---|-----|---|---|---|--------|
| 0 | 0 | $-\frac{19}{5}$ | 1 | $-\frac{3}{5}$ | 0 | 10 |
| 1 | 1 | $\frac{3}{5}$ | 0 | $\frac{1}{5}$ | 0 | 30 |
| 0 | 0 | $\frac{26}{5}$ | 0 | $\frac{2}{5}$ | 1 | 60 |

and we see that one optimal solution occurs when x = 30, y = 0, z = 0, and P = 60. Similarly, pivoting about the y-column, we obtain another optimal solution: x = 0, y = 30, z = 0, and P = 60.

26. We tabulate the given information

|  | Product A | Product B | Time available |
|---|---|---|---|
| Machine I | 6 | 9 | 300 |
| Machine II | 5 | 4 | 180 |
| Profit per unit ($) | 3 | 4 | |

Let x and y denote the number of units of Product A and Product B to be produced. Then the required linear programming problem is:

Maximize the objective function

$$P = 3x + 4y$$

subject to the constraints

$$6x + 9y \leq 300$$

$$5x + 4y \leq 180$$

$$x \geq 0, \ y \geq 0$$

The initial simplex tableau is

| x | y | u | v | P | Const. |
|---|---|---|---|---|---|
| 6 | 9 | 1 | 0 | 0 | 300 |
| 5 | 4 | 0 | 1 | 0 | 180 |
| -3 | -4 | 0 | 0 | 1 | 0 |

Using the following sequence of row operations

1. $\frac{1}{9}R_1$.

2. $R_2 - 4R_1$; $R_3 + 4R_1$

3. $\frac{3}{7}R_2$

4. $R_1 - \frac{2}{3}R_2$; $R_3 + \frac{1}{3}R_2$

we obtain the final tableau

| x | y | u | v | P | Const. |
|---|---|---|---|---|---|
| 0 | 1 | $\frac{15}{63}$ | $-\frac{2}{7}$ | 0 | 20 |
| 1 | 0 | $-\frac{4}{21}$ | $\frac{3}{7}$ | 0 | 20 |
| 0 | 0 | $\frac{8}{21}$ | $\frac{1}{7}$ | 1 | 140 |

and conclude that x = 20, y = 20, and P = 140.

27. Let the number of model A and model B fax machines made each month be x and y, respectively. Then we have the following linear programming problem:

$$\text{Maximize } P = 25x + 40y \text{ subject to}$$

$$200x + 300y \le 600{,}000$$

$$x + y \le 2{,}500$$

$$x \ge 0, \ y \ge 0.$$

Using the simplex method, we obtain the following sequence of tableaus:

| x | y | u | v | P | Const. | --Ratio-- | |
|---|---|---|---|---|---|---|---|
| 200 | (300) | 1 | 0 | 0 | 600,000 | 2000 | $\frac{1}{300}R_1$ |
| 1 | 1 | 0 | 1 | 0 | 2,500 | 2500 | |
| −25 | −40 | 0 | 0 | 1 | 0 | | |

| x | y | u | v | P | Const. | |
|---|---|---|---|---|---|---|
| $\frac{2}{3}$ | 1 | $\frac{1}{300}$ | 0 | 0 | 2000 | $R_2 - R_1$ |
| 1 | 1 | 0 | 1 | 0 | 2500 | $R_3 + 40R_1$ |
| −25 | −40 | 0 | 0 | 1 | 0 | |

| x | y | u | v | P | Const. |
|---|---|---|---|---|---|
| $\frac{2}{3}$ | 1 | $\frac{1}{300}$ | 0 | 0 | 2,000 |
| $\frac{1}{3}$ | 0 | $-\frac{1}{300}$ | 1 | 0 | 500 |
| $\frac{5}{3}$ | 0 | $\frac{2}{15}$ | 0 | 1 | 80,000 |

We conclude that the maximum monthly profit is $80,000, and this occurs when 0 model A and 2000 model B fax machines are produced.

28. Let x denote the number of model A hibachis and y the number of model B hibachis to be manufactured. Then the problem is equivalent to the following linear programming problem:

$$\text{Maximize } P = 2x + 1.5y \text{ subject to}$$

$$3x + 4y \leq 1000$$

$$6x + 3y \leq 1200$$

$$x \geq 0, \ y \geq 0.$$

The initial simplex tableau is

| x | y | u | v | P | Const. |
|---|---|---|---|---|--------|
| 3 | 4 | 1 | 0 | 0 | 1000 |
| 6 | 3 | 0 | 1 | 0 | 1200 |
| -2 | $-\frac{3}{2}$ | 0 | 0 | 1 | 0 |

Using the following sequence of row operations,

1. $\frac{1}{6}R_2$     2. $R_1 - 3R_2$; $R_3 + 2R_2$

3. $\frac{2}{5}R_1$     4. $R_2 - \frac{1}{2}R_1$; $R_3 + \frac{1}{2}R_1$

we obtain the final tableau

| x | y | u | v | P | Const. |
|---|---|---|---|---|--------|
| 0 | 1 | $\frac{2}{5}$ | $-\frac{1}{5}$ | 0 | 160 |
| 1 | 0 | $-\frac{1}{5}$ | $\frac{4}{15}$ | 0 | 120 |
| 0 | 0 | $\frac{1}{5}$ | $\frac{7}{30}$ | 1 | 480 |

We conclude that the company should produce 120 model A and 160 model B hibachis to realize a profit of $480.

29. Suppose the farmer plants x acres of Crop A and y acres of crop B. Then the problem is

$$\text{Maximize } P = 150x + 200y \text{ subject to}$$

$$40x + 60y \leq 7400$$

$$20x + 25y \leq 3300$$

$$x \geq 0, \ y \geq 0.$$

Using the simplex method, we obtain the following sequence of tableaus:

$$\text{p.r.} \rightarrow$$

| x | y | u | v | P | Const. | --Ratio-- |
|---|---|---|---|---|---|---|
| 40 | (60) | 1 | 0 | 0 | 7400 | 7400/60 = 370/3 |
| 20 | 25 | 0 | 1 | 0 | 3300 | 3300/25 = 132 |
| −150 | −200 | 0 | 0 | 1 | 0 | |

$$\xrightarrow{\frac{1}{60}R_1}$$

p.c. (under y)

| x | y | u | v | P | Const. |
|---|---|---|---|---|---|
| $\frac{2}{3}$ | 1 | $\frac{1}{60}$ | 0 | 0 | $\frac{370}{3}$ |
| 20 | 25 | 0 | 1 | 0 | 3300 |
| −150 | −200 | 0 | 0 | 1 | 0 |

$$\xrightarrow[R_3 + 200R_1]{R_2 - 25R_1}$$

$$\text{p.r.} \rightarrow$$

| x | y | u | v | P | Const. | --Ratio-- |
|---|---|---|---|---|---|---|
| $\frac{2}{3}$ | 1 | $\frac{1}{60}$ | 0 | 0 | $\frac{370}{3}$ | 185 |
| $\left(\frac{10}{3}\right)$ | 0 | $-\frac{5}{12}$ | 1 | 0 | $\frac{650}{3}$ | 65 |
| $-\frac{50}{3}$ | 0 | $\frac{10}{3}$ | 0 | 1 | $\frac{74,000}{3}$ | |

$$\xrightarrow{\frac{3}{10}R_2}$$

p.c. (under x)

| x | y | u | v | P | Const. |
|---|---|---|---|---|---|
| $\frac{2}{3}$ | 1 | $\frac{1}{60}$ | 0 | 0 | $\frac{370}{3}$ |
| 1 | 0 | $-\frac{1}{8}$ | $\frac{3}{10}$ | 0 | 65 |
| $-\frac{50}{3}$ | 0 | $\frac{10}{3}$ | 0 | 1 | $\frac{74,000}{3}$ |

$$\xrightarrow[R_3 + \frac{50}{3}R_2]{R_1 - \frac{2}{3}R_2}$$

| x | y | u | v | P | Const. |
|---|---|---|---|---|---|
| 0 | 1 | $\frac{1}{10}$ | $-\frac{1}{5}$ | 0 | 80 |
| 1 | 0 | $-\frac{1}{8}$ | $\frac{3}{10}$ | 0 | 65 |
| 0 | 0 | $\frac{5}{4}$ | 5 | 1 | 25,750 |

The last tableau is in final form. We find x = 65, y = 80, and P = 25,750. So the maximum profit of $25,750 is realized by planting 65 acres of Crop A and 80 acres of Crop B.

30. We wish to maximize $P = 18x + 12y + 15z$ subject to

$$2x + y + 2z \leq 900$$

$$3x + y + 2z \leq 1080$$

$$2x + 2y + z \leq 840.$$

The initial simplex tableau is

| x | y | z | u | v | w | P | Const |
|---|---|---|---|---|---|---|---|
| 2 | 1 | 2 | 1 | 0 | 0 | 0 | 900 |
| 3 | 1 | 2 | 0 | 1 | 0 | 0 | 1080 |
| 2 | 2 | 1 | 0 | 0 | 1 | 0 | 840 |
| -18 | -12 | -15 | 0 | 0 | 0 | 1 | 0 |

Using the following sequence of row operations,

1. $\frac{1}{3}R_2$  
2. $R_1 - 2R_2$; $R_3 - 2R_2$; $R_4 + 18R_2$

3. $\frac{3}{4}R_3$  
4. $R_1 - \frac{1}{3}R_3$; $R_2 - \frac{1}{3}R_3$; $R_4 + 6R_3$

4. $\frac{4}{3}R_1$  
5. $R_2 - \frac{3}{4}R_1$; $R_3 + \frac{1}{4}R_1$; $R_4 + \frac{9}{2}R_1$

we obtain the final tableau

| x | y | z | u | v | w | P | Const |
|---|---|---|---|---|---|---|---|
| 0 | 0 | 1 | $\frac{4}{3}$ | $-\frac{2}{3}$ | $-\frac{1}{3}$ | 0 | 200 |
| 1 | 0 | 0 | -1 | 1 | 0 | 0 | 180 |
| 0 | 1 | 0 | $\frac{1}{3}$ | $-\frac{2}{3}$ | $\frac{2}{3}$ | 0 | 140 |
| 0 | 0 | 0 | 6 | 0 | 3 | 1 | 7920 |

and conclude that the company will realize a maximum profit of $7920 if they produce 180 units of product A, 140 units of product B, and 200 units of product C.

31. Suppose the Excelsior Company buys x, y, and z minutes of morning, afternoon, and evening commercials, respectively. Then we wish to maximize

$$P = 200{,}000x + 100{,}000y + 600{,}000z$$

subject to $3000x + 1000y + 12{,}000z \leq 102{,}000$

$$z \leq 6$$

$$x + y + z \leq 25$$

$$x \geq 0, \; y \geq 0, \; z \geq 0.$$

Using the simplex method, we obtain the following sequence of tableaus.

| x | y | z | u | v | w | P | Constant | Ratio |
|---|---|---|---|---|---|---|---|---|
| 3000 | 1000 | 12,000 | 1 | 0 | 0 | 0 | 102,000 | 17/2 |
| 0 | 0 | 1 | 0 | 1 | 0 | 0 | 6 | 6 |
| 1 | 1 | 1 | 0 | 0 | 1 | 0 | 25 | 25 |
| −200,000 | −100,000 | −600,000 | 0 | 1 | 0 | 0 | 0 | |

$$\xrightarrow[\begin{array}{c} R_3 - R_2 \\ R_4 + 600{,}000R_2 \end{array}]{R_1 - 12{,}000R_2}$$

| x | y | z | u | v | w | P | Constant | Ratio |
|---|---|---|---|---|---|---|---|---|
| 3000 | 1000 | 0 | 1 | −12000 | 0 | 0 | 30,000 | 10 |
| 0 | 0 | 1 | 0 | 1 | 0 | 0 | 6 | -- |
| 1 | 1 | 0 | 0 | −1 | 1 | 0 | 19 | 19 |
| −200,000 | −100,000 | 0 | 0 | 600,000 | 0 | 1 | 3,600,000 | |

$$\xrightarrow{\frac{1}{3000} R_1}$$

| x | y | z | u | v | w | P | Constant |
|---|---|---|---|---|---|---|---|
| 1 | $\frac{1}{3}$ | 0 | $\frac{1}{3000}$ | -4 | 0 | 0 | 10 |
| 0 | 0 | 1 | 0 | 1 | 0 | 0 | 6 |
| 1 | 1 | 0 | 0 | -1 | 1 | 0 | 19 |
| -200,000 | -100,000 | 0 | 0 | 600,000 | 0 | 1 | 3,600,000 |

$$\xrightarrow[\;R_4 + 200000R_1\;]{\;R_3 - R_1\;}$$

| x | y | z | u | v | w | P | Constant |
|---|---|---|---|---|---|---|---|
| 1 | $\frac{1}{3}$ | 0 | $\frac{1}{3000}$ | -4 | 0 | 0 | 10 |
| 0 | 0 | 1 | 0 | 1 | 0 | 0 | 6 |
| 0 | $\frac{2}{3}$ | 0 | $-\frac{1}{3000}$ | ③ | 1 | 0 | 9 |
| 0 | $\frac{-100,000}{3}$ | 0 | $\frac{200}{3}$ | -200,000 | 0 | 1 | 5,600,000 |

$$\xrightarrow{\;\frac{1}{3}R_3\;}$$

| x | y | z | u | v | w | P | Constant |
|---|---|---|---|---|---|---|---|
| 1 | $\frac{1}{3}$ | 0 | $\frac{1}{3000}$ | -4 | 0 | 0 | 10 |
| 0 | 0 | 1 | 0 | 1 | 0 | 0 | 6 |
| 0 | $\frac{2}{9}$ | 0 | $-\frac{1}{9000}$ | 1 | $\frac{1}{3}$ | 0 | 3 |
| 0 | $\frac{-100,000}{3}$ | 0 | $\frac{200}{3}$ | -200,000 | 0 | 1 | 5,600,000 |

$$\begin{array}{l} R_1 + 4R_3 \\ R_2 - R_3 \\ \xrightarrow{\hspace{3cm}} \\ R_4 + 200000R_3 \end{array}$$

| x | y | z | u | v | w | P | Constant |
|---|---|---|---|---|---|---|---|
| 1 | $\frac{11}{9}$ | 0 | $-\frac{1}{9000}$ | 0 | $\frac{4}{3}$ | 0 | 22 |
| 0 | $-\frac{2}{9}$ | 1 | $\frac{1}{9000}$ | 0 | $-\frac{1}{3}$ | 0 | 3 |
| 0 | $\frac{2}{9}$ | 0 | $-\frac{1}{9000}$ | 1 | $\frac{1}{3}$ | 0 | 3 |
| 0 | $\frac{100,000}{9}$ | 0 | $\frac{400}{9}$ | 0 | $\frac{200,000}{3}$ | 1 | 6,200,000 |

We conclude that $x = 22$, $y = 0$, $z = 3$, $u = 0$, $v = 3$, and $P = 6,200,000$. Therefore, the company should buy 22 minutes of morning and 3 minutes of evening advertising time, thereby maximizing their exposure to 6,200,000 viewers.

32. The problem is to maximize

$$x + y - z \le 0$$

$$x - 3y + z \le 0$$

$$5x + y - 3z \le 0$$

$$x + y + z \le 200,000.$$

The initial simplex tableau is

| x | y | z | t | u | v | w | P | Const. |
|---|---|---|---|---|---|---|---|---|
| 1 | 1 | -1 | 1 | 0 | 0 | 0 | 0 | 0 |
| 1 | -3 | 1 | 0 | 1 | 0 | 0 | 0 | 0 |
| 5 | 1 | -3 | 0 | 0 | 1 | 0 | 0 | 0 |
| 1 | 1 | 1 | 0 | 0 | 0 | 1 | 0 | 200,000 |
| -.12 | -.10 | -.06 | 0 | 0 | 0 | 0 | 1 | 0 |

Using the following sequence of row operations,

1. $R_2 - R_1$, $R_3 - 5R_1$, $R_4 - R_1$, $R_5 + 0.12R_1$     2. $\frac{1}{2}R_2$

3. $R_1 + R_2$, $R_3 - 2R_2$, $R_4 - 2R_2$, $R_5 + 0.18R_2$

4. $\frac{1}{4}R_4$  5. $R_1 + R_4$; $R_2 + 2R_4$; $R_5 + 0.34R_4$

we obtain the final tableau

| x | y | z | t | u | v | w | P | Const. |
|---|---|---|---|---|---|---|---|--------|
| 1 | 0 | 0 | .5 | .25 | 0 | .25 | 0 | 50,000 |
| 0 | 0 | 1 | -.5 | 0 | 0 | .5 | 0 | 100,000 |
| 0 | 0 | 0 | -4 | -1 | 1 | 0 | 0 | 0 |
| 0 | 1 | 0 | 0 | -.25 | 0 | .25 | 0 | 50,000 |
| 0 | 0 | 0 | .03 | .005 | 0 | .085 | 1 | 17,000 |

Therefore, the maximum return on the investment each year is $17,000 when Sharon invests $50,000 in growth funds, $50,000 in balanced funds, and $100,000 in income funds.

33. We first tabulate the given information:

**MODELS**

| Dept. | A | B | C | Time available |
|-------|---|---|---|----------------|
| Fabrication | $\frac{5}{4}$ | $\frac{3}{2}$ | $\frac{3}{2}$ | 310 |
| Assembly | 1 | 1 | $\frac{3}{4}$ | 205 |
| Finishing | 1 | 1 | $\frac{1}{2}$ | 190 |
| Profit | 26 | 28 | 24 | |

Let x, y, and z denote the number of units of model A, model B, and model C to be produced, respectively. Then the required linear programming problem is

Maximize $P = 26x + 28y + 24z$ subject to

$$\frac{5}{4}x + \frac{3}{2}y + \frac{3}{2}z \leq 310$$

$$x + y + \frac{3}{4}z \leq 205$$

$$x + y + \frac{1}{2}z \leq 190$$

$$x \geq 0, \ y \geq 0, \ z \geq 0.$$

Using the simplex method, we obtain the following tableaus

| | x | y | z | u | v | w | P | Const. | Ratio | |
|---|---|---|---|---|---|---|---|---|---|---|
| | $\frac{5}{4}$ | $\frac{3}{2}$ | $\frac{3}{2}$ | 1 | 0 | 0 | 0 | 310 | 248 | $R_1 -\frac{3}{2}R_3$ |
| | 1 | 1 | $\frac{3}{4}$ | 0 | 1 | 0 | 0 | 205 | 205 | $R_2 - R_3$ |
| p.r.→ | 1 | ① | $\frac{1}{2}$ | 0 | 0 | 1 | 0 | 190 | 190 | $R_4 +28R_3$ |
| | -26 | -28 | -24 | 0 | 0 | 0 | 1 | 0 | | |

p.c. (under y column)

| | x | y | z | u | v | w | P | Const. | Ratio | |
|---|---|---|---|---|---|---|---|---|---|---|
| p.r.→ | $-\frac{1}{4}$ | 0 | $\boxed{\frac{3}{4}}$ | 1 | 0 | $-\frac{3}{2}$ | 0 | 25 | $33\frac{1}{3}$ | $\frac{4}{3}R_1$ |
| | 0 | 0 | $\frac{1}{4}$ | 0 | 1 | -1 | 0 | 15 | 60 | |
| | 1 | 1 | $\frac{1}{2}$ | 0 | 0 | 1 | 0 | 190 | 380 | |
| | 2 | 0 | -10 | 0 | 0 | 28 | 1 | 5320 | | |

p.c. (under z column)

| | x | y | z | u | v | w | P | Const. | |
|---|---|---|---|---|---|---|---|---|---|
| | $-\frac{1}{3}$ | 0 | 1 | $\frac{4}{3}$ | 0 | -2 | 0 | $\frac{100}{3}$ | $R_2 - \frac{1}{4}R_1$ |
| | 0 | 0 | $\frac{1}{4}$ | 0 | 1 | -1 | 0 | 15 | $R_3 - \frac{1}{2}R_1$ |
| | 1 | 1 | $\frac{1}{2}$ | 0 | 0 | 1 | 0 | 190 | $R_4 + 10R_1$ |
| | 2 | 0 | -10 | 0 | 0 | 28 | 1 | 5320 | |

| | x | y | z | u | v | w | P | Const. | Ratio | |
|---|---|---|---|---|---|---|---|---|---|---|
| | $-\frac{1}{3}$ | 0 | 1 | $\frac{4}{3}$ | 0 | -2 | 0 | $\frac{100}{3}$ | -- | |
| p.r.→ | $\boxed{\frac{1}{12}}$ | 0 | 0 | $-\frac{1}{3}$ | 1 | $-\frac{1}{2}$ | 0 | $\frac{20}{3}$ | 80 | $12R_2$ |
| | $\frac{7}{6}$ | 1 | 0 | $-\frac{2}{3}$ | 0 | 2 | 0 | $\frac{520}{3}$ | $148\frac{4}{7}$ | |
| | $-\frac{4}{3}$ | 0 | 0 | $\frac{40}{3}$ | 0 | 8 | 1 | $\frac{16960}{3}$ | | |

p.c. (under x column)

| x | y | z | u | v | w | P | Const. |
|---|---|---|---|---|---|---|---|
| $-\frac{1}{3}$ | 0 | 1 | $\frac{4}{3}$ | 0 | -2 | 0 | $\frac{100}{3}$ |
| 1 | 0 | 0 | -4 | 12 | -6 | 0 | 80 |
| $\frac{7}{6}$ | 1 | 0 | $-\frac{2}{3}$ | 0 | 2 | 0 | $\frac{520}{3}$ |
| $-\frac{4}{3}$ | 0 | 0 | $\frac{40}{3}$ | 0 | 8 | 1 | $\frac{16960}{3}$ |

$$R_1 + \tfrac{1}{3}R_2$$
$$\xrightarrow{\hspace{2cm}}$$
$$R_3 - \tfrac{7}{6}R_2$$
$$R_4 + \tfrac{4}{3}R_2$$

| x | y | z | u | v | w | P | Const. |
|---|---|---|---|---|---|---|---|
| 0 | 0 | 1 | 0 | 4 | -4 | 0 | 60 |
| 1 | 0 | 0 | -4 | 12 | -6 | 0 | 80 |
| 0 | 1 | 0 | 4 | -14 | 9 | 0 | 80 |
| 0 | 0 | 0 | 8 | 16 | 0 | 1 | 5760 |

The last tableau is in final form. We see that $x = 80$, $y = 80$, $z = 60$, and $P = 5760$. So, by producing 80 units each of Models A and B, and 60 units of Model C, the company stands to make a profit of $5760.

34. The linear programming problem is

Maximize $P = 3400x + 4000y + 5000z$   subject to

$$6x + 8y + 10z \le 8200$$
$$24x + 22y + 20z \le 21800$$
$$18x + 21y + 30z \le 23700$$
$$x \ge 0,\ y \ge 0,\ z \ge 0.$$

The initial simplex tableau is

| x | y | z | u | v | w | P | Const. |
|---|---|---|---|---|---|---|---|
| 6 | 8 | 10 | 1 | 0 | 0 | 0 | 8,200 |
| 24 | 22 | 20 | 0 | 1 | 0 | 0 | 21,800 |
| 18 | 21 | 30 | 0 | 0 | 1 | 0 | 23,700 |
| -3400 | -4000 | -5000 | 0 | 0 | 0 | 1 | 0. |

Using the sequence of row operations

1. $\frac{1}{30}R_3$;    2. $R_1 - 10R_3$; $R_2 - 20R_3$; $R_4 + 5000R_3$

3.  $R_2 - 8R_1$;  $R_3 - \frac{7}{10}R_1$;  $R_4 + 500R_1$    4.    $\frac{1}{12}R_2$

5.  $R_3 - \frac{3}{5}R_2$;  $R_4 + 400R_2$

we obtain the final simplex tableau

| x | y | z | u | v | w | P | Const. |
|---|---|---|---|---|---|---|---|
| 0 | 1 | 0 | 1 | 0 | $-\frac{1}{3}$ | 0 | 300 |
| 1 | 0 | 0 | $-\frac{2}{3}$ | $\frac{1}{12}$ | $\frac{1}{6}$ | 0 | 300 |
| 0 | 0 | 1 | $-\frac{3}{10}$ | $-\frac{1}{20}$ | $\frac{1}{6}$ | 0 | 400 |
| 0 | 0 | 0 | $\frac{700}{3}$ | $\frac{100}{3}$ | $\frac{200}{3}$ | 1 | 4,220,000 |

from which we conclude that maximum profit of \$4,220,000 is obtained if Boise produces 300 standard, 300 deluxe, and 400 luxury models.

35.  Let x, y, and z denote the number (in thousands) of bottles of formula I, formula II, and formula III, respectively, produced. The resulting linear programming problem is

Maximize $P = 180x + 200y + 300z$ subject to

$$\frac{5}{2}x + 3y + 4z \leq 70$$
$$x \leq 9$$
$$y \leq 12$$
$$z \leq 6$$

$x \geq 0$, $y \geq 0$, and $z \geq 0$.

Using the simplex method, we have

| | x | y | z | s | t | u | v | P | Const. | Ratio |
|---|---|---|---|---|---|---|---|---|---|---|
| | $\frac{5}{2}$ | 3 | 4 | 1 | 0 | 0 | 0 | 0 | 70 | $17\frac{1}{2}$ |
| | 1 | 0 | 0 | 0 | 1 | 0 | 0 | 0 | 9 | -- |
| | 0 | 1 | 0 | 0 | 0 | 1 | 0 | 0 | 12 | -- |
| p.r.→ | 0 | 0 | ①  | 0 | 0 | 0 | 1 | 0 | 6 | 6 |
| | -180 | -200 | -300 | 0 | 0 | 0 | 0 | 1 | 0 | |

↑
p.c.

$$\begin{array}{c} R_1 - 4R_4 \\ \hline R_5 + 300R_4 \end{array} \longrightarrow$$

| x | y | z | s | t | u | v | P | Const. | —Ratio— |
|---|---|---|---|---|---|---|---|---|---|
| $\frac{5}{2}$ | 3 | 0 | 1 | 0 | 0 | -4 | 0 | 46 | $15\frac{1}{3}$ |
| 1 | 0 | 0 | 0 | 1 | 0 | 0 | 0 | 9 | -- |
| 0 | ①  | 0 | 0 | 0 | 1 | 0 | 0 | 12 | 12 |
| 0 | 0 | 1 | 0 | 0 | 0 | 1 | 0 | 6 | -- |
| -180 | -200 | 0 | 0 | 0 | 0 | 300 | 1 | 1800 | |

p.r. → (third row)  
↑ p.c. (under -200)

$$\begin{array}{c} R_1 - 3R_3 \\ \hline R_5 + 200R_3 \end{array} \longrightarrow$$

| x | y | z | s | t | u | v | P | Const. | —Ratio— |
|---|---|---|---|---|---|---|---|---|---|
| $\frac{5}{2}$ | 0 | 0 | 1 | 0 | -3 | -4 | 0 | 10 | 4 |
| 1 | 0 | 0 | 0 | 1 | 0 | 0 | 0 | 9 | 9 |
| 0 | 1 | 0 | 0 | 0 | 1 | 0 | 0 | 12 | -- |
| 0 | 0 | 1 | 0 | 0 | 0 | 1 | 0 | 6 | -- |
| -180 | 0 | 0 | 0 | 0 | 200 | 300 | 1 | 4200 | |

$\frac{2}{5}R_1 \longrightarrow$

| x | y | z | s | t | u | v | P | Const. |
|---|---|---|---|---|---|---|---|---|
| 1 | 0 | 0 | $\frac{2}{5}$ | 0 | $-\frac{6}{5}$ | $-\frac{8}{5}$ | 0 | 4 |
| 1 | 0 | 0 | 0 | 1 | 0 | 0 | 0 | 9 |
| 0 | 1 | 0 | 0 | 0 | 1 | 0 | 0 | 12 |
| 0 | 0 | 1 | 0 | 0 | 0 | 1 | 0 | 6 |
| -180 | 0 | 0 | 0 | 0 | 200 | 300 | 1 | 4200 |

$$R_2 - R_1 \longrightarrow$$
$$R_5 + 180R_1$$

| x | y | z | s | t | u | v | P | Const. | Ratio |
|---|---|---|---|---|---|---|---|---|---|
| 1 | 0 | 0 | $\frac{2}{5}$ | 0 | $-\frac{6}{5}$ | $-\frac{8}{5}$ | 0 | 4 | -- |
| 0 | 0 | 0 | $-\frac{2}{5}$ | 1 | $\boxed{\frac{6}{5}}$ | $\frac{8}{5}$ | 0 | 5 | $4\frac{1}{6}$ |
| 0 | 1 | 0 | 0 | 0 | 1 | 0 | 0 | 12 | 12 |
| 0 | 0 | 1 | 0 | 0 | 0 | 1 | 0 | 6 | -- |
| 0 | 0 | 0 | 72 | 0 | -16 | 12 | 1 | 4920 | |

p.c.

$\xrightarrow{\frac{5}{6}R_2}$

| x | y | z | s | t | u | v | P | Const. |
|---|---|---|---|---|---|---|---|---|
| 1 | 0 | 0 | $\frac{2}{5}$ | 0 | $-\frac{6}{5}$ | $-\frac{8}{5}$ | 0 | 4 |
| 0 | 0 | 0 | $-\frac{1}{3}$ | $\frac{5}{6}$ | 1 | $\frac{4}{3}$ | 0 | $\frac{25}{6}$ |
| 0 | 1 | 0 | 0 | 0 | 1 | 0 | 0 | 12 |
| 0 | 0 | 1 | 0 | 0 | 0 | 1 | 0 | 6 |
| 0 | 0 | 0 | 72 | 0 | -16 | 12 | 1 | 4920 |

$$R_1 + \frac{6}{5}R_2$$
$$R_3 - R_2 \xrightarrow{\hspace{2cm}}$$
$$R_5 + 16R_2$$

| x | y | z | s | t | u | v | P | Const. |
|---|---|---|---|---|---|---|---|---|
| 1 | 0 | 0 | 0 | 1 | 0 | 0 | 0 | 9 |
| 0 | 0 | 0 | $-\frac{1}{3}$ | $\frac{5}{6}$ | 1 | $\frac{4}{3}$ | 0 | $\frac{25}{6}$ |
| 0 | 1 | 0 | $\frac{1}{3}$ | $-\frac{5}{6}$ | 0 | $-\frac{4}{3}$ | 0 | $\frac{47}{6}$ |
| 0 | 0 | 1 | 0 | 0 | 0 | 1 | 0 | 6 |
| 0 | 0 | 0 | $\frac{200}{3}$ | $\frac{40}{3}$ | 0 | $\frac{100}{3}$ | 1 | $4986\frac{2}{3}$ |

Therefore, $x = 9$, $y = 47/6$, $z = 6$, and $P \approx 4986.67$; that is, the company should manufacture 9000 bottles of formula I, 7833 bottles of formula II, and 6000 bottles of formula III for a maximum profit of $4986.67.

1. $x = 1.2$, $y = 0$, $z = 1.6$, $w = 0$, and $P = 8.8$

2. $x = 5.33$, $y = 0$, $z = 2.67$, $w = 0$, and $P = 21.33$.

3. $x = 1.6$, $y = 0$, $z = 0$, $w = 3.6$, and $P = 12.4$

4. $x = 0$, $y = 3.33$, $z = 1.33$, $w = 0$, and $P = 17.33$.

## EXERCISES 4.2, page 246

1. We solve the associated regular problem:

   Maximize $P = -C = 2x - y$ subject to
   $$x + 2y \leq 6$$
   $$3x + 2y \leq 12$$
   $$x \geq 0, \ y \geq 0.$$

   Using the simplex method where u and v are slack variables, we have

| x | y | u | v | P | Const. | Ratio |
|---|---|---|---|---|--------|-------|
| 1 | 2 | 1 | 0 | 0 | 6 | 6 |
| ③ | 2 | 0 | 1 | 0 | 12 | 4 |
| -2 | 1 | 0 | 0 | 1 | 0 | |

p.r.→ (on row 2)   p.c. (on column x)   $\frac{1}{3}R_2$ →

| x | y | u | v | P | Const. |
|---|---|---|---|---|--------|
| 1 | 2 | 1 | 0 | 0 | 6 |
| 1 | $\frac{2}{3}$ | 0 | $\frac{1}{3}$ | 0 | 4 |
| -2 | 1 | 0 | 0 | 1 | 0 |

$\begin{array}{c} R_1 - R_2 \\ \hline R_3 + 2R_2 \end{array}$ →

| x | y | u | v | P | Const. |
|---|---|---|---|---|--------|
| 0 | $\frac{4}{3}$ | 1 | $-\frac{1}{3}$ | 0 | 2 |
| 1 | $\frac{2}{3}$ | 0 | $\frac{1}{3}$ | 0 | 4 |
| 0 | $\frac{7}{3}$ | 0 | $\frac{2}{3}$ | 1 | 8 |

Therefore, $x = 4$, $y = 0$, and $C = -P = -8$.

2. The problem is equivalent to maximizing $P = -C = 2x + 3y$ subject to the given constraints. Using the simplex method for regular problems, we have

| | x | y | u | v | P | Const. | -- Ratio -- | |
|---|---|---|---|---|---|---|---|---|
| p.r.→ | 3 | ④ | 1 | 0 | 0 | 24 | 6 | |
| | 7 | -4 | 0 | 1 | 0 | 16 | -- | $\frac{1}{4}R_1$ |
| | -2 | -3 | 0 | 0 | 1 | 0 | | |

p.c.

| x | y | u | v | P | Const. | |
|---|---|---|---|---|---|---|
| $\frac{3}{4}$ | 1 | $\frac{1}{4}$ | 0 | 0 | 6 | $R_2 + 4R_1$ |
| 7 | -4 | 0 | 1 | 0 | 16 | $R_3 + 3R_1$ |
| -2 | -3 | 0 | 0 | 1 | 0 | |

| x | y | u | v | P | Const. |
|---|---|---|---|---|---|
| $\frac{3}{4}$ | 1 | $\frac{1}{4}$ | 0 | 0 | 6 |
| 10 | 0 | 1 | 1 | 0 | 40 |
| $\frac{1}{4}$ | 0 | $\frac{3}{4}$ | 0 | 1 | 18 |

The last tableau is in final form. We see that the solution is $x = 0$, $y = 6$, and $C = -P = -18$.

3. We maximize $P = -C = 3x + 2y$. Using the simplex method, we obtain

| | x | y | u | v | P | Const. | -- Ratio -- | |
|---|---|---|---|---|---|---|---|---|
| | 3 | 4 | 1 | 0 | 0 | 24 | 8 | |
| p.r.→ | ⑦ | -4 | 0 | 1 | 0 | 16 | $\frac{16}{7}$ | $\frac{1}{7}R_2$ |
| | -3 | -2 | 0 | 0 | 1 | 0 | | |

p.c.

| x | y | u | v | P | Const. |
|---|---|---|---|---|---|
| 3 | 4 | 1 | 0 | 0 | 24 |
| 1 | $-\frac{4}{7}$ | 0 | $\frac{1}{7}$ | 0 | $\frac{16}{7}$ |
| $-3$ | $-2$ | 0 | 0 | 1 | 0 |

$$R_1 - 3R_2$$
$$R_3 + 3R_2 \longrightarrow$$

| | x | y | u | v | P | Const. | Ratio |
|---|---|---|---|---|---|---|---|
| p.r. → | 0 | $\boxed{\frac{40}{7}}$ | 1 | $-\frac{3}{7}$ | 0 | $\frac{120}{7}$ | 3 |
| | 1 | $-\frac{4}{7}$ | 0 | $\frac{1}{7}$ | 0 | $\frac{16}{7}$ | — |
| | 0 | $-\frac{26}{7}$ | 0 | $\frac{3}{7}$ | 1 | $\frac{48}{7}$ | |

↑ p.c.

$$\frac{7}{40}R_1 \longrightarrow$$

| x | y | u | v | P | Const. |
|---|---|---|---|---|---|
| 0 | 1 | $\frac{7}{40}$ | $-\frac{3}{40}$ | 0 | 3 |
| 1 | $-\frac{4}{7}$ | 0 | $\frac{1}{7}$ | 0 | $\frac{16}{7}$ |
| 0 | $-\frac{26}{7}$ | 0 | $\frac{3}{7}$ | 1 | $\frac{48}{7}$ |

$$R_2 + \frac{4}{7}R_1 \longrightarrow$$
$$R_3 + \frac{26}{7}R_1$$

| x | y | u | v | P | Const. |
|---|---|---|---|---|---|
| 0 | 1 | $\frac{7}{40}$ | $-\frac{3}{40}$ | 0 | 3 |
| 1 | 0 | $\frac{1}{10}$ | $\frac{1}{10}$ | 0 | 4 |
| 0 | 0 | $\frac{13}{20}$ | $\frac{3}{20}$ | 1 | 18 |

The last tableau is in final form. We find x = 4, y = 3, and C = −P = −18.

4. We solve the associated regular problem:

$$\text{Maximize } P = -C = -x + 2y - z$$

subject to the given constraints. We obtain the following initial tableau:

| x | y | z | u | v | w | P | Const. |
|---|---|---|---|---|---|---|--------|
| 1 | -2 | 3 | 1 | 0 | 0 | 0 | 10 |
| 2 | 1 | -2 | 0 | 1 | 0 | 0 | 15 |
| 2 | 1 | 3 | 0 | 0 | 1 | 0 | 20 |
| 1 | -2 | 1 | 0 | 0 | 0 | 1 | 0 |

Using the following sequence of row operations;

1. $R_1 + 2R_2$; $R_3 - R_2$; $R_4 + 2R_2$

2. $\frac{1}{5}R_3$    3. $R_1 + R_3$; $R_2 + 2R_3$; $R_4 + 3R_3$

We obtain the final simplex tableau

| x | y | z | u | v | w | P | Const. |
|---|---|---|---|---|---|---|--------|
| 5 | 0 | 0 | 1 | $\frac{9}{5}$ | $\frac{1}{5}$ | 0 | 41 |
| 2 | 1 | 0 | 0 | $\frac{3}{5}$ | $\frac{2}{5}$ | 0 | 17 |
| 0 | 0 | 1 | 0 | $-\frac{1}{5}$ | $\frac{1}{5}$ | 0 | 1 |
| 5 | 0 | 0 | 0 | $\frac{7}{5}$ | $\frac{3}{5}$ | 1 | 33 |

from which we deduce that x = 0, y = 17, z = 1, u = 41, v = 0, w = 0, and C = -P = -33.

5.  We maximize P = -C = -2x + 3y + 4z subject to the given constraints. Using the simplex method we obtain

| | x | y | z | u | v | w | P | Const. | Ratio |
|---|---|---|---|---|---|---|---|--------|-------|
| | -1 | 2 | -1 | 1 | 0 | 0 | 0 | 8 | -- |
| p.r.→ | 1 | -2 | (2) | 0 | 1 | 0 | 0 | 10 | 5 |
| | 2 | 4 | -3 | 0 | 0 | 1 | 0 | 12 | -- |
| | 2 | -3 | -4 | 0 | 0 | 0 | 1 | 0 | |

$\frac{1}{2}R_2$

p.c. (at z column)

| x | y | z | u | v | w | P | Const. |
|---|---|---|---|---|---|---|--------|
| -1 | 2 | -1 | 1 | 0 | 0 | 0 | 8 |
| $\frac{1}{2}$ | -1 | 1 | 0 | $\frac{1}{2}$ | 0 | 0 | 5 |
| 2 | 4 | -3 | 0 | 0 | 1 | 0 | 12 |
| 2 | -3 | -4 | 0 | 0 | 0 | 1 | 0 |

$R_1 + R_2$
$R_3 + 3R_2$
$R_4 + 4R_2$

| | x | y | z | u | v | w | P | Const. | Ratio | |
|---|---|---|---|---|---|---|---|---|---|---|
| p.r. → | $-\frac{1}{2}$ | ① | 0 | 1 | $\frac{1}{2}$ | 0 | 0 | 13 | 13 | $R_2 + R_1$ |
| | $\frac{1}{2}$ | -1 | 1 | 0 | $\frac{1}{2}$ | 0 | 0 | 5 | -- | $R_3 - R_1$ |
| | $\frac{7}{2}$ | 1 | 0 | 0 | $\frac{3}{2}$ | 1 | 0 | 27 | 27 | $R_4 + 7R_1$ |
| | 4 | -7 | 0 | 0 | 2 | 0 | 1 | 20 | | |

p.c.

| x | y | z | u | v | w | P | Const. |
|---|---|---|---|---|---|---|---|
| $-\frac{1}{2}$ | 1 | 0 | 1 | $\frac{1}{2}$ | 0 | 0 | 13 |
| 0 | 0 | 1 | 1 | 1 | 0 | 0 | 18 |
| 4 | 0 | 0 | -1 | 1 | 1 | 0 | 14 |
| $\frac{1}{2}$ | 0 | 0 | 7 | $\frac{11}{2}$ | 0 | 1 | 111 |

The last tableau is in final form. We see that $x = 0$, $y = 13$, $z = 18$, $w = 14$, and $C = -P = -111$.

6.    We maximize $P = -C = 3x + 2y + z$ subject to the given constraints.

| x | y | z | u | v | w | P | Const. |
|---|---|---|---|---|---|---|---|
| -1 | 2 | -1 | 1 | 0 | 0 | 0 | 8 |
| 1 | -2 | 2 | 0 | 1 | 0 | 0 | 10 |
| 2 | 4 | -3 | 0 | 0 | 1 | 0 | 12 |
| -3 | -2 | -1 | 0 | 0 | 0 | 1 | 0 |

From the following sequence of row operations,

1. $\frac{1}{2}R_3$  2. $R_1 + R_3$; $R_2 - R_3$; $R_4 + 3R_3$  3. $\frac{2}{7}R_2$

4. $R_1 + \frac{5}{2}R_2$; $R_3 + \frac{3}{2}R_2$; $R_4 + \frac{11}{2}R_2$  5. $\frac{7}{8}R_1$

6. $R_2 + \frac{8}{7}R_1$; $R_3 - \frac{2}{7}R_1$; $R_4 + \frac{16}{7}R_1$

we obtain the final tableau

| x | y | z | u | v | w | P | Const. |
|---|---|---|---|---|---|---|--------|
| 0 | 1 | 0 | $\frac{7}{8}$ | $\frac{5}{8}$ | $\frac{1}{8}$ | 0 | $\frac{59}{4}$ |
| 0 | 0 | 1 | 1 | 1 | 0 | 0 | 18 |
| 1 | 0 | 0 | $-\frac{1}{4}$ | $\frac{1}{4}$ | $\frac{1}{4}$ | 0 | $\frac{7}{2}$ |
| 0 | 0 | 0 | 2 | 3 | 1 | 1 | 58 |

The last tableau is in final form. We find $x = 7/2$, $y = 59/4$, $z = 18$, and $C = -P = -58$.

7.  $x = 5/4$, $y = 1/4$, $u = 2$, $v = 3$, and $C = P = 13$.

8.  $x = 1$, $y = 5$, $u = \frac{1}{4}$, $v = \frac{7}{8}$, and $C = P = 13$.

9.  $x = 5$, $y = 10$, $z = 0$, $u = 1$, $v = 2$, and $C = P = 80$.

10.  $x = 4$, $y = 1$, $u = \frac{1}{3}$, $v = \frac{5}{3}$, and $C = P = 11$.

11.  We first write the tableau

| x | y | Constant |
|---|---|----------|
| 1 | 2 | 4 |
| 3 | 2 | 6 |
| 2 | 5 | |

Then obtain the following by interchanging rows and columns:

| u | v | Constant |
|---|---|----------|
| 1 | 3 | 2 |
| 2 | 2 | 5 |
| 4 | 6 | |

From this table we construct the dual problem:

Maximize the objective function

$$P = 4u + 6v$$

subject to the constraints

$$u + 3v \leq 2$$
$$2u + 2v \leq 5$$
$$u \geq 0, \ v \geq 0.$$

Solving the dual problem using the simplex method with x and y as the slack variables, we obtain

| | u | v | x | y | P | Const. | | --Ratio-- |
|---|---|---|---|---|---|---|---|---|
| p.r.→ | 1 | ③ | 1 | 0 | 0 | 2 | | $\frac{2}{3}$ |
| | 2 | 2 | 0 | 1 | 0 | 5 | | $\frac{5}{2}$ |
| | -4 | -6 | 0 | 0 | 1 | 0 | | |

$\xrightarrow{\frac{1}{3}R_1}$

$\uparrow$ p.c.

| u | v | x | y | P | Const. |
|---|---|---|---|---|---|
| $\frac{1}{3}$ | 1 | $\frac{1}{3}$ | 0 | 0 | $\frac{2}{3}$ |
| 2 | 2 | 0 | 1 | 0 | 5 |
| -4 | -6 | 0 | 0 | 1 | 0 |

$\xrightarrow[R_3 + 6R_1]{R_2 - 2R_1}$

| | u | v | x | y | P | Const. | | --Ratio-- |
|---|---|---|---|---|---|---|---|---|
| p.r.→ | $\frac{1}{3}$ | 1 | $\frac{1}{3}$ | 0 | 0 | $\frac{2}{3}$ | | 2 |
| | $\frac{4}{3}$ | 0 | $-\frac{2}{3}$ | 1 | 0 | $\frac{11}{3}$ | | $2\frac{3}{4}$ |
| | -2 | 0 | 2 | 0 | 1 | 4 | | |

$\xrightarrow{3R_1}$

$\uparrow$ p.c.

| u | v | x | y | P | Const. |
|---|---|---|---|---|---|
| 1 | 3 | 1 | 0 | 0 | 2 |
| $\frac{4}{3}$ | 0 | $-\frac{2}{3}$ | 1 | 0 | $\frac{11}{3}$ |
| -2 | 0 | 2 | 0 | 1 | 4 |

$\xrightarrow[R_3 + 2R_1]{R_2 - \frac{4}{3}R_1}$

| u | v | x | y | P | Const. |
|---|---|---|---|---|---|
| 1 | 3 | 1 | 0 | 0 | 2 |
| 0 | -4 | -2 | 1 | 0 | 1 |
| 0 | 6 | 4 | 0 | 1 | 8 |

Interpreting the final tableau, we see that x = 4, y = 0, and P = C = 8.

12.   The dual problem is

$$\text{Maximize } P = 90u + 120v \text{ subject to}$$

$$2u + 3v \le 3$$

$$3u + 2v \le 2$$

$$u \ge 0, \ v \ge 0.$$

The initial simplex tableau is

| u | v | x | y | P | Const. |
|---|---|---|---|---|--------|
| 2 | 3 | 1 | 0 | 0 | 3 |
| 3 | 2 | 0 | 1 | 0 | 2 |
| -90 | -120 | 0 | 0 | 1 | 0 |

$\dfrac{1}{2}R_2 \longrightarrow$

| u | v | x | y | P | Const. |
|---|---|---|---|---|--------|
| 2 | 3 | 1 | 0 | 0 | 3 |
| $\frac{3}{2}$ | 1 | 0 | $\frac{1}{2}$ | 0 | 1 |
| -90 | -120 | 0 | 0 | 1 | 0 |

$\begin{array}{c} R_1 - 3R_2 \\ \hline R_3 + 120R_2 \end{array} \longrightarrow$

| u | v | x | y | P | Const. |
|---|---|---|---|---|--------|
| $-\frac{5}{2}$ | 0 | 1 | $-\frac{3}{2}$ | 0 | 0 |
| $\frac{3}{2}$ | 1 | 0 | $\frac{1}{2}$ | 0 | 1 |
| 90 | 0 | 0 | 60 | 1 | 120 |

We conclude that $x = 0$, $y = 60$, and $C = P = 120$.

13.   We first write the tableau

| x | y | Constant |
|---|---|----------|
| 6 | 1 | 60 |
| 2 | 1 | 40 |
| 1 | 1 | 30 |
| 6 | 4 | |

Then obtain the following by interchanging rows and columns:

| u | v | w | Constant |
|---|---|---|----------|
| 6 | 2 | 1 | 6 |
| 1 | 1 | 1 | 4 |
| 60 | 40 | 30 | |

From this table we construct the dual problem:

Maximize $P = 60u + 40v + 30w$ subject to

$$6u + 2v + w \le 6$$
$$u + v + w \le 4$$
$$u \ge 0, \ v \ge 0, \ w \ge 0.$$

We solve the problem as follows.

| | u | v | w | x | y | P | Const. | --Ratio-- | |
|---|---|---|---|---|---|---|---|---|---|
| p.r.→ | (6) | 2 | 1 | 1 | 0 | 0 | 6 | 1 | $\frac{1}{6}R_1$ |
| | 1 | 1 | 1 | 0 | 1 | 0 | 4 | 4 | |
| | -60 | -40 | -30 | 0 | 0 | 1 | 0 | | |

↑
p.c.

| | u | v | w | x | y | P | Const. | |
|---|---|---|---|---|---|---|---|---|
| | 1 | $\frac{1}{3}$ | $\frac{1}{6}$ | $\frac{1}{6}$ | 0 | 0 | 1 | $R_2 - R_1$ |
| | 1 | 1 | 1 | 0 | 1 | 0 | 4 | $R_3 + 60R_1$ |
| | -60 | -40 | -30 | 0 | 0 | 1 | 0 | |

| | u | v | w | x | y | P | Const. | --Ratio-- | |
|---|---|---|---|---|---|---|---|---|---|
| | 1 | $\frac{1}{3}$ | $\frac{1}{6}$ | $\frac{1}{6}$ | 0 | 0 | 1 | 6 | $\frac{6R_2}{5}$ |
| p.r.→ | 0 | $\frac{2}{3}$ | $(\frac{5}{6})$ | $-\frac{1}{6}$ | 1 | 0 | 3 | $\frac{18}{5}$ | |
| | 0 | -20 | -20 | 10 | 0 | 1 | 60 | | |

↑
p.c.

| | u | v | w | x | y | P | Const. | |
|---|---|---|---|---|---|---|---|---|
| | 1 | $\frac{1}{3}$ | $\frac{1}{6}$ | $\frac{1}{6}$ | 0 | 0 | 1 | $R_1 - \frac{1}{6}R_2$ |
| | 0 | $\frac{4}{5}$ | 1 | $-\frac{1}{5}$ | $\frac{6}{5}$ | 0 | $\frac{18}{5}$ | $R_3 + 20R_2$ |
| | 0 | -20 | -20 | 10 | 0 | 1 | 60 | |

| | u | v | w | x | y | P | Const. | --Ratio-- | |
|---|---|---|---|---|---|---|---|---|---|
| p.r.→ | 1 | $(\frac{1}{5})$ | 0 | $\frac{1}{5}$ | $-\frac{1}{5}$ | 0 | $\frac{2}{5}$ | 2 | $5R_1$ |
| | 0 | $\frac{4}{5}$ | 1 | $-\frac{1}{5}$ | $\frac{6}{5}$ | 0 | $\frac{18}{5}$ | $\frac{9}{2}$ | |
| | 0 | -4 | 0 | 6 | 24 | 1 | 132 | | |

↑
p.c.

| u | v | w | x | y | P | Const. |
|---|---|---|---|---|---|---|
| 5 | 1 | 0 | 1 | -1 | 0 | 2 |
| 0 | $\frac{4}{5}$ | 1 | $-\frac{1}{5}$ | $\frac{6}{5}$ | 0 | $\frac{18}{5}$ |
| 0 | -4 | 0 | 6 | 24 | 1 | 132 |

$$\begin{array}{c} R_2 - \frac{4}{5}R_1 \\ \longrightarrow \\ R_3 + 4R_1 \end{array}$$

| u | v | w | x | y | P | Const. |
|---|---|---|---|---|---|---|
| 5 | 1 | 0 | 1 | -1 | 0 | 2 |
| -4 | 0 | 1 | -1 | 2 | 0 | 2 |
| 20 | 0 | 0 | 10 | 20 | 1 | 140 |

The last tableau is in final form. We find that $x = 10$, $y = 20$, and $C = 140$.

14.    We first write the tableau

| x | y | Constant |
|---|---|---|
| 4 | 1 | 16 |
| 1 | 2 | 12 |
| 1 | 0 | 2 |
| 10 | 1 | |

Then obtain the following by interchanging rows and columns:

| u | v | w | Constant |
|---|---|---|---|
| 4 | 1 | 1 | 10 |
| 1 | 2 | 0 | 1 |
| 16 | 12 | 2 | |

From this table we construct the dual problem:

Maximize $P = 16u + 12v + 2w$ subject to

$$4u + v + w \le 10$$
$$u + 2v \le 1$$
$$u \ge 0, \ v \ge 0, \ w \ge 0.$$

Solving the dual problem using the simplex method with $x$ and $y$ as slack variables, we obtain the following initial tableau.

| | u | v | w | x | y | P | Const. | Ratio |
|---|---|---|---|---|---|---|---|---|
| | 4 | 1 | 1 | 1 | 0 | 0 | 10 | $\frac{5}{2}$ |
| p.r.→ | ① | 2 | 0 | 0 | 1 | 0 | 1 | 1 |
| | -16 | -12 | -2 | 0 | 0 | 1 | 0 | |

$$\begin{array}{c} R_1 - 4R_2 \\ \longrightarrow \\ R_3 + 16R_2 \end{array}$$

↑
p.c.

| | u | v | w | x | y | P | Const. | Ratio |
|---|---|---|---|---|---|---|---|---|
| p.r.→ | 0 | -7 | (1) | 1 | -4 | 0 | 6 | 6 |
| | 1 | 2 | 0 | 0 | 1 | 0 | 1 | -- |
| | 0 | 20 | -2 | 0 | 16 | 1 | 16 | |

$R_3 + 2R_1$ →

↑ p.c.

| u | v | w | x | y | P | Const. |
|---|---|---|---|---|---|---|
| 0 | -7 | 1 | 1 | -4 | 0 | 6 |
| 1 | 2 | 0 | 0 | 1 | 0 | 1 |
| 0 | 6 | 0 | 2 | 8 | 1 | 28 |

Interpreting this tableau in the usual fashion, we see that $x = 2$, $y = 8$, and $C = 28$.

15.  We first write the tableau

| x | y | z | Constant |
|---|---|---|---|
| 20 | 10 | 1 | 10 |
| 1 | 1 | 2 | 20 |
| 200 | 150 | 120 | |

Then obtain the following by interchanging rows and columns:

| u | v | Constant |
|---|---|---|
| 20 | 1 | 200 |
| 10 | 1 | 150 |
| 1 | 2 | 120 |
| 10 | 20 | |

From this table we construct the dual problem:

Maximize $P = 10u + 20v$ subject to the constraints

$$20u + v \leq 200$$

$$10u + v \leq 150$$

$$u + 2v \leq 120$$

$$u \geq 0, \ v \geq 0.$$

Solving this problem, we obtain the following tableaus:

| | u | v | x | y | z | P | Const. | Ratio |
|---|---|---|---|---|---|---|---|---|
| | 20 | 1 | 1 | 0 | 0 | 0 | 200 | 200 |
| | 10 | 1 | 0 | 1 | 0 | 0 | 150 | 150 |
| p.r.→ | 1 | (2) | 0 | 0 | 1 | 0 | 120 | 60 |
| | −10 | −20 | 0 | 0 | 0 | 1 | 0 | |

$\frac{1}{2}R_3$ →

p.c. (under the v column)

| u | v | x | y | z | P | Const. |
|---|---|---|---|---|---|---|
| 20 | 1 | 1 | 0 | 0 | 0 | 200 |
| 10 | 1 | 0 | 1 | 0 | 0 | 150 |
| $\frac{1}{2}$ | 1 | 0 | 0 | $\frac{1}{2}$ | 0 | 60 |
| −10 | −20 | 0 | 0 | 0 | 1 | 0 |

$$R_1 - R_3$$
$$R_2 - R_3$$
$$R_4 + 20R_3$$
→

| u | v | x | y | z | P | Const. |
|---|---|---|---|---|---|---|
| $\frac{39}{2}$ | 0 | 1 | 0 | $-\frac{1}{2}$ | 0 | 140 |
| $\frac{19}{2}$ | 0 | 0 | 1 | $-\frac{1}{2}$ | 0 | 90 |
| $\frac{1}{2}$ | 1 | 0 | 0 | $\frac{1}{2}$ | 0 | 60 |
| 0 | 0 | 0 | 0 | 10 | 1 | 1200 |

This last tableau is in final form. We find that $x = 0$, $y = 0$, $z = 10$, and $C = 1200$.

16.   The dual problem is

Maximize $P = 8u + 6v$ subject to

$$2u + v \le 40$$

$$u + v \le 30$$

$$u - v \le 11$$

$$u \ge 0; \; v \ge 0.$$

The initial simplex tableau is

| u | v | x | y | z | P | Const. |
|---|---|---|---|---|---|---|
| 2 | 1 | 1 | 0 | 0 | 0 | 40 |
| 1 | 1 | 0 | 1 | 0 | 0 | 30 |
| 1 | -1 | 0 | 0 | 1 | 0 | 11 |
| -8 | -6 | 0 | 0 | 0 | 1 | 0 |

Using the following sequence of row operations

1. $R_1 - 2R_3$, $R_2 - R_3$, $R_4 + 8R_3$    2. $\frac{1}{3}R_1$

3. $R_2 - 2R_1$, $R_3 + R_1$, $R_4 + 14R_1$    4. $3R_2$

5. $R_1 + \frac{2}{3}R_2$, $R_3 - \frac{1}{3}R_2$, $R_4 + \frac{4}{3}R_2$

we obtain the final tableau

| u | v | x | y | z | P | Const. |
|---|---|---|---|---|---|---|
| 0 | 1 | -1 | 2 | 0 | 0 | 20 |
| 0 | 0 | -2 | 3 | 1 | 0 | 21 |
| 1 | 0 | 1 | -1 | 0 | 0 | 10 |
| 0 | 0 | 2 | 4 | 0 | 1 | 200 |

The last tableau is in final form. We find x = 2, y = 4, z = 0, and C = 200.

17.  We first write the tableau

| x | y | z | Constant |
|---|---|---|---|
| 1 | 2 | 2 | 10 |
| 2 | 1 | 1 | 24 |
| 1 | 1 | 1 | 16 |
| 6 | 8 | 4 | |

Then obtain the following by interchanging rows and columns:

| u | v | w | Constant |
|---|---|---|---|
| 1 | 2 | 1 | 6 |
| 2 | 1 | 1 | 8 |
| 2 | 1 | 1 | 4 |
| 10 | 24 | 16 | |

From this table we construct the dual problem:

Maximize the objective function

$P = 10u + 24v + 16w$ subject to

$$u + 2v + w \leq 6$$

$$2u + v + w \leq 8$$

$$2u + v + w \leq 4$$

$$u \geq 0, \ v \geq 0, \ w \geq 0.$$

Solving the dual problem using the simplex method with $x$, $y$, and $z$ as slack variables, we obtain

| | u | v | w | x | y | z | P | Const. | --Ratio-- |
|---|---|---|---|---|---|---|---|---|---|
| p.r.→ | 1 | ②| 1 | 1 | 0 | 0 | 0 | 6 | 3 |
| | 2 | 1 | 1 | 0 | 1 | 0 | 0 | 8 | 8 |
| | 2 | 1 | 1 | 0 | 0 | 1 | 0 | 4 | 4 |
| | −10 | −24 | −16 | 0 | 0 | 0 | 1 | 0 | |

$\uparrow$ p.c.

$\xrightarrow{\frac{1}{2}R_1}$

| u | v | w | x | y | z | P | Const. |
|---|---|---|---|---|---|---|---|
| $\frac{1}{2}$ | 1 | $\frac{1}{2}$ | $\frac{1}{2}$ | 0 | 0 | 0 | 3 |
| 2 | 1 | 1 | 0 | 1 | 0 | 0 | 8 |
| 2 | 1 | 1 | 0 | 0 | 1 | 0 | 4 |
| −10 | −24 | −16 | 0 | 0 | 0 | 1 | 0 |

$\xrightarrow{\begin{array}{c} R_2 - R_1 \\ R_3 - R_1 \\ R_4 + 24R_1 \end{array}}$

| | u | v | w | x | y | z | P | Const. | --Ratio-- |
|---|---|---|---|---|---|---|---|---|---|
| | $\frac{1}{2}$ | 1 | $\frac{1}{2}$ | $\frac{1}{2}$ | 0 | 0 | 0 | 3 | 6 |
| | $\frac{3}{2}$ | 0 | $\frac{1}{2}$ | $-\frac{1}{2}$ | 1 | 0 | 0 | 5 | 10 |
| p.r.→ | $\frac{3}{2}$ | 0 | ⑫ | $-\frac{1}{2}$ | 0 | 1 | 0 | 1 | 2 |
| | 2 | 0 | −4 | 12 | 0 | 0 | 1 | 72 | |

$\uparrow$ p.c.

$\xrightarrow{2R_3}$

| u | v | w | x | y | z | P | Const. |
|---|---|---|---|---|---|---|---|
| $\frac{1}{2}$ | 1 | $\frac{1}{2}$ | $\frac{1}{2}$ | 0 | 0 | 0 | 3 |
| $\frac{3}{2}$ | 0 | $\frac{1}{2}$ | $-\frac{1}{2}$ | 1 | 0 | 0 | 5 |
| 3 | 0 | 1 | -1 | 0 | 2 | 0 | 2 |
| 2 | 0 | -4 | 12 | 0 | 0 | 1 | 72 |

$$\begin{array}{l} R_1 - \frac{1}{2}R_3 \\ R_2 - \frac{1}{2}R_3 \\ R_4 + 4R_3 \end{array} \longrightarrow$$

| u | v | w | x | y | z | P | Const. |
|---|---|---|---|---|---|---|---|
| -1 | 1 | 0 | 1 | 0 | -1 | 0 | 2 |
| 0 | 0 | 0 | 0 | 1 | -1 | 0 | 4 |
| 3 | 0 | 1 | -1 | 0 | 2 | 0 | 2 |
| 14 | 0 | 0 | 8 | 0 | 8 | 1 | 80 |

The solution to the primal problem is $x = 8$, $y = 0$, $z = 8$, and $C = 80$.

18.  The dual problem is

Maximize $P = 6u + 2v + 2w$ subject to

$$2u + 3v + 4w \le 12$$
$$4u + 2v + w \le 4$$
$$u + 2v + w \le 8$$
$$u \ge 0, \ v \ge 0, \ w \ge 0.$$

The initial simplex tableau is

| u | v | w | x | y | z | P | Const. |
|---|---|---|---|---|---|---|---|
| 2 | 3 | 4 | 1 | 0 | 0 | 0 | 12 |
| 4 | 2 | 1 | 0 | 1 | 0 | 0 | 4 |
| 1 | 2 | 1 | 0 | 0 | 1 | 0 | 8 |
| -6 | -2 | -2 | 0 | 0 | 0 | 1 | 0 |

Using the following sequence of row operations,

1. $\frac{1}{4}R_2$     2. $R_1 - 2R_2$, $R_3 - R_2$, $R_4 + 6R_2$

3. $\frac{2}{7}R_1$      4. $R_2 - \frac{1}{4}R_1$, $R_3 - \frac{3}{4}R_1$, $R_4 + \frac{1}{2}R_1$

we obtain the final tableau

| u | v | w | x | y | z | P | Const. |
|---|---|---|---|---|---|---|--------|
| 0 | $\frac{4}{7}$ | 1 | $\frac{2}{7}$ | $-\frac{1}{7}$ | 0 | 0 | $\frac{20}{7}$ |
| 1 | $\frac{5}{14}$ | 0 | $-\frac{1}{14}$ | $\frac{2}{7}$ | 0 | 0 | $\frac{2}{7}$ |
| 0 | $\frac{15}{14}$ | 0 | $-\frac{3}{14}$ | $-\frac{1}{7}$ | 1 | 0 | $\frac{34}{7}$ |
| 0 | $\frac{9}{7}$ | 0 | $\frac{1}{7}$ | $\frac{10}{7}$ | 0 | 1 | $\frac{52}{7}$ |

From the table, we deduce that x = 1/7, y = 10/7, z = 0, and
C = 52/7.

19. We first write

Maximize P = 6u + 2v + 4w subject to the constraints

| x | y | z | Constant |
|---|---|---|----------|
| 2 | 4 | 3 | 6 |
| 6 | 0 | 1 | 2 |
| 0 | 6 | 2 | 4 |
| 30 | 12 | 20 | |

Then obtain the following by interchanging rows and columns:

| u | v | w | Constant |
|---|---|---|----------|
| 2 | 6 | 0 | 30 |
| 4 | 0 | 6 | 12 |
| 3 | 1 | 2 | 20 |
| 6 | 2 | 4 | |

From this table we construct the dual problem:

Maximize P = 6u + 2v + 4w subject to

$$2u + 6v \le 30$$
$$4u + 6w \le 12$$
$$3u + v + 2w \le 20$$
$$u \ge 0, \ v \ge 0, \ w \ge 0.$$

Using the simplex method, we obtain

|  | u | v | w | x | y | z | P | Const. | Ratio |
|---|---|---|---|---|---|---|---|---|---|
|  | 2 | 6 | 0 | 1 | 0 | 0 | 0 | 30 | 15 |
| p.r.→ | ④ | 0 | 6 | 0 | 1 | 0 | 0 | 12 | 3 |
|  | 3 | 1 | 2 | 0 | 0 | 1 | 0 | 20 | $\frac{20}{8}$ |
|  | -6 | -2 | -4 | 0 | 0 | 0 | 1 | 0 |  |

$\xrightarrow{\frac{1}{4}R_2}$

p.c. (under u)

| u | v | w | x | y | z | P | Const. |
|---|---|---|---|---|---|---|---|
| 2 | 6 | 0 | 1 | 0 | 0 | 0 | 30 |
| 1 | 0 | $\frac{3}{2}$ | 0 | $\frac{1}{4}$ | 0 | 0 | 3 |
| 3 | 1 | 2 | 0 | 0 | 1 | 0 | 20 |
| -6 | -2 | -4 | 0 | 0 | 0 | 1 | 0 |

$$\frac{R_1 - 2R_2}{R_3 - 3R_2}$$
$$R_4 + 6R_2$$

|  | u | v | w | x | y | z | P | Const. | Ratio |
|---|---|---|---|---|---|---|---|---|---|
| p.r.→ | 0 | ⑥ | -3 | 1 | $-\frac{1}{2}$ | 0 | 0 | 24 | 4 |
|  | 1 | 0 | $\frac{3}{2}$ | 0 | $\frac{1}{4}$ | 0 | 0 | 3 | --- |
|  | 0 | 1 | $-\frac{5}{2}$ | 0 | $-\frac{3}{4}$ | 1 | 0 | 11 | 11 |
|  | 0 | -2 | 5 | 0 | $\frac{3}{2}$ | 0 | 1 | 18 |  |

$\xrightarrow{\frac{1}{6}R_1}$

p.c. (under v)

| u | v | w | x | y | z | P | Const. |
|---|---|---|---|---|---|---|---|
| 0 | 1 | $-\frac{1}{2}$ | $\frac{1}{6}$ | $-\frac{1}{12}$ | 0 | 0 | 4 |
| 1 | 0 | $\frac{3}{2}$ | 0 | $\frac{1}{4}$ | 0 | 0 | 3 |
| 0 | 1 | $-\frac{5}{2}$ | 0 | $-\frac{3}{4}$ | 1 | 0 | 11 |
| 0 | -2 | 5 | 0 | $\frac{3}{2}$ | 0 | 1 | 18 |

$$\frac{R_3 - R_1}{R_4 + 2R_1}$$

| u | v | w | x | y | z | P | Const. |
|---|---|---|---|---|---|---|---|
| 0 | 1 | $-\frac{1}{2}$ | $\frac{1}{6}$ | $-\frac{1}{12}$ | 0 | 0 | 4 |
| 1 | 0 | $\frac{3}{2}$ | 0 | $\frac{1}{4}$ | 0 | 0 | 3 |
| 0 | 0 | -2 | $-\frac{1}{6}$ | $-\frac{2}{3}$ | 1 | 0 | 7 |
| 0 | 0 | 4 | $\frac{1}{3}$ | $\frac{4}{3}$ | 0 | 1 | 26 |

The last tableau is in final form. We find x = 1/3, y = 4/3, z = 0, and C = 26.

20.  The dual problem is

Maximize P = 6u + 4v + 2w subject to

$$2u + v + w \leq 8$$

$$3u + 2v + w \leq 6$$

$$u - 2v + 2w \leq 4$$

$$u \geq 0, \ v \geq 0, \ w \geq 0.$$

The initial tableau is

| u | v | w | x | y | z | P | Const. |
|---|---|---|---|---|---|---|--------|
| 2 | 1 | 1 | 1 | 0 | 0 | 0 | 8 |
| 3 | 2 | 1 | 0 | 1 | 0 | 0 | 6 |
| 1 | -2 | 2 | 0 | 0 | 0 | 1 | 4 |
| -6 | -4 | -2 | 0 | 0 | 0 | 1 | 0 |

Using the following sequence of row operations

1. $\frac{1}{3}R_2$          2. $R_1 - 2R_2, \ R_3 - R_2, \ R_4 + 6R_2$

we obtain the final tableau

| u | v | w | x | y | z | P | Const. |
|---|---|---|---|---|---|---|--------|
| 0 | $-\frac{1}{3}$ | $\frac{1}{3}$ | 1 | $-\frac{2}{3}$ | 0 | 0 | 4 |
| 1 | $\frac{2}{3}$ | $\frac{1}{3}$ | 0 | $\frac{1}{3}$ | 0 | 0 | 2 |
| 0 | $-\frac{8}{3}$ | $\frac{5}{3}$ | 0 | $-\frac{1}{3}$ | 1 | 0 | 2 |
| 0 | 0 | 0 | 0 | 2 | 0 | 1 | 12 |

Interpreting the tableau, we see that the solution to the primal problem is x = 0, y = 2, z = 0, and C = 12.

21.  This problem was formulated in Exercise 12, Section 3.2, page 218. We rewrite the constraints in the form

$$-x_1 - x_2 - x_3 \geq -800$$
$$- x_4 - x_5 - x_6 \geq -600$$
$$x_1 + x_4 \geq 500$$
$$x_2 + x_5 \geq 400$$
$$x_3 + x_6 \geq 400.$$

We solve this problem using duality. We first write

| $x_1$ | $x_2$ | $x_3$ | $x_4$ | $x_5$ | $x_6$ | Constant |
|---|---|---|---|---|---|---|
| $-1$ | $-1$ | $-1$ | $0$ | $0$ | $0$ | $-800$ |
| $0$ | $0$ | $0$ | $-1$ | $-1$ | $-1$ | $-600$ |
| $1$ | $0$ | $0$ | $1$ | $0$ | $0$ | $500$ |
| $0$ | $1$ | $0$ | $0$ | $0$ | $1$ | $400$ |
| $0$ | $0$ | $1$ | $0$ | $0$ | $1$ | $400$ |
| $16$ | $20$ | $22$ | $18$ | $16$ | $14$ | |

Interchanging the rows with the columns, we obtain

| $u_1$ | $u_2$ | $u_3$ | $u_4$ | $u_5$ | Constant |
|---|---|---|---|---|---|
| $-1$ | $0$ | $1$ | $0$ | $0$ | $16$ |
| $-1$ | $0$ | $0$ | $1$ | $0$ | $20$ |
| $-1$ | $0$ | $0$ | $0$ | $1$ | $22$ |
| $0$ | $-1$ | $1$ | $0$ | $0$ | $18$ |
| $0$ | $-1$ | $0$ | $1$ | $0$ | $16$ |
| $0$ | $-1$ | $0$ | $0$ | $1$ | $14$ |
| $-800$ | $-600$ | $500$ | $400$ | $400$ | |

from which we obtain the dual problem:

Maximize $P = -800u_1 - 600u_2 + 500u_3 + 400u_4 + 400u_5$ subject to

$$-u_1 \quad + u_3 \qquad\qquad \le 16$$

$$-u_1 \qquad\quad + u_4 \qquad \le 20$$

$$-u_1 \qquad\qquad\quad + u_5 \ \le 22$$

$$- u_2 + u_3 \qquad\qquad \le 18$$

$$-u_2 \qquad + u_4 \qquad \le 16$$

$$-u_2 \qquad\qquad +u_5 \ \le 14$$

$$u_1 \ge 0, \ u_2 \ge 0, \ \ldots, \ u_5 \ge 0.$$

The initial simplex tableau is

| $u_1$ | $u_2$ | $u_3$ | $u_4$ | $u_5$ | $x_1$ | $x_2$ | $x_3$ | $x_4$ | $x_5$ | $x_6$ | P | Constant |
|---|---|---|---|---|---|---|---|---|---|---|---|---|
| −1 | 0 | 1 | 0 | 0 | 1 | 0 | 0 | 0 | 0 | 0 | 0 | 16 |
| −1 | 0 | 0 | 1 | 0 | 0 | 1 | 0 | 0 | 0 | 0 | 0 | 20 |
| −1 | 0 | 0 | 0 | 1 | 0 | 0 | 1 | 0 | 0 | 0 | 0 | 22 |
| 0 | −1 | 1 | 0 | 0 | 0 | 0 | 0 | 1 | 0 | 0 | 0 | 18 |
| 0 | −1 | 0 | 1 | 0 | 0 | 0 | 0 | 0 | 1 | 0 | 0 | 16 |
| 0 | −1 | 0 | 0 | 1 | 0 | 0 | 0 | 0 | 0 | 1 | 0 | 14 |
| 800 | 600 | −500 | −400 | −400 | 0 | 0 | 0 | 0 | 0 | 0 | 1 | 0 |

Using the sequence of row operations

1. $R_4 - R_1$, $R_7 + 500R_1$        2. $R_2 - R_5$, $R_7 + 400R_5$

3. $R_3 - R_6$, $R_7 + 400R_6$

4. $R_3 - R_2$, $R_4 + R_2$, $R_5 + R_2$, $R_6 + R_2$, $R_7 + 200R_2$

we obtain the final tableau

| $u_1$ | $u_2$ | $u_3$ | $u_4$ | $u_5$ | $x_1$ | $x_2$ | $x_3$ | $x_4$ | $x_5$ | $x_6$ | P | Constant |
|---|---|---|---|---|---|---|---|---|---|---|---|---|
| −1 | 0 | 1 | 0 | 0 | 1 | 0 | 0 | 0 | 0 | 0 | 0 | 16 |
| −1 | 1 | 0 | 0 | 0 | 0 | 1 | 0 | 0 | −1 | 0 | 0 | 4 |
| 0 | 0 | 0 | 0 | 0 | 0 | −1 | 1 | 0 | 1 | −1 | 0 | 4 |
| 0 | 0 | 0 | 0 | 0 | −1 | 1 | 0 | 1 | −1 | 0 | 0 | 6 |
| −1 | 0 | 0 | 1 | 0 | 0 | 1 | 0 | 0 | 0 | 0 | 0 | 20 |
| −1 | 0 | 0 | 0 | 1 | 0 | 1 | 0 | 0 | −1 | 1 | 0 | 18 |
| 100 | 0 | 0 | 0 | 0 | 500 | 200 | 0 | 0 | 200 | 400 | 1 | 20,800 |

We find $x_1 = 500$, $x_2 = 200$, $x_3 = 0$, $x_4 = 0$, $x_5 = 200$, $x_6 = 400$, and $C = 20,800$. So the schedule is

Location I:  500 to warehouse A, 200 to warehouse B
Location II: 200 to warehouse B, 400 to warehouse C.
Shipping costs: $20,800.

22.  Refer to Exercise 3.2 (Problem 13).

The dual problem is

Maximize $P = -300u_1 - 250u_2 + 200u_3 + 150u_4 + 200u_5$ subject to

$$-u_1 \quad\;\; + u_3 \qquad\qquad\quad \leq 60$$
$$-u_1 \qquad\quad + u_4 \qquad\qquad \leq 60$$
$$-u_1 \qquad\qquad\quad + u_5 \;\; \leq 80$$
$$-u_2 + u_3 \qquad\qquad\qquad \leq 80$$
$$-u_2 \qquad + u_4 \qquad\qquad \leq 70$$
$$-u_2 \qquad\qquad + u_5 \;\; \leq 50$$

$$u_1 \geq 0, \; u_2 \geq 0, \; \ldots, \; u_5 \geq 0.$$

The initial tableau is

| $u_1$ | $u_2$ | $u_3$ | $u_4$ | $u_5$ | $x_1$ | $x_2$ | $x_3$ | $x_4$ | $x_5$ | $x_6$ | P | Constant |
|---|---|---|---|---|---|---|---|---|---|---|---|---|
| -1 | 0 | 1 | 0 | 0 | 1 | 0 | 0 | 0 | 0 | 0 | 0 | 60 |
| -1 | 0 | 0 | 1 | 0 | 0 | 1 | 0 | 0 | 0 | 0 | 0 | 60 |
| -1 | 0 | 0 | 0 | 1 | 0 | 0 | 1 | 0 | 0 | 0 | 0 | 80 |
| 0 | -1 | 1 | 0 | 0 | 0 | 0 | 0 | 1 | 0 | 0 | 0 | 80 |
| 0 | -1 | 0 | 1 | 0 | 0 | 0 | 0 | 0 | 1 | 0 | 0 | 70 |
| 0 | -1 | 0 | 0 | 1 | 0 | 0 | 0 | 0 | 0 | 1 | 0 | 50 |
| 300 | 250 | -200 | -150 | -200 | 0 | 0 | 0 | 0 | 0 | 0 | 1 | 0 |

Using the following sequence of row operations,

1. $R_4 - R_1$, $R_7 + 200R_1$         2. $R_3 - R_6$, $R_7 + 200R_6$

3. $R_5 - R_2$, $R_7 + 150R_2$

4. $R_1 + R_5$, $R_2 + R_5$, $R_3 + R_5$, $R_4 - R_5$, $R_7 + 50R_5$

we obtain the final tableau

| $u_1$ | $u_2$ | $u_3$ | $u_4$ | $u_5$ | $x_1$ | $x_2$ | $x_3$ | $x_4$ | $x_5$ | $x_6$ | $P$ | Constant |
|---|---|---|---|---|---|---|---|---|---|---|---|---|
| 0 | -1 | 1 | 0 | 0 | 1 | -1 | 0 | 0 | 1 | 0 | 0 | 70 |
| 0 | -1 | 0 | 1 | 0 | 0 | 0 | 0 | 0 | 1 | 0 | 0 | 70 |
| 0 | 0 | 0 | 0 | 0 | 0 | -1 | 1 | 0 | 1 | -1 | 0 | 40 |
| 0 | 0 | 0 | 0 | 0 | -1 | 1 | 0 | 1 | -1 | 0 | 0 | 10 |
| 1 | -1 | 0 | 0 | 0 | 0 | -1 | 0 | 0 | 1 | 0 | 0 | 10 |
| 0 | -1 | 0 | 0 | 1 | 0 | 0 | 0 | 0 | 0 | 1 | 0 | 50 |
| 0 | 0 | 0 | 0 | 0 | 200 | 100 | 0 | 0 | 50 | 200 | 0 | 31,500 |

We see that $x_1 = 200$, $x_2 = 100$, $x_3 = 0$, $x_4 = 0$, $x_5 = 50$, $x_6 = 200$, and C = 31,500. So the schedule is

Location I:   200 to warehouse A, 100 to warehouse B
Location II: 50 to warehouse B,   200 to warehouse C.
Shipping costs: $31,500.

23. The given data may be summarized as follows:

|  | Orange Juice | Grapefruit Juice |
|---|---|---|
| Vitamin A | 60 I.U. | 120 I.U. |
| Vitamin C | 16 I.U. | 12 I.U. |
| Calories | 14 | 11 |

Suppose x ounces of orange juice and y ounces of pink-grapefruit juice are required for each glass of the blend. Then the problem is

Minimize C = 14x + 11y subject to

$$60x + 120y \geq 1200$$

$$16x + 12y \geq 200$$

$$x \geq 0, \ y \geq 0.$$

To construct the dual problem, we first write down the tableau

| x | y | Constant |
|---|---|---|
| 60 | 120 | 1200 |
| 16 | 12 | 200 |
| 14 | 11 |  |

Then obtain the following by interchanging rows and columns:

| u | v | Constant |
|---|---|---|
| 60 | 16 | 14 |
| 120 | 12 | 11 |
| 1200 | 200 | |

From this table we construct the dual problem:

Maximize $P = 1200u + 200v$ subject to

$$60u + 16v \leq 14$$

$$120u + 12v \leq 11$$

$$u \geq 0, \ v \geq 0.$$

The initial tableau is

| u | v | x | y | P | Const. |
|---|---|---|---|---|---|
| 60 | 16 | 1 | 0 | 0 | 14 |
| 120 | 12 | 0 | 1 | 0 | 11 |
| -1200 | -200 | 0 | 0 | 1 | 0 |

Using the following sequence of row operations,

1. $\frac{1}{120}R_2$       2. $R_1 - 60R_2$, $R_3 + 1200R_2$

3. $\frac{1}{10}R_1$      4. $R_2 - \frac{1}{10}R_1$, $R_3 + 80R_1$

we obtain the final tableau

| u | v | x | y | P | Const. |
|---|---|---|---|---|---|
| 0 | 1 | $\frac{1}{10}$ | $-\frac{1}{20}$ | 0 | $\frac{17}{20}$ |
| 0 | 0 | $-\frac{1}{100}$ | $\frac{1}{75}$ | 0 | $\frac{1}{150}$ |
| 0 | 0 | 8 | 6 | 1 | 178 |

We conclude that the owner should use 8 ounces of orange juice and 6 ounces of grapefruit juice per glass of the blend for a minimal calorie count of 178.

**24.** We first tabulate the data as follows:

| | OUTPUT | | | Operating Cost per day ($) |
| | Low | Medium | High | |
|---|---|---|---|---|
| Refinery I | 200 | 100 | 100 | 200 |
| Refinery II | 100 | 200 | 600 | 300 |
| Minimum Requirement (barrels) | 1000 | 1400 | 3000 | |

Let x and y denote the number of days refinery I and refinery II should be operated. Then we have the following linear programming problem.

Minimize $C = 200x + 300y$ subject to

$$200x + 100y \geq 1000$$

$$100x + 200y \geq 1400$$

$$100x + 600y \geq 3000$$

$$x \geq 0, \ y \geq 0.$$

To construct the dual problem, we first write down the tableau

| x | y | Constant |
|---|---|---|
| 200 | 100 | 1000 |
| 100 | 200 | 1400 |
| 100 | 600 | 300 |
| 200 | 300 | |

Then obtain the following by interchanging rows and columns:

| u | v | w | Constant |
|---|---|---|---|
| 200 | 100 | 100 | 200 |
| 100 | 200 | 600 | 300 |
| 1000 | 1400 | 3000 | |

From this table we construct the dual problem:

Maximize $P = 1000u + 1400v + 3000w$ subject to

$$200u + 100v + 100w \leq 200$$

$$100u + 200v + 600w \leq 300$$

$$u \geq 0, \ v \geq 0, \ w \geq 0.$$

The initial tableau is

| u | v | w | x | y | P | Const. |
|------|------|------|---|---|---|--------|
| 200 | 100 | 100 | 1 | 0 | 0 | 200 |
| 100 | 200 | 600 | 0 | 1 | 0 | 300 |
| −1000 | −1400 | −3000 | 0 | 0 | 1 | 0 |

.

Using the following sequence of row operations,

1. $\frac{1}{600}R_2$        2. $R_1 - 100R_2$, $R_3 + 3000R_2$

3. $\frac{3}{550}R_1$        4. $R_2 - \frac{1}{6}R_1$, $R_3 + 500R_1$

5. $\frac{11}{3}R_2$        6. $R_1 - \frac{4}{11}R_2$, $R_3 + \frac{2400}{11}R_2$

we obtain the final tableau

| u | v | w | x | y | P | Const. |
|---|---|------|------|------|---|--------|
| 1 | 0 | $-\frac{4}{3}$ | $\frac{1}{150}$ | $-\frac{1}{300}$ | 0 | $\frac{1}{3}$ |
| 0 | 0 | $\frac{11}{3}$ | $-\frac{1}{300}$ | $\frac{1}{150}$ | 0 | $\frac{4}{3}$ |
| 0 | 1 | 800 | 2 | 6 | 1 | 2200 |

We conclude that $x = 2$, $y = 6$, and $C = P = 2200$, So the company should operate refinery I for 2 days and refinery II for 6 days at a minimum cost of $2200.

## USING TECHNOLOGY EXERCISES 4.2, page 252

1.    $x = \frac{4}{3}$, $y = \frac{10}{3}$, $z = 0$, and $C = \frac{14}{3}$.

2. $x = \frac{36}{7}$, $y = 0$, $z = \frac{66}{7}$, and $C = \frac{138}{7}$.

3. $x = 0.9524$, $y = 4.2857$, $z = 0$, and $C = 6.0952$.

4. $x = 5.8154$, $y = 0$, $z = 0.6154$, and $C = 12.8277$

# EXERCISES 4.3, page 265

1. Maximize $C = -P = -2x + 3y$ subject to

$$-3x - 5y \leq -20$$
$$3x + y \leq 16$$
$$-2x + y \leq 1$$
$$x \geq 0, \ y \geq 0.$$

2. Maximize $P = -C = -2x - 3y$ subject to

$$x + y \leq 10$$
$$-x - 2y \leq -12$$
$$-2x - y \leq -12$$
$$x \leq 0, \ y \leq 0 .$$

3. Maximize $P = -C = -5x - 10y - z$ subject to

$$-2x - y - z \leq -4$$
$$-x - 2y - 2z \leq -2$$
$$2x + 4y + 3z \leq 12$$
$$x \geq 0, \ y \geq 0, \text{ and } z \geq 0.$$

4. Maximize $P = 2x + y - 2z$ subject to

$$-x - 2y - z \leq -10$$
$$-3x - 4y - 2z \leq -5$$
$$2x + 5y + 12z \leq 20$$
$$x \geq 0, \ y \geq 0, \text{ and } z \geq 0.$$

5. We set up the tableau and solve the problem using the simplex method:

| x | y | u | v | P | Const. | Ratio | |
|---|---|---|---|---|---|---|---|
| 2 | ⑤ | 1 | 0 | 0 | 20 | 4 | $-\frac{1}{5}R_2$ |
| p.r.→ 1 | -5 | 0 | 1 | 0 | -5 | 1 | $\longrightarrow$ |
| -1 | -2 | 0 | 0 | 1 | 0 | | |

p.c. (under y)

| x | y | u | v | P | Const. | |
|---|---|---|---|---|---|---|
| 2 | 5 | 1 | 0 | 0 | 20 | |
| $-\frac{1}{5}$ | 1 | 0 | $-\frac{1}{5}$ | 0 | 1 | $R_1 - 5R_2$ |
| -1 | -2 | 0 | 0 | 1 | 0 | $R_3 + 2R_2$ |

| x | y | u | v | P | Const. | Ratio | |
|---|---|---|---|---|---|---|---|
| 3 | 0 | 1 | 1 | 0 | 15 | 5 | $\frac{1}{3}R_1$ |
| $-\frac{1}{5}$ | 1 | 0 | $-\frac{1}{5}$ | 0 | 1 | -- | $\longrightarrow$ |
| $-\frac{7}{5}$ | 0 | 0 | $-\frac{2}{5}$ | 1 | 2 | | |

| x | y | u | v | P | Const. | |
|---|---|---|---|---|---|---|
| 1 | 0 | $\frac{1}{3}$ | $\frac{1}{3}$ | 0 | 5 | $R_2 + \frac{1}{5}R_1$ |
| $-\frac{1}{5}$ | 1 | 0 | $-\frac{1}{5}$ | 0 | 1 | $R_3 + \frac{7}{5}R_1$ |
| $-\frac{7}{5}$ | 0 | 0 | $-\frac{2}{5}$ | 1 | 2 | |

| x | y | u | v | P | Const. |
|---|---|---|---|---|---|
| 1 | 0 | $\frac{1}{3}$ | $\frac{1}{3}$ | 0 | 5 |
| 0 | 1 | $\frac{1}{15}$ | $-\frac{2}{15}$ | 0 | 2 |
| 0 | 0 | $\frac{7}{15}$ | $\frac{1}{15}$ | 1 | 9 |

The maximum value of P is 9 when x = 5 and y = 2.

6. The initial tableau is

| x | y | u | v | P | Const. |
|---|---|---|---|---|--------|
| 1 | 2 | 1 | 0 | 0 | 8 |
| 1 | -1 | 0 | 1 | 0 | -2 |
| -2 | -3 | 0 | 0 | 1 | 0 |

.

Using the following sequence of row operations

1. $-R_2$          2. $R_1 - 2R_2$; $R_3 + 3R_2$

3. $\frac{1}{3}R_1$          4. $R_2 + R_1$; $R_3 + 5R_1$

we obtain the final tableau

| x | y | u | v | P | Const. |
|---|---|---|---|---|--------|
| 1 | 0 | $\frac{1}{3}$ | $\frac{2}{3}$ | 0 | $\frac{4}{3}$ |
| 0 | 1 | $\frac{1}{3}$ | $-\frac{1}{3}$ | 0 | $\frac{10}{3}$ |
| 0 | 0 | $\frac{5}{3}$ | $\frac{1}{3}$ | 1 | $\frac{38}{3}$ |

from which we deduce that the maximum value of P is 38/3 attained when x = 4/3 and y = 10/3.

7. We first rewrite the problem as a maximization problem with inequality constraints using $\leq$ , obtaining the following equivalent problem:

Maximize $P = -C = 2x - y$ subject to

$$x + 2y \leq 6$$

$$3x + 2y \leq 12.$$

$$x \geq 0,\ y \geq 0.$$

Following the procedure outlined for nonstandard problems, we have

| | x | y | u | v | P | Const. | ⌐ Ratio ⌐ | |
|---|---|---|---|---|---|--------|------|---|
| | 1 | 2 | 1 | 0 | 0 | 6 | 6 | |
| p.r.→ | ③ | 2 | 0 | 1 | 0 | 12 | 4 | $\xrightarrow{\frac{1}{3}R_2}$ |
| | -2 | 1 | 0 | 0 | 1 | 0 | | |

        ↑
       p.c.

| x | y | u | v | P | Const. |
|---|---|---|---|---|---|
| 1 | 2 | 1 | 0 | 0 | 6 |
| 1 | $\frac{2}{3}$ | 0 | $\frac{1}{3}$ | 0 | 4 |
| -2 | 1 | 0 | 0 | 1 | 0 |

$$\xrightarrow[R_3 + 2R_2]{R_1 - R_2}$$

| x | y | u | v | P | Const. |
|---|---|---|---|---|---|
| 0 | $\frac{4}{3}$ | 1 | $-\frac{1}{3}$ | 0 | 2 |
| 1 | $\frac{2}{3}$ | 0 | $\frac{1}{3}$ | 0 | 4 |
| 0 | $\frac{7}{3}$ | 0 | $\frac{2}{3}$ | 1 | 8 |

.

We conclude that C attains a minimum value of $-8$ when $x = 4$ and $y = 0$.

8.  We first rewrite the problem as a maximization problem with inequality constraints using $\leq$ , obtaining the following equivalent problem:

Maximize $P = -C = 2x - 3y$ subject to

$$x + 3y \leq 60$$
$$-2x - y \leq -45$$
$$x \leq 40$$
$$x \geq 0, \ y \geq 0.$$

The initial tableau is

| x | y | u | v | w | P | Const. |
|---|---|---|---|---|---|---|
| 1 | 3 | 1 | 0 | 0 | 0 | 60 |
| -2 | -1 | 0 | 1 | 0 | 0 | -45 |
| 1 | 0 | 0 | 0 | 1 | 0 | 40 |
| -2 | 3 | 0 | 0 | 0 | 1 | 0 |

.

Using the following sequence of row operations

1.  $-\frac{1}{2}R_2$      2.  $R_1 - R_2$; $R_3 - R_2$; $R_4 + 2R_2$

3.  $2R_3$      4.  $R_1 - \frac{1}{2}R_3$; $R_2 + \frac{1}{2}R_3$; $R_4 + R_3$

we obtain the final tableau

| x | y | u | v | w | P | Const. |
|---|---|---|---|---|---|--------|
| 0 | 3 | 1 | 0 | -1 | 0 | 20 |
| 1 | 0 | 0 | 0 | 1 | 0 | 40 |
| 0 | -1 | 0 | 1 | 2 | 0 | 35 |
| 0 | 3 | 0 | 0 | 2 | 1 | 80 |

,

from which we deduce that C attains a minimum value of $-80$ when $x = 40$ and $y = 0$.

9. Using the simplex method we have

| x | y | u | v | P | Const. | -- Ratio -- |
|---|---|---|---|---|--------|-------------|
| 1 | 3 | 1 | 0 | 0 | 6 | 6 |
| -2 | 3 | 0 | 1 | 0 | -6 | 3 |
| -1 | -4 | 0 | 0 | 1 | 0 | |

p.r.→ (-2)   p.c. ↑   $\xrightarrow{-\frac{1}{2}R_2}$

| x | y | u | v | P | Const. |
|---|---|---|---|---|--------|
| 1 | 3 | 1 | 0 | 0 | 6 |
| 1 | $-\frac{3}{2}$ | 0 | $-\frac{1}{2}$ | 0 | 3 |
| -1 | -4 | 0 | 0 | 1 | 0 |

$\xrightarrow[R_3 + R_2]{R_1 - R_2}$

| x | y | u | v | P | Const. |
|---|---|---|---|---|--------|
| 0 | $\frac{9}{2}$ | 1 | $\frac{1}{2}$ | 0 | 3 |
| 1 | $-\frac{3}{2}$ | 0 | $-\frac{1}{2}$ | 0 | 3 |
| 0 | $-\frac{11}{2}$ | 0 | $-\frac{1}{2}$ | 1 | 3 |

$\xrightarrow{\frac{2}{9}R_1}$

| x | y | u | v | P | Const. |
|---|---|---|---|---|--------|
| 0 | 1 | $\frac{2}{9}$ | $\frac{1}{9}$ | 0 | $\frac{2}{3}$ |
| 1 | $-\frac{3}{2}$ | 0 | $-\frac{1}{2}$ | 0 | 3 |
| 0 | $-\frac{11}{2}$ | 0 | $-\frac{1}{2}$ | 1 | 3 |

$\xrightarrow[R_3 + \frac{11}{2}R_1]{R_2 + \frac{3}{2}R_1}$

| x | y | u | v | P | Const. |
|---|---|---|---|---|---|
| 0 | 1 | $\frac{2}{9}$ | $\frac{1}{9}$ | 0 | $\frac{2}{3}$ |
| 1 | 0 | $\frac{1}{3}$ | $-\frac{1}{3}$ | 0 | 4 |
| 0 | 0 | $\frac{11}{9}$ | $\frac{1}{9}$ | 1 | $\frac{20}{3}$ |

We conclude that P attains a maximum value of 20/3, when x = 4 and y = 2/3.

10. We rewrite the problem as

Maximize P = 5x + y subject to

$$2x + y \leq 8$$

$$x - y \leq -2$$

$$x \geq 0, \ y \geq 0.$$

The initial tableau is

| x | y | u | v | P | Const. |
|---|---|---|---|---|---|
| 2 | 1 | 1 | 0 | 0 | 8 |
| 1 | -1 | 0 | 1 | 0 | -2 |
| -5 | -1 | 0 | 0 | 1 | 0 |

Using the following sequence of row operations

1. $-R_2$
2. $R_1 - R_2$; $R_3 + R_2$
3. $\frac{1}{3}R_1$
4. $R_2 + R_1$; $R_3 + 6R_1$

we obtain the final tableau

| x | y | u | v | P | Const. |
|---|---|---|---|---|---|
| 0 | 1 | $\frac{1}{3}$ | $\frac{1}{3}$ | 0 | 2 |
| 1 | 0 | $\frac{1}{3}$ | $-\frac{2}{3}$ | 0 | 4 |
| 0 | 0 | 2 | 1 | 1 | 14 |

We conclude that P attains a maximum value of 14 when x = 2, and y = 4.

11. We rewrite the problem as

Maximize $P = x + 2y$ subject to

$$2x + 3y \leq 12$$
$$-x + 3y \leq 3$$
$$-x + 3y \geq 3$$
$$x \geq 0, \ y \geq 0.$$

The initial tableau is

| x | y | u | v | w | P | Const. |
|---|---|---|---|---|---|--------|
| 2 | 3 | 1 | 0 | 0 | 0 | 12 |
| -1 | 3 | 0 | 1 | 0 | 0 | 3 |
| 1 | -3 | 0 | 0 | 1 | 0 | -3 |
| -1 | -2 | 0 | 0 | 0 | 1 | 0 . |

Using the following sequence of row operations

1. $-\frac{1}{3}R_3$            2. $R_1 - 3R_3$, $R_2 - 3R_3$, $R_4 + 2R_3$

3. $\frac{1}{3}R_1$            4. $R_3 + \frac{1}{3}R_1$, $R_4 + \frac{5}{3}R_1$

5. $R_1 - \frac{1}{3}R_2$, $R_3 + \frac{2}{9}R_2$, $R_4 + \frac{1}{9}R_2$

we obtain the final tableau

| x | y | u | v | w | P | Const. |
|---|---|---|---|---|---|--------|
| 1 | 0 | $\frac{1}{3}$ | $-\frac{1}{3}$ | 0 | 0 | 3 |
| 0 | 0 | 0 | 1 | 1 | 0 | 0 |
| 0 | 1 | $\frac{1}{9}$ | $\frac{2}{9}$ | 0 | 0 | 2 |
| 0 | 0 | $\frac{5}{9}$ | $\frac{1}{9}$ | 0 | 1 | 7 |

We conclude that P attains a maximum value of 7 when $x = 3$ and $y = 2$.

12. We rewrite the problem as

$$C = -P = -x - 2y \text{ subject to}$$

$$4x + 7y \le 70$$

$$2x + y \le 20$$

$$-2x - y \le -20$$

$$x \ge 0, \ y \ge 0.$$

The initial tableau is

| x | y | u | v | w | C | Const. |
|---|---|---|---|---|---|--------|
| 4 | 7 | 1 | 0 | 0 | 0 | 70 |
| 2 | 1 | 0 | 1 | 0 | 0 | 20 |
| -2 | -1 | 0 | 0 | 1 | 0 | -20 |
| 1 | 2 | 0 | 0 | 0 | 1 | 0 . |

Using the following sequence of row operations

1. $-\frac{1}{2}R_3$          2. $R_1 - 4R_3$, $R_2 - 2R_3$, $R_4 - R_3$

we obtain the final tableau

| x | y | u | v | w | C | Const. |
|---|---|---|---|---|---|--------|
| 0 | 5 | 1 | 0 | 2 | 0 | 30 |
| 0 | 0 | 0 | 1 | 1 | 0 | 0 |
| 1 | $\frac{1}{2}$ | 0 | 0 | $-\frac{1}{2}$ | 0 | 10 |
| 0 | $\frac{3}{2}$ | 0 | 0 | $\frac{1}{2}$ | 0 | -10 . |

We conclude that P attains a minimum value of 10 when x = 10 and y = 0.

13. We rewrite the problem as

$$\text{Maximize } P = 5x + 4y + 2z \text{ subject to}$$

$$x + 2y + 3z \le 24$$

$$-x + y - z \le -6$$

$$x \ge 0, \ y \ge 0, \ z \ge 0.$$

The initial tableau is

| x | y | z | u | v | P | Const. |
|---|---|---|---|---|---|--------|
| 1 | 2 | 3 | 1 | 0 | 0 | 24 |
| -1 | 1 | -1 | 0 | 1 | 0 | -6 |
| -5 | -4 | -2 | 0 | 0 | 1 | 0 |

.

Using the following sequence of row operations

1. $-R_2$     2. $R_1 - R_2$, $R_3 + 5R_2$     3. $\frac{1}{3}R_1$

4. $R_2 + R_1$, $R_3 + 9R_1$     5. $3R_1$    6. $R_2 + \frac{2}{3}R_1$; $R_3 + 2R_1$

we obtain the final tableau

| x | y | z | u | v | P | Const. |
|---|---|---|---|---|---|--------|
| 0 | 3 | 2 | 1 | 1 | 0 | 18 |
| 1 | 2 | 3 | 1 | 0 | 0 | 24 |
| 0 | 6 | 13 | 5 | 0 | 1 | 120 |

,

from which we deduce that P attains a maximum value of 120 when
$x = 24$, $y = 0$, and $z = 0$.

14.  We rewrite the problem as

Maximize $P = x - 2y + z$ subject to

$$2x + 3y + 2z \leq 12$$

$$-x - 2y + 3z \leq -6$$

$$x \geq 0, \; y \geq 0, \; z \geq 0.$$

The initial tableau is

| x | y | z | u | v | P | Const. |
|---|---|---|---|---|---|--------|
| 2 | 3 | 2 | 1 | 0 | 0 | 12 |
| -1 | -2 | 3 | 0 | 1 | 0 | -6 |
| -1 | 2 | -1 | 0 | 0 | 1 | 0 |

.

Using the following sequence of row operations

1. $-R_2$          2. $R_1 - 2R_2$, $R_3 + R_2$

3. $\frac{1}{8}R_1$         4. $R_2 + 3R_1$, $R_3 + 4R_1$

we obtain the final tableau

| x | y | z | u | v | P | Const. |
|---|---|---|---|---|---|---|
| 0 | $-\frac{1}{8}$ | 1 | $\frac{1}{8}$ | $\frac{1}{4}$ | 0 | 0 |
| 1 | $\frac{13}{8}$ | 0 | $\frac{3}{8}$ | $-\frac{1}{4}$ | 0 | 6 |
| 0 | $\frac{7}{2}$ | 0 | $\frac{1}{2}$ | 0 | 1 | 6 |

Thus, P attains a maximum value of 6 when x = 6, y = 0, and z = 0.

15. The problem is to maximize P = −C = −x + 2y − z subject to the given constraints. The initial tableau is

| x | y | z | u | v | w | P | Const. |
|---|---|---|---|---|---|---|---|
| 1 | -2 | 3 | 1 | 0 | 0 | 0 | 10 |
| 2 | 1 | -2 | 0 | 1 | 0 | 0 | 15 |
| 2 | 1 | 3 | 0 | 0 | 1 | 0 | 20 |
| 1 | -2 | 1 | 0 | 0 | 0 | 1 | 0 |

Using the following sequence of row operations,

1. $R_1 + 2R_2$, $R_3 - R_2$, $R_4 + 2R_2$   2. $\frac{1}{5}R_3$

3. $R_1 + R_3$, $R_2 + 2R_3$, $R_4 + 3R_3$

we obtain the final tableau

| x | y | z | u | v | w | P | Const. |
|---|---|---|---|---|---|---|---|
| 5 | 0 | 0 | 1 | $\frac{9}{5}$ | $\frac{1}{5}$ | 0 | 41 |
| 2 | 1 | 0 | 0 | $\frac{3}{5}$ | $\frac{2}{5}$ | 0 | 17 |
| 0 | 0 | 1 | 0 | $-\frac{1}{5}$ | $\frac{1}{5}$ | 0 | 1 |
| 5 | 0 | 0 | 0 | $\frac{7}{5}$ | $\frac{3}{5}$ | 1 | 33 |

We conclude that C attains a minimum value of −33 when x = 0, y = 17, z = 1, and C = −P = −33.

16. The problem is to maximize $P = -C = -2x + 3y - 4z$ subject to the given constraints. The initial tableau is

| x | y | z | u | v | w | P | Const. |
|---|---|---|---|---|---|---|--------|
| -1 | 2 | -1 | 1 | 0 | 0 | 0 | 8 |
| 1 | -2 | 2 | 0 | 1 | 0 | 0 | 10 |
| 2 | 4 | -3 | 0 | 0 | 1 | 0 | 12 |
| 2 | -3 | 4 | 0 | 0 | 0 | 1 | 0 |

Using the following sequence of row operations

1. $\frac{1}{4}R_3$    2. $R_1 - 2R_3$, $R_2 + 2R_3$, $R_4 + 3R_3$

we obtain the final tableau

| x | y | z | u | v | w | P | Const. |
|---|---|---|---|---|---|---|--------|
| -2 | 0 | $\frac{1}{2}$ | 1 | 0 | $-\frac{1}{2}$ | 0 | 2 |
| 2 | 0 | $\frac{1}{2}$ | 0 | 1 | $\frac{1}{2}$ | 0 | 16 |
| $\frac{1}{2}$ | 1 | $-\frac{3}{4}$ | 0 | 0 | $\frac{1}{4}$ | 0 | 3 |
| $\frac{7}{2}$ | 0 | $\frac{7}{4}$ | 0 | 0 | $\frac{3}{4}$ | 1 | 9 |

from which we deduce that C attains a minimum value of $-9$ when $x = 0$, $y = 3$, and $z = 0$.

17. Rewriting the third constraint as $-x + 2y - z \leq -4$, we obtain the following initial tableau

| x | y | z | u | v | w | P | Const. |
|---|---|---|---|---|---|---|--------|
| 1 | 2 | 3 | 1 | 0 | 0 | 0 | 28 |
| 2 | 3 | -1 | 0 | 1 | 0 | 0 | 6 |
| -1 | 2 | -1 | 0 | 0 | 1 | 0 | -4 |
| -2 | -1 | -1 | 0 | 0 | 0 | 1 | 0 |

Using the following sequence of row operations

1. $\frac{1}{2}R_2$

2. $R_1 - R_2$, $R_3 + R_2$, $R_4 + 2R_2$

3. $-\frac{2}{3}R_3$

4. $R_1 - \frac{7}{2}R_3$, $R_2 + \frac{1}{2}R_3$, $R_4 + 2R_3$

5. $\frac{3}{26}R_1$

6. $R_2 - \frac{1}{3}R_1$, $R_3 + \frac{7}{3}R_1$, $R_4 + \frac{8}{3}R_1$

7. $\frac{26}{7}R_1$

8. $R_2 + \frac{11}{26}R_1$, $R_3 + \frac{1}{26}R_1$, $R_4 + \frac{8}{13}R_1$

we obtain the final tableau

| x | y | z | u | v | w | P | Const. |
|---|---|---|---|---|---|---|--------|
| 0 | $\frac{26}{7}$ | 0 | $\frac{3}{7}$ | $\frac{2}{7}$ | 1 | 0 | $\frac{68}{7}$ |
| 1 | $\frac{11}{7}$ | 0 | $\frac{1}{7}$ | $\frac{3}{7}$ | 1 | 0 | $\frac{46}{7}$ |
| 0 | $\frac{1}{7}$ | 1 | $\frac{2}{7}$ | $-\frac{1}{7}$ | 0 | 0 | $\frac{50}{7}$ |
| 0 | $\frac{16}{7}$ | 0 | $\frac{4}{7}$ | $\frac{5}{7}$ | 0 | 1 | $\frac{142}{7}$ |

from which we deduce that P attains a maximum value of 142/7 when
x = 46/7, y = 0, and z = 50/7.

18. We first rewrite the problem in the form

$$\text{Maximize } P = -C = -2x + y - 3z$$

$$-2x - y - z \leq -2$$

$$-x - 3y - z \leq -6$$

$$2x + y + 2z \leq 12$$

$$x \geq 0, \ y \geq 0, \text{ and } z \geq 0.$$

The initial tableau is

| x | y | z | u | v | w | P | Const. |
|---|---|---|---|---|---|---|--------|
| -2 | -1 | -1 | 1 | 0 | 0 | 0 | -2 |
| -1 | -3 | -1 | 0 | 1 | 0 | 0 | -6 |
| 2 | 1 | 2 | 0 | 0 | 1 | 0 | 12 |
| 2 | -1 | 3 | 0 | 0 | 0 | 1 | 0 |

Using the following sequence of row operations

1. $-R_1$        2. $R_2 + 3R_1$, $R_3 - R_1$, $R_4 + R_1$

3. $R_1 + R_3$, $R_2 + 3R_3$, $R_4 + R_3$

we obtain the final tableau

| x | y | z | u | v | w | P | Const. |
|---|---|---|---|---|---|---|--------|
| 2 | 1 | 2 | 0 | 0 | 1 | 0 | 12 |
| 5 | 0 | 5 | 0 | 1 | 3 | 0 | 30 |
| 0 | 0 | 1 | 1 | 0 | 1 | 0 | 10 |
| 4 | 0 | 5 | 0 | 0 | 1 | 1 | 12 |

Thus, C attains a minimum value of $-12$ when $x = 0$, $y = 12$, and $z = 0$.

19. Rewriting the third constraint ($2x + y + z = 10$) in the form

$$2x + y + z \geq 10 \quad \text{and} \quad -2x - y - z \leq -10,$$

we obtain the following initial tableau.

| x | y | z | t | u | v | w | P | Const. |
|---|---|---|---|---|---|---|---|--------|
| 1 | 2 | 1 | 1 | 0 | 0 | 0 | 0 | 20 |
| 3 | 1 | 0 | 0 | 1 | 0 | 0 | 0 | 30 |
| 2 | 1 | 1 | 0 | 0 | 1 | 0 | 0 | 10 |
| -2 | -1 | -1 | 0 | 0 | 0 | 1 | 0 | -10 |
| -1 | -2 | -3 | 0 | 0 | 0 | 0 | 1 | 0 |

Using the following sequence of row operations

1. $-R_4$        2. $R_1 - R_4$, $R_3 - R_4$, $R_5 + 3R_4$

3. $R_1 - R_3$, $R_4 + R_3$, $R_5 + 3R_3$

we obtain the final tableau

| x | y | z | t | u | v | w | P | Const. |
|---|---|---|---|---|---|---|---|--------|
| -1 | 1 | 0 | 1 | 0 | -1 | 0 | 0 | 10 |
| 3 | 1 | 0 | 0 | 1 | 0 | 0 | 0 | 30 |
| 0 | 0 | 0 | 0 | 0 | 1 | 1 | 0 | 0 |
| 2 | 1 | 1 | 0 | 0 | 1 | 0 | 0 | 10 |
| 5 | 1 | 0 | 0 | 0 | 3 | 0 | 1 | 30 |

We conclude that P attains a maximum value of 30 when $x = 0$, $y = 0$, and $z = 10$.

20. The problem is to maximize $P = -Q = -3x - 2y - z$ subject to the same constraints as given in Exercise 19. The initial simplex tableau is

| x | y | z | t | u | v | w | P | Const. |
|---|---|---|---|---|---|---|---|--------|
| 1 | 2 | 1 | 1 | 0 | 0 | 0 | 0 | 20 |
| 3 | 1 | 0 | 0 | 1 | 0 | 0 | 0 | 30 |
| 2 | 1 | 1 | 0 | 0 | 1 | 0 | 0 | 10 |
| -2 | -1 | -1 | 0 | 0 | 0 | 1 | 0 | -10 |
| 3 | 2 | 1 | 0 | 0 | 0 | 0 | 1 | 0 |

Using the sequence of row operations

1. $-R_4$      2. $R_1 - R_4$, $R_3 - R_4$, $R_5 - R_4$

we obtain the final tableau

| x | y | z | t | u | v | w | P | Const. |
|---|---|---|---|---|---|---|---|--------|
| -1 | 1 | 0 | 1 | 0 | 0 | 1 | 0 | 10 |
| 3 | 1 | 0 | 0 | 1 | 0 | 0 | 0 | 30 |
| 0 | 0 | 0 | 0 | 0 | 1 | 1 | 0 | 0 |
| 2 | 1 | 1 | 0 | 0 | 0 | -1 | 0 | 10 |
| 1 | 1 | 0 | 0 | 0 | 0 | 1 | 1 | -10 |

from which we deduce that Q attains a minimum value of 10, when $x = 0$, $y = 0$, and $z = 10$.

21. Let x and y denote the number of acres of crops A and B, respectively to be planted. Then the problem is

Maximize $P = 150x + 200y$ subject to the constraints

$$x + y \le 150$$

$$40x + 60y \le 7400$$

$$20x + 25y \le 3300$$

$$x \ge 80$$

$$x \ge 0, \quad y \ge 0.$$

Using the simplex method, we obtain

| x | y | u | v | w | z | P | Const. | --Ratio-- | |
|---|---|---|---|---|---|---|--------|-----------|---|
| 1 | 1 | 1 | 0 | 0 | 0 | 0 | 150 | 150 | |
| 40 | 60 | 0 | 1 | 0 | 0 | 0 | 7400 | 185 | $-R_4$ |
| 20 | 25 | 0 | 0 | 1 | 0 | 0 | 3300 | 165 | $\longrightarrow$ |
| (-1) | 0 | 0 | 0 | 0 | 1 | 0 | -80 | -80 | |
| -150 | -200 | 0 | 0 | 0 | 0 | 1 | 0 | | |

| x | y | u | v | w | z | P | Const. |
|---|---|---|---|---|---|---|---|
| 1 | 1 | 1 | 0 | 0 | 0 | 0 | 150 |
| 40 | 60 | 0 | 1 | 0 | 0 | 0 | 7400 |
| 20 | 25 | 0 | 0 | 1 | 0 | 0 | 3300 |
| 1 | 0 | 0 | 0 | 0 | -1 | 0 | 80 |
| -150 | -200 | 0 | 0 | 0 | 0 | 1 | 0 |

$$R_1 - R_4$$
$$R_2 - 40R_4$$
$$R_3 - 20R_4 \qquad 150R_4$$
$$R_5 + 150R_4$$

| x | y | u | v | w | z | P | Const. |
|---|---|---|---|---|---|---|---|
| 0 | 1 | 1 | 0 | 0 | 1 | 0 | 70 |
| 0 | 60 | 0 | 1 | 0 | 40 | 0 | 4200 |
| 0 | 25 | 0 | 0 | 1 | 20 | 0 | 1700 |
| 1 | 0 | 0 | 0 | 0 | -1 | 0 | 80 |
| 0 | -200 | 0 | 0 | 0 | -150 | 1 | 12000 |

$$\tfrac{1}{25}R_3$$

| x | y | u | v | w | z | P | Const. |
|---|---|---|---|---|---|---|---|
| 0 | 1 | 1 | 0 | 0 | 1 | 0 | 70 |
| 0 | 60 | 0 | 1 | 0 | 40 | 0 | 4200 |
| 0 | 1 | 0 | 0 | $\frac{1}{25}$ | $\frac{4}{5}$ | 0 | 68 |
| 1 | 0 | 0 | 0 | 0 | -1 | 0 | 80 |
| 0 | -200 | 0 | 0 | 0 | -150 | 1 | 12000 |

$$R_1 - R_3$$
$$R_2 - 60R_3$$
$$R_5 + 200R_3$$

| x | y | u | v | w | z | P | Const. |
|---|---|---|---|---|---|---|---|
| 0 | 0 | 1 | 0 | $-\frac{1}{25}$ | $\frac{1}{5}$ | 0 | 2 |
| 0 | 0 | 0 | 1 | $-\frac{12}{25}$ | -8 | 0 | 120 |
| 0 | 1 | 0 | 0 | $\frac{1}{25}$ | $\frac{4}{5}$ | 0 | 68 |
| 1 | 0 | 0 | 0 | 0 | -1 | 0 | 80 |
| 0 | 0 | 0 | 0 | 8 | 10 | 1 | 25600 |

.

We conclude that the farmer should plant 80 acres of crop A and 68 acres of crop B to realize a maximum profit of $25,600.

22. Let x and y denote the amount (in dollars) invested in company A and company B, respectively. Then the problem is

Maximize $P = 0.10x + 0.20y$ subject to

$$x + y \leq 50,000$$

$$-x + y \leq -20,000.$$

The initial tableau is

| x | y | u | v | P | Const. |
|---|---|---|---|---|---|
| 1 | 1 | 1 | 0 | 0 | 50,000 |
| -1 | 1 | 0 | 1 | 0 | -20,000 |
| -.10 | -.20 | 0 | 0 | 1 | 0 |

Using the following sequence of row operations

1. $-R_2$

2. $R_1 - R_2$, $R_3 + 10R_2$

3. $\frac{1}{2}R_1$

4. $R_2 + R_1$, $R_3 + .3R_1$

we obtain the final tableau

| x | y | u | v | P | Const. |
|---|---|---|---|---|---|
| 1 | 1 | .5 | .5 | 0 | 15,000 |
| 1 | 0 | .5 | -.5 | 0 | 35,000 |
| 0 | 0 | .15 | 0.5 | 1 | 6,500 |

Thus, William should invest $35,000 in the stocks of company A and $15,000 in the stocks of company B to attain a maximum return of $6,500 on his investment.

23. Let x and y denote the amount (in dollars) invested in company A and company B, respectively. Then the problem is

Maximize $P = 0.08x + 0.06y$ subject to

$$-x + 3y \leq 0$$

$$y \geq 10,000,000$$

$$x + y \geq 60,000,000$$

$$x \geq 0, \ y \geq 0.$$

Substituting $x = 60,000,000 - y$ into the first equation and the first and second inequalities, we have

Maximize $P = 0.08(60,000,000 - y) + 0.06y$

$$= 4,800,000, \ - 0.02y \text{ subject to}$$

$$y \le 15{,}000{,}000$$

$$y \ge 10{,}000{,}000$$

$$x \ge 0, \ y \ge 0.$$

Using the simplex method, we have

| y | u | v | P | Const. |
|---|---|---|---|--------|
| 1 | 1 | 0 | 0 | 15,000,000 |
| -1 | 0 | 1 | 0 | -10,000,000 |
| .02 | 0 | 0 | 1 | 4,800,000 |

p.r.→ circled (−1)   p.c. (under .02)   $\xrightarrow{-R_2}$

| y | u | v | P | Const. |
|---|---|---|---|--------|
| 1 | 1 | 0 | 0 | 15,000,000 |
| 1 | 0 | -1 | 0 | 10,000,000 |
| .02 | 0 | 0 | 1 | 4,800,000 |

$\xrightarrow[R_5 - .02R_2]{R_1 - R_2}$

| y | u | v | P | Const. |
|---|---|---|---|--------|
| 0 | 1 | 1 | 0 | 5,000,000 |
| 1 | 0 | -1 | 0 | 10,000,000 |
| 0 | 0 | .02 | 1 | 4,600,000 |

We conclude that the bank should extend $50 million in home loans, $10 million of commercial-development loans to attain a maximum return of $4.6 million.

24. Let x and y denote the number of standard and deluxe models produced at location II, respectively. Then the number of standard and deluxe models produced at location I is $600 - x$ and $300 - y$, respectively; and $P = 30(600 - x) + 20(300 - y) + 34x + 18y$. The linear programming problem is

Maximize $P = 4x - 2y + 24{,}000$ subject to

$$-x - y \le -300$$

$$x + y \le 400$$

$$-x + y \le 50$$

$$x \ge 0, \ y \ge 0.$$

The initial tableau is

| x | y | u | v | w | z | P | Const. |
|---|---|---|---|---|---|---|--------|
| -1 | -1 | 1 | 0 | 0 | 0 | 0 | -300 |
| 1 | 1 | 0 | 1 | 0 | 0 | 0 | 400 |
| -1 | 1 | 0 | 0 | 1 | 0 | 0 | 50 |
| 0 | 1 | 0 | 0 | 0 | 1 | 0 | 300 |
| -4 | 2 | 0 | 0 | 0 | 0 | 1 | 24,000 |

Using the following sequence of row operations

1. $-R_1$         2. $R_2 - R_1$, $R_3 + R_1$, $R_5 + 4R_1$

3. $R_1 + R_2$, $R_3 + R_2$, $R_5 + 4R_2$

we obtain the final tableau

| x | y | u | v | w | z | P | Const. |
|---|---|---|---|---|---|---|--------|
| 1 | 1 | 0 | 1 | 0 | 0 | 0 | 400 |
| 0 | 0 | 1 | 1 | 0 | 0 | 0 | 100 |
| 0 | 2 | 0 | 1 | 1 | 0 | 0 | 450 |
| 0 | 1 | 0 | 0 | 0 | 1 | 0 | 300 |
| 0 | 6 | 0 | 4 | 0 | 0 | 1 | 25,600 |

The solution is P = 25,600 when x = 400 and y = 0. This means that 200 standard and 300 deluxe futons should be produced at location I and 400 standard and 0 deluxe futons should be produced at location II to realize a maximum profit of $25,600.

25. Let x, y, and z denote the number of units of products A, B, and C manufactured by the company. Then the linear programming problem is

$$\text{Maximize } P = 18z + 12y + 15z \text{ subject to}$$

$$2x + y + 2z \leq 900$$

$$3x + y + 2z \leq 1080$$

$$2x + 2y + z \leq 840$$

$$x - y + z \leq 0$$

$$x \geq 0, \ y \geq 0, \ z \geq 0.$$

The initial tableau is

| x | y | z | t | u | v | w | P | Const. |
|---|---|---|---|---|---|---|---|--------|
| 2 | 1 | 2 | 1 | 0 | 0 | 0 | 0 | 900 |
| 3 | 1 | 2 | 0 | 1 | 0 | 0 | 0 | 1080 |
| 2 | 2 | 1 | 0 | 0 | 1 | 0 | 0 | 840 |
| 1 | -1 | 1 | 0 | 0 | 0 | 1 | 0 | 0 |
| -18 | -12 | -15 | 0 | 0 | 0 | 0 | 1 | 0 |

Using the following sequence of row operations,

1. $R_1 - 2R_4$, $R_2 - 3R_4$, $R_3 - 2R_4$, $R_5 + 18R_4$

2. $\frac{1}{4}R_3$

3. $R_1 - 3R_3$, $R_2 - 4R_3$, $R_4 + R_3$, $R_5 + 30R_3$,

4. $\frac{4}{3}R_4$

5. $R_1 - \frac{3}{4}R_4$ $R_3 + \frac{1}{4}R_4$, $R_5 + \frac{9}{2}R_4$

we obtain the final tableau

| x | y | z | t | u | v | w | P | Const. |
|---|---|---|---|---|---|---|---|--------|
| -1 | 0 | 0 | 1 | 0 | -1 | -1 | 0 | 60 |
| 0 | 0 | 0 | 0 | 1 | -1 | -1 | 0 | 240 |
| $\frac{1}{3}$ | 1 | 0 | 0 | 0 | $\frac{1}{3}$ | $-\frac{1}{3}$ | 0 | 280 |
| $\frac{4}{3}$ | 0 | 1 | 0 | 0 | $\frac{1}{3}$ | $\frac{2}{3}$ | 0 | 280 |
| -6 | 0 | 0 | 0 | 0 | 9 | 6 | 1 | 7560 |

and conclude that the company should produce 0 units of product A, 280 units of product B, and 280 units of product C to realize a maximum profit of $7,560.

26. Let x, y, and z, denote the number of pianos shipped from plant I to location A, B, and C, respectively. Then, the number of pianos shipped from plant II to location A, B, and C is 200 − x, 150 − y, and 200 − z, respectively. Then the function to be minimized is

$$C = 60x + 60y + 80z + 80(200 - x) + 70(150 - y) + 50(200 - z)$$

$$= 36500 - 20x - 10y + 30z.$$

and the linear programming problem is

Minimize C = 36500 − 20x − 10y + 30z

$$x \le 200$$
$$y \le 150$$
$$z \le 200$$
$$x + y + z \le 300$$
$$-x - y - z \le -300$$
$$x \ge 0, \ y \ge 0, \text{ and } z \ge 0.$$

The initial tableau is

| x | y | z | s | t | u | v | w | P | Const. |
|---|---|---|---|---|---|---|---|---|--------|
| 1 | 0 | 0 | 1 | 0 | 0 | 0 | 0 | 0 | 200 |
| 0 | 1 | 0 | 0 | 1 | 0 | 0 | 0 | 0 | 150 |
| 0 | 0 | 1 | 0 | 0 | 1 | 0 | 0 | 0 | 200 |
| 1 | 1 | 1 | 0 | 0 | 0 | 1 | 0 | 0 | 300 |
| −1 | −1 | −1 | 0 | 0 | 0 | 0 | 1 | 0 | −300 |
| −20 | −10 | 30 | 0 | 0 | 0 | 0 | 0 | 1 | −36,500 |

Using the following sequence of row operations

1. $R_4 - R_1$, $R_5 + R_1$, $R_6 + 20R_1$

2. $R_2 - R_4$, $R_5 + R_4$, $R_6 + 10R_4$

we obtain the final tableau

| x | y | z | s | t | u | v | w | P | Const. |
|---|---|---|---|---|---|---|---|---|--------|
| 1 | 0 | 0 | 1 | 0 | 0 | 0 | 0 | 0 | 200 |
| 0 | 0 | −1 | 1 | 1 | 0 | −1 | 0 | 0 | 50 |
| 0 | 0 | 1 | 0 | 0 | 1 | 0 | 0 | 0 | 200 |
| 0 | 1 | 1 | −1 | 0 | 0 | 1 | 0 | 0 | 100 |
| 0 | 0 | 0 | 0 | 0 | 0 | 1 | 1 | 0 | 0 |
| 0 | 0 | 40 | 10 | 0 | 0 | 10 | 0 | 1 | −31,500 |

Thus, the optimal solution is x = 200, y = 100, z = 0, and
C = 31,500. This means that the minimum shipping cost is $31,500
when 200 pianos are shipped from plant I to warehouse A, 100 from
plant I to warehouse B, and 0 from plant I to warehouse C; and 0
pianos are shipped from plant II to warehouse A, 50 from plant II
to warehouse B, and 200 from plant II to warehouse C.

27. Let x denote the number of ounces of food A  and y denote the
number of ounces of food B used in the meal. Then the problem is

to minimize the amount of cholesterol in the meal.  Thus, the linear programming problem is

Maximize $P = -C = -2x - 5y$ subject to

$$30x + 25y \geq 400$$

$$x + \tfrac{1}{2}y \geq 10$$

$$2x + 5y \geq 40.$$

$$x \geq 0, \; y \geq 0.$$

The initial tableau is

| x | y | u | v | w | P | Const. |
|---|---|---|---|---|---|--------|
| -30 | -25 | 1 | 0 | 0 | 0 | -400 |
| -1 | $-\tfrac{1}{2}$ | 0 | 1 | 0 | 0 | -10 |
| -2 | -5 | 0 | 0 | 1 | 0 | -40 |
| 2 | 5 | 0 | 0 | 0 | 1 | 0 |

Using the following sequence of row operations

1. $-R_2$       2. $R_1 + 30R_2$; $R_3 + 2R_2$; $R_4 - 2R_2$       3. $-\tfrac{1}{4}R_3$

4. $R_1 + 10R_3$; $R_2 - \tfrac{1}{2}R_3$; $R_4 - 4R_3$     5. $-\tfrac{1}{25}R_1$     6. $R_2 + \tfrac{5}{4}R_1$; $R_3 - \tfrac{1}{2}R_1$

we obtain the final tableau

| x | y | u | v | w | P | Const. |
|---|---|---|---|---|---|--------|
| 0 | 0 | $-\tfrac{1}{25}$ | 1 | $\tfrac{1}{10}$ | 0 | 2 |
| 1 | 0 | $-\tfrac{1}{20}$ | 1 | $\tfrac{1}{4}$ | 0 | 10 |
| 0 | 1 | $\tfrac{1}{50}$ | 0 | $-\tfrac{3}{10}$ | 0 | 4 |
| 0 | 0 | 0 | 0 | 1 | 1 | -40 |

Thus, the minimum content of cholesterol is 40mg when 10 ounces of food A and 4 ounces of food B are used.(Since the  u-column is not in unit form, we see that the problem has multiple solutions.)

# CHAPTER 4  REVIEW EXERCISES, page 270

1.   This is a regular linear programming problem. Using the simplex method with u and v as slack variables, we obtain the following sequence of tableaus:

| | x | y | u | v | P | Const. | Ratio |
|---|---|---|---|---|---|---|---|
| p.r.→ | 1 | ③ | 1 | 0 | 0 | 15 | 5 |
| | 4 | 1 | 0 | 1 | 0 | 16 | 16 |
| | -3 | -4 | 0 | 0 | 1 | 0 | |

$\uparrow$
p.c.

$\xrightarrow{\frac{1}{3}R_1}$

| x | y | u | v | P | Const. |
|---|---|---|---|---|---|
| $\frac{1}{3}$ | 1 | $\frac{1}{3}$ | 0 | 0 | 5 |
| 4 | 1 | 0 | 1 | 0 | 16 |
| -3 | -4 | 0 | 0 | 1 | 0 |

$\xrightarrow{\begin{array}{c} R_2 - R_1 \\ R_3 + 4R_1 \end{array}}$

| | x | y | u | v | P | Const. |
|---|---|---|---|---|---|---|
| | $\frac{1}{3}$ | 1 | $\frac{1}{3}$ | 0 | 0 | 5 |
| p.c.→ | $\textcircled{\frac{11}{3}}$ | 0 | $-\frac{1}{3}$ | 1 | 0 | 11 |
| | $-\frac{5}{3}$ | 0 | $\frac{4}{3}$ | 0 | 1 | 20 |

$\uparrow$
p.c.

$\xrightarrow{\frac{3}{11}R_2}$

| x | y | u | v | P | Const. |
|---|---|---|---|---|---|
| $\frac{1}{3}$ | 1 | $\frac{1}{3}$ | 0 | 0 | 5 |
| 1 | 0 | $-\frac{1}{11}$ | $\frac{3}{11}$ | 0 | 3 |
| $-\frac{5}{3}$ | 0 | $\frac{4}{3}$ | 0 | 1 | 20 |

$\xrightarrow{\begin{array}{c} R_1 - \frac{1}{3}R_2 \\ R_3 + \frac{5}{3}R_2 \end{array}}$

| x | y | u | v | P | Const. |
|---|---|---|---|---|---|
| 0 | 1 | $\frac{4}{11}$ | $-\frac{1}{11}$ | 0 | 4 |
| 1 | 0 | $-\frac{1}{11}$ | $\frac{3}{11}$ | 0 | 3 |
| 0 | 0 | $\frac{13}{11}$ | $\frac{5}{11}$ | 1 | 25 |

$\xrightarrow{R_3 + \frac{5}{3}R_2}$

and conclude that x = 3, y = 4, and P = 25.

2. This is a regular linear programming problem. The initial tableau is

| x | y | u | v | w | P | Const. |
|---|---|---|---|---|---|---|
| 2 | 1 | 1 | 0 | 0 | 0 | 16 |
| 2 | 3 | 0 | 1 | 0 | 0 | 24 |
| 0 | 0 | 0 | 0 | 1 | 0 | 6 |
| -2 | -5 | 0 | 0 | 0 | 1 | 0 |

Using the following sequence of row operations

1. $R_1 - R_3$, $R_2 - 3R_3$, $R_4 + 5R_3$   2. $\frac{1}{2}R_2$

3. $R_1 - 2R_2$, $R_4 + 2R_2$

we obtain the final tableau

| x | y | u | v | w | P | Const. |
|---|---|---|---|---|---|---|
| 0 | 0 | 1 | -1 | 2 | 0 | 4 |
| 1 | 0 | 0 | $\frac{1}{2}$ | $-\frac{3}{2}$ | 0 | 3 |
| 0 | 1 | 0 | 0 | 1 | 0 | 6 |
| 0 | 0 | 0 | 1 | 2 | 1 | 36 |

and conclude that $P = 36$ when $x = 3$ and $y = 6$.

3. Using the simplex method to solve this regular linear programming problem we have

| | x | y | z | u | v | P | Const. | Ratio | |
|---|---|---|---|---|---|---|---|---|---|
| p.r.→ | 1 | 2 | ③ | 1 | 0 | 0 | 12 | 4 | $\frac{1}{3}R_1$ |
| | 1 | -3 | 2 | 0 | 1 | 0 | 10 | 5 | → |
| | -2 | -3 | -5 | 0 | 0 | 1 | 0 | | |

p.c. (under z column)

| x | y | z | u | v | P | Const. | |
|---|---|---|---|---|---|---|---|
| $\frac{1}{3}$ | $\frac{2}{3}$ | 1 | $\frac{1}{3}$ | 0 | 0 | 4 | $R_2 - 2R_1$ |
| 1 | -3 | 2 | 0 | 1 | 0 | 10 | $R_3 + 5R_1$ |
| -2 | -3 | -5 | 0 | 0 | 1 | 0 | |

| x | y | z | u | v | P | Const. | Ratio |
|---|---|---|---|---|---|---|---|
| $\frac{1}{3}$ | $\frac{2}{3}$ | 1 | $\frac{1}{3}$ | 0 | 0 | 4 | 12 |
| $\left(\frac{1}{3}\right)$ | $-\frac{13}{3}$ | 0 | $-\frac{2}{3}$ | 1 | 0 | 2 | 6 |
| $-\frac{1}{3}$ | $\frac{1}{3}$ | 0 | $\frac{5}{3}$ | 0 | 1 | 20 | |

p.r.→ (second row)   p.c. ↑ (x column)   $\xrightarrow{3R_2}$

| x | y | z | u | v | P | Const. |
|---|---|---|---|---|---|---|
| $\frac{1}{3}$ | $\frac{2}{3}$ | 1 | $\frac{1}{3}$ | 0 | 0 | 4 |
| 0 | -13 | 0 | -2 | 3 | 0 | 6 |
| $-\frac{1}{3}$ | $\frac{1}{3}$ | 0 | $\frac{5}{3}$ | 0 | 1 | 20 |

$$\xrightarrow[R_3 + \frac{1}{3}R_2]{R_1 - \frac{1}{3}R_2}$$

| x | y | z | u | v | P | Const. | Ratio |
|---|---|---|---|---|---|---|---|
| 0 | (5) | 1 | 1 | -1 | 0 | 2 | 2/5 |
| 0 | -13 | 0 | -2 | 3 | 0 | 6 | -- |
| 0 | -4 | 0 | 1 | 1 | 1 | 22 | |

p.r.→ (first row)   p.c. ↑ (y column)   $\xrightarrow{\frac{1}{5}R_1}$

| x | y | z | u | v | P | Const. |
|---|---|---|---|---|---|---|
| 0 | 1 | $\frac{1}{5}$ | $\frac{1}{5}$ | $-\frac{1}{5}$ | 0 | $\frac{2}{5}$ |
| 0 | -13 | 0 | -2 | 3 | 0 | 6 |
| 0 | -4 | 0 | 1 | 1 | 1 | 22 |

$$\xrightarrow[R_3 + 4R_1]{R_2 + 13R_1}$$

| x | y | z | u | v | P | Const. |
|---|---|---|---|---|---|---|
| 0 | 1 | $\frac{1}{5}$ | $\frac{1}{5}$ | $-\frac{1}{5}$ | 0 | $\frac{2}{5}$ |
| 1 | 0 | $\frac{13}{5}$ | $\frac{3}{5}$ | $\frac{2}{5}$ | 0 | $\frac{56}{5}$ |
| 0 | 0 | $\frac{4}{5}$ | $\frac{9}{5}$ | $\frac{1}{5}$ | 1 | $\frac{118}{5}$ |

We conclude that the P attains a maximum value of 23.6 when $x = 11.2$, $y = 0.4$ and $z = 0$.

4. This is a regular linear programming problem. The initial tableau is

| x | y | z | u | v | w | P | Const. |
|---|---|---|---|---|---|---|--------|
| 2 | 1 | 1 | 1 | 0 | 0 | 0 | 14 |
| 3 | 2 | 4 | 0 | 1 | 0 | 0 | 24 |
| 2 | 5 | -2 | 0 | 0 | 1 | 0 | 10 |
| -1 | -2 | -3 | 0 | 0 | 0 | 1 | 0 |

Using the following sequence of row operations;

1. $\frac{1}{4}R_2$    2. $R_1 - R_2$, $R_3 + 2R_2$, $R_4 + 3R_2$

3. $\frac{1}{6}R_3$    4. $R_1 - \frac{1}{2}R_3$, $R_2 - \frac{1}{2}R_3$, $R_4 + \frac{1}{2}R_3$

we obtain the final tableau

| x | y | z | u | v | w | P | Const. |
|---|---|---|---|---|---|---|--------|
| $\frac{23}{24}$ | 0 | 0 | 1 | $-\frac{7}{24}$ | $-\frac{1}{12}$ | 0 | $\frac{37}{6}$ |
| $\frac{11}{24}$ | 0 | 1 | 0 | $\frac{5}{24}$ | $-\frac{1}{12}$ | 0 | $\frac{25}{6}$ |
| $\frac{7}{24}$ | 1 | 0 | 0 | $\frac{1}{12}$ | $\frac{1}{6}$ | 0 | $\frac{11}{3}$ |
| $\frac{37}{24}$ | 0 | 0 | 0 | $\frac{19}{24}$ | $\frac{1}{12}$ | 1 | $\frac{119}{6}$ |

and conclude that $x = 0$, $y = 11/3$, $z = 25/6$, and $P = 119/6$.

5. We first write the tableau

| x | y | Constant |
|---|---|----------|
| 2 | 3 | 6 |
| 2 | 1 | 4 |
| 3 | 2 | |

Then obtain the following by interchanging rows and columns:

| u | v | Constant |
|---|---|----------|
| 2 | 2 | 3 |
| 3 | 1 | 2 |
| 6 | 4 | |

From this table we construct the dual problem:

Maximize the objective function

$$P = 6u + 4v$$

subject to the constraints

$$2u + 2v \le 3$$

$$3u + \phantom{2}v \le 2$$

$$u \ge 0, \ v \ge 0.$$

Using the simplex method, we have

| u | v | x | y | P | Const. | Ratio |
|---|---|---|---|---|--------|-------|
| 2 | 2 | 1 | 0 | 0 | 3 | 3/2 |
| ③ | 1 | 0 | 1 | 0 | 2 | 2/3 |
| -6 | -4 | 0 | 0 | 1 | 0 | |

p.r. → ③ , $\frac{1}{3}R_2$

p.c. ↑ (u column)

| u | v | x | y | P | Const. |
|---|---|---|---|---|--------|
| 2 | 2 | 1 | 0 | 0 | 3 |
| 1 | $\frac{1}{3}$ | 0 | $\frac{1}{3}$ | 0 | $\frac{2}{3}$ |
| -6 | -4 | 0 | 0 | 1 | 0 |

$$R_1 - 2R_2$$
$$R_3 + 6R_2$$

| u | v | x | y | P | Const. | Ratio |
|---|---|---|---|---|--------|-------|
| 0 | $\frac{4}{3}$ | 1 | $-\frac{2}{3}$ | 0 | $\frac{5}{3}$ | 3/4 |
| 1 | $\frac{1}{3}$ | 0 | $\frac{1}{3}$ | 0 | $\frac{2}{3}$ | 2 |
| 0 | -2 | 0 | 2 | 1 | 4 | |

$$\tfrac{3}{4}R_1$$

| u | v | x | y | P | Const. |
|---|---|---|---|---|--------|
| 0 | 1 | $\frac{3}{4}$ | $-\frac{1}{2}$ | 0 | $\frac{5}{4}$ |
| 1 | $\frac{1}{3}$ | 0 | $\frac{1}{3}$ | 0 | $\frac{2}{3}$ |
| 0 | -2 | 0 | 2 | 1 | 4 |

$$R_2 - \tfrac{1}{3}R_1$$
$$R_3 + 2R_1$$

| u | v | x | y | P | Const. |
|---|---|---|---|---|---|
| 0 | 1 | $\frac{3}{4}$ | $-\frac{1}{2}$ | 0 | $\frac{5}{4}$ |
| 1 | 0 | $-\frac{1}{4}$ | $\frac{1}{2}$ | 0 | $\frac{1}{4}$ |
| 0 | 0 | $\frac{3}{2}$ | 1 | 1 | $\frac{13}{2}$ |

Therefore, C attains a minimum value of 13/2 when x = 3/2 and y = 1.

6.    We first write the tableau

| x | y | Constant |
|---|---|---|
| 3 | 1 | 12 |
| 1 | 4 | 16 |
| 1 | 2 | |

Then obtain the following by interchanging rows and columns:

| u | v | Constant |
|---|---|---|
| 3 | 1 | 1 |
| 1 | 4 | 2 |
| 12 | 16 | |

From this table we construct the dual problem:

Maximize the objective function

$$P = 12u + 16v$$

subject to the constraints

$$3u + v \leq 1$$

$$u + 4v \leq 2$$

$$u \geq 0, \ v \geq 0.$$

The initial tableau is

| u | v | x | y | P | Const. |
|---|---|---|---|---|---|
| 3 | 1 | 1 | 0 | 0 | 1 |
| 1 | 4 | 0 | 1 | 0 | 2 |
| -12 | -16 | 0 | 0 | 1 | 0 |

Using the following sequence of row operations,

1. $\frac{1}{4}R_2$          2. $R_1 - R_2$, $R_3 + 16R_2$

3. $\frac{4}{11}R_1$          4. $R_2 - \frac{1}{4}R_1$, $R_3 + 8R_1$

we obtain the following tableau

| u | v | x | y | P | Const. |
|---|---|---|---|---|--------|
| 1 | 0 | $\frac{4}{11}$ | $-\frac{1}{11}$ | 0 | $\frac{2}{11}$ |
| 0 | 1 | $-\frac{1}{11}$ | $\frac{3}{11}$ | 0 | $\frac{5}{11}$ |
| 0 | 1 | $\frac{32}{11}$ | $\frac{36}{11}$ | 1 | $\frac{104}{11}$ |

Thus, C attains a minimum value of 104/11 when x = 32/11 and y = 36/11.

7.    We first write the tableau

| x | y | z | Const. |
|---|---|---|--------|
| 3 | 2 | 1 | 4 |
| 1 | 1 | 3 | 6 |
| 24 | 18 | 24 | |

Then obtain the following by interchanging rows and columns:

| u | v | Const. |
|---|---|--------|
| 3 | 2 | 24 |
| 2 | 1 | 18 |
| 1 | 3 | 24 |
| 4 | 6 | |

From this table we construct the dual problem:

Maximize the objective function P = 4u + 6v

subject to

$$3u + v \le 24$$
$$2u + v \le 18$$
$$u + 3v \le 24$$
$$u \ge 0, \ v \ge 0.$$

The initial tableau is

| u | v | x | y | z | P | Const. |
|---|---|---|---|---|---|--------|
| 3 | 1 | 1 | 0 | 0 | 0 | 24 |
| 2 | 1 | 0 | 1 | 0 | 0 | 18 |
| 1 | 3 | 0 | 0 | 1 | 0 | 24 |
| -4 | -6 | 0 | 0 | 0 | 1 | 0 |

Using the following sequence of row operations,

1. $\frac{1}{3}R_3$

2. $R_1 - R_3$, $R_2 - R_3$, $R_4 + 6R_3$

3. $\frac{3}{8}R_1$

4. $R_2 - \frac{5}{3}R_1$, $R_3 - \frac{1}{3}R_1$, $R_4 + 2R_1$

we obtain the final tableau

| u | v | x | y | z | P | Const. |
|---|---|---|---|---|---|--------|
| 1 | 0 | $\frac{3}{8}$ | 0 | $-\frac{1}{8}$ | 0 | 6 |
| 0 | 0 | $-\frac{5}{8}$ | 1 | $-\frac{1}{8}$ | 0 | 0 |
| 0 | 1 | $-\frac{1}{8}$ | 0 | $\frac{3}{8}$ | 0 | 6 |
| 0 | 0 | $\frac{3}{4}$ | 0 | $\frac{7}{4}$ | 0 | 60 |

.

We conclude that C attains a minimum value of 60 when $x = 3/4$, $y = 0$, and $z = 7/4$.

8. The dual problem is

Maximize $P = 4u + 2v + 3w$ subject to

$$u + 2v + 3w \le 4$$

$$2u + v + 2w \le 2$$

$$u + 2v + w \le 6$$

$$u \ge 0, \ v \ge 0, \text{ and } w \ge 0.$$

Using the simplex method, we obtain the following sequence of tableaus

| u | v | w | x | y | z | P | Const. |
|---|---|---|---|---|---|---|--------|
| 1 | 2 | 3 | 1 | 0 | 0 | 0 | 4 |
| ②| 1 | 2 | 0 | 1 | 0 | 0 | 2 |
| 1 | 2 | 1 | 0 | 0 | 0 | 1 | 6 |
| -4 | -2 | -3 | 0 | 0 | 0 | 1 | 0 |

$\xrightarrow{\frac{1}{2}R_2}$

| u | v | w | x | y | z | P | Const. | |
|---|---|---|---|---|---|---|---|---|
| 1 | 2 | 3 | 1 | 0 | 0 | 0 | 4 | $R_1 - R_2$ |
| 1 | $\frac{1}{2}$ | 1 | 0 | $\frac{1}{2}$ | 0 | 0 | 1 | $R_3 - R_2$ |
| 1 | 2 | 1 | 0 | 0 | 0 | 1 | 6 | $R_4 + 4R_2$ |
| -4 | -2 | -3 | 0 | 0 | 0 | 1 | 0 | |

| u | v | w | x | y | z | P | Const. |
|---|---|---|---|---|---|---|---|
| 0 | $\frac{3}{2}$ | 2 | 1 | $-\frac{1}{2}$ | 0 | 0 | 3 |
| 1 | $\frac{1}{2}$ | 1 | 0 | $\frac{1}{2}$ | 0 | 0 | 1 |
| 0 | $\frac{3}{2}$ | 0 | 0 | $-\frac{1}{2}$ | 1 | 0 | 5 |
| 0 | 0 | 1 | 0 | 2 | 0 | 1 | 4 |

Interpreting this last tableau, we find that the solution is $x = 0$, $y = 2$, $z = 0$, and $P = C = 4$.

9.  Rewriting the problem, we have

Maximize $P = 3x - 4y$ subject to

$$x + y \leq 45$$

$$-x + 2y \leq -10$$

$$x \geq 0, \; y \geq 0.$$

Using the simplex method, we have

| x | y | u | v | P | Const. | --Ratio-- | |
|---|---|---|---|---|---|---|---|
| 1 | 1 | 1 | 0 | 0 | 45 | 45 | |
| (-1) | 2 | 0 | 1 | 0 | -10 | 10 | $-R_2$ |
| -3 | 4 | 0 | 0 | 1 | 0 | | |

| x | y | u | v | P | Const. | |
|---|---|---|---|---|---|---|
| 1 | 1 | 1 | 0 | 0 | 45 | $R_1 - R_2$ |
| 1 | -2 | 0 | -1 | 0 | 10 | $R_3 + 3R_2$ |
| -3 | 4 | 0 | 0 | 1 | 0 | |

| x | y | u | v | P | Const. | |
|---|---|---|---|---|---|---|
| 0 | 3 | 1 | 1 | 0 | 35 | $R_2 + R_1$ |
| 1 | -2 | 0 | -1 | 0 | 10 | $R_3 + 3R_1$ |
| 0 | -2 | 0 | -3 | 1 | 30 | |

| x | y | u | v | P | Const. |
|---|---|---|---|---|---|
| 0 | 3 | 1 | 1 | 0 | 35 |
| 1 | 1 | 1 | 0 | 0 | 45 |
| 0 | 7 | 3 | 0 | 1 | 135 |

We conclude that P attains a maximum value of 135 when x = 45 and y = 0.

10. Write the linear programming problem as

Maximize $P = -C = -2x - 3y$ subject to

$$x + y \leq 10$$

$$-x - 2y \leq -12$$

$$-2x - y \leq -12$$

$$x \geq 0, \ y \geq 0 \quad .$$

The initial tableau is

| x | y | u | v | w | P | Const. |
|---|---|---|---|---|---|---|
| 1 | 1 | 1 | 0 | 0 | 0 | 10 |
| -1 | -2 | 0 | 1 | 0 | 0 | -12 |
| -2 | -1 | 0 | 0 | 1 | 0 | -12 |
| 2 | 3 | 0 | 0 | 0 | 1 | 0 |

Using the following sequence of row operations

1. $-\frac{1}{2}R_3$    2. $R_1 - R_3, \ R_2 + R_3, \ R_4 - 2R_3$

3. $-\frac{2}{3}R_2$    4. $R_1 - \frac{1}{2}R_2, \ R_3 - \frac{1}{2}R_2, \ R_4 - 2R_2$

we obtain the final tableau

| x | y | u | v | w | P | Const. |
|---|---|---|---|---|---|---|
| 0 | 0 | 1 | $\frac{1}{3}$ | $\frac{1}{3}$ | 0 | 2 |
| 0 | 1 | 0 | $-\frac{2}{3}$ | $\frac{1}{3}$ | 0 | 4 |
| 1 | 0 | 0 | $\frac{1}{3}$ | $-\frac{2}{3}$ | 0 | 4 |
| 0 | 0 | 0 | $\frac{4}{3}$ | $\frac{1}{3}$ | 1 | -20 |

We conclude that C attains a minimum value of 20 when x = 4 and y = 4.

11. We first write the problem in the form

Maximize P = 2x + 3y subject to

$$2x + 5y \leq 20$$

$$x - 5y < -5$$

$$x \geq 0, \ y \geq 0 \quad .$$

The initial tableau is

| x | y | u | v | P | Const. |
|---|---|---|---|---|--------|
| 2 | 5 | 1 | 0 | 0 | 20 |
| 1 | -5 | 0 | 1 | 0 | -5 |
| -2 | -3 | 0 | 0 | 1 | 0 |

Using the sequence of row operations

1. $\frac{1}{5}R_1$

2. $R_2 + 5R_1$, $R_3 + 3R_1$

3. $\frac{1}{3}R_2$

4. $R_1 - \frac{2}{5}R_2$, $R_3 + \frac{4}{5}R_2$

we obtain the final tableau

| x | y | u | v | P | Const. |
|---|---|---|---|---|--------|
| 0 | 1 | $\frac{1}{15}$ | $-\frac{2}{15}$ | 0 | 2 |
| 1 | 0 | $\frac{1}{3}$ | $\frac{1}{3}$ | 0 | 5 |
| 0 | 0 | $\frac{13}{15}$ | $\frac{4}{15}$ | 1 | 16 |

We conclude that P attains a maximum value of 16 when x = 5 and y = 2.

12. We solve the linear programming problem

Maximize P = -C = 3x + 4y subject to

$$x + y \leq 45$$

$$-x - y \leq -15$$

$$x \leq 30$$

$$y \leq 25$$

$$x \geq 0, \ y \geq 0.$$

The initial tableau is

| x | y | u | v | w | z | P | Const. |
|---|---|---|---|---|---|---|--------|
| 1 | 1 | 1 | 0 | 0 | 0 | 0 | 45 |
| -1 | -1 | 0 | 1 | 0 | 0 | 0 | -15 |
| 1 | 0 | 0 | 0 | 1 | 0 | 0 | 30 |
| 0 | 1 | 0 | 0 | 0 | 1 | 0 | 25 |
| -3 | -4 | 0 | 0 | 0 | 0 | 1 | 0 |

Using the following sequence of row operations,

1. $-R_2$          2. $R_1 - R_2$, $R_4 - R_2$, $R_5 + 4R_2$

3. $R_1 - R_4$, $R_2 + R_4$, $R_5 + 4R_4$

4. $R_3 - R_1$, $R_4 + R_1$, $R_5 + 3R_1$,

we obtain the final tableau

| x | y | u | v | w | z | P | Const. |
|---|---|---|---|---|---|---|--------|
| 1 | 0 | 1 | 0 | 0 | -1 | 0 | 20 |
| 0 | 1 | 0 | 0 | 0 | 1 | 0 | 25 |
| 0 | 0 | -1 | 0 | 1 | 1 | 0 | 10 |
| 0 | 0 | 1 | 1 | 0 | 0 | 0 | 30 |
| 0 | 0 | 3 | 0 | 0 | 1 | 1 | 160 |

and conclude that C attains a minimum value of $-160$ when $x = 20$ and $y = 25$.

13. Let $x$, $y$, and $z$ denote the number of units of products A, B, and C made, respectively. Then the problem is to maximize the profit

$$P = 4x + 6y + 8z \text{ subject to}$$

$$9x + 12y + 18z \leq 360$$

$$6x + 6y + 10z \leq 240$$

where          $x \geq 0$, $y \geq 0$, and $z \geq 0$.

The initial tableau is

| x | y | z | u | v | P | Const. |
|---|---|---|---|---|---|--------|
| 9 | 12 | 18 | 1 | 0 | 0 | 360 |
| 6 | 6 | 10 | 0 | 1 | 0 | 240 |
| -4 | -6 | -8 | 0 | 0 | 1 | 0 |

Using the sequence of row operations

1. $\frac{1}{18}R_1$          2. $R_2 - 10R_1$

3. $R_3 + 8R_1$       4. $\frac{3}{2}R_1$             5. $R_2 + \frac{2}{3}R_1, \; R_3 + \frac{2}{3}R_1$

we obtain the final tableau

| x | y | z | u | v | P | Const. |
|---|---|---|---|---|---|---|
| $\frac{3}{4}$ | 1 | $\frac{3}{2}$ | $\frac{1}{12}$ | 0 | 0 | 30 |
| $\frac{3}{2}$ | 0 | 1 | $-\frac{1}{2}$ | 1 | 0 | 60 |
| $\frac{1}{2}$ | 0 | 1 | $\frac{1}{2}$ | 0 | 1 | 180 |

and conclude that the company should produce 0 units of product A, 30 units of product B, and 0 units of product C to realize a maximum profit of $180.

14. Let the amount invested in blue chip, growth, and speculative stocks be x, y, and z, respectively. Then, the problem is to maximize

$$P = 0.10x + 0.15y + 0.20z \text{ subject to}$$

$$-0.3x + 0.7y + 0.7z \le 0$$

$$-0.5x + 0.5y - 0.5z \le 0$$

$$x \ge 0, \; y \ge 0, \text{ and } z \ge 0.$$

The initial tableau is

| x | y | z | u | v | w | P | Const. |
|---|---|---|---|---|---|---|---|
| 1 | 1 | 1 | 1 | 0 | 0 | 0 | 100,000 |
| $-\frac{3}{10}$ | $\frac{7}{10}$ | $\frac{7}{10}$ | 0 | 1 | 0 | 0 | 0 |
| $-\frac{5}{10}$ | $\frac{5}{10}$ | $-\frac{5}{10}$ | 0 | 0 | 1 | 0 | 0 |
| $-\frac{1}{10}$ | $-\frac{15}{100}$ | $-\frac{2}{10}$ | 0 | 0 | 1 | 0 | 0 |

Using the following sequence of row operations,

1. $\frac{10}{7}R_2$      2. $R_1 - R_2, \; R_3 + 0.5R_2, \; R_4 + 0.2R_2$

3. $\frac{7}{10}R_1$      4. $R_2 + \frac{3}{7}R_1, \; R_3 + \frac{5}{7}R_1, \; R_4 + \frac{13}{70}R_1$

we obtain the final tableau

| x | y | z | u | v | w | P | Const. |
|---|---|---|---|---|---|---|---|
| 1 | 0 | 0 | $\frac{7}{10}$ | -1 | 0 | 0 | 70,000 |
| 0 | 1 | 1 | $\frac{3}{10}$ | 1 | 0 | 0 | 30,000 |
| 0 | 1 | 0 | $\frac{1}{2}$ | 0 | 1 | 0 | 50,000 |
| 0 | $\frac{1}{20}$ | 0 | $\frac{13}{100}$ | $\frac{1}{10}$ | 0 | 1 | 13,000 |

and conclude that Mr. Moody should invest $70,000 in blue-chip stocks, $0 in growth stocks, and $30,000 in speculative stocks to realize a maximum return of $13,000 on his investments.

15. Let x, y, and z, denote the amount invested in stocks, bonds, and money-market funds, respectively. Then the problem is

Maximize $P = 0.15x + 0.10y + 0.08z$ subject to

$$x + y + z \le 200,000$$

$$-z \le -50,000$$

$$y - x + z \le 0$$

$$x \ge 0, \ y \ge 0, \text{ and } z \ge 0.$$

The initial tableau is

| x | y | z | u | v | w | P | Const. |
|---|---|---|---|---|---|---|---|
| 1 | 1 | 1 | 1 | 0 | 0 | 0 | 200,000 |
| 0 | 0 | -1 | 0 | 1 | 0 | 0 | -50,000 |
| 1 | -1 | 1 | 0 | 0 | 1 | 0 | 0 |
| -.15 | -.10 | -.08 | 0 | 0 | 0 | 1 | 0 |

Using the following sequence of row operations,

1. $-R_2$   2. $R_1 - R_2, \ R_3 - R_2, \ R_4 + 0.08R_2$,

3. $-R_3$   4. $R_1 - R_3, \ R_4 + \frac{1}{10}R_3$

5. $\frac{1}{2}R_1$   5. $R_3 + R_1, \ R_4 + \frac{1}{4}R_1$

we obtain the final tableau

| x | y | z | u | v | w | P | Const. |
|---|---|---|---|---|---|---|---|
| 1 | 0 | 0 | $\frac{1}{2}$ | 1 | $\frac{1}{2}$ | 0 | 50,000 |
| 0 | 0 | 1 | 0 | -1 | 0 | 0 | 50,000 |
| 0 | 1 | 0 | $\frac{1}{2}$ | 0 | $-\frac{1}{2}$ | 0 | 100,000 |
| 0 | 0 | 0 | $\frac{1}{8}$ | $\frac{7}{100}$ | $\frac{1}{40}$ | 1 | 21,500 |

and we conclude that Sandra should invest \$50,000 in stocks, \$100,000 in bonds, and \$50,000 in money-market funds to realize a maximum return of \$21,500 per year on her investments.

## GROUP DISCUSSION QUESTIONS

**Page 223**

1.  a.

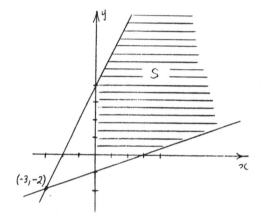

Observe that we can find points (x,y) in S with x and y that are arbitrarily large. This implies that P = x + 2y can be made as large as we please by taking x and/or y sufficiently large. So the problem has an unbounded solution

b.  (i)

| | x | y | u | v | P | Const. | Ratio | |
|---|---|---|---|---|---|---|---|---|
| p.r.→ | -2 | ① | 1 | 0 | 0 | 4 | 4 | $R_2 + 3R_1$ |
| | 1 | -3 | 0 | 1 | 0 | 3 | -- | $R_3 + 2R_1$ |
| | -1 | -2 | 0 | 0 | 1 | 0 | | |

↑
p.c.

| x | y | u | v | P | Const. |
|---|---|---|---|---|--------|
| -2 | 1 | 1 | 0 | 0 | 4 |
| -5 | 0 | 3 | 1 | 0 | 15 |
| -5 | 0 | 2 | 0 | 1 | 8 |

Interpreting the last tableau, we see that $x = 0$, $y = 4$, and $P = 8$. So, after one iteration, we are at the point $A(0,4)$.

(ii)  Referring to the last tableau, you can see that the x-column is the pivot column. Since the entries in that column are all negative, no ratios can be computed. Therefore, there is no pivot element and the Simplex Method breaks down.

(iii) Proceeding, in spite of the negative ratios, we find

| | x | y | u | v | P | Const. | Ratio |
|---|---|---|---|---|---|--------|-------|
| | -2 | 1 | 1 | 0 | 0 | 4 | -2 $\quad -\frac{1}{5}R_2$ |
| p.r.→ | (-5) | 0 | 3 | 1 | 0 | 15 | -3 |
| | -5 | 0 | 2 | 0 | 1 | 8 | |

p.c.

| x | y | u | v | P | Const. | |
|---|---|---|---|---|--------|---|
| -2 | 1 | 1 | 0 | 0 | 4 | $R_1 + 2R_2$ |
| 1 | 0 | $-\frac{3}{5}$ | $-\frac{1}{5}$ | 0 | -3 | $R_3 + 5R_2$ |
| -5 | 0 | 2 | 0 | 1 | 8 | |

| x | y | u | v | P | Const. |
|---|---|---|---|---|--------|
| 0 | 1 | $-\frac{1}{5}$ | $-\frac{2}{5}$ | 0 | -2 |
| 1 | 0 | $-\frac{3}{5}$ | $-\frac{1}{5}$ | 0 | -3 |
| 0 | 0 | -1 | -1 | 1 | -7 |

Interpreting the last tableau, we find $x = -3$ and $y = -2$. So, this iteration takes us from the feasible point $(0,4)$ to the nonfeasible point $(-3,-2)$!

**Page 226**

1.  a. The feasible set is the same as that for the Group Discussion Problem on page 196 in the text (see page 249 of this manual).

b. From the table

| Vertex | P = 4x + 6y |
|--------|-------------|
| A(0,0) | 0 |
| B(5,0) | 20 |
| C(3,4) | 36 |
| D(0,6) | 36 |

we see that there are infinitely many solutions lying on the line segment joining the vertices C and D. The optimal value of P is 36.

c. (i)

| x | y | u | v | P | Const. | Ratio |
|---|---|---|---|---|--------|-------|
| 2 | 1 | 1 | 0 | 0 | 10 | 10 |
| 2 | ③ | 0 | 1 | 0 | 18 | 6 |
| -4 | -6 | 0 | 0 | 1 | 0 | |

p.r.→ points to second row; p.c. points to y column. $\frac{1}{3}R_2 \longrightarrow$

| x | y | u | v | P | Const. |
|---|---|---|---|---|--------|
| 2 | 1 | 1 | 0 | 0 | 10 |
| $\frac{2}{3}$ | 1 | 0 | $\frac{1}{3}$ | 0 | 6 |
| -4 | -6 | 0 | 0 | 1 | 0 |

$R_1 - R_2$
$\longrightarrow$
$R_3 + 6R_2$

| x | y | u | v | P | Const. |
|---|---|---|---|---|--------|
| $\frac{4}{3}$ | 0 | 1 | $-\frac{1}{3}$ | 0 | 4 |
| $\frac{2}{3}$ | 1 | 0 | $\frac{1}{3}$ | 0 | 6 |
| 0 | 0 | 0 | 2 | 1 | 36 |

Interpreting the last tableau, which is in final form, we see that x = 0, y = 6, and P = 36. So after one iteration, we have arrived at the optimal solution occurring at D(0,6) with an optimal value of 36. This is compatible with the result obtained in part (b).

(ii)

| x | y | u | v | P | Const. | | Ratio | |
|---|---|---|---|---|---|---|---|---|
| $\left(\frac{4}{3}\right)$ | 0 | 1 | $-\frac{1}{3}$ | 0 | 4 | | 3 | $\frac{3}{4}R_1$ $\longrightarrow$ |
| $\frac{2}{3}$ | 1 | 0 | $\frac{1}{3}$ | 0 | 6 | | 9 | |
| 0 | 0 | 0 | 2 | 1 | 36 | | | |

| x | y | u | v | P | Const. | | |
|---|---|---|---|---|---|---|---|
| 1 | 0 | $\frac{3}{4}$ | $-\frac{1}{4}$ | 0 | 3 | | $R_2 - \frac{2}{3}R_1$ |
| $\frac{2}{3}$ | 1 | 0 | $\frac{1}{3}$ | 0 | 6 | | $\longrightarrow$ |
| 0 | 0 | 0 | 2 | 1 | 36 | | |

| x | y | u | v | P | Const. |
|---|---|---|---|---|---|
| 1 | 0 | $\frac{3}{4}$ | $-\frac{1}{4}$ | 0 | 3 |
| 0 | 1 | $-\frac{1}{2}$ | $\frac{1}{6}$ | 0 | 4 |
| 0 | 0 | 0 | 2 | 1 | 36 |

Interpreting the last tableau, which is in final form, we see
that x = 3, y = 4, and P = 36. This shows that an optimal
solution to the problem is also attained at the vertex C(3,4).
Thus, there are infinitely many solutions lying on the line
segment joining C and O. The optimal value of P is 36.

**Page 237**

1. a.

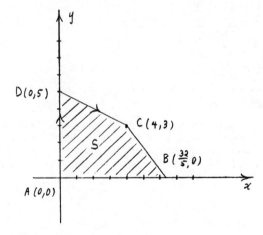

b.

| Vertex | $P = -2x - 3y$ |
|--------|----------------|
| A(0,0) | 0 |
| B($\frac{32}{5}$,0) | $-\frac{64}{5} = -12\frac{4}{5}$ |
| C(4,3) | $-17$ |
| D(0,5) | $-15$ |

we see that the minimum value of C is $-17$ occurring at the point C(4,3).

c.  See the figure for part (a).

# CHAPTER 5

## EXERCISES 5.1, page 283

1.    The interest is given by I = (500)(2)(0.08) = 80, or $870.

The accumulated amount is 500 + 80, or $580.

2.    The interest is given by I = (1000)(3)(0.05) = 150, or $150.

The accumulated amount is 1000 + 150, or $1150.

3.    The interest is given by I = (800)(0.06)(0.75) = 36, or $36.

The accumulated amount is 800 + 36, or $836.

4.    The interest is given by

$$I = (1200)\left(\frac{7}{100}\right)\left(\frac{2}{3}\right) = 56, \text{ or } \$56.$$

The accumulated amount is 1200 + 56, or $1256.

5.    We are given that A = 1160, t = 2, and r = 0.08, and we are asked to find P. Since

$$A = P(1 + rt)$$

we see that

$$P = \frac{A}{1 + rt} = \frac{1160}{1 + (0.08)(2)} = 1000,$$

or $1000.

6.    We are given that a = 3100, t = 10/12, and r = 0.05, and we are asked to find P. Since

$$A = P(1 + rt)$$

we see that

$$P = \frac{A}{1 + rt} = \frac{3100}{1 + (0.05)\left(\frac{5}{6}\right)} = 2976,$$

or $2976.

7.    We use the formula I = Prt and solve for t when I = 20, P = 1000, and r = 0.05. Thus,

$$20 = 1000(0.05)\left(\frac{t}{365}\right)$$

and
$$t = \frac{365(20)}{50} = 146,$$

or 146 days.

8.  We use the formula $I = Prt$ and solve for $t$ when $I = 25$, $P = 1500$, and $r = 0.05$. Thus,

$$25 = 1500(0.05)\left(\frac{t}{365}\right)$$

and
$$t = \frac{365(25)}{75} \approx 122,$$

or 122 days.

9.  We use the formula $A = P(1 + rt)$ with $A = 1075$, $P = 1000$, $t = 0.75$, and solve for $r$. Thus,

$$1075 = 1000(1 + 0.75r)$$

$$75 = 750r$$

or
$$r = 0.10.$$

Therefore, the interest rate is 10 percent per year.

10.  We use the formula $A = P(1 + rt)$ with $A = 1250$, $P = 1200$, $t = 2/3$, and solve for $r$. Thus

$$1250 = 1200(1 + \tfrac{2}{3}r)$$

$$50 = 800r$$

or
$$r = 0.0625.$$

Therefore, the interest rate is 6.25 percent per year.

11.  $A = 1000(1 + 0.07)^8 = 1718,19$, or \$1718.19.

12.  $A = 1000(1 + 0.085)^6 = 1631.47$, or \$1631.47.

13.  $A = 2500(1 + \frac{0.07}{2})^{20} = 4974.47$, or \$4974.47.

14.  $A = 2500(1 + \frac{0.09}{2})^{21} = 6300.60$, or \$6300.60.

15.  $A = 12000(1 + \frac{0.08}{4})^{42} = 27,566.93$, or \$27,566.93.

16.  $A = 42000(1 + \dfrac{0.0775}{4})^{32} = 77{,}613.38$, or \$77,613.38.

17.  $A = 150{,}000(1 + \dfrac{0.14}{12})^{48} = 261{,}751.04$ or \$261,751.04.

18.  $A = 180{,}000(1 + \dfrac{0.09}{12})^{75} = 315{,}247.47$, or \$315,247.47.

19.  $A = 150{,}000(1 + \dfrac{0.12}{365})^{1095} = 214{,}986.69$, or \$214,986.69.

20.  $A = 200{,}000(1 + \dfrac{0.08}{365})^{4(365)} = 275{,}518$, or \$275,518.

21.  Using the formula
$$r_{eff} = (1 + \frac{r}{m})^m - 1$$

with $r = 0.10$ and $m = 2$, we have
$$r_{eff} = (1 + \frac{0.10}{2})^2 - 1$$
$$= 0.1025, \text{ or } 10.25 \text{ percent.}$$

22.  Using the formula
$$r_{eff} = (1 + \frac{r}{m})^m - 1$$

with $r = 0.09$ and $m = 4$, we have

$$r_{eff} = (1 + \frac{0.09}{4})^4 - 1$$
$$= 0.09308, \text{ or } 9.308 \text{ percent.}$$

23.  Using the formula
$$r_{eff} = (1 + \frac{r}{m})^m - 1$$

with $r = 0.08$ and $m = 12$, we have
$$r_{eff} = (1 + \frac{0.08}{12})^{12} - 1$$
$$= 0.08300, \text{ or } 8.3 \text{ percent per year.}$$

24. The effective rate is given by

$$R = (1 + \frac{0.08}{365})^{365} - 1 = 0.08328,$$

or 8.328 percent per year.

25. The present value is given by

$$P = 40,000(1 + \frac{0.08}{2})^{-8} = 29,227.61, \text{ or } \$29,227.61.$$

26. The present value is given by

$$P = 40,000(1 + \frac{0.08}{4})^{-16} = 29,137.83, \text{ or } \$29,137.83.$$

27. The present value is given by

$$P = 40,000(1 + \frac{0.07}{12})^{-48} = 30,255.95, \text{ or } \$30,255.95.$$

28. The present value is given by

$$P = 40,000(1 + \frac{0.09}{365})^{-(365)(4)} = 27,908.29, \text{ or } \$27,908.29.$$

29. Think of $4300 as the principal and $306 as the accumulated amount at the end of 30 days. If r denotes the simple interest rate per annum, then we have P = 300, A = 306, n = 1/12, and we are required to find r. Using (8b) we have

$$306 = 300(1 + \frac{r}{12}) = 300 + r(\frac{300}{12})$$

and $\quad r = (\frac{12}{300})6 = 0.24,$

30. Equation (1b), A = P(1 + rn), may be rewritten in the form

$$A = (Pr)n + P \qquad \text{(Think of A as a function of n.)}$$

This equation is in the slope-intercept form. The slope of the equation is equal to Pr and the A-intercept is equal to P.

31. The rate that you would expect to pay is

$$A = 380(1 + 0.08)^5 = 558.34,$$

or $558.34 per day.

32. The amount that the typical family of four would expect to pay for food six years from now is

$$A = 600(1 + 0.04)^6 = 759.19,$$

or \$759.19.

33. The amount that they can expect to pay is given by

$$A = 150,000(1 + 0.05)^4 = 182,325.94,$$

or approximately \$182,326.

34. The generating capacity at the end of the decade will have to be

$$A = P(1.08)^{10} = 2.1589P,$$

or 215.89 percent of the current generating capacity.

Therefore, the utility company will have to increase its generating capacity by an amount of 115.89 percent of its current generating capacity.

35. The investment will be worth

$$A = 1.5(1 + \frac{0.095}{2})^{20} = 3.794651,$$

or approximately \$3.8 million dollars.

36. a. If the money has earned interest at the rate of 8 percent compounded annually, he will receive

$$A = (1.08)^{21}(10,000) = 50,338.34,$$

or \$50,338.34.

   b. If the money has earned interest at the rate of 8 percent compounded quarterly, he will receive

$$A = (1 + \frac{0.08}{4})^{4(21)}(10,000) = 52,773.32,$$

or \$52,773.32.

   c. If the money has earned interest at the rate of 8 percent compounded monthly, he will receive

$$A = (1 + \frac{0.08}{12})^{12(21)}(10,000) = 53,357.25,$$

or \$53,357.25.

37. Using the formula

$$P = A\left(1 + \frac{r}{m}\right)^{-mt}$$

we have

$$P = 40,000\left(1 + \frac{0.085}{4}\right)^{-20} = 26,267.49,$$

or \$26,267.49.

38. Using the formula

$$P = A\left(1 + \frac{r}{m}\right)^{-mt}$$

we see that she purchased the note for

$$P = 10,000\left(1 + \frac{0.085}{2}\right)^{-8} = 7167.89, \quad \text{or } \$7167.89.$$

39. a. They should set aside

$$P = 100,000(1 + 0.085)^{-13} = 34,626.88, \quad \text{or } \$34,626.88.$$

b. They should set aside

$$P = 100,000\left(1 + \frac{0.085}{2}\right)^{-26} = 33,886.16, \quad \text{or } \$33,886.16.$$

c. They should set aside

$$P = 100,000\left(1 + \frac{0.085}{4}\right)^{-52} = 33,506.76, \quad \text{or } \$33,506.76.$$

40. Mr. Kaplan originally invested

$$P = 22,289.22\left(1 + \frac{0.08}{4}\right)^{-20} = 15,000, \quad \text{or } \$15,000.$$

41. The present value of the \$8000 loan due in 3 years is given by

$$P = 8000\left(1 + \frac{0.10}{2}\right)^{-6} = 5969.72, \quad \text{or } \$5969.72.$$

The present value of the \$15,000 loan due in 6 years is given by

$$P = 15,000\left(1 + \frac{0.10}{2}\right)^{-12} = 8352.56.$$

Therefore, the amount the proprietors of the inn will be required to pay at the end of 5 years is given by

$$A = 14{,}322.28\left(1 + \frac{0.10}{2}\right)^{10} = 23{,}329.48,$$

or $23,329.48.

42.  a. Using the formula

$$r_{eff} = \left(1 + \frac{r}{m}\right)^m - 1$$

with $r = 0.09$ and $m = 1$, we have

$$r_{eff} = (1 + 0.09)^1 - 1 = 0.09$$

or 9 percent per year.

b. Using the formula

$$r_{eff} = \left(1 + \frac{r}{m}\right)^m - 1$$

with $r = 0.09$ and $m = 2$, we have

$$r_{eff} = \left(1 + \frac{0.09}{2}\right)^2 - 1 = 0.092025,$$

or 9.2025 percent per annum.

c. $r_{eff} = \left(1 + \frac{0.09}{4}\right)^4 - 1 = 0.093083,$

or 9.3083 percent per annum.

d. $r_{eff} = \left(1 + \frac{0.09}{12}\right)^{12} - 1 = 0.093807,$ or

9.3807 percent per annum.

43.  Using the compound interest formula with $A = 108{,}000$, $P = 80{,}000$

and $t = 6$, we have

$$128{,}000 = 100{,}000(1 + R)^6$$

$$(1 + R)^{1/6} = (1.28)^{1/6}$$

$$1 + R = 1.042,$$

$$R = 0.042,$$

or 4.2 percent.

44.  Take $A = 32{,}100$, $P = 25{,}250$, $m = 1$, and $t = 2$, so that
$n = 2$. We solve the equation

$$32,100 = 25,250(1 + i)^2$$

$$1 + i = \left(\frac{32,100}{25,250}\right)^{1/2}$$

and $\qquad i = 0.127514.$

This gives $r = i = 0.127514$ since $m = 1$. Also, since $m = 1$, the effective rate is 12.7514 percent per annum.

45. Let the <u>effective rate</u> of interest be R. Then R satisfies

$$A = P(1 + R)^t$$

or $\qquad 10,000 = 6595.37(1 + \frac{R}{2})^{\cancel{10}\ 5}$

$$1 + \frac{R}{\cancel{2}} = (1.51621516)^{1/\cancel{10}\ 5}$$

$$= \cancel{1.0425}\ 1.0868$$

and $\qquad R = \cancel{0.085},\ .0868$

or $\cancel{8.5}$ percent.
$\qquad 8.68$

46. Let the <u>effective rate</u> of interest be R. Then R satisfies

$$A = P(1 + R)^t$$

or

$$5347.09 = 5000(1 + R)^{245/365}$$

$$1 + R = (1.069418)^{365/245}$$

$$= 1.105156573$$

and $\qquad R = 0.105156573$, or approximately 10.5157 percent.

47. a. We obtain a family of straight lines with varying slope and P-intercept as P increases. For a fixed rate of interest, the accumulated amount A grows at the rate of Pr units per year starting initially with an amount of \$P.

b. We obtain a family of straight lines emanating from the point (0,P) and with varying slope as r increases. For a fixed principal, the accumulated amount A grows at the rate Pr units per year starting initially with an amount of \$P.

## USING TECHNOLOGY EXERCISES, page 287

1.  $5872.78        2.  $3,712.07        3.  $475.49

4.  $567.35         5.  8.95%/yr         6.  11.158%

7.  10.20%/yr

8.  4.447%

9.  :PROGRAM: PREVAL
    :Disp "A"
    :Input A
    :Disp "r"
    :Input r
    :Disp "t"
    :Input t
    :Disp "m"
    :Input m
    :A(1 + r/m)^(-m*t)→P
    :Disp "PRESENT VALUE IS"
    :Disp P

10. $29,743.30       11.  $94,038.74       12.  $53,303.25.

13. $62,244.96

## EXERCISES 5.2, page 295

1.  $S = 1000\left[\dfrac{(1 + 0.1)^{10} - 1}{0.1}\right] = 15{,}937.42$, or $15,937.42.

2.  $S = 1500\left[\dfrac{(1 + \frac{0.09}{2})^{16} - 1}{\frac{0.09}{2}}\right] = 34{,}079.01$, or $34,079.01.

3.  $S = 1800\left[\dfrac{(1 + \frac{0.08}{4})^{24} - 1}{\frac{0.08}{4}}\right] = 54{,}759.35$, or $54,759.35.

4.  $S = 500\left[\dfrac{(1 + \frac{0.11}{2})^{24} - 1}{\frac{0.11}{2}}\right] = 23{,}769.00$, or $23,769.00.

5. $S = 600 \left[\dfrac{(1 + \frac{0.12}{4})^{36} - 1}{\frac{0.12}{4}}\right] = 37{,}965.57$, or $37,965.57.

6. $S = 150 \left[\dfrac{(1 + \frac{0.10}{12})^{180} - 1}{\frac{0.10}{12}}\right] = 62{,}170.55$, or $62,170.55.

7. $P = 5000\left[\dfrac{1 - (1 + 0.08)^{-8}}{0.08}\right] = 28{,}733.19$, or $28,733.19.

8. $P = 1200\left[\dfrac{1 - (1 + \frac{0.10}{2})^{-12}}{\frac{0.10}{2}}\right] = 10{,}635.90$, or $10,635.90.

9. $P = 4000\left[\dfrac{1 - (1 + 0.09)^{-5}}{0.09}\right] = 15{,}558.61$, or $15,558.61.

10. $P = 3000\left[\dfrac{1 - (1 + \frac{0.11}{2})^{-12}}{\frac{0.11}{2}}\right] = 25{,}855.55$, or $25,855.55.

11. $P = 800\left[\dfrac{1 - (1 + \frac{0.12}{4})^{-28}}{\frac{0.12}{4}}\right] = 15{,}011.29$, or $15,011.29.

12. $P = 150\left[\dfrac{1 - (1 + \frac{0.08}{12})^{-120}}{\frac{0.08}{12}}\right] = 12{,}363.22$, or $12,363.22.

13. She will have

$$S = 1500\left[\dfrac{(1 + 0.08)^{25} - 1}{0.08}\right] = 109{,}658.91, \text{ or } \$109{,}658.91.$$

14. Mr. Pruitt will have

$$S = 100\left[\dfrac{(1 + \frac{0.08}{12})^{72} - 1}{\frac{0.08}{12}}\right] = 9{,}202.53, \text{ or } \$9{,}202.53.$$

15. On October 31, Mrs Lynde's account will be worth
$$S = 40\left[\frac{(1 + \frac{0.07}{12})^{11} - 1}{\frac{0.07}{12}}\right] = 453.06, \text{ or } \$453.06.$$

One month later, this account will be worth
$$A = (453.06)(1 + \frac{0.07}{12}) = 455.70, \text{ or } \$455.70.$$

16. He will have an amount given by
$$S = 5000\left[\frac{(1 + 0.085)^{25} - 1}{0.085}\right] = 393,338.96, \text{ or } \$393,338.96.$$

17. The amount in Mr. Collin's employee retirement account is given by
$$S = 100\left[\frac{(1 + \frac{0.07}{12})^{144} - 1}{0.0058333}\right] = 22,469.60, \text{ or } \$22,469.60.$$

The amount in Mr. Collin's IRA is given by
$$S = 2000\left[\frac{(1 + 0.09)^{8} - 1}{0.09}\right] = 22,056.85, \text{ or } \$22,056.85.$$

Therefore, the total amount in his retirement fund is given by

22,469.60 + 22,056.85 = 44,526.45, or \$44,526.45.

18. They will have
$$S = 150\left[\frac{(1 + \frac{0.08}{12})^{36} - 1}{\frac{0.08}{12}}\right] = 6,080.33, \text{ or } \$6080.33.$$

19. The equivalent cash payment is given by
$$P = 450\left[\frac{1 - (1 + \frac{0.09}{12})^{-24}}{\frac{0.09}{12}}\right] = 9850.12, \text{ or } \$9850.12.$$

20. We use the formula for the present value of an annuity obtaining
$$P = 210\left[\frac{1 - (1 + \frac{0.12}{12})^{-36}}{\frac{0.12}{12}}\right] = 6322.58, \text{ or } \$6322.58.$$

Since her down payment was \$2000, the cash price of the car was \$8322.58.

21. We use the formula for the present value of an annuity obtaining

$$P = 22\left[\frac{1 - (1 + \frac{0.18}{12})^{-36}}{\frac{0.18}{12}}\right] = 608.54, \text{ or } \$608.54.$$

22. We first find the present value of the 19 future payments. Thus,

$$P = 50{,}000\left[\frac{1 - (1 + 0.08)^{-19}}{0.08}\right] = 480{,}179.96, \text{ or } \$480{,}179.96.$$

Therefore, the commission should have

$$\$480{,}179.96 + \$50{,}000,$$

or \$530,179.96 in the bank initially.

23. With an \$800 monthly payment, the present value of their loan would be

$$P = 800\left[\frac{1 - (1 + \frac{0.095}{12})^{-360}}{\frac{0.095}{12}}\right] = 95{,}141.34, \text{ or } \$95{,}141.34.$$

With a \$1000 monthly payment, the present value of their loan would be

$$P = 1000\left[\frac{1 - (1 + \frac{0.095}{12})^{-360}}{\frac{0.095}{12}}\right] = 118{,}926.68, \text{ or } \$118{,}926.68.$$

Since they intend to make a \$25,000 down payment, the range of homes they should consider is \$120,141 to \$143,927.

24. With an \$800 monthly payment, the present value of their loan would be

$$P = 800\left[\frac{1 - (1 + \frac{0.10}{12})^{-360}}{\frac{0.10}{12}}\right] = 91{,}160.66, \text{ or } \$91{,}160.66$$

With a \$1000 monthly payment, the present value of their loan would be

$$P = 1000\left[\frac{1 - (1 + \frac{0.010}{12})^{-360}}{\frac{0.10}{12}}\right] = 113{,}950.82, \text{ or } \$113{,}950.82.$$

Since they intend to make a \$25,000 down payment, the range of homes they should consider is approximately \$116,161 to \$138,951.

25. The lower limit of their investment is

$$A = 800\left[\frac{1 - (1 + \frac{0.09}{12})^{-180}}{0.0075}\right] + 25{,}000 = 103{,}874.73$$

or approximately $103,875. The upper limit of their investment is

$$A = 1000\left[\frac{1 - (1 + \frac{0.09}{12})^{-180}}{0.0075}\right] + 25{,}000 = 123{,}593.41$$

or approximately $123,593. Therefore, the price range of houses they should consider is $103,875 to $123,593.

## USING TECHNOLOGY EXERCISES 5.2, page 297

1. $59,622.15        2. $55,718.57        3. $8453.59

4. $20,460.98

5. :PROGRAM: PVAN
   :Disp "R"
   :Input R
   :Disp "i"
   :Input i
   :Disp "N"
   :Input N
   :(R/i)(1-(1+i)^(-N))→P
   :Disp "AMOUNT IS"
   :Disp P

6. $35,607.23        7. $45,983.53        8. $13,828.60

9. $18,344.08

## EXERCISES 5.3, page 305

1. The size of each installment is given by

   $$R = \frac{100{,}000(0.08)}{1 - (1.08)^{-10}} = 14{,}902.95, \text{ or } \$14{,}902.95.$$

2. The size of each installment is given by

   $$R = \frac{40{,}000(0.015)}{1 - (1.015)^{-30}} = 1{,}665.57, \text{ or } \$1{,}665.57.$$

3. The size of each installment is given by

$$R = \frac{5000(0.01)}{1 - (1 + 0.01)^{-12}} = 444.24, \text{ or } \$444.24.$$

4. The size of each installment is given by

$$R = \frac{16000(0.0075)}{1 - (1 + 0.0075)^{-48}} = 398.16, \text{ or } \$398.16.$$

5. The size of each installment is given by

$$R = \frac{25000(0.0075)}{1 - (1 + 0.0075)^{-48}} = 622.13, \text{ or } \$622.13.$$

6. The size of each installment is given by

$$R = \frac{80000(0.00875)}{1 - (1 + 0.00875)^{-180}} = 884.32, \text{ or } \$884.32.$$

7. The size of each installment is

$$R = \frac{80,000(0.00875)}{1 - (1 + 0.00875)^{-360}} = 731.79, \text{ or } \$731.79.$$

8. The size of each installment is

$$R = \frac{100,000(0.00875)}{1 - (1 + 0.00875)^{-300}} = 944.18, \text{ or } \$944.18.$$

9. The periodic payment that is required is

$$R = \frac{20,000(0.02)}{(1 + 0.02)^{12} - 1} = 1491.19, \text{ or } \$1491.19.$$

10. The periodic payment that is required is

$$R = \frac{40,000(0.01)}{(1 + 0.01)^{36} - 1} = 928.57, \text{ or } \$928.57.$$

11. The periodic payment that is required is

$$R = \frac{100,000(0.0075)}{(1 + 0.0075)^{120} - 1} = 516.76, \text{ or } \$516.76$$

12. The periodic payment that is required is

$$R = \frac{120,000(0.0075)}{(1 + 0.0075)^{180} - 1} = 317.12, \text{ or } \$317.12.$$

13. The periodic payment that is required is

$$R = \frac{250,000(0.00875)}{(1.00875)^{300} - 1} = 172.95, \quad \text{or } \$172.95.$$

14. The periodic payment that is required is

$$R = \frac{350,000(0.00625)}{(1.00625)^{120} - 1} = 1967.06, \quad \text{or } \$1967.06.$$

15. The size of each installment is given by

$$R = \frac{100,000(0.10)}{1 - (1 + 0.10)^{-10}} = 16,274.53, \quad \text{or } \$16,274.53.$$

16. The monthly payment that is required is given by

$$R = \frac{30,000\left(\frac{0.12}{12}\right)}{1 - \left(1 + \frac{0.12}{12}\right)^{-120}} = 430.41, \quad \text{or } \$430.41.$$

17. The monthly payment in each case is given by

$$R = \frac{100,000\left(\frac{r}{12}\right)}{1 - \left(1 + \frac{r}{12}\right)^{-360}}.$$

Thus, if r = 0.08, then

$$R = \frac{100,000\left(\frac{0.08}{12}\right)}{1 - \left(1 + \frac{0.08}{12}\right)^{-360}} = 733.76, \quad \text{or } \$733.76$$

If r = 0.09, then

$$R = \frac{100,000\left(\frac{0.09}{12}\right)}{1 - \left(1 + \frac{0.09}{12}\right)^{-360}} = 804.62, \quad \text{or } \$804.62$$

If r = 0.10, then

$$R = \frac{100,000\left(\frac{0.10}{12}\right)}{1 - \left(1 + \frac{0.10}{12}\right)^{-360}} = 877.57, \quad \text{or } \$877.57.$$

If r = 0.11, then

$$R = \frac{100,000(\frac{0.11}{12})}{1 - (1 + \frac{0.11}{12})^{-360}} = \$952.32.$$

a. The difference in monthly payments in the two loans is

$\$877.57 - \$665.30 = \$212.27.$

b. The monthly mortgage payment on a \$150,000 mortgage would be

$1.5(\$877.57) = \$1316.36.$

The monthly mortgage payment on a \$50,000 mortgage would be

$0.5(\$877.57) = \$438.79.$

18. The monthly payment will be

$$\frac{96000(\frac{0.09}{12})}{1 - (1 + \frac{0.09}{12})^{-300}} \approx 805.63, \text{ or } \$805.63.$$

19. a. The amount of the loan required is $16000 - (0.25)(12000)$ or 13000 dollars. If the car is financed over 36 months, the payment will be

$$\frac{12000(\frac{0.1}{12})}{1 - (1 + \frac{0.1}{12})^{-36}} \approx 387.21, \text{ or } \$387.21 \text{ per month.}$$

If the car is financed over 48 months, the payment will be

$$\frac{12000(\frac{0.1}{12})}{1 - (1 + \frac{0.1}{12})^{-48}} \approx 304.35, \text{ or } \$304.35 \text{ per month.}$$

b. The interest charges for the 36-month plan are

$36(387.21) - 12000 = 1939.56,$

or \$1939.56. The interest charges for the 48-month plan are

$48(304.35) - 12000 = 2608.80, \text{ or } \$2608.80.$

20. Since the down payment is .10(\$2 million), the amount financed is \$1.8 million. The required quarterly payment is

$$R = \frac{1{,}800{,}000(\frac{0.12}{4})}{1 - (1 + \frac{0.12}{4})^{-60}} \approx 65{,}039.33, \text{ or } \$65{,}039.33.$$

21. The amount borrowed is 180,000 − 20,000 = 160,000 dollars. The size of the monthly installment is

$$R = \frac{160{,}000(\frac{0.08}{12})}{1 - (1 + \frac{0.08}{12})^{-360}} \approx 1174.0233, \text{ or } \$1174.0233.$$

To find their equity after five years, we compute

$$P = 1174.0233 \left[\frac{1 - (1 + \frac{0.08}{12})^{-300}}{\frac{0.08}{12}}\right] \approx 152{,}112$$

or $152,112, and so their equity is

$$180{,}000 - 152{,}112 = 27{,}888,$$

or $27,888.

To find their equity after ten years, we compute

$$P = 1174.0233 \left[\frac{1 - (1 + \frac{0.08}{12})^{-240}}{\frac{0.08}{12}}\right] \approx 140{,}360, \text{ or } \$140{,}360.$$

and their equity is

$$180{,}000 - 140{,}360 = 39{,}640, \text{ or } \$39{,}640.$$

To find their equity after twenty years, we compute

$$P = 1174.0233 \left[\frac{1 - (1 + \frac{0.08}{12})^{-120}}{\frac{0.08}{12}}\right] = 96{,}765, \text{ or } \$96{,}765,$$

and their equity is 180,000 − 96,765, or $83,235.

22. The amount that must be deposited annually into this fund is given by

$$R = \frac{(0.07)(2.5)}{(1 + 0.07)^{20} - 1} = 0.06098241 \text{ million},$$

or $60,982.41 annually.

23. The amount that must be deposited quarterly into this fund is

$$R = \frac{(\frac{0.09}{4})200,000}{(1 + \frac{0.09}{4})^{40} - 1} = 3,135.48$$

or $3,135.48.

24. He will receive

$$R = \frac{20,000(0.09)}{1 - (1 + 0.09)^{-5}} = 5141.85,$$

or $5141.85 each year.

25. The size of each quarterly installment is given by

$$R = \frac{(\frac{0.1}{4})20,000}{(1 + \frac{0.1}{4})^{12} - 1} = 1449.74,$$

or $1449.74.

26. The size of each monthly installment is given by

$$R = \frac{(\frac{0.085}{12})250,000}{(1 + \frac{0.085}{12})^{300} - 1} = 242.23,$$

or $242.23.

27. The value of the IRA account after 20 years is

$$S = 375 \left[\frac{(1 + \frac{0.08}{4})^{80} - 1}{0.02}\right] = 72,664.48, \text{ or } \$72,664.48.$$

The payment he would receive at the end of each quarter for the next 15 years is given by

$$R = \frac{(\frac{0.08}{4})72,664.48}{1 - (1 + \frac{0.08}{4})^{-60}} = 2090.41, \text{ or } \$2090.41.$$

If he continues working and makes quarterly payments until age 65, the monthly payment he will receive is

$$S = 375 \left[\frac{(1 + \frac{0.08}{4})^{100} - 1}{0.02}\right] = 117,087.11, \text{ or } \$117,087.11.$$

The payment he would receive at the end of each quarter for the next 10 years is given by

$$R = \frac{(\frac{0.08}{4})117{,}087.11}{1 - (1 + \frac{0.08}{4})^{-40}} = 4280.21, \text{ or } \$4280.21.$$

28. If she secures the loan from the manufacturer her monthly payment will be

$$R_1 = \frac{10{,}000(\frac{0.079}{12})}{1 - (1 + \frac{0.079}{12})^{-36}} \approx 312.902 \qquad \text{or } \$312.90$$

If she secures the loan from the bank, her monthly payment will be

$$R_2 = \frac{10{,}000(\frac{0.115}{12})}{1 - (1 + \frac{0.115}{12})^{-36}} \approx 329.7601$$

or $329.76. Therefore, her savings in interest will be

$$36(329.76 - 312.90) = 606.96, \text{ or } \$606.96.$$

29. The monthly payment the Sandersons are required to make under the terms of their original loan is given by

$$R = \frac{100{,}000(\frac{0.10}{12})}{1 - (1 + \frac{0.10}{12})^{-240}} \approx 965.02, \text{ or } \$965.02.$$

The monthly payment the Sandersons are required to make under the terms of their new loan is given by

$$R = \frac{100{,}000(\frac{0.078}{12})}{1 - (1 + \frac{0.078}{12})^{-240}} \approx 824.04, \text{ or } \$824.04.$$

The amount of money that the Sandersons can expect to save over the life of the loan by refinancing is given by

$$240(965.02 - 824.04) = 33{,}835.20, \text{ or } \$33{,}835.20.$$

30. The amount of the loan the Meyers need to secure is $90,000. Using the bank's financing, the monthly payment would be

$$R = \frac{90{,}000(\frac{0.11}{12})}{1 - (1 + \frac{0.11}{12})^{-300}} \approx 882.10, \text{ or } \$882.10.$$

Using the seller's financing, the monthly payment would be

$$R = \frac{90{,}000\left(\dfrac{0.098}{12}\right)}{1 - \left(1 + \dfrac{0.098}{12}\right)^{-300}} \approx 805.18, \text{ or } \$805.18.$$

By choosing the seller's financing rather than the bank's, the Meyers would save

(882.10 - 805.18)(300) = 23,076, or \$23,076 in interest.

### USING TECHNOLOGY, page 309

1. \$3645.40     2. \$12,682.60     3. \$18,443.75     4. \$11,062.50

5. :PROGRAM: SINKFD
   :Disp "S"
   :Input S
   :Disp "i"
   :Input i
   :Disp "N"
   :Input N
   :S*i/((1+i)^N-1)→R
   :Disp "R is"
   :Disp R

6. \$1863.99     7. \$916.26   8. \$707.96   9. \$809.31

10. \$18,288.92.   The amortization schedule is shown below.

| End of Period | Interest charged | Repayment made | Payment toward principal | Outstanding Principal |
|---|---|---|---|---|
| 0 | | | | 120,000.00 |
| 1 | 10,200.00 | 18,288.92 | 8,088.92 | 111,911.08 |
| 2 | 9,512.44 | 18,288.92 | 8,776.48 | 103,134.60 |
| 3 | 8,766.44 | 18,288.92 | 9,522.48 | 93,612.12 |
| 4 | 7,957.03 | 18,288.92 | 10,331.89 | 83,280.23 |
| 5 | 7,078.82 | 18,288.92 | 11,210.10 | 72,070.13 |
| 6 | 6,125.96 | 18,288.92 | 12,162.96 | 59,907.17 |
| 7 | 5,092.11 | 18,288.92 | 13,196.81 | 46,710.36 |
| 8 | 3,970.38 | 18,288.92 | 14,318.54 | 32,391.82 |
| 9 | 2,753.30 | 18,288.92 | 15,535.62 | 16,856.20 |
| 10 | 1,432.78 | 18,288.98 | 16,856.14 | .00 |

11. $45,069.31. The amortization schedule is shown below.

| End of Period | Interest charged | Repayment made | Payment toward principal | Outstanding Principal |
|---|---|---|---|---|
| 0 | | | | 265,000.00 |
| 1 | 19,610.00 | 45,069.31 | 25,459.31 | 239,540.69 |
| 2 | 17,726.01 | 45,069.31 | 27,343.30 | 212,197.39 |
| 3 | 15,702.61 | 45,069.31 | 29,366.70 | 182,830.69 |
| 4 | 13,529.47 | 45,069.31 | 31,539.84 | 151,290.85 |
| 5 | 11,195.52 | 45,069.31 | 33,873.79 | 117,417.06 |
| 6 | 8,688.86 | 45,069.31 | 36,380.45 | 81,036.61 |
| 7 | 5,996.71 | 45,069.31 | 39,072.60 | 41,964.01 |
| 8 | 3,105.34 | 45,069.35 | 41,964.01 | .00 |

# EXERCISES 5.4, page 316

1.  $a_9 = 6 + (9 - 1)3 = 30$

2  $a_7 = -5 + (7 - 1)3 = 13$

3.  $a_8 = -15 + (8 - 1)(\frac{3}{2}) = -\frac{9}{2} = -4.5.$

4.  $a_{98} = 1.2 + (98 - 1)(0.4) = 40.$

5.  $a_{11} - a_4 = (a_1 + 10d) - (a_1 + 3d) = 7d.$

Also, $a_{11} - a_4 = 107 - 30 = 77.$

Therefore, $7d = 77$, and $d = 11.$

Next,

$$a_4 = a + 3d = a + 3(11) = a + 33 = 30.$$

and     $a = -3.$

Therefore, the first five terms are -3, 8, 19, 30, 41.

6.  $a_{23} - a_7 = (a_1 + 22d) - (a_1 + 6d) = 16d.$

Also, $a_{23} - a_7 = -29 - (-5) = -24$.

Therefore, $16d = -24$, and $d = -1.5$.

Next,

$$a_7 = a + 6d = a + 6(-1.5) = a - 9 = -5.$$

and $\quad a = 4$.

Therefore, the first five terms are 4, 2.5, 1, -0.5, -2.

7.  Here $a = x$, $n = 7$, and $d = y$. therefore, the required term   is

$$a_7 = x + (7 - 1)y = x + 6y.$$

8.  The common difference is

$$d = 2a - (a + b) \qquad \text{(The second term minus the first term.)}$$

$$= a - b$$

The eleventh term is

$$a_{11} = a + b + (11 - 1)(a - b) = a + b + 10a - 10b = 11a - 9b.$$

9.  Using the formula for the sum of the terms of an arithmetic progression with $a = 4$, $d = 7$ and $n = 15$,   we have

$$S_n = \frac{n}{2}[2a + (n - 1)d]$$

$$= \frac{15}{2}[2(4) + (15 - 1)7] = \frac{15}{2}(106) = 795.$$

10.  The common difference is $d = -1 - 5 = -6$. The first term is $a = 5$ and $n = 20$. Therefore, the required sum is

$$S_{20} = \frac{20}{2}[2(5) + (20 - 1)(-6)] = 10(10 - 114) = -1040.$$

11.  The common difference is $d = 2$ and the first term is $a = 15$. Using the formula for the nth term

$$a_n = a + (n - 1)d,$$

we have

$$57 = 15 + (n - 1)(2) = 13 + 2n$$

$$2n = 44,$$

and         n = 22.

Using the formula for the sum of the terms of an arithmetic progression with a = 15, d = 2 and n = 22, we have

$$S_n = \frac{n}{2}[2a + (n - 1)d]$$

$$= \frac{22}{2}[2(15) + (22 - 1)2] = 11(72) = 792.$$

12.  The common difference is d = 2 and the first term is a = 22. Using the formula for the nth term

$$a_n = a + (n - 1)d,$$

we have

$$98 = 22 + (n - 1)(2) = 20 + 2n$$

$$2n = 78, \text{ and } n = 39.$$

Using the formula for the sum of the terms of an arithmetic progression with a = 22, d = 2 and n = 39, we have

$$S_n = \frac{n}{2}[2a + (n - 1)d]$$

$$= \frac{39}{2}[2(22) + (39 - 1)2] = \frac{39}{2}(120) = 2340.$$

13.  $f(1) + f(2) + f(3) + \cdots + f(20)$

$$= [3(1) - 4] + [3(2) - 4] + [3(3) - 4] + \cdots + [3(20) - 4]$$

$$= 3(1 + 2 + 3 + \cdots + 20) + 20(-4)$$

$$= 3(\frac{20}{2})[2(1) + (20 - 1)1] - 80$$

$$= 550.$$

14.  $g(1) + g(2) + g(3) + \cdots + g(50)$

$$= [12 - 4(1)] + [12 - 4(2)] + [12 - 4(3)] + \cdots + [12 - 4(50)]$$

$$= 12(50) - 4(1 + 2 + 3 + \cdots + 50)$$

$$= 600 - 4(\frac{50}{2})[2(1) + (50 - 1)(1)]$$

$$= -4500.$$

15.  $$S_n = \frac{n}{2}[2a_1 + (n - 1)d]$$

$$= \frac{n}{2}(a_1 + a_1 + (n-1)d]$$

$$= \frac{n}{2}(a_1 + a_n).$$

a.  $S_{11} = \frac{11}{2}(3 + 47) = 275.$

b.  $S_{20} = \frac{20}{2}[5 + (-33)] = -280.$

16. Put a = 150,000, d = 16,000. Then the sales in the fifth year is given by

$$a_5 = 150,000 + (5 - 1)16,000 = 214,000,$$

or \$214,000. The total sales over the first five years is

$$S_5 = \frac{5}{2}[2(150,000) + (5 - 1)16,000] = 910,000$$

or \$910,000.

17. Let n be the number of weeks till she reaches 10 miles. Then

$$a_n = 1 + (n - 1)\frac{1}{4} = 1 + \frac{1}{4}n - \frac{1}{4} = \frac{1}{4}n + \frac{3}{4} = 10.$$

Therefore, n + 3 = 40, and n = 37; that is, it will take Karen 37 weeks to meet her goal.

18. Using the formula for the sum of the terms of an arithmetic progression with a = 6, d = 2.50 and n = 100, we have

$$S_n = \frac{n}{2}[2a + (n - 1)d]$$

$$= \frac{100}{2}[2(6) + (100 - 1)2.50] = 50(259.50) = 12,975, \quad \text{or } \$12,975.$$

19. To compute the tourist's fare by taxi, take a = 1, d = 0.60, and n = 25. Then the required fare is given by

$$a_{25} = 1 + (25 - 1)0.60 = 15.4,$$

or \$15.40. Therefore, by taking the airport limousine, the tourist will save

$$15.40 - 7.50 = 7.90, \text{ or } \$7.90.$$

20. a. In the fifth year of employment, the salary offered by Company A will be

$$a_5 = 24,800 + (5 - 1)1250 = 29,800, \text{ or } \$29,800.$$

Similarly, the salary offered by Company B will be

$$a_5 = 26,400 + (5 - 1)1100 = 30,800 \text{ , or } \$30,800.$$

We conclude that Company B is offering the higher salary for the fifth year.

b. The total salary for the first five years of employment at Company A would be

$$S_5 = \frac{5}{2}[2(24,800) + (5 - 1)(1250)] = 136,500, \text{ or } \$136,500,$$

while that at Company B would be

$$S_5 = \frac{5}{2}[2(26,400) + (5 - 1)(1100)] = 143,000, \text{ or } \$143,000.$$

Therefore, Company B is offering more money for the first five years of employment.

21.  a. Using the formula for the sum of an arithmetic progression, we have

$$S_n = \frac{n}{2}[2a + (n - 1)d]$$

$$= \frac{N}{2}[2(1) + (N - 1)(1)]$$

$$= \frac{N}{2}(N + 1).$$

b. $S_{10} = \frac{10}{2}(10 + 1) = 5(11) = 55.$

$$D_3 = (C - S)\frac{N - (n - 1)}{S_N} = (6000 - 500)\frac{10 - (3 - 1)}{55} = 5500\frac{8}{55}$$

$$= 800, \text{ or } \$800.$$

22.  We first compute

$$S_5 = \frac{5(6)}{2} = 15.$$

We then compute $D_1 = 100,000 \left[\frac{5 - (1 - 1)}{15}\right] = 33,333.33.$

Thus, the amount depreciated using the sum-of-the-years digits method in the first year is $33,333.33; certainly greater than the $20,000 allowed by the straight line method.

23. This is a geometric progression with $a = 4$ and $r = 2$. Next,

$$a_7 = 4(2)^6 = 256.$$

and $\quad S_7 = \dfrac{4(1 - 2^7)}{1 - 2} = 508.$

24. This is a geometric progression with $a = 1$ and $r = -1/2$. Next,

$$a_7 = 1(-1/2)^6 = 1/64.$$

and $\quad S_7 = \dfrac{1(1 - (-1/2)^7)}{1 - (-1/2)} = 0.671875.$

25. If we compute the ratios

$$\frac{a_2}{a_1} = \frac{-3/8}{1/2} = -\frac{3}{4}.$$

and

$$\frac{a_3}{a_2} = \frac{1/4}{-3/8} = -\frac{2}{3}.$$

we see that the given sequence is not geometric since the ratios are not equal.

26. This is a geometric progression with $a = 0.004$, and $r = 10$.

$$a_7 = (0.004)(10)^6 = 4000$$

$$S_7 = \frac{0.004(1 - 10^7)}{1 - 10} = 4{,}444.444.$$

27. This is a geometric progression with $a = 243$, and $r = 1/3$.

$$a_7 = 243(1/3)^6 = 1/3.$$

$$S_7 = \frac{243(1 - (1/3)^7)}{1 - 1/3} = 364\frac{1}{3}.$$

28. This is not a geometric progression because $a_2/a_1 = -1$ and $a_3/a_2 = 3$.

29. First, we compute

$$r = \frac{a_2}{a_1} = \frac{-3}{3} = -1.$$

Next,
$$a_{20} = -3(-1)^{19} = 3$$

and so

$$S_{20} = \frac{-3[1 - (-1)^{20}]}{[1 - (-1)]} = 0.$$

30. The 23rd term is

$$a_{23} = (0.1)2^{23-1} = (0.1)2^{22} = 419430.4.$$

31. The population in five years is expected to be

$$200,000(1.08)^{6-1} = 200,000(1.08)^5$$

$$= 293,866.$$

32. Using the formula for the nth term of a geometric progression with $a = 2,500,000$, $n = 5$, and $r = 1.12$, we find that the sales in the fifth year were

$$a_5 = 2,500,000(1.12)^{5-1} = 3,933,798.40$$

or approximately $3,933,798.

Using the formula for the sum of a geometric progression, we find that the total sales for the first five years were

$$S_5 = \frac{2,500,000[1 - (1.12)^5]}{1 - 1.12} = 15,882,118.40$$

or approximately $15,882,118.

33. The salary of a union member whose salary was $22,000 six years ago is given by the 7th term of a geometric progression whose first term is 22,000 and whose common ratio is 1.11. Thus

$$a_7 = (22,000)(1.11)^6 = 41,149.12,$$

or $41,149.12.

34. a. The amount to be deposited on his 18th birthday is

$$a_9 = 10(2^8) = 2560, \text{ or } \$2560.$$

b. By his 18th birthday, they would have

$$S_9 = \frac{10(1 - 2^9)}{1 - 2} = 5110, \text{ or } \$5110.$$

35. With 8 percent raises per year, the employee would make

$$S_4 = 28,000\left[\frac{1 - (1.08)^4}{1 - 1.08}\right] = 126,171.14,$$

or $126,171.14 over the next four years.

With $1500 raises per year, the employee would make

$$S_4 = \frac{4}{2}[2(28,000) + (4 - 1)1500] = 121,000$$

or $121,000 over the next four years.

We conclude that the employee should choose the 8 percent per year raises.

36. At the end of 24 hours, the number of bacteria in the culture will be

$$a_9 = 20(2)^8 = 5120.$$

37. a. During the sixth year, she will receive

$$a_6 = 10,000(1.15)^5 = 20,113.57, \text{ or } \$20,113.57.$$

b. The total amount of the six payments will be given by

$$S_6 = \frac{10,000[1 - (1.15)^6]}{1 - (1.15)} = 87,537.38, \text{ or } \$87,537.38.$$

38. The book value of the office equipment at the end of the fourth year is given by

$$V(4) = 20,000\left(1 - \frac{2}{10}\right)^4 = 8,192, \text{ or } \$8192.$$

39. The book value of the office equipment at the end of the eighth year is given by

$$V(8) = 150,000\left(1 - \frac{2}{10}\right)^8 = 25,165.82, \text{ or } \$25,165.82.$$

40. The book value of the office equipment at the end of the seventh year is given by

$$V(7) = 80,000\left(1 - \frac{2}{10}\right)^7 = 16,777.22,$$

or $16,777.22.

41. The book value of the restaurant equipment at the end of six years is given by

$$V(6) = 150,000(0.8)^6 = 39,321.60,$$

or \$39,321.60. By the end of the sixth year, the equipment will have depreciated by

$$D(n) = 150,000 - 39,321.60 = 110,678.40, \text{ or } \$110,678.40.$$

42. Using the straight-line method the amount of depreciation allowed in the first year is \$20,000; using the sum-of-the-years-digits method the amount of depreciation allowed in the first year is \$33,333. Using the double declining-balance method, the book value of the printing machine after the first year is

$$V(1) = 100,000(1 - \frac{2}{5})^1 = 60,000$$

or \$60,000. Therefore, the amount of depreciation for the first year is

$$100,000 - 60,000,$$

or \$40,000. We conclude that the double declining-balance method results in the largest depreciation at the end of the first year of use.

# CHAPTER 5, REVIEW EXERCISES, page 320

1.  a. Here P = 5000, r = 0.1, and m = 1. Thus, i = r = 0.1 and n = 4. So

$$A = 5000(1.1)^4 = 7320.5, \text{ or } \$7320.50.$$

   b. Here m = 2 so that i = 0.1/2 = 0.05 and n = (4)(2) = 8. So

$$A = 5000(1.05)^8 = 7387.28 \text{ or } \$7387.28.$$

   c. Here m = 4, so that i = 0.1/4 = 0.025 and n = (4)(4) = 16. So

$$A = 5000(1.025)^{16} = 7,422.53, \text{ or } \$7422.53.$$

   d. Here m = 12, so that i = 0.1/12 and n = (4)(12) = 48. So

$$A = 5000(1 + \frac{0.10}{12})^{48} = 7446.77, \text{ or } \$7446.77.$$

2.  a. Here P = 12000, r = 0.065, m = 1. Thus, i = r = 0.065 and n = 8. So

$$A = 12000(1.065)^8 = 19,859.95, \text{ or } \$19,859.95.$$

   b. Here m = 2, r = 0.065, and n = (8)(2) = 16. So

$$A = 12000(1 + \frac{0.065}{2})^{16} = 20,018.07, \text{ or } \$20,018.07.$$

c. Here m = 4, r = 0.065, and n =(4)(8) = 32. So

$$A = 12000(1 + \frac{0.065}{4})^{32} = 20,100.14, \text{ or } \$20,100.14.$$

d. Here m = 12, r = 0.065, and n = (8)(12) = 96. So

$$A = 12000(1 + \frac{0.065}{12})^{96} = 20,156.03, \text{ or } \$20,156.03.$$

3.  a. The effective rate of interest is given by

$$R = (1 + \frac{r}{m})^{m} - 1 = (1 + 0.12) - 1 = 0.12, \text{ or } 12 \text{ percent.}$$

b. The effective rate of interest is given by

$$R = (1 + \frac{r}{m})^{m} - 1 = (1 + \frac{0.12}{2})^{2} - 1 = 0.1236$$

or 12.36 percent.

c. The effective rate of interest is given by

$$R = (1 + \frac{r}{m})^{m} - 1 = (1 + \frac{0.12}{4})^{4} - 1 = 0.125509$$

or 12.5509 percent.

d. The effective rate of interest is given by

$$R = (1 + \frac{r}{m})^{m} - 1 = (1 + \frac{0.12}{12})^{12} - 1 = 0.126825$$

or 12.6825 percent.

4.  a. The effective rate of interest is given by

$$R = (1 + \frac{r}{m})^{m} - 1 = (1 + 0.115) - 1 = 0.115$$

or 11.5 percent.

b. The effective rate of interest is given by

$$R = (1 + \frac{r}{m})^{m} - 1 = (1 + \frac{0.115}{2})^{2} - 1 = 0.118306$$

or 11.8306 percent.

c. The effective rate of interest is given by

$$R = (1 + \frac{r}{m})^{m} - 1 = (1 + \frac{0.115}{4})^{4} - 1 = 0.120055$$

or 12.0055 percent.

d. The effective rate of interest is given by

$$R = (1 + \frac{r}{m})^m - 1 = (1 + \frac{0.115}{12})^{12} - 1 = 0.121259$$

or 12.1259 percent.

5. The present value is given by

$$P = 41,413(1 + \frac{0.065}{4})^{-20} = 30,000.29,$$

or approximately \$30,000.

6. The present value is given by

$$P = 64,540(1 + \frac{0.08}{12})^{-72} = 39,999.95, \text{ or approximately } \$40,000.$$

7.

$$S = 150 \left[\frac{(1 + \frac{0.08}{4})^{28} - 1}{\frac{0.08}{4}}\right] = 5557.68, \text{ or } \$5557.68$$

8.

$$S = 120 \left[\frac{(1 + \frac{0.09}{12})^{120} - 1}{\frac{0.09}{12}}\right] = 23,221.71, \text{ or } \$23,221.71.$$

9. Using the formula for the present value of an annuity with $R = 250$, $n = 36$, $i = 0.09/12 = 0.0075$, we have

$$P = 250 \left[\frac{1 - (1.0075)^{-36}}{0.0075}\right] \approx 7861.70, \text{ or } \$7861.70.$$

10. Using the formula for the present value of an annuity with $R = 5000$, $n = 60$, and $i = 0.08/4$, we have

$$P = 5000 \left[\frac{1 - (1 + \frac{0.08}{4})^{-60}}{\frac{0.08}{4}}\right] = 173,804.43, \text{ or } \$173,804.43.$$

11. Using the amortization formula with $P = 22,000$, $n = 36$, and $i = 0.085/12$, we find

$$R = \frac{22,000(\frac{0.085}{12})}{1 - (1 + \frac{0.085}{12})^{-36}} \approx 694.49, \text{ or } \$694.49.$$

12. Using the amortization formula with $P = 10,000$, $n = 36$, and $i = 0.092/12$, we find

$$R = \frac{10,000(\frac{0.092}{12})}{1 - (1 + \frac{0.092}{12})^{-36}} \approx 318.93, \text{ or } \$318.93.$$

13. Using the sinking fund formula with S = 18,000, n = 48, and i = 0.06/12, we have

$$R = \frac{(\frac{0.06}{12})18,000}{(1 + \frac{0.06}{12})^{48} - 1} = 332.73, \text{ or } \$332.73.$$

14. Using the sinking fund formula with S = 15,000, n = 60, and i = 0.072/12 = 0.006, we find

$$R = \frac{(0.006)(15,000)}{(1.006)^{60} - 1} \approx 208.44, \text{ or } \$208.44.$$

15. We are asked to find r such that

$$(1 + \frac{r}{365})^{365} = (1 + \frac{0.072}{12})^{12} = 1.074424168.$$

Then

$$1 + \frac{r}{365} = (1.074424168)^{1/365}$$

$$\frac{r}{365} = (1.074424168)^{1/365} - 1$$

and

$$r = 365[1.074424168)^{1/365} - 1]$$

$$= 0.071791886, \text{ or approximately 7.179 percent.}$$

16. We are asked to find r such that

$$(1 + \frac{r}{365})^{365} = (1 + \frac{0.096}{12})^{12} = 1.100338694.$$

Then

$$1 + \frac{r}{365} = (1.100338694)^{1/365}$$

$$\frac{r}{365} = (1.100338694)^{1/365} - 1$$

and

$$r = 365[1.100338694)^{1/365} - 1]$$

$$= 0.095630547, \text{ or approximately 9.563 percent.}$$

17. Let $a_n$ denote the sales during the nth year of operation. Then

$$a_{n+1}/a_n = 1.14 = r.$$

Therefore, the sales during the fourth year of operation were

$$a_4 = a_1 r^{n-1} = 1,750,000(1.14)^{4-1} = 2,592,702,$$

or $2,592,702.

The total sales over the first four years of operation are given by

$$S_4 = \frac{a(1 - r^4)}{1 - r} = \frac{1,750,000[1 - (1.14)^4]}{1 - (1.14)} = 8,612,002.$$

or $8,612,002.

18. At the end of five years, the investment will be worth

$$A = P(1 + \frac{r}{m})^{mt} = 4.2(1 + \frac{0.054}{4})^{4(5)} = 5.491,922,$$

or $5,491,922.

19. Using the present value formula for compound interest, we have

$$P = A(1 + \frac{r}{m})^{-mt} = 19,440.31(1 + \frac{0.065}{12})^{-12(4)} = 15,000.00$$

or $15,000.

20. The future value of his investment is given by

$$A = P(1 + r_{eff})^t.$$

Therefore,

$$34,616 = 24,000(1 + r_{eff})^5$$

and

$$1 + r_{eff} = (1.4423)^{1/5}$$

$$r_{eff} = (1.4423)^{1/5} - 1 = 0.0760021$$

or approximately 7.600 percent.

21. Using the sinking fund formula with $S = 40,000$, $n = 120$, and $i = 0.08/12$, we find

$$R = \frac{(\frac{0.08}{12})40,000}{(1 + \frac{0.08}{12})^{120} - 1} = 218.64, \text{ or } \$218.64.$$

*5   Mathematics of Finance*

22. Using the formula for the future value of an annuity with R = 400, n = 120, and i = 0.08/12, we have

$$S = 400\left[\dfrac{(1 + \frac{0.08}{12})^{120} - 1}{\frac{0.08}{12}}\right] = 73{,}178.41, \text{ or } \$73{,}178.41.$$

23. Using the formula for the present value of an annuity, we see that the equivalent cash payment of Ms. Lemsky's auto lease is

$$P = 300\left[\dfrac{1 - (1 + \frac{0.05}{12})^{-48}}{\frac{0.05}{12}}\right] = 13{,}026.89, \text{ or } \$13{,}026.89.$$

24. Using the formula for the present value of an annuity, we see that the purchase price of the furniture is

$$400 + P = 400 + 75.32\left[\dfrac{1 - (1 + \frac{0.12}{12})^{-24}}{\frac{0.12}{12}}\right] = 400 + 1600.05$$

or approximately $2000.

25. a. The monthly payment is given by

$$P = \dfrac{(120{,}000)(0.0075)}{1 - (1 + 0.0075)^{-360}} = 965.55,$$

or $965.55.

b. We can find the total interest payment by computing

$$360(965.55) - 120{,}000 = 227{,}598$$

or $227,598.

c. We first compute the present value of their remaining payments. Thus,

$$P = 965.55\left[\dfrac{1 - (1 + 0.0075)^{-240}}{0.0075}\right] = 107{,}316.01.$$

or $107,316.01. Then their equity is

$$150{,}000 - 107{,}316.01,$$

or approximately $42,684.

26. a. The monthly payment is given by

$$P = \dfrac{(120{,}000)(0.0075)}{1 - (1 + 0.0075)^{-180}} = 1217.1199,$$

or $1217.12.

b. We can find the total interest payment by computing

$$180(1217.12) - 120,000 = 99,081.60,$$

or \$99,081.60.

c. We first compute the present value of their remaining payments. Thus,

$$P = 1217.12 \left[ \frac{1 - (1 + 0.0075)^{-60}}{0.0075} \right] = 58632.78.$$

or \$58,632.78. Then their equity is

$150,000 - 58,632.78$, or approximately \$91367.

27. Using the sinking fund formula with $S = 500,000$, $n = 20$, and $i = 0.10/4$, we find that the amount of each installment should be

$$R = \frac{(\frac{0.10}{4})500,000}{(1 + \frac{0.10}{4})^{20} - 1} = 19,573.56, \text{ or } \$19,573.56.$$

28. Using the sinking fund formula with $S = 120,000$, $n = 24$, and $i = 0.058/12$, we find that the amount of each installment should be

$$R = \frac{(\frac{0.058}{12})120,000}{(1 + \frac{0.058}{12})^{24} - 1} = 4727.67, \text{ or } \$4727.67.$$

29. Using the amortization formula, we find that Mr. Baker's monthly payment will be

$$R = \frac{3200(\frac{0.186}{12})}{1 - (1 + \frac{0.186}{12})^{-18}} \approx 205.09, \text{ or } \$205.09.$$

30. Using the formula for computing the effective rate of interest with $r = 0.186$ and $m = 12$, we have

$$r_{eff} = (1 + \frac{0.186}{12})^{12} - 1 = 0.2027,$$

or 20.27 percent per year.

**Page 275**

1.

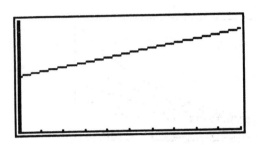

a. The A-intercept of the straight line is 1000 and it represents the principal.

b. The slope of the straight line is 1000(0.08) = 80. [Write A = 1000(1 + 0.08t) as A = 1000 + 1000(0.08)t , which is the slope-intercept form]. The slope represents the rate ($80 per year) at which the accumulated amount is increasing per year.

**Page 277**

1.   a.   $A_1(t) = 100(1 + 0.1t)$

     b.

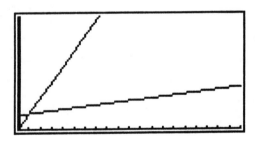

c. The growth rate of both $A_1$ and $A_2$ appear to be about the same for small values of t but $A_2(t)$ grows much faster than $A_1(t)$ when t is large.

**Page 279**

1.   a.   $A_1(t) = 10,000(1.04)^t$

         $A_2(t) = 10,000(1.06)^t$

$$A_3(t) = 10,000(1.08)^t$$

$$A_4(t) = 10,000(1.1)^t$$

$$A_5(t) = 10,000(1.12)^t$$

b.

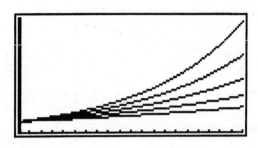

c.  $A_1(20) = 21,911.23$, $A_2(20) = 32,071.35$, $A_3(20) = 446,609.57$,

$A_4(20) = 67,275.00$ and $A_5(20) = 96,462.93$,

and  give the accumulated amounts after 20 years when $10,000 is invested at 4%, 6%, ..., 12% per year compounded annually.

# CHAPTER 6

## EXERCISES 6.1, page 332

1. {x | x is gold medalist in the 1996 Summer Olympic Games}

2. {x | x is a football team in the NFL}

3. {x| x is an integer greater than 2 and less than 8}

4. {x| x = 2n − 1;n, an integer between 1 and 20 inclusive}

5. {2,3,4,5,6}

6. {A,H,I,M,O,P,S,T,U}

7. {−2}

8. $\{\frac{-2}{1}\}$

9. a. True--the order in which the elements are listed is not important.
   b. False-- A is a set, not an element.

10. a. False--the symbol $\phi$ refers to the empty *set*. $\phi$ is not an element of any set.

    b. False. A set cannot be a proper subset of itself.

11. a. False. The empty set has no elements.

    b. False. 0 is an element and $\phi$ is a set.

12. a. False. {$\phi$} contains an element but $\phi$ has no elements.

    b. False. {a,b} is a set and not an element of another set.

13. True.

14. False. There were no 1996 Summer Olympic Games.

15.  a. True. 2 belongs to A.

b. False. For example, 5 belongs to A but 5 $\notin$ {2,4,6}.

16.  a. False. A does not contain the number 0.
b. False. It is a subset, not an element.

17.  a. and b.

18.  a. b. and c.

19.  a. $\phi$, {1}, {2}, {1,2}

b. $\phi$, {1}, {2}, {3}, {1,2}, {1,3}, {2,3}, {1,2,3}

c. $\phi$, {1}, {2}, {3}, {4}, {1,2}, {1,3}, {1,4}, {2,3}, {2,4},

{3,4}, {1,2,3}, {1,2,4}, {2,3,4}, {1,3,4}, {1,2,3,4}

20.  $\phi$, {IBM}, {U.S.Steel}, {Union Carbide}, {Boeing},{IBM,U.S.Steel},

{IBM, Union Carbide}, {IBM, Boeing}, {U.S. Steel, Union Carbide},

{U.S.Steel, Boeing}, {Union Carbide, Boeing},

{IBM, U.S. Steel, Union Carbide}, {IBM, Union Carbide, Boeing},

{IBM, U.S. Steel, Boeing},{U.S.Steel,Union Carbide, Boeing},

{IBM, U.S. Steel, Union Carbide, Boeing}.

All except the last subset listed above are proper subsets.

21.  {1,2,3,4,6,8,10}

22.  {1,2,4,a,b}

23.  {Jill, John, Jack, Susan, Sharon}

24.  {GM, Ford, Chrysler, Daimler-Benz, Volkswagen, Toyota, Datsun}.

25.  a.                                        b.

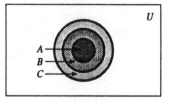        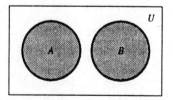

c.

26. a.

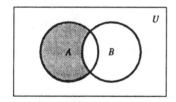

b. (i) False    (ii) True    (iii) False

27. a.                                    b.

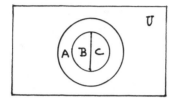    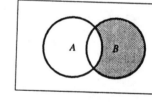

28. a.                                    b.

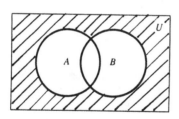    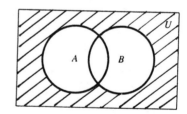

29. a.                                    b.

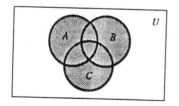    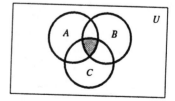

30. a.

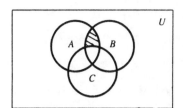

b.

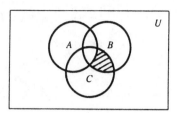

31. a.

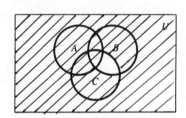

b.

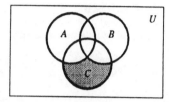

32. a.

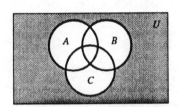

b.

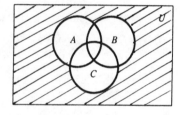

33.  a. $A^c = \{2,4,6,8,10\}$

b. $B \cup C = \{2,4,6,8,10\} \cup \{1,2,4,5,8,9\} = \{1,2,4,5,6,8,9,10\}$

c. $C \cup C^c = U = \{1,2,3,4,5,6,7,8,9,10\}$

34.  a. $C \cap C^c = \phi$

b. $(A \cap C)^c = \{1,5,9\}^c = \{2,3,4,6,7,8,10\}$

c. $A \cup (B \cap C) = \{1,3,5,7,9\} \cup \{2,4,8\} = \{1,2,3,4,5,7,8,9\}$

35.  a. $(A \cap B) \cup C = C = \{1,2,4,5,8,9\}$

b. $(A \cup B \cup C)^c = \phi$

c. $(A \cap B \cap C)^c = U = \{1,2,3,4,5,6,7,8,9,10\}$

36.  a.  $A^c = \{2,4,6,8,10\}$ and $C^c = \{3,6,7,10\}$. Therefore,

$B \cap C^c = \{6,10\}$ and so $A^c \cap (B \cap C^c) = \{6,10\}$.

b.  A $\cup$ B$^C$ = {1,3,5,7,9}, and B $\cap$ C$^C$ = {6,10}, and

(A $\cup$ B$^C$) $\cup$ (B $\cap$ C$^C$) = {1,3,5,6,7,9,10}.

c.  (A $\cup$ B) = {1,2,3,4,5,6,7,8,9,10} = U. Therefore,

(A $\cup$ B)$^C$ = $\phi$ and so (A $\cup$ B)$^C$ $\cap$ C$^C$ = $\phi$ $\cap$ C$^C$ = $\phi$.

37.  a. The sets are not disjoint. 4 is an element of both sets.

b. The sets are disjoint as they have no common elements.

38.  a. The sets are disjoint as they do not contain any common elements.

b. The sets are not disjoint as 0 is an element of both sets.

39.  a. The set of all employees at the Universal Life Insurance Company who do not drink tea.

b. The set of all employees at the Universal Life Insurance Company who do not drink coffee.

40.  a. The set of all employees at the Universal Life Insurance Company who drink tea and/or coffee.

b. The set of all employees at the Universal Life Insurance Company who drink both tea and coffee.

41.  a. The set of all employees at the Universal Life Insurance Company who drink tea but not coffee.

b. The set of all employees at the Universal Life Insurance Company who drink coffee but not tea.

42.  a. The set of all employees at the Universal Life Insurance Company who drink neither tea nor coffee.

b. The set of all employees at the Universal Life Insurance Company who drink neither tea nor coffee.

43.  a. The set of all employees at the hospital who are not doctors.

b. The set of all employees at the hospital who are not nurses.

44.  a. The set of all employees at the hospital who are nurses and/or doctors.

b. The set of all employees at the hospital who are male nurses.

45.  a. The set of all employees at the hospital who are female doctors.

b. The set of all employees at the hospital who are both doctors and administrators.

46. a. The set of all employees at the hospital who are female nurses.

b. The set of all employees at the hospital who are neither doctors nor nurses.

47. a. $D \cap F$    b. $R \cap F^C \cap L^C$

48. a. $D \cap (F \cup L)$    b. $D^C \cup L$

49. a. $B^C$    b. $A \cap B$    c. $A \cap B \cap C^C$

50. a. $A^C \cap B \cap C^C$    b. $A \cup B \cup C$    c. $A \cap B \cap C$

51. a. Region 1: $A \cap B \cap C$ is the set of tourists who used all three modes of transportation over a 1-week period in London.

b. Regions 1 and 4: $A \cap C$ is the set of tourists who have taken a underground and a bus over a 1-week period in London.

c. Regions 4, 5, 7, and 8: $B^c$ is the set of tourists who have not taken a cab over a 1-week period in London.

52. a. Region 3: $A \cap B \cap C^c$ is the set of tourist who have taken the underground and a cab but not a bus over a 1-week period in London.

b. Regions 4 and 6: $(A \cap B^c \cap C) \cup (A^c \cap B \cap C^c)$ is the set of tourists who have taken the underground and a bus but have not taken a cab or those tourists who have taken a cab but have not taken the underground or a bus.

c. Regions 5, 6, and 7:

$$(C \cap A^c \cap B^c) \cup (B \cap C^c \cap A^c) \cup (A \cap B^c \cap C^c)$$

The set of tourists who have taken a bus only, a cab only, or the underground only.

53.    $A \subset A \cup B$                $B \subset A \cup B$

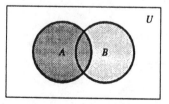        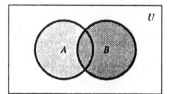

54. $A \cap B \subseteq A$          $A \cap B \subseteq B$

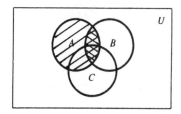 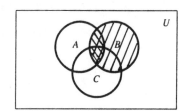

55. $A \cup (B \cup C) = (A \cup B) \cup C$

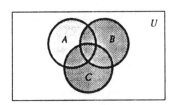   =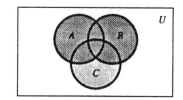

56. $A \cap (B \cap C) = (A \cap B) \cap C$

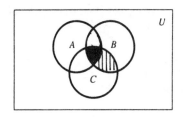 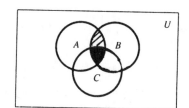

57. $A \cap (B \cup C) = (A \cap B) \cup (A \cap C)$

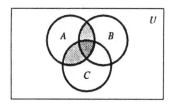   =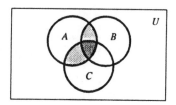

58. $(A \cup B)^c = A^c \cap B^c$

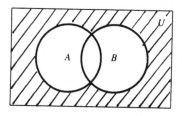

59. a. $A \cup (B \cup C) = \{1,3,5,7,9\} \cup (\{1,2,4,7,8\} \cup \{2,4,6,8\})$

$= \{1\ 3,5,7,9\} \cup \{1,2,4,6,7,8\}$

$$= \{1,2,3,4,5,6,7,8,9\}$$

$$(A \cup B) \cup C = (\{1,3,5,7,9\} \cup \{1,2,4,7,8\}) \cup \{2,4,6,8\}$$

$$= \{1,2,3,4,5,7,8,9\} \cup \{2,4,6,8\}$$

$$= \{1,2,3,4,5,6,7,8,9\}$$

b. $A \cap (B \cap C) = \{1,3,5,7,9\} \cap (\{1,2,4,7,8\} \cap \{2,4,6,8\})$

$$= \{1,3,5,7,9\} \cap (\{2,4,8\}$$

$$= \phi$$

$$(A \cap B) \cap C = (\{1,3,5,7,9\} \cap \{1,2,4,7,8\}) \cap \{2,4,6,8\}$$

$$= \{1,7\} \cap \{2,4,6,8\}$$

$$= \phi.$$

60.  a. $A \cap (B \cup C) = \{1,3,5,7,9\} \cap (\{1,2,4,7,8\} \cup \{2,4,6,8\})$

$$= \{1,3,5,7,9\} \cap \{1,2,4,6,7,8\}$$

$$= \{1,7\}.$$

$(A \cap B) \cup (A \cap C) = (\{1,3,5,7,9\} \cap \{1,2,4,7,8\})$
$$\cup (\{1,3,5,7,9\} \cap \{2,4,6,8\}$$

$$= \{1,7\} \cup \phi = \{1,7\}.$$

b. $(A \cup B)^C = (\{1,3,5,7,9\} \cup \{1,2,4,7,8\})^C$

$$= \{1,2,3,4,5,7,8,9\}^C$$

$$= \{6,10\}.$$

$A^C \cap B^C = \{1,3,5,7,9\}^C \cap \{1,2,4,7,8\}^C$

$$= \{2,4,6,8,10\} \cap \{3,5,6,9,10\}$$

$$= \{6,10\}.$$

61.  a. r, u, v, w, x, y     b. v,r

62.  a. r,u,v          b. t,x,u,z,v,y,s

63.  a. t,y,s          b. t,s,w,x,z

64.  a. v          b. t,s

65.  $A \subseteq C$

66.  If $A = B$, then $A \subseteq B$ and $B \subseteq A$. Next, if $A \subseteq B$ and $B \subseteq A$, then $A$ and $B$ contain exactly the same elements and so $A = B$.

# EXERCISES 6.2, page 339

1. A ∪ B = {a,e,g,h,i,k,l,m,o,u}, and so n(A ∪ B) = 10.

   Next, n(A) + n(B) = 5 + 5 = 10.

2. A ∪ B = {0,1,2,3,4} ∪ {-3,-2,-1} = {-3,-2,-1,0,1,2,3,4} and so

   n(A ∪ B) = 8.

   Next, n(A) + n(B) = 5 + 3 = 8.

3. a. A = {2,4,6,8} and n(A) = 4.

   b. B = {6,7,8,9,10} and n(B) = 5

   c. A ∪ B = {2,4,6,7,8,9,10} and n(A ∪ B) = 7.

   d. A ∩ B = {6,8} and n(A ∩ B) = 2.

4. Using the results of Exercise 3, we see that n(A ∪ B) = 7

   and   n(A) + n(B) - n(A ∩ B) = 4 + 5 - 2 = 7.

5. A ∪ B = {a,e,i,o,u} ∪ {b,d,e,o,u} = {a,b,d,e,i,o,u} and n(A ∪ B) = 7

   A = {a,e,i,o,u} so n(A) = 5, B = {b,d,e,o,u} and n(B) = 5, and

   (A ∩ B) = {a,e,i,o,u} ∩ {b,d,e,o,u} = {e,o,u} so that n(A ∩ B) = 3.

   Therefore, n(A ∪ B) = n(A) + n(B) - n(A ∩ B) = 5 + 5 - 3 = 7.

6. Since   n(A ∪ B) = n(A) + n(B) - n(A ∩ B)

   $$n(B) = n(A ∪ B) + n(A ∩ B) - n(A)$$

   $$= 30 + 5 - 15 = 20.$$

7. n(A ∩ B) = n(A) + n(B) - n(A ∪ B) = 10 + 8 - 15 = 3.

8. Refer to the Venn diagram at the right.

   a. n(A ∪ B) = 60 + 40 + 40 = 140.

   b. n(A$^c$) = 40 + 60 = 100.

   c. n(A ∩ B$^c$) = 60.

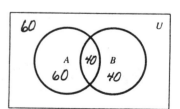

9. **Refer to the Venn diagram at the right.**

   a. $n(A^c \cap B) = 40$.

   b. $n(B^c) = 60 + 60 = 120$.

   c. $n(A^c \cap B^c) = n(A \cup B)^c = 60$.

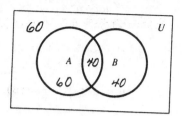

10. $n(A \cup B) = n(A) + n(B) - n(A \cap B) = 6 + 10 - 3 = 13$.

11. $n(A \cup B) = n(A) + n(B) - n(A \cap B)$, so

   $n(A) = n(A \cup B) + n(A \cap B) - n(B)$

   $\quad\quad = 14 + 3 - 6 = 11$.

12. $n(A \cup B) = n(A) + n(B) - n(A \cap B)$, so

   $n(A \cap B) = n(A) + n(B) - n(A \cup B)$

   $\quad\quad = 4 + 5 - 9 = 0$.

13. $n(A \cap B \cap C)$

   $= n(A \cup B \cup C) - n(A) - n(B) - n(C) + n(A \cap B) + n(A \cap C)$
   $\quad + n(B \cap C)$

   $= 31 - 16 - 16 - 14 + 6 + 5 + 6$

   $= 2$.

14. $n(A \cap B \cap C)$

   $= n(A \cup B \cup C) - n(A) - n(B) - n(C) + n(A \cap B) + n(A \cap C)$
   $\quad + n(B \cap C)$

   so

   $n(C) = n(A \cup B \cup C) - n(A \cap B \cap C) - n(A) - n(B) + n(A \cap B)$
   $\quad\quad + n(A \cap C) + n(B \cap C)$

   $= 25 - 2 - 12 - 12 + 5 + 5 + 4 = 13$.

15. Let $A = \{x \mid x$ is a subscriber to the Sunday L.A. Times$\}$. Then, we are given that $n(A) = 900$, $n(A \cap B) = 500$, and $n(A \cup B = 1000$. Refer to the Venn diagram on the next page.

*6 Sets and Counting*

Since $n(A \cup B) = n(A) + n(B) - n(A \cap B)$, we see that

$$n(B) = n(A \cup B) + n(A \cap B) - n(A)$$

$$= 1000 + 500 - 900 = 600.$$

Next, $(B \cap A^C) = n(B) - n(A \cap B)$

$$= 600 - 500 = 100.$$

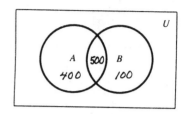

16. Let A = {x | x has FM circuitry}

    B = {x | x has AM circuitry}.

Then $n(A) = 70$, $n(B) = 90$, and $n(A \cup B) = 100$.

Refer to the Venn diagram at the right.

The number of radios with both FM and AM circuitry is given by

$$n(A \cap B) = n(A) + n(B) - n(A \cup B)$$

$$= 70 + 90 - 100 = 60.$$

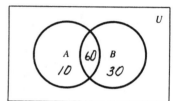

The number of radios that could receive FM transmission only is given by

$$n(A \cap B^C) = n(A) - n(A \cap B)$$

$$= 70 - 60 = 10.$$

The number of radios that could receive AM transmission only is given by

$$n(A^C \cap B) = n(B) - n(A \cap B)$$

$$= 90 - 60 = 30.$$

17. Let A denote the set of prisoners in the Wilton County Jail who were accused of a felony and B the set of prisoners in that jail who were accused of a misdemeanor. Then we are given that

    n(A ∪ B) = 190.

Refer to the diagram at the right. Then the number of prisoners who were accused of both a felony and a

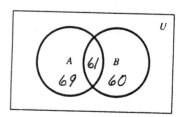

misdemeanor is given by

$$(A \cap B) = n(A) + n(B) - n(A \cup B)$$

$$= 130 + 121 - 190 = 61.$$

18. Let U denote the set of all members of the sports club who were surveyed, and let

A = {x ∈ U| x plans to attend the Summer Olympic Games}

B = {x ∈ U| x plans to attend the Winter Olympic Games}.

Then n(U) = 200, n(A) = 100, n(B) = 60, and n(A ∩ B) = 40.

Refer to the diagram at the right.

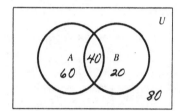

a. The number of members who plan to attend at least one of the two games is

$$n(A \cup B) = n(A) + n(B) - n(A \cap B)$$

$$= 100 + 60 - 40 = 120.$$

b. The number of members who plan to attend exactly one of the games is

$$n(A \cap B^C) + n(A^C \cap B) = 60 + 20 = 80.$$

c. The number of members who plan to attend the Summer Olympic Games only is

$$n(A \cap B^C) = 60.$$

d. The number of members who do not plan to attend either of the games is

$$U - n(A \cup B) = 200 - 120 = 80.$$

19. Let U denote the set of all customers surveyed, and let

A = {x ∈ U| x buys brand A}

B = {x ∈ U| x buys brand B}.

Then n(U) = 120, n(A) = 80,

n(B) = 68, and n(A ∩ B) = 42.

Refer to the diagram at the right.

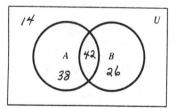

a. The number of customers who buy at least one of these brands is $n(A \cup B) = 80 + 68 - 42 = 106$.

b. The number who buy exactly one of these brands is
$$n(A \cap B^c) + n(A^c \cap B) = 38 + 26 = 64.$$

c. The number who buy only brand A is $n(A \cap B^c) = 38$.

d. The number who buy none of these brands is
$$n[(A \cup B)^c] = 120 - 106 = 14.$$

20. Let U denote the set of 50 employees at the downtown store, and let
$$A = \{x \in U \mid x \text{ takes the subway to work}\}$$
$$B = \{x \in U \mid x \text{ takes the bus to work}\}.$$

Then we are given that $n(A) = 18$, $n(B) = 12$, and $n(A \cap B) = 7$.

Refer to the diagram at the right.

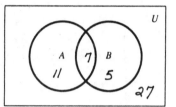

a. $n(A \cup B) = n(A) + n(B) - n(A \cap B)$
$$= 18 + 12 - 7 = 23.$$

b. $n(B \cap A^c) = 5$.

c. $n[(B \cap A^c) \cup (A \cap B^c)] = 11 + 5 = 16$.

d. $n(U) - n(A \cup B) = 50 - 23 = 27$.

21. Let U denote the set of 200 investors and let
$$A = \{x \in U \mid x \text{ uses a discount broker}\}$$
$$B = \{x \in U \mid x \text{ uses a full-service broker}\}.$$

Refer to the diagram at the right.

a. The number of investors who use at least one kind of broker is
$$n(A \cup B) = n(A) + n(B) - n(A \cap B)$$
$$= 120 + 126 - 64$$
$$= 182.$$

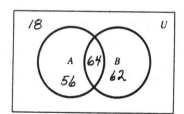

b. The number of investors who use exactly one kind of broker is

$$n(A \cap B^C) + n(A^C \cap B) = 56 + 62$$

$$= 118.$$

c. The number of investors who use only discount brokers is

$$n(A \cap B^C) = 56.$$

d. The number of investors who don't use a broker is

$$n(A \cup B)^C = n(U) - n(A \cup B)$$

$$= 200 - 182$$

$$= 18.$$

In Exercises 22 - 25, refer to the accompanying figure.

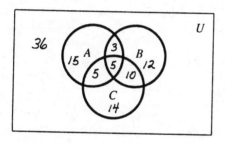

22.  a. $n(A \cup B \cup C) = 64$

b. $n(A^C \cap B \cap C) = 10$

23.  a. $n[A \cap (B \cup C)] = 13$

b. $n[A \cap (B \cup C)^C] = 15$

24.  a. $n(A^C \cap B^C \cap C^C) = n[(A \cup B \cup C)^C]$

$$= 36$$

b. $n[A^C \cap (B \cup C)] = 36$

25. a. $n[A \cup (B \cap C)] = 38$

b. $n(A^c \cap B^c \cap C^c)^c = n[(A \cup B \cup C)] = 64.$

26. Let U denote the set of 50 states and let

A = {x|x had an increase in the dropout rate during the past 2 years}

and

B = {x|x had a dropout rate of at least 30 percent during the past 2 years}.

Refer to the diagram at the right.

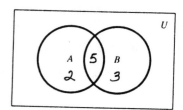

a. The number of states that had both a dropout rate of at least 30 percent and an increase in the dropout rate over the two-year period is

$n(A \cap B) = 6.$

b. The number of states that had a dropout rate that was less than 30 percent but that had increased over the two-year period is

$n(B^c \cap A) = 6.$

27. Let U denote the set of all economists surveyed, and let

A = {x ∈ U| x had lowered his estimate of the consumer inflation rate}

B = {x ∈ U| x had raised his estimate of the GNP growth rate}.

Refer to the diagram at the right. Then $n(U) = 10$, $n(A) = 7$, $n(B) = 8$, and $n(A \cap B^c) = 2$. Then the number of economists who had both lowered their estimate of the consumer inflation rate and raised their estimate of the GNP rate is given by

$n(A \cap B) = 5.$

28. Let U denote the set of states surveyed, and let

A = {x ∈ U| x is a state that had an average composite test score of at least 900}

B = {x ∈ U| x is a state that had an increase
    of at least 10 points in the average
    composite score}

Then n(U) = 22, n(A) = 10, n(B) = 15,
and (A ∩ B) = 8.

Refer to the diagram at the right.

a. n(B ∩ A^c) = 7

b. n(A ∩ B^c) = 2.

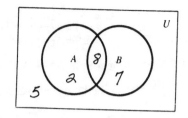

29.  Let U denote the set of 100 college students
     who were surveyed and let

A = {x ∈ U| x is a student who reads Time
    magazine}

B = {x ∈ U| x is a student who reads
    Newsweek magazine}

and

C = {x ∈ U| x is a student who reads
    U.S. News and World Report magazine}

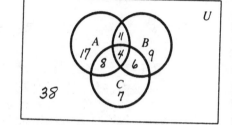

Then n(A) = 40, n(B) = 30, n(C) = 25, n(A ∩ B) = 15,
n(A ∩ C) = 12, n(B ∩ C) = 10, and n(A ∩ B ∩ C) = 4.

Refer to the diagram at the right.
a. The number of students surveyed
   who read at least one magazine is

   n(A ∪ B ∪ C) = 17 + 11 + 4 + 8 + 6 + 7 + 9

              = 62.

b. The number of students surveyed who read exactly one magazine
is

   n(A ∩ B^c ∩ C^c) + n(A^c ∩ B ∩ C^c) + n(A^c ∩ B^c ∩ C)

          = 17 + 9 + 7 = 33.

c. The number of students surveyed who read exactly two magazines
is

   n(A ∩ B ∩ C^c) + n(A^c ∩ B ∩ C) + n(A ∩ B^c ∩ C)

              = 11 + 6 + 8 = 25.

d. The number of students surveyed who did not read any of these
   magazines is

$$n(A \cup B \cup C)^C = 100 - 62 = 38.$$

30. Let A = {x | x ate breakfast}
    B = {x | x ate lunch}
    C = {x | x ate dinner}

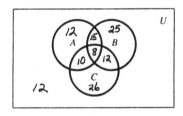

Then n(A) = 130, n(B) = 180, n(C) = 275,

$n(A \cap B) = 68$, $n(A \cap C) = 112$,

$n(B \cap C) = 90$, and $n(A \cap B \cap C) = 58$.

Refer to the diagram at the right.

a. n(A $\cup$ B $\cup$ C) = 80 + 10 + 8 + 131 + 54 + 58 + 32 = 373.

b. $n(A \cap B^c \cap C^c) + n(A^c \cap B^c \cap C) + n(A^c \cap B \cap C^c)$

   = 8 + 80 + 131 = 219.

   $n(A \cap B \cap C^c) + n(A^c \cap B \cap C) + n(A \cap B^c \cap C)$

   = 10 + 32 + 54 = 96.

c. $n(A^c \cap B^c \cap C) = 131$.

31. Let U denote the set of all customers surveyed, and let

    A = {x ∈ U| x buys brand A}

    B = {x ∈ U| x buys brand B}.

    C = {x ∈ U| x buys brand C}.

    Then n(U) = 120, $n(A \cap B \cap C^c) = 15$,

    $n(A^c \cap B \cap C^c) = 25$, $n(A^c \cap B^c \cap C) = 26$,

    $n(A \cap B \cap C^c) = 15$, $n(A \cap B^c \cap C) = 10$,

    $n(A^c \cap B \cap C) = 12$, and $n(A \cap B \cap C) = 8$.

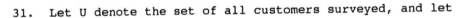

Refer to the diagram at the right.

a. The number of customers who buy at least one of these brands is

   n(A $\cup$ B $\cup$ C) = 12 + 15 + 25 + 12 + 8 + 10 + 26 = 108.

b. The number who buy labels A and B but not C is

   $n(A \cap B \cap C^c)$ = 15.

c. The number who buy brand A is

   n(A) = 12 + 10 + 15 + 8 = 45.

d. The number who buy none of these brands is

$$n[(A \cup B \cup C)^c] = 120 - 108 = 12.$$

32. Write Equation (4) as $n(D \cup E) = n(D) + n(E) - n(D \cap E)$. Then let $D = A \cup B$ and $E = C$ so that

$$n(A \cup B \cup C) = n(A \cup B) + n(C) - n[(A \cup B) \cap C]$$

$$= n(A) + n(B) - n(A \cap B) + n(C) - n[(A \cup B) \cap C]$$

$$= n(A) + n(B) - n(A \cap B) + n(C) - \{n(A \cap C) \cup (B \cap C)]\}$$

$$= n(A) + n(B) - n(A \cap B) + n(C) \\ -[n(A \cap C) + n(B \cap C) - n(A \cap C \cap B \cap C)]$$

$$= n(A) + n(B) + n(C) - n(A \cap B) - n(A \cap C) - n(B \cap C) \\ + n(A \cap B \cap C)$$

## EXERCISES 6.3, page 347

1. By the multiplication principle, the number of rates is given by

$$(4)(3) = 12.$$

2. By the multiplication principle, the number of kinds of passes is

$$(5)(3) = 15.$$

3. By the multiplication principle, the number of ways that a blackjack hand can be dealt is

$$(4)(16) = 64.$$

4. a. The number of outcomes is $2 \cdot 2 \cdot 2 \cdot 2$, or 16.

   b.

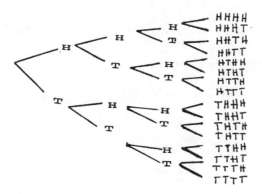

From the tree diagram, we see that the possible sequences are HHHH, HHHT, HHTH, HHTT, HTHH, HTHT, HTTH, HTTT, THHH, THHT, THTH, THTT, TTHH, TTHT, TTTH, and TTTT.

5.  By the multiplication principle, she can create

    $$(2)(4)(3) = 24$$

    different ensembles.

6.  By the multiplication principle, there are

    $$(7)(6) = 42$$

    ways that a commuter can compete a daily round trip using bus and/or train.

7.  The number of paths is $2 \cdot 4 \cdot 3$, or 24.

8.  The number of possible responses to the survey is given by

    | Number of responses to the first question | x | Number of responses to the second question | x | Number of responses to the third question |
    |---|---|---|---|---|
    | 5 | • | 5 | • | 5 |

    = 125.

9.  By the multiplication principle, we see that the number of ways a health-care plan can be selected is

    $$(10)(3)(2) = 60.$$

10. Using the multiplication principle, we see that the number of three-letter code words that can be formed is

    $$(10)(9)(8) = 720,$$

    or 720 ways.

11. The number of different responses is

    $$\underbrace{(5)\ (5)\ \cdots\ (5)}_{50\ terms} = 5^{50}.$$

12. The number of sets that have already been manufactured is

$$(26)(10)(10)(10)(10) = 260,000.$$

13. The number of selections is given by

$$(2)(5)(3), \quad \text{or } 30 \text{ selections.}$$

14. The number of selections a customer can make is

$$(3)(3)(4)(3) = 108.$$

15. The number of different selections is

$$(10)(10)(10)(10) - 10 = 10000 - 10 = 9990.$$

16. The number of ways the viewer can complete the poll is

$$(4)(4)(4)(4)(4)(4), \quad \text{or } 4096 \text{ ways.}$$

17. a. The number of possible classifications is

$$(2)(3)(6) = 36.$$

b.

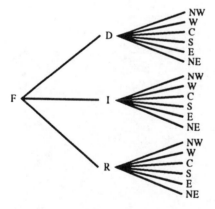

18. The number of license plate numbers that may be formed is

$$(26)(26)(26)(10)(10)(10), \quad \text{or } 17,576,000.$$

19. If every question is answered, there are $2^{10}$, or 1024, ways.
In the second case, there are 3 ways to answer each question, and so we have $3^{10}$, or 59,049, ways.

20. The number of possible identification numbers are

$$(26)(9)(10)(10)(10)(10) = 2,340,000.$$

21. The number of ways the first, second and third prizes can be awarded is

$$(15)(14)(13) = 2730.$$

22. a. If the first digit must be nonzero, then there are 9 possible choices for the first digit and 10 possible choices for the remaining 6 digits. Thus, the number of possible seven-digit numbers is given by

$$(9)(10)(10)(10)(10)(10)(10) = 9,000,000.$$

b. Using the multiplication principle, we find that the number of international direct-dialing numbers is given by

$$(9)(10)(10) \times 9,000,000 = 8,100,000,000.$$

23. The number of ways in which the nine symbols on the wheels can appear in the window slot is $(9)(9)(9)$, or 729. The number of ways in which the eight symbols other than the "lucky dollar" can appear in the window slot is $(8)(8)(8)$ or 512. Therefore, the number of ways in which the "lucky dollars" can appear in the window slot is $729 - 512$, or 217.

## EXERCISES 6.4, page 360

1. $3(5!) = 3(5)(4)(3)(2)(1) = 360.$

2. $2(7!) = 2(7)(6)(5)(4)(3)(2)(1) = 10,080.$

3. $\dfrac{5!}{2!3!} = 5(2) = 10.$

4. $\dfrac{6!}{4!2!} = 3(5) = 15.$

5. $P(5,5) = \dfrac{5!}{(5-5)!} = \dfrac{5!}{0!} = 120.$

6. $P(6,6) = \dfrac{6!}{0!} = 6! = 720.$

7. $P(5,2) = \dfrac{5!}{(5-2)!} = \dfrac{5!}{3!} = (5)(4) = 20.$

8. $P(5,3) = \dfrac{5!}{(5-3)!} = \dfrac{5!}{2!} = (5)(4)(3) = 60.$

9. $P(n,1) = \dfrac{n!}{(n-1)!} = n.$

10. $P(k,2) = \dfrac{k!}{(k-2)!} = k(k-1).$

11. $C(6,6) = \dfrac{6!}{6!0!} = 1.$

12. $C(8,8) = \dfrac{8!}{8!0!} = 1.$

13. $C(7,4) = \dfrac{7!}{4!3!} = \dfrac{7 \cdot 6 \cdot 5}{3 \cdot 2} = 35.$

14. $C(9,3) = \dfrac{9!}{6!3!} = \dfrac{9 \cdot 8 \cdot 7}{3 \cdot 2} = 84.$

15. $C(5,0) = \dfrac{5!}{5!0!} = 1.$

16. $C(6,5) = \dfrac{6!}{5!1!} = 6.$

17. $C(9,6) = \dfrac{9!}{3!6!} = \dfrac{9 \cdot 8 \cdot 7}{3 \cdot 2} = 84.$

18. $C(10,3) = \dfrac{10!}{3!7!} = \dfrac{10 \cdot 9 \cdot 8}{3 \cdot 2} = 120.$

19. $C(n,2) = \dfrac{n!}{(n-2)!2!} = \dfrac{n(n-1)}{2}.$

20. $C(7,r) = \dfrac{7!}{r!(7-r)!}$

21. $P(n,n-2) = \dfrac{n!}{(n-(n-2))!} = \dfrac{n!}{(n-n+2)!} = \dfrac{n!}{2}$

22. $C(n,n-2) = \dfrac{n!}{[n-(n-2]!(n-2)!} = \dfrac{n!}{2!(n-2)!} = \dfrac{n(n-1)}{2}.$

23. Order is important here since the word "glacier" is different from "reicalg", so this is a permutation.

24. Order is not important here since the order in which the pairs are chosen is not important; that is, it does not matter if a dance couple AB is the first pair or the last pair chosen.

25. Order is not important here. Therefore, we are dealing with a combination. If we consider a sample of three record-o-phones of which one is defective, it does not matter whether the defective record-o-phone is the first member of our sample, the second member of our sample, or the third member of our sample. The net result is a sample of three record-o-phones of which one is defective.

26. Order is important here since 327 is different from 732, so we are dealing with a permutation.

27. The order is important here. Therefore, we are dealing with a permutation. Consider, for example, 9 books on a library shelf. Each of the 9 books would have a call number, and the books would be placed in order of their call numbers; that is, a call number of 902 would come before a call number of 910.

28. The order is not important here as the selection AB would be considered the same as the selection BA. Therefore, we are dealing with a combination.

29. The order is not important here, and consequently we are dealing with a combination. It would not matter if the hand Q Q Q 5 5 were dealt or the hand 5 5 Q Q Q. In each case the hand would consist of three queens and a pair.

30. This is a permutation since the order in which the couples are seated is important. For example, an arrangement where couple A sat at the head of the table would be considered different from an arrangement where couple B sat at the head of the table.

31. The number of 4-letter permutations is

$$P(4,4) = \frac{4!}{0!} = 4 \cdot 3 \cdot 2 \cdot 1 = 24.$$

32. The number of 3-letter permutations is

$$P(5,3) = \frac{5!}{2!} = 5 \cdot 4 \cdot 3 = 60.$$

33. The number of seating arrangements is

$$P(4,4) = \frac{4!}{0!} = 24.$$

34. The number of different ways they can line up is

$$P(5,5) = \frac{5!}{0!} = 120.$$

35. The number of different batting orders is

$$P(9,9) = \frac{9!}{0!} = 362,880.$$

36. The number of different voting lists is

$$P(6,6) = \frac{6!}{0!} = 720.$$

37. The number of different ways the 3 candidates can be selected is

$$C(12,3) = \frac{12!}{9!3!} = \frac{12 \cdot 11 \cdot 10}{3 \cdot 2 \cdot 1} = 220.$$

38. The number of different ways the investor can select the four mutual funds is

$$C(8,4) = \frac{8!}{4!4!} = \frac{8 \cdot 7 \cdot 6 \cdot 5}{4 \cdot 3 \cdot 2 \cdot 1} = 70.$$

39. There are 10 letters in the word ANTARCTICA, 3As, 1N, 2Ts, 1R, 2Cs, and 1I. Therefore, we use the formula for the permutation of n objects, not all distinct:

$$\frac{n!}{n_1!n_2! \cdots n_r!} = \frac{10!}{3!2!2!} = 151,200.$$

40. There are 11 letters in the word PHILIPPINES, 3Ps, 1H, 3Is, 1Ls, 1N, 1E, and 1S. Therefore, we use the formula for the permutation of n objects, not all distinct:

$$\frac{n!}{n_1!n_2! \cdots n_r!} = \frac{11!}{3!3!} = 1,108,800.$$

41. The number of ways the 3 sites can be selected is

$$C(12,3) = \frac{12!}{9!3!} = \frac{12 \cdot 11 \cdot 10}{3 \cdot 2 \cdot 1} = 220.$$

42. The number of ways the student can select the two books is

$$C(10,2) = \frac{10!}{8!2!} = \frac{10 \cdot 9}{2 \cdot 1} = 45.$$

43. The number of ways in which the sample of 3 transistors can be selected is

$$C(100,3) = \frac{100!}{97!3!} = \frac{100 \cdot 99 \cdot 98}{3 \cdot 2 \cdot 1} = 161,700.$$

44. The five courses can be assigned to the members of the group in

$$P(5,5) = \frac{5!}{0!} = 5!,$$

or 120 ways.

45. In this case order is important, as it makes a difference whether a commercial is shown first, last, or in between. The number of ways that the director can schedule the commercials is given by

$$P(6,6) = 6! = 720.$$

46. The number of ways they can line up to purchase their ticket is

$$P(7,7) = 7! = 5040.$$

47. The inquiries can be directed in

$$P(12,6) = \frac{12!}{6!} = 12 \cdot 11 \cdot 10 \cdot 9 \cdot 8 \cdot 7,$$

or 665,280 ways.

48. The driver can be selected in $C(4,1) = 4$ ways. Next, the 5 remaining passengers can then be arranged in $P(5,5) = 120$ ways. Then by the multiplication principle, the number of possible seating arrangements is given by

$$C(4,1) \cdot P(5,5) = 4 \times 120 = 480.$$

49. a. The ten books can be arranged in

$$P(10,10) = 10! = 3,628,800 \text{ ways.}$$

b. If books on the same subject are placed together, then they can be arranged on the shelf

$$P(3,3) \bullet P(4,4) \bullet P(3,3) \bullet P(3,3) = 5184 \text{ ways.}$$

Here we have computed the number of ways the mathematics books can be arranged times the number of ways the social science books can be arranged times the number of ways the biology books can be arranged times the number of ways the 3 sets of books can be arranged.

50. a. The number of ways is

$$P(8,8) = \frac{8!}{0!} = 8!, \text{ or } 40,320 \text{ ways.}$$

b. The four married couples can be seated in

$$P(4,4) \bullet 2^4 = \frac{4!}{0!}(16), \text{ or } 384, \text{ ways.}$$

c. The number of ways is

$$P(4,4) \bullet P(4,4) \bullet 2, \text{ or } 1152 \text{ ways.}$$

a. The number of ways that the 20 featured items can be arranged is given by

$$P(20,20) = 20! = 2.43 \times 10^{18}.$$

b. If items from the same department must appear in the same row, then the number of ways they can be arranged on the page is

Number of ways of    x    Number of ways of arranging
arranging the rows          the items in each of the 5 rows

$$P(5,5) \qquad x \qquad P(4,4) \cdot P(4,4) \cdot P(4,4) \cdot P(4,4) \cdot P(4,4)$$

$$= 5! \times (4!)^5 = 955,514,880.$$

52. Using the formula for the permutation of n objects, not all distinct, with n = 12, and $n_1 = n_2 = n_3 = n_4 = 3$, we see that the number of ways the inquiries can be directed to the agents is

$$\frac{12!}{3!3!3!3!}, \quad \text{or } 369,600.$$

53. The number of ways is given by

$$2 \{C(2,2) + [C(3,2) - C(2,2)]\} = 2[1 + (3 - 1)] = 2 \cdot 3 = 6$$

(number of players)[number of ways to win in exactly 2 sets - number of ways to win in exactly 3 sets]

54. The number of ways is given by

$$2\{C(3,3) + [C(4,3) - C(3,3)] + [C(5,3) - C(4,3)]\} = 20$$

(number of players)[(number of ways to win in exactly 3 sets)+(number of ways to win in exactly 4

sets)+(number of ways to win in exactly 5 sets)]

55. The number of ways the measure can be passed is

$$C(3,3) \cdot [C(8,6) + C(8,7) + C(8,8)] = 37.$$

Here three of the three permanent members must vote for passage of the bill and this can be done in C(3,3) = 1 way. Of the 8 nonpermanent members who are voting 6 can vote for passage of the bill, or 7 can vote for passage, or 8 can vote for passage. Therefore, there are

$$C(8,6) + C(8,7) + C(8,8) = 37 \text{ ways}$$

that the nonpermanent members can vote to ensure passage of the measure. This gives 1 • 37 = 37 ways that the members can vote so that the nonpermanent members can vote to ensure passage of the measure. This gives 1 • 37 = 37 ways that the members can vote so that the bill is passed.

56. The number of ways of selecting a panel of 12 jurors and 2 alternate jurors is given by

$$C(30,12) \cdot C(18,2) = \frac{30!}{12!16!2!} = 1.32 \times 10^{10}.$$

57. a. If no preference is given to any student, then the number of ways of awarding the 3 teaching assistantships is

$$C(12,3) = \frac{12!}{3!9!} = 220.$$

b. If it is stipulated that one particular student receive one of the assistantships, then the remaining two assistantships must be awarded to two of the remaining 11 students. Thus, the number of ways is

$$C(11,2) = \frac{11!}{2!9!} = 55.$$

c. If at least one woman is to be awarded one of the assistantships, and the group of students consists of seven men and five women, then the number of ways the assistantships can be awarded is given by

$$C(5,1) \cdot C(7,2) + C(5,2) \cdot C(7,1) + C(5,3)$$

$$= \frac{5!}{4!1!} \cdot \frac{7!}{5!2!} + \frac{5!}{3!2!} \cdot \frac{7!}{6!1!} + \frac{5!}{3!2!}$$

$$= 105 + 70 + 10$$

$$= 185.$$

58. a. The number of ways that the 10 questions can be selected from the 15 questions is

$$C(15,10) = \frac{15!}{10!5!} = 3003.$$

b. The number of ways the 10 questions can be selected if exactly 2 of the first 3 questions must be answered is

$$C(3,2) \cdot C(12,8) = \frac{3!}{1!2!} \frac{12!}{4!8!} = 1485.$$

59. The number of ways of awarding the 7 contracts to 3 different firms is given by

$$P(7,3) = \frac{7!}{4!} = 210.$$

The number of ways of awarding the 3 contracts to 2 different firms is

$$C(7,2) \cdot P(3,2) = 126.$$   (First pick the two firms, and then award the 3 contracts.)

Therefore, the number of ways the contracts can be awarded if no firm is to receive more than 2 contracts is given by

$$210 + 126 = 336.$$

60.  a. The number of ways the subcommittee can be chosen is

$$C(9,4) = \frac{9!}{5!4!} = 126.$$

b. The number of ways the subcommittee can be chosen if it must include 2 Republicans and 2 Democrats is

$$C(5,2) \cdot C(4,2) = \frac{5!}{3!2!} \cdot \frac{4!}{2!2!} = 60.$$

61.  The number of different curricula that are available for the student's consideration is given by

$$C(5,1) \cdot C(3,1) \cdot C(6,2) \cdot C(4,1) + C(5,1) \cdot C(3,1) \cdot C(6,2) \cdot C(3,1)$$

$$= \frac{5!}{4!1!} \cdot \frac{3!}{2!1!} \cdot \frac{6!}{4!2!} \cdot \frac{4!}{3!1!} + \frac{5!}{4!1!} \cdot \frac{3!}{2!1!} \cdot \frac{6!}{4!2!} \cdot \frac{3!}{2!1!}$$

$$= (5)(3)(15)(4) + (5)(3)(15)(3) = 900 + 675 = 1575.$$

62.  a. The number of ways of choosing the 5 executive trainees is

$$C(20,5) = \frac{20!}{15!5!} = 15,504.$$

b. The number of ways of choosing 2 male and 3 female trainees is

$$C(10,2) \cdot C(10,3) = \frac{10!}{8!2!} \cdot \frac{10!}{7!3!} = 5400.$$

63.  The number of ways is given by

$$P(10,2) + P(10,1) + P(10,0) = 45 + 10 + 1 = 56$$

or

$$C(10,8) + C(10,9) + C(10,10) = 56.$$

64. a. The number of different sets is

$$C(32,4) = \frac{32!}{28!4!} = 35,960.$$

b. The number of sets that can be selected that do not contain any defective tires is

$$C(30,4) = \frac{30!}{26!4!} = 27,405.$$

65. The number of ways of dealing a straight flush (5 cards in sequence in the same suit) is given by

| the number of ways of selecting 5 cards in sequence in the same suit | • | the number of ways of selecting a suit |
|---|---|---|
| 10 | • | $C(4,1) = $  40. |

66. The number of ways of dealing a straight (but not a straight flush) is

| the number of ways a card of each suit can be selected | • | the number of ways of selecting 5 cards in sequence | — | the number of ways of selecting a straight flush |
|---|---|---|---|---|
| $[C(4,1)C(4,1)C(4,1)C(4,1)C(4,1)](10)$ | | | − | 40 |

$$= 4^5(10) - 40 = 10,200$$

67. The number of ways of dealing a flush (5 cards in one suit that are not all in sequence) is given by

| the number of ways of selecting 5 cards in one suit | — | the number of ways of selecting 5 cards in one suit in sequence |
|---|---|---|
| $4C(13,5)$ | − | $4(10)$ |

$$= 5148 - 40 = 5108.$$

68. The number of ways of dealing 4 of a kind is

| the number of different cards in one suit | • | the number of ways of selecting four cards from four cards | • | the number of ways of picking the remaining card |
|---|---|---|---|---|
| 13 | • | $C(4,4)$ | • | $C(48,1)$ |

$$= 624.$$

69. The number of ways of dealing a full house (3 of a kind and a pair) is given by

| the number of ways of picking 3 of a kind from a given rank | • | the number of ways of picking a pair from the 12 remaining ranks |
|---|---|---|
| $13C(4,3)$ | • | $12C(4,2)$ |

$$= 13(4) \cdot (12)(6) = 3744.$$

70. The number of ways of dealing 2 pairs is

| the number of ways of picking 2 of a kind from a given rank | the number of ways of picking the first pair | the number of ways of picking the second pair | the number of ways the remaining card |
|---|---|---|---|

$$C(13,2) \bullet \qquad C(4,2) \quad \bullet \quad C(4,2) \qquad \bullet \quad C(44,1)$$

$$= 123,552.$$

71. The bus will travel a total of 6 blocks. Each route must include 2 blocks running north and south and 4 blocks running east and west. To compute the total number of possible routes, it suffices to compute the number of ways the 2 blocks running north and south can be selected from the six blocks. Thus,

$$C(6,2) = \frac{6!}{2!4!} = 15.$$

72. The number of ways the series can be completed is

$$C(4,0) \bullet 2 + C(4,1) \bullet 2 + C(5,2) \bullet 2 + C(6,3) \bullet 2 = 70.$$

In each case we are computing the number of ways a team can lose-- 0, 1, 2, and 3 games to win the series.

73. The number of ways that the quorum can be formed is given by

$$C(12,6) + C(12,7) + C(12,8) + C(12,9) + C(12,10) + C(12,11) + C(12,12)$$

$$= \frac{12!}{6!6!} + \frac{12!}{7!5!} + \frac{12!}{8!4!} + \frac{12!}{9!3!} + \frac{12!}{10!2!} + \frac{12!}{11!1!} + \frac{12!}{12!0!}$$

$$= 924 + 792 + 495 + 220 + 66 + 12 + 1 = 2510.$$

74. In the case of the circular permutation of 5 objects A, B, C, D, and E, observe that the permutations ABCDE, BCDEA, CDEAB, DEABC, and EABCD are not distinguishable. Therefore, if there are N different arrangements of the five objects on a circle, there are 5N permutations of these objects on the line. But there are n! ways of permuting 5 objects on the line. So 5N = 5!, or N! = 4!.

Generalizing this result, we see that there are n (beginning with any of the n objects) permutations on a circle that are not distinguishable.
Therefore, if there are N different arrangements of the n objects on a circle, there are Nn permutations of these objects on the line. So,

$$Nn = n! \text{ , or } N = n!/n = (n - 1)!.$$

75. Using the formula given in Exercise 74, we see that the number of ways of seating the 5 commentators at a round table is

$$(5 - 1)! = 4! = 24.$$

76. The number of ways of seating the guests is

$$\frac{4!4!}{2!2!} = 144.$$

77. The number of possible corner points is

$$C(8,3) = \frac{8!}{5!3!} = 56.$$

78. The number of possible corner points is

$$C(15,5) = \frac{15!}{10!5!} = 3003.$$

## USING TECHNOLOGY EXERCISES, page 365

1.  $1.307674368 \times 10^{12}$

2.  $2.43290200818 \times 10^{18}$

3.  $2.56094948229 \times 10^{16}$

4.  $4.14303931642 \times 10^{16}$

5.  $674,274,182,400$

6.  $29,654,109,720$

7.  $133,784,560$

8.  $1,562,275$

9.  $4,656,960$

10.  $10,939,622,400$

11. Using the multiplication principle, the number of 10-question exams she can set is given by

$$C(25,3) \cdot C(40,5) \cdot C(30,2) = 658,337,004,000$$

12. The number of inquiries that can be handled is

$$\frac{100!}{20!20!20!20!20!}$$

or, $1.09491541553 \times 10^{66}$ , ways.

## CHAPTER 6, REVIEW EXERCISES, page 367

1.  {3}. The set consists of all solutions to the equation
   $3x - 2 = 7$.

2.   {A,E,H,L,S,T}

3.   {4,6,8,10}

4.   {-4}. The set consists of all solutions to the equation
     (x − 3)(x + 4) = 0 which are negative in value.

5.   Yes.

6.   Yes.

7.   Yes.

8.   No.

9.

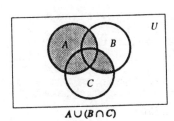

$A \cup (B \cap C)$

10.

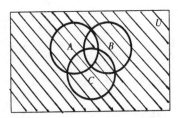

11.

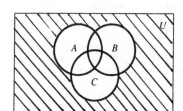

$A^c \cap B^c \cap C^c$

12.

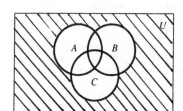

13.   A ∪ (B ∪ C) = {a,b} ∪ [{b,c,d} ∪ {a,d,e}] = {a,b} ∪ {a,b,c,d,e}

            = {a,b,c,d,e}.

     (A ∪ B) ∪ C = [{a,b} ∪ {b,c,d}] ∪ {a,d,e} = {a,b,c,d} ∪ {a,d,e}

            = {a,b,c,d,e}.

14.   A ∩ (B ∩ C) = {a,b} ∩ [{b,c,d} ∩ {a,d,e}] = {a,b} ∩ {d}

                = φ.

     (A ∩ B) ∩ C = [{a,b} ∩ {b,c,d}] ∩ {a,d,e} = {b} ∩ {a,d,e}

                = φ.

15. A ∩ (B ∪ C) = {a,b} ∩ [{b,c,d} ∪ {a,d,e}] = {a,b} ∩ {a,b,c,d,e}

    = {a,b}.

    (A ∩ B) ∪ (A ∩ C) = [{a,b} ∩ {b,c,d}] ∪ [{a,b} ∩ {a,d,e}]

    = {b} ∪ {a} = {a,b}.

16. A ∪ (B ∩ C) = {a,b} ∪ [{b,c,d} ∩ {a,d,e}]

    = {a,b} ∪ {d} = {a,b,d}.

    (A ∪ B) ∩ (A ∪ C) = [{a,b} ∪ {b,c,d}] ∩ [{a,b} ∪ {a,d,e}]

    = {a,b,c,d} ∩ {a,b,d,e}

    = {a,b,d}.

17. The set of all participants in a consumer behavior survey who both avoided buying a product because it is not recyclable and boycotted a company's products because of its record on the environment.

18. The set of all participants in a consumer behavior survey who avoided buying a product because it is not recyclable and/or voluntarily recycled their garbage.

19. The set of all participants in a consumer behavior survey who both did not use cloth diapers rather than disposable diapers and voluntarily recycled their garbage.

20. The set of all participants in a consumer behavior survey who do not boycott a company's products because of their record on the environment and/or who do not voluntarily recycle their garbage.

In Exercises 21-26, refer to the following Venn diagram.

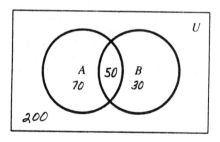

21. n(A ∪ B) = n(A) + n(B) − n(A ∩ B) = 120 + 80 − 50 = 150.

22. n(A^c) = n(U) − n(A) = 350 − 120 = 230.

23.  $n(B^c) = n(U) - n(B) = 350 - 80 = 270.$

24.  $n(A^c \cap B) = n(B) - n(A \cap B) = 80 - 50 = 30.$

25.  $n(A \cap B^c) = n(A) - n(A \cap B) = 120 - 50 = 70.$

26.  $n(A^c \cap B^c) = n(U) - n(A \cup B) = 350 - 150 = 200.$

27.  $C(20,18) = \dfrac{20!}{18!2!} = 190$

28.  $P(9,7) = \dfrac{9!}{2!} = 181,440$

29.  $C(5,3) \cdot P(4,2) = \dfrac{5!}{3!2!} \cdot \dfrac{4!}{2!} = 10 \cdot 12 = 120$

30.  $4 \cdot P(5,3) \cdot C(7,4) = 4 \dfrac{5!}{2!} \cdot \dfrac{7!}{3!4!} = 4 \cdot 60 \cdot 35 = 8400.$

31.  Let U denote the set of 5 major cards, and let

   $A = \{x \in U \mid x \text{ offered cash advances}\}$

   $B = \{x \in U \mid x \text{ offered extended payments for all goods and services purchased}\}$

   $C = \{x \in U \mid x \text{ required an annual fee that was less than \$35}\}$

   Thus,  $n(A) = 3$, $n(B) = 3$, $n(C) = 2$

   $n(A \cap B) = 2$, $n(B \cap C) = 1$

   and    $n(A \cap B \cap C) = 0.$

   Using the Venn diagram that accompanies this exercise, we have

   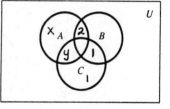

   $x + y + 2 = 3$

   $y + 2 = 2$

   Solving the system, we find $x = 1$, and $y = 0$. Therefore, the number of cards that offer cash advances and have an annual fee which is less than \$35 is given by

   $n(A \cap C) = y = 0.$

32. Refer to the Venn diagram shown at the right.

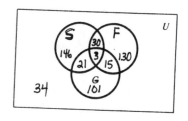

a. The number of graduates who had at least one year of at least one of the three languages is given by

$$S \cup F \cup G = 146 + 30 + 130 + 21 \\ + 3 + 15 + 101 \\ = 446$$

b. The number of graduates who had at least one year of exactly one of the three languages is

$$(S \cap F^C \cap G^C) \cup (S^C \cap F \cap G^C) \cup (S^C \cap F^C \cap G)$$

$$= 146 + 130 + 101 = 377.$$

c. The number of graduates who had less than a year of any of the three languages is

$$(S \cap F \cap G)^C = 477.$$

33. The number of ways the compact discs can be arranged on a shelf is

$$P(6,6) = 6! = 720.$$

34. The three pictures can be selected in

$$C(6,3) = \frac{6!}{3!3!} = 20.$$

35. The number of possible outcomes is

$$(6)(4)(5)(6) = 720.$$

36. a. If repetition of digits is not allowed, the number of three-digit numbers is

$$P(5,3) = \frac{5!}{2!} = 60.$$

b. If repetition of digits is allowed, the number of three-digit numbers is

$$(5)(5)(5) = 125.$$

37. a. Since there is repetition of the letters C, I, and N, we use the formula for the permutation of n objects, not all distinct, with $n = 10$, $n_1 = 2$, $n_2 = 3$, and $n_3 = 3$. Then the number of

permutations that can be formed is given by

$$\frac{10!}{2!3!3!} = 50,400.$$

b. Here, again, we use the formula for the permutation of n objects, not all distinct, this time with $n = 8$, $n_1 = 2$, $n_2 = 2$, and $n_3 = 2$. Then the number of permutations is given by

$$\frac{8!}{2! \ 2! \ 2!} = 5040.$$

38.  a. The number of hands that can be dealt is given by

$$C(13,5) = \frac{13!}{5!8!} = \frac{13 \cdot 12 \cdot 11 \cdot 10 \cdot 9}{5 \cdot 4 \cdot 3 \cdot 2},$$

or 1287.

b. The number of ways of picking 3 kings from 4 is $C(4,3)$. There are $C(4,2)$ ways of picking a pair and there are 12 such possibilities. By the multiplication principle, there are

$$C(4,3) \cdot C(4,2) \cdot 12 = \frac{4!}{3!1!} \cdot \frac{4!}{2!2!} \cdot 12 = 288 \text{ ways.}$$

39.  a. The number of ways the 7 students can be assigned to seats is

$$P(7,7) = 7! = 5040.$$

b. The number of ways 2 specified students can be seated next to each other is

$$2(6) = 12.$$

(Think of seven numbered seats. Then the students can be seated in seats 1–2, or 2–3, or 3–4, or 4–5, or 5–6, or 6–7. Since there are 6 such possibilities and the pair of students can be seated in 2 ways, we conclude that there are 2(6) possible arrangements.)

Then the remaining 5 students can be seated in $P(5,5) = 5!$ ways. Therefore, the number of ways the 7 students can be seated if two specified students sit next to each other is

$$2(6)5! = 1440.$$

Finally, the number of ways the students can be seated if the two students do not sit next to each other is

$$P(7,7) - 2(6)5! = 5040 - 1440 = 3600.$$

40.  The math team can be selected in

$$C(8,4) \cdot C(6,2) = \frac{8!}{4!4!} \cdot \frac{6!}{4!2!} = 1050 \text{ ways.}$$

41.    a. The number of samples that can be selected is

$$C(15,4) = \frac{15!}{4!11!} = 1365.$$

b. There are

$$C(10,4) = \frac{10!}{4!6!} = 210$$

ways of selecting 4 balls none of which are white. Therefore, there are

$$1365 - 210,$$

or 1155 ways of selecting 4 balls of which at least one is white.

42.    a. The number of different ways the sample can be selected is given by

$$C(60,4) = \frac{60!}{56!\ 4!} = 487,365.$$

b. The number of samples that contain 3 defective transistors is given by

$$C(5,3) \cdot C(55,1) = \frac{5!}{3!2!} \cdot \frac{55!}{54!1!} = 10(55) = 550.$$

c. The number of samples that do not contain any defective transistors is given by

$$C(55,4) = \frac{55!}{51!4!} = 341,055.$$

 **GROUP DISCUSSION QUESTIONS**

**Page 324**

1.    a. A is not a set because the condition "approximately 75°F" is too vague to make the collection well-defined.

b. B is a set because the rule for admission to the set is precise.

**Page 329**

1.    a.  No. Let A = {1,2,3}, B = {3,4,5}, and C = {2,5}.

b.  Yes. If A ∩ B ∩ C = $\phi$, then there is at least one element that is in A, B, and C simultaneously. Such an element must therefore be in A and B, in A and C, and in B and C, simultaneously, giving A ∩ B ≠ $\phi$, A ∩ C ≠ $\phi$ and B ∩ C ≠ $\phi$, simultaneously.

**Page 337**

1.  Refer to the diagram below.

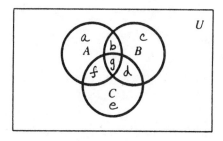

The left-hand side of (5) is

$$n(A \cup B \cup C) = a + b + c + d + e + f + g$$

The right-hand side of (5) is

$$n(A) + n(B) + n(C) - n(A \cap B) - n(A \cap C) - n(B \cap C) + n(A \cap B \cap C)$$

$$= (a + b + f + g) + (b + c + d + g) + (d + e + f + g)$$

$$- (b + g) - (f + g) - (d + g) + g$$

$$= a + b + c + d + e + f + g$$

and it is equal to the left-hand side of (5). The proof is complete.

**Page 344**

1.  a.

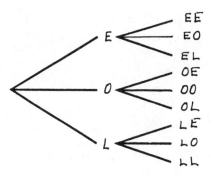

There are 9 outcomes.

b.  The number of outcomes is 3•3•3. or 29 outcomes.

# CHAPTER 7

## EXERCISES 7.1, page 379

1.  $E \cup F = \{a,b,d,f\}$; $E \cap F = \{a\}$

2.  $F \cup G = \{a,b,c,d,e,f\}$; $F \cap G = \phi$

3.  $F^c = \{b,c,e\}$; $E \cap G^c = \{a,b\} \cap \{a,d,f\} = \{a\}$.

4.  $E^c = \{c,d,e,f\}$; $F^c \cap G = \{b,c,e\} \cap \{b,c,e\} = \{b,c,e\}$.

5.  Since $E \cap F = \{a\}$ is not a null set, we conclude that E and F are not mutually exclusive.

6.  $E \cup F = \{a,b,d,f\}$ and $E \cap F^c = \{a,b\} \cap \{b,c,e\} = \{b\}$. Since $\{b\}$ is an element of both sets, they are not mutually exclusive.

7.  $E \cup F \cup G = \{2,4,6\} \cup \{1,3,5\} \cup \{5,6\} = \{1,2,3,4,5,6\}$.

8.  $E \cap F \cap G = \{2,4,6\} \cap \{1,3,5\} \cap \{5,6\} = \phi$.

9.  $(E \cup F \cup G)^c = \{1,2,3,4,5,6\}^c = \phi$.

10. $(E \cap F \cap G)^c = \{1,2,3,4,5,6\}$.

11. Yes, $E \cap F = \phi$; that is, E and F do not contain any common elements.

12. No. 5 is an element of both sets.

13. $E \cup F$

14. $E \cap F$

15. $G^c$

16. $(E \cap F^c)$

17. $(E \cup F \cup G)^c$

18. $(E \cap F^c \cap G^c)$

19. $\phi$, {a}, {b}, {c}, {a,b}, {a,c}, {b,c}, {a,b,c}.

20. a. $\phi$, {1}, {2}, {3}, {1,2}, {1,3}, {2,3}, {1,2,3}.
    b. 4
    c. 4

21. a. $S = \{R,B\}$
    b. $\phi$, {B}, {R}, {B,R}

22. a. {A,C,E,H,M,S,T,U}
    b. {A,E,U}

23. a. $S = \{(H,1), (H,2), (H,3), (H,4), (H,5), (H,6), (T,1), (T,2), (T,3), (T,4), (T,5), (T,6)\}$
    b. $E = \{(H,2), (H,4), (H,6)\}$

24. a. $S = \{1,2,3,4,5\}$
    b. $E = \{2\}$
    c. $F = \{1,3,5\}$

25. $S = \{(d,d,d), (d,d,n), (d,n,d), (n,d,d), (d,n,n), (n,d,n), (n,n,d), (n,n,n)\}$

26. $S = \{A^+, A^-, B^+, B^-, AB^+, AB^-, O^+, O^-\}$

27. a. {ABC, ABD, ABE, ACD, ACE, ADE, BCD, BCE, BDE, CDE};
    b. 6    c. 3       d. 6

28. a. $S = \{t \mid t > 0\}$                    b. $E = \{t \mid 2 \le t \le 3\}$

29. a. $E^c$   b. $E^c \cap F^c$   c. $E \cup F$    d. $(E \cap F^c) \cup (E^c \cap F)$

30. a. $S = \{t \mid t \geq 0\}$
    b. $E = \{t \mid 0 \leq t < 90\}$
    c. $F = \{t \mid t \geq 365\}$

31. a. $S = \{x \mid x > 0\}$
    b. $E = \{x \mid 0 < x \leq 2\}$
    c. $F = \{x \mid x > 2\}$

32. a. $S = \{(L,f), (L,o), (L,u), (M,f), (M,o), (M,u), (U,f), (U,o), (U,u)\}$

    b. $E_1 = \{(L,f), (M,f), (U,f)\}$

    c. $E_2 = \{(M,o), (U,o)\}$

    d. $E_3 = \{(L,o),(L,u),(M,o),(M,u)\}$

33. a. $S = \{0,1,2,3,\ldots,10\}$

    b. $E = \{0,1,2,3\}$

    c. $F = \{5,6,7,8,9,10\}$

34. a. $S = \{(L,R), (L,D), (L,I), (M,R), (M,D), (M,I), (U,R), (U,D), (U,I)\}$

    b. $E_1 = \{(L,D), (M,D), (U,D)\}$

    c. $E_2 = \{(U,R)$

    d. $E_3 = \{(M,R), (M,I)\}$

35. a. $S = \{0,1,2,\ldots,20\}$    b. $E = \{0,1,2,\ldots,9\}$    c. $F = \{20\}$

36. $\{(A,E), (A,F), (A,G), (A,H), (B,E), (B,F), (B,G), (B,H),$

    $(C,E), (C,F), (C,G), (C,H), (D,E), (D,F), (D,G), (D,H)\}$

37. If E is an event of an experiment then $E^c$ is the event containing the elements in S that are not in E. Therefore $E \cap E^c = \phi$ and the two sets are mutually exclusive.

38. $E^c \cap F^c = (E \cup F)^c$ by DeMorgan's Law.

    Since $(E \cup F) \cap (E \cup F)^c = \phi$, they    are mutually exclusive.

39. The number of events of this experiment is $2^n$.

1.  {(H,H)}, {(H,T)}, {(T,H)}, {(T,T)}.

2.  {h}, {d}, {s}, {c}

3.  {(D,m)}, {(D,f)}, {(R,m)}, {(R,f)}, {(I,m)}, {(I,f)}

4.  {0}, {1}, {2}, {3}, {4}, {5}, {6}, {7}, {8}.

5.  {(1,i)}, {(1,d)}, {(1,s)}, {(2,i)}, {(2,d)}, {(2,s)}, ...,
    {(5,i)}, {(5,d)},{(5,s)}

6.  {(1,i)}, {(1,d)}, {(1,u)}, {(2,i)}, {(2,d)}, {(2,u)}, ...,
    {(12,i)}, {(12,d)}, {(12,u)}

7.  {(A,Rh$^+$)}, {(A,Rh$^-$)}, {(B,Rh$^+$)}, {(B,Rh$^-$)}, {(AB,Rh$^+$)}, {(AB,Rh$^-$)},
    {(O,Rh$^+$)}, {(O,Rh$^-$)}

8.  {(1,a)}, {(1,b)}, {(1,c)}, {(1,d)}, ..., {(5,a)}, {(5,b)},
    {(5,c)}, {(5,d)}.

9.  The probability distribution associated with this data is

| Grade       | A    | B    | C    | D    | F    |
|-------------|------|------|------|------|------|
| Probability | 0.10 | 0.25 | 0.45 | 0.15 | 0.05 |

10. The probability distribution associated with this data is

| Bloodtype   | A    | B    | AB   | O    |
|-------------|------|------|------|------|
| Probability | 0.41 | 0.12 | 0.03 | 0.44 |

11. a. S = {$(0 < x \le 200)$, $(200 < x \le 400)$, $(400 < x \le 600)$,
    $(600 < \overline{x} \le 800)$, $(800 < \overline{x} \le 1000)$, $(x > 1\overline{0}00)$}

b.

| Number of cars (x) | Probability |
|---|---|
| $0 < x \leq 200$ | 0.075 |
| $200 < x \leq 400$ | 0.1 |
| $400 < x \leq 600$ | 0.175 |
| $600 < x \leq 800$ | 0.35 |
| $800 < x \leq 1000$ | 0.225 |
| $x > 1000$ | 0.075 |

12. The probability distribution associated with this data is

| Rating | A | B | C | D | F |
|---|---|---|---|---|---|
| Probability | 0.19 | 0.61 | 0.15 | 0.02 | 0.03 |

13. The probability distribution associated with this data is

| Rating | A | B | C | D | F |
|---|---|---|---|---|---|
| Probability | 0.026 | 0.199 | 0.570 | 0.193 | 0.012 |

14. The probability distribution is

| Number of calls received/minute | 10 | 11 | 12 | 13 | 14 |
|---|---|---|---|---|---|
| Probability | 0.05 | 0.125 | 0.1 | 0.025 | 0.1 |

| Number of calls received/minute | 15 | 16 | 17 | 18 | 19 |
|---|---|---|---|---|---|
| Probability | 0.3 | 0.2 | 0 | 0.05 | 0.05 |

15. The probability distribution is

| Number of figures produced (in dozens) | 30 | 31 | 32 | 33 | 34 | 35 | 36 |
|---|---|---|---|---|---|---|---|
| Probability | .125 | 0 | .1875 | .25 | .1875 | .125 | .125 |

16. The probability distribution is

| Company | A | B | C | D | E |
|---|---|---|---|---|---|
| Probability | 0.395 | 0.263 | 0.158 | 0.105 | 0.079 |

17. The probability is
$$\frac{84,000,000}{179,000,000} = 0.469.$$

18. The probability is
$$\frac{163,605}{1,778,314} = 0.092$$

19. a. The probability that a person killed by lightning is a male is
$$\frac{376}{439} \approx 0.856.$$

b. The probability that a person killed by lightning is a female is
$$\frac{439 - 376}{439} = \frac{63}{439} \approx 0.144.$$

20. The probability that a defective bulb is chosen is
$$\frac{6}{120} = 0.05.$$

21. The probability that the retailer uses electronic tags as antitheft devices is
$$\frac{81}{179} \approx 0.46.$$

22. The probability that it will be a white ball is

$$P(W) = \frac{2}{3 + 2 + 5} = \frac{2}{10} = 0.2.$$

23.    a. $P(D) = \frac{13}{52} = \frac{1}{4}$      b. $P(B) = \frac{26}{52} = \frac{1}{2}$      c. $P(A) = \frac{4}{52} = \frac{1}{13}$

24.    Refer to Example 3, page 386.

     a. The required event is $E = \{(1,1),(1,2),(1,3),(2,1),(2,2),(3,1)\}$ and so

$$P(E) = P[\{(1,1)\}] + P\{(1,2)\} + \cdots + P\{(3,1)\}]$$

$$= \frac{1}{36} + \frac{1}{36} + \cdots + \frac{1}{36} \qquad \text{(six terms)}$$

     b. The required event is

$$F = \{(1,6), (2,6), \ldots, (5,6), (6,1), \ldots, (6,6)\},$$

and so

$$P(F) = P[(1,6)] + \cdots + P[(6,6)]$$

$$= \frac{1}{36} + \frac{1}{36} + \cdots + \frac{1}{36} \qquad \text{(eleven terms)}$$

$$= \frac{11}{36}.$$

25.    The probability of arriving at the traffic light when it is red is

$$\frac{30}{80} = 0.375.$$

26.    The required event is $E = \{2,4,\ldots, 36\}$. So

$$P(E) = \frac{1}{38} + \frac{1}{38} + \cdots + \frac{1}{38} \qquad \text{(eighteen terms)}$$

$$= \frac{18}{38}, \text{ or } \frac{9}{19}.$$

27.    The probability is

$$P(D) + P(C) + P(B) + P(A) = 0.15 + 0.45 + 0.25 + 0.10 = 0.95.$$

28. The probability is

$$P(600 < x \le 800) + P(800 < x \le 1000) + P(x > 1000)$$
$$= 0.35 + 0.225 + 0.075 = 0.65.$$

29. a. $P(E) = \dfrac{62}{9 + 62 + 27} = \dfrac{62}{98} \approx 0.633.$

   b. $P(E) = \dfrac{27}{98} \approx 0.276.$

30. a. $P(E) = \dfrac{1}{100,000} = 0.00001$

   b. $P(E) = \dfrac{531,000}{100,000} = 0.00531.$

31. There are two ways of getting a 7, one die showing a 3 and the other die showing a 4, and vice versa.

32. No. Since the die is loaded the outcomes are not equally likely.

33. No, the outcomes are not equally likely.

34. Yes, the outcomes are equally likely.

35. No. Since the coin is weighted, the outcomes are not equally likely.

36. a. $P(A) = P(s_1) + P(s_2) + P(s_4) = \dfrac{1}{14} + \dfrac{3}{14} + \dfrac{2}{14} = \dfrac{3}{7}.$

   b. $P(B) = P(s_1) + P(s_5) = \dfrac{1}{14} + \dfrac{2}{14} = \dfrac{3}{14}.$

   c. $P(C) = P(S) = 1.$

37. a. $P(A) = P(s_1) + P(s_2) = \dfrac{1}{12} + \dfrac{1}{12} = \dfrac{1}{6}.$

   b. $P(B) = P(s_2) + P(s_4) + P(s_5) + P(s_6) = \dfrac{1}{4} + \dfrac{1}{6} + \dfrac{1}{3} + \dfrac{1}{12} = \dfrac{5}{6}.$

   c. $P(C) = 1.$

38. a. The probability that a registered voter favors the proposition is 0.35.

b. The probability that a registered voter is undecided about the proposition is 1 - 0.35 - 0.32 = 0.33.

39. Let G denote a female birth and let B denote a male birth. Then the eight equally likely outcomes of this experiment are

   GGG GGB GBG BGG BGB BBG GBB BBB.

   a. The event that there are two girls and a boy in the family is

      E = {GGB, GBG, BGG}.

   Since there are three favorable outcomes, P(E) = 3/8.

   b. The event that the oldest child is a girl is

      F = {GGG, GGB, GBG, GBB}.

   Since there are 4 favorable outcomes, P(F) = 1/2.

   c. The event that the oldest child is a girl and the youngest child is a boy is

      G = {GGB, GBB}.

   Since there are two favorable outcomes, P(F) = 1/4.

40. a. The required probability is $\frac{50}{295} \approx 0.17$.

    b. The required probability is $\frac{50 + 40 + 31 + 29 + 25}{295 + 325 + 167 + 50 + 248} \approx 0.16$.

## EXERCISES 7.3, page 398

1. Refer to Example 3, page 386. Let E denote the event of interest. Then
   $$P(E) = \frac{18}{36} = \frac{1}{2}.$$

2. Refer to Example 3, page 386. The event of interest is

   E = {(1,6),(2,5),(3,4),(4,3),(5,2),(5,6),(6,1),(6,5)}

   and so

   $$P(E) = \frac{8}{36} = \frac{2}{9}.$$

3. Refer to Example 3, page 386. The event of interest is

   E = {1,1},

and P(E) = 1/36.

4. Let E denote the event of interest. Then

$$E = (1,1),(2,2),\ldots,(6,6)\}.$$

Therefore,

$$P(E) = \frac{6}{36} = \frac{1}{6}.$$

5. Let E denote the event of interest.

Then E = {(6,2),(6,1),(1,6),(2,6)}

and $P(E) = \frac{4}{36} = \frac{1}{9}.$

6. Let E denote the event of interest. Then

$$E^c = \{(1,1),\ (1,2),\ (2,1)\},$$

and $P(E^c) = \frac{3}{12} = \frac{1}{12}.$

The $P(E) = 1 - \frac{1}{12} = \frac{11}{12}.$

7. Let E denote the event that the card drawn is a king, and let F denote the event that the card drawn is a diamond. Then the required probability is

$$P(E \cap F) = \frac{1}{52}.$$

8. Let E denote the event that the card drawn is a diamond and let F denote the event that the card drawn is a king. Then the required probability is

$$P(E \cup F) = P(E) + P(F) - P(E \cap F) = \frac{1}{4} + \frac{1}{13} - \frac{1}{52}$$

$$= \frac{16}{52} = \frac{4}{13}.$$

9. Let E denote the event that a face card is drawn. Then

$$P(E) = \frac{12}{52} = \frac{3}{13}.$$

10. The required probability is $\frac{6}{52}$, or $\frac{3}{26}$.

11. Let E denote the event that an ace is drawn. Then P(E) = 1/13. Then $E^c$ is the event that an ace is not drawn and

$$P(E^c) = 1 - P(E) = \frac{12}{13}.$$

12. Let E denote the event that a black face card is not drawn. Then $P(E) = 6/52 = 3/26$. Then $E^c$ is the event that a black face card is not drawn and

$$P(E^c) = 1 - P(E) = \frac{23}{26}.$$

13. Let E denote the event that a ticket holder will win first prize, then

$$P(E) = \frac{1}{500} = 0.002,$$

and the probability of the event that a ticket holder will not win first prize is

$$P(E^c)\ 1 - 0.002 = 0.998.$$

14. Let E denote the event that a TV household has at least 1 remote control, then

$$P(E) = 0.87,$$

and the probability of the event that a TV household does not have at least 1 remote control is

$$P(E^c) = 0.13.$$

15. Property 2 of the laws of probability is violated. The sum of the probabilities must add up to 1. In this case $P(S) = 1.1$, which is not possible.

16. This violates Property 2: The sum of the probabilities must add up to 1.

17. The five events are not mutually exclusive; the probability of winning at least one purse is

$$1 - \text{probability of losing all 5 times} = 1 - \frac{9^5}{10^5} = 1 - 0.5905$$
$$= 0.4095.$$

18. The two events are not necessarily complementary events; that is, the stock's value could stay the same.

19. The two events are not mutually exclusive; hence, the probability of the given event is

$$\frac{1}{6} + \frac{1}{6} - \frac{1}{36} = \frac{11}{36}.$$

20. These events are not mutually exclusive; she could be accepted by all four colleges, or three, or two, or one, or none.

21. $E^c \cap F^c = \{c,d,e\} \cap \{a,b,e\} = \{e\} \neq \phi.$

22. $A \cap B \neq \phi$, since it is possible to obtain a straight and a flush—a straight flush.

23. Let G denote the event that a customer purchases a pair of glasses and let C denote the event that the customer purchases a pair of contact lenses. Then

$$P(G \cup C)^c \neq 1 - P(G) - P(C).$$

Mr. Owens has not considered the case in which the customer buy both glasses and contact lenses.

24. The sample space is not necessarily uniform; that is, there may be different numbers of students in each grade.

25. a. $P(E \cap F) = 0$ since E and F are mutually exclusive.

b. $P(E \cup F) = P(E) + P(F) - P(E \cap F) = 0.2 + 0.5 = 0.7.$

c. $P(E^c) = 1 - P(E) = 1 - 0.2 = 0.8.$

d. $P(E^c \cap F^c) = P[(E \cup F)^c] = 1 - P(E \cup F) = 1 - 0.7 = 0.3.$

26. a. $P(E \cup F) = P(E) + P(F) - P(E \cap F) = 0.6 + 0.4 - 0.2 = 0.8.$

b. $P(E^c) = 1 - P(E) = 1 - 0.6 = 0.4.$

c. $P(F^c) = 1 - P(F) = 1 - 0.4 = 0.6.$

d. $P(E^c \cap F) = P(F) - P(E \cap F) = 0.4 - 0.2 = 0.2.$

27. a. $P(A) = P(s_1) + P(s_2) = \frac{1}{8} + \frac{3}{8} = \frac{1}{2}.$

$P(B) = P(s_1) + P(s_3) = \frac{1}{8} + \frac{1}{4} = \frac{3}{8}.$

b. $P(A^c) = 1 - P(A) = 1 - \frac{1}{2} = \frac{1}{2}.$

$$P(B^c) = 1 - P(B) = 1 - \frac{3}{8} = \frac{5}{8}.$$

c. $P(A \cap B) = P(s_1) = \frac{1}{8}.$

d. $P(A \cup B) = P(A) + P(B) - P(A \cap B) = \frac{1}{2} + \frac{3}{8} - \frac{1}{8} = \frac{3}{4}.$

28. a. $P(A) = P(s_1) + P(s_2) = \frac{1}{3} + \frac{1}{8} = \frac{11}{24}.$

$$P(B) = P(s_1) + P(s_5) + P(s_{6)} = \frac{1}{3} + \frac{1}{12} + \frac{1}{8} = \frac{6}{24} = \frac{13}{24}.$$

b. $P(A^c) = 1 - P(A) = 1 - \frac{11}{24} = \frac{13}{24}.$

$$P(B^c) = 1 - P(B) = 1 - \frac{13}{24} = \frac{11}{24}.$$

c. $P(A \cap B) = P(s_1) = \frac{1}{3}.$

d. $P(A \cup B) = P(A) + P(B) - P(A \cap B) = \frac{11}{24} + \frac{13}{24} - \frac{1}{3} = \frac{2}{3}.$

e. $P(A^c \cap B^c) = P[(A \cup B)^c] = 1 - \frac{2}{3} = \frac{1}{3}.$

f. $P(A^c \cup B^c) = P(A^c) + P(B^c) - P(A^c \cap B^c) = \frac{13}{24} + \frac{11}{24} - \frac{1}{3} = \frac{2}{3}.$

29. Referring to the following diagram we see that

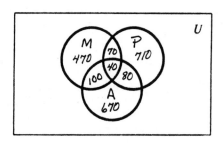

P: lack of parental support
M: malnutrition or poor health
A: abused or neglected

the probability that a teacher selected at random from this group said that lack of parental support is the only problem hampering a student's schooling is

$$\frac{710}{2140} = 0.33.$$

30. Referring to the following Venn diagram, we see that

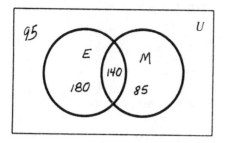

a. the probability that a freshman selected at random from the group is enrolled in an economics and/or a mathematics course is

$$P(E \cup M) = \frac{405}{500} = 0.81.$$

b. the probability that a freshman selected at random from the group is enrolled in exactly one of these two courses is

$$P(E^c \cap M) + P(E \cap M^c) = \frac{180}{500} + \frac{85}{500} = \frac{265}{500} = 0.53$$

c. the probability that a freshman selected at random from the group is not enrolled in a mathematics or economics course is

$$P(E \cup M)^c = 1 - P(E \cup M) = 1 - 0.81 = 0.19.$$

31. Let E and F denote the events that the person surveyed learned of the products from "Good Housekeeping" and "The Ladies Home Journal," respectively. Then

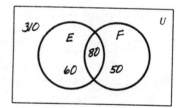

$$P(E) = \frac{140}{500} = \frac{7}{25}, \quad P(F) = \frac{130}{500} = \frac{13}{50}$$

and $P(E \cap F) = \frac{80}{500} = \frac{4}{25}.$

a. $P(E \cap F) = \frac{4}{19} = 0.16$        b. $P(E \cup F) = \frac{14}{50} + \frac{13}{50} - \frac{8}{50} = \frac{19}{50}$

$$= 0.38$$

c. $P(E \cap F^c) + P(E^c \cap F) = \frac{60}{500} + \frac{50}{500} = \frac{110}{500} = 0.22.$

32. The probability distribution is

| Time spent in hours (x) | Probability |
|---|---|
| $0 \leq x \leq 1$ | 0.323 |
| $1 < x \leq 4$ | 0.407 |
| $4 < x \leq 10$ | 0.165 |
| $x > 10$ | 0.105 |

a. The probability that a student selected at random at the university studied in the library more than 4 hours per week is

$$0.165 + 0.105 = 0.27.$$

b. The probability that a student selected at random at the university studied in the library no more than 10 hours per week is
$$1 - 0.105 = .895.$$

33.  Let $A = \{t \mid t < 3\}$, $B = \{t \mid t \leq 4\}$, $C = \{t \mid t > 5\}$

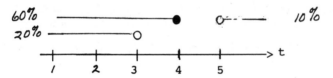

a. $D = \{t \mid t \leq 5\}$ and $P(D) = 1 - P(C) = 1 - 0.1 = 0.9$.

b. $E = \{t \mid t > 4\}$ and $P(E) = 1 - P(B) = 1 - 0.6 = 0.4$.

c. $F = \{t \mid 3 \leq t \leq 4\}$ and $P(F) = P(A^c \cap B) = 0.4$.

34.  The probability distribution associated with this data is

| Number of years car is kept (x) | Probability |
|---|---|
| $0 \leq x \leq 1$ | 0.03 |
| $1 \leq x < 3$ | 0.22 |
| $3 \leq x < 5$ | 0.18 |
| $5 \leq x < 7$ | 0.17 |
| $7 \leq x < 10$ | 0.12 |
| $x \geq 10$ | 0.28 |

a. The probability that an automobile owner selected at random from those surveyed plans to keep his or her present car less than five years is

$$0.18 + 0.22 + 0.03 = 0.43.$$

b. The probability that an automobile owner selected at random from those surveyed plans to keep his or her present car more than three years is

$$0.18 + 0.17 + 0.12 + 0.28 = 0.75.$$

35.   a. The probability that the participant favors tougher gun-control laws is
$$\frac{150}{250} = 0.6.$$

b. The probability that the participant owns a handgun is

$$\frac{58 + 25}{250} = 0.332.$$

c. The probability that the participant owns a handgun but not a rifle is
$$\frac{58}{250} = 0.232.$$

d. The probability that the participant favors tougher gun-control laws and does not own a handgun is

$$\frac{12 + 138}{250} = 0.6.$$

36.   The probability that Bill will fail to solve the problem is $1 - p_1$, and the probability that Mike will fail to solve the problem is $1 - p_2$. Therefore, the probability that both Bill and Mike will

fail to solve the problem is $(1 - p_1)(1 - p_2)$. So, the probability that at least one of them will solve the problem is

$$1 - (1 - p_1)(1 - p_2) = 1 - (1 - p_2 - p_1 + p_1p_2) = p_1 + p_2 - p_1p_2$$

37. The event E that a multiple of 5 is drawn and the event F that a multiple of 7 is drawn are not mutually exclusive. In fact, the correct answer is

$$\frac{16}{50} = \frac{8}{25}.$$

38. True. Write $B = A \cup (B - A)$. Since A and $B - A$ are mutually exclusive, we have

$$P(B) = P(A) + P(B - A).$$

Since $P(B) = 0$, we have $P(A) + P(B - A) = 0$. If $P(A) > 0$, then $P(B - A) < 0$ and this is not possible. Therefore, $P(A) = 0$.

39. True. As in Exercise 38, we have $P(A) = P(B) - P(B - A)$. Since $P(B - A) \geq 0$, we see that $P(A) \leq P(B)$.

## EXERCISES 7.4, page 407

1. Let E denote the event that the coin lands heads all five times. Then

$$P(E) = \frac{1}{2^5} = \frac{1}{32}.$$

2. $P(F) = 5\left(\frac{1}{2^5}\right) = \frac{5}{32}.$

3. Let E denote the event that the coin lands tails all 5 times, then

$$P(E^c) = 1 - P(E) = 1 - \frac{1}{32} = \frac{31}{32},$$

where $E^c$ is the event that the coin lands heads at least once.

4. Let E denote the event that the coin lands heads more than once, then $E^c$ is the event that the coin lands tails all five times or four times.

Then $n(E^c) = C(5,5) + C(5,4) = 1 + 5 = 6.$

So $P(E^c) = \frac{6}{32}$ and $P(E) = 1 - \frac{6}{32} = 0.8125.$

5. $P(E) = \dfrac{13 \cdot C(4,2)}{C(52,2)} = \dfrac{78}{1326} \approx 0.0588.$

6. Refer to Exercise 5. $P(E^c) = 1 - P(E) = 1 - 0.0588 = 0.9412.$

7. $P(E) = \dfrac{C(26,2)}{C(52,2)} = \dfrac{325}{1326} \approx 0.2451.$

8. $P(E) = \dfrac{4 \cdot C(13,2)}{C(52,2)} = \dfrac{312}{1326} \approx 0.2353.$

9. The probability of the event that two of the balls will be white and two will be blue is

$$P(E) = \dfrac{n(E)}{n(S)} = \dfrac{C(3,2) \cdot C(5,2)}{C(8,4)} = \dfrac{(3)(10)}{70} = \dfrac{3}{7}.$$

10. The probability of the event that all of the balls will be blue is

$$P(E) = \dfrac{n(E)}{n(S)} = \dfrac{C(5,4)}{C(8,4)} = \dfrac{5}{70} = \dfrac{1}{14}.$$

11. The probability of the event that exactly three of the balls are blue is

$$P(E) = \dfrac{n(E)}{n(S)} = \dfrac{C(5,3)C(3,1)}{C(8,4)} = \dfrac{30}{70} = \dfrac{3}{7}.$$

12. The probability of the event that two or three of the balls are white is

$$P(E) = \dfrac{n(E)}{n(S)} = \dfrac{C(3,2)C(5,2) + C(3,3)C(5,1)}{C(8,4)} = \dfrac{35}{70} = \dfrac{1}{2}.$$

13. $P(E) = \dfrac{C(3,2) \cdot C(1,1)}{8} = \dfrac{3}{8}.$

14. $P(E^c) = \dfrac{1}{8};\ P(E) = 1 - P(E^c) = 1 - \dfrac{1}{8} = \dfrac{7}{8}.$

15. $P(E) = 1 - \dfrac{C(3,3)}{8} = \dfrac{1}{8}.$

16. $P(E) = \dfrac{C(1,1) \cdot C(1,1) \cdot C(2,1)}{8} = \dfrac{(1)(1)(2)}{8} = \dfrac{1}{4}.$

*7 Probability*

17. The number of elements in the sample space is $2^{10}$. There are
$$C(10,6) = \frac{10!}{6!4!},$$

or 210 ways of answering exactly six questions correctly. Therefore, the required probability is
$$\frac{210}{2^{10}} = \frac{210}{1024} \approx 0.205.$$

18. The probability that 3 CPAs will be selected is
$$P(E) = \frac{C(8,3)}{C(14,3)} = \frac{2}{13} = 0.154.$$

19. a. Let E denote the event that both of the bulbs are defective. Then
$$P(E) = \frac{C(4,2)}{C(24,2)} = \frac{\frac{4!}{2!2!}}{\frac{24!}{22!2!}} = \frac{4 \cdot 3}{24 \cdot 23} = \frac{1}{46} \approx 0.022.$$

b. Let F denote the event that none of the bulbs are defective. then
$$P(F) = \frac{C(20,2)}{C(24,2)} = \frac{20!}{18!2!} \cdot \frac{22!2!}{24!} = \frac{20}{24} \cdot \frac{19}{23} = 0.6884.$$

Therefore, the probability that at least one of the light bulbs is defective is given by
$$1 - P(F) = 1 - 0.6884 = 0.3116.$$

20. Let E denote the event that there is at least one rotten orange in the sample. Then $E^c$ is the event that there are no rotten oranges in the sample and
$$P(E^c) = \frac{C(56,3)}{C(60,3)} = \frac{166320}{205320} \approx 0.81,$$

and $P(E) = 1 - P(E^c) = 1 - 0.81 = 0.19.$

21. a. The probability that both of the cartridges are defective is
$$P(E) = \frac{C(6,2)}{C(80,2)} = \frac{30}{6320} = 0.0048.$$

b. Let F denote the event that none of the cartridges are defective. Then
$$P(F) = \frac{C(74,2)}{C(80,2)} = \frac{5402}{6320} = 0.855.$$

and $P(F^c) = 1 - P(F) = 1 - 0.855 = 0.145,$

is the probability that at least 1 of the cartridges is defective.

22. The required probability is given by

$$\frac{C(22,8)}{C(24,8)} = \frac{\frac{22!}{14!8!}}{\frac{24!}{16!8!}} = \frac{30}{69} = \frac{10}{23} \approx 0.4348.$$

23. a. The probability that Mary's name will be selected is

$$P(E) = \frac{12}{100} = 0.12;$$

The probability that both Mary's and John's names will be selected is

$$P(F) = \frac{C(98,10)}{C(100,12)} = \frac{\frac{98!}{88!10!}}{\frac{100!}{88!12!}} = \frac{12 \cdot 11}{100 \cdot 99} \approx 0.013.$$

b. The probability that Mary's name will be selected is

$$P(M) = \frac{6}{40} = 0.15.$$

The probability that both Mary's and John's names will be selected is

$$P(M) \cdot P(J) = \frac{6}{60} \cdot \frac{6}{40} = \frac{36}{2400} = 0.015.$$

24. a. The probability that a specific qualified applicant will be selected for one of the apartments is

$$\frac{8}{50} = 0.16.$$

b. The probability that two specific qualified applicants will be selected for apartments on the same side of town is

$$\frac{C(48,6)}{C(50,8)} \cdot \frac{C(3,2) + C(5,2)}{C(8,2)} = \frac{4}{175} \cdot \frac{13}{28} = \frac{13}{1225} \approx 0.0106.$$

25. The probability is given by

$$\frac{C(12,8) \cdot C(8,2)}{C(20,10)} + \frac{C(12,9)C(8,1)}{C(20,10)} + \frac{C(12,10)}{C(20,10)}$$

$$= \frac{(28)(495) + (220)(8) + 66}{184,756} \approx 0.085.$$

26. a. The probability that exactly two of the five will take the same test is

$$\frac{C(5,2)3!}{4^5} = \frac{60}{1024} \approx 0.0586.$$

b. The probability that the two women will take the same test is

$$\frac{C(4,1)4^3}{4^5} = \frac{4}{16} = \frac{1}{4}.$$

27. a. The probability that he will select brand B is

$$\frac{C(4,2)}{C(5,3)} = \frac{6}{15} = \frac{3}{5}. \qquad \left(\frac{\text{the number of selections that include brand B}}{\text{the number of possible selections}}\right)$$

b. The probability that he will select brands B and C is

$$\frac{C(3,1)}{C(5,3)} = 0.3$$

c. The probability that he will select at least one of the two brands, B and C is

$$1 - \frac{C(3,3)}{C(5,3)} = 0.9. \qquad \begin{array}{c}\text{(1 - probability that he does not select}\\\text{brands B and C.)}\end{array}$$

28. a. The required probability is given by

$$\frac{C(4,1) \cdot C(16,1)}{C(52,2)} = \frac{4 \cdot 16}{1326} \approx 0.0483.$$

b. The required probability is given by

$$\frac{C(8,1) \cdot C(32,1)}{C(104,2)} = \frac{8 \cdot 32}{5356} \cdot 0.0478.$$

29. The probability that the three "Lucky Dollar" symbols will appear in the window of the slot machine is

$$P(E) = \frac{n(E)}{n(S)} = \frac{(1)(1)(1)}{C(1,9)C(1,9)C(1,9)} = \frac{1}{729}.$$

30. The probability that the number 10 will appear 6 times in a row is

$$P(E) = \frac{n(E)}{n(S)} = \frac{1}{38^6} = 3.32 \times 10^{-10}.$$

31. The probability of a ticket holder having all four digits in exact order is

$$\frac{1}{C(10,1) \cdot C(10,1) \cdot C(10,1) \cdot C(10,1)} = \frac{1}{10,000} = 0.0001.$$

32. The probability of a ticket holder having two specified, consecutive digits in exact order is

$$\frac{(1)(1) \cdot C(10,1) \cdot C(10,1)}{(10)^4} = \frac{1}{100}.$$

33. The probability of a ticket holder having a specified digit in exact order is

$$\frac{C(1,1)C(10,1)C(10,1),C(10,1)}{10^4} = 0.10.$$

34. The probability of a ticket holder having all four digits in any order is

$$\frac{P(4,4)}{10^4} = \frac{24}{10000} = 0.0024.$$

35. The number of ways of selecting a 5-card hand from 52 cards is given by

$$C(52,5) = 2,598,960.$$

The number of straight flushes that can be dealt in each suit is 10, so there are 4(10) possible straight flushes. Therefore, the probability of being dealt a straight flush is

$$\frac{4(10)}{C(52,5)} = \frac{40}{2,598,960} = 0.0000154.$$

36. The number of ways of selecting a 5-card hand from 52 cards is given by

$$C(52,5) = 2,598,960.$$

Since there are 10 possible straights in each suit, there are

$$10 \cdot C(4,1) \cdot C(4,1) \cdot C(4,1) \cdot C(4,1) = 10,240$$

ways of being dealt a straight of which 40 hands are a straight flush. Thus, the required probability is

$$\frac{10,280 - 40}{2,598,960} = \frac{10,200}{2,598,960} = 0.00392.$$

37. The number of ways of being dealt a flush in one suit is C(13,5), and, since there are four suits, the number of ways of being dealt a flush is 4• C(13,5). Since we wish to exclude the hands that are straight flushes we subtract the number of possible straight flushes from 4 • C(13,5). Therefore, the probability of being drawn a flush, but not a straight flush, is

$$\frac{4 \cdot C(13,5) - 40}{C(52,5)} = \frac{5108}{2,598,960} = 0.0019654.$$

38. The number of ways of being dealt four of a kind is C(13,1) • C(48,1). Therefore, the probability of being dealt four of a kind is

$$\frac{C(13,1) \cdot C(48,1)}{C(52,5)} = 0.000240.$$

39. The total number of ways to select three cards of one rank is

13 • C(4,3).

The remaining two cards must form a pair of another rank and there are

12 • C(4,2)

ways of selecting these pairs.
Next, the total number of ways to be dealt a full house is

13 • C(4,3) • 12 • C(4,2) = 3744.

Hence, the probability of being dealt a full house is

$$\frac{3,744}{2,598,960} \approx 0.0014406.$$

40. The number of ways of being dealt two pairs is

$$\frac{C(13,2) \cdot C(4,2) \cdot C(4,2) \cdot C(44,1)}{C(52,5)} = \frac{123,552}{2,598,960} = 0.04754.$$

41. a. Let E denote the event that in a group of 5, no two will have the same sign. Then

$$P(E) = \frac{12 \cdot 11 \cdot 10 \cdot 9 \cdot 8}{12^5} \approx 0.381944.$$

Therefore, the probability that at least two will have the same sign is given by

1 - P(E) = 1 - 0.381944 ≈ 0.618.

b.　$P(\text{no Aries}) = \dfrac{11 \cdot 11 \cdot 11 \cdot 11 \cdot 11}{12^5} \approx 0.647228.$

$P(1 \text{ Aries}) = \dfrac{C(5,1) \cdot (1)(11)(11)(11)(11)}{12^5} \approx 0.2941945.$

Therefore, the probability that at least two will have the sign Aries is given by

$1 - [P(\text{no Aries}) + P(1 \text{ Aries})] = 1 - 0.9414225 \approx 0.059.$

42.　Recall that there are 9 Justices on the Supreme Court. Next, let E denote the event that in a group of 9 people, no two will have the same birthday. Then,

$P(E) = \dfrac{365 \cdot 364 \cdot 363 \cdot 362 \cdot 361 \cdot 360 \cdot 359 \cdot 358 \cdot 357}{365^9}$

$\approx 0.9053762.$

Therefore, the probability that at least two will have the same birthday is given by

$1 - P(E) = 1 - 0.9053762 = 0.0946238 \approx 0.095.$

43.　Referring to the table on page 406, we see that in a group of 50 people, the probability that none of the people will have the same birthday is $1 - 0.970 = 0.03$.

44.　The required probability is

$P(E) = 1 - \dfrac{365 \cdot 364 \cdot 363 \cdot \; \cdots \; \cdot (365 - 42 + 1)}{365^{42}}$

$= 1 - \dfrac{365 \cdot 364 \cdot 363 \cdot \; \cdots \; \cdot 324}{365^{42}} \approx 0.914$

## EXERCISES 7.5, page 422

1.　a. $P(A|B) = \dfrac{P(A \cap B)}{P(B)} = \dfrac{0.2}{0.5} = \dfrac{2}{5}.$

　　b. $P(B|A) = \dfrac{P(A \cap B)}{P(A)} = \dfrac{0.2}{0.6} = \dfrac{1}{3}.$

2.　a. $P(A|B) = \dfrac{P(A \cap B)}{P(B)} = \dfrac{0.3}{0.6} = \dfrac{1}{2}.$

b. $P(B|A) = \dfrac{P(A \cap B)}{P(A)} = \dfrac{0.3}{0.4} = \dfrac{3}{4}.$

3.  $P(A \cap B) = P(A)P(B) = (0.6)(0.5) = 0.3.$

4.  a. $P(A|B^c) = \dfrac{P(A \cap B^c)}{P(B^c)} = \dfrac{P(A) - P(A \cap B)}{P(B^c)} = \dfrac{0.6 - 0.2}{1 - 0.5} = \dfrac{0.4}{0.5} = \dfrac{4}{5}.$

    b. $P(B|A^c) = \dfrac{P(B \cap A^c)}{P(A^c)} = \dfrac{P(B) - P(A \cap B)}{P(A^c)} = \dfrac{0.5 - 0.2}{1 - 0.6} = \dfrac{0.3}{0.5} = \dfrac{3}{4}.$

5.  $P(A) \cdot P(B) = (0.3)(0.6) = 0.18 = P(A \cap B).$

Therefore the events are independent.

6.  $P(A) \cdot P(B) = (0.6)(0.8) = 0.48 \neq 0.2 = P(A \cap B).$

Therefore, A and B are not independent events.

7.  $P(A \cap B) = P(A) + P(B) - P(A \cup B) = 0.5 + 0.7 - 0.85 = 0.35$

                     $= P(A) \cdot P(B),$

so they are independent events.

8.  $P(A) = 1 - P(A^c) = 1 - 0.3 = 0.7.$ $P(B) = 1 - P(B^c) = 1 - 0.4 = 0.6.$

$P(A) \cdot P(B) = (0.7)(0.6) = 0.42 = P(A \cap B).$ Therefore, the events are independent.

9.  a. $P(A \cap B) = P(A)P(B) = (0.4)(0.6) = 0.24.$

    b. $P(A \cup B) = P(A) + P(B) - P(A \cap B) = 0.4 + 0.6 - 0.24 = 0.76.$

10.  a. $P(A \cap B) = P(A)P(B) = (0.35)(0.45) = 0.1575.$

     b. $P(A \cup B) = P(A) + P(B) - P(A \cap B)$

                   $= 0.35 + 0.45 - 0.1575 = 0.6425.$

11.  a. $P(A) = 0.5$                 b. $P(E|A) = 0.4.$

     c. $P(A \cap E) = P(A)P(E|A) = (0.5)(0.4) = 0.2.$

     d. $P(E) = (0.5)(0.4) + (0.5)(0.3) = 0.35.$

e. No. $P(A \cap E) \neq P(A) \cdot P(E) = (0.5)(0.35)$

f. A and E are not independent events.

12.  a. $P(A) = 0.4$                    b. $P(E|A) = 0.5$.

c. $P(A \cap E) = P(A)P(E|A) = (0.5)(0.4) = 0.2$.

d. $P(E) = (0.4)(0.5) + (0.4)(0.3) + (0.2)(0.4) = 0.4$.

e. No. $P(A \cap E) \neq P(A) \cdot P(E) = (0.4)(0.4)$

f. A and E are not independent events.

13.

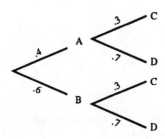

a. $P(A) = 0.4$                    b. $P(C|A) = 0.3$

c. $P(A \cap C) = P(A)P(C|A) = (0.4)(0.3) = 0.12$

d. $P(C) = (0.4)(0.3) + (0.6)(0.3) = 0.3$

e. Yes. $P(A \cap C) = 0.12 = P(A)P(C)$

f. Yes.

14.

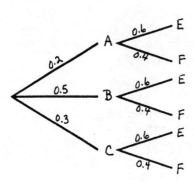

From the tree diagram, we see that

a. $P(B) = 0.5$

b. $P(F|B) = 0.4$

c. $P(B \cap F) = (0.5)(0.4) = 0.2$

d. $P(F) = (0.2)(0.4) + (0.5)(0.4) + (0.3)(0.4) = 0.4$

e. $P(B)P(F) = (0.5)(0.4) = 0.2 = P(B \cap F)$. Yes.

f. Yes.

15. Let A denote the event that the sum of the numbers is less than 9 and let B denote the event that one of the numbers is a 6.

Then, $P(A|B) = \dfrac{P(A \cap B)}{P(B)}$

$$= \dfrac{\frac{4}{36}}{\frac{11}{36}} = \frac{4}{11}.$$

16. Let A denote the event that the battery lasts 10 or more hours and let B denote the event that the battery lasts 15 or more hours.

Then $\qquad P(A) = 0.8, \qquad P(B) = 0.15$

and $\qquad P(A \cap B) = 0.15.$

Therefore, the probability that the battery will last 15 hours or more is

$$P(B|A) = \frac{P(A \cap B)}{P(A)} = \frac{0.15}{0.8} = \frac{3}{16} = 0.1875.$$

17. a. The probability that the first card drawn is a heart is

$$P(H) = \frac{13}{52} = \frac{1}{4}.$$

b. The probability that the second card drawn is a heart given that the first card drawn was not a heart is

$$P(H|H^c) = \frac{13}{51}.$$

c. The probability that the second card drawn is a heart given that the first card drawn was a heart is

$$P(H|H) = \frac{12}{51}.$$

18.  Refer to the following tree diagram:

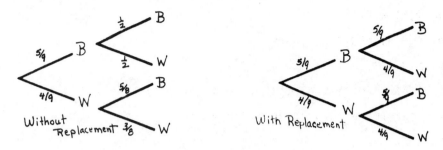

a. The probability that the second ball drawn is a white ball if the second ball is drawn without replacing the first is

$$P(B)P(W|B) + P(W)P(W|W) = \left(\frac{5}{9}\right)\left(\frac{1}{2}\right) + \left(\frac{4}{9}\right)\left(\frac{3}{8}\right)$$

$$= \frac{4}{9}.$$

b. The probability that the second ball drawn is a white ball if the first ball is replaced before the second is drawn is

$$\left(\frac{5}{9}\right)\left(\frac{4}{9}\right) + \left(\frac{4}{9}\right)\left(\frac{4}{9}\right) = \frac{4}{9}.$$

19.  Referring to the following tree diagram, we see that

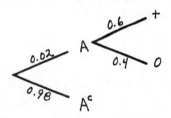

the probability that a tax return selected at random will result in additional assessments being levied on the taxpayer is

$$(0.02)(0.6) = 0.012.$$

20. Refer to the following tree diagram:

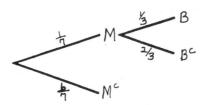

a. The probability that a student selected at random from this medical school is black is

$$\left(\frac{1}{7}\right)\left(\frac{1}{3}\right) = \frac{1}{21}.$$

b. The probability that a student selected at random from this medical school is black if it is known that the student is a member of a minority group is $P(B|M) = 1/3$.

21. Let $C = \{x | x$ is an eligible voter with a college degree$\}$ and $V = \{x | x$ is an eligible voter who voted$\}$.

Referring to the following tree diagram, we see that

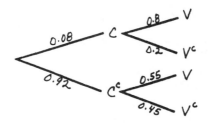

a. the probability that an eligible voter selected at random has a college degree and voted in the last presidential election is

$$P(C \cap V) = (0.08)(0.8) = 0.064.$$

b. the probability that an eligible voter selected at random does not have a college degree and did not vote in the last presidential election is

$$P(C^c \cap V^c) = (0.92)(0.45) = 0.414.$$

c. the probability that an eligible voter selected at random voted in the last presidential election is

$$P(C \cap V) + P(C^c \cap V) = (0.08)(0.8) + (0.92)(0.55)$$

$$= 0.57$$

d. the probability that an eligible voter selected at random did not vote in the last presidential election is

$$P(V^c) = 1 - P(V) = 1 - 0.57 = 0.43.$$

22. Let D denote the event that the card drawn is a diamond. Consider the tree diagram that follows.

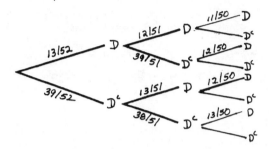

Then the required probability is

$$\left(\frac{13}{52}\right)\left(\frac{12}{51}\right)\left(\frac{11}{50}\right) + \left(\frac{13}{52}\right)\left(\frac{39}{51}\right)\left(\frac{12}{50}\right) + \left(\frac{39}{52}\right)\left(\frac{13}{51}\right)\left(\frac{12}{50}\right) + \left(\frac{39}{52}\right)\left(\frac{38}{51}\right)\left(\frac{13}{50}\right)$$

$$= 0.25.$$

23. Refer to the following tree diagram.

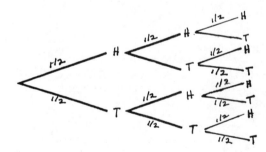

a. The probability that the coin will land heads at least twice is

$$\frac{4}{8} = \frac{1}{2}.$$

b. The probability that the coin will land heads on the second toss given that heads were thrown on the first toss is

$$\frac{2}{4} = \frac{1}{2}.$$

c. The probability that the coin will land heads on the third toss given that tails were thrown on the first toss is

$$\frac{2}{4} = \frac{1}{2}.$$

24. The sample space for a three-child family is

$$S = \{GGG,\ GGB,\ GBG,\ GBB,\ BGG,\ BGB,\ BBG,\ BBB\}.$$

Since we know that there is at least one girl in the three-child family we are dealing with a reduced sample space

$$S_1 = \{GGG,\ GGB,\ GBG,\ GBB,\ BGG,\ BGB,\ BBG\}$$

in which there are 7 outcomes. Then the probability that all three children are girls is

$$P(E) = \frac{n(E)}{n(S)} = \frac{1}{7}.$$

25. $P(D) = P(A \cap D) + P(B \cap D) + P(C \cap D)$

$$= (0.45)(0.01) + (0.25)(0.02) + (0.30)(0.015)$$

$$= 0.014.$$

26. a.

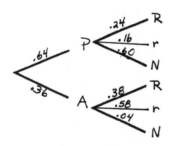

R = recovered within 48 hrs.
r = recovered after 48 hrs.
N = never recovered

b. The required probability is 0.24.

c. The required probability is

$$(0.64)(0.60) + (0.36)(0.04) \approx 0.40.$$

27. a.

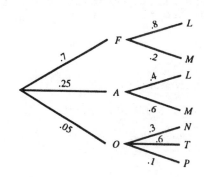

L = 30-year loan
M = 15-year loan
N = 20-year loan
T = 10-year loan
P = "5-year or less" loan

b. The required probability is P(A ∩ M) = (0.25)(0.6) = 0.15.

c. The required probability is

P(F ∩ M) + P(A ∩ M) = (0.7)(0.2) + (0.25)(0.6)

= 0.29.

28. Refer to the following tree diagram.

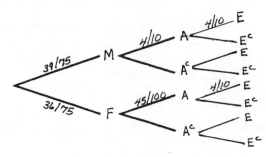

a. P(A ∩ E|M) = (0.4)(0.4) = 0.16.

b. $P(A) = P(M \cap A) + P(F \cap A) = \frac{39}{75} \cdot \frac{4}{10} + \frac{36}{75} \cdot \frac{45}{100} = 0.424$

c. $P(M \cap A \cap E) + P(F \cap A \cap E) = \frac{39}{75} \cdot \frac{4}{10} \cdot \frac{4}{10} + \frac{36}{75} \cdot \frac{45}{100} \cdot \frac{4}{10}$

= 0.0832 + 0.0864

= 0.1696.

29. Let D denote the event that a light is defective and $D^c$ the event that a light is nondefective. Referring to the following tree diagram

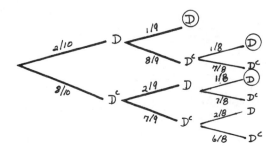

we see that the probability that both defective lights will be found after three trails is

$$P(D \cap D) + P(D \cap D^c \cap D) + P(D^c \cap D \cap D)$$

$$= \frac{2}{10} \cdot \frac{1}{9} + \frac{2}{10} \cdot \frac{8}{9} \cdot \frac{1}{8} + \frac{8}{10} \cdot \frac{2}{9} \cdot \frac{1}{8} = \frac{16 + 16 + 16}{720}$$

$$= \frac{1}{15}.$$

30. a. The probability that none of the dozen eggs is broken is

   $(0.992)^{12} = 0.908.$

   Therefore, the probability that at least one egg is broken is

   $1 - 0.908 = 0.092.$

   b. Using the results of (a), we see that the required probability is

   $(0.092)(0.092)(0.908) \approx 0.008.$

31. a. $P(A) = \dfrac{8120}{10730} = 0.757$; $P(B) = \dfrac{6101}{10730} = 0.569$;

   $P(A \cap B) = \dfrac{4222}{10730} = 0.393$

   $P(B|A) = \dfrac{P(A \cap B)}{P(A)} = \dfrac{n(A \cap B)}{n(A)} = \dfrac{4222}{8120} = 0.520.$

   $P(B|A^c) = \dfrac{P(A^c \cap B)}{P(A^c)} = \dfrac{n(A^c \cap B)}{n(A^c)} = \dfrac{1879}{2610} = 0.720.$

   b. $P(B|A) \neq P(B)$, so A and B are not independent events.

32.  a. $P(A) = \frac{1120}{4000} = 0.280$; $P(B) = \frac{1560}{4000} = 0.390$;

$P(A \cap B) = \frac{720}{4000} = 0.180$.

$P(B|A) = \frac{P(A \cap B)}{P(A)} = \frac{n(A \cap B)}{n(A)} = \frac{720}{1120} = 0.643$.

$P(B|A^c) = \frac{P(A^c \cap B)}{P(A^c)} = \frac{n(A^c \cap B)}{n(A^c)} = \frac{840}{2880} = 0.292$.

b. $P(B|A) \neq P(B)$, so A and B are not independent events.

33.  $P(A \cap B) = \frac{1}{4} \cdot \frac{25}{51} = \frac{25}{204}$.

$P(A) \cdot P(B) = \frac{1}{4} \cdot \frac{1}{2} = \frac{1}{8}$.

Since $P(A \cap B) \neq P(A) \cdot P(B)$, A and B are dependent events.

34.  Let C denote the event that a person in the survey was a heavy coffee drinker and Pa denote the event that a person in the survey had cancer of the pancreas. Then

$P(C) = \frac{3200}{10000} = 0.32$ and $P(Pa) = \frac{160}{10000} = 0.016$.

$P(C \cap Pa) = \frac{132}{160} = 0.825$.

and $P(C) \cdot P(Pa) = 0.00512 \neq P(A \cap Pa)$. Therefore the events are not independent.

35.  a. These are independent events. Therefore, the probability is

$(0.9)(0.9) = 0.81$.

b. The probability that the mail will be delivered before 2 P.M. is

$(0.9)(0.9)(0.9) = 0.729$.

36.  The probability that the first test will fail is 0.03, that the second test will fail is 0.015, and the third test will fail is 0.015. Since these are independent events the probability that all three tests will fail is

$(0.03)(0.015)(0.015) = 0.0000068$.

37.  The probability that on a particular day

a. all four machines will break down is

$$P(A) \cdot P(B) \cdot P(C) \cdot P(D) = \frac{1}{50} \cdot \frac{1}{60} \cdot \frac{1}{75} \cdot \frac{1}{40} = 0.0000001.$$

b. none of the machines will break down is

$$P(A^c) \cdot P(B^c) \cdot P(C^c) \cdot P(D^c) = \frac{49}{50} \cdot \frac{59}{60} \cdot \frac{74}{75} \cdot \frac{39}{40} = 0.9270473 \approx 0.927.$$

c. exactly one machine will break down is

$$P(A) \cdot P(B^c) \cdot P(C^c) \cdot P(D^c) + P(A^c) \cdot P(B) \cdot P(C^c) \cdot P(D^c)$$

$$+ P(A^c) \cdot P(B^c) \cdot P(C) \cdot P(D^c) + P(A^c) \cdot P(B^c) \cdot P(C^c) \cdot P(D)$$

$$= \frac{1}{50} \cdot \frac{59}{60} \cdot \frac{74}{75} \cdot \frac{39}{40} + \frac{49}{50} \cdot \frac{1}{60} \cdot \frac{74}{75} \cdot \frac{39}{40} + \frac{49}{50} \cdot \frac{59}{60} \cdot \frac{1}{75} \cdot \frac{39}{40} + \frac{49}{50} \cdot \frac{59}{60} \cdot \frac{74}{75} \cdot \frac{1}{40}$$

$$= 0.0189193 + 0.0157126 + 0.0125276 + 0.2737704$$

$$= 0.0709299 \approx 0.071.$$

38. Let A denote the event that at least one of the floodlights remain functional over the one-year period. Then

$$P(A) = 0.99999 \quad \text{and} \quad P(A^c) = 1 - P(A) = 0.00001.$$

Letting n represent the minimum number of floodlights needed, we have

$$(0.1)^n = 0.00001$$

$$n \log (0.01) = -5$$

$$n(-2) = -5$$

$$n = \frac{5}{2} = 2.5.$$

Therefore, the minimum number of floodlights needed is 3.

39. a. No, because $E \cap S = E \neq \phi$ unless $E = \phi$.

b. Yes, because $E \cap \phi = \phi$.

40. The probability that the event will not occur in one trial is $1 - p$. Therefore, the probability that it will not occur in $n$ independent trials is $(1 - p)^n$. Therefore, the probability that it will occur at least once in n independent trials is $1 - (1 - p)^n$.

41. Using Formula (2), we find

$$P(A | A \cup B) = \frac{P(A \cap (A \cup B))}{P(A \cup B)}$$

Since A and B are mutually exclusive, $A \cap (A \cup B) = A$ and

$$P(A \cup B) = P(A) + P(B).$$

Therefore, $P(A|A \cup B) = \dfrac{P(A)}{P(A) + P(B)}$.

## EXERCISES 7.6, page 431

1.

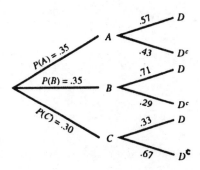

2. a. $P(D) = \dfrac{20 + 25 + 10}{35 + 35 + 30} = 0.55$.

   b. $P(A|D) = \dfrac{20}{20 + 25 + 10} = 0.36$.

3. a. $P(D^c) = \dfrac{15 + 10 + 20}{35 + 35 + 30} = 0.45$.

   b. $P(B|D^c) = \dfrac{10}{15 + 10 + 20} = 0.22$.

4.

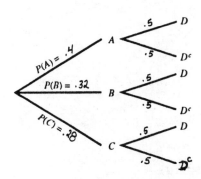

5. a. $P(D) = \dfrac{25 + 20 + 15}{50 + 40 + 35} = 0.48$.

   b. $P(B|D) = \dfrac{20}{25 + 20 + 15} = 0.33$.

6.  a. $P(D^c) = \dfrac{25 + 20 + 20}{50 + 40 + 35} = 0.52.$

    b. $P(B|D^c) = \dfrac{20}{25 + 20 + 20} = 0.308.$

7.  a. $P(A) \cdot P(D|A) = (0.4)(0.2) = 0.08.$

    b. $P(B) \cdot P(D|B) = (0.6)(0.25) = 0.15.$

    c. $P(A|D) = \dfrac{P(A) \cdot P(D|A)}{P(A) \cdot P(D|A) + P(B) \cdot P(D|B)} = \dfrac{(0.4)(0.2)}{0.08 + 0.15} \approx 0.35.$

8.  a. $P(A) \cdot P(D|A) = (0.35)(0.7) = 0.245.$

    b. $P(B) \cdot P(D|B) = (0.65)(0.6) = 0.39.$

    c. $P(A|D) = \dfrac{P(A) \cdot P(D|A)}{P(A) \cdot P(D|A) + P(B) \cdot P(D|B)} = \dfrac{0.245}{0.245 + 0.39} \approx 0.386.$

9.  a. $P(A) \cdot P(D|A) = \dfrac{1}{3} \cdot \dfrac{1}{4} = \dfrac{1}{12}.$

    b. $P(B) \cdot P(D|B) = \dfrac{1}{2} \cdot \dfrac{1}{2} = \dfrac{1}{4}.$

    c. $P(C) \cdot P(D|C) = \dfrac{1}{6} \cdot \dfrac{1}{3} = \dfrac{1}{18}.$

    d. $P(A|D) = \dfrac{P(A)\,P(D|A)}{P(A)P(D|A) + P(B)P(D|B) + P(C)P(D|C)}$

$$= \dfrac{1/12}{1/12 + 1/4 + 1/18} = \dfrac{1}{12} \cdot \dfrac{36}{14} = \dfrac{3}{14}.$$

10. a. $P(A \cap D) = \dfrac{1}{5} \cdot \dfrac{1}{2} = \dfrac{1}{10}.$

    b. $P(B \cap D) = \dfrac{1}{5} \cdot \dfrac{1}{3} = \dfrac{1}{15}.$

    c. $P(C \cap D) = \dfrac{2}{5} \cdot \dfrac{3}{4} = \dfrac{6}{20} = \dfrac{3}{10}.$

    d. $P(D) = \dfrac{1}{10} + \dfrac{2}{15} + \dfrac{3}{10} = \dfrac{16}{30} = \dfrac{8}{15}.$

    e. $\dfrac{P(A \cap D)}{P(D)} = \dfrac{\frac{1}{10}}{\frac{8}{15}} = \dfrac{3}{16} = \dfrac{\left(\frac{1}{5}\right)\left(\frac{1}{2}\right)}{\left(\frac{1}{5}\right)\left(\frac{1}{2}\right) + \left(\frac{2}{5}\right)\left(\frac{1}{3}\right) + \left(\frac{2}{5}\right)\left(\frac{3}{4}\right)}.$

11. Let A denote the event that the first card drawn is a heart and B the event that the second card drawn is a heart. Then

$$P(A|B) = \frac{P(A) \cdot P(B|A)}{P(A) \cdot P(B|A) + P(A^c) \cdot P(B|A^c)}$$

$$= \frac{(\frac{1}{4})(\frac{12}{51})}{(\frac{1}{4})(\frac{12}{51}) + (\frac{3}{4})(\frac{13}{51})} = \frac{4}{17}.$$

12. Let A denote the event that the first card drawn is a heart and B the event that the second card drawn is a diamond. Then

$$P(A|B) = \frac{P(A) \cdot P(B|A)}{P(B)}$$

$$= \frac{(\frac{1}{4})(\frac{13}{51})}{(\frac{1}{4})(\frac{13}{51}) + (\frac{1}{4})(\frac{4}{17}) + (\frac{13}{51})(\frac{1}{2})} = \frac{13}{51}.$$

13. Using the following tree diagram, we see that

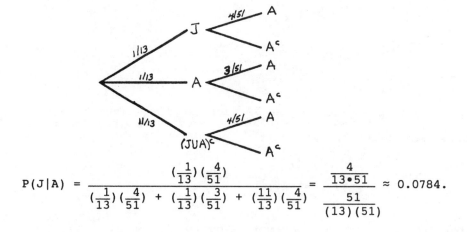

$$P(J|A) = \frac{(\frac{1}{13})(\frac{4}{51})}{(\frac{1}{13})(\frac{4}{51}) + (\frac{1}{13})(\frac{3}{51}) + (\frac{11}{13})(\frac{4}{51})} = \frac{\frac{4}{13 \cdot 51}}{\frac{51}{(13)(51)}} \approx 0.0784.$$

14.  Using the following tree diagram, we see that

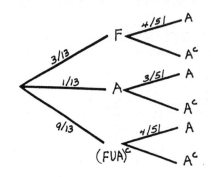

$$P(F|A) = \frac{(\frac{3}{13})(\frac{4}{51})}{(\frac{3}{13})(\frac{4}{51}) + (\frac{1}{13})(\frac{3}{51}) + (\frac{9}{13})(\frac{4}{51})} = \frac{12}{51} \approx 0.2353.$$

15.  The probabilities associated with this experiment are represented in the following tree diagram.

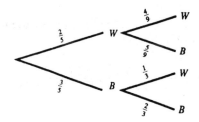

16.  Referring to the tree diagram in Exercise 15, we see that the probability that the transferred ball was white given that the second ball drawn was white is

$$P(W|W) = \frac{(\frac{2}{5})(\frac{4}{9})}{(\frac{2}{5})(\frac{4}{9}) + (\frac{3}{5})(\frac{1}{3})} = \frac{8}{17}.$$

17.  Referring to the tree diagram in Exercise 15, we see that the probability that the transferred ball was black given that the second ball was white is

$$P(B|W) = \frac{(\frac{3}{5})(\frac{1}{3})}{(\frac{2}{5})(\frac{4}{9}) + (\frac{3}{5})(\frac{1}{3})} = \frac{9}{17}.$$

18.  Referring to the tree diagram in Exercise 15, we see that the probability that the transferred ball was black given that the

second ball was black is

$$P(B|B) \;=\; \frac{\left(\frac{3}{5}\right)\left(\frac{2}{3}\right)}{\left(\frac{2}{5}\right)\left(\frac{5}{9}\right) + \left(\frac{3}{5}\right)\left(\frac{2}{3}\right)} \;=\; \frac{9}{14}.$$

19. Let D denote the event that a senator selected at random is a Democrat, R denote the event that a senator selected at random is a Republican, and M the event that a senator has served in the military. From the following tree diagram

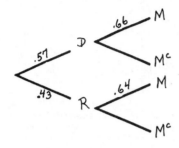

we see that the probability that a senator selected at random who has served in the military is a Republican is

$$P(R|M) \;=\; \frac{P(R)P(M|R)}{P(M)} \;=\; \frac{(0.64)(0.43)}{(0.66)(0.57) + (0.64)(0.43)}$$

$$= 0.4225.$$

20. a. $P(D) = P(I) \cdot P(D|I) + P(II) \cdot P(D|II) + P(III) \cdot P(D|III)$
$\qquad + P(IV) \cdot P(D|IV)$

$\qquad = (0.15)(0.04) + (0.3)(0.02) + (0.35)(0.02)$
$\qquad + (0.2)(0.03)$

$\qquad = 0.025.$

b. $P(D|I) = \dfrac{P(I)P(D|I)}{P(D)} = \dfrac{(0.15)(0.04)}{0.025} = 0.24.$

c. $P(D|II) = \dfrac{P(II)P(D|II)}{P(D)} = \dfrac{(0.3)(0.02)}{0.025} = 0.24.$

21. Let $H_2$ denote the event that the coin tossed is the two-headed coin, $H_B$ denote the event that the coin tossed is the biased coin, and $H_F$ denote the event that the coin tossed is the fair coin.

Referring to the following tree diagram, we see that

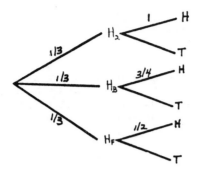

a.  $P(H) = (\frac{1}{3})(1) + (\frac{1}{3})(\frac{3}{4}) + (\frac{1}{3})(\frac{1}{2}) = \frac{1}{3} + \frac{1}{4} + \frac{1}{6} = \frac{9}{12} = \frac{3}{4}.$

b.  $P(H_F|H) = \dfrac{(\frac{1}{3})(\frac{1}{2})}{(\frac{3}{4})} = \dfrac{2}{9}.$

22.  Refer to the following tree diagram:

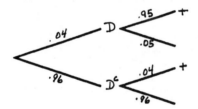

a.  $P(D|+) = \dfrac{(0.04)(0.95)}{(0.04)(0.95) + (0.96)(0.04)}$

   $\approx 0.497.$

b. From part (a), we know that 49.7% of those who test positive have the disease; whereas, 50.3% of those who test positive do not have the disease. Using this information, we construct the second tree diagram. Then,

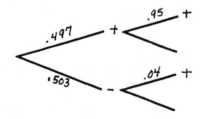

Second test for those who test positive on the 1st test.

$$P(D|++) = \frac{(0.497)(0.95)}{(0.497)(0.95) + (0.503)(0.04)}$$

$$\approx 0.959.$$

23. Let D denote the event that the person has the disease, and let Y denote the event that the test is positive. Referring to the following tree diagram, we see that the required probability is

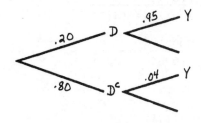

$$P(D|Y) = \frac{P(D) \cdot P(Y|D)}{P(D) \cdot P(Y|D) + P(D^c) \cdot P(Y|D^c)}$$

$$= \frac{(0.2)(0.95)}{(0.2)(0.95) + (0.8)(0.04)}$$

$$\approx 0.856.$$

24. $$P(III|D) = \frac{(0.30)(0.02)}{(0.35)(0.015) + (0.35)(0.01) + (0.30)(0.02)}$$

$$= \frac{0.006}{0.01475} \approx 0.407.$$

25. Let x denote the age of an insured driver, and let A denote the event that an insured driver is in an accident. Using the tree diagram we find,

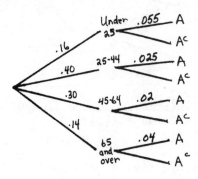

a. $P(A) = (0.16)(0.055) + (0.4)(0.025) + (0.3)(0.02)$
$+ (0.14)(0.04)$

$\approx 0.03.$

b. $P(x < 25 | A) = \dfrac{(0.16)(0.055)}{(0.03)}$

$\approx 0.29.$

26. a. $P(I | S) = \dfrac{P(I) \bullet P(S | I)}{P(I) \bullet P(S | I) + P(II) \bullet P(S | II)}$

$= \dfrac{(0.64)(0.0002)}{(0.64)(0.002) + (0.36)(0.005)}$

$\approx 0.42.$

b. $P(II | S) = \dfrac{P(II) \bullet P(S | II)}{P(I) \bullet P(S | I) + P(II) \bullet P(S | II)}$

$= \dfrac{(0.36)(0.005)}{(0.64)(0.002) + (0.36)(0.005)}$

$\approx 0.58.$

27. Let E, F, and G denote the events that the child selected at random is 12 years old, 13 years old, or 14 years old, respectively; and let $C^c$ denote the event that the child does not have a cavity. Using the following tree diagram, we see that

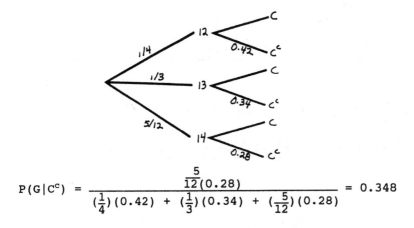

$$P(G | C^c) = \dfrac{\frac{5}{12}(0.28)}{(\frac{1}{4})(0.42) + (\frac{1}{3})(0.34) + (\frac{5}{12})(0.28)} = 0.348$$

28. Let D, R, and I denote the events that a voter selected at random

was a registered Democrat, Republican, or Independent, respectively; and let V denote the voters who voted for the incumbent senator. Using the following tree diagram

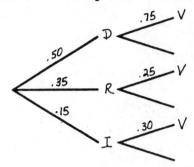

we see that the probability that a randomly selected voter who voted for the incumbent was a registered Republican is

$$P(R|V) = \frac{(0.35)(0.25)}{(0.5)(0.75) + (0.35)(0.25) + (0.15)(0.30)}$$

$$\approx 0.1724$$

29. Let M and F denote the events that a person arrested for crime in 1988 was male or female, respectively; and let U denote the event that the person was under the age of 18. Using the following tree diagram, we have

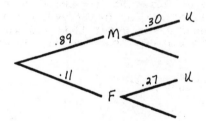

a. $P(U) = (0.89)(0.30) + (0.11)(0.27) = 0.2967$.

b. $P(F|U) = \frac{(0.11)(0.27)}{(0.89)(0.30) + (0.11)(0.27)} = 0.1001$.

30. Using the tree diagram shown below, we see that

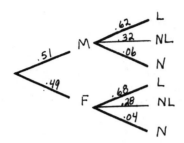

    a. $P(F|L) = \dfrac{(0.49)(0.68)}{(0.51)(0.62) + (0.49)(0.68)} = 0.513$

    b. $P(F|N) = \dfrac{(0.49)(0.04)}{(0.51)(0.06) + (0.49)(0.04)} = 0.390$

31. Let I and II denote a customer who purchased the drug in capsule or tablet form, respectively; and let E denote a customer in Group I and II who purchased the extra-strength dosage of the drug. Then using the following tree diagram, we see that

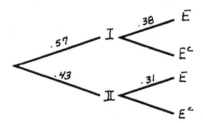

$$P(I|E) = \dfrac{(0.57)(0.38)}{(0.57)(0.38) + (0.43)(0.31)} = 0.619.$$

32. Using the tree diagram shown below, we find

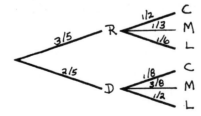

$$P(D|C) = \frac{P(D) \cdot P(C|D)}{P(R) \cdot P(C|R) + P(D) \cdot P(C|D)}$$

$$= \frac{(\frac{2}{5})(\frac{1}{8})}{(\frac{3}{5})(\frac{1}{2}) + (\frac{2}{5})(\frac{1}{8})} = 0.143$$

33. Let D and N denote the events that a employee was placed by Ms. Dwyer or Ms. Newberg, respectively; and let S denote the event that the employee  placed by one of these women was satisfactory. Using the following tree diagram, we see that

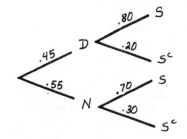

$$P(N|S^c) = \frac{(0.55)(0.3)}{(0.45)(0.2) + (0.55)(0.3)} = 0.647.$$

34. Referring to the following tree diagram, we see that

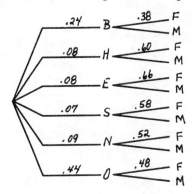

a. P(F) = (0.24)(0.38) + (0.08)(0.60) + (0.08)(0.66)
         + (0.07)(0.58) + (0.09)(0.52) + (0.44)(0.48)

   = 0.4906.

b. P(M|B) = 0.62.

c. $P(B|F) = \frac{(0.24)(0.38)}{(0.4906)} \approx 0.186.$

35. Using the tree diagram shown below, we see that

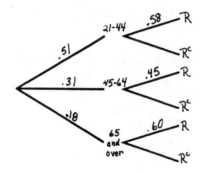

$$P(S_2|S) = \frac{(0.95)(0.8)}{(0.95)(0.8) + (0.2)(0.3)}$$

$$\approx 0.93.$$

36. Let x denote the age of an adult selected at random from the population, and let R denote the event that the adult is a renter. Then

a. $P(R) = (0.51)(0.58) + (0.31)(0.45) + (0.18)(0.60)$

$$\approx 0.543.$$

b. $P(21 \leq x \leq 44|R) = \dfrac{(0.51)(0.58)}{0.543}$

$$\approx 0.545.$$

c. $P(E) = 1 - P(21 \leq x \leq 44|R)$

$$= 1 - 0.545$$

$$= 0.455.$$

# CHAPTER 7, REVIEW EXERCISES, page 437

1.  a. $P(E \cap F) = 0$ since E and F are mutually exclusive.

    b. $P(E \cup F) = P(E) + P(F) - P(E \cap F) = 0.4 + 0.2 = 0.6.$

    c. $P(E^c) = 1 - P(E) = 1 - 0.4 = 0.6.$

    d. $P(E^c \cap F^c) = P(E \cup F)^c = 1 - P(E \cup F) = 1 - 0.6 = 0.4.$

    e. $P(E^c \cup F^c) = P(E \cap F)^c = 1 - P(E \cap F) = 1 - 0 = 1.$

2.  a. $P(E \cup F) = 0.3 + 0.2 - 0.15 = 0.35.$

    b. $P(E^c \cap F^c) = P(E \cup F)^c = 1 - P(E \cup F) = 1 - 0.35 = 0.65.$

    c. $P(E^c \cap F) = P(F) - P(E \cap F) = 0.2 - 0.15 = 0.05.$

3.  a. The probability of the number being even is

    $$P(2) + P(4) + P(6) = 0.12 + 0.18 + 0.19 = 0.49.$$

    b. The probability that the number is either a 1 or a 6 is

    $$P(1) + P(6) = 0.20 + 0.19 = 0.39.$$

    c. The probability that the number is less than 4 is

    $$P(1) + P(2) + P(3) = 0.20 + 0.12 + 0.16 = 0.48.$$

4.  The required probability is given by

    $$P(R \cap B) + P(B \cap R) = \left(\frac{6}{15}\right)\left(\frac{5}{14}\right) + \left(\frac{5}{15}\right)\left(\frac{6}{14}\right)$$
    $$= \frac{2}{7}.$$

5.  Let A denote the event that a video-game cartridge has an audio defect and let V denote the event that a video-game cartridge has a video defect. Then using the following Venn diagram, we have

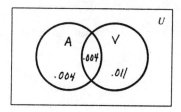

a. the probability that a cartridge purchased by a customer will have a video or audio defect is

$$P(A \cup V) = P(A \cap V^c) + P(V \cap A^c) + P(A \cap V)$$

$$= 0.004 + 0.004 + 0.011 = 0.019.$$

b. the probability that a cartridge purchased by a customer will have not have a video or audio defect is

$$P(A \cup V)^c = 1 - P(A \cup V) = 1 - 0.019 = 0.981.$$

6.  $$P(E|F) = \frac{P(E \cap F)}{P(F)} = \frac{P(E) + P(F) - P(E \cup F)}{P(F)}$$

$$= \frac{0.35 + 0.55 - 0.70}{0.55} = 0.364.$$

7.  $P(A \cap E) = (0.3)(0.6) = 0.18.$

8.  $P(B \cap E) = (0.5)(0.5) = 0.25.$

9.  $P(C \cap E) = (0.2)(0.3) = 0.06.$

10. $P(A|E) = \frac{0.18}{0.49} \approx 0.367.$

11. $P(E) = 0.18 + 0.25 + 0.06 = 0.49$

12. a. $P(A) = 1 - P(A^c) = 1 - \frac{1}{8} = \frac{7}{8}.$

b. $P(B) = 1 - P(B^c) = 1 - \frac{1}{8} = \frac{7}{8}.$

c. $P(A \cap B) = \frac{7}{8}$; $P(A) \cdot P(B) = \frac{7}{8} \cdot \frac{7}{8} = \frac{49}{64}.$

Since $P(A \cap B) \neq P(A) \cdot P(B)$, they are not independent events.

13. a. The probability that none of the pens in the sample are defective is

$$\frac{C(18,3)}{C(20,3)} = \frac{\frac{18!}{15!3!}}{\frac{20!}{17!3!}} = \frac{18!}{15!} \cdot \frac{17!}{20!} = \frac{68}{95} \approx 0.7159.$$

Therefore, the probability that at least one is defective is given by

$$1 - 0.71579 \approx 0.284.$$

b. The probability that two are defective is given by

$$\frac{C(2,2) \cdot C(18,1)}{C(20,3)} = \frac{18}{\frac{20!}{17!3!}} = \frac{6}{380} \approx 0.0158.$$

Therefore, the probability that no more than 1 is defective is given by

$$1 - \frac{6}{380} = \frac{374}{380} \approx 0.984.$$

14.  $P(E) = \dfrac{7 \cdot 6 \cdot 5 \cdot 4 \cdot 3}{7^5} \approx 0.150.$

15.  Let E denote the event that the sum of the numbers is 8 and let D denote the event that the numbers appearing on the face of the two dice are different. Then

$$P(E|D) = \frac{P(E \cap D)}{P(D)} = \frac{4}{30} = \frac{2}{15}.$$

16.  The probability that all three cards are aces is

$$\frac{C(4,3)}{C(52,3)} = 0.00018.$$

17.  The probability that all three cards are face cards is

$$\frac{C(12,3)}{C(52,3)} = 0.00995.$$

18.  Referring to the tree diagram at the right, we see that the required probability is

$$\left(\tfrac{1}{2}\right)\left(\tfrac{25}{51}\right)\left(\tfrac{24}{50}\right) + \left(\tfrac{1}{2}\right)\left(\tfrac{26}{51}\right)\left(\tfrac{25}{50}\right) = \frac{1250}{5100}$$

$$= 0.2451.$$

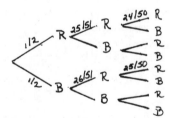

19.  The probability that the second card is black, given that the first card was red is

$$\frac{26}{51} = 0.510.$$

20. Referring to the tree diagram at the right, we see that the probability that the second card is a club, given that the first card was black is

$$(\tfrac{1}{2})(\tfrac{12}{51}) + (\tfrac{1}{2})(\tfrac{13}{51}) = 0.2451.$$

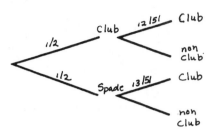

21. Let M denote the event that an employee at the insurance company is a male and let F denote the event that an employee at the insurance company is on flex time. Then

$$P(M|F) = \dfrac{\dfrac{320}{600} \cdot \dfrac{160}{320}}{\dfrac{320}{600} \cdot \dfrac{160}{320} + \dfrac{280}{600} \cdot \dfrac{190}{280}}$$

$$= 0.4571.$$

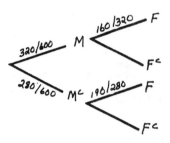

22. Referring to the following tree diagram,

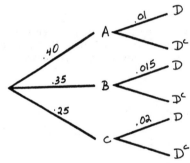

we see that

$$P(B|D) = \dfrac{(0.35)(0.015)}{(0.40)(0.01) + (0.35)(0.015) + (0.25)(0.02)}$$

$$= \dfrac{(0.35)(0.015)}{0.01425}$$

$$\approx 0.368.$$

23. Let E denote the event that an applicant selected at random is eligible for admission, and let Pa denote the event that an applicant selected at random passes the admission exam. Using the following tree diagram

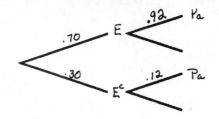

we see that

a.   P(Pa) = (0.70)(0.92) + (0.30)(0.12) = 0.68.

b.   $P(E^c|Pa) = \dfrac{(0.30)(0.12)}{(0.70)(0.92) + (0.30)(0.12)} = 0.053.$

## GROUP DISCUSSION QUESTIONS

**Page 374**

1.   a.   Since E and F are complementary events, $E \cap F = \phi$ and so E and F are mutually exclusive.

b.   E and F need not be complementary. For example, let $U = \{1,2,3,4,5\}$, $E = \{1,2\}$, and $F = \{4,5\}$. Then E and F are not complementary, but $E \cap F = \phi$ and so they are mutually exclusive.

**Page 377**

Answers to this question will vary.

**Page 384**

1.   a. Cast the die a large number of times (the larger the better) and record the outcome after each throw. Compute the relative frequencies as follows: Suppose the number 1 lands $m_1$ times, the number 2 lands $m_2$ times, ..., and the number 6 lands $m_6$ times. Let $n = m_1 + m_2 + m_n$, be the total number of tosses. Then the relative frequencies are $m_1/n$, $m_2/n$, ..., $m_6/n$. If the die is biased, then not all of the relative frequencies will approach 1/6.

b.   Assuming n is reasonably large, we can assign the probabilities

$$P(1) = \frac{m_1}{n}, \ P(2) = \frac{m_2}{n}, \ \dots, \ P(6) = \frac{m_6}{n}$$

1. $P(E \cup F \cup G) = \dfrac{n(E \cup F \cup G)}{n(S)}$

   $= \dfrac{1}{n(S)} [n(E) + n(F) + n(G) - n(E \cap F) - n(E \cap G) - n(F \cap G)$
   $\qquad + n(E \cap F \cap G)]$

   $= \dfrac{n(E)}{n(S)} + \dfrac{n(F)}{n(S)} + \dfrac{n(G)}{n(S)} + \cdots + \dfrac{n(E \cap F \cap G)}{n(S)}$

   $= P(E) + P(F) + P(E) - P(E \cap F) - P(E \cap G) - P(F \cap G)$
   $\qquad + P(E \cap F \cap G)$

   If E, F, and G are mutually exclusive, then

   $P(E \cup F \cup G) = P(E) + P(F) + P(E) - P(E \cap F) - P(E \cap G)$
   $\qquad\qquad\qquad - P(F \cap G).$

## Page 406

1. In the first episode, Mr. Carson was illustrating the probability that two people in the audience had **one specific date** as their birthday; i.e. the probability that two people in the audience were born on January 1.

   To illustrate the point he was trying to make, he would have to ask each person in the audience to write down their birthday-- and from this list he would then have to find the number of people that have the same birthday; i.e. the probability that two people in the audience were born on the same day.

## Page 413

1. a. Since we are given that A has occurred, we use the reduced sample space consisting of the elements of A, of which there are $n(A) = m$. Therefore, the relative frequency of the event B given the event A is equal to

   $$\dfrac{\text{the number of outcomes favorable to A and B}}{\text{the number of outcomes in A}} = \dfrac{n(A \cap B)}{n(A)} = \dfrac{\ell}{m}.$$

   b. The right-hand side of the equation is equal to

   $$\dfrac{\ell}{n} \cdot \dfrac{n}{m} = \dfrac{\ell}{m}$$

   which is the left-hand side.

   c. As more and more trials are carried out, the relative

frequencies $\frac{\ell}{m}$ approach P(B|A), while the values of $\frac{\ell}{n}$ approach P(A ∩ B) and the values of $\frac{m}{n}$ approach P(A).

**Page 415**

1.  a.  The probability of the three events A, B, and C occurring simultaneously is equal to the product of the probability of A and the probability of B given A and the probability of C given that A and B occurred simultaneously.

b. Let A denote the event that the first card drawn is an ace, B the event that the second card drawn is an ace, and C the event that the third card drawn is an ace. Then the required probability is given by

$$P(A \cap B \cap C) = P(A)P(B|A)P(C|A \cap B)$$

$$= (\tfrac{4}{52})(\tfrac{3}{51})(\tfrac{2}{50}) \approx 0.000181.$$

**Page 420**

1.  Yes. To prove the assertion, we compute

$$P(E^c \cap F^c) = P[(E \cup F)^c] \qquad \text{(By De Morgans' Law)}$$

$$= 1 - P(E \cup F)$$

$$= 1 - [P(E) + P(F) - P(E \cap F)] \qquad \text{(Property 4, page 393)}$$

$$= 1 - P(E) - P(F) + P(E \cap F)$$

$$= 1 - P(E) - P(F) + P(E) \bullet P(F) \qquad \text{(E and F are independent.)}$$

$$= [1 - P(E)] - P(F)[1 - P(E)]$$

$$= [1 - P(F)][1 - P(E)]$$

$$= P(F^c)P(E^c) = P(E^c) \bullet P(F^c)$$

and the prove is complete.

7  *Probability*

# CHAPTER 8

## EXERCISES 8.1, page 448

1. a. See part (b).
   b.

   c. {GGG}

   | Outcome | GGG | GGR | GRG | RGG |
   |---------|-----|-----|-----|-----|
   | Value   | 3   | 2   | 2   | 2   |

   | Outcome | GRR | RGR | RRG | RRR |
   |---------|-----|-----|-----|-----|
   | Value   | 1   | 1   | 1   | 0   |

2. a. See part (b).
   b.

   | Outcome | HHHH | HHHT | HHTH | HHTT | HTHH | HTHT | HTTH | HTTT |
   |---------|------|------|------|------|------|------|------|------|
   | Value   | 0    | 1    | 1    | 2    | 1    | 2    | 2    | 3    |

   | Outcome | THHH | THHT | THTH | THTT | TTHH | TTHT | TTTH | TTTT |
   |---------|------|------|------|------|------|------|------|------|
   | Value   | 1    | 2    | 2    | 3    | 2    | 3    | 3    | 4    |

   c. E = {HHTT, HTHT, HTTH, THHT, THTH, TTHH}

3. X may assume the values in the set S = {1,2,3,...}.

4. X may assume the values in the set S = {1, 2, ..., 49}.

5. The event that the sum of the dice is 7 is

   $$E = \{(1,6),(2,5),(3,4),(4,3),(5,2),(6,1)\}$$

   and $P(E) = \frac{6}{36} = \frac{1}{6}$.

6.   $P(X = 2) = \dfrac{C(4,2)}{C(52,2)} = \dfrac{6}{1326} = 0.00452.$

7.   X may assume the value of any positive integer. The random variable is infinite discrete.

8.   {0,1,2,3,4,5,6,7,8}; The random variable is finite discrete.

9.   {d|d ≥ 0}. The random variable is continuous.

10.  X may assume the value of any real number between 0 and 24 inclusive. The random variable is continuous.

11.  X may assume the value of any positive integer. The random variable is infinite discrete.

12.  {0,1,2,3,4}. The random variable is finite discrete.

13.  a. P(X = −10) = 0.20

     b. P(X ≥ 5) = 0.1 + 0.25 + 0.1 + 0.15 = 0.60

     c. P(−5 ≤ X ≤ 5) = 0.15 + 0.05 + 0.1 = 0.30

     d. P(X ≤ 20) = 0.20 + 0.15 + 0.05 + 0.1 + 0.25 + 0.1 + 0.15 = 1

14.  a. P(X ≤ 0) = 0.17 + 0.13 + 0.33 + 0.16 = 0.79

     b. P(X ≤ −3) = 0.17 + 0.13 = 0.30

     c. P(−2 ≤ X ≤ 2) = 0.33 + 0.16 + 0.11 = 0.60.

15.

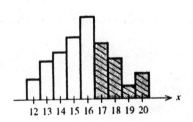

16.  The height should be 0.35.

17. a.

| x | 1 | 2 | 3 | 4 | 5 | 6 |
|---|---|---|---|---|---|---|
| P(X = x) | $\frac{1}{6}$ | $\frac{1}{6}$ | $\frac{1}{6}$ | $\frac{1}{6}$ | $\frac{1}{6}$ | $\frac{1}{6}$ |

| y | 1 | 2 | 3 | 4 | 5 | 6 |
|---|---|---|---|---|---|---|
| P(Y = y) | $\frac{1}{6}$ | $\frac{1}{6}$ | $\frac{1}{6}$ | $\frac{1}{6}$ | $\frac{1}{6}$ | $\frac{1}{6}$ |

b.

| x + y | 2 | 3 | 4 | 5 | 6 | 7 | 8 | 9 | 10 | 11 | 12 |
|---|---|---|---|---|---|---|---|---|---|---|---|
| P(X + Y = x + y) | $\frac{1}{36}$ | $\frac{2}{36}$ | $\frac{3}{36}$ | $\frac{4}{36}$ | $\frac{5}{36}$ | $\frac{6}{36}$ | $\frac{5}{36}$ | $\frac{4}{36}$ | $\frac{3}{36}$ | $\frac{2}{36}$ | $\frac{1}{36}$ |

18. a.

| x | 2 | 3 | 4 | 5 | 6 | 7 | 8 |
|---|---|---|---|---|---|---|---|
| P(X = x) | .35 | .20 | .245 | .125 | .066 | .01 | .004 |

b.

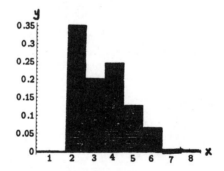

19. a.

| x | 0 | 1 | 2 | 3 | 4 | 5 |
|---|---|---|---|---|---|---|
| P(X = x) | .017 | .067 | .033 | .117 | .233 | .133 |

| x | 6 | 7 | 8 | 9 | 10 |
|---|---|---|---|---|---|
| P(X = x) | .167 | .1 | .05 | .067 | .017 |

b.

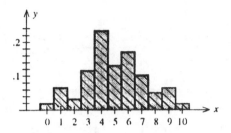

20.

| x | 6 | 6.25 | 6.55 | 6.56 | 6.58 | 6.6 | 6.65 | 6.85 |
|---|---|------|------|------|------|-----|------|------|
| P(X = x) | $\frac{1}{30}$ | $\frac{7}{30}$ | $\frac{7}{30}$ | $\frac{1}{30}$ | $\frac{1}{30}$ | $\frac{8}{30}$ | $\frac{3}{30}$ | $\frac{2}{30}$ |

21.

| x | 1 | 2 | 3 | 4 | 5 |
|---|---|---|---|---|---|
| P(X = x) | .007 | .029 | .021 | .079 | .164 |

| x | 6 | 7 | 8 | 9 | 10 |
|---|---|---|---|---|---|
| P(X = x) | .15 | .20 | .207 | .114 | .029 |

## USING TECHNOLOGY EXERCISES, page 451

1.                                          2.

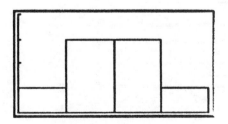     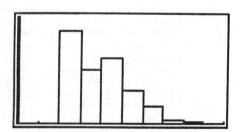

**3.**

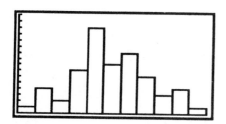

**4.**

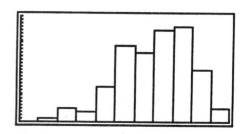

## EXERCISES 8.2, page 463

1.  a. The student's grade-point average is given by
$$\frac{(2)(4)(3) + (3)(3)(3) + (4)(2)(3) + (1)(1)(3)}{(10)(3)}$$

or 2.6.

b.

| x | 0 | 1 | 2 | 3 | 4 |
|---|---|---|---|---|---|
| P(X = x) | 0 | 0.1 | 0.4 | 0.3 | 0.2 |

$$E(X) = 1(0.1) + 2(0.4) + 3(0.3) + 4(0.2)$$
$$= 2.6.$$

2.  a. The average number of gallons of milk consumed per week is
$$\frac{3(200) + 4(205) + 6(210) + 5(215) + 4(220) + 3(225) + 2(230) + 2(235) + 240}{30}$$
$$= 216.$$

b.

| x | 200 | 205 | 210 | 215 | 220 |
|---|---|---|---|---|---|
| P(X = x) | .1 | .133 | .2 | .167 | .133 |

| x | 225 | 230 | 235 | 240 |
|---|---|---|---|---|
| P(X = x) | .1 | .067 | .067 | .033 |

c. $E(X) = 0.1(200) + 0.133(205) + 0.2(210) + 0.167(215) + 0.133(220)$
$\quad\quad + (0.1)(225) + (.067)(230) + (.067)(235) + (.033)(240)$

$\quad = 216.$

3.  $E(X) = -5(0.12) + -1(0.16) + 0(0.28) + 1(0.22) + 5(0.12) + 8(0.1)$

$\quad\quad = 0.86.$

4.  $E(X) = (0)(\frac{1}{8}) + (1)(\frac{1}{4}) + (2)(\frac{3}{16}) + (3)(\frac{1}{4}) + (4)(\frac{1}{16}) + (5)(\frac{1}{8})$

$\quad\quad = \frac{1}{4} + \frac{3}{8} + \frac{3}{4} + \frac{1}{4} + \frac{5}{8} = \frac{18}{8} = \frac{9}{4}$, or $2.25$.

5.  $E(X) = 0(0.07) + 25(0.12) + 50(0.17) + 75(0.14) + 100(0.28)$
$\quad\quad + 125(0.18) + 150(0.04)$

$\quad\quad = 78.5,$

or \$78.50.

6.  The outcomes and random values associated with each outcome are listed below.

| Outcome | GGGG | GGGB | GGBG | GGBB | GBGG | GBGB | GBBG | GBBB |
|---------|------|------|------|------|------|------|------|------|
| Value   | 0    | 1    | 1    | 2    | 1    | 2    | 2    | 3    |

| Outcome | BGGG | BGGB | BGBG | BGBB | BBGG | BBGB | BBBG | BBBB |
|---------|------|------|------|------|------|------|------|------|
| Value   | 1    | 2    | 2    | 3    | 2    | 3    | 3    | 4    |

Then $E(X) = 0(\frac{1}{16}) + 1(\frac{4}{16}) + 2(\frac{6}{16}) + 3(\frac{4}{16}) + 4(\frac{1}{16}) = \frac{32}{16} = 2.$

7.  A customer entering the store is expected to buy

$E(X) = (0)(0.42) + (1)(0.36) + (2)(0.14) + (3)(0.05) + (4)(0.03)$

$\quad\quad = 0.91,$

or 0.91 videocassettes.

8.  The probability that there are no defective batteries in the sample is

$$\frac{C(8,3)}{C(10,3)} = \frac{7}{15}.$$

The probability that there is one defective battery in the sample is

$$\frac{C(8,2)C(2,1)}{C(10,3)} = \frac{7}{15}.$$

The probability that there are two defective batteries in the sample is

$$\frac{C(8,1)C(2,2)}{C(10,3)} = \frac{1}{15}.$$

Therefore, the expected number of defective batteries is

$$0\left(\frac{7}{15}\right) + 1\left(\frac{7}{15}\right) + 2\left(\frac{1}{15}\right) = 0.6$$

9.  The expected number of accidents is given by

$$E(X) = (0)(0.935) + (1)(0.03) + (2)(0.02) + (3)(0.01) + (4)(0.005)$$

$$= 0.12.$$

10.  The owner should expect to sell

$$E(X) = (10)(0.05) + (11)(0.15) + (12)(0.25) + (13)(0.30)$$

$$+ (14)(0.20) + (15)(0.05)$$

$$= 12.6,$$

that is, 12.6 issues of the magazine per week.

11.  The expected number of machines that will break down on a given day is given by

$$E(X) = (0)(0.43) + (1)(0.19) + (2)(0.12) + (3)(0.09) + (4)(0.04)$$
$$+ (5)(0.03) + (6)(0.03) + (7)(0.02) + (8)(0.05)$$

$$= 1.73.$$

12.  The expected net earnings of a person who buys one ticket are

$$-1(0.997) + 24(0.002) + 99(0.0006) + 499(0.0002) + 1999(0.0002)$$

$$= -0.39,$$

or a loss of $0.39 per ticket.

13.  The expected gain of the insurance company is given by

$$E(X) = 0.96P - (20,000 - P)(0.04),$$

where P is the amount the man can expect to pay. We want $E(X) = 0$, that is,

$$P - (0.04)(20,000) = 0.$$

Solving for P, we find

$$P = 800$$

so the minimum he can expect to pay is $800.

14. The expected gain of the insurance company is given by

$$E(X) = 0.992(130) - (9870)(0.008) = 50,$$

or $50.

15. The expected gain of the insurance company is given by

$$E(X) = 0.9935P - (25,000 - P)0.0065 \geq 0,$$

where P is the amount that Mr. Taylor can expect to pay. Since $E(X) \geq 0$,

$$P - 0.0065(25,000) \geq 0.$$

Solving for P, we find

$$P \geq 162.50$$

so the minimum Mr. Taylor can expect to pay is $162.50.

16. The company's expected gross profit is given by

$$E(X) = (0.3)(80,000) + (0.60)(75,000) + (0.10)(70,000) - 64,000$$

$$= 12,000, \text{ or } \$12,000.$$

17. The expected value of the first project is

$$(0.7)(180,000) + (0.3)(150,000) = 171,000, \text{ or } \$171,000$$

and the expected value of the second project is

$$(0.6)(220,000) + (0.4)(80,000) = 164,000, \text{ or } \$164,000.$$

He should choose the first project if he wants to maximize his expected profits.

18. City A: $E(X) = (10,000,000)(0.2) - 250,000 = 1,750,000$,

or $1.75 million.

City B: $E(X) = (7,000,000)(0.3) - 200,000 = 1,900,000$,

or $1.9 million.

We see that the company should bid for the rights in city B.

19. a. DAHL MOTORS

$$E(X) = 5(0.05) + 6(0.09) + 7(0.14) + 8(0.24) + 9(0.18)$$
$$+ 10(0.14) + 11(0.11) + 12(0.05) = 8.52.$$

FARTHINGTON AUTO SALES

$$E(X) = 5(0.08) + 6(0.21) + 7(0.31) + 8(0.24) + 9(0.10)$$
$$+ 10(0.06)$$

$$= 7.25.$$

b. The expected weekly profit from Dahl Motors is

$$8.52(362) = 3084.24,$$

or \$3084.24.

The expected weekly profit from Farthington Auto Sales is

$$7.25(436)$$

or \$3161.

We conclude that Mr. Hunt should purchase Farthington Auto Sales.

20. The expected number of houses sold per year at company A is given by

$$E(X) = (12)(.02) + (13)(.03) + (14)(.05) + (15)(.07) + (16)(.07)$$
$$+ (17)(.16) + (18)(.17) + (19)(.13) + (20)(.11)$$
$$+ (21)(.09) + (22)(.06) + (23)(.03) + (24)(.01)$$

$$= 18.09.$$

The expected number of houses sold per year at company B is given by

$$E(X) = (6)(.01) + (7)(.04) + (8)(.07) + (9)(.06) + (10)(.11)$$
$$+ (11)(.12) + (12)(.19) + (13)(.17) + (14)(.13)$$
$$+ (15)(.04) + (16)(.03) + (17)(.02) + (18)(.01)$$

$$= 11.77.$$

Then, Ms. Leonard's expected commission at company A is given by

$$(0.03)(104,000)(18.09) = 56,440.80,$$

or \$56,440.80.

Her expected commission at company B is given by

$$(0.03)(177,000)(11.77) = 62,498.70,$$

or $62.498.70. Based on these expectations, she should accept the job offer with company B.

21.  a. The odds that it will rain tomorrow are 3 to 7.

     b. The odds that it will not rain tomorrow are 7 to 3.

22.  The expected value of the winnings on a $1 bet placed on a split is

$$E(X) = 17\frac{2}{38} + (-1)\frac{36}{38} = -0.0526,$$

or a loss of 5.3 cents.

23.  The expected value of the player's winnings are given by

$$E(X) = (1)(\frac{18}{38}) + (-1)(\frac{18}{38}) + (-2)(\frac{2}{38})$$

$$= -\frac{4}{38}$$

$$\approx -0.105,$$

or a loss of $10\frac{1}{2}$ cents.

24.  The expected value of a player's winnings are

$$1(\frac{18}{37}) + (-1)(\frac{19}{37}) = -\frac{1}{37} = -0.027,$$

or a loss of 2.7 cents per bet.

25.  The odds in favor of E occurring are

$$\frac{P(E)}{P(E^c)} = \frac{0.8}{0.2},$$

or 4 to 1.

The odds against E occurring are 1 to 4.

26.  The odds in favor of E occurring are

$$\frac{P(E)}{P(E^c)} = \frac{0.4}{0.6},$$

or 2 to 3.

The odds against E occurring are 3 to 2.

27.  The probability of E occurring is given by

$$P(E) = \frac{9}{9 + 7} = \frac{9}{16} \approx 0.5625.$$

28. The probability of E not occurring is given by
$$P(E) = \frac{2}{3 + 2} = \frac{2}{5} \approx 0.4.$$

29. The probability that Joan will make the sale is given by
$$P(E) = \frac{8}{8 + 5} = \frac{8}{13} \approx 0.6154.$$

30. The probability that she will win her match is
$$P(E) = \frac{7}{7 + 5} = \frac{7}{12} = 0.5833.$$

31. The probability that the boxer will win the match is given by
$$P(E) = \frac{4}{3 + 4} = \frac{4}{7} \approx 0.5714.$$

32. The probability that the business deal will not go through is
$$P(E) = \frac{5}{5 + 9} = \frac{5}{14} \approx 0.3571.$$

33. a. $E(cX) = (cx_1)p_1 + (cx_2)p_2 + \cdots + (cx_n)p_n$

$\qquad = c(x_1p_1 + x_2p_2 + \cdots + x_np_n)$

$\qquad = cE(X).$

b. The expected loss is $(300)(-\frac{2}{38}) = -15.79$, or a loss of \$15.79.

34. a. The mean is given by
$$\frac{40 + 45 + 2(50) + 55 + 2(60) + 2(75) + 2(80) + 4(85) + 2(90) + 2(95) + 100}{20}$$

$\qquad = 74.$

The mode is 85 (the value that appears most frequently).

The median is 80 (the middle value).

b. The mode is the least representative of this set of test scores.

35. The mean-wage rate is given by

$$(\tfrac{60}{450})(10.70) + (\tfrac{90}{450})(10.80) + (\tfrac{75}{450})(10.90) + (\tfrac{120}{450})(11.00)$$

$$+ (\tfrac{60}{450})(11.10) + (\tfrac{45}{450})(11.20)$$

$$= 10.94$$

or $10.94.

The mode is $11.00, and the median is

$$\frac{10.90 + 11.00}{2} = 10.95,$$

or $10.95.

## EXERCISES 8.3, page 474

1. $\mu = (1)(0.4) + (2)(0.3) + 3(0.2) + (4)(0.1) = 2.$

Var $(X) = (0.4)(1 - 2)^2 + (0.3)(2 - 2)^2 + (0.2)(3 - 2)^2 + (0.1)(4 - 2)^2$

$$= 0.4 + 0 + 0.2 + 0.4 = 1$$

$$\sigma = \sqrt{1} = 1.$$

2. $\mu = (-4)(0.1) + (-2)(0.2) + 0(0.3) + (2)(0.1) + (4)(0.3) = 0.6.$

Var $(X) = (0.1)(-4 - 0.6)^2 + (0.2)(-2 - 0.6)^2 + (0.3)(0 - 0.6)^2$

$$+ (0.1)(2 - 0.6)^2 + (0.3)(4 - 0.6)^2$$

$$= 7.24$$

$$\sigma = \sqrt{7.24} \approx 2.69.$$

3. $\mu = -2(\tfrac{1}{16}) + -1(\tfrac{4}{16}) + 0(\tfrac{6}{16}) + 1(\tfrac{4}{16}) + 2(\tfrac{1}{16})$

$$= \frac{0}{16} = 0.$$

Var $(X) = \tfrac{1}{16}(-2 - 0)^2 + \tfrac{4}{16}(-1 - 0)^2 + \tfrac{6}{16}(0 - 0)^2 + \tfrac{4}{16}(1 - 0)^2 + \tfrac{1}{16}(2 - 0)^2$

$$= 1.$$

$$\sigma = \sqrt{1} = 1.$$

4.  $$\mu = 10(\tfrac{1}{8}) + 11(\tfrac{2}{8}) + 12(\tfrac{1}{8}) + 13(\tfrac{2}{8}) + 14(\tfrac{1}{8}) + 15(\tfrac{1}{8})$$

$$= \frac{99}{8} = 12.375.$$

$$\text{Var } (X) = \tfrac{1}{8}(10 - 12.375)^2 + \tfrac{2}{8}(11 - 12.375)^2 + \tfrac{1}{8}(12 - 12.375)^2$$

$$+ \; \tfrac{2}{8}(13 - 12.375)^2 + \tfrac{1}{8}(14 - 12.375)^2 + \tfrac{1}{8}(15 - 12.375)^2$$

$$= 0.7051 + 0.4727 + 0.0176 + 0.0977 + 0.3301 + 0.8613$$

$$= 2.4845.$$

$$\sigma = \sqrt{2.4845} = 1.58.$$

5.  $$\mu = 0.1(430) + (0.2)(480) + (0.4)(520) + (0.2)(565) + (0.1)(580)$$

$$= 518.$$

$$\text{Var } (X) = 0.1(430 - 518)^2 + (0.2)(480 - 518)^2 + (0.4)(520 - 518)^2$$
$$+ \; (0.2)(565 - 518)^2 + (0.1)(580 - 518)^2$$

$$= 1891.$$

$$\sigma = \sqrt{1891} \approx 43.49.$$

6.  $$\mu = (0.15)(-198) + (0.30)(-195) + (0.10)(-193) + (0.25)(-188)$$
$$+ \; (0.20)(-185)$$

$$= -191.5.$$

$$\text{Var } (X) = (0.15)(-198 + 191.5)^2 + (0.30)(-195 + 191.5)^2$$
$$+ \; (0.25)(-188 + 191.5)^2 + (0.20)(-185 + 191.5)^2$$

$$= 21.525.$$

$$\sigma = \sqrt{21.525} \approx 4.64.$$

7.  The mean of the histogram in Figure (b) is more concentrated about its mean than the histogram in Figure (a). Therefore, the histogram in Figure (a) has the larger variance.

8.  a.

9.  $$E(X) = 1(0.1) + 2(0.2) + 3(0.3) + 4(0.2) + 5(0.2) = 3.2.$$

$$\text{Var } (X) = (0.1)(1 - 3.2)^2 + (0.2)(2 - 3.2)^2 + (0.3)(3 - 3.2)^2$$
$$+ \; (0.2)(4 - 3.2)^2 + (0.2)(5 - 3.2)^2$$

$$= 1.56$$

10. $E(X) = 0.05(1) + (0.1)(2) + (0.15)(3) + (0.2)(4) + (0.15)(5)$
$\qquad\quad + (0.1)(6) + (0.15)(7) + (0.1)(8)$

$\quad = 4.7$

$\text{Var }(X) = (0.05)(1 - 4.7)^2 + (0.1)(2 - 4.7)^2 + (0.15)(3 - 4.7)^2$
$\qquad\qquad + (0.2)(4 - 4.7)^2 + (0.15)(5 - 4.7)^2 + (0.1)(6 - 4.7)^2$
$\qquad\qquad + (0.15)(7 - 4.7)^2 + (0.1)(8 - 4.7)^2$

$\qquad = 4.01.$

11. $\mu = \dfrac{1 + 2 + 3 + \cdots + 8}{8} = 4.5$

$V(X) = \frac{1}{8}(1 - 4.5)^2 + \frac{1}{8}(2 - 4.5)^2 + \cdots + \frac{1}{8}(8 - 4.5)^2 = 5.25.$

12. a. X gives the minimum age requirement for a regular driver's license.

b.

| x | 15 | 16 | 17 | 18 | 19 | 21 |
|---|---|---|---|---|---|---|
| P(X = x) | .02 | .30 | .08 | .56 | .02 | .02 |

c. $\mu = E(X)$

$\quad = (0.02)(15) + (0.3)(16) + (0.08)(17) + (0.56)(18) + (0.02)(19)$
$\qquad + (0.02)(21)$

$\quad = 17.34.$

$V(X) = (0.02)(15 - 17.34)^2 + (0.3)(16 - 17.34)^2$
$\qquad\quad + (0.08)(17 - 17.34)^2 + (0.56)(18 - 17.34)^2$
$\qquad\quad + (0.02)(19 - 17.34)^2 + (0.02)(21 - 17.34)^2$

$\qquad = 1.2244$

$\sigma = \sqrt{1.2244} \approx 1.11.$

13. a. Let X be the annual birth rate during the years 1981 − 1990.

b.

| x | 15.5 | 15.6 | 15.7 | 15.9 | 16.2 | 16.7 |
|---|---|---|---|---|---|---|
| P(X = x) | .2 | .1 | .3 | .2 | .1 | .1 |

c.

$$E(X) = (0.2)(15.5) + (0.1)(15.6) + (0.3)(15.7) + (0.2)(15.9)$$
$$+ (0.1)(16.2) + (0.1)(16.7)$$

$$= 15.84.$$

$$V(X) = (0.2)(15.5 - 15.84)^2 + (0.1)(15.6 - 15.84)^2$$
$$+ (0.3)(15.7 - 15.84)^2 + (0.2)(15.9 - 15.84)^2$$
$$+ (0.1)(16.2 - 15.84)^2 + (0.1)(16.7 - 15.84)^2$$

$$= 0.1224$$

$$\sigma = \sqrt{0.1224} \approx 0.350.$$

14.  a.

Venture A

$$\mu = (-20,000)(0.3) + (40,000)(0.4) + (50,000)(0.3)$$

$$= 25,000.$$

$$V(X) = (0.3)(-20,000 - 25,000)^2 + (0.4)(40,000 - 25,000)^2$$
$$+ (0.3)(50,000 - 25,000)^2$$

$$= 8.85 \times 10^8.$$

Venture B

$$\mu = (-15,000)(0.2) + (30,000)(0.5) + (40,000)(0.3)$$

$$= 24,000.$$

$$V(X) = (0.2)(-15,000 - 24,000)^2 + (0.5)(30,000 - 24,000)^2$$
$$+ (0.3)(40,000 - 24,000)^2$$

$$= 3.99 \times 10^8.$$

b.  Venture A

c.  Venture B

15.  a.

Mutual Fund A

$$\mu = (0.2)(-4) + (0.5)(8) + (0.3)(10) = 6.2, \text{ or } \$620.$$

$$V(X) = (0.2)(-4 - 6.2)^2 + (0.5)(8 - 6.2)^2 + (0.3)(10 - 6.2)^2$$

$$= 26.76, \text{ or } \$267,600.$$

Mutual Fund B

$$\mu = (0.2)(-2) + (0.4)(6) + (0.4)(8)$$

$$= 5.2, \text{ or } \$520.$$

$$V(X) = (0.2)(-2 - 5.2)^2 + (0.4)(6 - 5.2)^2 + (0.4)(8 - 5.2)^2$$

$$= 13.76, \text{ or } \$137,600.$$

b. Mutual Fund A

c. Mutual Fund B

16. $\mu = (0.01)(0) + (0.03)(1) + (0.05)(2) + (0.11)(3) + (0.13)(4)$
$\qquad + (0.24)(5) + (0.22)(6) + (0.16)(7) + (0.05)(8)$
$\quad = 5.02$

$V(X) = (0.01)(0 - 5.02)^2 + (0.03)(1 - 5.02)^2 + (0.05)(2 - 5.02)^2$
$\qquad + (0.11)(3 - 5.02)^2 + (0.13)(4 - 5.02)^2 + (0.24)(5 - 5.02)^2$
$\qquad + (0.22)(6 - 5.02)^2 + (0.16)(7 - 5.02)^2 + (0.05)(8 - 5.02)^2$

$\qquad = 3.0596.$

17. $\text{Var } (X) = (0.4)(1)^2 + (0.3)(2)^2 + (0.2)(3)^2 + (0.1)(4)^2 - (2)^2 = 1.$

18. $\text{Var } (X) = (0.01)(0)^2 + (0.03)(1)^2 + (0.05)(2)^2 + (0.11)(3)^2$
$\qquad\qquad\quad + (0.13)(4)^2 + (0.24)(5)^2 + (0.22)(6)^2 + (0.16)(7)^2$
$\qquad\qquad\quad + (0.05)(8)^2 - (5.02)^2$

$\qquad\qquad = 3.0596.$

19. $\mu = \dfrac{10}{500}(80) + \dfrac{20}{500}(90) + \cdots + \dfrac{5}{500}(200) = 139.6, \text{ or } \$139,600.$

$V(X) = [\dfrac{10}{500}(80 - 13.96)^2 + \dfrac{20}{500}(90 - 13.96)^2 + \cdots$

$\qquad\qquad + \dfrac{5}{500}(200 - 13.96)^2][(1000)^2]$

$\qquad = 1443.84 \times 10^6 \text{ dollars}$

$\sigma = \sqrt{1443.84 \times 10^6} = 37.998 \times 10^3, \text{ or } \$37,998.$

20. a. Using Chebychev's inequality we have

$$P(\mu - k\sigma \leq X \leq \mu + k\sigma) \geq 1 - 1/k^2.$$

$$\mu - k\sigma = 20 - k(3) = 15, \text{ and } k = 5/3,$$

and $P(\mu - k\sigma \leq X \leq \mu + k\sigma) \geq 1 - 1/(5/3)^2$

$$\geq 1 - 9/25$$

$$\geq 16/25, \text{ or at least } 0.64.$$

b. Using Chebychev's inequality we have

$$P(\mu - k\sigma \leq X \leq \mu + k\sigma) \geq 1 - 1/k^2.$$

$\mu - k\sigma = 20 - k(3) = 10$, and $k = 10/3$,

and $P(\mu - k\sigma \leq X \leq \mu + k\sigma) \geq 1 - 1/(10/3)^2$

$$\geq 1 - 9/100$$

$$\geq 91/100, \text{ or at least } 0.91.$$

21.  a. Using Chebychev's inequality we have

$$P(\mu - k\sigma \leq X \leq \mu + k\sigma) \geq 1 - 1/k^2.$$

$\mu - k\sigma = 42 - k(2) = 38$ , and $k = 2$,

and      $P(\mu - k\sigma \leq X \leq \mu + k\sigma) \geq 1 - 1/(2)^2$

$$\geq 1 - 1/4$$

$$\geq 3/4, \text{ or at least } 0.75.$$

b. Using Chebychev's inequality we have

$$P(\mu - k\sigma \leq X \leq \mu + k\sigma) \geq 1 - 1/k^2.$$

$\mu - k\sigma = 42 - k(2) = 32$, and $k = 5$,

and      $P(\mu - k\sigma \leq X \leq \mu + k\sigma) \geq 1 - 1/(5)^2$

$$\geq 1 - 1/25$$

$$\geq 24/25, \text{ or at least } 0.96.$$

22.  Here $\mu = 50$ and $\sigma = 1.4$. Now, we require that $c = k\sigma$, or $k = \dfrac{c}{1.4}$.

Next, we solve

$$0.96 = 1 - \left(\frac{1.4}{c}\right)^2$$

$$\frac{1.96}{c^2} = 0.04$$

$$c^2 = \frac{1.96}{0.04} = 49, \text{ or } c = 7.$$

23. Using Chebychev's inequality we have

$$P(\mu - k\sigma \le X \le \mu + k\sigma) \ge 1 - 1/k^2.$$

Here k = 2, so

$$P(\mu - k\sigma \le X \le \mu + k\sigma) \ge 1 - 1/2^2 = 3/4.$$

This means that at least 75 percent of the values are expected to lie between $\mu - 2\sigma$ and $\mu + 2\sigma$.

24. Here $\mu = 200$ and $\sigma = 2$.

a. In this case k satisfies

$$200 - 2k = 190 \text{ and } 200 + 2k = 210$$

from which we deduce that $k = \dfrac{10}{2} = 5$. Therefore,

$$P(190 \le X \le 210) \ge 1 - \frac{1}{(5)^2}$$

$$= \frac{96}{100}, \quad \text{or } 0.96.$$

b. In this case k satisfies

$$200 - 2k = 180 \text{ and } 200 + 2k = 220$$

from which we deduce that $k = 20/2 = 10$. Therefore,

$$P(180 \le X \le 220) \ge 1 - \frac{1}{(10)^2} = \frac{99}{100}$$

or 0.01. Then the estimated number of Christmas tree lights that will burn out is given by

$$(0.01)(150,000) = 1500.$$

25. Using Chebychev's inequality we have

$$P(\mu - k\sigma \le X \le \mu + k\sigma) \ge 1 - 1/k^2.$$

Here, $\mu - k\sigma = 24 - k(3) = 20$, and $k = 4/3$.

So $P(\mu - k\sigma \le X \le \mu + k\sigma) \ge 1 - 1/(4/3)^2$

$$\ge 1 - 9/16 = 7/16.$$

or at least 0.4375.

26. Using Chebychev's inequality we have

$$P(\mu - k\sigma \le X \le \mu + k\sigma) \ge 1 - 1/k^2.$$

Here, $\mu - k\sigma = 30{,}000 - k(500) = 28{,}000$, and $k = 4$.

So $\quad P(\mu - k\sigma \le X \le \mu + k\sigma) \ge 1 - 1/(4)^2 \ge 1 - 1/16$

$$\ge 15/16,$$

or at least 0.9375.

27.  Here $\mu = 5$ and $\sigma = 0.02$. Next, we require that $c = k\sigma$, or $k = \dfrac{c}{0.02}$.

Next, solve

$$0.96 = 1 - \left(\frac{0.02}{c}\right)^2$$

$$0.04 = \frac{0.0004}{c^2}$$

$$c^2 = \frac{0.0004}{0.04} = 0.01$$

and $\qquad c = 0.1$.

We conclude that for $P(5 - c \le X \le 5 + c) \ge 0.96$, we require that $c \ge 0.1$.

## USING TECHNOLOGY EXERCISES, page 479

1.  a.

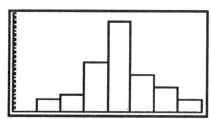

b. $\mu = 4$ and $\sigma = 1.40$

2.  a.

b. $\mu = 4$ and $\sigma = 2.28$

3.  a.

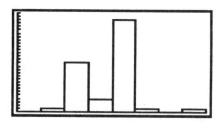

b. $\mu = 17.34$ and $\sigma = 1.11$

4.  a.

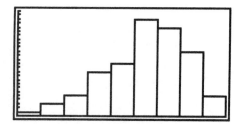

b. $\mu = 5.02$ and $\sigma = 1.749$

5. a. Let X denote the random variable that gives the weight of a carton of sugar.

   b. The probability distribution for the random variable X is

| x | 4.96 | 4.97 | 4.98 | 4.99 | 5.00 | 5.01 | 5.02 | 5.03 |
|---|------|------|------|------|------|------|------|------|
| P(X = x) | $\frac{3}{30}$ | $\frac{4}{30}$ | $\frac{4}{30}$ | $\frac{1}{30}$ | $\frac{1}{30}$ | $\frac{5}{30}$ | $\frac{3}{30}$ | $\frac{3}{30}$ |

| x | 5.04 | 5.05 | 5.06 |
|---|------|------|------|
| P(X = x) | $\frac{4}{30}$ | $\frac{1}{30}$ | $\frac{1}{30}$ |

   $\mu = 5.00467 \approx 5.00$.

   $V(X) = 0.0009 \approx 0.03$.

   $\sigma = 0.03$

6. a. Let X be the random variable that is the score of a student in a mathematics examination.

   b. The probability distribution for the random variable X is

| x | 58 | 66 | 68 | 69 | 70 | 71 | 72 | 73 |
|---|----|----|----|----|----|----|----|----|
| P(X = x) | .04 | .08 | .12 | .04 | .08 | .04 | .08 | .04 |

| x | 74 | 75 | 85 | 87 | 88 | 90 | 92 | 94 | 98 |
|---|----|----|----|----|----|----|----|----|----|
| P(X = x) | .08 | .04 | .08 | .04 | .04 | .08 | .04 | .04 | .04 |

   c. $\mu = 76.92$; $V(X) = 110.9536$; $\sigma \approx 10.533$.

## EXERCISES 8.4, page 489

1. Yes. The number of trials is fixed, there are two outcomes of the experiment, the probability in each trial is fixed ($p = \frac{1}{6}$), and the trials are independent of each other.

2. No. The number of trials is not fixed.

3. No. There are more than 2 outcomes in each trial.

4. No. The probability of "success" in the two trials is not the same. Also, the trials are not independent of each other.

5. No. There are more than 2 outcomes in each trial and the probability of success (an accident) in each trial is not the same.

6. Yes. The number of trials is fixed, there are two outcomes of the experiment, the probability in each trial is fixed ($p = 0.325$), and the trials are independent of each other.

7. $C(4,2)(\frac{1}{3})^2(\frac{2}{3})^2 = \frac{4!}{2!2!}(\frac{4}{81}) \approx 0.296.$

8. $C(6,4)(\frac{1}{4})^4(\frac{3}{4})^2 = \frac{6!}{2!4!}(\frac{9}{4096}) \approx 0.03296.$

9. $C(5,3)(0.2)^3(0.8)^2 = \frac{5!}{2!3!}(0.2)^3(0.8)^2 \approx 0.0512.$

10. $C(6,5)(0.4)^5(0.6) = \frac{6!}{1!5!}(0.4)^5(0.6) \approx 0.036864.$

11. The required probability is given by
$$P(X = 0) = C(5,0)(\tfrac{1}{3})^0(\tfrac{2}{3})^5 \approx 0.132.$$

12. The required probability is given by
$$P(X = 3) = C(6,3)(\tfrac{1}{2})^3(\tfrac{1}{2})^3 = 0.3125.$$

13. The required probability is given by
$$P(X \geq 3) = C(6,3)(\tfrac{1}{2})^3(\tfrac{1}{2})^{6-3} + C(6,4)(\tfrac{1}{2})^4(\tfrac{1}{2})^{6-4} + C(6,5)(\tfrac{1}{2})^5(\tfrac{1}{2})^{6-5}$$
$$+ C(6,6)(\tfrac{1}{2})^6(\tfrac{1}{2})^{6-6}$$
$$= \frac{6!}{3!3!}(\tfrac{1}{2})^6 + \frac{6!}{4!2!}(\tfrac{1}{2})^6 + \frac{6!}{5!1!}(\tfrac{1}{2})^6 + \frac{6!}{6!0!}(\tfrac{1}{2})^6$$
$$= \frac{1}{64}(20 + 15 + 6 + 1) = \frac{21}{32}.$$

14. The required probability is given by
$$P(X = 0) = C(6,0)(\tfrac{1}{3})^0(\tfrac{2}{3})^6 \approx 0.088.$$

15. The probability of no failures, or, equivalently, the probability of five successes is
$$P(X = 5) = C(5,5)(\tfrac{1}{3})^5(\tfrac{2}{3})^{5-5} = \frac{1}{243} \approx 0.00412.$$

16. The probability of at least one failure in five trials is $P(X \geq 1)$ which is equal to $1 - P(X = 5)$ or

$$1 - C(5,5)\left(\frac{1}{3}\right)^5\left(\frac{2}{3}\right)^0 = \frac{242}{243} \approx = 0.996.$$

17. Here $n = 4$, and $p = 1/6$. Then

$$P(X = 2) = C(4,2)\left(\frac{1}{6}\right)^2\left(\frac{5}{6}\right)^2 = \frac{25}{216} \approx 0.116.$$

18. Here $n = 5$ and $p = 0.4$. Using Table 2 in the Appendix, we have

a. $P(X = 4) = 0.077$.

b. $P(2 \leq X \leq 4) = P(X = 2) + P(X = 3) + P(X = 4)$

$$= 0.346 + 0.230 + 0.077$$

$$= 0.653.$$

19. Here $n = 5$, $p = 0.4$, and therefore, $q = 1 - 0.4 = 0.6$.

a. Using Table 2 in the Appendix, we see that

$$P(X = 0) = 0.078, \; P(X = 1) = 0.259, \; P(X = 2) = 0.346,$$

$$P(X = 3) = 0.230, \; P(X = 4) = 0.077, \; P(X = 5) = 0.010.$$

b.

| x | 0 | 1 | 2 | 3 | 4 | 5 |
|---|---|---|---|---|---|---|
| P(x = x) | 0.078 | 0.259 | 0.346 | 0.230 | 0.077 | 0.010 |

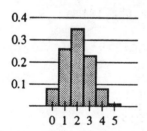

c.　$\mu = np = 5(0.4) = 2$

$\sigma = \sqrt{npq} = \sqrt{5(0.4)(0.6)} = \sqrt{1.2} = 1.095$.

20. Here n = 5, p = 0.5, and therefore, q = 1 - 0.5 = 0.5.

a. Using Table 2 in the Appendix, we see that

$$P(X = 0) = 0.031, \ P(X = 1) = 0.156, \ P(X = 2) = 0.312,$$

$$P(X = 3) = 0.312, \ P(X = 4) = 0.156, \ P(X = 5) = 0.031.$$

b.

| x | 0 | 1 | 2 | 3 | 4 | 5 |
|---|---|---|---|---|---|---|
| P(x = x) | 0.031 | 0.156 | 0.312 | 0.312 | 0.156 | 0.031 |

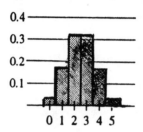

c. $\mu = np = 5(0.5) = 2.5$

$\sigma = \sqrt{npq} = \sqrt{5(0.5)(0.5)} = \sqrt{1.25} = 1.118$.

21. Here $1 - p = 1/50$ or $p = 49/50$. So the probability of obtaining 49 or 50 nondefective fuses is

$$P(X = 49) + P(X = 50) = C(50,49)\left(\frac{49}{50}\right)^{49}\left(\frac{1}{50}\right) + C(50,50)\left(\frac{49}{50}\right)^{50}\left(\frac{1}{50}\right)^{0}$$

$$\approx 0.74.$$

This is also the probability of at most one defective fuse. So the inference is incorrect.

22. The required probability is given by

$$P(X = 2) = C(5,2)\left(\frac{1}{4}\right)^{2}\left(\frac{3}{4}\right)^{3} \approx 0.264.$$

23. The required probability is given by

$$P(X = 6) = C(6,6)\left(\frac{1}{4}\right)^{6}\left(\frac{3}{4}\right)^{0} \approx 0.0002.$$

24. The required probability is given by

$$P(X \geq 3) = 1 - P(X \leq 2)$$

$$= 1 - [C(10,0)(.4)^{0}(.6)^{10} + C(10,1)(.4)^{1}(.6)^{9}$$
$$+ \ C(10,2)(.4)^{2}(.6)^{8}]$$

$$= 1 - (0.006 + 0.040 + 0.12) \approx 0.834.$$

25.  a. The probability that six or more people stated a preference for brand A is

$$P(X \geq 6) = C(10,6)(.6)^6(.4)^4 + C(10,7)(.6)^7(.4)^3$$
$$+ C(10,8)(.6)^8(.4)^2 + C(10,9)(.6)^9(.4)^1$$
$$+ C(10,10)(.6)^{10}(.4)^0$$

$$\approx 0.251 + 0.215 + 0.121 + 0.040 + 0.006$$

$$= 0.633.$$

(Use Table 2 in Appendix C.)

b. The required probability is $1 - 0.633 = 0.367$.

26.  The required probability is

$$P(X = 4) = C(10,4)(.4)^4(.6)^6 \approx 0.251$$

27.  This is a binomial experiment with $n = 9$, $p = 1/3$, and $q = 2/3$.

a. The probability is given by

$$P(X = 3) = C(9,3)\left(\tfrac{1}{3}\right)^3\left(\tfrac{2}{3}\right)^6$$

$$= \frac{9!}{6!3!}\left(\tfrac{1}{3}\right)^3\left(\tfrac{2}{3}\right)^6$$

$$\approx 0.273.$$

b. The probability is given by

$$P(X = 0) + P(X = 1) + P(X = 2) + P(X = 3)$$
$$= C(9,0)\left(\tfrac{1}{3}\right)^0\left(\tfrac{2}{3}\right)^9 + C(9,1)\left(\tfrac{1}{3}\right)\left(\tfrac{2}{3}\right)^8 + C(9,2)\left(\tfrac{1}{3}\right)^2\left(\tfrac{2}{3}\right)^7$$
$$+ C(9,3)\left(\tfrac{1}{3}\right)^3\left(\tfrac{2}{3}\right)^6$$
$$= 0.026 + 0.117 + 0.234 + 0.273$$
$$\approx 0.650.$$

28.  The probability of "success" is 1/5. The probability that he will pass the examination through random guesses is

$$P(X \geq 5) = C(8,5)(.2)^5(.8)^3 + C(8,6)(.2)^6(.8)^2 + C(8,7)(.2)^7(.8)^1$$
$$+ C(8,8)(.2)^8(.8)^0$$

$$= 0.009 + 0.001 + 0.0000 + 0.0000$$

$$\approx 0.01. \qquad \text{(Use Table 2 in Appendix C.)}$$

29. In order to obtain a score of at least 90 percent the student needs to answer 3 or 4 of the remaining questions correctly. The probability of doing this is

$$P(X \geq 3) = C(4,3)(.5)^3(.5) + C(4,4)(.5)^4(.5)^0 = 0.3125.$$

30. This is a binomial experiment with $n = 10$, $p = 0.02$, and $q = 0.98$.

a. The probability that the sample contains no defectives is given by
$$P(X = 0) = C(10,0)(0.02)^0(0.98)^{10} \approx 0.817.$$

b. The probability that the sample contains at most 2 defective sets is given by
$$P(X \leq 2) = (10,0)(.02)^0(.98)^{10} + C(10,1)(.02)(0.98)^9$$
$$+ C(10,2)(.02)^2(.98)^8$$
$$\approx 0.817 + 0.167 + 0.015$$
$$= 0.999.$$

31. Here $1 - p = 0.015$ and $p = 0.985$. The probability that the sample will be accepted, or, equivalently, that the sample contains all six nondefective cartridges is given by

$$P(X = 6) = C(6,6)(0.985)^6(0.015)^0 \approx 0.913.$$

32. a. The required probability is
$$P(X = 2) = C(10,2)(.05)^2(.95)^8 \approx 0.075.$$

b. The required probability is
$$P(X \geq 3) = 1 - P(X \leq 2)$$
$$= 1 - [C(10,2)(.05)^2(.95)^8 + C(10,1)(.05)(.95)^9$$
$$+ C(10,0)(.05)^0(.95)^{10}]$$
$$\approx 0.012.$$

33. This is a binomial experiment with $n = 4$, $p = 0.001$, and $q = 0.999$.

a. The probability that exactly one engine will fail is given by
$$P(X = 1) = C(4,1)(0.001)(0.999)^3 = 4(0.001)(0.999)^3$$
$$= 0.003988.$$

b. The probability that exactly two engines will fail is given by
$$P(X = 2) = C(4,2)(0.001)^2(0.999)^2$$

$$= 6(0.001)^2(0.999)^2$$

$$= 0.000006.$$

c. The probability that more than two engines will fail is given by

$$P(X > 2) = P(X = 3) + P(X = 4)$$

$$= C(4,3)(0.001)^3(0.999) + C(4,4)(0.001)^4(0.999)^0$$

$$= 3.996 \times 10^{-9} + 1 \times 10^{-12}$$

$$\approx 3.997 \times 10^{-9}.$$

34.  a. The required probability is

$$P(X = 0) = C(20,0)(.1)^0(.9)^{20} \approx 0.1216.$$

b. The required probability is

$$P(X = 0) = C(20,0)(.05)^0(.95)^{20} \approx 0.3585.$$

35.  The required probability is

$$P(X \leq 1) = P(X = 0) + P(X = 1)$$

$$= C(20,0)(.1)^0(.9)^{20} + C(20,1)(.1)^1(.9)^{19}$$

$$\approx 0.3917.$$

36.  The required probability is

$$P(X = 0) = C(10,0)(.1)^0(.9)^{10} \approx 0.3487.$$

37.  Take $p = 1/2$. The probability of obtaining no heads in n tosses is

$$P(X = n) = C(n,n)\left(\tfrac{1}{2}\right)^n\left(\tfrac{1}{2}\right)^0 = \left(\tfrac{1}{2}\right)^n.$$

The probability of obtaining at least one head is $1 - \left(\tfrac{1}{2}\right)^n$.
We want this to exceed 0.99. Thus,

$$1 - \left(\tfrac{1}{2}\right)^n \geq 0.99$$

$$\frac{1}{2^n} \geq 0.01$$

$$2^n \geq 100$$

or

$$n \geq \frac{\ln 100}{\ln 2} = 6.64.$$

So one must toss the coin at least 7 times.

38.    The mean number of people for whom the drug is effective is

$$\mu = np = (500)(0.75) = 375.$$

The standard deviation of the number of people for whom the drug can be expected to be effective is

$$\sigma = \sqrt{npq} = \sqrt{(500)(0.75)(0.25)} \approx 9.68.$$

39.    a. The expected number of students who will graduate within four years is

$$\mu = np = (0.6)(2000) = 1200.$$

b. The standard deviation of the number of students who will graduate within four years is

$$\sigma = \sqrt{npq} = \sqrt{(2000)(0.6)(0.4)} \approx 21.91.$$

## EXERCISES 8.5, page 500

1.    $P(Z < 1.45) = 0.9265.$

2.    $P(Z > 1.11) = 1 - P(Z < 1.11) = 1 - 0.8665 = 0.1335.$

3.    $P(Z < -1.75) = 0.0401.$

4.    $P(0.3 < Z < 1.83) = P(Z < 1.83) - P(Z < 0.3)$

$$= 0.9664 - 0.6179 = 0.3485.$$

5.    $P(-1.32 < Z < 1.74) = P(Z < 1.74) - P(Z < -1.32)$

$$= 0.9591 - 0.0934 = 0.8657.$$

6.    $P(-2.35 < Z < -0.51) = P(Z < -0.51) - P(Z < -2.35)$

$$= 0.3050 - 0.0094 = 0.2956.$$

7.    $P(Z < 1.37) = 0.9147.$

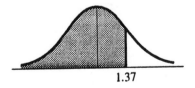

1.37

8.  $P(Z > 2.24) = 1 - P(Z < 2.24) = 1 - 0.9875 = 0.0125.$

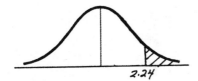

9.  $P(Z < -0.65) = 0.2578.$

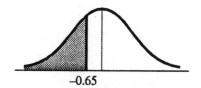

10. $P(0.45 < Z < 1.75) = P(Z < 1.75) - P(Z < 0.45)$

$$= 0.9599 - 0.6736$$

$$= 0.2863.$$

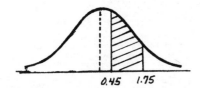

11. $P(Z > -1.25) = 1 - P(Z < -1.25) = 1 - 0.1056 = 0.8944$

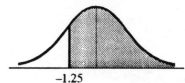

12. $P(-1.48 < Z < 1.54) = P(Z < 1.54) - P(Z < -1.48)$

$$= 0.9382 - 0.0694$$

$$= 0.8688.$$

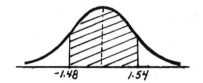

13.  P(0.68 < Z < 2.02) = P(Z < 2.02) − P(Z < 0.68)

= 0.9783 − 0.7517 = 0.2266.

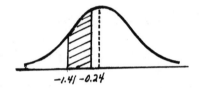

0.68  2.02

14.  P(−1.41 < Z < −0.24) = P(Z < −0.24) − P(Z < −1.41)

= 0.4052 − 0.0793 = 0.3259.

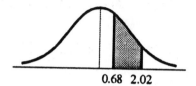

−1.41 −0.24

15.  a. Referring to Table 3, we see that P(Z < z) = 0.8907 implies that z = 1.23.

b. Referring to Table 3, we see that P(Z < z) = 0.2090 implies that z = −0.81.

16.  a. P(Z > z) = 0.9678 implies

P(Z > z) = 1 − P(Z < z)

= 1 − 0.9678  = 0.0322.

Therefore, z = −1.85.

b. P(−z < Z < z) = 0.8354 implies

P(Z < z) − P(Z < −z) = 0.8354.

Therefore, P(Z < −z) = $\dfrac{1 - 0.8354}{2}$

$$= 0.0823,$$

and $\qquad -z = -1.39$

so $\qquad z = 1.39.$

17. a. $P(Z > -z) = 1 - P(Z < -z) = 1 - 0.9713 = 0.0287$ implies $z = 1.9$.

    b. $P(Z < -z) = 0.9713$ implies that $z = -1.9$.

18. a. $P(X < 405) = P(Z < \dfrac{405 - 380}{20}) = P(Z < 1.25) = 0.8944.$

    b. $P(400 < X < 430) = P(\dfrac{400 - 380}{20} < Z < \dfrac{430 - 380}{20}) = P(1 < Z < 2.5)$

$$= P(Z < 2.5) - P(Z < 1)$$

$$= 0.9938 - 0.8413 = 0.1525.$$

    c. $P(X > 400) = P(Z > \dfrac{400 - 380}{20}) = P(Z > 1) = 1 - P(Z < 1)$

$$= 1 - 0.8413 = 0.1587.$$

19. a. $P(X < 60) = P(Z < \dfrac{60 - 50}{5}) = P(Z < 2) = 0.9772.$

    b. $P(X > 43) = P(Z > \dfrac{43 - 50}{5}) = P(Z > -1.4) = P(Z < 1.4) = 0.9192.$

    c. $P(46 < X < 58) = P(\dfrac{46 - 50}{5} < Z < \dfrac{58 - 50}{5}) = P(-0.8 < Z < 1.6)$

$$= P(Z < 1.6) - P(Z < -0.8)$$

$$= 0.9452 - 0.2119 = 0.7333.$$

20. a. $P(X < 750) = P(Z < \dfrac{750 - 500}{75}) = P(Z < 3.333) = 0.9996.$

    b. $P(X > 350) = P(Z > \dfrac{350 - 500}{75}) = P(Z > -2) = 0.9772.$

    c. $P(400 < X < 600) = P(\dfrac{400 - 500}{75} < Z < \dfrac{600 - 500}{75})$

$$= P(-1.333 < Z < 1.333)$$

$$= 0.9082 - 0.0918 = 0.8164.$$

## EXERCISES 8.6, page 510

1. $\mu = 20$ and $\sigma = 2.6$.

   a. $P(X > 22) = P(Z > \dfrac{22 - 20}{2.6}) = P(Z > 0.77) = P(Z < -0.77) = 0.2206$.

   b. $P(X < 18) = P(Z < \dfrac{18 - 20}{2.6}) = P(Z < -0.77) = 0.2206$.

   c. $P(19 < X < 21) = P(\dfrac{19 - 20}{2.6} < Z < \dfrac{21 - 20}{2.6}) = P(-0.39 < Z < 0.39)$

   $$= P(Z < 0.39) - P(Z < -0.39)$$

   $$= 0.6517 - 0.3483 = 0.3034.$$

2. $\mu = 400$ and $\sigma = 50$.

   a. $P(X < 300) = P(Z < \dfrac{300 - 400}{50}) = P(Z < -2) = 0.0228$.

   b. $P(X > 460) = P(Z > \dfrac{460 - 400}{50})$

   $$= P(Z > 1.2) = P(Z < -1.2) = 0.1151.$$

   c. $P(350 < X < 450) = P(\dfrac{350 - 400}{50} < Z < \dfrac{450 - 400}{50}) = P(-1 < Z < 1)$

   $$= P(Z < 1) - P(Z < -1)$$

   $$= 0.8413 - 0.1587 = 0.6826.$$

3. $\mu = 750$ and $\sigma = 75$.

   a. $P(X > 900) = P(Z > \dfrac{900 - 750}{75}) = P(Z > 2) = P(Z < -2) = 0.0228$.

   b. $P(X < 600) = P(Z < \dfrac{600 - 750}{75}) = P(Z < -2) = 0.0228$.

   c. $P(750 < X < 900) = P(\dfrac{750 - 750}{75} < Z < \dfrac{900 - 750}{75})$

   $$= P(0 < Z < 2) = P(Z < 2) - P(Z < 0)$$

   $$= 0.9772 - 0.5000 = 0.4772.$$

   d. $P(600 < X < 800) = P(\dfrac{600 - 750}{75} < Z < \dfrac{800 - 750}{75})$

   $$= P(-2 < Z < .667) = P(Z < .667) - P(Z < -2)$$

   $$= 0.7486 - 0.0228 = 0.7258.$$

4.  $\mu = 100$ and $\sigma = 20$.

a. $P(X > 120) = P(Z > \dfrac{120 - 100}{20}) = P(Z > 1) = P(Z < -1) = 0.1587$.

b. $P(80 < X < 120) = P(\dfrac{80 - 100}{20} < Z < \dfrac{120 - 100}{20}) = P(-1 < Z < 1)$.

$$= P(Z < 1) - P(Z < -1)$$

$$= 0.8413 - 0.1587 = 0.6826.$$

c. $P(X < 80) = P(Z < \dfrac{80 - 100}{20}) = P(Z < -1) = 0.1587$.

5.  $\mu = 100$ and $\sigma = 15$.

a. $P(X > 140) = P(Z > \dfrac{140 - 100}{15}) = P(Z > 2.667) = P(Z < -2.667)$

$$= 0.0038.$$

b. $P(X > 120) = P(Z > \dfrac{120 - 100}{15}) = P(Z > 1.33) = P(Z < -1.33)$

$$= 0.0918.$$

c. $P(100 < X < 120) = P(\dfrac{100 - 100}{15}) < Z < \dfrac{120 - 100}{15})$

$$= P(0 < Z < 1.333).$$

$$= P(Z < 0) - P(Z < 1.333)$$

$$= 0.9082 - 0.5000 = 0.4082.$$

d. $P(X < 90) = P(Z < \dfrac{90 - 100}{15}) = P(Z < -0.667) = 0.2514$.

6.  Here $\mu = 40,000$ and $\sigma = 2000$.

$$P(X > 35,000) = P(Z > \dfrac{35,000 - 40,000}{2000}) = P(Z > -2.5) = P(Z < 2.5)$$

$$= 0.9938.$$

The probability that all four tires will still have useful tread lives after 35,000 miles of driving is

$$(0.9938)(0.9938)(0.9938)(0.9938) \approx 0.9754$$

7.  Here $\mu = 375$ and $\sigma = 50$.

$$P(350 < X < 450) = P(\frac{350 - 375}{50}) < Z < \frac{450 - 375}{50}) = P(-0.5 < Z < 1.5)$$

$$= P(Z < 1.5) - P(Z < -0.5)$$

$$= 0.9332 - 0.3085 = 0.6247.$$

8. Here $\mu = 60$ and $\sigma = 10$.

$$P(X \geq 70) = = P(Z > \frac{70 - 60}{10}) = P(Z > 1) = P(Z < -1) = 0.1587,$$

or 15.87 percent.

9. Here $\mu = 22$ and $\sigma = 4$.

$$P(X < 12) = P(Z < \frac{12 - 22}{4}) = P(Z < -2.5) = 0.0062, \text{ or } 0.62 \text{ percent.}$$

10. $\mu = 72$ and $\sigma = 16$.

We solve $P(Y < y) = 0.90$ for y. Now

$$P(Y < y) = P(Z < \frac{Y - 72}{16}) = 0.90 \text{ implies } \frac{Y - 72}{16} = 1.28,$$

or $y \approx 92.5$.

11. $\mu = 70$ and $\sigma = 10$.

To find the cut-off point for an A, we solve $P(Y < y) = 0.85$ for y. Now

$$P(Y < y) = P(Z < \frac{Y - 70}{10}) = 0.85 \text{ implies } \frac{Y - 70}{10} = 1.04$$

or $y = 80.4 \approx 80$.

For a B: $P(Y < y) = P(Z < \frac{Y - 70}{10}) = 0.60 \text{ implies } \frac{Y - 70}{10} = 0.25,$
or $y \approx 73$.

For a C: $P(Z \leq \frac{Y - 70}{10}) = 0.2 \text{ implies } \frac{Y - 70}{10} = -0.84 \text{ or } y \approx 62.$

For a D: $P(Z < \frac{Y - 70}{10}) = 0.05 \text{ implies } \frac{Y - 70}{10} = -1.65, \text{ or } y \approx 54.$

12. Let X denote the number of heads in 20 tosses of the coin. Then X is a binomial random variable. Also, n = 20, p = 0.5 and q = 0.5.

$$\mu = (20)(0.5) = 10$$

$$\sigma = \sqrt{(20)(0.5)(0.5)} \approx 2.24.$$

Approximating the binomial distribution by a normal distribution with a mean of 10 and a standard deviation of 2.24, we find upon letting Y denote the associated normal random variable.

a. $P(X < 8) \approx P(Y < 7.5)$

$$= P(Z < \frac{7.5 - 10}{2.24})$$

$$= P(Z < -1.12)$$

$$= 0.1314.$$

b. $P(X > 6) \approx P(Y \geq 6.5)$

$$= P(Z > \frac{6.5 - 10}{2.24})$$

$$= P(Z > -1.56) = P(Z < 1.56)$$

$$= 0.9406.$$

c. $P(6 \leq X \leq 10) \approx P(5.5 < Y < 10.5)$

$$= P(\frac{5.5 - 10}{2.24} < Z < \frac{10.5 - 10}{2.24})$$

$$= P(Z < 0.22) - P(Z < -2.01)$$

$$= 0.5871 - 0.0222 = 0.5649.$$

13. Let X denote the number of heads in 25 tosses of the coin. Then X is a binomial random variable. Also, n = 25, p = 0.4, and q = 0.6. So

$$\mu = (25)(0.4) = 10$$

$$\sigma = \sqrt{(25)(0.4)(0.6)} \approx 2.45.$$

Approximating the binomial distribution by a normal distribution with a mean of 10 and a standard deviation of 2.45, we find upon letting Y denote the associated normal random variable,

a. $P(X < 10) \approx P(Y < 9.5)$

$$= P(Z < \frac{9.5 - 10}{2.45})$$

$$= P(Z < -0.20)$$

$$= 0.4207.$$

b. $P(10 \leq X \leq 12) \approx P(9.5 < Y < 12.5)$

$$= P(\frac{9.5 - 10}{2.45} < Z < \frac{12.5 - 10}{2.45})$$

$$= P(Z < 1.02) - P(Z < -0.20)$$

$$= 0.8461 - 0.4207 = 0.4254.$$

c. $P(X > 15) \approx P(Y \geq 15)$

$$= P(Z > \frac{15.5 - 10}{2.45})$$

$$= P(Z > 2.25) = P(Z < -2.25)$$

$$= 0.0122.$$

14. This is a binomial experiment. Approximating the distribution by a normal distribution with n = 120, p = 0.75, and q = 0.25, we have

$$\mu = (120)(0.75) = 90, \; \sigma = \sqrt{(120)(0.75)(0.25)} = 4.74$$

and the required probability is given by

$$P(X \geq 100) = P(Z > \frac{99.5 - 90}{4.74}) = P(Z > 2) = P(Z < -2)$$

$$\approx 0.0228.$$

15. Let X denote the number of times the marksman hits his target. Then X has a binomial distribution with n = 30, p = 0.6 and q = 0.4. Therefore,

$$\mu = (30)(0.6) = 18, \; \sigma = \sqrt{(30)(0.6)(0.4)} = 2.68.$$

a. $P(X \geq 20) \approx P(Y \geq 19.5)$

$$= P(Z > \frac{19.5 - 18}{2.68})$$

$$= P(Z > 0.56) = P(Z < -0.56)$$

$$= 0.2877.$$

b. $P(X < 10) \approx P(Y < 9.5)$

$$= P(Z < \frac{9.5 - 18}{2.68})$$

$$= P(Z < -3.17)$$

$$= 0.0008.$$

c. $P(15 \leq X \leq 20) \approx P(14.5 < Y < 20.5)$

$$= P(\frac{14.5 - 18}{2.68} < Z < \frac{20.5 - 18}{2.68})$$

$$= P(Z < 0.93) - P(Z < -1.31)$$

$$= 0.8238 - 0.0951 = 0.7287.$$

16. Let X denote the number of substandard ball bearings. Then X has a binomial distribution with n = 200, p = 0.06, and q = 0.94, so

$$\mu = (200)(0.06) = 12$$

$$\sigma = \sqrt{(200)(0.06)(0.94)} \approx 3.36.$$

Approximating the binomial distribution by a normal distribution with a mean of 12 and a standard deviation of 3.36, we find that the probability that more than 10 ball bearings are defective in a shipment of 200 is

$$P(X > 10) \approx P(Y > 10.5)$$

$$= P(Z > \frac{10.5 - 12}{3.36})$$

$$= P(Z > -0.45) = P(Z < 0.45) = 0.6736.$$

17. Let X denote the number of "seconds." Then X has a binomial distribution with n = 200, p = 0.03, and q = 0.97. Then

$$\mu = (200)(0.03) = 6$$

$$\sigma = \sqrt{(200)(0.03)(0.97)} \approx 2.41,$$

and $P(X < 10) \approx P(Y < 9.5) = P(Z < \frac{9.5 - 6}{2.41}) = P(Z < 1.45) = 0.9265.$

18. Let X denote the number of workers who meet with an accident during a 1-year period. Then

$$\mu = (800)(0.1) = 80$$

$$\sigma = \sqrt{(800)(0.1)(0.9)} \approx 8.49,$$

and $\quad P(X > 70) \approx P(Y > 70.5)$

$$= P(Z > \frac{70.5 - 80}{8.49})$$

$$= P(Z > -1.12) = P(Z < 1.12) = 0.8686.$$

19. a. Let X denote the number of mice that recovered from the disease. Then X has a binomial distribution with n = 50, p = 0.5, and q = 0.5, so

$$\mu = (50)(0.5) = 25$$

$$\sigma = \sqrt{(50)(0.5)(0.5)} \approx 3.54.$$

Approximating the binomial distribution by a normal distribution with a mean of 25 and a standard deviation of 3.54, we find that the probability that 35 or more of the mice would recover from the disease without benefit of the drug is

$$P(X \geq 35) \approx P(Y > 34.5)$$

$$= P(Z > \frac{34.5 - 25}{3.54})$$

$$= P(Z > 2.68) = P(Z < -2.68) = 0.0037.$$

b. The drug is very effective.

20. This is a binomial experiment with $n = 400$, $p = 0.05$, and $q = 0.95$. Therefore,

$$\mu = (400)(0.05) = 20 \quad \text{and} \quad \sigma = \sqrt{(400)(0.05)(0.95)} \approx 4.36.$$

The required probability is approximated by

$$P(X \geq 25) = P(Z > \frac{24.5 - 20}{4.36}) = P(Z > 1.03) = P(Z < -1.03)$$

$$\approx 0.1515.$$

21. Let $n$ denote the number of reservations the company should accept. Then we need to find

$$P(X \geq 2000) \approx P(Y > 1999.5) = 0.01$$

or equivalently,

$$P(Z \geq \frac{1999.5 - np}{\sqrt{npq}}) = 0.01$$

$$P(Z \geq \frac{1999.5 - 0.92n}{\sqrt{(0.92)(0.08)n}}) = 0.01 \qquad \text{[Here } p = 0.92 \text{ and } q = 0.08.\text{]}$$

Using Table 3 in Appendix C, we find

$$\frac{1999.5 - 0.92n}{\sqrt{0.0736n}} = -2.33$$

$$(1999.5 - 0.92n)^2 = (-2.33)^2(0.0736n)$$

$$3{,}998{,}000.25 - 3679.08n + 0.8464n^2 = 0.39956704n,$$

or $\quad 0.8464n^2 - 3679.479567n + 3{,}998{,}000.25 = 0.$

Using the quadratic formula, we obtain

$$n = \frac{3679.479567 \pm \sqrt{2940.2375}}{1.6928} \approx 2142,$$

or 2142. [You can verify that 2206 is not a root of the original equation (before squaring).] Therefore, the company should accept no more than 2142 reservations.

22. Let n denote the number of tickets the company should send out. Then we solve the problem

$$P(X \geq 500) \approx P(Y > 499.5) = 0.01,$$

or equivalently,

$$P\left(Z \geq \frac{499.5 - np}{\sqrt{npq}}\right) = 0.01$$

$$P\left(Z \geq \frac{499.5 - 0.8n}{\sqrt{(0.2)(0.8)n}}\right) = 0.01 \quad \text{[Here } p = 0.8 \text{ and } q = 0.2.\text{]}$$

Using Table 3 in Appendix C, we find

$$\frac{499.5 - 0.8n}{\sqrt{0.16n}} = -2.33$$

$$(499.5 - 0.8n)^2 = (-2.33)^2(0.16n)$$

$$0.64n^2 - 800.068624n + 249500.25 = 0,$$

Using the quadratic formula, we obtain

$$n = \frac{800.068624 \pm \sqrt{1389.163109}}{1.28} \approx 596,$$

or 596 (654 is extraneous.) Therefore, the company should send out no more than 596 tickets.

## CHAPTER 8, REVIEW EXERCISES, page 450

1.  a. S = {WWW, WWB, WBW, WBB, BWW, BWB, BBW, BBB}

    b.

    | Outcome | WWW | WWB | WBW | WBB |
    |---------|-----|-----|-----|-----|
    | Value   | 0   | 1   | 1   | 2   |

| Outcome | BWW | BWB | BBW | BBB |
|---------|-----|-----|-----|-----|
| Value   | 1   | 2   | 2   | 3   |

c.

| x | 0 | 1 | 2 | 3 |
|---|---|---|---|---|
| P(X = x) | $\frac{1}{35}$ | $\frac{12}{35}$ | $\frac{18}{35}$ | $\frac{4}{35}$ |

d.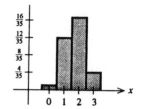

2.    The company's expected gain is given by

$$E(X) = (0.989)(375) - (0.011)(24{,}625)$$

$$= 370.88 - 270.88 = 100, \text{ or } \$100.$$

3.    a. $P(1 \le X \le 4) = 0.1 + 0.2 + 0.3 + 0.2 = 0.8.$

b. $\mu = 0(0.1) + 1(0.1) + 2(0.2) + 3(0.3) + 4(0.2) + 5(0.1) = 2.7.$

$$V(x) = .1(0 - 2.7)^2 + .1(1 - 2.7)^2 + .2(2 - 2.7)^2 + .3(3 - 2.7)^2$$

$$+ .2(4 - 2.7)^2 + .1(5 - 2.7)^2$$

$$= 2.01$$

$$\sigma = \sqrt{2.01} = 1.418.$$

4.    a.

| x | 0 | 1 | 2 | 3 | 4 |
|---|---|---|---|---|---|
| P(X = x) | .1296 | .3456 | .3456 | .1536 | .0256 |

b. $\mu = 0(.1296) + 1(.3456) + 2(.3456) + 3(.1536) + 4(.0256) = 1.6.$

$$V(X) = .1296(0 - 1.6)^2 + .3456(1 - 1.6)^2 + .3456(2 - 1.6)^2$$

$$+ .1536(3 - 1.6)^2 + .0256(4 - 1.6)^2$$

$$= 0.96$$

$$\sigma = \sqrt{0.96} = 0.9798$$

5.    $P(Z < 0.5) = 0.6915.$

6. $P(Z < -0.75) = 0.2266$

7.   $P(-0.75 < Z < 0.5) = P(Z < 0.5) - P(Z < -0.75)$

$$= 0.6915 - 0.2266 = 0.4649.$$

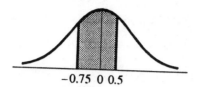

$$-0.75 \ 0 \ 0.5$$

8.   $P(-0.42 < Z < 0.66) = P(Z < 0.66) - P(Z < -0.42) = 0.7454 - 0.3372$

$$= 0.4082.$$

$$-.42 \quad .66$$

9.   If $P(Z < z) = 0.9922$, then $z = 2.42$.

10.  If $P(Z < z) = 0.1469$, then $z = -1.05$.

11.  If $P(Z > z) = 0.9788$, then $P(Z < -z) = 0.9788$, and $-z = 2.03$,

or $z = -2.03$.

12.  If $P(-z < Z < z) = 0.8444$, then

$$P(Z < z) - P(Z < -z) = 2P(Z < z) - 1 = 0.8444.$$

and   $P(Z < z) = 0.9222$, and $z = 1.42$.

13.  $P(X < 11) = P(Z < \dfrac{11 - 10}{2}) = P(Z < 0.5) = 0.6915.$

14.  $P(X > 8) = P(Z > \dfrac{8 - 10}{2}) = P(Z > -1) = P(Z < 1) = 0.8413.$

15.  $P(7 < X < 9) = P(\dfrac{7 - 10}{2} < z < \dfrac{9 - 10}{2}) = P(-1.5 < Z < -0.5)$

$$= P(Z < -0.5) - P(Z < -1.5)$$

$$= 0.3085 - 0.0668 = 0.2417.$$

16.  $P(6.5 < X < 11.5) = P(\dfrac{6.5 - 10}{2} < z < \dfrac{11.5 - 10}{2})$

$$= P(-1.75 < Z < 0.75)$$

$$= P(Z < 0.75) - P(Z < -1.75) = 0.7734 - 0.0401$$

$$= 0.7333.$$

17. This is a binomial experiment with $p = 0.7$, and so $q = 0.3$. The probability that he will get exactly two strikes in four attempts is given by

$$P(X = 2) = C(4,2)(0.7)^2(0.3)^2 \approx 0.2646.$$

The probability that he will get at least two strikes in four attempts is given by

$$P(X = 2) + P(X = 3) + P(X = 4)$$

$$= C(4,2)(0.7)^2(0.3)^2 + C(4,3)(0.7)^3(0.3)$$
$$+ C(4,4)(0.7)^4(0.3)^0$$

$$= 0.2646 + 0.4116 + 0.2401 \approx 0.9163.$$

18. Here $\mu = 64.5$ and $\sigma = 2.5$. Next,

$$P(X \geq 67) = P\left(Z \geq \frac{67 - 64.5}{2.5}\right) = P(Z \geq 1) = P(Z \leq -1) = 0.1587,$$

or 15.87 percent.

19. Here $\mu = 64.5$ and $\sigma = 2.5$. Next,

$$64.5 - 2.5k = 59.5 \quad \text{and} \quad 64.5 + 2.5k = 69.5$$

and $k = 2$. Therefore, the required probability is given by

$$P(59.5 \leq X \leq 69.5) \geq 1 - \frac{1}{2^2} = 0.75.$$

20. This is a binomial experiment with $n = 20$, $p = 0.1$, and $q = 0.9$. We compute

$$P(X \leq 2) = P(X = 0) + P(X = 1) + P(X = 2)$$

$$= C(20,0)(.1)^0(.9)^{20} + C(20,1)(.1)(.9)^{19}$$
$$+ C(20,2)(.1)^2(.9)^{18}$$

$$= 0.12158 + 0.27017 + 0.28518 \approx 0.677.$$

21. Let the random variable X be the number of people for whom the drug is effective. Then

$$\mu = (0.15)(800) = 120 \text{ and } \sigma = \sqrt{800(0.15)(0.85)} = \sqrt{102} \approx 10.1.$$

22. Let X denote the diameter of the steel rods. Then the probability that a rod will be accepted by the buyer is

$$P(0.995 < X < 1.005) = P(\frac{0.9945 - 1}{0.002}) < Z < \frac{1.0055 - 1}{0.002})$$

$$= P(Z < 2.75) - P(Z < -2.75)$$

$$= 0.9970 - 0.0030 = 0.9940.$$

Then the probability that a rod will be rejected by the buyer is

$$1 - 0.9940 = 0.006,$$

and the percentage of rods that will be rejected by the buyer is 0.6 percent.

23. Here $\mu = (0.6)(100) = 60$ and $\sigma = \sqrt{100(0.6)(0.4)} = 4.899$.

Then $P(X > 50) \approx P(Y > 50.5) = P(Z > \frac{50.5 - 60}{4.899}) = P(Z > -1.94)$

$$= P(Z < 1.94) = 0.9738.$$

24. This is a binomial experiment with n = 200, p = 0.05, and q = 0.95. Next,

$$\mu = (0.05)(200) = 10$$

$$\sigma = \sqrt{(0.05)(200)(0.95)} = 3.08.$$

Then

$$P(X \leq 20) = P(Z < \frac{20.5 - 10}{3.08}) = P(Z < 3.41) = 0.9997.$$

 **GROUP DISCUSSION QUESTIONS**

**Page 462**

1. Hitting jackpots in the three machines are independent events. Therefore, the probability of hitting three jackpots in a row is given by

$$(\frac{1}{1,500,000})^3 = 2.963 \times 10^{-19},$$

or virtually impossible.

**Page 472**

1. a. We have

$$\sigma^2 = \text{Var}(X) = p_1(x_1 - \mu)^2 + p_2(x_2 - \mu)^2 + \cdots + p_n(x_n - \mu)^2$$
$$= p_1(x_1^2 - 2x_1\mu + \mu^2) + p_2(x_2^2 - 2x_2\mu + \mu^2) + \cdots$$
$$+ p_n(x_n - 2x_n\mu + \mu^2)$$
$$= x_1^2 p_1 + x_2^2 p_2 + \cdots + x_n^2 p_n - 2\mu(p_1 x_1 + p_2 x_2 + \cdots + p_n x_n)$$
$$+ \mu^2(p_1 + p_2 + \cdots + p_n)$$
$$= E(X^2) - 2\mu^2 + \mu^2 = E(X^2) - \mu^2$$

Observe that $p_1 + p_2 + \cdots + p_n = 1$.

b. $\sigma_X^2 = (0.1)(15.8)^2 + (0.2)(15.9)^2 + (0.4)(16.0)^2 + (0.2)(16.1)^2$
$$+ (0.1)(16.2)^2 - 16^2 \approx 0.012$$

and so $\sigma_X^2 \approx 0.11$, as obtained before.

The value for $\sigma_Y$ is verified in a similar manner.

**Page 485**

1. a. $P(X = x) = C(n,x)p^x q^{n-x}$

With $n = 5$ and $p = 0.2$, we have $P(X = x) = C(5,x)(0.2)^x(0.8)^{5-x}$

So, $P(X = 0) = 0.32768$, $P(X = 1) = 0.4096$, $P(X = 2) = 0.2048$,

$P(X = 3) = 0.0512$, $P(X = 4) = 0.0064$, $P(X = 5) = 0.00032$.

The histogram follows:

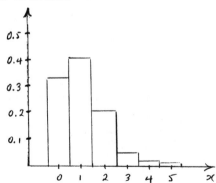

Next, with $n = 5$ and $p = 0.5$, we have

$$P(X = x) = C(5,x)(0.5)^x(0.5)^{5-x} = \frac{1}{32}C(5,x)$$

So, $P(X = 0) = \frac{1}{32}$, $p(X = 1) = \frac{5}{32}$, $p(X = 2) = \frac{10}{32}$, $P(X = 3) = \frac{10}{32}$

$P(X = 4) = \frac{5}{32}$, and $P(X = 5) = \frac{1}{32}$.

The histogram follows:

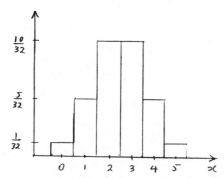

Finally, with n = 5 and p = 0.8, we have

$$P(X = x) = C(5,x)(0.8)^x(0.2)^{5-x}$$

So $P(X = 0) = 0.00032$, $P(X = 1) = 0.0064$, $P(X = 2) = 0.0512$, $P(X = 3) = 0.2048$, $P(X = 4) = 0.4096$, and $P(X = 5) = 0.32768$.

The histogram follows:

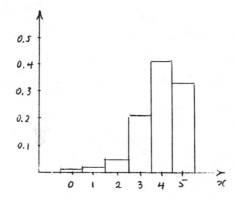

c.   The binomial distribution with n = 5 and p = 0.5 is symmetrical. The binomial distribution with n = 5 and p = 0.2 is skewed to one side, whereas the binomial distribution with n = 5 and p = 0.8 is skewed to the other side.

**Page 495**

1.   a.

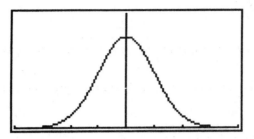

2.   The area of the region on the interval $[-1,1]$ is approximately 0.6827; the area on the interval $[-2,2]$ is approximately 0.9545, and the area on the interval $[-3,3]$ is approximately 0.9973. These results are compatible with those stated in Property 5 of the normal distributions for the special case where $\mu = 0$ and $\sigma = 1$.

# CHAPTER 9

## EXERCISES 9.1, page 461

1. Yes. All entries are nonnegative and the sum of the entries in each row is equal to 1.

2. No. The sum of the entries in each row is not equal to 1.

3. Yes.

4. No. The sum of the entries in the first row is not equal to 1.

5. No. The sum of the entries of the third row is not 1.

6. No. There is a negative entry in third row.

7. Yes.

8. Yes.

9. No. It is not a square (n x n) matrix.

10. No. It is not a square matrix.

11. a. The conditional probability that the outcome state 1 will occur given that the outcome state 1 has occurred is 0.3.

    b. 0.7

    c. We compute

$$X_1 = X_0T = [.4 \quad .6] \begin{bmatrix} .3 & .7 \\ .6 & .4 \end{bmatrix} = [.48 \quad .52]$$

12. a. The conditional probability that the outcome state 2 will occur given that the outcome state 2 has occurred is 1/3.

    b. 5/6

    c. We compute

$$X_1 = X_0T = [\tfrac{1}{4} \quad \tfrac{3}{4}] \begin{bmatrix} \tfrac{1}{6} & \tfrac{5}{6} \\ \tfrac{2}{3} & \tfrac{1}{3} \end{bmatrix} = [\tfrac{13}{24} \quad \tfrac{11}{24}].$$

13. We compute

$$X_0T = [.5 \quad .5] \begin{bmatrix} .6 & .4 \\ .2 & .8 \end{bmatrix} = [.4 \quad .6]$$

Thus, after 1 stage of the experiment, the probability of state 1 occurring is 0.4 and the probability of state 2 occurring is 0.6. The tree diagram describing this process follows.

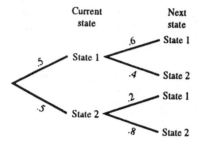

Using this diagram, we see that the probabilities of state 1 and state 2 occurring in the next stage of the experiment are given by

$$P(S_1) = (.5)(.6) + (.5)(.2) = .4$$

$$P(S_2) = (.5)(.4) + (.5)(.8) = .6$$

Observe that these probabilities are precisely those represented in the probability distribution vector $X_0T$.

14. $X_1 = X_0T = [\ \frac{2}{3} \quad \frac{1}{3}\ ]$.

The tree diagram is shown below.

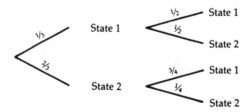

15.

$$X_1 = X_0T = [.6 \quad .4] \begin{bmatrix} .4 & .6 \\ .8 & .2 \end{bmatrix} = [.56 \quad .44]$$

$$X_2 = X_1T = [.56 \quad .44] \begin{bmatrix} .4 & .6 \\ .8 & .2 \end{bmatrix} = [.576 \quad .424]$$

16.

$$X_1 = [\tfrac{1}{2} \quad \tfrac{1}{2} \quad 0] \begin{bmatrix} \tfrac{1}{2} & 0 & \tfrac{1}{2} \\ \tfrac{1}{3} & \tfrac{1}{3} & \tfrac{1}{3} \\ \tfrac{1}{2} & \tfrac{1}{4} & \tfrac{1}{4} \end{bmatrix} = [\tfrac{5}{12} \quad \tfrac{1}{6} \quad \tfrac{5}{12}]$$

$$X_2 = [\tfrac{5}{12} \quad \tfrac{1}{6} \quad \tfrac{5}{12}] \begin{bmatrix} \tfrac{1}{2} & 0 & \tfrac{1}{2} \\ \tfrac{1}{3} & \tfrac{1}{3} & \tfrac{1}{3} \\ \tfrac{1}{2} & \tfrac{1}{4} & \tfrac{1}{4} \end{bmatrix} = [\tfrac{17}{36} \quad \tfrac{23}{144} \quad \tfrac{53}{144}]$$

17.

$$X_1 = [\tfrac{1}{4} \quad \tfrac{1}{2} \quad \tfrac{1}{4}] \begin{bmatrix} \tfrac{1}{4} & \tfrac{1}{4} & \tfrac{1}{2} \\ \tfrac{1}{4} & \tfrac{1}{2} & \tfrac{1}{4} \\ \tfrac{1}{2} & \tfrac{1}{2} & 0 \end{bmatrix} = [\tfrac{5}{16} \quad \tfrac{7}{16} \quad \tfrac{1}{4}].$$

$$X_2 = [\tfrac{5}{16} \quad \tfrac{7}{16} \quad \tfrac{1}{4}] \begin{bmatrix} \tfrac{1}{4} & \tfrac{1}{4} & \tfrac{1}{2} \\ \tfrac{1}{4} & \tfrac{1}{2} & \tfrac{1}{4} \\ \tfrac{1}{2} & \tfrac{1}{2} & 0 \end{bmatrix} = [\tfrac{5}{16} \quad \tfrac{27}{64} \quad \tfrac{17}{64}].$$

18.

$$X_1 = [.25 \quad .40 \quad .35] \begin{bmatrix} .1 & .8 & .1 \\ .1 & .7 & .2 \\ .3 & .2 & .5 \end{bmatrix} = [.17 \quad .55 \quad .28]$$

$$X_2 = [.17 \quad .55 \quad .28] \begin{bmatrix} .1 & .8 & .1 \\ .1 & .7 & .2 \\ .3 & .2 & .5 \end{bmatrix} = [.156 \quad .577 \quad .267]$$

**19.** **a.**

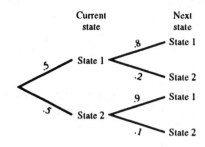

**b.**

$$T = \begin{array}{c} \\ L \\ R \end{array} \begin{array}{cc} L & R \\ \begin{bmatrix} .8 & .2 \\ .9 & .1 \end{bmatrix} \end{array}$$

**c.**

$$X_0 = \begin{array}{cc} L & R \\ [.5 & .5] \end{array}$$

**d.**

$$X_1 = [.5 \quad .5] \begin{array}{c} \\ L \\ R \end{array} \begin{array}{cc} L & R \\ \begin{bmatrix} .8 & .2 \\ .9 & .1 \end{bmatrix} \end{array} = \begin{array}{cc} L & R \\ [.85 & .15] \end{array}$$

so the required probability is 0.85.

**20.**

**a.**

$$T = \begin{array}{c} \\ P \\ A \end{array} \begin{array}{cc} P & A \\ \begin{bmatrix} .8 & .2 \\ .3 & .7 \end{bmatrix} \end{array}$$

**b.**

$$X_0 = [.20 \quad .80]$$

**c.**

$$X_0 T = [.20 \quad .80] \begin{bmatrix} .8 & .2 \\ .3 & .7 \end{bmatrix} = [.40 \quad .60]$$

We conclude that the expected percentage of commuters using public transportation six months from now is 40 percent.

**21.** **a.**

$$X_1 = [.6 \quad .4] \begin{array}{c} \\ D \\ R \end{array} \begin{array}{cc} D & R \\ \begin{bmatrix} .7 & .3 \\ .2 & .8 \end{bmatrix} \end{array} = \begin{array}{cc} D & R \\ [.5 & .5] \end{array}$$

so if the election were held now, it would be a tie.

b.

$$X_1 = [.5 \quad .5] \quad \begin{array}{c} \\ D \\ R \end{array} \overset{\begin{array}{cc} D & R \end{array}}{\begin{bmatrix} .7 & .3 \\ .2 & .8 \end{bmatrix}} = \begin{array}{cc} D & R \end{array} \atop [.45 \quad .55] \, ,$$

which means that the Republican is expected to win if the trend continues.

22.

$$X_1 = X_0 T = [.80 \quad .20] \begin{bmatrix} .97 & .03 \\ .06 & .94 \end{bmatrix} = [.788 \quad .212]$$

$$X_2 = X_1 T = [.788 \quad .212] \begin{bmatrix} .97 & .03 \\ .06 & .94 \end{bmatrix} = [.777 \quad .223]$$

So after one year, 78.8 percent will be in the city and 21.2 percent in the suburb. After two years, 77.7 percent will be in the city and 22.3 percent in the suburb.

23. After one pickup and discharge the distribution will be

$$X_1 = [.6 \quad .2 \quad .2] \begin{bmatrix} .6 & .3 & .1 \\ .4 & .3 & .3 \\ .3 & .3 & .4 \end{bmatrix} = [.5 \; .3 \; .2]$$

or 50% will be in Zone I, 30% will be in Zone II, and 20 percent will be in Zone III.

24.

$$X_1 = X_0 T = [.6 \quad .3 \quad .1] \begin{bmatrix} .75 & .15 & .10 \\ .05 & .90 & .05 \\ .05 & .10 & .85 \end{bmatrix} = [.47 \quad .37 \quad .16]$$

$$X_2 = X_1 T = [.47 \; .37 \; .16] \begin{bmatrix} .75 & .15 & .10 \\ .05 & .90 & .05 \\ .05 & .10 & .85 \end{bmatrix} = [.379 \; .420 \; .202]$$

After 1 year A has 47%, B has 37%, and C has 16%; after 2 years A has 38%, B has 42%, and C has 20%.

25.  The expected distribution is given by

$$X_1 = X_0T = [.4 \quad .4 \quad .2] \begin{bmatrix} .80 & .10 & .10 \\ .10 & .75 & .15 \\ .05 & .05 & .90 \end{bmatrix} = [.37 \quad .35 \quad .28]$$

and we conclude that at the beginning of the second quarter the University Bookstore will have 37 percent of the market, the Campus Bookstore will have 35 percent, and the Book Mart will have 28 percent of the market.

Similarly,

$$X_2 = X_1T = [.37 \quad .35 \quad .28] \begin{bmatrix} .80 & .10 & .10 \\ .10 & .75 & .15 \\ .05 & .05 & .90 \end{bmatrix} = [.345 \quad .3135 \quad .3415]$$

implies that the University Bookstore will have 34.5% of the market, the Campus Bookstore will have 31.35% of the market, and the Book Mart will have 34.15% of the market at the beginning of the third quarter.

26.

$$X_1 = X_0T = [.20 \quad .35 \quad .40 \quad .05] \begin{bmatrix} .70 & .15 & .05 & .10 \\ 0 & .90 & .02 & .08 \\ 0 & .20 & .75 & .05 \\ 0 & .05 & 0 & .95 \end{bmatrix}$$

$$= [.14 \quad .4275 \quad .317 \quad .1155].$$

27.

$$X_1 = X_0T = [.3 \quad .3 \quad .2 \quad .2] \begin{bmatrix} .80 & .10 & .05 & .05 \\ .10 & .70 & .10 & .10 \\ .20 & .10 & .60 & .10 \\ .10 & .05 & .05 & .80 \end{bmatrix}$$

$$= [.33 \quad .27 \quad .175 \quad .225].$$

Similarly,

$$X_2 = X_1 T = [.3485 \quad .25075 \quad .15975 \quad .241]$$

and

$$X_3 = X_2 T = [.3599 \quad .2384 \quad .1504 \quad .2513].$$

Assuming that the present trend continues, 36% of the students in their senior year will major in business, 23.8% will major in the humanities, 15% will major in education, and 25.1% will major in the natural sciences.

## USING TECHNOLOGY EXERCISES 9.1, page 529

1.  $X_5 = [.204489 \quad .131869 \quad .261028 \quad .186814 \quad .2158].$

2.  $X_5 = [.199755 \quad .162005 \quad .200009 \quad .218011 \quad .22022]$

3.  Manufacturer A will have 23.95% of the market, Manufacturer B will have 49.71% of the market share, and Manufacturer C will have 26.34 percent of the market share.

## EXERCISES 9.2, page 538

1.  Since all entries in the matrix are positive, it is regular.

2.  Regular

3.  $$T^2 = \begin{bmatrix} 1 & 0 \\ .8 & .2 \end{bmatrix} \begin{bmatrix} 1 & 0 \\ .8 & .2 \end{bmatrix} = \begin{bmatrix} 1 & 0 \\ .96 & .04 \end{bmatrix}$$

    $$T^3 = \begin{bmatrix} 1 & 0 \\ .96 & .04 \end{bmatrix} \begin{bmatrix} 1 & 0 \\ .8 & .2 \end{bmatrix} = \begin{bmatrix} 1 & 0 \\ .992 & .008 \end{bmatrix}$$

    and we see that the $a_{12}$ entry will always be zero, so T is not regular.

4.  $$T^2 = \begin{bmatrix} \frac{1}{3} & \frac{2}{3} \\ 0 & 1 \end{bmatrix} \begin{bmatrix} \frac{1}{3} & \frac{2}{3} \\ 0 & 1 \end{bmatrix} = \begin{bmatrix} \frac{1}{9} & \frac{8}{9} \\ 0 & 1 \end{bmatrix}$$

    $$T^3 = \begin{bmatrix} \frac{1}{9} & \frac{8}{9} \\ 0 & 1 \end{bmatrix} \begin{bmatrix} \frac{1}{3} & \frac{2}{3} \\ 0 & 1 \end{bmatrix} = \begin{bmatrix} \frac{1}{27} & \frac{26}{27} \\ 0 & 1 \end{bmatrix} \quad \text{and so forth.}$$

and we see that the $a_{21}$ entry will always be zero, so T is not regular.

5.

$$T^2 = \begin{bmatrix} \frac{1}{2} & \frac{1}{2} & 0 \\ \frac{3}{4} & 0 & \frac{1}{4} \\ 0 & \frac{1}{2} & \frac{1}{2} \end{bmatrix} \begin{bmatrix} \frac{1}{2} & \frac{1}{2} & 0 \\ \frac{3}{4} & 0 & \frac{1}{4} \\ 0 & \frac{1}{2} & \frac{1}{2} \end{bmatrix} = \begin{bmatrix} \frac{5}{8} & \frac{1}{4} & \frac{1}{8} \\ \frac{3}{8} & \frac{1}{2} & \frac{1}{8} \\ \frac{3}{8} & \frac{1}{4} & \frac{3}{8} \end{bmatrix}.$$

and so the matrix is regular.

6.     T is not regular.

7.

$$T^2 = \begin{bmatrix} .7 & .3 & 0 \\ .2 & .8 & 0 \\ .3 & .3 & .4 \end{bmatrix} \begin{bmatrix} .7 & .3 & 0 \\ .2 & .8 & 0 \\ .3 & .3 & .4 \end{bmatrix} = \begin{bmatrix} .55 & .45 & 0 \\ .3 & .7 & 0 \\ .39 & .45 & .16 \end{bmatrix}$$

and so forth.

Continuing, we see that $T^3$, $T^4$, ..., will have the $a_{13}$ and $a_{23}$ entries equal to zero and T is not regular.

8.     $T^4$ has entries which are all positive so T is regular.

9.     We solve the matrix equation

$$[x \quad y] = \begin{bmatrix} \frac{1}{3} & \frac{2}{3} \\ \frac{1}{4} & \frac{3}{4} \end{bmatrix} = [x \quad y]$$

or equivalently, the system of equations

$$\frac{1}{3}x + \frac{1}{4}y = x$$

$$\frac{2}{3}x + \frac{3}{4}y = y$$

$$x + y = 1.$$

Solving this system of equations, we find the required vector to be

$$[\frac{3}{11} \quad \frac{8}{11}].$$

10. We solve the matrix equation

$$[x \quad y] = \begin{bmatrix} \dfrac{4}{5} & \dfrac{1}{5} \\ \dfrac{3}{5} & \dfrac{2}{5} \end{bmatrix} = [x \quad y]$$

or equivalently, the system of equations

$$\frac{4}{5}x + \frac{3}{5}y = x$$

$$\frac{1}{5}x + \frac{2}{5}y = y$$

$$x + y = 1.$$

Solving this system of equations, we find the required vector to be

$$[\frac{3}{4} \quad \frac{1}{4}].$$

11. We have XT = X, that is,

$$[x \quad y] \begin{bmatrix} .5 & .5 \\ .2 & .8 \end{bmatrix} = [x \quad y]$$

or equivalently, the system of equations

$$.5x + .2y = x$$

$$.5x + .8y = y.$$

These two equations are equivalent to the single equation $0.5x - 0.2y = 0$. We must also have $x + y = 1$. So we have the system

$$.5x - .2y = 0$$

$$x + \quad y = 1.$$

The second equation gives $y = 1 - x$, which when substituted into the first equation yields

$$0.5x - 0.2(1 - x) = 0, \quad 0.7x - 0.2 = 0, \quad \text{or } x = 2/7.$$

Therefore $y = 5/7$ and the steady-state distribution vector is

$$[\frac{2}{7} \quad \frac{5}{7}].$$

12. We solve the matrix equation

$$[x \quad y] \begin{bmatrix} .9 & .1 \\ 1 & 0 \end{bmatrix} = [x \quad y]$$

or equivalently, the system of equations

$$.9x + y = x$$
$$.1x \quad\quad = y$$
$$x + y = 1.$$

Solving this system of equations, we find the required vector to be

$$[\tfrac{10}{11} \quad \tfrac{1}{11}].$$

13. We solve the system

$$[x \quad y \quad z] \begin{bmatrix} 0 & 1 & 0 \\ \frac{1}{8} & \frac{5}{8} & \frac{1}{4} \\ 1 & 0 & 0 \end{bmatrix} = [x \quad y \quad z]$$

together with the equation $x + y + z = 1$; that is, the system

$$-x + \tfrac{1}{8}y + z = 0$$
$$x - \tfrac{3}{8}y \quad\quad = 0$$
$$\tfrac{1}{4}y - z = 0$$
$$x + y + z = 1.$$

Using the Gauss-Jordan Elimination Method, we find that the required steady-state vector is

$$[\tfrac{3}{13} \quad \tfrac{8}{13} \quad \tfrac{2}{13}]$$

14. We solve the system

$$[x \quad y \quad z] = \begin{bmatrix} .6 & .4 & 0 \\ .3 & .4 & .3 \\ 0 & .6 & .4 \end{bmatrix} = [x \quad y \quad z]$$

together with the equation x + y + z = 1, or equivalently, the system

$$-0.4x + 0.3y \qquad\quad = 0$$

$$0.4x - 0.6y + 0.6z = 0$$

$$0.3y - 0.6z = 0$$

$$x + \quad y + \quad z = 1.$$

Using the Gauss-Jordan Elimination Method, we find that the required steady-state vector is

$$[\tfrac{1}{3} \quad \tfrac{4}{9} \quad \tfrac{2}{9}].$$

15.  We solve the system

$$[x \quad y \quad z] = \begin{bmatrix} .2 & 0 & .8 \\ 0 & .6 & .4 \\ .3 & .4 & .3 \end{bmatrix} = [x \quad y \quad z]$$

together with the equation x + y + z = 1, or equivalently, the system

$$-0.8x \qquad\quad + 0.3z = 0$$

$$- 0.4y + 0.4z = 0$$

$$.8x + 0.4y - 0.7z = 0$$

$$x + \quad y + \quad z = 1.$$

Using the Gauss-Jordan Elimination Method, we find that the required steady-state vector is [3/19   8/19   8/19].

16.  We solve the system

$$[x \quad y \quad z] = \begin{bmatrix} .1 & .1 & .8 \\ .2 & .2 & .6 \\ .3 & .3 & .4 \end{bmatrix} = [x \quad y \quad z]$$

together with the equation x + y + z = 1, or equivalently, the system

$$-0.9x + 0.2y + 0.3z = 0$$

$$0.1x - 0.8y + 0.3z = 0$$

$$0.8x + 0.6y - 0.6z = 0$$

$$x + \quad y + \quad z = 1.$$

Using the Gauss-Jordan Elimination Method, we find that the required steady-state vector is $[\frac{3}{13} \quad \frac{3}{13} \quad \frac{7}{13}]$.

17. We want to solve

$$[x \quad y] \begin{bmatrix} .8 & .2 \\ .9 & .1 \end{bmatrix} = [x \quad y]$$

or, equivalently, the system

$$.8x + .9y = x$$

$$.2x + .1y = y$$

$$x + y = 1.$$

Solving this system, we find that the required steady-state vector is

$$[\frac{2}{11} \quad \frac{9}{11}],$$

and conclude that in the long run, the mouse will turn left 81.8% of the time.

18. We want to solve

$$[x \quad y] \begin{bmatrix} .8 & .2 \\ .3 & .7 \end{bmatrix} = [x \quad y]$$

or, equivalently, the system

$$.8x + .3y = x$$

$$.2x + .7y = y$$

$$x + y = 1.$$

Solving this system, we find that the required steady-state vector is

$$[.6 \quad .4],$$

and conclude that in the long run, 60% of the commuters will use public transportation.

19. a. We compute

$$X_1 = [.48 \quad .52] \begin{bmatrix} .72 & .28 \\ .12 & .88 \end{bmatrix} = [.408 \quad .592],$$

and conclude that, ten years from now, there will be 40.8 percent 1-wage earner and 59.2% 2-wage earners.

b.   We solve the system

$$[x \quad y] \begin{bmatrix} .72 & .28 \\ .12 & .88 \end{bmatrix} = [x \quad y],$$

together with the equation $x + y = 1$.

$$-0.28x + 0.12y = 0$$

$$0.28x - 0.12y = 0$$

$$x + \quad y = 1.$$

Solving, we find $x = 0.3$ and $y = 0.7$, and conclude that in the long run, there will be 30% 1-wage earner and 70% 2-wage earners.

20.   We solve the system

$$[x \quad y] \begin{bmatrix} .95 & .05 \\ .04 & .96 \end{bmatrix} = [x \quad y],$$

together with the equation $x + y = 1$.

$$-0.05x + 0.04y = 0$$

$$x + \quad y = 1.$$

Solving, we find $x = 4/9$ and $y = 5/9$, and conclude that in the long run 55.6% of professional jobs will be held by women.

21.   a. If this trend continues, the percentage of homeowners in this city who will own single-family homes or condominiums two years from now will be given by $X_2 = X_1 T$. Thus,

$$X_1 = X_0 T = [.8 \quad .2] \begin{bmatrix} .85 & .15 \\ .35 & .65 \end{bmatrix} = [.75 \quad .25]$$

$$X_2 = X_1 T = [.75 \quad .25] \begin{bmatrix} .85 & .15 \\ .35 & .65 \end{bmatrix} = [.725 \quad .275]$$

and we conclude that 72.5% will own single-family homes and 27.5% will own condominiums at that time.

b.   We solve the system

$$[x \quad y] \begin{bmatrix} .85 & .15 \\ .35 & .65 \end{bmatrix} = [x \quad y],$$

together with the equation $x + y = 1$. Thus,

$$-0.15x + 0.35y = 0$$

$$0.15x - 0.35y = 0$$

$$x + \quad y = 1.$$

Solving, we find $x = 0.7$ and $y = 0.3$, and conclude that in the long run 70% will own single family homes and 30% will own condominiums.

22. We wish to solve the system

$$[x \quad y \quad z \quad w] = \begin{bmatrix} .70 & .15 & .05 & .10 \\ 0 & .90 & .02 & .08 \\ .10 & .10 & .75 & .05 \\ 0 & .05 & .05 & .90 \end{bmatrix} = [x \quad y \quad z \quad w]$$

together with the equation $x + y + z + w = 1$; equivalently, the system

$$-0.30x \qquad + 0.10z \qquad = 0$$

$$0.15x - 0.10y + 0.10z + 0.05w = 0$$

$$0.05x + 0.02y - 0.25z + 0.05w = 0$$

$$0.10x + 0.08y + 0.05z - 0.10w = 0$$

$$x + \quad y + \quad z + \quad w = 1.$$

Using the Gauss-Jordan Method of elimination, we find that

$$x = 0.042, \ y = 0.404, \ z = 0.126, \text{ and } w = 0.428,$$

and conclude that in the long run 42.8% of the homeowners will be using solar energy.

23. a.

$$X_1 = X_0T = [.3 \quad .4 \quad .3] \begin{bmatrix} .8 & .1 & .1 \\ .1 & .85 & .05 \\ .1 & .05 & .85 \end{bmatrix} = [.31 \quad .385 \quad .305]$$

$$X_2 = X_1T = [.31 \quad .385 \quad .305] \begin{bmatrix} .8 & .1 & .1 \\ .1 & .85 & .05 \\ .1 & .05 & .85 \end{bmatrix} = [.317 \quad .3735 \quad .3095]$$

From our computations, we conclude that after two weeks 31.7% of the viewers will watch the ABC news, 37.35% will watch the CBS news, and 30.95% will watch the NBC news.

b. We solve the system

$$[x \quad y \quad z] = \begin{bmatrix} .8 & .1 & .1 \\ .1 & .85 & .05 \\ .1 & .05 & .85 \end{bmatrix} = [x \quad y \quad z]$$

together with the equation $x + y + z = 1$, or equivalently, the system

$$-0.2x + 0.1y + 0.1z = 0$$
$$0.1x - 0.15y + 0.05z = 0$$
$$0.1x + 0.05y - 0.15z = 0$$
$$x + y + z = 1.$$

Using the Gauss–Jordan Elimination Method, we find that the required steady-state vector is $[1/3 \quad 1/3 \quad 1/3]$, and conclude that each network will command 33.333% of the audience in the long run.

24. In the long-run each network will command 33.333% of the audience. Observe that the same steady state is reached regardless of the initial state of the system.

25. We wish to solve the system

$$[x \quad y \quad z] \begin{array}{c} \\ R \\ P \\ W \end{array} \begin{array}{ccc} R & P & W \\ \begin{bmatrix} \frac{1}{2} & \frac{1}{2} & 0 \\ \frac{1}{4} & \frac{1}{2} & \frac{1}{4} \\ 0 & \frac{1}{2} & \frac{1}{2} \end{bmatrix} \end{array} = [x \quad y \quad z]$$

together with the equation $x + y + z = 1$, or, equivalently, the system of equations

$$\frac{1}{2}x + \frac{1}{4}y = x$$

$$\frac{1}{2}x + \frac{1}{2}y + \frac{1}{2}z = y$$

$$\frac{1}{4}y + \frac{1}{2}z = z$$

$$x + y + z = 1.$$

Solving this system, we find that

$$x = \frac{1}{4}, \ y = \frac{1}{2}, \ \text{and} \ z = \frac{1}{4}.$$

Thus, in the long run, 25% of the plants will have red flowers, 50% will have pink flowers and 25% will have white flowers.

26. We wish to solve the system

$$[x \quad y \quad z] = \begin{bmatrix} .75 & .15 & .10 \\ .05 & .90 & .05 \\ .05 & .10 & .85 \end{bmatrix} = [x \quad y \quad z],$$

or, equivalently,

$$.75x + .05y + .05z = x$$

$$.15x + .90y + .10z = y$$

$$.10x + .05y + .85z = z$$

$$x + y + z = 1.$$

Using the Gauss–Jordan Method to solve this system of equations, we find that the steady-state vector is

$$[.167 \quad .542 \quad .292]$$

and conclude that in the long run manufacturer A will have 16.7% of the market, manufacturer B will have 54.2% of the market, and manufacturer C will have 29.2% of the market.

27. Let T be a regular stochastic matrix and X the steady-state distribution vector that satisfies the equation $XT = X$ and assume that the sum of the elements of X are equal to 1. Then $X = XT$ implies that $XT = XT^2$, or $X = XT^2$, ... . So we have $X = XT^n$.

Next, let L be the steady-state distribution vector, then

$$L = \lim_{m \to \infty} X_m = \lim_{m \to \infty} X_0 T^m \approx X_0 T^m$$

when m is large. Multiplying both sides by T, we obtain

$$LT \approx X_0 T^{m+1} \approx L.$$

Thus, L also satisfies LT = L together with the condition that the sum of the elements in L be equal to 1. Since the matrix equation XT = X has a unique solution, we conclude that X = L.

## USING TECHNOLOGY EXERCISES 9.2, page 543

1.  X = [0.2045    0.1319    0.2610    0.1868    0.2158]

2.  X = [0.1998    0.1620    0.2000    0.2180    0.2202]

## EXERCISES 9.3, page 549

1.  The given matrix is an absorbing stochastic matrix.

$$
\begin{array}{cc}
 & \begin{array}{cc} 1 & 2 \end{array} \\
T = \begin{array}{c} 1 \\ 2 \end{array} & \left[\begin{array}{cc} \frac{2}{5} & \frac{3}{5} \\ 0 & 1 \end{array}\right]
\end{array}
$$

State 2 is an absorbing state. State 1 is nonabsorbing, but an object in this state has a probability of 3/5 of going to the absorbing state 2.

2.  Yes. It is an absorbing stochastic matrix.

3.  The given matrix is

$$
\begin{array}{c}
 & \begin{array}{ccc} 1 & 2 & 3 \end{array} \\
\begin{array}{c} 1 \\ 2 \\ 3 \end{array} & \left[\begin{array}{ccc} 1 & 0 & 0 \\ .5 & 0 & .5 \\ 0 & 1 & 0 \end{array}\right]
\end{array}
$$

States 1 and 3 are absorbing states. State 2 is not absorbing, but an object in this state has a probability of .5 of going to the absorbing state 1 and .5 of going to the absorbing state 3. Thus, the matrix is an absorbing matrix.

4.  The given matrix is

$$
\begin{array}{c}
 & \begin{array}{ccc} 1 & 2 & 3 \end{array} \\
\begin{array}{c} 1 \\ 2 \\ 3 \end{array} & \left[\begin{array}{ccc} 1 & 0 & 0 \\ 0 & .7 & .3 \\ 0 & .2 & .8 \end{array}\right]
\end{array}
$$

State 1 is an absorbing state. But it is impossible for an object to go from the nonabsorbing states 2 and 3 to the absorbing state 1. Therefore, the given matrix is not an absorbing matrix.

5. Yes. It is an absorbing stochastic matrix since it is possible to go from state 1 to the absorbing states 2 and 3.

6. No. It is not an absorbing stochastic matrix since it is not possible to go from the nonabsorbing state 2 or the nonabsorbing state 4 to the absorbing state 1 no matter how many stages occur.

7. The given matrix is

$$
\begin{array}{c}
\begin{array}{cccc} 1 & 2 & 3 & 4 \end{array} \\
\begin{array}{c} 1 \\ 2 \\ 3 \\ 4 \end{array}
\left[
\begin{array}{cccc}
1 & 0 & 0 & 0 \\
0 & 1 & 0 & 0 \\
.3 & .2 & .1 & .4 \\
0 & 0 & .5 & .5
\end{array}
\right]
\end{array}
$$

States 1 and 2 are absorbing states. States 3 and 4 are not. However, it is possible for an object to go from state 3 to state 1 with probability 0.3. Furthermore, it is also possible for an object to go from the non-absorbing state 4 to an absorbing state. For example, via state 3 with a probability of 0.5. Therefore, the given matrix is an absorbing matrix.

8. No. It is not an absorbing stochastic matrix, since it is not possible to go from the nonabsorbing state 3 or the nonabsorbing state 4 to the absorbing state 1 or the absorbing state 2.

9. The required matrix is

$$
\begin{array}{c}
\begin{array}{cc} 2 & 1 \end{array} \\
\begin{array}{c} 2 \\ 1 \end{array}
\left[
\begin{array}{c|c}
1 & 0 \\
\hline
.4 & .6
\end{array}
\right]
\end{array}
$$

where $R = [.4]$ and $S = [.6]$.

10. The required matrix is

$$
\begin{array}{c}
\begin{array}{ccc} 2 & 3 & 1 \end{array} \\
\begin{array}{c} 2 \\ 3 \\ \\ 1 \end{array}
\left[
\begin{array}{cc|c}
1 & 0 & 0 \\
0 & 1 & 0 \\
\hline
\frac{1}{4} & \frac{1}{2} & \frac{1}{4}
\end{array}
\right]
\end{array}
$$

where R = $[\frac{1}{4} \quad \frac{1}{2}]$ and S = $[\frac{1}{4}]$, or

$$\begin{array}{c} \\ 3 \\ 2 \\ 1 \end{array} \begin{array}{ccc} 3 & 2 & 1 \\ \left[\begin{array}{cc|c} 1 & 0 & 0 \\ 0 & 1 & 0 \\ \hline \frac{1}{2} & \frac{1}{4} & \frac{1}{4} \end{array}\right] \end{array}$$

where R = $[\frac{1}{2} \quad \frac{1}{4}]$ and S = $[\frac{1}{4}]$.

11.

$$\begin{array}{c} \\ 3 \\ 2 \\ 1 \end{array} \begin{array}{ccc} 3 & 2 & 1 \\ \left[\begin{array}{c|cc} 1 & 0 & 0 \\ \hline .4 & .4 & .2 \\ .5 & .5 & 0 \end{array}\right] \end{array},$$

where R = $\begin{bmatrix} .4 \\ .5 \end{bmatrix}$ and S = $\begin{bmatrix} .4 & .2 \\ .5 & 0 \end{bmatrix}$

or

$$\begin{array}{c} \\ 3 \\ 1 \\ 2 \end{array} \begin{array}{ccc} 3 & 1 & 2 \\ \left[\begin{array}{c|cc} 1 & 0 & 0 \\ \hline .5 & 0 & .5 \\ .4 & .2 & .4 \end{array}\right] \end{array},$$

where R = $\begin{bmatrix} .5 \\ .4 \end{bmatrix}$ and S = $\begin{bmatrix} 0 & .5 \\ .2 & .4 \end{bmatrix}$

12. The required matrix is

$$\begin{array}{c} \\ 2 \\ 1 \\ 3 \end{array} \begin{array}{ccc} 2 & 1 & 3 \\ \left[\begin{array}{c|cc} 1 & 0 & 0 \\ \hline 0 & .5 & .5 \\ .1 & .3 & .6 \end{array}\right] \end{array},$$

where R = $\begin{bmatrix} 0 \\ .1 \end{bmatrix}$ and S = $\begin{bmatrix} .5 & .5 \\ .3 & .6 \end{bmatrix}$

13.
$$
\begin{bmatrix}
1 & 0 & \vdots & 0 & 0 \\
0 & 1 & \vdots & 0 & 0 \\
\hdashline
.2 & .3 & \vdots & .3 & .2 \\
.4 & 0 & \vdots & .2 & .4
\end{bmatrix}, \quad
R = \begin{bmatrix} .2 & .3 \\ .4 & 0 \end{bmatrix}, \quad
S = \begin{bmatrix} .3 & .2 \\ .2 & .4 \end{bmatrix}
$$

or,
$$
\begin{bmatrix}
1 & 0 & \vdots & 0 & 0 \\
0 & 1 & \vdots & 0 & 0 \\
\hdashline
.4 & 0 & \vdots & .4 & .2 \\
.2 & .3 & \vdots & .2 & .3
\end{bmatrix}, \quad
R = \begin{bmatrix} .4 & 0 \\ .2 & .3 \end{bmatrix}, \quad
S = \begin{bmatrix} .4 & .2 \\ .2 & .3 \end{bmatrix}
$$

and so forth.

14.
$$
\begin{bmatrix}
1 & 0 & \vdots & 0 & 0 \\
0 & 1 & \vdots & 0 & 0 \\
\hdashline
.2 & .3 & \vdots & .1 & .4 \\
.2 & 0 & \vdots & 0 & .8
\end{bmatrix}, \quad
R = \begin{bmatrix} .2 & .3 \\ .2 & 0 \end{bmatrix}, \quad
S = \begin{bmatrix} .1 & .4 \\ 0 & .8 \end{bmatrix}
$$

15. Rewriting the matrix so that the absorbing states appear first, we have

$$
\begin{array}{cc}
 & \begin{array}{cc} 2 & \ \ 1 \end{array} \\
\begin{array}{c} 2 \\ 1 \end{array} &
\begin{bmatrix}
1 & \vdots & 0 \\
\hdashline
.45 & \vdots & .55
\end{bmatrix}
\end{array}
$$

where $R = [.45]$ and $S = [.55]$. Then

$$(I - S) = [.45] \quad \text{and} \quad (I - S)^{-1}R = [\tfrac{1}{.45}][.45] = 1.$$

Therefore, the steady-state matrix is

$$
\begin{array}{cc}
 & \begin{array}{cc} 2 & \ \ 1 \end{array} \\
\begin{array}{c} 2 \\ 1 \end{array} &
\begin{bmatrix}
1 & \vdots & 0 \\
\hdashline
1 & \vdots & 0
\end{bmatrix}
\end{array} .
$$

16. Here we have

$$\left[\begin{array}{c|c} 1 & 0 \\ \hline \dfrac{2}{5} & \dfrac{3}{5} \end{array}\right] \qquad \text{where } R = [\tfrac{2}{5}] \text{ and } S = [\tfrac{3}{5}].$$

Next, we compute

$$I - S = [\tfrac{2}{5}] \text{ and so } (I - S)^{-1} = \tfrac{5}{2}.$$

Then

$$(I - S)^{-1}R = [\tfrac{5}{2}][\tfrac{2}{5}] = 1.$$

Therefore, the steady-state matrix is

$$\left[\begin{array}{c|c} 1 & 0 \\ \hline 1 & 0 \end{array}\right].$$

17. Here we have

$$\left[\begin{array}{c|cc} 1 & 0 & 0 \\ \hline .2 & .4 & .4 \\ .3 & .2 & .5 \end{array}\right] \qquad \text{where } R = \begin{bmatrix} .2 \\ .3 \end{bmatrix} \text{ and } S = \begin{bmatrix} .4 & .4 \\ .2 & .5 \end{bmatrix}$$

Next,

$$I - S = \begin{bmatrix} 1 & 0 \\ 0 & 1 \end{bmatrix} - \begin{bmatrix} .4 & .4 \\ .2 & .5 \end{bmatrix} = \begin{bmatrix} .6 & -.4 \\ -.2 & .5 \end{bmatrix}$$

using the formula for finding the inverse of a 2 x 2 matrix, we have

$$(I - S)^{-1} = \begin{bmatrix} 2.27 & 1.8 \\ .91 & 2.73 \end{bmatrix}.$$

Then

$$(I - S)^{-1}R = \begin{bmatrix} 2.27 & 1.8 \\ .91 & 2.73 \end{bmatrix} \begin{bmatrix} .2 \\ .3 \end{bmatrix} = \begin{bmatrix} .994 \\ 1 \end{bmatrix} \approx \begin{bmatrix} 1 \\ 1 \end{bmatrix}$$

We conclude that the steady-state matrix is

$$\left[\begin{array}{c|cc} 1 & 0 & 0 \\ \hline 1 & 0 & 0 \\ 1 & 0 & 0 \end{array}\right]$$

18. Rewriting the given matrix so that the absorbing states appear first, we have,

$$\begin{bmatrix} 1 & 0 & 0 \\ \hline 0 & \frac{1}{5} & \frac{4}{5} \\ \frac{3}{8} & 0 & \frac{5}{8} \end{bmatrix}$$

where $R = \begin{bmatrix} 0 \\ \frac{3}{8} \end{bmatrix}$ and $S = \begin{bmatrix} \frac{1}{5} & \frac{4}{5} \\ 0 & \frac{5}{8} \end{bmatrix}$.

Now, $I - S = \begin{bmatrix} \frac{4}{5} & -\frac{4}{5} \\ 0 & \frac{3}{8} \end{bmatrix}$ and $(I - S)^{-1} = \begin{bmatrix} \frac{5}{4} & -\frac{8}{3} \\ 0 & \frac{8}{3} \end{bmatrix}$,

and therefore, $(I - S)^{-1}R = \begin{bmatrix} 1 \\ 1 \end{bmatrix}$.

So the steady-state matrix is given by

$$\begin{bmatrix} 1 & 0 & 0 \\ \hline 1 & 0 & 0 \\ 1 & 0 & 0 \end{bmatrix}.$$

19. Upon rewriting the given matrix so that the absorbing states appear first, we have

$$\begin{array}{c} \\ 2 \\ 4 \\ 1 \\ 3 \end{array} \begin{array}{cccc} 2 & 4 & 1 & 3 \\ \begin{bmatrix} 1 & 0 & 0 & 0 \\ 0 & 1 & 0 & 0 \\ \hline \frac{1}{2} & 0 & \frac{1}{2} & 0 \\ 0 & 0 & \frac{1}{3} & \frac{2}{3} \end{bmatrix} \end{array}$$

where

$$R = \begin{bmatrix} \frac{1}{2} & 0 \\ 0 & 0 \end{bmatrix} \text{ and } S = \begin{bmatrix} \frac{1}{2} & 0 \\ \frac{1}{3} & \frac{2}{3} \end{bmatrix}$$

Next, we compute

$$I - S = \begin{bmatrix} 1 & 0 \\ 0 & 1 \end{bmatrix} - \begin{bmatrix} \frac{1}{2} & 0 \\ \frac{1}{3} & \frac{2}{3} \end{bmatrix} = \begin{bmatrix} \frac{1}{2} & 0 \\ -\frac{1}{3} & \frac{1}{3} \end{bmatrix}$$

Using the formula for finding the inverse of a 2 x 2 matrix, we have

$$(I - S)^{-1} = \begin{bmatrix} 2 & 0 \\ 2 & 3 \end{bmatrix} \text{ and so } (I - S)^{-1}R = \begin{bmatrix} 2 & 0 \\ 2 & 3 \end{bmatrix} \begin{bmatrix} \frac{1}{2} & 0 \\ 0 & 0 \end{bmatrix} = \begin{bmatrix} 1 & 0 \\ 1 & 0 \end{bmatrix}$$

Therefore, the steady-state matrix is

$$\begin{bmatrix} 1 & 0 & 0 & 0 \\ 0 & 1 & 0 & 0 \\ 1 & 0 & 0 & 0 \\ 1 & 0 & 0 & 0 \end{bmatrix}$$

20. Upon rewriting the given matrix, we have

$$\begin{array}{c} \\ 1 \\ 4 \\ 2 \\ 3 \end{array} \begin{array}{cccc} 1 & 4 & 2 & 3 \end{array} \\ \begin{bmatrix} 1 & 0 & 0 & 0 \\ 0 & 1 & 0 & 0 \\ \frac{1}{8} & \frac{1}{2} & \frac{1}{8} & \frac{1}{4} \\ \frac{1}{3} & 0 & 0 & \frac{2}{3} \end{bmatrix}$$

where

$$R = \begin{bmatrix} \frac{1}{8} & \frac{1}{2} \\ \frac{1}{3} & 0 \end{bmatrix} \text{ and } S = \begin{bmatrix} \frac{1}{8} & \frac{1}{4} \\ 0 & \frac{2}{3} \end{bmatrix} .$$

Next,

$$I - S = \begin{bmatrix} \frac{7}{8} & -\frac{1}{4} \\ 0 & \frac{1}{3} \end{bmatrix} .$$

Using the formula for finding the inverse of a 2 x 2 matrix, we have

$$(I - S)^{-1} = \begin{bmatrix} \frac{8}{7} & \frac{6}{7} \\ 0 & 3 \end{bmatrix} \quad \text{and} \quad (I - S)^{-1}R = \begin{bmatrix} \frac{3}{7} & \frac{4}{7} \\ 1 & 0 \end{bmatrix}.$$

Therefore, the steady-state matrix is

$$\begin{bmatrix} 1 & 0 & \vdots & 0 & 0 \\ 0 & 1 & \vdots & 0 & 0 \\ - & - & - & - & - \\ \frac{3}{7} & \frac{4}{7} & \vdots & 0 & 0 \\ 1 & 0 & \vdots & 0 & 0 \end{bmatrix}.$$

21. Here

$$\begin{bmatrix} 1 & 0 & \vdots & 0 & 0 \\ 0 & 1 & \vdots & 0 & 0 \\ - & - & - & - & - \\ \frac{1}{4} & \frac{1}{4} & \vdots & \frac{1}{2} & 0 \\ \frac{1}{3} & \frac{1}{3} & \vdots & 0 & \frac{1}{3} \end{bmatrix}$$

$$R = \begin{bmatrix} \frac{1}{4} & \frac{1}{4} \\ \frac{1}{3} & \frac{1}{3} \end{bmatrix} \qquad \begin{bmatrix} \frac{1}{2} & 0 \\ 0 & \frac{1}{3} \end{bmatrix}$$

and

$$I - S = \begin{bmatrix} 1 & 0 \\ 0 & 1 \end{bmatrix} - \begin{bmatrix} \frac{1}{2} & 0 \\ 0 & \frac{1}{3} \end{bmatrix} = \begin{bmatrix} \frac{1}{2} & 0 \\ 0 & \frac{2}{3} \end{bmatrix}.$$

Using the formula for finding the inverse of a 2 x 2 matrix, we find

$$(I - S)^{-1} = \begin{bmatrix} 2 & 0 \\ 0 & \frac{3}{2} \end{bmatrix}$$

$$(I - S)^{-1}R = \begin{bmatrix} 2 & 0 \\ 0 & \frac{3}{2} \end{bmatrix} \begin{bmatrix} \frac{1}{4} & \frac{1}{4} \\ \frac{1}{3} & \frac{1}{3} \end{bmatrix} = \begin{bmatrix} \frac{1}{2} & \frac{1}{2} \\ \frac{1}{2} & \frac{1}{2} \end{bmatrix}.$$

We conclude that the steady-state matrix is given by

$$\begin{bmatrix} 1 & 0 & | & 0 & 0 \\ 0 & 1 & | & 0 & 0 \\ \hline \frac{1}{2} & \frac{1}{2} & | & 0 & 0 \\ \frac{1}{2} & \frac{1}{2} & | & 0 & 0 \end{bmatrix}$$

22. Here
$$\begin{bmatrix} 1 & 0 & | & 0 & 0 \\ 0 & 1 & | & 0 & 0 \\ \hline .2 & .4 & | & 0 & .4 \\ .1 & .2 & | & .4 & .3 \end{bmatrix}$$

$$R = \begin{bmatrix} .2 & .4 \\ .1 & .2 \end{bmatrix} \quad \text{and } S = \begin{bmatrix} 0 & .4 \\ .4 & .3 \end{bmatrix}.$$

We find

$$I - S = \begin{bmatrix} 1 & 0 \\ 0 & 1 \end{bmatrix} - \begin{bmatrix} 0 & .4 \\ .4 & .3 \end{bmatrix} = \begin{bmatrix} 1 & -.4 \\ -.4 & .7 \end{bmatrix}$$

$$(I - S)^{-1} = \begin{bmatrix} \frac{35}{27} & \frac{20}{27} \\ \frac{20}{27} & \frac{50}{27} \end{bmatrix}$$

so that

$$(I - S)^{-1}R = \begin{bmatrix} \frac{35}{27} & \frac{20}{27} \\ \frac{20}{27} & \frac{50}{27} \end{bmatrix} \begin{bmatrix} .2 & .4 \\ .1 & .2 \end{bmatrix} = \begin{bmatrix} \frac{1}{3} & \frac{2}{3} \\ \frac{1}{3} & \frac{2}{3} \end{bmatrix}$$

Therefore, the steady-state matrix is given by

$$\begin{bmatrix} 1 & 0 & | & 0 & 0 \\ 0 & 1 & | & 0 & 0 \\ \hline \frac{1}{3} & \frac{2}{3} & | & 0 & 0 \\ \frac{1}{3} & \frac{2}{3} & | & 0 & 0 \end{bmatrix}$$

23. The absorbing states already appear first in the matrix, so it need not be rewritten. Next,

$$(I - S) = \begin{bmatrix} .8 & -.2 \\ -.2 & .6 \end{bmatrix}.$$

and

$$(I - S)^{-1} = \begin{bmatrix} \dfrac{15}{11} & \dfrac{5}{11} \\ \dfrac{5}{11} & \dfrac{20}{11} \end{bmatrix}.$$

so that

$$(I - S)^{-1}R = \begin{bmatrix} \dfrac{15}{11} & \dfrac{5}{11} \\ \dfrac{5}{11} & \dfrac{20}{11} \end{bmatrix} \begin{bmatrix} .2 & .1 & .3 \\ .1 & .2 & .1 \end{bmatrix} = \begin{bmatrix} \dfrac{7}{22} & \dfrac{5}{22} & \dfrac{5}{11} \\ \dfrac{3}{11} & \dfrac{9}{22} & \dfrac{7}{22} \end{bmatrix}.$$

Therefore, the steady-state matrix is given by

$$\left[ \begin{array}{ccc|cc} 1 & 0 & 0 & 0 & 0 \\ 0 & 1 & 0 & 0 & 0 \\ 0 & 0 & 1 & 0 & 0 \\ \hline \dfrac{7}{22} & \dfrac{5}{22} & \dfrac{5}{11} & 0 & 0 \\ \dfrac{3}{11} & \dfrac{9}{22} & \dfrac{7}{22} & 0 & 0 \end{array} \right].$$

24.

$$S = \begin{bmatrix} \dfrac{1}{4} & \dfrac{1}{2} & 0 \\ \dfrac{1}{3} & 0 & 0 \\ 0 & \dfrac{1}{2} & 0 \end{bmatrix}$$

$$I - S = \begin{bmatrix} \dfrac{3}{4} & -\dfrac{1}{2} & 0 \\ -\dfrac{1}{3} & 1 & 0 \\ 0 & -\dfrac{1}{2} & 1 \end{bmatrix}$$

and $(I - S)^{-1} = \begin{bmatrix} \dfrac{12}{7} & \dfrac{6}{7} & 0 \\ \dfrac{4}{7} & \dfrac{9}{7} & 0 \\ \dfrac{2}{7} & \dfrac{9}{14} & 1 \end{bmatrix}.$

Therefore, $(I - S)^{-1}P =$ $\begin{bmatrix} \frac{5}{7} & \frac{2}{7} \\ \frac{4}{7} & \frac{3}{7} \\ \frac{2}{7} & \frac{5}{7} \end{bmatrix}.$

So, the steady-state matrix is

$$\left[\begin{array}{ccccc} 1 & 0 & 0 & 0 & 0 \\ 0 & 1 & 0 & 0 & 0 \\ \frac{5}{7} & \frac{2}{7} & 0 & 0 & 0 \\ \frac{4}{7} & \frac{3}{7} & 0 & 0 & 0 \\ \frac{2}{7} & \frac{5}{7} & 0 & 0 & 0 \end{array}\right]$$

25.  a. State 2 is absorbing. State 1 is not absorbing, but it is possible for an object to go from state 1 to state 2 with probability 0.8. Therefore, the matrix is absorbing. Rewriting, we obtain

$$\begin{array}{c} \phantom{1}\ \ \ \ 2\ \ \ \ \ 1 \\ \begin{array}{c} 1 \\ 2 \end{array} \left[\begin{array}{cc} 1 & 0 \\ .2 & .8 \end{array}\right] \end{array} \quad \text{where } R = [0.2] \text{ and } S = [0.8].$$

b. We compute $I - S = [1] - [0.8] = [0.2]$. So, $(I - S)^{-1} = [5]$.

Therefore, $(I - S)^{-1}R = [5][0.2] = [1]$ and the steady-state matrix is
$$\left[\begin{array}{cc} 1 & 0 \\ 1 & 0 \end{array}\right]$$

This result tells us that in the long run only unleaded gas will be used.

26.  Here

$$\begin{array}{c} \phantom{\$0}\ \ \$0\ \ \ \ \$3\ \ \ \ \$1\ \ \ \$2 \\ \begin{array}{c} \$0 \\ \$3 \\ \$1 \\ \$2 \end{array} \left[\begin{array}{cccc} 1 & 0 & 0 & 0 \\ 0 & 1 & 0 & 0 \\ \frac{1}{2} & 0 & 0 & \frac{1}{2} \\ 0 & \frac{1}{2} & \frac{1}{2} & 0 \end{array}\right] \end{array}$$

where

$$R = \begin{bmatrix} \frac{1}{2} & 0 \\ 0 & \frac{1}{2} \end{bmatrix} \quad \text{and} \quad S = \begin{bmatrix} 0 & \frac{1}{2} \\ \frac{1}{2} & 1 \end{bmatrix}.$$

Next,

$$I - S = \begin{bmatrix} 1 & 0 \\ 0 & 1 \end{bmatrix} - \begin{bmatrix} 0 & \frac{1}{2} \\ \frac{1}{2} & 1 \end{bmatrix} = \begin{bmatrix} 1 & -\frac{1}{2} \\ -\frac{1}{2} & 1 \end{bmatrix}$$

$$(I - S)^{-1}R = \begin{bmatrix} \frac{4}{3} & \frac{2}{3} \\ \frac{2}{3} & \frac{4}{3} \end{bmatrix} \begin{bmatrix} \frac{1}{2} & 0 \\ 0 & \frac{1}{2} \end{bmatrix} = \begin{bmatrix} \frac{2}{3} & \frac{1}{3} \\ \frac{1}{3} & \frac{2}{3} \end{bmatrix}$$

Therefore, the steady-state matrix is given by

$$\begin{array}{c} \\ \$0 \\ \$3 \\ \$1 \\ \$2 \end{array} \begin{array}{cccc} \$0 & \$3 & \$1 & \$2 \\ \begin{bmatrix} 1 & 0 & 0 & 0 \\ 0 & 1 & 0 & 0 \\ \frac{2}{3} & \frac{1}{3} & 0 & 0 \\ \frac{1}{3} & \frac{2}{3} & 0 & 0 \end{bmatrix} \end{array}.$$

We conclude that if Diane started out with \$1, the probability that she would leave the game a winner would be 1/3. Similarly, if she started out with \$2, the probability that she would leave the game a winner is 2/3.

27. Here

$$\begin{array}{c} \\ \$0 \\ \$4 \\ \$1 \\ \$2 \\ \$3 \end{array} \begin{array}{ccccc} \$0 & \$4 & \$1 & \$2 & \$3 \\ \begin{bmatrix} 1 & 0 & 0 & 0 & 0 \\ 0 & 1 & 0 & 0 & 0 \\ \frac{1}{2} & 0 & 0 & \frac{1}{2} & 0 \\ 0 & 0 & \frac{1}{2} & 0 & \frac{1}{2} \\ 0 & \frac{1}{2} & 0 & \frac{1}{2} & 0 \end{bmatrix} \end{array}$$

where

$$R = \begin{bmatrix} \frac{1}{2} & 0 \\ 0 & 0 \\ 0 & \frac{1}{2} \end{bmatrix} \quad \text{and} \quad S = \begin{bmatrix} 0 & \frac{1}{2} & 0 \\ \frac{1}{2} & 0 & \frac{1}{2} \\ 0 & \frac{1}{2} & 0 \end{bmatrix}.$$

Next,

$$I - S = \begin{bmatrix} 1 & -\frac{1}{2} & 0 \\ -\frac{1}{2} & 1 & -\frac{1}{2} \\ 0 & -\frac{1}{2} & 1 \end{bmatrix} \quad \text{and} \quad (I - S)^{-1} = \begin{bmatrix} \frac{3}{2} & 1 & \frac{3}{2} \\ 1 & 2 & 1 \\ \frac{3}{2} & 1 & \frac{3}{2} \end{bmatrix}.$$

$$(I - S)^{-1}R = \begin{bmatrix} \frac{3}{4} & \frac{1}{4} \\ \frac{1}{2} & \frac{1}{2} \\ \frac{1}{4} & \frac{3}{4} \end{bmatrix}.$$

Therefore, the steady-state matrix is given by

|      | $0 | $4 | $1 | $2 | $3 |
|------|-----|-----|-----|-----|-----|
| $0  | 1   | 0   | 0   | 0   | 0   |
| $4  | 0   | 1   | 0   | 0   | 0   |
| $1  | $\frac{3}{4}$ | $\frac{1}{4}$ | 0 | 0 | 0 |
| $2  | $\frac{1}{2}$ | $\frac{1}{2}$ | 0 | 0 | 0 |
| $3  | $\frac{1}{4}$ | $\frac{3}{4}$ | 0 | 0 | 0 |

We conclude that if Diane started out with $1, the probability that she would leave the game a winner is 1/4. Similarly, if she started out with $2, the probability that she would leave the game a winner is 1/2, and if she started out with $3, the probability that she would leave as a winner is 3/4.

28. a.

|   | W | M | E |
|---|-----|-----|-----|
| W | 1   | 0   | 0   |
| M | .20 | .10 | .70 |
| E | .40 | 0   | .60 |

b.

$$I - S = \begin{bmatrix} 1 & 0 \\ 0 & 1 \end{bmatrix} - \begin{bmatrix} .1 & .7 \\ 0 & .6 \end{bmatrix} = \begin{bmatrix} .9 & -.7 \\ 0 & .4 \end{bmatrix}.$$

Next, using the formula for the inverse of a 2 x 2 matrix, we find that

$$(I - S)^{-1} = \begin{bmatrix} 1.11 & 1.95 \\ 0 & 2.5 \end{bmatrix}$$

and

$$(I - S)^{-1}R = \begin{bmatrix} 1.11 & 1.95 \\ 0 & 2.5 \end{bmatrix} \begin{bmatrix} .2 \\ .4 \end{bmatrix} = \begin{bmatrix} 1 \\ 1 \end{bmatrix}.$$

Therefore, the steady-state matrix is

$$\begin{bmatrix} 1 & 0 & 0 \\ \hline 1 & 0 & 0 \\ 1 & 0 & 0 \end{bmatrix}$$

So, eventually all companies will use electric typewriters with some form of word-processing capability.

29.  a.

$$\begin{array}{c} \\ D \\ G \\ 1 \\ 2 \end{array}
\begin{array}{cccc} D & G & 1 & 2 \end{array}
\begin{bmatrix} 1 & 0 & 0 & 0 \\ 0 & 1 & 0 & 0 \\ \hline .25 & 0 & 0 & .75 \\ .1 & .9 & 0 & 0 \end{bmatrix}$$

b.

$$I - S = \begin{bmatrix} 1 & -.75 \\ 0 & 1 \end{bmatrix} \quad \text{and} \quad (I - S)^{-1} = \begin{bmatrix} 1 & .75 \\ 0 & 1 \end{bmatrix}.$$

and

$$(I - S)^{-1}R = \begin{bmatrix} 1 & .75 \\ 0 & 1 \end{bmatrix} \begin{bmatrix} .25 & 0 \\ .1 & .9 \end{bmatrix} = \begin{bmatrix} .325 & .675 \\ .1 & .9 \end{bmatrix}.$$

Therefore, the steady-state matrix is

$$
\begin{bmatrix}
1 & 0 & 0 & 0 \\
0 & 1 & 0 & 0 \\
.325 & .675 & 0 & 0 \\
.1 & .9 & 0 & 0
\end{bmatrix}.
$$

c. From the steady-state matrix, we see that the probability that a beginning student enrolled in the program will complete the course successfully is 0.675.

30. a.

$$
\begin{array}{c}
\quad\;\; D \quad\; G \quad\; 1 \quad\; 2 \quad\; 3 \\
\begin{array}{c} D \\ G \\ 1 \\ 2 \\ 3 \end{array}
\begin{bmatrix}
1 & 0 & 0 & 0 & 0 \\
0 & 1 & 0 & 0 & 0 \\
.15 & 0 & 0 & .85 & 0 \\
.08 & 0 & 0 & 0 & .92 \\
.02 & .98 & 0 & 0 & 0
\end{bmatrix}
\end{array}
$$

b.

$$
I - S = \begin{bmatrix}
1 & -.85 & 0 \\
0 & 1 & -.92 \\
0 & 0 & 1
\end{bmatrix}
\quad \text{and} \quad (I - S)^{-1} = \begin{bmatrix}
1 & .85 & .782 \\
0 & 1 & .92 \\
0 & 0 & 1
\end{bmatrix}.
$$

and

$$
(I - S)^{-1}R = \begin{bmatrix}
.2336 & .7664 \\
.0984 & .9016 \\
.02 & .98
\end{bmatrix}.
$$

Therefore, the steady-state matrix is

$$
\begin{bmatrix}
1 & 0 & 0 & 0 & 0 \\
0 & 1 & 0 & 0 & 0 \\
.2336 & .7664 & 0 & 0 & 0 \\
.0984 & .9016 & 0 & 0 & 0 \\
.02 & .98 & 0 & 0 & 0
\end{bmatrix}.
$$

**c.** From the steady-state matrix, we see that the probability that a student will graduate is 0.7664.

31.  The transition matrix is

$$
T = \begin{array}{c} \\ aa \\ Aa \\ AA \end{array}
\begin{array}{ccc} aa & Aa & AA \end{array}
\left[
\begin{array}{c:c:c}
1 & 0 & 0 \\ \hdashline
\frac{1}{2} & \frac{1}{2} & 0 \\ \hdashline
0 & 1 & 0
\end{array}
\right] .
$$

Since the entries in T are exactly the same as those in Example 4, the steady-state matrix is

$$
\begin{array}{c} \\ aa \\ Aa \\ AA \end{array}
\begin{array}{ccc} aa & Aa & AA \end{array}
\left[
\begin{array}{c:cc}
1 & 0 & 0 \\ \hdashline
1 & 0 & 0 \\
1 & 0 & 0
\end{array}
\right] .
$$

Interpreting the steady-state matrix, we see that in the long run all the flowers produced by the plants will be white.

## EXERCISES 9.4, page 562

1.  We first determine the minimum of each row and the maxima of each column of the payoff matrix. Next, we find the larger of the row minima and the smaller of the column maxima as shown below.

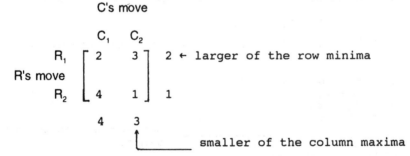

From the above results, we conclude that the row player's maximum strategy is to play row 1, whereas the column player's minimax strategy is to play column 2.

2.  We first determine the minimum of each row and the maxima of each column of the payoff matrix. Next, we find the larger of the row

minima and the smaller of the column maxima as shown below.

C's move

$$
\begin{array}{cc}
 & C_1 \quad C_2 \\
R_1 \\
R's\ move \\
R_2
\end{array}
\begin{bmatrix}
-1 & 3 \\
2 & 5
\end{bmatrix}
\begin{array}{l}
-1 \\
2 \leftarrow \text{larger of the row minima}
\end{array}
$$

2   5

↑_____ smaller of the column maxima

From the above results, we conclude that the row player's maximum strategy is to play row 2, whereas the column player's minimax strategy is to play column 1.

3.  We first obtain the following matrix, where the larger of the row minima and the smallest of the column maxima are displayed.

$$
\begin{array}{c}
C_1 \quad C_2 \quad C_3 \\
R_1 \\
R_2
\end{array}
\begin{bmatrix}
1 & 3 & 2 \\
0 & -1 & 4
\end{bmatrix}
\begin{array}{l}
1 \leftarrow \text{larger of the row minima} \\
-1
\end{array}
$$

1   3   4

↑_____ smallest of the column maxima

We conclude that the row player's maximun strategy is to play row 1, whereas the column player's minimax strategy is to play column 1.

4.  We first obtain the following matrix, where the larger of the row minima and the smallest of the column maxima are displayed.

$$
\begin{array}{c}
C_1 \quad C_2 \quad C_3 \\
R_1 \\
R_2
\end{array}
\begin{bmatrix}
1 & 4 & -2 \\
4 & 6 & -3
\end{bmatrix}
\begin{array}{l}
-2 \longleftarrow \text{larger of the row minima} \\
-3
\end{array}
$$

4   6   -2

↑_____ smallest of the column maxima

We conclude that the row player's maximun strategy is to play row 1, whereas the column player's minimax strategy is to play column 3.

5.  From the following payoff matrix where the largest of the row minima and the smallest of the column maxima are displayed

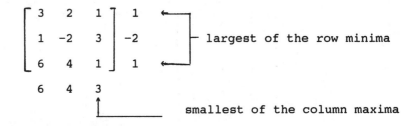

largest of the row minima

smallest of the column maxima

we conclude that the row player's maximin strategy is to play either row 1 or row 3, whereas the column player's minimax strategy is to play column 3.

6. We first obtain the following matrix, where the largest of the row minima and the smaller of the column maxima are displayed.

$$\begin{bmatrix} 1 & 4 \\ 2 & -2 \\ 3 & 0 \end{bmatrix} \begin{matrix} 1 & \leftarrow \text{ largest of the row minima} \\ -2 \\ 0 \end{matrix}$$

3   4

smaller of the column maxima

We conclude that the row player's maximin strategy is to play row 1, and the column player's minimax strategy is to play column 1.

7. From the following payoff matrix where the largest of the row minima and the smallest of the column maxima are displayed

$$\begin{bmatrix} 4 & 2 & 1 \\ 1 & 0 & -1 \\ 2 & 1 & 3 \end{bmatrix} \begin{matrix} 1 & \leftarrow \\ -1 \\ 1 & \leftarrow \end{matrix}$$

4   2   3

largest of the row minima

smallest of the column maxima

we conclude that the row player's maximin strategy is to play either row 1 or row 3, whereas the column player's minimax strategy is to play column 2.

8. From the following payoff matrix where the largest of the row minima and the smallest of the column maxima are displayed,

$$\begin{bmatrix} -1 & 1 & 2 \\ 3 & 1 & 1 \\ -1 & 1 & 2 \\ 3 & 2 & -1 \end{bmatrix} \begin{array}{c} -1 \\ 1 \\ -1 \\ -1 \end{array} \longleftarrow \text{largest of the row minima}$$

$$\begin{array}{ccc} 3 & 2 & 2 \end{array}$$

smallest of the column maxima

we conclude that the row player's maximin strategy is to play row 2, whereas the column player's minimax strategy is to play either column 2 or column 3.

9.  From

$$\begin{bmatrix} ②& 3 \\ 1 & -4 \end{bmatrix} \begin{array}{c} 2 \\ -4 \end{array} \longleftarrow \text{larger of the row minima}$$

$$\begin{array}{cc} 2 & 3 \end{array}$$

smaller of the column maxima

we see that the game is strictly determined, and

a. the saddle point is 2.

b. the optimum strategy for the row player is to play row 1, whereas the optimum strategy for the column player is to play column 1.

c. the value of the game is 2.

d. the game favors the row player.

10.  From

$$\begin{bmatrix} 1 & ⓪ \\ 0 & -1 \end{bmatrix} \begin{array}{c} 0 \\ -1 \end{array} \longleftarrow \text{larger of the row minima}$$

$$\begin{array}{cc} 1 & 0 \end{array}$$

smaller of the column maxima

we see that the game is strictly determined, and

a. the saddle point is 0.

b. the optimum strategy for the row player is to play row 1, whereas the optimum strategy for the column player is to play column 2.

c. the value of the game is zero.

d. the game does not favor either player.

11. From

$$
\begin{bmatrix} \boxed{①} & 3 & 2 \\ -1 & 4 & -6 \end{bmatrix} \quad \begin{matrix} 1 \\ -6 \end{matrix} \longleftarrow \text{larger of the row minima}
$$

$$
\begin{matrix} 1 & 4 & 2 \end{matrix}
$$

↑ ⎯⎯⎯⎯⎯⎯⎯ smallest of the column maxima

we see that the game is strictly determined, and

a. the saddle point is 1.

b. the optimum strategy for the row player is to play row 1, whereas, the optimum strategy for the column player is to play column 1.

c. the value of the game is 1.

d. the game favors the row player.

12. From

$$
\begin{bmatrix} 3 & ② \\ -1 & -2 \\ 4 & 1 \end{bmatrix} \quad \begin{matrix} 2 \\ -2 \\ 1 \end{matrix} \longleftarrow \text{largest of the row minima}
$$

$$
\begin{matrix} 4 & 2 \end{matrix}
$$

↑ ⎯⎯⎯⎯⎯⎯⎯ smaller of the column maxima

we see that the game is strictly determined, and

a. the saddle point is 2.

b. the optimum strategy for the row player is to play row 1, whereas the optimum strategy for the column player is to play column 2.

c. the value of the game is 2.

d. the game favors the row player.

13. From

$$\begin{bmatrix} \textcircled{1} & 3 & 4 & 2 \\ 0 & 2 & 6 & -4 \\ -1 & -3 & -2 & 1 \end{bmatrix} \quad \begin{matrix} 1 \\ -4 \\ -3 \end{matrix}$$ ← largest of the row minima

$$\begin{matrix} 1 & 3 & 6 & 2 \\ \uparrow & & & \end{matrix}$$ smallest of the column maxima

we conclude that the game is strictly determined, and

a. the saddle point is 1.

b. the optimum strategy for the row player is to play row 1, while the optimum strategy for the column player is to play column 1.

c. the value of the game is 1.

d. the game favors the row player.

14. From

$$\begin{bmatrix} \textcircled{2} & 4 & \textcircled{2} \\ 0 & 3 & 0 \\ -1 & -2 & 1 \end{bmatrix} \quad \begin{matrix} 2 \\ 0 \\ -2 \end{matrix}$$ ← largest of the row minima

$$\begin{matrix} 2 & 4 & 2 \\ \uparrow & & \uparrow \end{matrix}$$ smallest of the column maxima

we conclude that the game is strictly determined, and

a. the saddle point is 2.

b. the optimum strategy for the row player is to play row 1, while the optimum strategy for the column player is to play column 1 or column 3.

c. the value of the game is 2.

d. the game favors the row player.

**15.** From

$$\begin{bmatrix} 1 & 2 \\ 0 & 3 \\ -1 & 2 \\ 2 & -2 \end{bmatrix} \quad \begin{matrix} 1 \\ 0 \\ -1 \\ -2 \end{matrix}$$

$1$ ←——— larger of the row minima

$$\begin{matrix} 2 & 3 \end{matrix}$$

↑_____ smaller of the column maxima

we see that the game is not strictly determined and consequently has no saddle point.

**16.** From

$$\begin{bmatrix} -1 & 2 & 4 \\ ② & 3 & 5 \\ 0 & 1 & -3 \\ -2 & 4 & -2 \end{bmatrix} \quad \begin{matrix} -1 \\ 2 \\ -3 \\ -2 \end{matrix}$$

$2$ ←——— largest of the row minima

$$\begin{matrix} 2 & 4 & 5 \end{matrix}$$

↑_____ smallest of the column maxima

we conclude that the game is strictly determined, and

a. the saddle point is 2.

b. the optimum strategy for the row player is to play row 2, whereas the optimum strategy for the column player is to play column 1.

c. the value of the game is 2.

d. it favors the row player.

**17.** From

$$\begin{bmatrix} 1 & -1 & 3 & 2 \\ 1 & 0 & 2 & 2 \\ -2 & 2 & 3 & -1 \end{bmatrix} \quad \begin{matrix} -1 \\ 0 \\ -2 \end{matrix}$$

$0$ ←——— largest of the row minima

$$\begin{matrix} 1 & 2 & 3 & 2 \end{matrix}$$

↑_____ smallest of the column maxima

we conclude that the game is not strictly determined since there is no entry that is simultaneously the largest of the row minima and the smallest of the column maxima.

18. From

$$\begin{bmatrix} 3 & -1 & 0 & -4 \\ 2 & 1 & \boxed{0} & 2 \\ -3 & 1 & -2 & 1 \\ -1 & -1 & -2 & 1 \end{bmatrix} \begin{matrix} -4 \\ 0 \\ -3 \\ -2 \end{matrix}$$

0 ⟵ largest of the row minima

3  1  0  2

smallest of the column maxima

we conclude that the game is strictly determined, and

a. the saddle point is 0.

b. the optimum strategy for the row player is to play row 2, whereas the optimum strategy for the column player is to play column 3.

c. the value of the game is 0.

d. it does not favor either player.

19. a.

$$\begin{matrix} & 1 & 2 & 3 \\ 1 & \begin{bmatrix} 2 & -3 & 4 \\ 2 & -3 & 4 & -5 \\ 3 & 4 & -5 & 6 \end{bmatrix} \end{matrix}$$

b. From

$$\begin{bmatrix} 2 & -3 & 4 \\ -3 & 4 & -5 \\ 4 & -5 & 6 \end{bmatrix} \begin{matrix} -3 \\ -5 \\ -5 \end{matrix}$$

−3 ⟵ largest of the row minima

4  4  6

smaller of the column maxima

we conclude that the maximin strategy for Robin is to play row 1 (extend 1 finger), whereas the minimax strategy for Cathy is to play column 1 or column 2 (extend 1 or 2 fingers).

20.  a. From

$$\begin{bmatrix} 2 & \boxed{-2} \\ 3 & -4 \end{bmatrix} \begin{array}{l} -2 \longleftarrow \\ -4 \end{array} \quad \text{larger of the row minima}$$

$$\begin{array}{cc} 3 & -2 \\ & \uparrow \\ & \text{\rule{0.6cm}{0.4pt}} \end{array} \quad \text{smaller of the column maxima.}$$

We conclude that the game is strictly determined.

b. The value of the game is -2.

c. The ideal location for Brady's is the Civic Center and the ideal location for the Value Mart is the North Shore Plaza.

21.  a. The following is the payoff matrix for the game.

Economy

|  | good | recess. | |
|---|---|---|---|
| expand | 200,000 | 120,000 | 120,000 ← larger of the row minima |
| not expand | 50,000 | 150,000 | 50,000 |
|  | 200,000 | 150,000 | |

smaller of the column maxima

b. The row player's (management) minimax strategy is to play row 1, that is, to expand its line of conventional speakers.

22.  a. The following is the payoff matrix for this game.

|  | G | O | R | |
|---|---|---|---|---|
| Expand | 442,000 | 40,000 | -108,000 | -108,000 |
| Do not expand | 280,000 | 190,000 | (100,000) | 100,000 ← largest of row maxima |
|  | 442,000 | 190,000 | 100,000 | |

smallest of column maxima

b. From the payoff matrix, we see that the game is strictly determined, and the row player should play row 2; that is, the restaurant should not expand.

23. a. The following is the payoff matrix for this game.

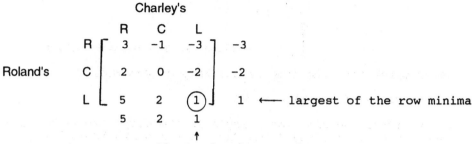

Charley's

|  |  | R | C | L |  |
|---|---|---|---|---|---|
| | R | 3 | −1 | −3 | −3 |
| Roland's | C | 2 | 0 | −2 | −2 |
| | L | 5 | 2 | ①1 | 1 ← largest of the row minima |
| | | 5 | 2 | 1 | |

↑
smallest of column maxima

b. From the payoff matrix, we see that the game is strictly determined,
c. If neither party is willing to lower their price, the payoff matrix would be

Charley's

|  |  | R | C |  |
|---|---|---|---|---|
| | R | 3 | −1 | −1 |
| Roland's | C | 2 | ⓪0 | 0 ← larger of the row minima |
| | | 3 | 0 | |

↑
smaller of column maxima

and we see that the game is strictly determined, so that the optimal strategy for each barber is to charge his current price for a haircut.

## EXERCISES 9.5, page 574

1. We compute

$$E = PAQ = \begin{bmatrix} \frac{1}{2} & \frac{1}{2} \end{bmatrix} \begin{bmatrix} 3 & 1 \\ -4 & 2 \end{bmatrix} \begin{bmatrix} \frac{3}{5} \\ \frac{2}{5} \end{bmatrix}$$

$$\begin{bmatrix} -\frac{1}{2} & \frac{3}{2} \end{bmatrix} \begin{bmatrix} \frac{3}{5} \\ \frac{2}{5} \end{bmatrix} = -\frac{3}{10} + \frac{6}{10} = \frac{3}{10}.$$

Thus, in the long run, the row player may be expected to win 0.3 units in each play of the game.

2. The expected payoff is given by

$$E = PAQ = [.8 \quad .2] \begin{bmatrix} -1 & 4 \\ 3 & -2 \end{bmatrix} \begin{bmatrix} 0.6 \\ 0.4 \end{bmatrix} = 1.$$

3. We compute

$$E = PAQ = [\ \tfrac{1}{3} \quad \tfrac{2}{3}\ ] \begin{bmatrix} -4 & 3 \\ 2 & 1 \end{bmatrix} \begin{bmatrix} \tfrac{3}{4} \\ \tfrac{1}{4} \end{bmatrix}$$

$$= [\ 0 \quad \tfrac{5}{3}\ ] \begin{bmatrix} \tfrac{3}{4} \\ \tfrac{1}{4} \end{bmatrix} = \tfrac{5}{12}.$$

Thus, in the long run, the row player may be expected to win 0.4167 units in each play of the game.

4. We compute

$$E = PAQ = [\ \tfrac{3}{5} \quad \tfrac{2}{5}\ ] \begin{bmatrix} 1 & 2 \\ -3 & 1 \end{bmatrix} \begin{bmatrix} \tfrac{1}{3} \\ \tfrac{2}{3} \end{bmatrix} = \tfrac{13}{15}$$

5. We compute

$$E = PAQ = [0.2 \quad 0.6 \quad 0.2] \begin{bmatrix} 2 & 0 & -2 \\ 1 & -1 & 3 \\ 2 & 1 & -4 \end{bmatrix} \begin{bmatrix} 0.2 \\ 0.6 \\ 0.2 \end{bmatrix}$$

$$= [\ 1.4 \quad -0.4 \quad 0.6] \begin{bmatrix} 0.2 \\ 0.6 \\ 0.2 \end{bmatrix} = 0.16.$$

6. We compute

$$E = PAQ = [0.2 \quad 0.3 \quad 0.5] \begin{bmatrix} 1 & -4 & 2 \\ 2 & 1 & -1 \\ 2 & -2 & 0 \end{bmatrix} \begin{bmatrix} 0.6 \\ 0.2 \\ 0.2 \end{bmatrix}$$

$$= [\ 1.8 \quad -1.5 \quad 0.1] \begin{bmatrix} 0.6 \\ 0.2 \\ 0.2 \end{bmatrix} = 0.8.$$

**7.**    **a.**

$$E = PAQ = \begin{bmatrix} 1 & 0 \end{bmatrix} \begin{bmatrix} 1 & -2 \\ -2 & 3 \end{bmatrix} \begin{bmatrix} 1 \\ 0 \end{bmatrix} = \begin{bmatrix} 1 & -2 \end{bmatrix} \begin{bmatrix} 1 \\ 0 \end{bmatrix} = 1.$$

**b.**

$$E = PAQ = \begin{bmatrix} 0 & 1 \end{bmatrix} \begin{bmatrix} 1 & -2 \\ -2 & 3 \end{bmatrix} \begin{bmatrix} 1 \\ 0 \end{bmatrix} = \begin{bmatrix} -2 & 3 \end{bmatrix} \begin{bmatrix} 1 \\ 0 \end{bmatrix} = -2.$$

**c.**

$$E = PAQ = \begin{bmatrix} \tfrac{1}{2} & \tfrac{1}{2} \end{bmatrix} \begin{bmatrix} 1 & -2 \\ -2 & 3 \end{bmatrix} \begin{bmatrix} \tfrac{1}{2} \\ \tfrac{1}{2} \end{bmatrix} = \begin{bmatrix} -\tfrac{1}{2} & \tfrac{1}{2} \end{bmatrix} \begin{bmatrix} \tfrac{1}{2} \\ \tfrac{1}{2} \end{bmatrix} = 0.$$

**d.**

$$E = PAQ = \begin{bmatrix} 0.5 & 0.5 \end{bmatrix} \begin{bmatrix} 1 & -2 \\ -2 & 3 \end{bmatrix} \begin{bmatrix} 0.8 \\ 0.2 \end{bmatrix}$$

$$= \begin{bmatrix} -0.5 & 0.5 \end{bmatrix} \begin{bmatrix} 0.8 \\ 0.2 \end{bmatrix}$$

$$= -0.3.$$

(a) is the most advantageous.

**8.**    We compute

**a.**    $E = PAQ = \dfrac{8}{9} = 0.8889.$

**b.**    $E = PAQ = \dfrac{29}{32} = 0.90625.$

**c.**    $E = PAQ = 0.94$          d. $E = PAQ = 0.66.$

The strategy in part (c) is most advantageous to R.

**9.**    **a.** From the payoff matrix

$$\begin{bmatrix} -3 & 3 & 2 \\ -3 & 1 & 1 \\ 1 & -2 & 1 \end{bmatrix} \begin{matrix} -3 \\ -3 \\ -2 \end{matrix} \longleftarrow \text{largest of the row minima}$$

$$\begin{matrix} 1 & 3 & 2 \end{matrix}$$

$\uparrow$_____ smallest of the column maxima

we see that the expected payoff to a row player using the minimax strategy is 1.

b. The expected payoff is given by

$$E = PAQ = [.25 \quad .25 \quad .5] \begin{bmatrix} -3 & 3 & 2 \\ -3 & 1 & 1 \\ 1 & -2 & 1 \end{bmatrix} \begin{bmatrix} .6 \\ .2 \\ .2 \end{bmatrix} = -0.35.$$

c. The minimax strategy (part (a)) is the better strategy for the row player.

10. a. From the payoff matrix

$$\begin{bmatrix} 4 & -3 & 3 \\ -4 & 2 & 1 \\ 3 & -5 & 2 \end{bmatrix} \begin{matrix} -3 \leftarrow \\ -4 \\ -5 \end{matrix} \qquad \text{largest of the row minima}$$

$$\begin{matrix} 4 & 2 & 3 \end{matrix}$$

$$\uparrow \text{_____} \qquad \text{smallest of the column maxima}$$

we see that the expected payoff to a row player using the minimax strategy is -3.

b. The expected payoff is given by

$$E = PAQ = [.40 \quad .30 \quad .30] \begin{bmatrix} 4 & -3 & 3 \\ -4 & 2 & 1 \\ 3 & -5 & 2 \end{bmatrix} \begin{bmatrix} .25 \\ .50 \\ .25 \end{bmatrix} = [-0.2].$$

c. The mixed strategy (part (b)) is the better strategy for the row player.

11. The game under consideration has no saddle point and is accordingly nonstrictly determined. Using the formulas for determining the optimal mixed strategies for a 2 x 2 game with a = 4, b = 1, c = 2, and d = 3, we find that

$$p_1 = \frac{d - c}{a + d - b - c} = \frac{3 - 2}{4 + 3 - 1 - 2} = \frac{1}{4}$$

$$p_2 = 1 - p_1 = 1 - \frac{1}{4} = \frac{3}{4}$$

so that the row player's optimal mixed strategy is given by

$$p = [\tfrac{1}{4} \quad \tfrac{3}{4}].$$

Next, we compute

$$q_1 = \frac{d - b}{a + d - b - c} = \frac{3 - 1}{4 + 3 - 1 - 2} = \frac{2}{4} = \frac{1}{2}.$$

$$q_2 = 1 - q_1 = 1 - \frac{1}{2} = \frac{1}{2}.$$

Thus, the optimal strategy for the column player is given by

$$Q = \begin{bmatrix} \dfrac{1}{2} \\[2mm] \dfrac{1}{2} \end{bmatrix}.$$

To determine whether the game favors one player over the other, we compute the expected value of the game which is given by

$$E = \frac{ad - bc}{a + d - b - c} = \frac{(4)(3) - (1)(2)}{4 + 3 - 1 - 2} = \frac{10}{4} = \frac{5}{2}.$$

or 5/2 units for each play of the game. These results imply that the game favors the row player.

12. Since the game is not strictly determined, we use the formulas for determining the optimal mixed strategies for a 2 x 2 game. We obtain

$$P = [\tfrac{3}{4} \quad \tfrac{1}{4}] \quad \text{and} \quad Q = \begin{bmatrix} \dfrac{11}{12} \\[2mm] \dfrac{1}{12} \end{bmatrix}$$

and $E = PAQ = 2.25$. We conclude that the game favors the row player.

13. Since the game is not strictly determined, we use the formulas for determining the optimal mixed strategies for a 2 x 2 game. We obtain

$$p_1 = \frac{d - c}{a + d - b - c} = \frac{-3 - 1}{-1 - 3 - 2 - 1} = \frac{4}{7}$$

$$p_2 = 1 - p_1 = 1 - \frac{4}{7} = \frac{3}{7}$$

Thus, the optimal mixed strategy for the row player is given by

$$P = [\tfrac{4}{7} \quad \tfrac{3}{7}]$$

To find the optimal mixed strategy for the column player, we compute

$$q_1 = \frac{d - b}{a + d - b - c} = \frac{-3 - 2}{-1 - 3 - 2 - 1} = \frac{5}{7}.$$

$$q_2 = 1 - q_1 = 1 - \frac{5}{7} = \frac{2}{7}.$$

Hence,

$$Q = \begin{bmatrix} \frac{5}{7} \\ \frac{2}{7} \end{bmatrix}.$$

The expected value of the game is given by

$$E = \frac{ad - bc}{a + d - b - c} = \frac{(-1)(-3) - (2)(1)}{-1 - 3 - 2 - 1} = -\frac{1}{7}.$$

Since the value of the game is negative, we conclude that the game favors the column player.

14. Since the game is not strictly determined, we use the formulas for determining the optimal mixed strategies for a 2 x 2 game. We obtain

$$p_1 = \frac{d - c}{a + d - b - c} = \frac{0 - 2}{-1 + 0 - 3 - 2} = \frac{1}{3}$$

$$p_2 = 1 - p_1 = 1 - \frac{1}{3} = \frac{2}{3}$$

Thus, the optimal mixed strategy for the row player is given by

$$P = \begin{bmatrix} \frac{1}{3} & \frac{2}{3} \end{bmatrix}$$

To find the optimal mixed strategy for the column player, we compute

$$q_1 = \frac{d - b}{a + d - b - c} = \frac{0 - 3}{-1 + 0 - 3 - 2} = \frac{1}{2}.$$

$$q_2 = 1 - q_1 = 1 - \frac{1}{2} = \frac{1}{2}.$$

Hence,

$$Q = \begin{bmatrix} \frac{1}{2} \\ \frac{1}{2} \end{bmatrix}.$$

The expected value of the game is given by

$$E = \frac{ad - bc}{a + d - b - c} = \frac{(-1)(0) - (3)(2)}{-1 + 0 - 3 - 2} = \frac{-6}{-6} = 1$$

Since the value of the game is positive, we conclude that the game favors the row player.

15. Since the game is not strictly determined, we use the formulas for determining the optimal mixed strategies for a 2 x 2 game. We obtain

$$P = \begin{bmatrix} \frac{1}{2} & \frac{1}{2} \end{bmatrix} \quad \text{and} \quad Q = \begin{bmatrix} \frac{1}{4} \\ \frac{3}{4} \end{bmatrix}$$

and $E = PAQ = -5$. We conclude that the game favors the column player.

16. From

$$\begin{bmatrix} \textcircled{2} & 5 \\ -2 & 4 \end{bmatrix} \quad \begin{matrix} 2 \\ -2 \end{matrix} \longleftarrow \text{larger of the row minima}$$

$$\begin{matrix} 2 & 5 \end{matrix}$$

smaller of the column maxima.

We conclude that the game is strictly determined and the row player should play row 1 and the column player should play column 1. The expected value of the game is 2 and the game favors the row player.

17. a. Since the game is not strictly determined, we employ the formulas for determining the optimal mixed strategies for a 2 x 2 games. We find that

$$p_1 = \frac{d - c}{a + d - b - c} = \frac{1 - (-2)}{4 + 1 - (-2) - (-2)} = \frac{3}{9} = \frac{1}{3},$$

$$p_2 = 1 - p_1 = 1 - \frac{1}{3} = \frac{2}{3}$$

so that Richie's optimal mixed strategy is given by

$$P = \begin{bmatrix} \frac{1}{3} & \frac{2}{3} \end{bmatrix}.$$

Next, we compute

$$q_1 = \frac{d - b}{a + d - b - c} = \frac{1 - (-2)}{4 + 1 - (-2) - (-2)} = \frac{3}{9} = \frac{1}{3}.$$

$$q_2 = 1 - q_1 = 1 - \frac{1}{3} = \frac{2}{3}.$$

Thus, Chuck's optimal strategy is given by

$$Q = \begin{bmatrix} \frac{1}{3} \\ \frac{2}{3} \end{bmatrix}.$$

b. The expected value of the game is given by

$$E = \frac{ad - bc}{a + d - b - c} = \frac{(4)(1) - (-2)(-2)}{4 + 1 - (-2) - (-2)} = 0$$

and conclude that in the long run the game will end in a draw.

18.  a. The required payoff matrix for this game is given by

|  | Expanding economy | Economic recession |
|---|---|---|
| Stock market investment | 20 | −5 |
| Commodity investment | 10 | 15 |

Since the game is not strictly determined, we use the formulas for finding the optimal mixed strategies for a 2 x 2 nonstrictly determined game. Then

$$p_1 = \frac{d - c}{a + d - b - c} = \frac{5}{35 + 5 - 10} = \frac{5}{30} = \frac{1}{6},$$

$$p_2 = 1 - p_1 = 1 - \frac{1}{6} = \frac{5}{6},$$

so that Carrington's optimal mixed strategy is

$$P = \begin{bmatrix} \frac{1}{6} & \frac{5}{6} \end{bmatrix}$$

Thus, Carrington should invest \$16,667 in stocks, and \$83,333 in commodities.

b. The profit that the Carrington's can expect to make is given by

$$E = \frac{ad - bc}{a + d - b - c} = \frac{(20)(15) - (-5)(10)}{30} = \frac{350}{30} = 11.667.$$

We conclude that the Carringtons will realize a profit of \$11,667 by employing their optimal mixed strategy.

19. a. The required payoff matrix for this game is given by

|  | Expanding economy | Economic recession |
|---|---|---|
| Hotel Stock | 25 | −5 |
| Brewery Stock | 10 | 15 |

Since the game is not strictly determined, we use the formulas for finding the optimal mixed strategies for a 2 x 2 nonstrictly determined game. Then

$$p_1 = \frac{d - c}{a + d - b - c} = \frac{15 - 10}{25 + 15 + 5 - 10} = \frac{5}{35} = \frac{1}{7},$$

$$p_2 = 1 - p_1 = 1 - \frac{1}{7} = \frac{6}{7},$$

so that the Maxwell's optimal mixed strategy is

$$P = [\frac{1}{7} \quad \frac{6}{7}]$$

Thus, the Maxwells should invest $(1/7)(\$40,000) = \$5,714$ in hotel stocks and $(6/7)(\$40,000) = \$34,286$ in brewery stocks.

b. The profit that the Maxwell's can expect to make is given by

$$E = \frac{ad - bc}{a + d - b - c} = \frac{(25)(15) - (-5)(10)}{35} = \frac{425}{35} = 12.142$$

We conclude that the Maxwells will realize a profit of

$$(.12142)(\$40,000) = \$4,867$$

by employing their optimal mixed strategy.

20. a. The required payoff matrix for this game is given by

|  | Mr. Carson City | Rural |  |
|---|---|---|---|
| City | .6 | .4 | .4 |
| Mr. Robinson Rural | .45 | .55 | (.45) |
|  | .6 | (.55) |  |

Note that the larger of the row minima and the smaller of the column maxima are circled. Since there is no saddle point, we conclude that the game is not strictly determined.

b. Employing the formulas for finding the optimal mixed strategies for a 2 x 2 nonstrictly determined game, we find that

$$p_1 = \frac{d - c}{a + d - b - c} = \frac{.55 - .45}{.6 + .55 - .4 - .45} = \frac{1}{3} \; .$$

$$p_2 = 1 - p_1 = 1 - \frac{1}{3} = \frac{2}{3}.$$

So Mr. Robinson's optimal mixed strategy is given by

$$R = [\frac{1}{3} \quad \frac{2}{3}]$$

that is, he should spend 1/3 of his time campaigning in the city and 2/3's of his time campaigning in the rural area. Similarly, we find

$$q_1 = \frac{d - b}{a + d - b - c} = \frac{.55 - .4}{.6 + .55 - .4 - .45} = \frac{1}{2} \; ,$$

$$q_2 = 1 - q_1 = 1 - \frac{1}{2} = \frac{1}{2},$$

so that Mr. Carson's optimal mixed strategy is given by

$$Q = \begin{bmatrix} \frac{1}{2} \\ \frac{1}{2} \end{bmatrix}$$

that is, Mr. Carson should spend 1/2 of his time campaigning in the city and 1/2 of his time campaigning in the rural area.

21.  a. The required payoff matrix for this game is given by

$$\begin{array}{c} \\ \\ R \end{array} \begin{array}{cc} & \begin{array}{cc} \text{C} \\ \text{N} \quad\quad \text{F} \end{array} \\ \begin{array}{c} \text{N} \\ \text{F} \end{array} & \begin{bmatrix} .48 & .65 \\ .50 & .45 \end{bmatrix} \begin{array}{c} .48 \\ .45 \end{array} \\ & \;\; .50 \quad\; .65 \end{array} \quad\quad \begin{array}{l} \text{N = local newspaper,} \\ \\ \text{F = flyer} \end{array}$$

Since there is no saddle point, we conclude that the game is not strictly determined.

b. Employing the formulas for finding the optimal mixed **strategies** for a 2 x 2 nonstrictly determined game, we find that

$$p_1 = \frac{d - c}{a + d - b - c} = \frac{.45 - .50}{.48 + .45 - .65 - .50} = .227$$

$$p_2 = 1 - p_2 = 1 - .227 = .773$$

$$q_1 = \frac{d - b}{a + d - b - c} = \frac{.45 - .65}{.48 + .45 - .65 - .50} = .909$$

$$q_2 = 1 - q_1 = 1 - .909 = .091$$

We conclude that Dr. Russell's strategy is given by

$$P = [.227 \quad .773]$$

and Dr. Carlton's strategy is given by

$$Q = \begin{bmatrix} .909 \\ .091 \end{bmatrix}.$$

Also Dr. Russell should place 22.7% of his advertisements in the local newspaper and 77.3% in fliers; whereas, Dr. Carton should place 90.9% of his advertisements in the local newspaper and 9.1% of his advertisements in fliers.

22.
$$E = PAQ = [p_1 \quad p_2] \begin{bmatrix} a_{11} & a_{12} \\ a_{21} & a_{22} \end{bmatrix} \begin{bmatrix} q_1 \\ q_2 \end{bmatrix}$$

$$= [p_1 a_{11} + p_2 a_{21} \quad p_1 a_{12} + p_2 a_{22}] \begin{bmatrix} q_1 \\ q_2 \end{bmatrix}$$

$$= p_1 a_{11} q_1 + p_2 a_{21} q_1 + p_1 a_{12} q_2 + p_2 a_{22} q_2$$

$$= p_1 q_1 a_{11} + p_1 q_2 a_{12} + p_2 q_1 a_{21} + p_2 q_2 a_{22}$$

and this is equal to the value of the game.

23. The optimal strategies for the row and column players are

$$P = [p_1 \quad p_2]$$

where

$$p_1 = \frac{d - c}{a + d - b - c} \quad \text{and}$$

$$p_2 = 1 - p_1 = 1 - \frac{d - c}{a + d - b - c}$$

$$= \frac{a - b}{a + d - b - c},$$

and

$$Q = \begin{bmatrix} q_1 \\ q_2 \end{bmatrix}$$

where

$$q_1 = \frac{d - b}{a + d - b - c}$$

and

$$q_2 = 1 - q_1 = 1 - \frac{d - b}{a + d - b - c} = \frac{a - c}{a + d - b - c}.$$

Therefore, the expected value of the game is

$$E = PAQ = \begin{bmatrix} p_1 & p_2 \end{bmatrix} \begin{bmatrix} a & b \\ c & d \end{bmatrix} \begin{bmatrix} q_1 \\ q_2 \end{bmatrix}$$

$$= \begin{bmatrix} ap_1 + cp_2 & bp_1 + dp_2 \end{bmatrix} \begin{bmatrix} q_1 \\ q_2 \end{bmatrix}$$

$$= (ap_1 + cp_2)q_1 + (bp_1 + dp_2)q_2$$

$$= \left[ \left[ \frac{a(d - c)}{a + d - b - c} \right] + \left[ \frac{c(a - b)}{a + d - b - c} \right] \right] \left[ \frac{d - b}{a + d - b - c} \right]$$

$$+ \left[ \left[ \frac{b(d - c)}{a + d - b - c} + \frac{d(a - b)}{a + d - b - c} \right] \right] \left[ \frac{a - c}{a + d - b - c} \right]$$

$$= \frac{(ad - bc)(d - b)}{(a + d - b - c)^2} + \frac{(ad - bc)(a - c)}{(a + d - b - c)^2}$$

$$= \frac{(ad - bc)(a + d - b - c)}{(a + d - b - c)^2} = \frac{ad - bc}{a + d - b - c},$$

as was to be shown.

## CHAPTER 9, REVIEW EXERCISES, page 580

1. Since the entries $a_{21} = -2$ and $a_{22} = -8$ are negative, the given matrix is not stochastic and is hence not a regular stochastic matrix.

2. The matrix is regular since the second power of the matrix has entries which are all positive.

3.

$$T^2 = \begin{bmatrix} \frac{1}{2} & 0 & \frac{1}{2} \\ 0 & 0 & 1 \\ \frac{1}{3} & \frac{1}{3} & \frac{1}{3} \end{bmatrix} \begin{bmatrix} \frac{1}{2} & 0 & \frac{1}{2} \\ 0 & 0 & 1 \\ \frac{1}{3} & \frac{1}{3} & \frac{1}{3} \end{bmatrix} = \begin{bmatrix} \frac{5}{12} & \frac{1}{6} & \frac{5}{12} \\ \frac{1}{3} & \frac{1}{3} & \frac{1}{3} \\ \frac{5}{18} & \frac{1}{9} & \frac{11}{18} \end{bmatrix}.$$

and so the matrix is regular.

4. Since the entries in the first row of the given matrix do not equal 1, that is,

$$a_{11} + a_{12} + a_{12} = .3 + .2 + .1 = .6 \neq 1$$

the given matrix is not stochastic. Consequently, it is not a regular stochastic matrix.

5.

$$X_1 = [\tfrac{1}{2} \quad \tfrac{1}{2} \quad 0] \begin{bmatrix} 0 & \frac{2}{5} & \frac{3}{5} \\ \frac{1}{4} & \frac{1}{2} & \frac{1}{4} \\ \frac{3}{5} & \frac{1}{5} & \frac{1}{5} \end{bmatrix} = [\tfrac{1}{8} \quad \tfrac{9}{20} \quad \tfrac{17}{40}].$$

$$X_2 = [\tfrac{1}{8} \quad \tfrac{9}{20} \quad \tfrac{17}{40}] \begin{bmatrix} 0 & \frac{2}{5} & \frac{3}{5} \\ \frac{1}{4} & \frac{1}{2} & \frac{1}{4} \\ \frac{3}{5} & \frac{1}{5} & \frac{1}{5} \end{bmatrix} = [\tfrac{147}{400} \quad \tfrac{9}{25} \quad \tfrac{109}{400}]$$

$$= [0.3675 \quad 0.36 \quad 0.2725].$$

6. $X_1 = X_0T = [0.215 \quad 0.435 \quad 0.350]$

$X_2 = X_1T = [0.1915 \quad 0.4215 \quad 0.387].$

7. This is an absorbing matrix since state 1 is an absorbing state and it is possible to go from any nonabsorbing state to state 1.

8. This is not an absorbing stochastic matrix since there is no absorbing state.

9. This is not an absorbing stochastic matrix since there is no absorbing state.

10. This is an absorbing matrix since State 3 is an absorbing state and it is possible to go from any nonabsorbing state to state 3 in 1 stage.

11. We solve the matrix equation

$$[x \quad y] \begin{bmatrix} .6 & .4 \\ .3 & .7 \end{bmatrix} = [x \quad y]$$

or equivalently, the system of equations

$$-.4x + .3y = 0$$
$$.4x - .3y = 0$$
$$x + y = 1.$$

Solving this system of equations, we find the steady-state distribution vector to be

$$[\tfrac{3}{7} \quad \tfrac{4}{7}],$$

and the steady-state matrix to be

$$\begin{bmatrix} \tfrac{3}{7} & \tfrac{4}{7} \\ \tfrac{3}{7} & \tfrac{4}{7} \end{bmatrix},$$

12. We solve the matrix equation

$$[x \quad y] \begin{bmatrix} .5 & .5 \\ .4 & .6 \end{bmatrix} = [x \quad y]$$

or equivalently, the system of equations

$$-.5x + .4y = 0$$
$$.5x - .4y = 0$$
$$x + y = 1.$$

Solving this system of equations, we find the steady-state distribution vector to be

$$[\tfrac{4}{9} \quad \tfrac{5}{9}],$$

and the steady-state matrix to be

$$\begin{bmatrix} \dfrac{4}{9} & \dfrac{5}{9} \\ \dfrac{4}{9} & \dfrac{5}{9} \end{bmatrix},$$

13. We solve the system

$$[x \quad y \quad z] \begin{bmatrix} .6 & .2 & .2 \\ .4 & .2 & .4 \\ .3 & .2 & .5 \end{bmatrix} = [x \quad y \quad z]$$

together with the equation x + y + z = 1, or, equivalently, the system

$$.6x + .4y + .3z = x$$

$$.2x + .2y + .2z = y$$

$$.2x + .4y + .5z = z$$

$$x + \quad y + \quad z = 1.$$

Upon solving the system, we find that

$$x = .457, \ y = .20 \text{ and } z = .343,$$

and the steady-state distribution vector is given by

$$[.457 \quad .20 \quad .343].$$

Therefore, the steady-state matrix is

$$\begin{bmatrix} .457 & .20 & .343 \\ .457 & .20 & .343 \\ .457 & .20 & .343 \end{bmatrix}.$$

14. We solve the system

$$[x \quad y \quad z] \begin{bmatrix} .1 & .3 & .6 \\ .2 & .4 & .4 \\ .6 & .2 & .2 \end{bmatrix} = [x \quad y \quad z]$$

together with the equation x + y + z = 1, or, equivalently, the system

$$-.9x + .2y + .6z = 0$$

$$.3x - .6y + .2z = 0$$

$$.6x + .4y - .8z = 0$$

$$x + y + z = 1.$$

Upon solving the system, we find that

$$x = .323, \quad y = .290 \text{ and } z = .387,$$

and the steady-state distribution vector is given by

$$[.323 \quad .290 \quad .387].$$

Therefore, the steady-state matrix is

$$\begin{bmatrix} .323 & .290 & .387 \\ .323 & .290 & .387 \\ .323 & .290 & .387 \end{bmatrix}.$$

15. a. The transition matrix for the Markov Chain is given by

$$\begin{array}{c} \\ \\ T = \end{array} \quad \begin{array}{c} \\ A \\ U \\ N \end{array} \begin{array}{ccc} A & U & N \\ \begin{bmatrix} .85 & .10 & .05 \\ 0 & .95 & .05 \\ .10 & .05 & .85 \end{bmatrix}. \end{array}$$

b. The probability vector describing the distribution of land 10 years ago is given by

$$\begin{array}{ccc} A & U & N \end{array}$$

$$[.50 \quad .15 \quad .35].$$

c. To find the required probability vector, we compute

$$X_0T = [.50 \ .15 \ .35] \begin{bmatrix} .85 & .10 & .05 \\ 0 & .95 & .05 \\ .10 & .05 & .85 \end{bmatrix} = [.46 \ .21 \ .33]$$

$$X_1T = [.46 \; .21 \; .33] \begin{bmatrix} .85 & .10 & .05 \\ 0 & .95 & .05 \\ .10 & .05 & .85 \end{bmatrix} = [.424 \; .262 \; .314]$$

Thus, the probability vector describing the distribution of land 10 years from now is

[.424     .262     .314].

16.  Let x = [x    y    z] be the steady-state distribution vector associated with the Markov process under consideration, where x, y, and z are to be determined. Then, the given information translates into the system

$$[x \quad y \quad z] \begin{bmatrix} .3 & .3 & .4 \\ .1 & .5 & .4 \\ .1 & .2 & .7 \end{bmatrix} = [x \quad y \quad z]$$

together with the equation x + y + z = 1, or, equivalently, the system of equations

$$.3x + .1y + .1z = x$$

$$.3x + .5y + .2z = y$$

$$.4x + .4y + .7z = z$$

$$x + \quad y + \quad z = 1.$$

Solving the system, we find

x = .125, y = .3036, and z = .5714,

and the steady-state distribution vector is given by

X = [.125    .3036    .5714].

That is, in the long run 12.5% of the cars in this area will be large cars, 30.36% of the cars will be intermediate in size and 57.14% of the cars will be small.

17. From

$$\begin{bmatrix} 1 & 2 \\ 3 & 5 \\ \boxed{4} & 6 \end{bmatrix} \begin{matrix} 1 \\ 3 \\ 4 \end{matrix} \quad \leftarrow \text{largest of the row minima}$$

$$\begin{matrix} 4 & 6 \end{matrix}$$

↑_____ smaller of the column maxima

we see that the game is strictly determined, and

a. the saddle point is 4.

b. the optimum strategy for the row player is to play row 3, whereas the optimum strategy for the column player is to play column 1.

c. the value of the game is 4.

d. the game favors the row player.

18. From

$$\begin{bmatrix} 1 & \boxed{0} & 3 \\ 2 & -1 & -2 \end{bmatrix} \begin{matrix} 0 \\ -2 \end{matrix} \quad \leftarrow \text{larger of the row minima}$$

$$\begin{matrix} 2 & 0 & 3 \end{matrix}$$

↑_____ smallest of the column maxima

we see that the game is strictly determined, and

a. the saddle point is 0.

b. the optimum strategy for the row player is to play row 1, whereas, the optimum strategy for the column player is to play column 2.

c. the value of the game is 0.

d. the game does not favor either player.

19. We first determine the largest of the row minima and the smallest of the column maxima and display these elements as shown below.

$$\begin{bmatrix} \boxed{1} & 3 & 6 \\ -2 & 4 & 3 \\ -5 & -4 & -2 \end{bmatrix} \begin{matrix} 1 \\ -2 \\ -5 \end{matrix} \longleftarrow \text{the largest of the row minima}$$

$$\begin{matrix} 1 & \ 4 & \ 6 \end{matrix}$$

$\uparrow$ the smallest of the column maxima

The entry $a_{11} = 1$ is the saddle point of the game and we conclude that the game is strictly determined. The row player's optimal strategy is to play row 1 and the column player's optimal strategy is to play column 1.

20. The payoff matrix for this game is

$$\begin{bmatrix} 4 & 3 & 2 \\ -6 & 3 & -1 \\ 2 & 3 & 4 \end{bmatrix} \begin{matrix} 2 \\ -6 \\ 2 \end{matrix} \longleftarrow \text{larger of the row minima}$$

$$\begin{matrix} 4 & \ 3 & \ 4 \end{matrix}$$

$\uparrow$ smaller of the column maxima

Since there is no saddle point, we conclude that the game is not strictly determined.

21. We compute

$$E = PAQ = \begin{bmatrix} \frac{1}{2} & \frac{1}{2} \end{bmatrix} \begin{bmatrix} 4 & 8 \\ \frac{3}{6} & -12 \end{bmatrix} \begin{bmatrix} \frac{1}{4} \\ 4 \end{bmatrix} = -\frac{1}{4}$$

22. The expected value of the game is given by

$$E = PAQ = \begin{bmatrix} \frac{1}{3} & \frac{2}{3} \end{bmatrix} \begin{bmatrix} 3 & 0 & -3 \\ 2 & 1 & 2 \end{bmatrix} \begin{bmatrix} \frac{1}{3} \\ \frac{1}{3} \\ \frac{1}{3} \end{bmatrix} = \frac{10}{9}.$$

23. We compute

$$E = PAQ = \begin{bmatrix} 0.2 & 0.4 & 0.4 \end{bmatrix} \begin{bmatrix} 3 & -1 & 2 \\ 1 & 2 & 4 \\ -2 & 3 & 6 \end{bmatrix} \begin{bmatrix} 0.2 \\ 0.6 \\ 0.2 \end{bmatrix}$$

$$= [0.2 \quad 1.8 \quad 4.4] \begin{bmatrix} 0.2 \\ 0.6 \\ 0.2 \end{bmatrix} = [2].$$

The expected payoff for the game is 2.

24. We compute

$$E = PAQ = [0.2 \quad 0.4 \quad 0.4] \begin{bmatrix} 2 & -2 & 3 \\ 1 & 2 & -1 \\ -1 & 2 & 3 \end{bmatrix} \begin{bmatrix} 0.3 \\ 0.3 \\ 0.4 \end{bmatrix}$$

$$= [.4 \quad 1.2 \quad 1.4] \begin{bmatrix} 0.3 \\ 0.3 \\ 0.4 \end{bmatrix} = [1.04].$$

The expected payoff for the game is 1.04.

25. The game under consideration has no saddle point and is accordingly nonstrictly determined. Using the formulas for determining the optimal mixed strategies for a 2 x 2 game with $a = 1$, $b = -2$, $c = 0$, and $d = 3$, we find that

$$p_1 = \frac{d - c}{a + d - b - c} = \frac{3 - 0}{1 + 3 + 2 - 0} = \frac{3}{6} = \frac{1}{2}.$$

$$p_2 = 1 - p_1 = 1 - \frac{1}{2} = \frac{1}{2}$$

so that the row player's optimal mixed strategy is given by

$$P = [\tfrac{1}{2} \quad \tfrac{1}{2}].$$

Next, we compute

$$q_1 = \frac{d - b}{a + d - b - c} = \frac{3 + 2}{1 + 3 + 2 - 0} = \frac{5}{6}.$$

$$q_2 = 1 - q_1 = 1 - \frac{5}{6} = \frac{1}{6}.$$

Thus, the optimal strategy for the column player is given by

$$Q = \begin{bmatrix} \frac{5}{6} \\ \frac{1}{6} \end{bmatrix}.$$

To determine whether the game favors one player over the other, we compute the expected value of the game which is given by

$$E = \frac{ad - bc}{a + d - b - c} = \frac{(1)(3) - (-2)(0)}{1 + 3 + 2 - 0} = \frac{3}{6} = \frac{1}{2}.$$

or 1/2 units for each play of the game. These results imply that the game favors the row player.

26. Using the formulas for the optimal mixed strategies in a 2 x 2 non strictly determined game, we see that the optimal mixed strategy for the row player is

$$p = [\tfrac{1}{2} \quad \tfrac{1}{2}] \, ,$$

and the optimal mixed strategy for the column player is

$$q = \begin{bmatrix} \dfrac{13}{22} \\ \dfrac{9}{22} \end{bmatrix}.$$

The value of the game is PAQ = $[-\tfrac{1}{2}]$.

The game favors the column player.

27. Using the formulas for the optimal mixed strategies in a 2 x 2 non strictly determined game, we see that the optimal mixed strategy for the row player is

$$p = [\tfrac{1}{10} \quad \tfrac{9}{10}] \, ,$$

and the optimal mixed strategy for the column player is

$$q = \begin{bmatrix} \dfrac{4}{5} \\ \dfrac{1}{5} \end{bmatrix}.$$

The value of the game is PAQ = [1.2] and the game favors the row player.

28. Using the formulas for the optimal mixed strategies in a 2 x 2 non strictly determined game, we see that the optimal mixed strategy for the row player is

$$p = [\tfrac{4}{5} \quad \tfrac{1}{5}] \, ,$$

and the optimal mixed strategy for the column player is

$$q = \begin{bmatrix} \frac{2}{5} \\ \frac{3}{5} \end{bmatrix}.$$

The value of the game is PAQ = [10.8] and the game favors the row player.

29.  a. The required payoff matrix is given by

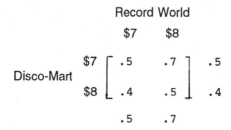

b. Upon finding the larger of the row minima and the smaller of the column maxima, we see that the entry $a_{11}$ = .5 is a saddle point, and, consequently, that the game is strictly determined. Thus, the optimal price that each company should sell the record

label for is $7.

30.  The required payoff matrix is given by

|  | Higher than Normal Rate | Normal Rate |
|---|---|---|
| Compact | 1500 | 3000 |
| Subcompact | 2500 | 2000 |

Since this is a nonstrictly determined game, we employ the formulas for finding the mixed strategies for a 2 x 2 game with a = 1500, b = 3000, c = 2500 and d = 2000. We find

$$p_1 = \frac{d - c}{a + d - b - c} = \frac{2000 - 2500}{1500 + 2000 - 3000 - 2500} = -\frac{500}{-2000} = \frac{1}{4}.$$

$$p_2 = 1 - p_1 = 1 - \frac{1}{4} = \frac{3}{4}.$$

Thus,  $p = [\frac{1}{4} \quad \frac{3}{4}]$.

We conclude that the optimal strategy for the company is to produce a line consisting of 25 percent of their compact models and 75 percent of their subcompact models.

## GROUP DISCUSSION QUESTIONS

**Page 521**

1.  a.
$$AB = \begin{bmatrix} p & 1-p \\ q & 1-q \end{bmatrix} \begin{bmatrix} r & 1-r \\ s & 1-s \end{bmatrix}$$

$$= \begin{bmatrix} pr + s(1-p) & p(1-r) + (1-p)(1-s) \\ qr + s(1-q) & q(1-r) + (1-q)(1-s) \end{bmatrix}$$

Since $0 \leq p \leq 1$, $0 \leq q \leq 1$, $0 \leq r \leq 1$, and $0 \leq s \leq 1$, we see that each element in the matrix AB is nonnegative. For example, the element $p(1-r) + (1-p)(1-s) \geq 0$ because $p \geq 0$, $1-r \geq 0$ because $0 \leq r \leq 1$, $1-p \geq 0$ because $0 \leq p \leq 1$; and $1-s \geq 0$ because $0 \leq s \leq 1$, so that $p(1-r) \geq 0$ and $(1-p)(1-s) \geq 0$ and therefore $p(1-r) + (1-p)(1-s) \geq 0$. Next, the sum of the elements in the first row of AB is

$$pr + s(1-p) + p(1-r) + (1-p)(1-s)$$

$$= pr + s - sp + p - pr + 1 - s - p + ps$$

$$= 1.$$

Therefore, AB is a stochastic matrix.

b.  The result of part (a) shows that, in general, the product of two 2 x 2 stochastic matrices is itself a stochastic matrix. Therefore, $A^2 = AA$ is a stochastic matrix. Similarly, $A^3 = A^2$, and so is stochastic. In general, $A^n = A^{n-1}A$ is a stochastic matrix since $A^{n-1}$ and A are stochastic matrices.

**page 535**

1.  The required matrices are

$$\begin{bmatrix} 0 & 1 \\ 0 & 1 \end{bmatrix} \quad \begin{bmatrix} 0 & 1 \\ 1 & 0 \end{bmatrix} \quad \begin{bmatrix} 1 & 0 \\ 0 & 1 \end{bmatrix} \quad \text{and} \quad \begin{bmatrix} 1 & 0 \\ 1 & 0 \end{bmatrix}$$

1. a.

$$
\begin{bmatrix}
1 & 0 & 0 \\
0 & 1 & 0 \\
\hline
a & b & 1-a-b
\end{bmatrix}
$$

Here $R = [a \quad b]$ and $S = [1-a-b]$.

Therefore, $I - S = [1 - (1 - a - b)] = [a + b]$, and

$(I - S)^{-1} = [\frac{1}{a + b}]$ .

So, $(I - S)^{-1}R = [\frac{1}{a + b}][a \quad b] = [\frac{a}{a + b} \quad \frac{b}{a + b}]$.

Therefore, the required steady-state matrix of A is given by

$$
\begin{bmatrix}
I & 0 \\
\hline
(I-S)^{-1}R & 0
\end{bmatrix}
\begin{bmatrix}
1 & 0 & 0 \\
0 & 1 & 0 \\
\hline
\frac{a}{a + b} & \frac{b}{a + b} & 0
\end{bmatrix}.
$$

b. The probability that state 3 will be absorbed by State 2 is

$\frac{b}{a + b}$.

1. a. We consider the following cases:

(i)  c, d ≥ a. We may assume d ≥ c (The other case is treated similarly).

Row minima

$$
\begin{bmatrix}
a & a \\
\boxed{c} & d
\end{bmatrix}
\quad
\begin{array}{l}
a \\
c \longleftarrow \text{Larger of the row minima}
\end{array}
$$

Column
maxima       c       d

↑_____ Smaller of the column maxima

So c is a saddle point.

(ii) c < a < d (The case where d < a < c is treated similarly.)

Row minima

$$\begin{bmatrix} \textcircled{a} & a \\ c & d \end{bmatrix} \quad \begin{matrix} a \\ c \end{matrix}$$

a ⟵ Larger of the row minima

Column     a    d

maxima    ↑_____ Smaller of the column maxima

So a is a saddle point.

(iii) c, d ≤ a. We assume c ≤ d (the case where d ≥ c) is treated similarly.)

Row minima

$$\begin{bmatrix} \textcircled{a} & \textcircled{a} \\ c & d \end{bmatrix} \quad \begin{matrix} a \\ c \end{matrix}$$

a ⟵ Larger of the row minima

Column     a    a

maxima    ↑_____ Smaller of the column maxima

So a is a saddle point.

In each case there is a saddle point. Therefore, the game is strictly determined.

b. The game is strictly determined. The proof is similar to that for part (a).

**Page 574**

1. a. If x = 1/2, then

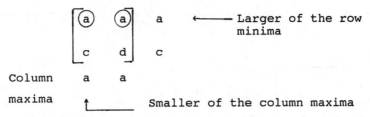

$$A = \begin{bmatrix} \frac{1}{2} & \frac{1}{2} \\ \frac{1}{2} & \frac{1}{2} \end{bmatrix}$$

and the game is seen to be strictly determined.

Next, suppose x ≠ 1/2. In particular, suppose x < 1/2. Then 1 − x > 1/2.  We find

$$\begin{bmatrix} x & 1 - x \\ \\ 1 - x & x \end{bmatrix} \quad \begin{matrix} x \\ \\ x \end{matrix}$$

Column
maxima    $1 - x \quad 1 - x$

Since $1 - x \neq x$ in this case, we see that there are no saddle points, and so the game is not strictly determined. The case where $x > 1/2$ is treated similarly. We conclude that if $x \neq 1/2$, the game is not strictly determined.

b. Using Formula (2c), we find that the value of the game is

$$E = \frac{ad - bc}{a + d - b - c} = \frac{x^2 - (1 - x)^2}{x + x - (1 - x) - (1 - x)}$$

$$= \frac{x^2 - 1 + 2x - x^2}{2x - 1 + x - 1 + x} = \frac{2x - 1}{4x - 2} = \frac{2x - 1}{2(2x - 1)} = \frac{1}{2}.$$